Victims of International Crimes: An Interdisciplinary Discourse

Thorsten Bonacker · Christoph Safferling
Editors

Victims of International Crimes: An Interdisciplinary Discourse

ASSER PRESS

Springer

Editors
Thorsten Bonacker
Institut für Soziologie
Philipps-Universität Marburg
Marburg
Germany

Christoph Safferling
Institut für Kriminalwissenschaften
Philipps-Universität Marburg
Marburg
Germany

ISBN 978-90-6704-911-5 ISBN 978-90-6704-912-2 (eBook)
DOI 10.1007/978-90-6704-912-2

Library of Congress Control Number: 2013934272

Published by T.M.C. ASSER PRESS, The Hague, The Netherlands www.asserpress.nl
Produced and distributed for T.M.C. ASSER PRESS by Springer-Verlag Berlin Heidelberg

Printed on acid-free paper

Springer is part of Springer Science+Business Media (www.springer.com)

Foreword

In the last 20 years we have seen new and successful global efforts to criminalise genocide, war crimes and crimes against humanity, and to prosecute and punish those responsible. The establishment of the *ad hoc* international criminal tribunals for the crimes committed in the former Yugoslavia and in Rwanda, and of the permanent International Criminal Court, is the most publicised outcome of these initiatives.

National courts are also beginning to exercise their universal jurisdiction over certain international crimes. The trial against a Rwandan national accused of participation in the killing of thousands of Tutsis in Rwanda that has begun this year before the Frankfurt Superior Court is just one example of these efforts.

As important as the punishment of perpetrators is, the suffering incurred by the victims should not be forgotten. The proportion of civilian casualties of war as opposed to military casualties has increased dramatically, up to 90 % by the end of the twentieth century.[1] At the end of 2010, the number of people forcibly uprooted by conflict and persecution worldwide stood at almost 34 million.[2] Therefore, this conference couldn't be timelier.

The welfare of crime victims is of special importance to the Ministry of Justice. Of course, I don't want to confound the special situation of victims of war crimes with crime victims in general. But it nevertheless seems that this conference's focus on victims of international crimes mirrors a growing interest in victims in national law.

Two of the upcoming panels will discuss the protection and participation of victims in criminal trials. Victim protection and victims' participation have also been special concerns of German criminal procedure law in recent years. Various changes in statutory law have been enacted to protect victims from further harm in their role as witnesses and to strengthen their rights as active participants in criminal proceedings.

But these legal protections for victims are not enough. They must be accompanied by counseling and practical assistance. In the State of Hessen, the Ministry of Justice

[1] UNICEF, Impact of Armed Conflict on Children, 1996, MN 24.

[2] Exactly 33.924.475—UNHCR, Global Trends Report 2010.

supports a network of crime victims support associations. They support victims while reporting the crime, giving testimony in court, pursuing claims for compensation and dealing with the psychological repercussions of the crime.

While the situation of victims of gross violations of international human rights law and victims of other crimes obviously differs, they also confront legal systems with a host of similar questions. How can the courts investigate a case effectively, with the help of the victim's testimony, while protecting the victim against further harm during the trial? How can victims become active participants in the proceedings while also recognising the right of the defendant to a fair trial?

How can the worst crimes ever be remedied? These problems are magnified and multiplied when we are trying to deal with mass violations of human rights.

Wiesbaden/Marburg
December 2012

Dr. Rudolf E. C. Kriszeleit
State Secretary
Hessian Ministry for Justice,
Integration and European Affairs

Acknowledgments

Since 1945 societies, but also the international community have developed different instruments to deal with massive past human rights abuses. Victims became significant actors in those so-called transitional justice processes. On that background we decided to conceptualise a conference that brought together international scholars from different disciplines to discuss the situation of victims of serious human rights violations and to further enhance their role in transition processes. The primary motivation for organising such a conference was to establish an interdisciplinary approach, which has been lacking in academic discourse to date.

Both organising institutions, the Center for Conflict Studies (CCS) and International Research and Documentation Centre War Crimes Trials (ICWC), conducted research on transitional justice, international criminal justice and the role of victims over the last years. The conference on "Victims of International Crimes" took place from October 6th to 8th 2011 at the University of Marburg.

This would not have been possible at all without many helping hands. Particular thanks are due to Wolfgang Form, Iain Fraser, Albrecht Kirschner and Daniela Ziegler who have contributed substantially to the success of the conference through their considerable dedication, expertise and creativity. Our thank goes in particular to Franziska Kowalski and Sebastian Kluckow who not only did tremendous work in organising the conference, but also were, together with Jana Groth, highly committed in assisting us to edit this volume.

Likewise, we are immensely grateful to Philip van Tongeren and Marjolijn Bastiaans at T.M.C. Asser Press for publishing this book.

Finally, we wish to thank the German Science Foundation (DFG) and the Foundation Remembrance, Responsibility and Future (EVZ) for sponsoring the conference and giving us the opportunity to bring together such a great variety of internationally renowned researchers and practitioners.

Marburg, December 2012

Thorsten Bonacker
Christoph Safferling

Contents

Part II Definition of Victims

Abbreviations

AC	Appeals Chamber
Afr J Int Comp Law	African Journal of International and Comparative Law
AHR	The American Historical Review
AIDS	Acquired Immunodeficiency Syndrome
AIJI	Asian International Justice Initiative
AJIL	American Journal of International Law
Am J Sociol	American Journal of Sociology
ANC	African National Congress
Ann Rev Political Sci	Annual Review of Political Science
Anthropol Theory	Anthropological Theory
APDH	Asamblea Permanente los Derechos Humanos
APR	Armée Patriotique Rwandaise
APSR	American Political Science Review
AQ	Anthropological Quarterly
Arab Stud Q	Arab Studies Quarterly
ARTS	The Journal of the Sydney University Arts Association
ASR	American Sociological Review
ASRIC	Applied Social Research Institute of Cambodia
AT	Anthropology Today
AUC	Autodefensas Unidas de Colombia
Aust J Anthropol	Austrian Journal of Anthropology
AVEGA	Association des Veuves du Génocide d'Avril
BCTWLJ	Boston College Third World Law Journal
BGBl.	Bundesgesetzblatt
BGHSt	Entscheidungen des Bundesgerichtshofs in Strafsachen
BHRLR	Buffalo Human Rights Law Review
Case West Reserv J Int Law	Case Western Reserve Journal of International Law

CEH	Comisión para el Esclarecimiento Histórico
CELS	Centro de Estudios Legales y Sociales
CICC	Coalition of the ICC
CICIG	Comisión Internacional contra la Impunidad en Guatemala
CJIL	Chicago Journal of International Law
CJR	Center for Justice and Reconciliation
CLF	Criminal Law Forum
CNPT	Comisión Nacional sobre Prisión Política y Tortura
CNRR	Comisión Nacional de Reparación y Reconciliación
Colum J Gener & L	Columbia Journal of Gender and Law
Comp Polit Stud	Comparative Political Studies
CONADEP	Comisión Nacional sobre la Desaparición de Personas
CPC	Cambodian Criminal Procedure Code
CSD	Journal of Conflict, Security and Development
DDR	Disarmament, Demobilization and Reintegration
DED	Deutscher Entwicklungsdienst (German Development Organisation), now GIZ
DJILP	Denver Journal of International Law and Policy
DLJ	The Denning Law Journal
DÖW	Dokumentationsarchiv des östereichischen Widerstandes
DRC	Democratic Republic of the Congo
DUP	Democratic Unionist Party
ECCC	Extraordinary Chambers in the Courts of Cambodia
ECHR	European Convention for Human Rights
ECtHR	European Court of Human Rights
EJCCLCJ	European Journal of Crime, Criminal Law and Criminal Justice
EJIL	European Journal of International Law
Ethics Int Aff	Ethics and International Affairs
Eur Rev Latin Am Caribb Stud	European Review of Latin American and Caribbean Studies
Europe-Asia Stud	Europe-Asia Studies
FAFG	Fundación de Antropología Forense de Guatemala
FAIR	Families Acting For Innocent Relatives
FARC	Fuerzas Armadas Revolucionarias de Colombia
FARG	Fonds d'Appui aux Rescapés du Génocide
FEDEFAM	Federación Latinoamericana de Asociaciones de Familiares de Detenidos-Desaparecidos

Fem LS	Feminist Legal Studies
FF Plus	Freedom Front Plus
FIS	Front Islamique du Salut
Fla Coast L Rev	Florida Coastal Law Review
FPR	Front Patriotique Rwandais
FRG	Frente Republicano Guatemalteco
Gen Dev	Gender & Development
GIZ	Deutsche Gesellschaft für Internationale Zusammenarbeit
GJIA	Georgetown Journal of International Affairs
Global Gov	Global Governance
Glob Soc	Global Society
GoJIL	Goettingen Journal of International Law
Hastings Law J	Hastings Law Journal
HHRJ	Harvard Human Rights Journal
HIV	Human Immunodeficiency Virus
Holocaust Genocide Stud	Holocaust and Genocide Studies
HRLR	Human Rights Law Review
HRQ	Human Rights Quarterly
HuV-I	Humanitäres Völkerrecht – Informations-schriften
ICC	International Criminal Court
ICJ	International Court of Justice
ICLR	International Criminal Law Review
ICRC	International Committee of the Red Cross
ICTR	International Criminal Tribunal for Rwanda
ICTY	International Criminal Tribunal for the Former Yugoslavia
ICWC	International Research and Documentation Centre War Crimes Trials
IDDRS	Integrated Disarmament, Demobilisation, and Reintegration Standards
IFJP	International Feminist Journal of Politics
IFP	Inkatha Freedom Party
IJCV	International Journal of Conflict and Violence
IJNL	International Journal of Non-for-Profit Law
IJTJ	The International Journal of Transitional Justice
ILJ	Cornell International Law Journal
ILSAJICL	ILSA Journal of International Comparative Law
IMT	International Military Tribunal
Int J Law Context	International Journal of Law in Context
Int Soc	International Sociology
IRA	Irish Republican Army
IRRC	International Review of the Red Cross
IRV	International Review of Victimology

ISQ	International Studies Quarterly
ITU	Interpretation and Translation Unit
J Appl Philos	Journal of Applied Philosophy
J Int Afr Inst	Journal of the International African Institute
J Intercult Stud	Journal of Intercultural Studies
J Per Soc Psychol	Journal of Personality and Social Psychology
JAMA	The Journal of the American Medical Association
JCLC	Journal of Criminal Law and Criminology
JCLP	Journal of Clinical Psychology
JHR	Journal of Human Rights
JHRP	Journal of Human Rights Practice
JICJ	Journal of International Criminal Justice
JIL	Case Western Reserve Journal of International Law
JILP	Journal of International Law and Politics
JLAS	Journal of Latin American Studies
JTS	Journal of Traumatic Stress
KLA	Kosovo Liberation Army
LJIL	Leiden Journal for International Law
LRA	Lord's Resistance Army
Mem Stud	Memory Studies
MJIL	Michigan Journal of International Law
MSLR	Michigan State Law Review
N Engl Law Rev	New England Law Review
NDJLEPP	Notre Dame Journal of Law, Ethics & Public Policies
NGO	Non-governmental Organisation
NJHR	Nordic Journal of Human Rights
NJIL	Nordic Journal of International Law
NJIHR	Northwestern Journal of International Human Rights
NJW	Neue Juristische Wochenschrift
NY Univ Law Rev	New York University Law Review
OCIJ	Office of the Co-Investigating Judges
ODHAG	Oficina de Derechos Humanos del Arzobispado de Guatemala
OHCHR	Office of the High Commissioner for Human Rights
OPCD	Office for Public Counsel for the Defence
OPCV	Office of Public Counsel for Victims
ORIL	Oregon Review of International Law
OUP	Oxford University Press
PAS	Public Affairs Section
Peace Rev	Peace Review

Peripherie	Peripherie – Zeitschrift für Politik und Ökonomie der Dritten Welt
POW	Prisoner of War
PTC	Pre-trial Chamber
R2P	Responsibility to Protect
REStat	Review of Economics and Statistics
RoC	Regulations of the Court
RPE	Rules of Procedure and Evidence
RPF	Rwandan Patriotic Front
RSC	Revue de Science Criminelle et de Droit Pénal Comparé
RUC	Royal Ulster Constabulary
RUF	Revolutionary United Front
Rutgers Law Rec	The Rutgers Law Record
S Afr J Mil Stud	South African Journal of Military Studies
SADF	South African Defence Force
Saint Louis Univ Public Law Rev	Saint Louis University Public Law Review
SCSL	Special Court for Sierra Leone
SJST	Scandinavian Journal of Social Theory
SLS	Social and Legal Studies
Smith Coll Stud Soc Work	Smith College Studies in Social Work
Soc Anal	Social Analysis
Soc Forces	Journal of Social Forces
Soc Legal Studies	Social & Legal Studies
Stat Abstr Lat Am	Statistical Abstract Latin America
STL	Special Tribunal for Lebanon
TC	Trial Chamber
TFV	Trust Fund for Victims
Third World Q	Third World Quarterly
TIG	Travaux d'Intérêt Général
TJ	Transitional Justice
TJLR	Thomas Jefferson Law Review
TLCP	Transnational Law & Contemporary Problems
TRC	Truth and Reconciliation Commission
Univ La Verne L Rev	University of La Verne Law Review
UC Davis JILP	U.C. Davis Journal of International Law and Policy
UN	United Nations
UNDF	United Nations Detention Facility
UNDP	United Nations Development Programme
UNESCO	United Nations Educational, Scientific and Cultural Organization
UNTAC	United Nations Transitional Authority in Cambodia
UVF	Ulster Volunteer Force

VJTL	Vanderbilt Journal of Transnational Law
VPRS	Victims Participation and Reparations Section
VSS	Victims Support Section
VTF	Victims Trust Fund
VWS	Victims and Witnesses Section
VWU	Victims and Witnesses Unit
WILJ	Wisconsin International Law Journal
WJILDR	Willamette Journal of International Law and Dispute Resolution
WSIF	Women's Studies International Forum
YHRDLJ	Yale Human Rights and Development Law Journal
YIHL	Yearbook of International Humanitarian Law
ZIB	Zeitschrift für Internationale Beziehungen
ZIS	Zeitschrift für Internationale Strafrechtsdogmatik
ZStW	Zeitschrift für die gesamte Strafrechtswissenschaft

Contributors

Raquel Aldana is Professor of Law and Director of the Inter-American Program at the Pacific McGeorge School of Law, email: raldana@pacific.edu

Brigitte Bailer-Galanda is Academic Director of the Documentation Center of Austrian Resistance in Vienna as well as Honorary Professor at the University of Vienna for Contemporary History, email: brigitte.bailer@doew.at

Boris Barth is Professor of Modern and Contemporary History at the University of Konstanz, email: boris.barth@uni-konstanz.de

Marcel M. Baumann is Lecturer and Senior Researcher at the Department of Political Science at the Albert-Ludwigs-Universität Freiburg, email: marcel.baumann@politik.uni-freiburg.de

Stefanie Bock is Senior Research Assistant of Professor Dr. Kai Ambos, Department for Foreign and International Criminal Law, and Assistant Professor at the Georg-August-Universität Göttingen, email: stefanie.bock@jura.uni-goettingen.de

Thorsten Bonacker is Professor of Peace and Conflict Studies at the Center for Conflict Studies at the Philipps-Universität Marburg, email: thorsten.bonacker@staff.uni-marburg.de

Susanne Buckley-Zistel is Professor of Peace and Conflict Studies at the Center for Conflict Studies at the Philipps-Universität Marburg, email: s.buckley-zistel@staff.uni-marburg.de

Mark A. Drumbl Class of 1975 Alumni Professor of Law and Director, Transnational Law Institute, Washington and Lee University, Lexington, Virginia, USA, email: drumblm@wlu.edu

Franziska C. Eckelmans is Legal Officer in the Appeals Chamber of the International Criminal Court, email: franziska.eckelmans@icc-cpi.int

Gerd Hankel is Guest Fellow at the Hamburg Institute for Social Research, email: Gerd.Hankel@his-online.de

Michael Humphrey holds the Chair in Sociology in the Department of Sociology and Social Policy at the University of Sydney, email: michael.humphrey@sydney.edu.au

H.E. Hans-Peter Kaul is a Judge at the International Criminal Court. From 1996 to 2003 he has been the Head of the German delegation for the negotiations for the ICC, before being elected in February 2003 as the First German Judge to the ICC for a period of three years. He was re-elected in 2006 for another period of nine years. From March 2009 to 2012 Judge Kaul has served for three years as the Second Vice-President of the ICC. He is assigned to the Pre-Trial Division, email: Hans-Peter.Kaul@icc-cpi.int

Michael J. Kelly is Professor of Law and Associate Dean for Faculty Research and International Programs, Creighton University School of Law, email: Michael-Kelly@creighton.edu

Daniela Kravetz Trial Attorney, Office of the Prosecution, International Criminal Tribunal for the Former Yugoslavia dkravetz@yahoo.com dkravetz@yahoo.com

Rudolf E. C. Kriszeleit is State Secretary in the Hessian Ministry for Justice, Integration and European Affairs

Anika Oettler is Professor for Sociology at the Philipps-Universität Marburg, email: anika.oettler@staff.uni-marburg.de

Katharina Peschke is Legal Advisor of the Trust Fund for Victims, The Hague, The Netherlands, email: Katharina.Peschke@icc-cpi.int

Christoph Safferling is Professor for Criminal Law, Criminal Procedure, International Criminal Law, and Public International Law at the Philipps-Universität Marburg as well as Director of the International Research and Documentation Centre War Crimes Trials, email: christoph.safferling@jura.uni-marburg.de

Christoph Sperfeldt is Regional Program Coordinator at the Asian International Justice Initiative, a collaborative project between the East–West Center and UC Berkeley's War Crimes Studies, email: Center csperfeldt@gmail.com

Chandra Lekha Sriram is Professor of Law at the School of Oriental and African Studies at the University of London, email: chandra.sriram@soas.ac.uk

Veit Strassner teaches at the Kurt Schumacher-School in Ingelheim, Germany. He holds a M.A. and a Ph.D. in Political Science and a postgraduate degree (Lic. theol.) in Theology, email: vstrassner@hotmail.com

Silke Studzinsky is a Criminal Defense Lawyer and Legal Representative for Civil Parties. Since February 2008, she has been working with the support of the Civil Peace Service of the German Development Organisation DED (now GIZ) in Cambodia to represent Civil Parties before the Extraordinary Chambers in the Courts of Cambodia, email: silke.eccc@googlemail.com

Theo C. van Boven is Professor Emeritus of International Law at Maastricht University, Faculty of Law (The Netherlands), and Former UN Special Rapporteur on torture and other cruel, inhuman or degrading treatment or punishment (2001–2004), email: th.vanboven@maastrichtuniversity.nl

Natalie von Wistinghausen is a self-employed Criminal Lawyer and admitted to the list of counsel at the ICC, STL and ICTR. Currently she is defending a Rwandan citizen before the Higher Regional Court of Frankfurt am Main who is accused of participation in the Rwandan genocide, email: office@nvw-law.com

Chapter 1
Introduction

Thorsten Bonacker and Christoph Safferling

1.1 Preliminary Remarks

Over a long period of time, victims and survivors of mass atrocities have not been in the focus of processes dealing with the past. Since the mid-1980 and especially over the last fifteen years there has been a notable global shift in regard to the relevance and participation of victims in national transitional justice processes. A greater recognition of victims' rights on the international level is observable, also referred to as the "humanization of international law".[1] In 2005, the United Nations General Assembly adopted the Resolution on *Basic Principles and Guidelines on the Right to a Remedy and Reparation for Victims of Gross Violations of International Human Rights Law and Serious Violations of International Humanitarian Law* that notes in its preamble "that victims should be treated with compassion and respect for their dignity, have their right to access to justice and redress mechanisms fully respected, and that the establishment, strengthening and expansion of national funds for compensation to victims should be encouraged, together with the expeditious development of appropriate rights and remedies for victims".[2] This is the strongest statement the United Nations (UN) ever made on victims' rights in the context of international crimes

Thorsten Bonacker is Professor of Peace and Conflict Studies at the Center for Conflict Studies at the University of Marburg. Christoph Safferling is Professor of Criminal Law, Criminal Procedure, International Criminal Law, and Public International Law at the University of Marburg as well as Director of the International Research and Documentation Center War Crimes Trials.

[1] Meron 2006.

[2] United Nations 2005.

T. Bonacker · C. Safferling (✉)
University of Marburg, Marburg, Germany
e-mail: christoph.safferling@jura.uni-marburg.de

T. Bonacker
e-mail: thorsten.bonacker@staff.uni-marburg.de

T. Bonacker and C. Safferling (eds.), *Victims of International Crimes: An Interdisciplinary Discourse*, DOI: 10.1007/978-90-6704-912-2_1,

and could be viewed as part of the last stage of the "justice cascade"[3] that now includes victims in international criminal law and especially in transitional justice processes.

As the resolution states the UN had developed several international instruments to provide victims' rights, like for instance Article 8 of the *Universal Declaration of Human Rights*, Article 2 of the *International Covenant on Civil and Political Rights*, Article 6 of the *International Convention on the Elimination of All Forms of Racial Discrimination*, Article 14 of the *Convention against Torture and Other Cruel, Inhuman or Degrading Treatment or Punishment*, Article 39 of the *Convention on the Rights of the Child*, and of course the Articles 68 and 75 of the *Rome Statute of the International Criminal Court*.

Twenty years before the UN decided on the *Basic Principles and Guidelines on the Right to a Remedy and Reparation for Victims of Gross Violations of International Human Rights Law and Serious Violations of International Humanitarian Law* it adopted the *Declaration of Basic Principles of Justice for Victims of Crime and Abuse of Power* that deals with individual victims of crimes in the context of national criminal law. At the end of the 1990s, victims' rights groups and the epistemic community of victimology began to expand the definition of victims in national law to international crimes.[4] That finally led to the resolution in 2005. Regarding this evolution of victims' rights one may speak of **victims' rights as an international norm** or at least as an international standard that obviously had and still has an impact on both the role of victims in international criminal law and especially in the procedural rights of victims of international crimes and the way victims are included in transitional justice approaches in postwar or postauthoritarian societies. In this volume we discuss these impacts, but also the several steps of a more victim centred way of dealing with past atrocities especially in international criminal law.

One great advantage of criminal proceedings dealing with international crimes is that they reduce the question of collective guilt to that of individual accountability on the side of the perpetrator. Mirroring that, victims usually are perceived as individuals that were harmed by individual perpetrators. In the context of macrocriminality the situation seems to be more complex. An international crime is usually characterised by a multitude of individual victims, who often do not even see themselves as victims but would call themselves "survivors", because they want to avoid the passive notion of the term "victim".[5] In some crimes, for example the crime of genocide, the perpetrator does not only aim at harming one or several individuals, his act is also directed towards an entire ethnic, racial, religious, or national group. The victim of an international crime thus carries an obvious collective aspect. Whereas the consequences of victimisation on the collective as such

[3] Sikkink 2011.

[4] Letschert 2010.

[5] Bouris 2007.

remain widely unclear, any integration of victims in the prosecution of international crimes has to cope with the issue of quantity in order to keep the process manageable. Nonetheless, international crimes, in particular with a view to this collective aspect, carry with them the need to deal with the past of conflicting groups not individuals. Transitional justice is therefore not satisfied by simply punishing the perpetrator; rather the victims' interests and perspectives need to be addressed and structured. Whereas at the UN *ad hoc* tribunals for the former Yugoslavia and for Rwanda the issue of victims has been brought to attention rather lately in the context of outreach and the question of acceptance of the trials in the societies concerned, the International Criminal Court (ICC) foresees a new and progressive victim participation scheme.

From a victim's point of view international criminal law is from its outset more than just a general tool of prevention. It is also supposed to document the suffering of victims and include them in the hearings. The latter is particularly mentioned in the Rome Statute and was practiced in the first trial against Thomas Lubanga. 123 victims participated in the proceeding and shared their experiences and opinions with the Court. The ICC assigns the victims with an important role at all stages of the proceedings. Besides the possibility to eventually obtain compensation they are further given the option to choose their own counsel. The Rules of Procedure of the ICC provide the victims with the opportunity to make an opening and final statement and to ask for permission to intervene in the proceeding e.g. through questions during witness hearings.[6] The participation of victims in criminal trials has been recognised as an elementary victims' right, not only by the ICC but also by other international and regional human rights bodies such as the European Court of Human Rights and the Inter-American Court of Human Rights. "In many parts of the world surviving victims already are participating in criminal trials or are promoting reforms to increase their standing to do so".[7] Aldana-Pindell identifies an evolving universality of victims' rights in criminal trials dealing with cases of violence supported or carried out by states. The international criminal law has established the inclusion of victims in the Rome Statute which provides a *Victims and Witnesses Unit* and points out that "the Unit shall include staff with expertise in trauma, including trauma related to crimes of sexual violence".[8] Furthermore, victims have the opportunity to participate in the proceedings. Article 68 (3) manifests this right:

> Where the personal interests of the victims are affected, the Court shall permit their views and concerns to be presented and considered at stages of the proceedings determined to be appropriate by the Court and in a manner which is not prejudicial to or inconsistent with the rights of the accused and a fair and impartial trial. Such views and concerns may be

[6] McKay 2008.

[7] Aldana-Pindell 2004, p. 686.

[8] Rome Statute, Article 43 (6); see ICC 2002b, p. 24.

presented by the legal representatives of the victims where the Court considers it appropriate, in accordance with the Rules of Procedure and Evidence.

Independent from the difficulties of victims' inclusion in criminal law proceedings regarding for instance the rights of the accused,[9] it can be noted that the ICC as well as the Extraordinary Chambers in the Courts of Cambodia (ECCC) have developed several instruments to involve victims in the processing of international crimes. Besides the *Victims and Witnesses Unit* of the ICC and the *Victims Unit* of the ECCC, outreach programs have been developed which inform and advise victims, often in cooperation with NGOs. At the same time, victims' lawyers are assigned with the task to present the victims' point of view in the proceedings. As a result of this global development the victim is now not only regarded as an individual whose rights and integrity have been violated but also as someone who has special rights due to the victim status itself. In recent years and as a result of the diffusion of victims' rights as an international norm these rights have been increasingly implemented by states and in international law.[10]

International criminal law also plays a crucial role in the discourse on **transitional justice** and victim participation. At its broadest, transitional justice "involves anything that a society devises to deal with a legacy of conflict and/or widespread human rights violations, from changes in criminal codes to those in high school textbooks, from creation of memorials, museums and days of mourning, to police and court reform, to tackling the distributional inequities that underlie conflict".[11] Reconstructing the historical development of the concept of transitional justice, Teitel distinguishes three phases demonstrating the focus shift from perpetrators to victims.[12] According to Teitel, the origins of modern transitional justice can be traced back to the First World War but are usually associated with the post-war history starting at 1945, especially with the Nuremberg Trials. The transitions from dictatorships to democracies in the mid-1980s mark the beginning of the second phase starting in Latin America, particularly Chile and Argentina, followed by the revolutions in Eastern Europe. In the still ongoing third phase internationalised transitional justice processes in the aftermath of civil wars and genocides are at the centre of attention, e.g. Sierra Leone, Rwanda, and Cambodia. The Nuremberg Trials are characterised by the effort to design a normative framework for a legal criminal prosecution and a criminal procedural law guaranteeing a fair trial. In contrast, the second and third phase have produced transitional justice mechanisms more aimed at the victims' needs, but also at national reconciliation.

The Nuremberg Trials, as well as the Tokyo Tribunal tried to identify individual responsibility of international crimes, thus their focus was on the perpetrators.[13]

---

9 Safferling 2003.

10 Letschert and Groenhuijsen 2011.

11 Roht-Arriaza 2006, p. 2.

12 Teitel 2003.

13 Ainley 2008.

Even in their function as witnesses, victims played a minor role. This started to change during the second phase, namely the democratic transitions in Latin America, South Africa and Eastern Europe. Approaches of *restorative justice,* especially Truth and Reconciliation Commissions in Chile and Argentina and later on in South Africa, were at the centre of attention during this second phase. The main objectives of restorative justice are on the one hand reconciliation between victims and actors and on the other hand truth-seeking, mostly achieved by public victims' testimonies. The participation of victims and the dialogue between perpetrators and victims has therefore become an important instrument of transitional justice. The perpetrator-orientation during the first phase becomes a victim-orientation during the second phase.

In the third phase, Truth and Reconciliation Commissions again play a major role in transitional justice processes after civil wars and genocides. Moreover, they are now being complemented by international criminal trials in the form of tribunals established by the UN Security Council, e.g. the International Tribunal for the former Yugoslavia (ICTY), the International Criminal Tribunal for Rwanda (ICTR), or hybrid courts such as those of Sierra Leone and Cambodia. Other important contributions were the founding and first legal prosecutions of the ICC, which can be seen as a consequence of the Nuremberg Trials and as important milestones for International Criminal Law manifesting the principle of responsibility for mass atrocities. In particular, strong criticism of the non-involvement of the victims and the local population in international criminal trials, both in the Yugoslavia and Rwanda Tribunals, has led to the focus on inclusion of victims and locals into the transitional justice processes, also to increase the legitimacy of the legal proceedings.

Hitherto criminal trials had been perceived as a mechanism of social control primarily aimed at marginalisation of the perpetrators, but from then on they aimed at a stronger and more active role of the victims. This idea was mainly manifested in the ICC Statute and practiced for the first time by the ECCC. The establishment of the ICC was also an important step for the international anchoring of the victims' right to reparations. This right, a common norm in national civil law which was applied to states only hesitantly, is now part of International Criminal Law.[14] The *Basic Principles and Guidelines of the Right to a Remedy and Reparation for Victims of Gross Violations of International Human Rights Law and Serious Violations of International Humanitarian Law* further define the Right to Reparation. In sum, the historical development of transitional justice shows a clear shift from the perpetrator-orientation and the identification of their responsibility for international crimes to the victim-orientation and their increased involvement in criminal proceedings as well as different mechanisms of restorative justice.

After focussing on individual accountability and different instruments of transitional justice as well as on the dilemma of peace versus justice and the limits of

[14] Tomuschat 2009.

legalistic approaches for national reconciliation, the research on transitional justice processes now also takes the victim as an individual and collective actor of transitional justice into account. So far, the victims' perception and judgement of transitional justice mechanisms,[15] negative consequences of transitional justice for victims,[16] collective mobilisation as well as instrumentalisation of victims,[17] and the construction of a victims' agency[18] are studied in more detail. Regarding the role of victims in international criminal law as a key element of transitional justice a controversial discussion on the possibilities and difficulties of victim participation in international criminal proceedings is going on.[19] Another debate stresses the limits of global transitional justice for victims' needs and the frictions and dilemmas of global justice.[20]

Taking these findings and debates on, this volume deals with the complex role victims are playing in transitional justice processes with a special focus on judicial or quasi-judicial instruments like criminal law or truth and reconciliation commissions. The overall aim thereby is to initiate and strengthen the interdisciplinary dialog on victims of international crimes. The volume brings together experts from different disciplines working on transitional justice and victims' rights. Over the last years, especially in peace and conflict studies, political science, and sociology, we can find an increasing interest in studying transitional justice processes and international criminal law in general and the role of victims in particular.

On the other hand criminal law traditionally focused more on perpetrators than on victims and treated victims in an abstract and individualised way. Criminological research has also been concentrated on the perpetrator, questioning the factors responsible for delinquency recidivism and resilience. Victimological research is a rather recent phenomenon, both in the national and international context. But like in social science research also in criminal law and criminology the victim became more and more the focus of research mirroring the development of victims' rights as an international norm. Bringing both streams of research on victims of international crimes together the volume shows first, that victims do play a more important role in transitional justice and international criminal law and that the increasing participation of victims in transitional justice and criminal proceedings seems to be due to the international evolution and distribution of victim rights. Second, the volume also discusses the multiple consequences this increasing inclusion of victims has, for instance concerning the concept of trials, the need of victims, and the reconciliation of former conflict parties.

---

15 Pham et al. 2009; Mallinder 2008; Bloomfield et al. 2003.

16 Madlingozi 2010.

17 Smyth 2003; Williams 2008.

18 Fassin and Rechtman 2009; Bonacker 2012; Bonacker et al. 2011.

19 Baumgartner 2008; Safferling 2010; Henham 2004; Glasius 2009.

20 Hinton 2011.

The contributions presented in this volume are separated into five different sections. In a rather general 1st part a view is being taken on a generally victim-oriented perspective of international law and on the chances and difficulties connected to putting a focus on victims. The 2nd part deals with the difficult issues of defining "victims", both in international law and social sciences. The 3rd part discusses the protection and participation of victims in criminal trials. The role and interests of victims in transitional justice processes is being addressed in the 4th part. In the final 5th part the focus lies on civil society actors and their role in dealing with victim issues. There will certainly be a considerable overlap between these different sections.

1.2 Part I: Victims in International Law

At the very beginning *Theo van Boven* speaks about "Victim-Oriented Perspectives: Rights and Realities". He looks back on the classical perspective of traditional international law and finds virtually no appraisal of the victim, e.g. by the International Court of Justice. Yet the transitional justice movement has changed that perspective. The right to reparation is now part of a trilogy of rights consisting of (1) the right to know, (2) the right to justice, and (3) the right to reparation.

Notwithstanding this development the author opines that it is still a long way to accept that reparation for the victims is a legal rather than a purely moral obligation on the side of the state. Even a World Conference Against Racism, Racial Discrimination, Xenophobia and Related Intolerance, which was held in Durban in 2001, could not establish such a legal obligation. Developing the concept of "reparative justice", however, is warranted in fulfilment of the UN Reparation Principles and Guidelines. The author rises two caveats in this regard: (1) It is difficult to describe collective reparations in particular with regards to other forms of social beneficiaries. (2) Reparations must not be mixed up with development. Victims have specific issues in which they separate themselves from the society in general, and reparations carry a constitutive character with regards to transitional justice goals. Thus the author calls for an inclusive approach and stresses that the future development of a country must not ignore the atrocities and wounds of the past.

In a second contribution in this first part, *Gerd Hankel* connects his understanding of victim issues with his experiences in Rwanda. In his chapter "On Victims and Non-Victims: Observations from Rwanda" he deals with the political implications in the definition of victims and the exclusionary power connected to this definition. The one-sided definition of victim has fatal consequences on the sustainability of the peace in Rwanda. The author describes how trials and Gacaca proceedings in Rwanda has in fact deepened the gap between the former belligerent groups and thus lowered the chances of establishing a peaceful society in freedom and equality of all citizens.

1.3 Part II: Definition of Victims

This part contains five contributions discussing different issues concerning the definition of victims. Whereas the first two chapters contain general discussions of the definition in international tribunals and truth commissions, the remaining contributions address three specific themes: gender, victims of Nazi crimes, and child soldiers.

Michael Kelly analyses the view of the ICC Statute on victims. Whereas both the ICTY and the ICTR Statute have largely ignored victim issues, the ICC Statute takes heed of the interests of victims. Yet the participation in the criminal trial at the ICC is depending on the certification as a victim. This certification requires the definition of "victim" contained in Rule 85 of the Rules of Procedure and Evidence (RPE). Several approaches to this definition are being discussed and questions are raised. The author tries to excavate a more precise answer by putting the definition into the context of other rights and obligations of victims in the ICC Statute. Finally the author argues in favour of a more collective approach in defining victims.

Victims in truth commissions and trials are the topic of *Michael Humphrey's* contribution. The author is not so much concerned with legal definitions as with the broader social context of constructing victimhood. He points out that trials and truth commissions produce a consensus about past violence and thereby change the social status both of the perpetrator and the victim. Thus, in transitional justice processes the "ritual victim" of criminal trials is the perpetrator, the one who is to be blamed for the violence which has occurred before, whereas the "ritual victim" of the truth commission is the victim of the previous violence, as it is in his victimhood that consensus is produced about the wrongs done. Furthermore, public trials and justice help to re-establish the "force of law"; whereas disputes about whom to prosecute, the amount of punishment, or about false allegations destabilise rather than help re-establishing the law. The author derives these results from an analysis of the historic context. The difficulties can be encapsulated in the antagonism of "war heroes vs. victims".

In the following chapter *Susanne Buckley-Zistel* concerns herself with gender issues in victimisation. She argues that sexual violence has changed from an ordinary, in a way unavoidable, by-product of armed conflict, quite similar to impunity, to a central focus of Transition Justice mechanisms. The author describes that both men and women become targets of sexual violence in armed conflicts due to their gender-specific roles within a society. This illustrates that the production and reproduction of hegemonic masculinities involves both men and woman. However, the concept of "the victim" is produced by transitional justice entrepreneurs and thus carries an inherent labelling aspect. Such narrative framing reproduces traditional models of active masculinity and passive femininity.

How victims of persecution disappear within a victimised nation is explained by *Brigitte Bailer-Galanda*. In her contribution about the dealing with the past in Austria she finds that the Austrian narrative of having been the first victim of

Nazi Germany, grounded in the 1943 Moscow Declaration and the impending State Treaty finally signed in 1955, annihilates the appreciation of real victimhood of the Nazi terror. This false self-perception—some 700,000 Austrians had been members of the NSDAP—also raised sentiments against the de-nazification process by the allied occupying powers. Austria was thus victimised twice: by Adolf Hitler's aggression and by the Allied powers. In the consequence of this narrative, the victims of perpetration—like Jews in exile—were marginalised and later disappeared from public opinion almost entirely.

In the final chapter of the section *Mark Drumbl* raises the difficult issue of child soldiers. This paradigmatic example illustrates the thin line between "perpetrator" and "victim". Legal attention arose with the foundation of the ICC and the implementation of child soldier recruitment as a war crime amongst Article 8 of the ICC Statute. The first trial ever held at the ICC against Thomas Lubanga Dyilo focused exclusively on child soldiers. The author revisits the general narrative of child soldiers as passive victimhood and raises the question whether all child soldiers (i.e. under 18s) are victims and are being forced to martial activity. For his analysis he brings together knowledge of several disciplines. The author concludes that although prosecuting child soldiers for such crimes is certainly not unlawful, such prosecutions are increasingly seen as inappropriate and even illegitimate. He himself agrees and is in favour of not trying child soldiers, however not because they are minors but because they are low ranking participants of military operations.

1.4 Part III: Victim Protection and Participation in Criminal Trials

Victim protection and participation in criminal trials is being discussed in this part of the book from five different angles of people involved in the prosecution process. This section starts out with "The Protection of Victims in War Crimes Trials" by an ICTY prosecutor, *Daniela Kravetz*. The author describes the victim protection scheme at the ICTY and opines that the necessity of protection depends also on cultural circumstances. Intimidation of witnesses both inside and outside the courtroom is one of the most pressing issues for the work of a prosecutor. Harmonising witness protection on the one hand and due process on the other is a highly problematic legal question. Finally the author points out that witness protection needs to continue despite closure of the ICTY and residual mechanism will be put into place.

From the defence lawyer's side things look different, as *Natalie von Wistinghausen* points out in the next contribution. The author looks mainly on victim participation issues and raises the question whether a participating victim is still an adequate witness. The principle of equality of arms is under scrutiny. Also an accused who has been detained for more than ten years at the ICTR and was then acquitted, as has happened, sees himself as a victim. Yet, he is still being called *génocidaire* and has no right to claim victim status. Furthermore, "story-telling" as a form of victim participation is not advisable; the trial is only concerned with charges and warrants testimony only relating to these. The right to a fair trial, the author concludes, is a right for the accused and not for victims.

The next contribution concerns itself with "Participation Rights of Victims as Civil Parties and the challenges of their implementation before the Extraordinary Chambers in the Courts of Cambodia". *Silke Studzinsky* gives an overview of the legal basis which is situated between national and international procedural law. Victims have the right to participate in the trial as civil party whose rights are even broader compared to the "personal interest"-approach taken by the Rome Statute of the ICC. The compensation scheme, however, is yet unclear. The author further reports of practical problems and challenges in implementing these rules taken from her personal experience in working with the victims. The authors personal "lessons learned" unfold a rather disillusioned account of victims' participation in criminal trials at the ECCC.

The ICC's participation scheme is still in the process of developing as *Franziska Eckelmans* explains. Compared to the ECCC the ICC system is slightly different, e.g. victims are being given numbers and are not present in the courtroom. Institutionally the ICC established a whole set of units and sections, like the Victims Participation and Reparations Section (VPRS), the Victims and Witnesses Unit (VWU), the Office of Public Counsel for Victims (OPCV), or the Office for Public Counsel for the Defence (OPCD). Before a victim can participate, s/he needs to register. The judges must be satisfied that the applicant is indeed a victim of the specific case at hand, which requires a special link between the person and a criminal charge.[21]

The following contribution by *H.E. Judge Hans-Peter Kaul* connects to the previous chapter and puts the victim participation scheme into the judge's perspective. The most pressing practical difficulty for the victim is proving his or her identification. It is usually a single judge who decides on the registration of a victim. In order to exercise rights during the prosecution process the victim needs to be represented by a counsel. Yet, the problem inherent to this approach is that the victim's legal representative acts like a second prosecutor which is not the role attributable to this function. Finally Judge Kaul points out that the best protection of human rights is the absence of violence, armed conflict, and war-making. Thus the ICC's primary goal would be to prevent mass violence in the first place.

1.5 Part IV: Victims in Transitional Justice Processes

This section of the book puts the issue of victims of macro-criminality into the context of the overall transitional justice process. In the first chapter of this part *Chandra Sriram* reflects about irreconcilable demands of victims, ex-combatants,

---

21 RPE, Rule 85; see ICC 2002a, p. 31.

and communities. These have to be seen as embedded in the "justice vs. peace"-debate. Promotions of victim-centred justice and DDR-programmes often intersect and contradict one another. Restorative justice is not per se victim-centred justice. Looking at examples like Sierra Leone and Columbia the author shows that former combatants are not interested in taking accountability while victims often request accountability. If one were to pay greater attentiveness to these intersections, as well as to the complexity of identities of beneficiaries, the practice of each might improve.

The following contribution by *Boris Barth* takes issue with victims of genocide. It is striking, as the author points out, that whereas the 19th century Europe experienced short wars it seems that genocide and ethnic cleansing are integral parts of the 20th century modernity and the process of modern nation building. The definition of victims in the Genocide Convention is ambiguous now; however in 1948, the author opines, everybody knew what was meant. A dilemma of interpretation; yet, genocide research was suppressed in particular in Germany, as argued by the author, because it bears a notion of relativisation of the holocaust. This has two consequences on our understanding of genocide victims: (1) The victim groups are arbitrarily defined by the perpetrator; (2) Remembrance is constructed either by a small number of survivors or by certain interest groups. In the end the author questions whether "genocide" is the right term after all. Crimes against humanity would be preferable as the legal term making all persecution punishable and avoiding hierarchies.

Contrasting genocide victims to victims of civil wars is the task to be fulfilled by the next author, *Stefanie Bock*. The emphasis is put on the importance of the Tadić decision for the law of war. The author attempts to explain violence between groups that share at least in part the same heritage, social bondage and statehood. In order to justify violence against former neighbours "de-individualisation" of these persons as opponents is necessary. Asymmetry between belligerent parties is most often one of the characteristics of civil war. In the consequence the entire civil society is being victimised.

These more specific thoughts pertain to different "types" of victims as they relate to international crimes. The following chapter by *Thorsten Bonacker*, *Anika Oettler* and *Christoph Safferling* presents the attempt to analyse the "rise of the victim", or in the words of the authors, the "valorisation of the victim" from an interdisciplinary viewpoint. The enhancement of the victim and the focus on international proceedings, in particular before the ICC, which can be observed in transitional justice discourses bears several ambiguities. The authors point at exclusionary mechanisms which could have a detrimental effect on those victims who do not fulfil the requirements of the ICC definition and cannot participate in the proceedings. Furthermore, the local and international needs are not necessarily the same. Expectations by victims are thus likely to be disappointed. Finally the authors call for more empirical research to back up the fulfilment of human rights expectations by victim participation and criminal prosecution.

After these rather general remarks *Raquel Aldana* presents a case study and reflects on transitional justice in Guatemala 15 years after the peace agreements.

The author focuses on the participation of victims in the transitional justice process and on the judicial system in Guatemala. Unlike other Latin American countries Guatemala did not adopt a general amnesty. It is argued that victims themselves have been burdened with the task of initiating criminal prosecution while the government has denied its responsibility. This is asking too much of the victims. Alternative ways of victim participation should be developed to free victims from having to ignite and keep burning a strenuous fight for justice. The individualised approach, which is the result of a victim driven prosecution, the author opines, hinders a general and systematic dealing with the past crimes.

The final chapter in this part is about the ICC Trust Fund for victims, written by *Katharina Peschke*. It is explained that the ICC-TFFV has two mandates: (1) Reparations to or in respect of victims. These can take many different forms such as restitution, compensation, or rehabilitation and can be individual or collective or both with a view to an individual case.

(2) General assistance mandate. This comprises physical and psychological as well as material support for victims. This mandate has already been under way for fourmckay years and there is no link to a specific ICC case necessary.

By this second mandate both transformation and empowerment of victims are intended. It is, however, different from general development aids as there needs to be a link to an international crime; an example is the victim of sexual abuse who gave birth to a child. In such a case the Trust Fund could help developing a motherly relationship to the child, providing support and child care. It is this double mandate which gives the necessary flexibility.

1.6 Part V: The Role of Civil Society Actors

In the fifth and final part of this book the focus shifts towards victim groups as civil society actors.

The first contribution in this section by *Veit Straßner* offers a typology of victims and victim groups focussing largely on Latin American peace processes. It holds that victim groups are important, even essential for the dealing with the past; yet due to their inherent inhomogeneous goals and interests their impact is limited and not sufficient for a general coping strategy. Furthermore, it is argued, victims groups also play a tragic role, as their fundamental goals can never be realised.

Two case studies complete the compendium of contributions. At first *Christoph Sperfeldt* deals with civil society, victims, and the ECCC. As has already been seen before (see Silke Studzinsky) Cambodia is a most interesting field of research as the ECCC have—to date—the most experience of all international tribunals in integrating victims into criminal prosecution. The reliance on NGOs to organise victim participation, as is the case in Cambodia, has led to a marginalisation of the Court in this regard. NGOs have or were forced to usurp the role of the Court in integrating some 8,000 victims into the trial. Many weaknesses in the ECCC's outreach and victim participation scheme were compensated during the early years by extensive contributions made by local NGOs. It is argued that courts must take a leading role in fostering coordination and collaboration of activities relating to victim participation.

The final chapter by *Marcel Baumann* looks at nationalism and victimhood in Northern Ireland and South Africa. The author concerns himself with collective memory and takes a stand for "critical memory studies". The main aim of this critical approach, based on the premise that "forgetting" is a cultural achievement while "remembering" is only advisable in exceptional circumstances, is the identification of the groups who benefit and those who suffer from remembrance. Focussing mainly on the societies of Northern Ireland and South Africa the author argues that "memory" is a social construction and, as such, policy driven. This is why in "divided societies" a "war on memory" can be observed concerning the question of who can claim to be the "real" victim.

Certainly not all issues concerning victims, victim participation, and the impact on a postwar society could be dealt with in this volume. Nevertheless it presents the attempt to look at "victims of international crimes" from different angles and in an interdisciplinary manner. It is our intimate conviction that a one-dimensional perspective will not help us further in cases of mass victimisation and the need for social rehabilitation in dealing with past crimes and present victims.

References

Ainley K (2008) Individual agency and responsibility for atrocity. In: Jeffery R (ed) Confronting evil in international relations: ethical responses to problems of moral agency. Palgrave, Basingstoke, pp. 37–60

Aldana-Pindell R (2004) An emerging universality of justiciable victims' rights in the criminal process to curtail impunity for state-sponsored crimes. Human Rights Q 26:605–686

Baumgartner E (2008) Aspects of victim participation in the proceedings of the International Criminal Court. Int Rev Red Cross 870:409–440

Bloomfield D, Barnes T, Huyse L (2003) Reconciliation after violent conflict: a handbook. International Institute for Democracy and Electoral Assistance, Stockholm

Bonacker T (2012) Globale Opferschaft. Zum Charisma des Opfers in Transitional-Justice-Prozessen. Zeitschrift für Internationale Beziehungen 19:5–36

Bonacker T, Form W, Pfeiffer D (2011) Transitional justice and victim participation in Cambodia: a world polity perspective. Glob Soc 25:113–134

Bouris E (2007) Complex political victims. Kumarian Press, Sterling

Fassin D, Rechtman R (2009) The empire of trauma: an inquiry into the condition of victimhood. Princeton University Press, Princeton

Glasius M (2009) What is global justice and who decides? Civil society and victim responses to the International Criminal Court's first investigations. Human Rights Q 31:496–520

Henham R (2004) Conceptualising access to justice and victims' rights in international sentencing. Soc Leg Stud 13:27–55

Hinton A (2011) Introduction. Toward an anthropology of transitional justice. In: Hinton A (ed) Transitional justice global mechanisms and local realities after genocide and mass violence. Rutgers University Press, Piscataway, pp. 1–22

ICC (2002a) Rules of procedure and evidence, Official Records ICC-ASP/1/3, 3–10 Sept 2002. http://www.uclalawforum.com/media/background/general/2002-09-09_ICC_Rules_of_Procedure_and_Evidence_%28English%29.pdf. Accessed 14 August 2012

ICC (2002b) Rome Statute of the International Criminal Court, Text of the Rome Statute circulated as document A/CONF.183/9 of 17 July 1998 and corrected by procès-verbaux of 10 Nov 1998, 12 July 1999, 30 Nov 1999, 8 May 2000, 17 Jan 2001 and 16 Jan 2002. http://www.untreaty.un.org/cod/icc/statute/english/rome_statute%28e%29.pdf. Accessed 14 August 2012
Letschert R (2010) Protecting and empowering victims of international crimes through the human security concept—a new challenge for victimologists? http://www.ssrn.com/abstract=1594250. Accessed 18 November 2012
Letschert R, Groenhuijsen M (2011) Global governance and global crime—Do victims fall in between? In: Letschert R, van Dijk J (eds) The new faces of victimhood. Globalization, transnational crimes and victim rights. Springer, New York, pp. 15–40
Madlingozi T (2010) On transitional justice entrepreneurs and the production of victims. J Hum Rights Pract 2:208–228
Mallinder L (2008) Amnesty, human rights and political transitions: bridging the peace and justice divide. Hart Publishing, Oxford
McKay F (2008) Victim participation in proceedings before the International Criminal Court. http://www.wcl.american.edu/hrbrief/15/3mckay.pdf. Accessed 16 March 2012
Meron T (2006) The humanization of international law. Martinus Nijhoff, Leiden
Pham P, Vinck P, Stover E (2009) So we will never forget. A population-based survey on attitudes about social reconstruction and the Extraordinary Chambers in the Courts of Cambodia. http://www.escholarship.org/uc/item/74x685xm. Accessed 30 May 2012
Roht-Arriaza N (2006) The new landscape of transitional justice. In: Roht-Arriaza N, Mariezcurrena J (eds) Transitional justice in the twenty-first century. Cambridge University Press, Cambridge, pp. 1–16
Safferling CJM (2003) Das Opfer völkerrechtlicher Verbrechen. Zeitschrift für die gesamte Strafrechtswissenschaft 115:352–384
Safferling CJM (2010) Die Rolle des Opfers im Strafverfahren: Paradigmenwechsel im nationalen und internationalen Recht? Zeitschrift für die gesamte Strafrechtswissenschaft 122:87–116
Sikkink K (2011) The justice cascade how human rights prosecutions are changing world politics. Norton, New York
Smyth M (2003) Truth, partial truth, and irreconcilable truths: Reflections on the prospects for truth recovery in Northern Ireland. Smith Coll Stud Soc Work 73:205–225
Teitel R (2003) Transitional justice genealogy. Harv Hum Rights J 16:69–94
Tomuschat C (2009) La protection internationale des droits des victimes. In: Flauss J-F (ed) La protection internationale des droits de l'homme et les droits des victimes. Bruylant, Bruxelles, pp. 1–29
United Nations (2005) Basic principles and guidelines on the right to a remedy and reparation for victims of gross violations of international human rights law and serious violations of international humanitarian law. Adopted and proclaimed by General Assembly resolution 60/147 of 16 Dec 2005. http://www2.ohchr.org/english/law/remedy.htm. Accessed 28 November 2012
Williams BG (2008) Commemorating 'The Deporation' in post-Soviet Chechnya: the role of memorialization and collective memory in the 1994–1996 and 1999–2000 Russo-Chechen Wars. Hist Mem 12(1):101–134

Part I
Victims in International Law

Chapter 2
Victim-Oriented Perspectives: Rights and Realities

Theo van Boven

Abstract For long the plight of victims of gross violations of human rights has been ignored because of legal shortcomings, political obstacles, economic factors and the incapacity of victims themselves to assert their rights and to pursue their claims. This is a reality at the domestic scene but it is also true that international law is not victim-oriented. However, there are recent, more positive, trends in the context of the humanisation of international law. These trends are reflected in the law and practice of international tribunals and in victim-related normative prescriptions, such as in the United Nations Basic Principles and Guidelines on the Right to a Remedy and Reparation for Victims of Gross Violations of International Human Rights Law and Serious Violations of International Humanitarian Law. One of the complex issues of reparative justice is the question to what extent historical wrongs, such as serious crimes committed under colonial or authoritarian rule, continue to incur liability in legal and/or moral terms. Another complex issue is posed by the massive proportions of gross violations and serious crimes which may well require resort to collective redress and collective means of reparation. Further, the question is raised of the relationship between reparation programmes and development programmes. It is finally observed that the wrongs of the past should be squarely faced in order to prevent their repetition.

Keywords Victims • Reparation • Human rights • Transitional justice • Reparative justice • Victim-oriented

---

The author is Professor emeritus of International Law at Maastricht University (Netherlands) and former UN Special Rapporteur on torture and other cruel, inhuman or degrading treatment or punishment (2001–2004).

T. van Boven (✉)
Faculty of Law, Maastricht University, Maastricht, The Netherlands
e-mail: th.vanboven@maastrichtuniversity.nl

T. Bonacker and C. Safferling (eds.), *Victims of International Crimes: An Interdisciplinary Discourse*, DOI: 10.1007/978-90-6704-912-2_2,

2.1 Silence and Disregard

More than forty years ago UNESCO—the United Nations Educational, Scientific and Cultural Organization—published a significant work, an anthology of texts on human values brought together from all periods, all continents and a wide variety of cultures under the title *Birthright of Man.*[1] The texts were drawn from every kind, from laws to proverbs, from political studies to religious invocations, from funerary inscriptions to tales and songs. This remarkable selection of texts was to mark the twentieth anniversary of the Universal Declaration of Human Rights. The preface was written by the then Director General of UNESCO, René Maheu. I am citing a few sentences from this preface:

> The groans and cries to be heard in these pages are never uttered by the most wretched victims. These, throughout the ages, have been mute. Wherever human rights are completely trampled underfoot, silence and immobility prevail, leaving no trace in history; for history records only the words and deeds of those who are capable, to however slight a degree, of ruling their own lives, or at least trying to do so. There have been – there still are – multitudes of men, women and children who, as a result of poverty, terror or lies, have been made to forget their inherent dignity, or to give up the effort to secure recognition of that dignity by others. They are silent. The lot of the victim who complains and is heard is already a better one.[2]

When I submitted in the early 1990s of the last century, in my capacity as Special Rapporteur of a UN Sub-Commission on Human Rights, a report on the right to restitution, compensation and rehabilitation for victims of gross violations of human rights and fundamental freedoms, I chose these words of René Maheu as the prologue of my study.[3] While making in that report the case for reparative justice for victims of gross violations of human rights, and thus laying the basis for UN basic principles and guidelines on this subject, I felt bound to point to the striking gap between, on the one hand, standards and aspirations and, on the other hand, the realities of leaving victims without redress and remedies. I noted that large categories of victims remain unnoticed, unacknowledged and unattended. Domestic legal and social orders disclose *legal* shortcomings such as inadequate laws, restrictions in the definition of the scope and nature of violations, the application of statutory limitations, the operation of amnesty laws, impediments in getting access to justice and restrictive attitudes of courts. Also *political* obstacles belittle the rights and interests of victims, notably the unwillingness of authorities and society to acknowledge that serious wrongs were committed. *Economic* factors also operate to the detriment of victims in view of alleged or actual shortage of economic and financial resources. And last but not least many victims suffer from the *incapacity*,

---

[1] Hersch 1969.

[2] Maheu R, Preface, in Hersch 1969, pp. 3, 4.

[3] UN Commission on Human Rights (1993) Study concerning the right to restitution, compensation and rehabilitation for victims of gross violations of human rights and fundamental freedoms, Final report submitted by Mr Theo van Boven, Special Rapporteur, UN doc. E/CN.4/Sub.2/1993/8, 2 July 1993.

the lack of means and methods at their disposal, to advance their interests and pursue their claims.[4]

Many examples can be cited, from the past till the present, about victims of serious breaches of the law and flagrant deprivation of rights who are ignored, neglected and who find themselves in permanent and hopeless states of denial.[5] They linger in different settings and situations: armed conflicts, situations of violence including domestic violence and sexual exploitation, as objects of crime and terror, or stricken by the misery of abject poverty and deprivation. For instance, the UN Special Rapporteur on Violence against Women, portrayed not so long ago a horrific picture of sexual violence after her visit to the Democratic Republic of Congo (DRC). These abuses are widespread and committed by non-State armed groups, the armed forces of the country, the national police and increasingly also by civilians. United Nations peace keepers were also involved, either as perpetrators or in their failure to prevent and protect. The Special Rapporteur concluded that in a handful of cases courts have ordered individual perpetrators as well as the State to pay modest reparations to the victims but so far the Government had not paid any reparations to a single victim who had suffered violence at the hands of State agents.[6]

In a survey drawn up by the London-based organisation REDRESS, on the basis of a study relating to law and practice on reparation for torture victims in thirty countries, a bleak portrait of impunity and lack of reparative justice was presented. I quote:

> The overall findings indicate that laws are inadequate and/or lacking in most of the countries under scrutiny and, even where present, rarely implemented. The absence of safeguards and the impunity afforded to perpetrators of torture contribute greatly to the prevalence of torture. Impunity is the result of a lack of political will and/or the failure to overcome severe institutional deficiencies to combat torture. The outcome is that torture remains unacknowledged, victims suffer in silence and there is little, if any, official support for survivors. This is especially true for those, for example minorities, who suffer torture more frequently than other groups.[7]

The overall perspective of the position of victims remains one of marginalisation, neglect and discard. The well-known international criminal law expert Cherif Bassiouni, with whom I worked together on the right to redress and reparation, wrote some years ago: “International law is not victim-oriented”.[8] He was right and let me mention a few examples from jurisprudence and practice of two principal organs of the United Nations. It appears that for them, as well as for many politicians and

---

[4] Idem, para 124.

[5] Cohen 2001.

[6] UN Human Rights Council (2008) Report of the Special Rapporteur on Violence against Women, its causes and consequences, Yakin Ertürk, Mission to the Democratic Republic of the Congo, UN doc. A/HRC/7/6/Add.4, 28 February 2008.

[7] REDRESS (2003) Reparation for Torture; A Survey of Law and Practice in Thirty Selected Countries, p. 41.

[8] Kristjánsd6ttir 2009, p. 167.

diplomats, the rights of victims and survivors are at best an afterthought. Thus, the International Court of Justice in its Bosnia-Genocide judgment (2007) showed a narrow victim approach and considered that a declaration of wrongfulness was a sufficient form of providing adequate reparation for the harm suffered by the victims and survivors of Srebrenica.[9] Another example was the handling by the UN Security Council of the findings and recommendations of the International Commission of Inquiry on Darfur, chaired by Antonio Cassese. One of the recommendations of this Commission was that the Security Council immediately refers the situation of Darfur to the International Criminal Court (ICC), pursuant to Article 13(b) of the ICC Statute.[10] And it was indeed at that time in 2005 a major step that the Security Council, in spite of the strong misgivings of the USA regarding the ICC, did refer the Darfur situation to the Prosecutor of the ICC.[11] However, another important recommendation of the International Commission of Inquiry on Darfur, which would provide for the establishment of a Compensation Commission designed to afford reparation to the victims of the crimes, irrespective whether or not the perpetrators of such crimes had been identified, was not acted upon by the Security Council.

2.2 New Trends

In spite of an overall depressive scene of victim's neglect, internationally and domestically, we are also witnessing hopeful signs that may indicate some change of mind, a re-orientation in the *opinion iuris* and morals. This re-orientation can be attributed to a reappraisal of values in societies that went through dark periods of conflict and contempt of human dignity. Here the notion of "transitional justice" came up. It comprises—to cite the UN Secretary-General in a significant report on the rule of law and transitional justice in conflict and post-conflict societies—"the full range of processes and mechanisms associated with a society's attempt to come to terms with a legacy of large-scale abuses, in order to ensure accountability, serve justice and achieve reconciliation."[12] In pursuing the quest for justice and reconciliation a victim-centered approach was taking shape. This implied the establishment of historical records as a crucial condition for meting out justice to perpetrators and affording reparations to victims.

In fact, only in recent times, reflecting a process of "humanisation of international law",[13] victims' rights are receiving wider recognition. This is evident in international human rights instruments and in opinions of international human rights

---

[9] ICJ *Bosnia Herzegovina v Serbia and Montenegro*, Application of the Convention on the Prevention of the Crime of Genocide, Judgment 26 February 2007, I.C.J. Reports 2007, p. 43.

[10] UN Commission of Inquiry (2005) Report of the International Commission of Inquiry on Darfur (established by Security Council Resolution 1564 of 18 September 2004), UN doc. S/2005/60, 11 February 2005.

[11] Security Council Resolution 1593 of 31 March 2005.

[12] Report of the Secretary-General (2004) The Rule of Law and Transitional Justice in Conflict and Post Conflict Societies, UN doc. S/2004/616, 23 August 2004, para 8.

[13] Meron 2006.

adjudicators, notably the European and Inter-American Courts of Human Rights. In the same spirit, the Statute of the International Criminal Court opened up ways and means for victims to participate in the proceedings before the Court and to be afforded reparations.[14] Along the same line, victims' rights were recognised in transitional justice processes, particularly in a number of countries in Latin America and in Africa. In the light of these developments, attempts were made to further spell out and create mechanisms and tools for combating impunity and strengthening the normative basis of reparative justice. Thus, the UN General Assembly adopted in 2005, after a lengthy process of preparations, the Basic Principles and Guidelines on the Right to a Remedy and Reparation for Victims of Gross Violations of International Human Rights Law and Serious Violations of International Humanitarian Law (Reparation Principles).[15] In the same year, the then UN Commission on Human Rights endorsed an Updated Set of Principles for the Protection and Promotion of Human Rights through Action to Combat Impunity (Impunity Principles).[16] Further, as an expression of strong interest and commitment on the part of national and international civil society, women's rights groups and activists adopted in 2007 the Nairobi Declaration on Women's and Girls' Rights to a Remedy and Reparation.[17]

Restoring the rule of law in societies that have been suffering from serious violations of basic norms of humanity requires the building of effective domestic justice capacities. Reparation to victims, in its various modalities and in individual and collective dimensions, was to be devised and materialised within the broader transitional justice context. In this regard the Impunity Principles, just referred to, provide important guidance in mapping out (i) The Right to Know, (ii) The Right to Justice, (iii) The Right to Reparation and Guarantees of Non-Recurrence, as a basic trilogy to serve the plight of victims.[18] The Right to Know as an inalienable right of people and as a right of victims and their families includes the right to learn the truth about heinous crimes committed and circumstances and reasons leading thereto as well as what happened to victims, individually and collectively. The Right to Justice entails the duty of States to carry out prompt and impartial investigations of violations of human rights and international humanitarian law and bring to justice those responsible for serious crimes under international law. The Right to Reparation completes this trilogy of basic justice. It is a victim-oriented right involving a duty on the part of the State to provide reparation and the possibility for victims to seek redress from the perpetrator. Obviously, the right to reparation is also the main thrust of the

[14] Article 68 ICC Statute (Protection of the victims and witnesses and their participation in the proceedings), Article 75 ICC Statute (Reparations to victims).

[15] Basic Principles and Guidelines on the Right to a Remedy and Reparation for Victims of Gross Violations of International Human Rights Law and Serious Violations of International Humanitarian Law, adopted by UN General Assembly Resolution 60/147, 16 December 2005.

[16] UN Commission on Human Rights (2005) Updated Set of principles for the protection and promotion of human rights through action to combat impunity, UN Doc. E/CN.4/2005/102/Add.1, 8 February 2005.

[17] www.womensrightscoalition.org/reparation

[18] See Impunity Principles, *supra* n. 16.

Reparation Principles. It includes the following modalities: restitution, compensation, rehabilitation, satisfaction and guarantees of non-repetition and prevention.[19] It fits in this pattern that the trilogy of basic justice, consisting of the right to know the truth, the right to justice and the right to reparation, finds clear expression in one of the newest core international human rights treaties: the 2006 International Convention for the Protection of All Persons from Enforced Disappearance.[20]

An illustrative, albeit somewhat rhetorical, expression of a victim-oriented approach reflecting an evolving *opinio iuris*, are the Declaration and Programme of Action adopted in 2001 at Durban by the World Conference Against Racism, Racial Discrimination, Xenophobia and Related Intolerance.[21] There is hardly any other United Nations document that gives so much prominence to the position and the interests of categories of victims, among them Africans and people of African descent, indigenous peoples, migrants, refugees, Roma and Sinti, persons belonging to ethnic, religious and linguistic minorities. The Durban texts are also explicit as regards the provision of effective remedies, recourse, redress, and compensatory measures at national, regional and international levels.

One of the major issues of discord causing deep political, legal and moral tensions in the Durban process, was the question of crimes committed in the past at the times of colonial rule and subjugation, slavery and slave trade. Western countries with a more than dubious record in this regard strongly opposed that this issue be taken up. They were most reluctant or rather unprepared to face legal and for that matter financial consequences for wrongs committed in the past that under contemporary international law would be categorised as crimes against humanity. Against this background the then German Minister for Foreign Affairs, Joschka Fischer, spoke enlightening words at Durban:

> … At this conference we must begin with the past. In many parts of the world the pain of the persisting consequences of slavery and colonial exploitation still sits deep. Past injustice cannot be undone. But to recognise guilt, assume responsibility and face up to historical obligations may at least give back to the victims and their descendants the dignity of which they were robbed. I should like therefore to do that here and now on behalf of the Federal Republic of Germany. Our historical responsibility in particular, but also the universal principles of humanity and justice therefore demand of Europe today a special solidarity with the developing countries.[22]

---

19 See Reparation Principles, *supra* n. 15; principles 18–23.

20 International Convention for the Protection of All Persons from Enforced Disappearance, adopted by UN General Assembly Resolution 61/177 of 20 December 2006 and entered into force on 23 December 2010, Article 24.

21 United Nations Department of Public Information (2002) World Conference Against Racism, Racial Discrimination, Xenophobia and Related Intolerance; Declaration and Programme of Action. Foreword by Mary Robinson, UN High Commissioner for Human Rights and Secretary-General of the World Conference.

22 Speech by Joschka Fischer, Minister of Foreign Affairs of the Federal Republic of Germany at the World Conference against Racism, Racial Discrimination, Xenophobia and Related Intolerance in Durban on 1 September 2001, Press release German delegation, 1 September 2001.

The spirit expressed in these words finally prevailed in the texts adopted in Durban by consensus, albeit in some instances in the form of skillful diplomatic acrobatics such as in the phrase: "We acknowledge that slavery and the slave trade are a crime against humanity *and should always have been so*" (my italics, TvB).[23] The same spirit also transpired in words included in the Durban Declaration: "We acknowledge and profoundly regret the untold suffering and evils inflicted on millions of men, women and children as a result of slavery, the slave trade, the transatlantic slave trade, apartheid, genocide and past tragedies".[24]

However, the Durban texts carefully avoided language that could be interpreted as supportive of *legal* obligations towards those peoples and nations that demand reparation including compensation for the historical wrongs their ancestors had undergone and the lasting effects thereof. Thus, texts referred to *moral* obligations along the following lines: "We are aware of the moral obligations on the part of all concerned States and call upon these States to take appropriate and effective measures to halt and reverse the lasting consequences of those practices".[25] In this excursion to Durban, some elements of the statement made by the Presidency of the European Union should be noted when he clarified the position of the EU Member States. He observed that the Durban texts were political and not legal documents and thus cannot impose obligations, a liability or a right to compensation. Neither can these texts, according to the same speaker, affect the legal principle which precludes retrospective application of international law in matters of State responsibility.[26] This leads one to remind again what Cherif Bassiouni said: "International law is not victim oriented".[27] Balancing between the legal and the moral implications of justice, the EU Presidency offered that the EU acknowledged and deplored the immense suffering caused by past and contemporary forms of slavery and slave trade wherever they have occurred as well as the most reprehensible aspects of colonialism.[28]

The World Conference Against Racism, Racial Discrimination, Xenophobia and Related Intolerance was held in Durban in 2001. A major follow-up event, a review conference, was convened eight years later in Geneva but did not further advance the issue of repairing historical wrongs. On my part, I do not want to go so far as to submit that repairing historical wrongs is a precondition for actively pursuing reparative justice, at domestic and international levels, in support of those victimised by recent and present-day serious crimes under international law. Yet, as was stated in Durban, echoing the words of the German Foreign Minister,

---

[23] Supra n. 21, Declaration, para 13.

[24] Ibid., para 100.

[25] Ibid, para 102.

[26] Report of the World Conference against Racism, Racial Discrimination, Xenophobia and Related Intolerance, Durban 31 August–8 September 2001, UN doc. A/CONF.189/12, Chapter VII, para 4.

[27] Supra n. 8.

[28] Supra n. 26, Chapter VIII, para 6.

remembrance of the crimes or wrongs of the past, wherever and whenever they occurred, and unequivocal condemnation of racist tragedies and telling the truth about history are essential elements for international reconciliation and the creation of societies based on justice, equality and solidarity.[29]

2.3 Towards an Inclusive Approach to Reparative Justice

Earlier in this presentation I recalled the state of silence and disregard that determined the fate of victims of gross violations of human rights and serious crimes under international law. I noted, however, positive new trends in the normative sphere and in the institutional domain to underscore the postulates of truth, justice and reparation. I further noted legal and moral dimensions and prescriptions as mutually supportive but equally divisive in the political discourse; legal obligations as enforceable demands of justice and moral obligations as voluntary undertakings and standards of achievement. In the dialectics of the tension between law and morality the perspective of the victim needs clarification and appraisal. With the recognition that victims have a basic right to a remedy and reparation, as spelled out in the earlier mentioned UN Reparation Principles and Guidelines,[30] its implementation requires common efforts on the part of governance, civil society groups and others working with and representing victims. It is encouraging that domestic courts and international tribunals, notably the Inter-American Court and the European Court of Human Rights, demonstrate an increasing readiness to afford reparative justice to victims, in particular in cases of violation of core rights such as the right to life and the right to be protected against torture and other cruel and inhuman treatment. Judicial mechanisms, meting out retributive justice and affording reparative justice, play a crucial role in effectively serving the plight of victims, individually and collectively. Equal and effective access to these mechanisms is an essential requirement. However, the most vulnerable segments among victimised groups and persons are encountering many obstacles depriving them of access to reparative justice. This underscores the need for providing special assistance to such groups and persons.

A major problem that complicates an inclusive approach to reparative justice is, as situations of repression, conflict and abuse dramatically bear out, the massive proportions of the harm inflicted on people. Thus, the types of situations referred to the International Criminal Court—Uganda, the Democratic Republic of Congo, Darfur, the Central African Republic, Kenya, Libya—all involve systematic and large-scale attacks against civilian populations, affecting many thousands if not hundreds of thousands of women, men and children. The reparative capacities of the Court and its Trust Fund for Victims are limited as regards the demarcation of beneficiaries and the entitlements to and modalities of reparation. The ICC

[29] Supra n. 21, Declaration, para 106.

[30] Reparation Principles, supra n. 15.

also faces complexities as to actual or potential numbers of victims who are to be allowed to participate in its proceedings. The ICC as an international complementarity organ of justice is a challenging project trying to come to grips with macro and massive criminality and the victims thereof. In this respect, it faces complex problems and dilemmas of inclusion and demarcation, equally encountered at national levels.

The question arises whether in situations where mass atrocities have occurred, reparative justice may be better served by collective programmes and measures rather than by litigation and court decisions on individual claims. In fact, there are no "one size fits all" solutions to reparative justice. The Reparation Principles provide a good deal of latitude in affording reparations to victims. While perceptions and policies of reparation are mostly discussed and understood in monetary terms, the importance of non-monetary forms of reparation, often referred to as "symbolic reparations",[31] must be appreciated as means to render satisfaction. Acknowledgement of harm inflicted and suffered and attribution of responsibility for grave abuses are important steps on the path of rendering justice. However, they cannot be considered a mere substitute for restitutional measures and compensatory schemes. Further, any margins or latitudes in shaping reparative policies and programmes may never ignore the principles of non-discrimination and non-exclusion.

In situations where gross and massive violations of human rights have occurred or are occurring, often amounting to serious crimes under international law, adequate and effective reparation may well imply and require a resort to collective redress and collective means of reparation.[32] The term "collective" applies to reparative measures and types of goods and services made available by way of reparations aiming at a victimised group or community as the beneficiary. Symbolic reparations, such as public apology and setting up memorials, are also collective reparations by way of satisfaction. And the provision of material goods and services so as to restore decent living conditions, and to secure health and educational facilities, may serve as a mode of collective reparations for the benefit of victimised groups or communities. However, this collective approach is not without hazards. Thus, what is being offered by way of reparation, for instance basic social services, is to be provided anyway to all persons as an entitlement under general human rights law. Reparations are a means to achieve justice for the benefit of individual and collective victims by offering redress for harm done, but they are no substitute for meeting targets that are pursued on other grounds. This also poses the question of the relationship between reparation programmes and development programmes.[33] Both what are considered "developing" and "developed" countries may prefer for expeditious policy reasons to avoid honouring obligations arising from the duty to afford reparations. "Developing" countries facing demands for

---

[31] Office of the United Nations High Commissioner for Human Rights (2008) Rule-of-Law Tools for Post-Conflict States, Reparations Programmes, HR/PUB/08/1, New York/Geneva, p. 23.

[32] Letschert and van Boven 2011, pp. 153, 169–173.

[33] Ibid., pp. 153, 177, 178.

reparations are often inclined to argue that development *is* reparation. Similarly, "developed" countries that are called upon to repair historical wrongs, may argue that compensatory measures are not appropriate means for redressing historical injustice, but that instead greater development efforts are needed to achieve a more just and equitable distribution of wealth and resources, in particular vis-à-vis disadvantaged, deprived and systematically injured groups. It is indeed enticing to make a shift from reparation to development. It avoids complex and agonising issues of accountability as well as troublesome classifications of people, as victims and as perpetrators. Such expeditious policy considerations appear to be attractive but fail to recognise the essential notion of reparation as constituting part of a process towards peace, justice and reconciliation. They also tend to loose sight of a victim-oriented perspective that keeps faith with the plight of victims and survivors.

2.4 Concluding Remarks

For long the plight of victims has been overlooked. Most victims have been suffering in anonymity. Their numbers are running into the thousands and millions in all continents. The Rome Statute of the International Criminal Court recalls in its preamble that during the last century millions of children, women and men have been made victims of unimaginable atrocities that deeply shock the conscience of humanity.[34] Deliberate and non-deliberate ignorance, neglect, denial, refusal to acknowledge, impunity, disrespect are components of patterns of injustice and inhumanity. But there are also counter forces at work. In the foregoing, I have tried to identify some positive trends in awareness building and in law. In doing so I was mindful of all the odds, the dilemmas and the deficiencies connected with rendering justice to victims and all the vulnerable. The United Nations Basic Principles and Guidelines on the Right to a Remedy and Reparation as well as the Impunity Principles have been shaped as new tools for victim-oriented policies and practices, setting out a range of modalities of reparation in the overall context of the right to truth and the prescriptions of retributive and restorative justice. Forward-looking policies should not ignore what happened in the past so as to see to it that the wrongs of the past will not be repeated. Therefore, squarely facing the past, opening up the truth, repairing harm done, restoring and upholding the rule of law must be a standing assignment in the implementation of the global agenda of peace and justice.

[34] ICC Statute, Preamble, para 2.

References

Cohen S (2001) States of denial—knowing about atrocities and suffering. Polity Press, Cambridge

Hersch J (ed) (1969) Birthright of man, A selection of Texts. UNESCO, Paris-New York

Kristjánsdóttir E (2009) International mass claims processes and the ICC Trust Fund for Victims. In: Ferstman C, Goetz M, Stephens A (eds) Reparations for victims of genocide, war crimes and crimes against humanity. Martinus Nijhoff Publishers, Leiden-Boston, p 167

Letschert R, van Boven T (2011) Providing reparation in situations of mass victimization; key challenges involved. In: Letschert R, Haveman R, de Brouwer A, Pemberton A (eds) Victimological approaches to international crimes: Africa. Intersentia, Cambridge/Antwerp/Portland, p 153

Meron T (2006) The humanization of international law. Martinus Nijhoff Publishers, Leiden-Boston

Chapter 3
On Victims and Non-Victims: Observations from Rwanda

Gerd Hankel

Abstract This chapter addresses the concept of the victim as it is used today, based on general perception, in international law. Used in this way, the term calls for legal and moral clarity, which ensure its significance and appellative force. And precisely because of this fact, as the Rwandan case shows, the concept can easily become an instrument used to maintain political power by defining a specific image of the victims in question. As a result, there is no space for other groups of victims, a fact that has fatal consequences for restoring a sustainable peace in countries whose populations were previously deeply divided.

Keywords Rwanda • Genocide • Victims • International law • Post-conflict transition • Reconciliation • ICTR • Gacaca

3.1 Introduction

By way of introduction, I would like to open with a few comments which provide some background to my subject.

As a topic of relevance to international law and politics, the concept of human beings as victims only emerged relatively recently. During and after the First World War, the vast numbers of victims disappeared behind state policies which gave priority to the safeguarding of national pride over the horror of the large-scale death of citizens. A victim was a number, a factor in the war propaganda, and something to be used to boost the home front; he or she was not a human being who had been

---

The author is Guest Fellow at the Hamburg Institute for Social Research.

G. Hankel (✉)
Hamburg Institute for Social Research, Hamburg, Germany
e-mail: Gerd.Hankel@his-online.de

T. Bonacker and C. Safferling (eds.), *Victims of International Crimes: An Interdisciplinary Discourse*, DOI: 10.1007/978-90-6704-912-2_3,

violently deprived of a future.[1] This understanding remained unchanged during and after the Second World War. During this war, the Allies showed little or no inclination to alter their strategies to protect the lives of the populations under threat.[2] And after the war, when it came to the international prosecution of the perpetrated crimes, attention was mainly focused on the crime of war of aggression, followed by war crimes and crimes against humanity, the latter being codified in such a way that the independent wrongfulness of the crimes was considerably reduced. Hence, the crucial factor for these crimes was not the significance of the object of protection, that is the human life to be shielded against violence and force, but its connection with the war which had disrupted the peaceful relations between the states and, as the first and greatest breach of the law, made all of the other breaches possible. Without the war there would be no crimes against humanity; without the breach of the peace, that is the direct attack on the sovereignty of other states, there would be no attack on the physical or psychological integrity of the person with relevance under international law.[3] There can be no doubt that this gave rise to a kind of hierarchy in the judicial treatment of the crimes. In cases in which, based on this traditional understanding, states believed themselves to be the main victims of the National Socialist aggression, all that remained for the millions upon millions of actual victims of the war was a kind of secondary role. Above all, the particular magnitude of the wrong committed, the mass murder of Europe's Jewish population, was lost.

The fact this did not have to be the case was demonstrated some years later by Israel with the trial of Adolf Eichmann. The focus here was on the victims. Survivors were given the opportunity to report on the injustices committed against them and their families and to gain recognition as victims through the collective, painful process of remembrance. The state as the superior instance of international law was subordinated, albeit under simpler circumstances than in 1945/1946 and, alas, temporarily: the *fait accompli* of Eichmann's abduction was quickly displaced again by the powerful resistance of the states—or their equally powerful indifference—to the focus on humans and their fates as influenced by crimes.[4] This situation prevailed for many

[1] This attitude is also evidenced by Article 3 of the Hague Convention of 1907 (Convention respecting the Laws and Customs of War on Land), which stipulated the obligation of a state to pay compensation in the event of the violation of the laws of war by members of its armed forces. Claims could only be made by states, i.e. the individual was mediatised in both directions by the state and disappeared behind its sovereignty.

[2] Breitman 1999, pp. 225–234.

[3] Robert Jackson, the head of the US delegation at the London Conference in July 1945 made the following comment in reference to the punishment of the National Socialist perpetrators: "Unless we have a war connection as a basis for reaching them, I would think we have no basis for dealing with atrocities" (Schabas 2000, p. 35).

[4] The acknowledgement of the "persecution of the Jews under the Nazis" and the general desirability of criminal proceedings against Adolf Eichmann only merited a few lines in the United Nations Security Council's Resolution 138, which was adopted by the Member States on 23 June 1960 following the abduction of Eichmann from Argentina (United Nations 1960). In contrast, the states protested at length about the breach of Argentinean sovereignty and lamented the threat to world peace posed by acts of that nature.

years of the Cold War until November 1985 when a declaration of the United Nations defined the concept of the victim for the first time and called on the states to take measures to improve the situation of victims of crime or abuses of power. This was followed by a process that has endured to the present day and testifies to the internationally increasing awareness of the role and associated rights of victims, particularly in international criminal law and the protection of human rights.[5] The state is no longer the defining subject of international law by a long chalk; as the holder of rights and obligations enshrined in international law, the individual has also become an—at least partial—subject of international law. He or she can be not only a perpetrator of crimes with a responsibility under international law but also enjoys increasing rights as a victim, which are intended to assist in the restoration of his or her dignity.

The general consensus is that this development represents progress—especially as internationally active institutions exist today, like the International Criminal Court and the regional courts of human rights that elevate the new legal position of the individual from the level of the merely declaratory—as an old reproach to international law would have it—to the level of the "right", i.e. that of enforceable law. And yet, certain doubts remain. They are not in any way directed against the associated normative achievements but against their simple capacity to be instrumentalised for the purposes of power politics. This comes as less of a surprise in the context of criminal prosecution than in relation to the legal status of the victims, as in the former case it arises indirectly and accompanied by high-sounding messages that obscure the reality. In other words: Under the guise of the acknowledgement and concern for victims, the other victim groups are excluded—the exclusion being involuntarily promoted by the anaesthetising effect of the victim semantics, a fatal phenomenon for post-conflict societies in particular. Admittedly, this point may appear rather cryptic at this juncture, hence I would now like to move on to the actual subject of my contribution and illustrate the problem discussed here based on the example of Rwanda.

3.2 Background: The Genocide of 1994 and the Subsequent Wars

Between April and July 1994, a genocide that claimed approximately 800,000 lives occurred in the small central-African country of Rwanda. The vast majority of the victims were members of the Tutsi, a minority ethnic group, while the perpetrators originated from the majority Hutu group.

The genocide involved the extreme escalation of a war that had broken out on 1 October 1990. On that day, the *Front Patriotique Rwandais* (FPR, Rwandan Patriotic Front)[6] crossed the Ugandan-Rwandan border to instigate the crucial military struggle

[5] See for an overview van Boven 2012.

[6] Actually the APR (*Armée Patriotique Rwandaise*), the military arm of the FPR. However, it is usual to refer to the FPR in general even when its military wing is intended.

with Rwandan President Juvénal Habyarimana's Hutu regime. The FPR, which had been established a few years earlier in Uganda and consisted mainly of exiled Tutsi and far fewer Hutu aimed to force the return of the Tutsi, who had been driven out of and fled Rwanda, through armed attack, and also bring about a change in regime. The FPR succeeded in penetrating the country to just outside the capital Kigali on several occasions, and was only prevented from advancing further by French military aid and international pressure.[7] Acts of revenge on the part of the threatened state power were not long in coming. Thousands of people were arrested in the capital Kigali, in particular, the vast majority of whom were Tutsi; however they also included many Hutu who had been identified as supporters of the opposition. Hundreds of those arrested died in prison.

This was followed by over three years of civil war which changed Rwandan society profoundly. The radicalisation of domestic politics was accompanied by an increasingly intense desire for annihilation. For many of Rwanda's Hutu, the enemy was no longer just the Tutsi who, in the form of the FPR fighters, were aiming to force their return by military means, instead the enemy was all of the country's Tutsi who, it was increasingly believed, supported the FPR's subversive actions and attacks as a fifth column. The signal for action was given by the shooting down of an aeroplane, which was approaching Kigali airport on the evening of 6 April 1994 and whose passengers included the Rwandan President Habyarimana, his Burundian presidential counterpart and a series of high-ranking officers. Based on the conviction that Tutsi, encouraged by the ambiguous attitude of moderate Hutu politicians, were responsible for the shooting down of the aeroplane and the death of its passengers, it was decided that revenge would be taken and an ethnic Rwanda established. In order to be able to act unhindered, extreme militias—including the *Interahamwe* ("those who stand together") and soldiers from the Presidential Guard and the Rwandan army—began to kill moderate Hutu (politicians), and then all Tutsi, whether young or old, men or women, that they could get their hands on. The murder spree only ended when the FPR had completely conquered the country in mid-July 1994. Many Hutu, including the perpetrators of the genocide, had fled by then. A lot of them went to Tanzania but around two million ended up in the Province of Kivu in the Congo, at the time still known as Zaire.[8]

Following the flight of the Hutu to Zaire or the Congo (Zaire was renamed Democratic Republic of the Congo in 1997), the war was also transferred there. To retaliate for the lost war and destabilise the new regime in Kigali, Hutu extremists attacked Rwandan localities near the border from the retreat area of the refugee camps. In response, the Rwandan army carried out punishment operations against these refugee camps and caused their large-scale dissolution through the use of armed violence. Almost half of the refugees, that is around one million people, actually returned to Rwanda. These were followed by another good 400,000 in

[7] Prunier 1999, pp. 127–137; Chrétien 2003, pp. 281, 282.

[8] Autesserre 2010, pp. 141, 142, 274.

autumn 1996 when the Rwandan army intervened again in eastern Zaire. Between 600,000 and 650,000 Hutu refugees retreated further into the jungle of eastern Zaire and were pursued by Rwandan special units whose mission was to eliminate this possible threat to Rwandan security.[9] It is not known exactly how many refugees were murdered at the turn of 1996/1997 and in the early months of 1997 although it is estimated that it may have been as many as 300,000.[10]

However, the horror for the Hutu refugees, very few of whom had participated in the genocide of the Tutsi and were innocent men, women and children, did not end there. Another war started in the Congo in 1998 and once again Rwanda assumed a leading role in this conflict. Officially this war is supposed to have lasted until the end of 2002, yet, in reality, apart from some short interruptions, it is being waged to the present day in the Kivu Provinces of eastern Congo.[11] Throughout this period there have been repeated massacres of the civil population, including the Hutu refugees. Although the massacres did not always involve Rwandan soldiers, they were carried out by militias that had the support of Rwanda.

As already noted, it is impossible to state the exact number of Hutu victims. It may justifiably be assumed that they run to several hundred thousand. A report compiled by the United Nations and published in late 2010 came to the following conclusion:

> Several incidents listed in this report point to circumstances and facts from which a court could infer the intention to destroy the Hutu ethnic group in the DRC in part, if these were established beyond all reasonable doubt. The apparently systematic and widespread nature of the attacks, which targeted very large numbers of Rwandan Hutu refugees and members of the Hutu civilian population, resulting in their death, reveal a number of damning elements that, if they were proven before a competent court, could be classified as crimes of genocide.[12]

3.3 How the Crimes were Punished

I would like to begin with the crimes committed during and around the time of the genocide. A distinction should be made here between different three levels in the criminal prosecution system. At international level there is the International Criminal Tribunal for Rwanda (ICTR) in Arusha (Tanzania), which was established by resolution of the UN Security Council in November 1994. Its material jurisdiction arises from the nature of the crimes, on which it would pass judgement, that is the crime of genocide, crimes against humanity, and war crimes (contraventions of

[9] Prunier 2009, pp. 121–123, 143.

[10] Prunier 2009, p. 148.

[11] The Guardian 2012.

[12] OHCHR 2010, para 515.

the Common Article 3 of the Geneva Conventions and its Additional Protocol II). In terms of its temporal jurisdiction, the court is responsible for the punishment of the specified crimes if they were committed between 1 January and 31 December 1994. Hence, acts related to the war that took place prior this period and the subsequent Rwandan wars in the Rwandan-Zairian/Rwandan-Congolese border area are outside the jurisdiction of this court, which is intended to focus its activities on the genocide and its immediate temporal context. Up to now (September 2012), the court has passed judgement on 72 cases (of which ten resulted in acquittals) against high-ranking or influential organisers of the genocide.[13]

The next level is the national one. This level is characterised by a series of courts which pass judgement on the perpetrators of the Rwandan genocide. Courts in several European states and in the USA and Canada have also conducted, or are still conducting, proceedings against suspected Rwandan perpetrators on the basis of the principle of universal jurisdiction. However, the vast majority of cases have been tried in Rwandan courts and, moreover, by the special chambers established specifically for this purpose in 1996. Up to 2001, a total of 6,000 defendants had to answer for their actions in these chambers.[14] Their material jurisdiction was a separate statute related to Rwandan criminal law, the Genocide Convention, and the legal sources for crimes against humanity. The temporal jurisdiction of the special chambers covered the period 1 October 1990 to 31 December 1994, i.e. the entire duration of the war preceding the genocide was included.[15]

The same temporal framework and the same legal material basis applied to the Gacaca justice system, the third and final level of prosecution. Gacaca is a form of traditional justice in Rwanda which combines retributive and restorative elements and does not base its punishments on the wrongfulness of the act alone but also makes them dependent on what would serve the restoration of the social peace in the community affected by the perpetrated crime.[16] Between 18 June 2002 (the day on which the reactivated Gacaca system commenced its activities having been adapted to the requirements of criminal proceedings for genocide) and 18 June 2012 (the day on which this activity came to an end) Rwanda's approximately 10,000 Gacaca courts prosecuted almost exactly one million people and sentenced them to the provision of compensation or prison terms.[17] Approximately 15 % of defendants were acquitted.[18]

With respect to the judicial proceedings dealing with the genocide and the associated crimes, it should, therefore, be noted that the crimes were prosecuted for the

---

[13] For information on the statute of the court and the current status of procedures, see its website: www.unictr.org/Home/tabid/36/Default.aspx.

[14] Republika y'u Rwanda 2012, p. 26.

[15] On the law of 1996 see Prevent Genocide International 2000.

[16] For more detail on the background, content and aims of Rwandan Gacaca justice and its adaptation to the requirements of the punishment of crimes of genocide, see Hankel 2012.

[17] Republika y'u Rwanda 2012, p. 37.

[18] According to an interview with the General Secretary of the National Service of Gacaca Courts, published on 17 June 2012 by the Rwandan press agency ARI-RNA.

most part in Rwanda itself, although some were also prosecuted abroad due to their dimension and the related international concern. This is good news as it demonstrates the solidarity with the victims shown by both the new Republic of Rwanda and, as expressed by the initiative taken by a number of states, the international community.

However, the question arises as to what has happened regarding the punishment of the crimes committed during the war, the genocide, and the months that followed, that is in the period 1 October 1990 to 31 December 1994, that is the crimes committed not against the Tutsi but against the Hutu. I refer here to the Hutu who lived in Rwanda at that time and did not participate in the genocide. The criminal proceedings held in Rwanda clearly showed that not all Hutu were perpetrators and that there was no collective Hutu guilt.[19] Moreover, it cannot be disputed either that, according to conservative estimations, approximately 25,000–45,000 Hutu were killed by the soldiers of the FPR liberation army between April and August 1994, not in combat but in planned systematic murder campaigns.[20] To this is added a still unknown but probably equally large number of Hutu who lost their lives in the course of the preceding war and the remaining months of 1994 in circumstances that would prompt suspicions of war crimes or crimes against humanity.[21] Were criminal proceedings held for these crimes? The answer to this question is a tentative "yes", which is overshadowed, however, by a resolute "no". A tentative "yes" because a few cases were brought before Rwandan military courts against FPR soldiers who were given custodial sentences. A decisive "no" because, despite the availability of proof of the perpetration of these acts, the punishments handed down were not at all severe, because the proceedings concentrated solely on the "small fish" among the perpetrators and the systematic nature of the crimes was not taken into account as a result, and, finally, because the small number of proceedings bore no relation to the number and scale of the crimes committed.[22] The "no" is further strengthened by the fact that the ICTR in Arusha also failed to initiate any judicial enquiry into possible FPR crimes,[23] and no such enquiry took place in any other country.

---

[19] Moreover, they also showed that in the first phase of the genocide in particular many Hutu, who were identified by the organisers of the genocide as opponents and as an obstacle to the implementation of their plans, were murdered.

[20] Prunier 2009, pp. 16–20; des Forges 1999, p. 728.

[21] See the final report of the International Commission of Inquiry of March 1993 entitled "Rapport de la Commission Internationale d'Enquête sur les violations des droits de l'homme au Rwanda depuis le 1er octobre 1990", Paris, 1993, pp. 71–75; for a summary of the report see USIP 2012.

[22] See Human Rights Watch 2011 as well as Bornkamm 2012, pp. 56, 57.

[23] When Carla del Ponte, the Chief Prosecutor of the International Criminal Tribunals for the Former Yugoslavia and for Rwanda, considered initiating a judicial enquiry into suspected APR crimes in spring 2003, at the instigation of Rwanda, which had the support of Great Britain and the USA, she was stripped of responsibility for the Rwanda Tribunal. Thereafter she was only prosecutor for the International Criminal Tribunal for the Former Yugoslavia (see del Ponte and Sudetic 2009, pp. 304–314).

This observation also applies to the crimes perpetrated against Hutu in the wars of 1996/97 and of 1998–2002/2003, and in subsequent conflicts. No national court or international court of justice became active on this matter.[24] The following conclusion may, therefore, be drawn: Crimes of genocide, crimes against humanity, and war crimes which were perpetrated by Hutu against Tutsi, in particular, were and are prosecuted both nationally and internationally. Crimes against humanity and possibly also crimes of genocide and war crimes, committed at the same time by Rwandan Tutsi and their allies against Rwandan Hutu and Congolese civilians, went and still go unpunished.

3.4 What Happened for the Victims

The mere formulation of the question as to what happened for the victims assumes that people existed, who were perceived as victims, not merely in a general sense, but, in keeping with the issue under discussion, in a judicially substantiated sense. Apart from those killed at the beginning of the genocide, this excludes the Hutu as victims, for, as already demonstrated, there were no court proceedings against the perpetrators of the crimes committed *prima facie* against them (and the Hutu victims also only featured peripherally in the genocide trials). Hence, with regard to the Tutsi as victims, a distinction should be made between their role as victims in the courts and the associated consequences for their individual and collective self-perception, on the one hand, and the political and/or social commitment towards this victim group, on the other.

With regard to the Tutsi as victims in the courts: The Statute of the ICTR (i.e. Articles 14 and 21 thereof) and the additional regulations adopted in association with it, i.e. the Rules of Procedure and Evidence, assign a merely subordinate role to victims in the tribunal proceedings. They could testify as witnesses for the prosecution but they could not themselves initiate procedural acts. The prosecutors represented the victims on a quasi fiduciary basis. This was due to the provisions of the Statute, and meant that they focused on the punishment of the perpetrators and dealt with the victims in accordance with the adversarial Anglo-American legal system, in other words all too often using them for purely dramatic procedural purposes.[25] It will come as no surprise to learn that this circumstance frequently provoked strong protests on the part of the victims in the course of the hearings which dealt with various forms of sexual violence.[26] Psychological help, financial support, and protection by the court, or the organisation behind it, i.e. the United Nations, was only made available to the victims following strong criticism

[24] The criminal proceedings against former Congolese warlords held or under way at the International Criminal Court concern a different event.

[25] de Hemptinne 2009, pp. 562, 563.

[26] Nowrojee 2005.

on the part of civil society organisations. These were voluntary services and not legally actionable and, as such, they also pursued the aim of improving the image of the ICTR among the predominantly female victims in Rwanda. This was all the more important as the ICTR referred to the events in Rwanda as a genocide as early as its first judgement of 1998[27] and had, therefore, confirmed to the victims that a very great injustice had been done to them. And, given that the world had to accept the convincing arguments as to how it had failed to prevent the genocide, this legal recognition also justified the demand for material recognition.

This conclusion that must be drawn in relation to the ICTR—i.e. confirmation of the crime of genocide, recognition of the victims, generation of awareness among the global public of the wrong that had been committed—can also be drawn in relation to the numerous national criminal courts that have become active in the application of the principle of universal jurisdiction against suspected perpetrators of genocide. On behalf of all states, they demonstrated and demonstrate (another trial started in Norway in September 2012)[28] that it is the task of the international community to safeguard and strengthen its own moral basis and to hold the perpetrators of crimes of genocide to account. For the victims, this means that they acquire an international presence and status that may help them in coming to terms with their traumatic experiences, both materially and immaterially.

However, whether the wounds of the past heal faster as a result of the judicial efforts than they would have done through the mere passage of time is another question. The Rwandan Gacaca justice system claims that this is true in its case as Gacaca is a form of justice that allocates a special place to the victim. In a Gacaca trial, victims can intervene at almost any time, they can ask the witnesses questions and can formulate or reject charges,[29] in short, they can do everything that may be necessary to clarify the facts of the case. Through their direct presence at the proceedings, the victims are an important yardstick for the determination of justice and punishment.

Regarding the political and social measures undertaken in support of the genocide victims: According to Rwanda's new constitution, which was passed by a significant majority in a referendum on 26 May 2003, Rwanda sees itself as a state that wishes to learn from the genocide, and fight for its unity and against negationism, revisionism, and divisionism.[30] To this end, a series of legislative measures have been implemented, the latest in July 2008, i.e. Law No 18/2008 relating to the Punishment of the Crime of Genocide Ideology.[31] These measures were not only intended to help with ensuring that the dignity of the genocide victims is respected but also to strengthen the activities aimed at managing their concerns.

---

27 The Prosecutor vs. Jean-Paul Akayesu, Case No. ICTR-96-4-T, 2 September 1998, para 129.

28 See the report by the Rwanda News Agency of 25 September 2012.

29 On the procedure for the Gacaca trials see Ministry of Justice 2012.

30 See Preamble and Articles 9 and 13 of the Constitution of the Republic of Rwanda.

31 For the full text of the law see UNHCR 2012.

The associated provisions include, first and foremost, *Ibuka* (Remember), a victims' organisation established as early as 1995, and AVEGA (*Association des Veuves du Génocide d'Avril*, Association of the Widows of the April Genocide), an organisation also established in 1995 that works on behalf of the female survivors of the genocide, in particular. These organisations are funded by both the Rwandan state—five percent of its budget goes to aid projects for genocide survivors—and foreign aid originating from both state and private sources. The support provided by FARG (*Fonds d'Appui aux Rescapés du Génocide*), a fund for school pupils whose parents were killed in the genocide, and TIG (*Travaux d'Intérêt Général*), a voluntary service provided by prisoners sentenced for crimes of genocide who cooperated with the legal system and can hence serve a part of their punishment in the form of active restitution (construction of roads and housing, digging of fields etc.), also merit a mention in this context.

The beneficiaries of the aid are the victims of the genocide. Up to 2008, this term was more broadly defined in Rwanda than it is today. Up to 2008, the constitution, laws, and statutes of the various victim organisations referred to "the genocide" in general. Following a change to the Constitution, this term was replaced by "genocide of the Tutsi",[32] and resulted in a stronger focus on the Tutsi as the actual victims of the genocide. The fact that an unknown but without doubt significant number of Hutu were killed in the early days of the genocide was relegated to the outer limits of memory and, ultimately, the realm of the forgotten. Apart from very few exceptions, which do not follow any identifiable rule, the national and international aid programmes, from the financing of schooling to the creation of places of commemoration, only benefit members of the Tutsi population.

3.5 What are the Consequences of the One-Sided Victim Perception for Rwandan Society?

Rwanda's new constitution no longer differentiates between Hutu and Tutsi. The equality of all Rwandans in terms of their rights and obligations is referred to in several of its articles. Article 11, for example, states that: "All Rwandans are born and remain free and equal in rights and duties. Discrimination of whatever kind based on, inter alia, ethnic origin, tribe, clan, colour [...] is prohibited and punishable by law."[33]

During the genocide proceedings and above all during the once or twice-weekly Gacaca trials, the terms Hutu and Tutsi were a permanent presence. For obvious reasons, no attempt to come to terms with the past judicially would be possible without the naming of the perpetrators and victims. Therefore, we have the "We are all Rwandans" flag-waving, on the one hand, and the division into

[32] See Official Gazette of the Republic of Rwanda 2008.

[33] Republic of Rwanda Parliament 2012, p. 10.

Hutu and Tutsi, on the other. The hope was that the court proceedings would generate a cathartic effect that would make the feeling of unity expressed in the statement "We are all Rwandans" possible. The reality was often very different, however. In early 2003, for example, I was in Bisesero, a large hill in western Rwanda, close to which several huts and a street village are located. When I reached the foot of the hill, on which a memorial to the genocide had been erected, three men approached me and offered to tell me the story of the genocide as it had unfolded in Bisesero. All three were Tutsi and had survived the genocide in Bisesero. Having listened to their impressive stories, I asked them how they got along with their Hutu neighbours at that point, not even ten years after the genocide. After all, the houses within view of the hill must also have been inhabited at the time when they feared for their lives on the hill. They replied without hesitation that life with the Hutu was completely unproblematic. People were trying to overcome the challenges posed by everyday life together. The poverty was the same everywhere and because many Tutsi women had been killed in the genocide, Tutsi men were now marrying Hutu women. As a result, the two groups were coming together again.

Five years later, in spring 2008, when the Gacaca justice system was active throughout the country, I was in Bisesero again. By coincidence I met two of the three genocide survivors again. This time their account of their situation was very different: They reported that they found it difficult to have to live alongside the perpetrators of the genocide. Many perpetrators had been shielded by the silence of the others and the confessions had not been honest. An atmosphere of widespread distrust prevailed and there were almost no more marriages between Hutu and Tutsi.

What had happened in the meantime? What explanation was there for the altered perception of the co-existence of the two groups? The obvious explanation was that the intensive preoccupation with the dark sides of the past had raised questions, to which controversial answers were being found and which could hence give rise to tensions or exacerbate existing ones. In this case, it would have been the task of the state, the courts, or the local administration to help smooth over these tensions. This was precisely what failed to happen. Instead, the organs of the state and state policy themselves were the cause of the tensions or, to be more precise, the divisions within society. As this was what occurred, not only in Bisesero but in many locations where Gacaca trials had taken place.[34] The reason for this is easy to identify: The dichotomous perpetrator-victim perception appears to be apart of the self-understanding of the new Rwanda. The perpetrators were the Hutu and the victims the Tutsi, and the self-understanding is formulated and implemented in accordance with this exclusiveness. However, the vast majority of Rwandans cannot identify themselves in this exclusiveness. Their experiences of war and genocide are absent from the official narrative. From the campaign carried out in the country at the beginning of the legal processing of the genocide, which

[34] See also Rettig 2011, pp. 200–204.

used the slogan "Truth heals" and encouraged Rwandans up and down the country to believe that "If we admit what we have done, if we say what we have seen, we close our wounds", just one version of the truth has remained, the one that was promoted by the new rulers.

It is obvious that the crimes of genocide perpetrated against the Tutsi cannot be equated with those suffered by the Hutu. With all due reservations regarding any form of death arithmetic, the fact remains that far more Tutsi than Hutu were killed during the genocide and the ensuing wars. However, to conclude from this that the Hutu victims are quasi inexistent involves *de facto* the acknowledgement that individual suffering based on the form of perpetration of the underlying crime is significant (in the case of genocide) and insignificant (in the case of crimes against humanity). And it means contributing to something that should actually be avoided, that is the equation of the victims. To refuse victims the victim status generally and inevitably causes them to compare and compensate, to insist on their own victim status and to reject or minimalise the suffering presented as dominant.[35] To put it another way, what happens is the exact opposite to the course of events desired by those in power in Rwanda today: The gap between Hutu and Tutsi gets bigger. Reinforced by the Hutu's experience of disadvantages in profession life, school, and education, the victim discourse, which is omnipresent in Rwanda and refers exclusively to the Tutsi, has long become a discourse that no longer reaches the vast majority of Rwandans.

3.6 Concluding Reflections

In 1985 and again in 2005 the General Assembly of the United Nations adopted a resolution in which the term "victims" was defined as follows:

> [...] victims are persons who individually or collectively suffered harm, including physical or mental injury, emotional suffering, economic loss or substantial impairment of their fundamental rights, through acts or omissions that constitute gross violations of international human rights law, or serious violations of international humanitarian law. Where appropriate, and in accordance with domestic law, the term 'victim' also includes the immediate family or dependants of the direct victim and persons who have suffered harm in intervening to assist victims in distress or to prevent victimisation.
>
> A person shall be considered a victim regardless of whether the perpetrator of the violation is identified, apprehended, prosecuted, or convicted and regardless of the familial relationship between the perpetrator and the victim.[36]

[35] See, for example, Roht-Arriaza 2006 as well as Hazan 2009.

[36] Paragraphs 1 and 2 of the Declaration of Basic Principles of Justice for Victims of Crime and Abuse of Power, UNGA Resolution 40/34 of 29 November 1985; paras 8 and 9 of the Basic Principles and Guidelines on the Right to a Remedy and Reparation for Victims of Gross Violations of International Human Rights Law and Serious Violations of International Humanitarian Law, UNGA Resolution 60/147 of 16 December 2005.

Hence, a victim is a victim. His or her capacity as such does not depend on the nature of the crime. However, the definition serves not only the purpose of substantive clarification, it also serves judicial-political purposes by demanding that it be considered specifically in post-conflict situations. This is not a problem when the distinction between perpetrators and victims is clear, either because there is only one group of victims or it is so big that victims in the group generally designated as perpetrators carry no weight. If neither of these cases apply, and if only one victim group is recognised, sooner or later a potentially conflictive situation can arise. This can be seen particularly clearly in Rwanda. Perpetrators and victims live there in one country and although, generally speaking, there are many victims among the perpetrators and there are a considerable number of perpetrators among the victims, officially there is only one perpetrator group, the Hutu, and one victim group, the genocide victims among the Tutsi. Shored up by the widespread perception of genocide as the "crime of crimes",[37] an international narrative of the events in Rwanda has emerged that contradicts the historical experience of most people in the country itself. The law that was developed for the punishment of the most serious mass crimes and is internationally recognised, was and is being abused for power-political reasons. And, fatally, it is the ICTR—i.e. a punishment body that is supposed to be a voice representing all of humanity—that made a crucial contribution to this situation. Although, according to the Preamble to its Statute it was intended to contribute "to national reconciliation",[38] it refrained, and refrains to the present day, from instigating a judicial enquiry into members of the current Rwandan nomenclature in politics and the military.

It may be assumed that behind this stance on the part of the ICTR lies political pressure from Great Britain and the USA, which are known to recognise Rwanda as a useful regional power.[39] This regional power must be kept stable; the minutest threat of fragility must be avoided. The subsequently openly practised mixture of law and politics, which was naturally willingly continued in Rwanda, has had a contrary effect: The one-sided judicial handling of the past has given rise to a social fragility that is steadily increasing. The rapprochement between the Hutu and Tutsi at individual level, which mainly arose through the Gacaca justice system, is being thwarted by the political tabooing of crimes that is the constant trigger of collective outrage and even fury among the Hutu. "Le baptême de l'Hutu est la prison" ("The Hutu's baptism is prison") is the bitter commentary frequently heard in reference to the regular outcome of a violation of this taboo. The taboo is maintained using draconian means and contradictory opinions are quickly denounced as the spreading of

---

[37] For the discussion on this see Schabas 2000, p. 9.

[38] See Resolution 955 of the United Nations Security Council (8 November 1994) in which the Security Council expresses its conviction "that in the particular circumstances of Rwanda, the prosecution of persons responsible for serious violations of international humanitarian law would enable this aim to be achieved and would contribute to the process of national reconciliation and to the restoration and maintenance of peace" (United Nations 1994).

[39] Prunier 2009, pp. 338–346; Zorbas 2011.

genocidal ideology.[40] In this way, the injustice towards the perpetrator group leads to the suppression of the entire Rwandan population. The media are under state control; political rights and civil liberties have been restricted for years to the extent that Rwanda is repeatedly classified as "not free".[41] Silence has spread over the country like a kind of mildew which renders serious open debate about the recent pasts impossible. What is expected is obedience and the absence of critical reflection and, therefore, precisely what resulted in the large-scale participation in the genocide in 1994. This is not a good sign in times, in which an increasingly radical counter-narrative is emerging in response to the official one, and raises a serious question as to the adequacy of a concept of genocide that has not ceased to cause division almost 20 years after the event.

References

Autesserre S (2010) The trouble with the Congo. Local violence and the failure of international peacebuilding. Cambridge University Press, Cambridge

Bornkamm PC (2012) Rwanda's Gacaca Courts. Between retribution and reparation. Oxford University Press, Oxford

Breitman R (1999) Official secrets—what the Nazis planned, what the British and Americans knew. Hill & Wang, New York

Chrétien J-P (2003) L'Afrique des grands lacs. Flammarion, Paris

de Hemptinne J (2009) Victims' participation in international proceedings. In: Cassese A (ed) The Oxford companion to international criminal justice. Oxford University Press, Oxford, pp. 562–564

del Ponte C, Sudetic C (2009) Im Namen der Anklage. Meine Jagd auf Kriegsverbrecher und die Suche nach Gerechtigkeit. Fischer, Frankfurt am Main

des Forges A (1999) Leave none to tell the story. Genocide in Rwanda. Human Rights Watch, New York

Hankel G (2012) Gacaca courts. In: Wolfrum R (ed) The Max Planck encyclopedia of public international law, vol 4. Oxford University Press, Oxford, pp. 279–284

Hazan P (2009) Reconciliation. In: Chetail V (ed) Post-conflict peacebuilding. A Lexicon. Oxford University Press, Oxford, pp. 256–267

Human Rights Watch (2011) Justice compromised. Selective justice and the failure to address Rwandan patriotic front crimes, 31 May 2011 http://www.hrw.org/node/99177/section/11. Accessed 28 Oct 2012

Ministry of Justice (2012) Organic Law N° 16/2004 of 19/6/2004 establishing the organisation, competence and functioning of Gacaca Courts charged with prosecuting and trying the perpetrators of the crime of genocide and other crimes against humanity, committed between 1 Oct 1990 and 31 Dec 1994. http://www.amategeko.net/display_rubrique.php?ActDo=ShowArt&Information_ID=1262&Parent_ID=30692916&type=public&Langue_ID=An&rubID=30692975#30692975. Accessed 28 Oct 2012

Nowrojee B (2005) "Your justice is too slow": will the ICTR fail Rwanda's rape victims? Occasional Paper 10 of the United Nations Research Institute for Social Development, Nov 2005. http://www.unrisd.org/80256B3C005BCCF9/(httpAuxPages)/56FE32D5C0F6DCE9C125710F0045D89F/$file/OP10%20Web.pdf. Accessed 28 Oct 2012

[40] Waldorf 2011.

[41] See www.freedomhouse.org/country/rwanda.

Official Gazette of the Republic of Rwanda (2008) Amendment of the Constitution, 13 Aug 2008. http://www.ddata.over-blog.com/xxxyyy/1/35/48/78/Rwanda/Rwanda-R-vision-2008.rtf. Accessed 28 Oct 2012

OHCHR (2010) Report of the Mapping Exercise documenting the most serious violations of human rights and international humanitarian law committed within the territory of the Democratic Republic of the Congo between March 1993 and June 2003 (Aug 2010). http://www.ohchr.org/Documents/Countries/ZR/DRC_MAPPING_REPORT_FINAL_EN.pdf. Accessed 28 Oct 2012

Prevent Genocide International (2000) Organic Law No. 08/96 of August 30, 1996 on the Organization of Prosecutions for Offences constituting the Crime of Genocide or Crimes against Humanity committed since 1 Oct 1990. http://www.preventgenocide.org/law/domestic/rwanda.htm. Accessed 28 Oct 2012

Prunier G (1999) Rwanda: le génocide. Dagorno, Paris

Prunier G (2009) From genocide to continental war: the 'Congolese' conflict and the crisis of contemporary Africa. Hurst, London

Republic of Rwanda Parliament (2012) Rwandan constitution. http://www.rwandaparliament.gov.rw/parliament/DF_DocumentViewer.aspx?id=73b3974e-12e8-497a-bb0b-e3411596deef. Accessed 28 Oct 2012

Republika y'u Rwanda (2012) National service of Gacaca Courts. Summary of the report presented at the closing of the Gacaca courts activities. Republika y'u Rwanda, Kigali

Rettig M (2011) The Sovu trials: the impact of genocide justice on one community. In: Strauss S, Waldorf L (eds) Remaking Rwanda. State building and human rights after mass violence. University of Wisconsin Press, Madison, pp. 194–209

Roht-Arriaza N (2006) The new landscape of transitional justice. In: Roht-Arriaza N, Mariezcurrena J (eds) Transitional justice in the twenty-first century. Cambridge University Press, Cambridge, pp. 1–16

Schabas WA (2000) Genocide in international law. Cambridge University Press, Cambridge

The Guardian (2012) Congo rebels capture key towns in east as conflict escalates, 9 July 2012. http://www.guardian.co.uk/world/2012/jul/09/congo-rebels-capture-key-towns-conflict. Accessed 28 Oct 2012

UNHRC (2012) Law N° 18/2008 of 23/07/2008 relating to the punishment of the crime of genocide ideology. http://www.unhcr.org/refworld/pdfid/4acc9a4e2.pdf. Accessed 28 Oct 2012

United Nations (1960) Resolution 138 (1960) of 23 June 1960. http://www.unhcr.org/refworld/country,,,RESOLUTION,ISR,,3b00f1cc74,0.html. Accessed 28 Oct 2012

United Nations (1994) Resolution 955 (1994), Adopted by the Security Council at its 3453rd meeting, on 8 Nov 1994. http://www.un.org/ga/search/view_doc.asp?symbol=S/RES/955%281994%29. Accessed 28 Oct 2012

USIP (2012) Commission of inquiry: Rwanda 93. http://www.usip.org/publications/commission-inquiry-rwanda-93. Accessed 28 Oct 2012

van Boven T (2012) Victim's rights. In: Wolfrum R (ed) The Max Planck encyclopedia of public international law, vol 10. Oxford University Press, Oxford, pp. 671–678

Waldorf L (2011) Instrumentalizing genocide: the RPF's campaign against "genocide ideology". In: Strauss S, Waldorf L (eds) Remaking Rwanda. State building and human rights after mass violence. University of Wisconsin Press, Madison, pp. 48–66

Zorbas E (2011) Aid dependence and policy independence. Explaining the Rwandan Paradox. In: Strauss S, Waldorf L (eds) Remaking Rwanda. State building and human rights after mass violence. University of Wisconsin Press, Madison, pp. 103–117

Part II
Definition of Victims

Chapter 4
The Status of Victims Under the Rome Statute of the International Criminal Court

Michael J. Kelly

Abstract This chapter analysis the three traditional foci of victim status under international criminal law: participation, protection, and reparation. Whereas, both the ICTY and ICTR statutes largely ignored victim issues, the Rome Statute of the ICC specifically addresses the interests of victims in cases against their persecutors. However, as a new body with little experience to draw upon, the process of bringing victims into the proceedings in a meaningful way is still under development. As a threshold matter, a person must meet the definition of "victim" under Rule 85 RPE ICC before they can qualify to participate. The author explores the parameters of "victimhood" by placing the definition in a variety of contexts—especially with respect to other rights and obligations victims may have under the Rome Statute. Victim safety is also addressed as well as the new Victim and Witness Unit within the ICC bureaucracy. With respect to reparations for victims, the author considers the options of restitution, compensation, and rehabilitation. To date the Trust Fund for Victims has not resolved key operational questions on reparations concerning the seizure and management of defendant assets, investment, return upon acquittal, and disbursement to qualified victims upon conviction.

Keywords Victim status • Participation • Protection • Reparation • Attaining victim status • Representation of victims • Personal interests • Preclusion • Victim and Witness Unit • Trust Fund for Victims

---

The author is Professor of Law and Associate Dean for Faculty Research & International Programs, Creighton University School of Law. B.A., J.D., Indiana University; LL.M., Georgetown University. The author wishes to thank his research assistant, Kathleen Pitts, for her diligent efforts in the research, preparation and initial drafting of this article.

M. J. Kelly (✉)
Creighton University School of Law, Creighton, Omaha, NE 68102, USA
e-mail: MichaelKelly@creighton.edu

T. Bonacker and C. Safferling (eds.), *Victims of International Crimes: An Interdisciplinary Discourse*, DOI: 10.1007/978-90-6704-912-2_4,

"Vic/tim" 2(a)(1) : One that is injured, destroyed, or sacrificed.... (2): one that is subjected to oppression, hardship, or mistreatment... (Merrium Webster Dictionary (2012), Encyclopædia Brittanica.)

4.1 Introduction

There is a symbiotic relationship between victims and international criminal tribunals. The courts are created to bring perpetrators of atrocities to justice. Surviving victims are witnesses. And a court needs witnesses to properly hear a criminal case. As Daniela Kravetz, a prosecutor at the International Criminal Tribunal for the former Yugoslavia (ICTY) noted at this Victims Conference, "At the ICTY, the vast majority of witnesses are themselves victims." The new International Criminal Court (ICC) created in 2002 by the Rome Statute is similarly situated. But this is not a new dynamic.

Justice Robert Jackson famously acknowledged the power of victim testimony during the trial of major Nazi war criminals at Nuremberg in 1945 before the International Military Tribunal (IMT). After stultifying the tribunal with thousands of pages of documentary evidence for weeks on end, Jackson's case was in jeopardy. He made the determination to switch to victim/witness testimony and electrified the court. International criminal tribunals since Nuremberg have followed that pattern.

But marshalling victims into witnesses is fraught with substantive and procedural difficulty. Vetting victims is a clearly subjective exercise on the part of the prosecution. Some victims may be selected to participate in the trial by virtue of their presentation abilities, even though they may not have suffered to the degree of other, less compelling, story-tellers. But there is an objective component as well. This side of the equation has two aspects—quantitative and qualitative.

In defining who is a victim (which is the key to this entire exercise), one encounters the quantitative aspect first. How many victims are enough for an atrocity to qualify as a crime under the jurisdiction of the ICC? What is the threshold number for each of the crimes: genocide, war crimes and crimes against humanity? Does this threshold number shift for distinct charges within the crime—for example, complicity to genocide versus bringing about conditions of life calculated to destroy the population in whole or in part? And which victims get counted—living or dead, or both?

Qualitatively, the matter becomes even more complex. Does victimhood become defined by the measure of the harm suffered—loss of life, loss of property, loss of family or loss of livelihood? Or is victimhood properly measured by typology of crime committed—raped victims, tortured victims, maimed victims, killed victims, illegally detained victims or forcibly relocated victims? In other words, does the gravity of harm suffered matter in a comparative sense? If this is so, then may genocide victims be considered greater victims than crimes against humanity victims?

May rape victims be considered greater victims that those who lost property? Does an empirical stratification of victims in a given conflict or atrocity correlate to a similar stratification of crimes or criminal acts within a crime? Should it?

This chapter, indeed this conference, cannot begin to consider or answer such questions in the vacuum of the academy. However, it can seek to explain the framework within which courts, states and actors on the international stage may consider such questions. The three foci of comprehensive justice schemes are (1) retributive justice, (2) reparative justice and (3) restorative justice. Retributive justice entails criminal law. Reparative justice entails victim compensation. Restorative justice entails societal restoration. International criminal law is a young discipline that has developed sporadically. It has really only dealt with retributive justice. But the adoption of the Rome Statute in 1999 moved this field squarely into the second area (and possibly a bit into the third) that requires a more considered view of victims.

The roles victims play in the International Criminal Court (ICC) are novel within the realm of international criminal proceedings. With a growing international human rights movement and the desire to promote restorative justice, the drafters of the Rome Statute established a scheme that contemplates remedies, participation rights and protections for victims whose cases come before the ICC. Earlier criminal tribunals, such as those for the former Yugoslavia and Rwanda, downplayed the importance of victim participation and reparation. It was observed that this disregard of victims' rights may have been more harmful to the process of resolving those conflicts.[1]

With that in mind, the ICC affords victims' different rights that can be grouped into three different components: participation, protection and reparation. Each will be explored in depth, with overviews of the Rome Statute's victim policies, procedural aspects of victims' rights and how the reparation scheme has been established by the Court and Assembly of States Parties through the Trust Fund for Victims.

4.2 Participation in Court Proceedings

Looking to prior criminal tribunals such as the International Criminal Tribunal for the former Yugoslavia (ICTY) and the International Criminal Tribunal for Rwanda (ICTR), the drafters of the Rome Statute were aware of the exclusion of victims in these courts and wanted to grant ICC victims participatory rights in proceedings.[2] Both the ICTY and ICTR were criticised for excluding victims, mostly because the lack of participation left a negative impression with the victims of these courts' motives, and frustrated the objectives of restoring peace and justice to the affected communities.[3] In contrast, the Rome Statute and implementing regulations of the ICC

[1] Kaoutzanis 2010, p. 116.

[2] Trumbull IV 2008, p. 788.

[3] Id.

give individuals or organisations who qualify as victims the ability to participate in almost every stage of ICC proceedings.[4] The drafters were cautious, however, as they wanted victims to take part but also wanted to ensure that the Court would still be able to do its job of enforcing the law and affording defendants' proper due process rights.[5]

4.2.1 Attaining Victim Status

Before the ICC can allow an individual to participate as a victim in a trial, the individual must be certified as a victim by meeting the criteria set out in the Rome Statute and in the Court's Rules of Procedure and Evidence. The definition of who is considered a victim is outlined in Rule 85 of the Rules of Procedure and Evidence; the ICC allows victims to be either (1) natural persons who have suffered harm resulting from crimes committed within the jurisdiction of the Court, or (2) institutions and organisations that have had property harmed that has been used for religious, educational, arts or science or charitable purposes, or any historic monuments, hospitals, or places or objects used for humanitarian purposes.[6] If an individual or organisation is claiming victim status under this definition, then the individual or organisation must file a written application with the ICC's Registry, while the case for which the individual wishes to apply for victim status is before the Pre-Trial Chamber (PTC).[7]

After the application has been filed, the information is forwarded to the PTC that is overseeing the case.[8] The PTC is the body of the ICC that officially grants or denies victim status, and begins the determination process by deciding if the applicant individual or organisation applying meets the definition of victim laid out in Rule 85.[9] The PTC will also determine whether the victim has provided appropriate identification to ensure that the victim is who he or she claims to be.[10] The Court has been fairly flexible as to what types of identification are acceptable, and has held that a lack of proper identification was an "insufficient reason" for dismissing a victim's application.[11]

If the applicant meets definitional criteria and provides sufficient identification, the PTC then must determine whether the crime the victim is claiming occurred falls under the Court's jurisdiction.[12] The crime alleged must be one identified as a

---

[4] Id. at p. 791.

[5] SaCouto and Cleary 2008, p. 83.

[6] Rule 85(a); Rule 85(b).

[7] Kaoutzanis 2010, p. 119.

[8] Id.

[9] Id.

[10] Id. at p. 120.

[11] Id. at p. 121.

[12] Id.

crime under the Rome Statute, occur post July 2002 when the Rome Statute was ratified, and must have occurred within the territory of States that are members of the ICC.[13] The PTC also has to determine if the victim suffered any harm; the ICC defines harm as including any "personal harm of a material, physical, or psychological nature" and applies this standard broadly.[14] If the crime alleged meets the jurisdictional requirements and the PTC determines that a harm has occurred, then the PTC has to determine that the harm has a causal connection to the alleged crime before the Court.[15] In various rulings by the PTC, it has been held that this causal link "is satisfied if the spatial and temporal circumstances surrounding the appearance of the harm and the occurrence of the incident seem to overlap, or at least appear compatible" and affects the personal interests of the victim.[16] If the victim's application does not meet any of these requirements set out above, then the Court may deny the application.[17]

Scholars have commented that the current victim certification process in place may defeat some of the objectives the drafters of the Rome Statute set out to accomplish. One scholar points out that the certification process is long and complicated, causing delays that could possibly lead to violations of defendants' due process rights and impact the overall effectiveness of the Court.[18] It has also been noted that due to the massive nature of most crimes that come before the ICC, the number of potential victims is also extensive.[19] Most victims do not or will not file an application to the ICC for victim status for a variety of reasons, including the lack of awareness amongst victims of the ICC's process or victims' lack of resources.[20] If victims do not formally apply for victim status, this limits any relief these individuals could potentially receive, as the ICC can only award reparations

---

[13] Id.

[14] Id., ICC *Prosecutor vMuthauraet al.*, PTC, ICC-01/09-02/11-267, 26 August 2011, Decision on Victims' Participation at the Confirmation of Charges Hearing and in the Related Proceedings, para 64.

[15] Kaoutzanis, supra note 5; ICC *Prosecutor vMuthauraet al.*, PTC, ICC-01/09-02/11-267, 26 August 2011, Decision on Victims' Participation at the Confirmation of Charges Hearing and in the Related Proceedings, para 60; ICC *Prosecutor v Lubanga,* AC, ICC-01/04-01/06-1432 OA 9 OA 10, 11 July 2008, Judgment on the appeals of The Prosecutor and The Defence against Trial Chamber I's Decision on Victims' Participation of 18 January 2008, para 62.

[16] Kaoutzanis, supra note 5, at p. 122; ICC *Situation in Uganda*, PTC, ICC-02/04-101, 10 August 2007, Decision on victims' applications for participation a/0010/06, a/0064/06 to a/0070/06, a/0081/06 to a/0104/06 and a/0111/06 to a/0127/06, paras 13, 14; Bemba, ICC-01/05-01/08-320, PTC III, para 75; Kony et al. ICC-02/04-01/05-252, para 14.

[17] Rule 89; ICC *Prosecutor v Bemba*, PTC, ICC-01/05-01/08-320, 12 December 2008, Fourth Decision on Victims' Participation, paras 31, 75.

[18] Kaoutzanis 2010, p. 128.

[19] ICC *Prosecutor v Bemba,* TC, ICC-01/05-01/08-1590-Corr, 21 July 2011, Decision on 47 applications by victims to participate in the proceedings.

[20] Id. at pp. 131–133.

to those whom the ICC has certified.[21] One scholar has suggested that the ICC should look to using a class action certification process instead of one that is focused on an individual basis to allow for more victims to participate and receive benefits from the process.[22]

4.2.2 Representation of Victims

Once an individual or organisation[23] has been certified as a victim, he or she is then entitled to representation before the Court. First, victims have the option of selecting their own representation.[24] If there is a large group of victims who apply and are certified by the Court, the Court may ask that they be represented as a group and have a common representative either selected by the Court or chosen by the victim group.[25] If the victim or group of victims is unable to fund their representative, the representative may be able to receive financial assistance from the Registry.[26]

After representation has been assigned, the legal representatives may participate in and attend proceedings of the Court, although the Court does maintain discretion to determine whether that participation is limited to only observations or written submissions.[27] The victims' representation may question witnesses, although this questioning is subject to approval by the Court. The Court has discretion to limit what victim representatives can and cannot do throughout most proceedings, although the limitations on victim participation in reparation proceedings are significantly less extensive.[28] Victims and their representatives are also entitled to notifications, including notifications that prosecutors will no longer continue an investigation or a prosecution, especially in cases where victims have already participated.[29] They are also entitled to notifications regarding dates and

---

[21] Id. at pp. 133, 134.

[22] Id. at p. 135.

[23] ICC *Prosecutor v Bemba*, PTC, ICC-01/05-01/08-320, 12 December 2008, Fourth Decision on Victims' Participation, para 53; ICC *Prosecutor v Lubanga*, TC, ICC-01/04-01/06-1119, 18 January 2008, Decision on victims' participation, para 89.

[24] Rule 90(1).

[25] Rule 90(2).

[26] Rule 90(4).

[27] Rule 91(2).

[28] Rule 91(3); Rule 91(4).

[29] Rule 92(2); ICC *Prosecutor v Muthauraet al.*, PTC, ICC-01/09-02/11-23, 30 March 2011, First Decision on Victims' Participation in the Case, para 23; ICC *Prosecutor v Lubanga*, TC, ICC-01/04-01/06-1211, 6 March 2008, paras 30–41; ICC *Prosecutor v Banda and Jerbo,* TC, ICC-02/05-03/09-231-Corr, 3 January 2012, Request for extension of time to submit complete applications, para 28.

times of Court proceedings and any decisions made by the Court in those proceedings.[30]

In September 2005, pursuant to Regulation 81 of the Regulations of the Court and to assist in implementing successful victim participation and representation, the Office for Public Counsel for Victims (OPCV) was established. This Office is an independent body whose job is to assist and support the legal representatives of victims before the Court.[31] Members of the Office can be appointed as legal representatives and participate directly in proceedings, in addition to providing legal research and advice to the legal representatives of victims.[32] The OPCV has developed into an Office that acts as the "go-between" for victims, their representatives and the Court, in addition to OPCV members serving as representatives for "underrepresented victims".[33]

4.2.3 Article 68(3): Victim Participation in Proceedings

Perhaps the most significant and at times, most ambiguous, article governing victim participation under the Rome Statute is Article 68(3):

> Where the personal interests of the victims are affected, the Court shall permit their views and concerns to be presented and considered at stages of the proceedings determined to be appropriate by the Court and in a manner which is not prejudicial to or inconsistent with the rights of the accused and a fair and impartial trial. Rome Statute, Art. 68(3).

Scholars have called this article "frustratingly vague", as it uses very general terms and provides no definition or guidance for interpretation.[34] The lack of direction Article 68(3) gives readers and the lack of implementing language in the Rules of Evidence and Procedure has created conflict amongst parties as to when and how victims should be able to participate.[35] Victims' representatives have asked that the Court include victims as often as possible, pushing against the objections to participation from both prosecutors and defense.[36] Leaving the interpretation of this article and the parameters of victim participation in the ICC to the Court, the Court has favoured the victims and their representatives by allowing

---

[30] Rule 93.

[31] Reg. of the Court, 81.

[32] International Criminal Court 2010, pp. 4–6.

[33] ICC *Prosecutor v Muthaura et al.*, PTC, ICC-01/09-02/11-23, 30 March 2011, First Decision on Victims' Participation in the Case, para 23; see also as to the role of the Office, ICC *Prosecutor v Lubanga*, TC, ICC-01/04-01/06-1211, 6 March 2008, paras 30–41; ICC *Prosecutor v Banda and Jerbo,* TC, ICC-02/05-03/09-231-Corr, 3 January 2012, Request for extension of time to submit complete applications, para 28.

[34] Trumbull 2008, pp. 793, 794.

[35] Pena 2010, p. 504.

[36] Trumbull 2008, p. 794.

victim participation in most proceedings and by interpreting most of the terms used in 68(3) broadly.[37]

4.2.3.1 Personal Interests

Despite its ambiguities, Article 68(3) defines how and when victims can participate in proceedings and leaves a great deal of discretion to the Court to decide how the article will be applied. The Court has had to issue rulings on almost every key phrase in Article 68(3) and institute specific rights that attach to victim participation. First, the Court ruled on the meaning of the first phrase of Article 68(3) "when the personal interests of the victims are affected", and has interpreted this phrase broadly in favour of victim participation.[38] Both Pre-Trial Chambers have ruled that personal interest requirements are met when "a victim applies for participation in proceedings following the issuance of a warrant of arrest or of a summons to appear for one or more individuals" and personal interests encompass "receiving reparations, expressing views and concerns, verifying particular facts, establishing the truth, protecting their dignity and ensuring their safety."[39] The Trial Chamber has upheld these broad definitions, and scholars have suggested that these interpretations "have effectively rendered the personal interest requirement superfluous."[40]

4.2.3.2 Proceedings

One of the first issues to be contested under Article 68(3) was over the definition of "proceedings" and whether investigations were included among the kinds of proceedings in which victims could participate. Despite objections from prosecutors, two Pre-Trial Chambers (PTC) have ruled that victims may participate in investigations, citing the precedent of other human rights courts that allow victim participation in investigations and giving consideration to the assisting roles

---

[37] Id.

[38] Early court decision, see ICC *Prosecutor v Lubanga*, ICC-01/04-01/06-925 OA 8, 13 June 2007, Decision of the Appeals Chamber on the Joint Application of Victims a/0001/06 to a/0003/06 and a/0105/06 concerning the "Directions and Decision of the Appeals Chamber" of 2 February 2007,ICC *Prosecutor v Lubanga*, ICC-01/04-01/06-925 OA 8, 13 June 2007, Decision of the Appeals Chamber on the Joint Application of Victims a/0001/06 to a/0003/06 and a/0105/06 concerning the "Directions and Decision of the Appeals Chamber" of 2 February 2007, Judge Song's separate opinion, p. 28, para 18; ICC *Prosecutor v Katanga and Chui,* PTC, ICC-01/04-01/07-474, 13 May 2008, Decision on the Set of Procedural Rights attached to Procedural Status of Victim at the Pre-Trial Stage of the Case, paras 37–44.

[39] Trumbull, supra note 36, at pp. 797, 798; ICC *Prosecutor v Katanga and Chui,* TC, ICC-01/04-01/07-1788, 22 January 2010, Decision on the Modalities of Victim Participation at Trial.

[40] Trumbull, supra note 36.

victims' can play in these investigations.[41] The academy has been critical of the Court in allowing victim participation during the investigatory stages. It has been pointed out that allowing victims to participate this early may give false hope to victims and inflate the role they play in such an early stage.[42] It is also argued that this kind of participation runs counter to what the drafters intended when they decided that victims would not have any rights to start investigations.[43] However, the Court has maintained, through its rulings, that victims do have rights under 68(3) to begin their participation in the investigatory stages.[44]

4.2.3.3 Presentation of Views and Concerns

The phrase, "the Court shall permit their views and concerns to be presented and considered" has also been contested in terms of when and in what manner victims can present views and concerns during proceedings.[45] Rule 91 allows for this kind of participation by victims based on the rulings of the Court and the Court may limit the presentation of views and concerns if it feels it necessary.[46] Pre-Trial Chambers, Trial Chambers and Appeals Chamber have all held that this phrase allows victims to question witnesses and present evidence to the Court, despite fierce objections from prosecutors to such a broad interpretation.[47] The Appeals Chamber even made it a point to specify that while the right to present evidence and challenge admissibility falls primarily to the possibility of the parties, that does not necessarily preclude victims from participating in these matters either.[48]

4.2.3.4 Additional Participation Rights Granted

In addition to the rights, the Court has also made other rulings that have expanded victim's participation rights. Victims and their representatives have always been able to access public records of the case and any public evidence presented. However, they were restricted from accessing any confidential filings.[49] This has

---

[41] Id., pp. 794, 795.

[42] SaCouto and Cleary 2008, p. 100.

[43] Id. at pp. 101, 102.

[44] See footnotes 41 and 42.

[45] Trumbull 2008, pp. 795, 796. ICC *Prosecutor v Lubanga,* PTC, ICC-01/04-01/06-678, Decision on the schedule and conduct of the confirmation hearing.

[46] Rule 91(2).

[47] Trumbull 2008, pp. 795, 796, ICC *Prosecutor v Lubanga,* PTC, ICC-01/04-01/06-678, Decision on the schedule and conduct of the confirmation hearing.

[48] Trumbull, supra note 47, at p. 797.

[49] Pena 2010, p. 504; ICC *Prosecutor v Lubanga*, TC, ICC-01/04-01/06-1119, 18 January 2008, Decision on victims' participation, paras 106, 107; ICC *Prosecutor v Lubanga,* PTC, ICC-01/04-01/06-462, 22 September 2006, Decision on the Arrangements for Participation of Victims a/0001/06, a/0002/06 and a/0003/06 at the Confirmation Hearing.

changed, as the Court can grant victims access to confidential materials and give representatives the ability to request to see confidential information that could impact a victim's personal interest.[50] The rights to question witnesses and present evidence have been upheld, and victims can also challenge the admission of evidence brought by both the Office of the Prosecutor or the defense.[51] Finally, in the case of *The Prosecutor v. Thomas Lubanga Dyilo*, the Court, upon hearing from victims that the charges against the defendant were too narrow, allowed victims to present a motion to expand the charges.[52] Although the Trial Chamber did not directly rule on this motion, it did specify to the parties that the charges could change, which indicates that victims may play a role in determining what charges may be brought against the accused.[53]

4.3 Protections

Beyond extensive participation rights outlined above, victims are also entitled to certain protections under the Rome Statute. These protections extend to both those who are certified as victims and those who are called as witnesses in proceedings.[54] The Rome Statute provides for the creation of the Victims and Witnesses Unit, an independent body within the ICC structure that falls under the purview of the ICC's Registry.[55] This Unit is in charge of implementing the security and support measures

---

[50] Pena, supra note 49, at pp. 504, 505; ICC *Prosecutor v Katanga and Chui,* PTC, ICC-01/04-01/07-537, 30 May 2008, Decision on Limitations of Set of Procedural Rights for Non-Anonymous Victims, paras 25, 26; ICC *Prosecutor v Katanga and Chui,* TC, ICC-01/04-01/07-1788, 22 January 2010, Decision on the Modalities of Victim Participation at Trial, paras 122, 123; ICC *Prosecutor v Abu Grada*, PTC, ICC-02/05-02/09-136, 06 October 2010, Decision on victims' modalities of participation at the Pre-Trial Stage of the Case, para 20.

[51] Pena, supra note 49, at p. 505.

[52] Pena, supra note 49, at p. 506; ICC *Prosecutor v Lubanga,* AC, ICC-01/04-01/06-1432, 11 July 2008, Judgment on the appeals of The Prosecutor and The Defence against Trial Chamber I's Decision on Victims' Participation of 18 January 2008, paras 97–104; this was a majority judgment, Judges Kirsch and Pikis dissented; see also ICC *Prosecutor v Katanga and Chui,* AC, ICC-01/04-01/07-2288, 16 July 2010, Judgment on the Appeal of Mr Katanga Against the Decision of Trial Chamber II of 22 January 2010 Entitled "Decision on the Modalities of Victim Participation at Trial", paras 37–48; 110–114.

[53] Pena, supra note 49, at p. 506; ICC *Prosecutor v Lubanga*, TC, ICC-01/04-01/06-1119, 18 January 2008, Decision on victims' participation, para 107; ICC *Prosecutor v Lubanga*, TC, ICC-01/04-01/06-2127, 16 September 2009, Decision on the Manner of Questioning Witnesses Representatives of Victims by the Legal, para 27; ICC *Prosecutor v Katanga and Chui,* TC, ICC-01/04-01/07-1788, 22 January 2010, Decision on the Modalities of Victim Participation at Trial, para 75.

[54] Greco 2007, p. 546; Rome Statute, Article 68.

[55] Rome Statute, Article 43.

mandated for victims and witnesses who come before the ICC.[56] The Court attempts to minimise the risks these individuals take to contribute to the process by affording them security and protective measures, and support them with various psychological and medical services.

4.3.1 Rome Statute Protections: Article 68

Article 68 of the Rome Statute is the primary source for the ICC's responsibilities in providing protections to victims, especially during the investigation and prosecution stages of the proceedings.[57] The first paragraph charges the Court with the task of protecting the "safety, physical and psychological well-being, dignity and privacy" of both victims and witnesses that come before the Court.[58] In assessing the type of protections to be provided, the Court has to take into account all "relevant factors", including age, gender, health of the victims and witnesses and the nature of the crime in which the victims and witnesses are involved.[59] The Rome Statute draws special attention to issuing protections when crimes involve sexual or gender violence or violence against children.[60]

Although the Court allows for public hearings, the Court may make exceptions to protect victims and witnesses by having proceedings in camera or allow evidence to be presented by alternative means.[61] Again, the Statute emphasises the use of these procedural exceptions when the crimes are of a sensitive nature and involve sexual violence or a child who is a victim or witness.[62] Article 68 leaves it to the discretion of the Court to decide when these exceptions will be used, taking into consideration all relevant circumstances.[63] Prior to the commencement of a trial, the Prosecutor is able to withhold evidence or information that could gravely endanger the safety of a witness or his or her family and instead submit a

---

[56] Rome Statute, Article 17; International Criminal Court (2012) Victims and Witnesses Unit. www.icc-cpi.int/Menus/ICC/Structure+of+the+Court/Protection/Victims+and+Witness+Unit.htm

[57] Rome Statute, Article 68(1).

[58] Id.

[59] Id; see also ICC *Prosecutor v Katanga and Chui,* AC, ICC-01/04-01/07-2288, 16 July 2010, Judgment on the Appeal of Mr Katanga Against the Decision of Trial Chamber II of 22 January 2010 Entitled "Decision on the Modalities of Victim Participation at Trial", para 114; the appealed decision is ICC *Prosecutor v Katanga and Chui,* TC, ICC-01/04-01/07-1788, 22 January 2010, Decision on the Modalities of Victim Participation at Trial.

[60] Id.

[61] Rome Statute, Article 68(2).

[62] Id.

[63] Id.

summary of the evidence or information.[64] But this must be balanced by the Court in such a way that will not unfairly prejudice the rights of the accused.[65]

4.3.2 Victims and Witnesses Unit

Under Article 43 of the Rome Statute, the Registry is mandated to create a Victims and Witnesses Unit which is the Unit in charge of implementing the protective measures guaranteed to victims and witnesses in Article 68.[66] This Unit is to include staff members who are experts in handling victims of trauma, especially including experts in trauma who specialise in trauma of crimes of sexual violence.[67] Expanding upon Article 43, the Rules of Evidence and Procedure further detail the responsibilities and functions of the Unit. These Rules cover the responsibility the Registry has to victims outside of the Unit, including providing notice or notifications to victims and their representatives and assisting and supporting legal representatives and organising legal representation of victims.

The functions and responsibilities of the Unit, in large part, are to assess and provide protective and support services to victims and witnesses.[68] The Unit is tasked with planning both long-term and short-term plans for protection and is the advocate of protective services before the Court. The Unit is also in charge of assisting in securing medical, psychological or trauma counselling services and providing training to the Court and parties to the Court on issues of trauma, sexual violence and confidentiality.[69] The Rules charge the Unit the responsibility to work with States to facilitate the security and support measures undertaken.[70] Children, the elderly and persons with disabilities are given special attention, and the Unit is able to appoint guardians for child victims or witnesses.[71]

4.3.3 The Court's Role in Victim Protection

In addition to the protections provided in the Rome Statute and the duties of the Victims and Witnesses Unit, the Court—through procedures and protocol of

---

[64] Rome Statute, Article 68(5).

[65] Id.

[66] Rome Statute, Article 43(5).

[67] Id.

[68] Key decision: *Prosecutor v Lubanga,* TC, ICC-01/04-01/06-1379, 5 June 2008, Decision on certain practicalities regarding individuals who have the dual status of witness and victim.

[69] Rule 17.

[70] Id.

[71] Id.

proceedings—is able to act to protect victims and witnesses. The Court may, after consultation with the Victims and Witnesses Unit, issue protective measures for victims, witnesses, or "another person at risk on account of testimony given by a witness."[72] Either the Office of the Prosecutor or defense counsel can make a motion for a protective order and the Court. In issuing these orders, the Court is to ensure the victim who is the subject of the protective order gives consent to the protections put in place.[73] As mentioned above, the Rome Statute also allows the Court to take special measures regarding the presentation of evidence that may endanger the safety of victims and witnesses.

4.4 Reparations

A third right granted to victims is the ability to receive reparations in the form of restitution, compensation or rehabilitation. Reparations were conceived by the ICC as a way to provide the victims of large-scale crimes a remedy beyond the conviction of the perpetrator, trying to assist those impacted in rebuilding and regaining what was lost as a result of harms suffered.[74] The drafters of the Rome Statute established an extensive structure for issuing reparations, including the creation of a trust fund that is to benefit not only victims directly impacted by crimes, but also their families.[75] This trust fund, known today as the Trust Fund for Victims, has established itself as its own institution and has supported rehabilitation efforts of communities impacted by crimes that meet jurisdictional requirements of the ICC.

4.4.1 Reparations Made Against a Convicted Person

Article 75 of the Rome Statute governs reparations to victims. As mentioned above, the Court is able to award reparations that include restitution, compensation or rehabilitation.[76] There are two main ways the Court can award these remedies against a convicted person; first, the Court can make a direct order against the convicted person to pay the appropriate reparations by fine or forfeiture of assets, or second, the Court can order the reparations that have been assessed to the convicted person to be paid through the Trust Fund for Victims.[77] This Article grants

[72] Rule 87(1).

[73] Id.; Greco 2007, p. 545.

[74] Keller 2007.

[75] Id.; Rome Statute, Article 75; Rome Statute, Article 79.

[76] Rome Statute, Article 75(1).

[77] Rome Statute, Article 75(2); Keller 2007, pp. 195, 196.

victims and their representatives the right to be heard during these reparation proceedings, and the Court has full discretion to determine the "scope and extent" of the damages and injuries the reparations are to remedy.[78] Article 75 also requires that States give effect to any reparation awards granted to victims and ensure the award is handed down to victims.[79]

Rules 94 through 99 in the Rules of Procedure and Evidence elaborate further upon the reparation scheme set out in the Rome Statute. In order to receive reparations, a victim has to file a formal request, in writing, with the Registrar.[80] The request needs to contain certain information, including the identity of the claimant, a description of the loss, injury or harm, the location and date of the incident and who the claimant believes is responsible and what kind of remedy is sought, among others.[81] When the trial begins, the Court is obligated to give notice to victims and all interested persons who filed reparation requests.[82] Pursuant to Article 75, the Court may also determine and separate any formal requests from victim.[83] In doing so, it must also notify the victims and interested persons so they make formal requests.[84]

The Registrar is to take measures to "give adequate publicity of the reparation proceedings before the Court" and can cooperate with States and intergovernmental organisations to publicise, as widely as possible, all reparation proceedings.[85] The Rules of Evidence and Procedure also allow the Court, after determining the scope and extent of damage, to award reparations to either individuals, collective groups of victims or both.[86] The Court has the option of hiring experts to help them determine the scope and extent of any damage, loss or injury and to help determine the appropriate remedy. The Rules require and seem to emphasise that the Court respect all rights of victims and convicted persons in making these determinations and should seek the cooperation of the States to take "protective measures for the purposes of forfeiture" in order to preserve potential property that could be used as reparations to victims.[87]

Scholars have commented extensively regarding the strengths and weaknesses of the ICC's reparations scheme. With respect to the role States Parties play in this reparation process, it has been noted that ICC reparations may conflict with how reparations are handled by States, and that their municipal laws may be impacted by the Court's decisions.[88] Indeed, it may be difficult to achieve compliance by

---

78 Rome Statute, Article 75(1).

79 Rome Statute, Article 75; Article 91.

80 Rule 94(1).

81 Rule 94(1)(a).

82 Rule 94(2).

83 Rule 95.

84 Id.

85 Rule 96.

86 Rule 97(1).

87 Rule 99.

88 Megret 2010, p. 11; Keller 2007, pp. 196, 197.

States in the enforcement of such judgments. Pursuant to the Rome Statute, States may not be fined or punished by the ICC despite any involvement the actor had with the State, or vice versa.[89] This may also be detrimental to victims trying to receive the complete reparation awarded by the Court for harms suffered because unlike most defendants in front of the ICC, States may have the funds and assets to supplement what those convicted cannot forfeit.[90] Additionally, there is, overall, an absence of the "responsible state" in most ICC proceedings, with States only playing a minimal role in the overall scheme of the Court.[91]

Nonetheless, reparations that can be awarded by the ICC are fewer than those that are traditionally utilised and recognised by other human rights tribunals.[92] The Rome Statute provides that victims can receive restitution, compensation and rehabilitation as potential reparations for loss and injury, but exclude satisfaction (such as an official state apology or recognition of harms caused by state or state actors) and guarantees of non-repetition (such as measures put in place to prevent reoccurrence) that human rights law often allows as remedies.[93] These may have been left out because they are often remedies required of States to provide, and as the ICC has no jurisdiction over States, they were not something the drafters wanted to include in the ICC's reparation scheme.[94]

Exclusion of such non-monetary remedies leaves the Court with only monetary remedies, which can be problematic given the lack of resources by those convicted, in addition to the large amount of victims the convicted individual's crimes may have impacted.[95] Scholars have suggested different ways to approach reparations under the ICC to maximise the goals of the Court regarding victims compensation, including shifting focus from individual monetary awards to the work that can be done by the Trust Fund for Victims.

4.4.2 The Trust Fund for Victims

The Trust Fund for Victims (TFV), established in 2002, serves two purposes. First, the TFV is the implementer of Court-ordered reparations against a convicted individual (as discussed above). Second, it provides general assistance to victims and their families funded through voluntary contributions from donors.[96] Article 79 of

89 Id.; Id.

90 Megret 2010, p. 11.

91 Id.; Keller 2007, p. 197.

92 Megret 2010, p. 15.

93 Id. at p. 16; Keller 2007, p. 194.

94 Keller 2007, p. 195.

95 Id.

96 The Trust Fund for Victims (2012) What We Do. http://www.trustfundforvictims.org/what-we-do.

the Rome Statute requires that a trust fund be established by the Assembly of States Parties "for the benefit of victims of crimes within the jurisdiction of the court, and of the families of such victims."[97] It also grants the Court the authority to order that money and property of a convicted individual collected as fines or forfeitures can be transferred to the TFV.[98] The third and final paragraph in Article 79 places the Assembly of States Parties in charge of managing and implementing the rules and regulations for the TFV.[99]

Under the Rules of Procedure and Evidence, the Court can order reparations issued against a convicted person to be deposited with the TFV for distribution to victims.[100] These reparation awards must be kept separate from other funding the TFV receives.[101] The Court may order that reparations against a convicted individual be made through the TFV if a collective award is needed due to the number of victims involved and the scope of reparations required.[102] The Court can order that an award be made to an intergovernmental, international or national organisation approved by the TFV, after consultations with the TFV and States involved.[103] Finally, the TFV can use "other resources" for the benefit of victims and their families.[104] It is through this final provision that the TFV has interpreted its power to provide general assistance to victims and families that allows it to focus on more community-oriented rebuilding projects with funds from voluntary contributions.[105]

The TFV receives funding from three primary sources. The first is through the fines and forfeitures awarded to victims pursuant to Court orders and to be used as dictated by the Court.[106] A second source of funding comes from allocations by the Assembly of States Parties. These funds are assessed in the Assembly's annual report and the use of these contributions is left to the discretion of the Assembly.[107] The third source of funding is through voluntary contributions that can be made by governments, international organisation, individuals, corporations and other entities.[108] The Board of the TFV is charged with making an annual

---

97 Rome Statute, Article 79(1).

98 Rome Statute, Article 79(2).

99 Rome Statute, Article 79(3).

100 Rule 98(1).

101 Id.

102 Rule 98(3).

103 Rule 98(4).

104 Rule 98(5).

105 Trust Fund for Victims (2012) Legal Basis. http://www.trustfundforvictims.org/legal-basis.

106 Dwertmann 2010, pp. 286–297.

107 Id. at p. 287.

108 Reg. of Trust Fund for Victims, 21.

appeal for voluntary contributions and soliciting these funds from organisations and individuals who can contribute.[109]

There are limitations placed on voluntary contributions as well as opportunities for donors to earmark for specific purposes. For example, a voluntary contribution cannot be accepted if it would be inconsistent with the "goals and activities" of the TFV or if it is inappropriately earmarked.[110] Any donations that would jeopardise the independence of the TFV also cannot be accepted.[111] Up to one-third of a contribution from organisations other than state governments may be earmarked for specific purposes, as long as those earmarked funds do not promote discrimination.[112] Other than these limitations, the funds can be used at the discretion of the TFV's Board to provide support and rehabilitation to victims and their families through means that are more difficult to achieve through Court-ordered reparations.[113]

The difficulties the Court faces when awarding reparations makes the TFV an important part of the reparation scheme, as it can use funds to supplement any awards issued by the Court, and can independently take on its own projects pursuant to Rule 98(5). While the Court is only able to grant awards post-conviction, the TFV is able to step in earlier in the proceedings and lend its assistance before and during trial.[114] While the Court's awards are limited as to who can receive them (only certified victims and families), the TFV is able to assist any victim or victim family who have suffered injury or harm committed by a crime that falls under the jurisdiction of the ICC, not just those directly involved in proceedings.[115] This allows the TFV to spread its resources to reach a larger group of individuals and can undertake projects that assist in rebuilding communities and a society that has been impacted by large-scale crime. Consequently, the effective and efficient functioning of the TFV is the best hope of realising the third traditional focus of criminal justice systems—societal restoration.

As of 2009, the TFV's income totalled over EUR 4.5 million. Of this, EUR 2.2 million was allocated for program grants and EUR 1 million was set aside for Court-ordered reparations.[116] All of the TFV's projects, so far, have been aimed at assisting victims in the Democratic Republic of Congo and Uganda.[117] The TFV's projects in these areas have four main foci: (1) to rebuild communities; (2) to provide assistance to victims of torture and mutilation; (3) to provide assistance to children and youth and (4) to provide assistance to victims of sexual violence.[118]

[109] Reg. of Trust Fund for Victims, 22, 23.

[110] Reg. of Trust Fund for Victims, 30(a), 30 (b).

[111] Reg. of Trust Fund for Victims, 30(d).

[112] Reg. of Trust Fund for Victims, 27.

[113] Dwertmann 2010, p. 287.

[114] Id.

[115] Id.

[116] The Trust Fund for Victims (2012) Projects. http://www.trustfundforvictims.org/projects.

[117] Id.

[118] Id.

The TFV estimates that its efforts have directly benefitted over 42,000 victims and over 180,000 of those victims' family members through thirty-one active projects in these areas.[119] In June 2001, the TFV announced that it would begin programs aimed at benefitting victims of crimes of sexual violence in the Central African Republic.[120]

The actions of the TFV, however, have escaped criticism. In January 2008, for example, the TFV decided to begin using voluntary contributions to fund projects independently of the Court's reparations orders.[121] After notifying the Court, the Office of Public Counsel for the Defense objected, claiming these actions went above and beyond what the TFV was empowered to undertake, and expressed concern that funding independent projects would damage the impartiality of the ICC.[122] In response, the Pre-Trial Chamber affirmed that the TFV was in fact empowered to fund projects independent of Court-ordered reparations, but could do so only so long as the TFV maintained sufficient funds to cover Court-ordered reparations that were made through the TFV.[123] The Pre-Trial Chamber's ruling has, in turn, been criticised for placing a limitation on the TFV that was not contemplated by the Rome Statute or TFV Regulations, thereby unjustifiably restricting some of the TFV's independence from the Court.[124]

That said, this decision and the protocol that governs the TFV indicate that while it is fairly independent, the TFV is still very much under the control of the Court. Scholars disagree as to whether increasing the independence of the TFV would be beneficial or would defeat some of the goals of the reparation scheme created under the Rome Statute. Some argue that further independence from the Court would allow the TFV to reach out to victims the ICC cannot reach, thereby maintaining the goals of restorative justice contemplated by the drafters of the ICC.[125] Others, however, cite the importance of maintaining funds in the TFV dedicated to Court-ordered reparation, and contend that complete independence from the ICC would defeat or effectively eliminate the ICC's reparation scheme.[126] Thus, it would be inappropriate, to use all voluntary contributions to fund independent projects if doing so would be detrimental to fulfilling Court-ordered remedies.[127]

---

119 Id.

120 International Criminal Court (2011) Trust Fund for Victims Launches Programmme in the Central African Republic. www.icc-cpi.int/menus/icc/press%20and%20media/press%20releases/pr685.

121 Dannenbaum 2010, pp. 242, 243.

122 Id.

123 Id. at p. 247; ICC *Situation in the Democratic Republic of Congo*, PTC, ICC-01/04-492, 11 April 2008, Decision on the Notification of the Board of Directors of the Trust Fund for Victims in accordance with Regulation 50 of the Regulations of the Trust Fund.

124 Id. at pp. 248, 249, 255, 256.

125 Id. at pp. 285, 286.

126 Dwertmann 2010, p. 293.

127 Id.

4.5 Conclusion

There are three main components to victim status under the ICC: participation, protection and reparation. The Court, so far, has used its discretion under the Rome Statute to rule in favour of expanding victims' rights despite objections made by other parties within the ICC. Not only are participation rights developing quickly, so too is the work carried out by the Trust Fund for Victims that has allowed the ICC to assist victims and communities in the rebuilding process. Although the ICC is still in the early stages of interpreting and animating these rights, the Court and the States Parties to the Rome Statute have committed to ensuring that victims would be heard and play an important part in how the Court operated and what kind of approach it would take to achieving justice for those most impacted by its decisions.

As this chapter began with several unanswerable questions, so to it concludes with further outstanding questions to consider. First, is the creation of "victim classes" a more efficient path for the ICC and the IFV than individualised application? A major problem with such a structure is victim qualification. Are all purported victims within the class qualified as victims for the crime alleged? In other words, the Court may be faced with the dilemma of only a portion of a victim class qualifying.

For example, assume the ICC could issue an indictment for Crimes Against Humanity and Genocide in Cambodia. Assume further, that only the genocide charge goes forward. Then, suddenly, the victim class of 1.7 million Cambodians shrinks to the 100,000 distinct population of Cham who were victims of genocide. The remainders are held not to be victims of genocide because they were not ethnically or religiously distinct from the perpetrators. Thus, a group could be stripped of its "victimhood"—a perverse operation of this system. Is that really what the drafters of the Rome Statute intended? And, if so, does this really further the goal of restorative justice?

Second, in a prolonged conflict, can those who are initially considered perpetrators become victims themselves? Dr. Baumann discusses this possibility in his chapter, but a further question, namely—are all victims innocent? remains. Does a perpetrator lose his or her chance to enter the victim class by virtue of the fact that they were guilty of a separate crime in a separate instance? And, if so, is the reverse true? Can victims become perpetrators and, thereby lose their status as victims? If a girl who is raped by a soldier then murders the soldier as he is departing the premises, is that girl stripped of her victimhood?

Third, what policies should be developed within the VTF for handling reparations? Katharina Peschke, legal advisor to the trust fund, confirmed at this conference that policies do not yet exist to resolve potentially vexing questions. Among them, whether a defendant who is acquitted will receive seized assets upon acquittal? Whether that same defendant would also be entitled to receive any interest gained on investments made by the VTF using the defendant's financial assets, or would the defendant only be entitled to the principal amount? What investment strategies will the VTF develop and what guidelines will govern such practices? Will the Court be able to overrule the VTF on use of all assets or only assets of persons currently with cases before the Court? Indeed an entire conference could be had on just this third question.

Of course, there are many more outstanding issues which must be resolved with respect to the status, rights and protection of victims. As the ICC moves forward, we await a lively debate in this area, as well as the issuance of resolutions based on justice and fair treatment.

References

Dannenbaum T (2010) The International Criminal Court, Article 79, and transitional justice: the case for an independent Trust Fund for Victims. WILJ 28:234–298

Dwertmann E (2010) The reparation system of the International Criminal Court: its implementation, possibilities and limitations. Brill, Leiden

Greco G (2007) Victims' Rights Overview under the ICC Legal Framework: a jurisprudential analysis. ICLR 7:531–547

International Criminal Court (2010) Helping victims make their voices heard—The Office of Public Counsel for Victims. http://www.icc-cpi.int/NR/rdonlyres/01A26724-F32B-4BE4-8B02-A65D6151E4AD/282846/LRBookletEng.pdf.Accessed11April2013.

Kaoutzanis C (2010) Two birds with one stone: how the use of the class action device for victim participation in the International Criminal Court can improve both the fight against impunity and victim participation. UC Davis JILP 17:111–150

Keller L (2007) Proceedings of the scholarly conference taking reparations seriously: seeking justice at the International Criminal Court: victims' reparations. TJLR 29:189–218

Megret F (2010) Article of shrines, memorials and museums: using the International Criminal Court's victim reparation and assistance regime to promote transitional justice. BHRLR 16:1–56

Pena M (2010) Victim participation in the International Criminal Court: Victim participation at the International Criminal Court: achievements made and challenges lying ahead. ILSAJICL 16:497–516

SaCouto S, Cleary K (2008) The war crimes symposium: Victims' participation in the investigations of the International Criminal Court. TCLP 17:73–106

Trumbull IV C (2008) The victims of victim participation in International Criminal Proceedings. MJIL 29:777–826

Chapter 5
The Individualising and Universalising Discourse of Law: Victims in Truth Commissions and Trials

Michael Humphrey

Abstract The increasing prominence of the role of the victim in managing post-conflict societies is the product of first, the attempt by the state to invert the project of the former regime from producing victims to redeeming victims and second, the framing of the effects of violence through the universalising and individualising discourses of human rights and trauma. Both are used to identify and recognise the victim. This process of selection and recognition of the victim is at the core of the truth, justice, and reconciliation narratives which set out the consensus around injustice and reconciliation. Through the recognition of victims, more than the prosecution of perpetrators, the state seeks to bind the individual to the state. In transitional justice the consensus is produced by the process of justice, in the case of trials by separating the guilty from the innocent and in the case of truth commissions by forging an alliance between the beneficiaries of previous injustice and the victims willing to accept moral victory and symbolic reparations.

Keywords Transitional justice • Ritual • Reconciliation • Human rights • Suffering • Trials • Truth commission • Victims

5.1 Introduction

On the way to a Human Rights Conference dinner in Buenos Aires in March 2010, I was made acutely aware of the layers of traumatised victims just below the surface of Argentine society. Travelling in a taxi with one of the very well-known members of the Mothers of the *Plaza de Mayo*, Nora Morales de Cortiñas, we said

---

The author holds the Chair in Sociology in the Department of Sociology and Social Policy at the University of Sydney, Australia.

M. Humphrey (✉)
University of Sydney, Sydney, Australia
e-mail: michael.humphrey@sydney.edu.au

T. Bonacker and C. Safferling (eds.), *Victims of International Crimes: An Interdisciplinary Discourse*, DOI: 10.1007/978-90-6704-912-2_5,

to the taxi driver, "Do you realise you are driving one of the Mother's to dinner?" He was very excited and immediately asked her. "I had an uncle who disappeared in 1959 [during an earlier period of repression in Argentina; author's note]. Have you been able to identify the remains of people you have found dating back that far?" The Mothers had become famous for their campaign to find out what had happened to their children, those whose disappearance nearly 20 years earlier (during the repression of 1976–1983) had never been investigated before. "What was the taxi driver imagining", I asked myself, "that the bones of victims of state repression were stacked in layers waiting to be identified?" For me his enquiry conjured up an image of Argentina haunted by the disappeared caused by many different violent events stretching back into the past. For him, the Mothers embodied the historical role of exhuming the entire past of state repression in Argentina. The taxi driver went on to reveal an even longer historical family experience of repression dating back to the Second World War in the Soviet Union where his family suffered deportation from a German colony in the Caucasus to Kazakhstan when the German army invaded in 1941. His family had arrived in Argentina as refugees from the Soviet Union. His family's memory had never entered the collective memory as victims of state repression.

This story highlights the problems transitional justice has confronted in trying to manage the historical complexity of political violence with unresolved layers of trauma and to promote national reconciliation in the face of persistent impunity. In Argentina transitional justice had included a truth commission investigating the fate of the disappeared (CONADEP) (1983–1984), the prosecution of the leading military figures of the dictatorship (1984–1986), amnesty laws which interrupted and stopped further prosecutions between 1986 and 2003, international prosecutions of Argentine military officers in Spanish courts, and the resumption of prosecutions of crimes against humanity in Argentine courts after 2003. However, largely excluded from these investigations was the history of endemic state violence and the forgotten layers of victims whose individual stories (or at least the memories of their relatives) had never been heard, let alone recognised and incorporated into the official (national) story. In other words, the human rights perspective on repression could identify the victims of violence but not its causes and structural dimensions or its relationship to "social traumatisation", the previous layers of trauma.[1]

The example of these forgotten layers of victims of political violence in Argentina raises important theoretical questions about the contemporary role of transitional justice project to reconstitute the legitimate state legal and political authority through justice measures, especially those focused on victims. Transitional justice has become a global project with a national focus. As a global legal project it employs the universalising and individualising discourses of human rights and suffering to make victims visible and legitimate their claims. Human rights are rights individuals have on the basis of a shared humanity and suffering is

[1] Robben 2005, p. 143.

an individual emotional experience shared on the basis of everyone having a sentient body. At the national level transitional justice seeks to reestablish legitimate legal and political authority through unification based on a political consensus about the illegality and immorality of past injustices. Transitional justice constructs the atemporal universalised victim of human rights violations and trauma on the one hand and the recovered citizen in the spatial and temporal present of the nation-state on the other.

The globalising legal project of transitional justice, which seeks to produce legal consensus about past human rights violations, confronts the political role of violence in founding and preserving the nation-state.[2] Nation-states are invariably constructed on a founding violence which they commemorate in the stories of their national heroes and martyrs in order to bind citizens to the national community. At the same time the conservative violence of regime maintenance and its victims often remain hidden. Transitional justice seeks to turn the violence of authoritarian state preservation—crimes against humanity, genocide, human rights violations—into the legitimating founding violence of the new democratic state by recognising the victims of state repression and prosecuting the perpetrators to forge a new unified national community. Transitional justice highlights the stories of victims to recover national unity by denouncing the perpetrators and redeeming the victims in the creation of the democratic order and reconciled (and unified) nation.

Trials and truth commissions have become the primary vehicles for revealing the past conservative violence of state repression through broad projects for justice and reconciliation. This chapter argues that the transitional justice project uses law as a vehicle for social transformation and in the process makes the victims of political violence (formulated as victims of human rights violations) the source of founding violence to legitimate the new democratic order. The mechanism at the centre of the project of social transformation through justice is the ritual structure of the scapegoat.[3] Trials aim to produce a legal judgement about the guilt of the accused which has the structural effect of separating the guilty from the innocent. However, because these trials are not just about individual criminal acts but large-scale collective political crimes—crimes against humanity, genocide, war crimes—they also produce a historical narrative in which to situate these individual acts. The trial becomes a vehicle to establish the guilt or innocence of an individual and to produce a unifying effect through a "moral consensus that the past was evil" in order to "to reach a political consensus that the evil is past".[4] The ritual structure of the trial seeks to separate the past from the present morally, politically, and legally.

While transitional justice strategies were developed to manage post-conflict settings they are also being deployed in the context of ongoing conflict. In this case

[2] Grandin 2005.

[3] Girard 1977, pp. 63–65.

[4] Meister 2002, p. 96.

the ritual scapegoat is used as a technique to construct violence as if it was in the past and available to produce a consensus. However, the consensus able to be produced in the context of ongoing conflict is often quite narrow and unstable. Even in post-conflict environments ongoing violence destabilises the attempt to construct violence as a past evil. Consequently the durability of the transitional justice project anchored in victims of large-scale repression is undermined by the demands of the new victims for protection, as is happening currently in Latin America where democratisation is witnessing a surge of criminal violence.[5]

5.2 Rights and Suffering

Transitional justice is an expression of increasing legal globalisation, in this case the resort to law as a solution for managing conflict and bringing about peace.[6] The term "lawfare", "the resort to legal instruments, to the violence inherent in the law, to commit acts of political coercion, even erasure",[7] points to intensification of judicialisation as both a defence of state legitimacy as well as a defence against the abuse of state power through human rights claims. As Talal Asad argues "*if* cruelty is increasingly represented in the language of rights (and especially of human rights), then it is because *perpetual legal struggle* has now become the dominant mode of moral engagement in an interconnected, uncertain and rapidly changing world".[8]

The international turn to law to manage political conflict is more than a response to growing "anxieties towards lawlessness" but the promotion of law as a framework and language in which to understand violence and lawlessness and to manage it. The greater the heterogeneity and diversity of violence, the greater the resort to law because "legal instruments appear to offer a means of commensuration [...] a repertoire of standardised terms and practices that permit the negotiation of values, beliefs, ideals and interests across otherwise intransitive lines of cleavage [...] Hence the effort to make human rights into an ever more global, ever more authoritative discourse".[9] Law is deployed as a technology to cut through the complexity underlying conflict and war in order to produce a narrative of culpability and justice—whether retributive or restorative.

Transitional justice emerged in the 1980s and 1990s in the context of third wave democratisation and in response to large-scale human rights violations that had occurred under authoritarian regimes in Latin America, in Eastern Europe and in intra-state conflicts in ethnically divided and/or failing states. Two trends emerged from this period of transition to democracy to manage the legacy of large-scale

5 Guerrero et al. 2009.

6 Hirschl 2008, p. 94.

7 Comaroff and Comaroff 2008, p. 144.

8 Asad 1997, pp. 304, 305.

9 Comaroff and Comaroff 2008, p. 145.

violence: first, the creation of the truth commission and second, the creation of new international criminal tribunals and courts.[10] The truth commission sought to balance accountability and amnesty and pursue broad justice and social goals rather than individual criminal accountability initially in the context of transition from authoritarianism. The expansion of international criminal justice through the establishment of the International Criminal Tribunal for the former-Yugoslavia (ICTY) in 1993 and International Criminal Tribunal for Rwanda (ICTR) in 1994, was followed by the establishment of a series of special courts and mixed tribunals[11] as well as the establishment of the ICC to respond to political crimes committed during armed conflicts and war. Underlying the expansion of transitional justice was the idea that societies ignored past political violence at their peril because the unresolved grievances of victims would very likely result in revenge.

While transitional justice has promoted accountability as the best way to overcome serious human rights violations the perceived political risk of trials produced a not too much, not too little justice solution.[12] Transitional justice became a complex political calculation translating conflict into crimes and justice into the pursuit of the "truth" about past violence as a pedagogic and therapeutic exercise.[13] Even international human rights conventions appear to acknowledge the problems of entrenched impunity by insisting on the rights of victims—e.g. the Convention on Enforced Disappearance gives the families of victims the "right to know" what happened to their loved ones even where amnesty laws continue to block investigations and prosecutions.[14]

Transitional justice must be contextualised as an outcome of the Cold War ideological divide over the politics of victimhood. As Robert Meister argues, "those who believe themselves to be victims of politically inflicted suffering face a choice about what to do with their grief: should it be harnessed as the politics of grievance or suppressed as the politics of resentment?".[15] On the one side there is the unreconciled revolutionary victim for whom justice became the removal of the perpetrator and the beneficiaries who were seen as a counter-revolutionary threat. On the other side of the Cold War ideological divide was the counter-revolutionary position fearful of being ruled by unreconciled victims. Transitional justice was put forward as a way to bridge this ideological divide, a way which "if practiced in

10 Bell et al. 2007.

11 The Special Court for Sierra Leone (2002), Special Tribunal for Lebanon (2007), Extraordinary Cambers in the Courts of Cambodia (2003), Ad-Hoc Court for East Timor (2006).

12 Meister 2002, p. 95.

13 Humphrey 2005.

14 International Convention for the Protection of All Persons from Enforced Disappearance (Article 24.2): "Each victim has the right to know the truth regarding the circumstances of the enforced disappearance, the progress and results of the investigation and the fate of the disappeared person. Each State Party shall take appropriate measures in this regard [victim includes both the disappeared person and any person who has suffered direct harm as a result of the disappearance; author's note]." (UN 2006, p. 9).

15 Meister 2002, p. 93.

just the right amount, and with just the right degree of restraint, can bring about a cultural transformation that will leave liberal democracy secure".[16]

Transitional justice developed as a strategy for managing counter-revolutionary fears by distinguishing the perpetrators from the beneficiaries of injustice and the reconciled from the unreconciled victims. The just enough justice solution addresses the counter-revolutionary fears of beneficiaries and the grievances of the victims. According to Robert Meister, reconciliation is produced between the beneficiaries (of previous injustice) who must acknowledge the injustice of victims' politically inflicted suffering and that the past was evil and the victims (the "good victims") who are willing to accept moral victory and compensation.[17] The perpetrators and unreconciled victims (the "bad victims") are excluded, the former through prosecution, or at least political marginalisation and stigmatisation, and the latter by being accused of being selfish and jeopardising the new political order by continuing their demands for justice. Through this compromise national unity and citizenship rights in the liberal democratic state promise—from that point on—accountability, rule of law and good governance.

As inclusive projects trials and truth commissions employ universalising and individualising discourses of human rights and suffering within a performative ritual structure to produce a consensus about past violence and thereby change the social status of perpetrator and victim. Pivotal to producing the consensus is the ritual scapegoat, the one blamed for the violence in order to bring cycles of violence to an end.[18] For Girard the scapegoat is the (ritual) victim constituted by the community that judge and exclude them. The (ritual) victim is made sacred through the ritual benefit of solidarity they engender in the community by their exclusion/sacrifice. Girard's "ritual victim" is not the same as the "victim" in transitional justice who—through the human rights lens—is constructed in relation to the perpetrator and reveals the perpetrator, the one responsible for their suffering. Thus in transitional justice the "ritual victim" of trials is the perpetrator, the one blamed for the violence, whereas the "ritual victim" of the truth commission is the victim of violence in whom consensus is produced about the wrongs done. The truth commissions seek to reverse the exclusion of the victim produced through violence by using them to produce a consensus about the wrongs done, if not who was responsible for them.

The universalising and individualising discourses of human rights and trauma address violence and suffering not just as social facts but "global plights to which the international community must respond".[19] The development of the international security and human rights norm "Responsibility to Protect" (R2P) has been based on the idea that we live in a world in a chronic state of emergency where globalised human rights need to be protected. Both lenses are inclusive, the human

---

[16] Meister 2002, p. 94.

[17] Meister 2005, p. 89.

[18] Girard 1977.

[19] Hastrup 2003, p. 310.

rights lens based on our shared humanity and the trauma lens based on the fact that we share the experience of having bodies (the site of pain).

The globalisation of the human rights lens is well appreciated. As Habermas observes, "human rights provide the sole recognised basis of legitimisation for the politics of the international community".[20] Moreover human rights consciousness has emerged as a subjectivity of legitimate grievance and discourse for claim making.[21] Yet the parallel globalisation of the trauma lens and its significance at the heart of transitional justice strategies is not well appreciated. Trauma is understood as both a bodily experience but also to refer to an underlying traumatic event. Clinical psychology constructs trauma as a symptom of a disturbing experience that has not been psychologically digested, an event unassimilable as memory that overthrows temporal sequence by collapsing the past into the present. But trauma is no longer simply a medical condition determined by clinicians but an expression of our humanity able to be recognised by the public. The victim is seen to embody our humanity. "It is in the name of this vestige of humanity that compensation is demanded for damage suffered, that witnesses testify against all forms of oppression, and that proofs of cruelty endured are brought forward".[22] Hence the truth commission ritual relies on the trauma of victims in determining the truth of suffering, not on experts such as lawyers or clinicians. Trauma has become a source of legitimacy derived from the authenticity of suffering, the truth of personal testimony and, as Paul Ricoeur argues, an expression of the affective roots of injustice.[23] Victims demand moral recognition and legal reparation in the name of unjust suffering and trauma connects them through a shared humanity. But while trauma becomes a source of political visibility it also introduces a moral economy of suffering which circumscribes who "deserves to be recognised as a victim".[24] No longer exclusively the lens of experts (lawyers and medical professionals) but a public discourse to frame, understand and relate to the world, trauma is integral to producing a consensus about past violence. Based on the ritual scapegoat structure transitional justice seeks to separate the past from the present, the guilty from the innocent, the deserving from undeserving and thereby turn the victims into a source of political legitimacy.

5.3 Truth Commissions

Truth commissions emerged as projects of national unity at a time of transition supporting the formation of a liberal democratic state hampered by political constraints on accountability. In Latin America these "state-sanctioned investigations

[20] Habermas 1998, p. 162.

[21] Humphrey and Valverde 2008; Grandin 2007.

[22] Fassin and Rechtman 2009, p. 97.

[23] Ricoeur 2000.

[24] Humphrey 2010.

into past episodes of political terror were one part of this transition's agenda to cultivate a notion of liberal citizenship that viewed the state not as a potential executor of social justice but as an arbiter of legal disputes and protector of individual rights".[25] However, this project came up against the reality that the militaries had won the counter-insurgency wars and were unwilling to give up their "self-assigned immunity". They forced the truth commissions away from "the legal arena into the realms of ethics and emotions".[26]

Truth commissions are projects for national unity produced by forging a consensus about the past. Truth in itself was seen as both a form of reparation and prevention. For José Zalaquett, a prominent member of the Rettig Commission in Chile, the role of the truth commission was to "help to create a consensus concerning events about which the community is deeply divided [...] The purpose of truth is to lay the groundwork for a shared understanding of the recent crisis and how to overcome it".[27] In general they aimed first, to repair the social trauma caused by repression and, second, to prevent repression from occurring again.

In Latin America truth commissions interpreted history "as a parable, not as politics".[28] Consequently they did not explain repression as reactions to the social democratic national project or agents creating the social conditions for the new neo-liberal economic order but as part of repetitive cycles of dictatorship. In this way truth commissions served as "modern-day instruments in the creation of nationalism and embody what Benedict Anderson describes as nationalism's enabling paradox: the need to forget acts of violence central to state formation that can never be forgotten".[29]

The role of truth commissions in producing a national consensus varied from case to case according to the way the trauma lens circumscribed who was included as a deserving victim. Here I will briefly consider two different political contexts in which truth commissions operated. First, situations where the military had defeated their opponents (insurgent groups) and largely dictated the terms of their handover of power to civilian government and granted themselves amnesty, and second, situations of ongoing conflict where a negotiated end to the conflict involved selective recognition of victims (depending on whether they were victims of state or insurgent violence).

In general in Latin America truth commissions were introduced as part of the transition from authoritarian to democratic rule in which militaries had prevailed over insurgencies and awarded themselves amnesties.

In Argentina the legalistic procedures of the Argentine truth commission (CONADEP) viewed violence through the human rights lens and turned everyone, the military defending the nation and the insurgents ideological struggles for

[25] Grandin 2005, p. 47.

[26] Grandin 2005, p. 47.

[27] Grandin 2005, p. 53.

[28] Grandin 2005, p. 47.

[29] Grandin 2005, p. 48.

greater justice, into "innocent or transgressing individuals with individual rights and obligations".[30] The collective motivations of both oppressors and political activists were omitted and reduced to a question of individuals whose human rights had been violated. What was significant in the Argentine case was the scale of the repression and the number of disappeared (30,000) which meant the families of the victims could not be easily ignored.

In Chile, where amnesty laws and the political prominence of the military prevented prosecutions, the main project of the *Comisión de Verdad y Reconciliación* (Commission of Truth and Reconciliation, also known as the Rettig Commission) became reconciliation. The Rettig Commission limited its aims to reinforcing social cohesion and not furthering accountability of those most responsible. The primary focus was the fate of the disappeared (around 3,000) and those recognised and compensated as official victims were the families of the disappeared, those constructed as most innocent. By contrast the many more thousands of political prisoners who survived imprisonment and torture were ignored. They were only recognised and given compensation in the form of pensions and health benefits in 2005, more than 15 years after the Rettig Commission, by the National Commission on Imprisonment and Torture which prevented full disclosure of the second part of its report by declaring it classified and closed for 50 years. The reconciliation focus of the Rettig Commission's mandate was based on "a conception of history that takes national cohesion as its starting premise and posits violence as resulting from the dissolution of that unity".[31] Consequently the commission report narrated the conflict and coup as the product of the normative breakdown of institutions and social relationships. While it addressed human rights violations committed by the Chilean dictatorship "the coup itself was redeemed as a tragic but necessary intervention that prevented complete national collapse".[32] In other words, the constitutive violence of national survival was the coup, not the redemption of the victims of repression whose suffering was merely a tragic consequence.

In Guatemala the *Comisión para el Esclarecimiento Histórico* (Commission for Historical Clarification) (CEH) was also limited by an environment where the military remained a dominant political force. The commission could not subpoena witnesses or records and its report (1999) could not individualise responsibility nor be used for prosecutions. However, it produced a quite comprehensive account of the causes of violence. First, it did not believe national reconciliation could be the basis for healing and a source of future protection against human rights abuses in a society so deeply divided by violence. Second, it found that the intensity of violence in Guatemala made the strategies of victim testimony inadequate to convey the reality of the experience of repression—in fact it found the violence against the Mayans was genocidal. The report constructed the intensity of terror and repression not as the product of the breakdown of state and society but "as a

---

30 Taylor 1994, p. 197.

31 Grandin 2005, p. 49.

32 Grandin 2005, p. 49.

component of state formation, as the foundation of the military's plan of national stabilisation through a return to constitutional rule".[33]

By shifting from accountability to ethics and suffering these victim-centred Latin American truth commissions in general accepted the military's justification of repression for national salvation to prevent chaos. This produced the contradictory outcome of their condemnation of human rights violations in general and their refusal, "despite the protests of victims and their families, to sanction the collective political projects that were defeated by the violence".[34]

Where truth commissions have been employed to forge a consensus about national reconciliation during ongoing conflict the selective and one-sided recognition of victims of the violence has been most pronounced. The cases of transitional justice in Algeria and Colombia highlight how the reconciliation process distinguished between victims of non-state and state violence to recognise and compensate the former and marginalise the latter. In both cases democratic consensus through elections and referenda also underpinned the legitimation of the differentiation of citizenship and the denial of human rights to particular categories of victims.[35]

In Algeria the Charter for Peace and National Reconciliation was enacted in 2006 to promote political peace after the state's decade long war against Islamist militias who had taken up armed struggle against the military coup which denied them their expected electoral victory after the strong showing of the FIS (Front Islamique du Salut) in the first round of the 1991 elections. The civil war that raged between 1991 and 2002 cost around 200,000 lives from Islamist terrorist violence on the one hand and military counter-insurgency on the other. The military described their counter-terrorism strategy as designed to "make fear change sides"—i.e. make the Islamists as fearful as they had made the rest of society.[36] State terror reciprocated non-state terror and both justified the use of terror in competing narratives of national renewal and salvation. Islamists represented themselves as "*mujahidin* fighting a holy war for the recovery of Algeria's "authentic values" and the popular sovereignty of the *mustad'afin* (the oppressed, the new "wretched of the earth") against the corruption and tyranny of those who have "betrayed" the promise of the revolution".[37] The army and the paramilitaries saw themselves as "fighting the alien and un-Algerian terror of "sons of *harkis*", who have betrayed the nation through their allegiance to the "Islamist international" and seek to destroy the republican state created by the revolution, condemning Algeria through "programmatic regression" to a barbaric medieval theocracy".[38]

---

[33] Grandin 2005, p. 50.

[34] Grandin 2005, p. 50.

[35] Humphrey 2012.

[36] Tlemçani 2008, p. 4.

[37] McDougall 2005, p. 127.

[38] McDougall 2005, p. 127.

The Charter was designed to bring peace by closing the past based on the formula of "no victor no vanquished". The Charter completed a process of amnesty initiated in the 1999 Civil Harmony Law. The Charter constituted transitional justice for the benefit of the majority—the Islamist insurgent groups, the military, the paramilitaries and the majority of the citizens who were largely untouched by the violence. Responsibility for the terrorist violence was narrowed to the most hardline Islamist groups and the state security forces and paramilitaries escaped practically all scrutiny. When the families of the 10,000 disappeared strongly objected to the Civil Harmony Law because of the lack of transparency in the amnesty process the government intimidated the families and even blamed survivors of massacres for not adequately defending themselves.[39] In 2003 President Bouteflika established the National Consultative Commission on the Promotion and Protection of Human Rights in response to the persistent demands of the families of the disappeared to know more about the fate of the disappeared. The outcome was to absolve the security forces from any responsibility and to compensate the families of the disappeared. By 2007 the Commission had considered 13,541 applications for compensation claims from families of terrorists and families of the disappeared and dispersed around $50 million in compensation.[40] No report of the Commission's findings was ever published.

The Charter for Peace and National Reconciliation was overwhelmingly affirmed by a democratic majority through referendum. The government also suppressed further public dissent by excluding Islamic parties from electoral politics, most notably the FIS and by criminalising further accusations by survivors and families of the disappeared of military or paramilitary culpability by making it a "criminal offence to speak of the disappearances in such a way as 'to undermine the good reputation of [state] agents who honorably served the country or to tarnish the image of Algeria internationally'".[41] The consensus narrative of transition was that the military saved the nation, that the victims of the Islamist terror deserved compensation and those who blamed the state/military and damaged their reputation should be punished. The founding violence of the new democracy was the military's victory over the extremist Islamists, not the victory of the victims of human rights violations—except those who suffered at the hands of Islamist terror. The "bad victims" were those who had rejected the Charter and continued their demands for truth and justice.

Another example of transitional justice launched in the context of an ongoing internal conflict between the Colombian state, FARC (Revolutionary Armed Forces of Colombia) and the paramilitaries. What distinguishes the Colombian conflict is the complexity and scale of the violence, the diversity of victims and the length of time—more than 40 years—the conflict has been going. Between 1964 and 2007 there was an estimated total of 674,000 homicides,[42] around 57,000 dis-

---

39 Ellyas and Hamani 1999.

40 Tlemçani 2008, p. 8.

41 Tlemçani 2008, p. 9.

42 García-Godos and Lid 2010, p. 490.

appeared[43] and between 1985 and 2011 around 5.3 million people internally displaced persons.[44] Even today, after the extensive efforts to address the injustices produced by widespread violence, the environment remains very violent with a homicide rate of 32 per 100,000 and ongoing internal displacement estimated at more than 300,000 in 2010.[45] Moreover human rights workers, journalists and trade unionists are frequent targets for kidnapping and murder.

In Colombia transitional justice became an extension of the government strategy to mobilise the population on the side of the military against non-state armed actors and to reconcile victims of non-state violence through reparations. The founding violence of the recovered Colombian state was security underwritten by the military and their paramilitary allies, not the recognition of victims of human rights violations and the prosecution of their perpetrators. President Uribe set out to militarise society in 2002 through the "Democratic Security" policy based on counter-terrorism, counter-narcotics and counter-insurgency in collaboration with US agencies. "Democratic Security" was designed to challenge the regional power of the FARC and the paramilitaries, the United Self-Defense Forces (AUC), where they had eroded state sovereignty and monopoly over the use of violence. The paramilitaries had begun as community militias and turned into private armies connected to business and corrupt politicians and managed to insert themselves into national politics as violent political brokers of local electoral politics. The logic of "Democratic Security" was a new recruitment of civilian cooperation with military goals to "defend democracy" in their own interest. The state promoted security as the basis for consolidating democracy and reaching peace.

The Peace and Justice Law (Law 975) established in 2005 spelled out the deal between the perpetrators and victims. Demobilisation of the paramilitaries—demobilisation, disarmament and reintegration (DDR)—was based on amnesty for full confession of their criminal activities and their victims received reparations. Government championed the success of Law 975 claiming 30,000 paramilitaries had demobilised and 155,000 victims had registered with the Justice and Peace Unit, largely victims of paramilitary violence, by 2008.[46] The National Commission for Reparations and Reconciliation (CNRR) processed the claims of victims and created forums for victims to ask paramilitary leaders about particular violations and events. The CNRR lists a wide range of violations experienced by victims: "forceful disappearances, kidnapping, murder, genocide, forced displacement, arbitrary detention and violation of due process, forced recruitment, torture, sexual and reproductive violence, inhuman and degrading treatment, terrorist acts, barbarism, destruction of cultural assets and sites, and use of antipersonnel mines".[47] The social diversity of victims, their geographical dispersal and the kind

43 Amnesty International 2011.

44 Human Rights Watch 2012.

45 Human Rights Watch 2012.

46 International Crisis Group 2008.

47 García-Godos and Lid 2010, p. 500.

of violence they had suffered left them fragmented and politically weak. Most did not belong to victim organisations.

Law 975 was strongly criticised by international human rights organisations because it served to grant paramilitaries amnesty and restricted the legal definition of "victim" to individuals who had suffered at the hand of non-state violence but not state violence.[48] The effect was to protect the paramilitaries (and the state) and neglect the victims. While officially more than 30,000 paramilitaries demobilised in practice many continued as paramilitaries in new organisations. Moreover at the point in CNRR hearings when a few paramilitary leaders began to cooperate by revealing the sites of massacres Uribe quickly had them extradited to the US where they faced lesser charges related to drug smuggling. Their extradition cut short the investigations of serious human rights violations, the potentially incriminating evidence against leading politicians, and the hope that families of the disappeared would learn the truth about what had happened to their family members.

Despite the breadth of transitional justice measures introduced under the Peace and Justice Law—truth commission, recognition of victims rights to compensation and to the truth, prosecution of corrupt Congressmen—security has prevailed over reconciliation in Colombia. Nevertheless the recent (2011) introduction of the Victims and Land Restitution Law (Law 1448) under President Santos has significantly expanded the victim category entitled to compensation. It is estimated some 4 million victims and/or their relatives will now be able to file for compensation claims until 2021 and millions of hectares are to be returned to internally displaced persons at an estimated $20 billion.[49] The Constitutional Court further extended the definition of victim to include "the third degree of kinship—relations such as nieces and nephews, grandparents and grandchildren, cousins and in some cases even friends".[50] While the Victims Law makes the transitional justice process potentially more inclusive it does not address the state's responsibility to find and identify the victims of the conflict. Where the funds for victim compensation are to come from is yet to be resolved. Transitional justice in Colombia has combined the normalisation of violence with the normalisation of law. As the Uruguayan writer Eduardo Galeano observes: "Nos quitaron la justicia y nos dejaron la ley"[51] (they took justice away from us and left us the law).

5.4 Trials

With the creation of the ICTY and ICTR in the early 1990s accountability came to the fore of the transitional justice agenda after an earlier period when justice had been balanced with political pragmatism. National and international trials after

[48] García-Godos and Lid 2010, p. 500.

[49] BBC 2011.

[50] Bittner 2012.

[51] Moores 2011.

mass atrocity have sought to produce consensus around the truth of the culpability of perpetrators and their crimes. However, the ability of trials to achieve the "force of law" in situations of political transition has been problematic. Prosecutions have been criticised as political because they were too selective (victors justice), too restricted (symbolic) or too few (impunity). Political divisions and social fragmentation have frequently prevented consensus about the meaning of outcomes. In national trials the hope that judicial accountability would help forge a political consensus has often been disappointing. In international trials establishing the force of (international) law and forging a consensus from trial outcomes has been problematic because perpetrators have often continued to be seen as national heroes and the victims as responsible for their own predicament. The problem of "new sovereignty" in the states of the former Yugoslavia has only compounded the accusation of political trials.[52]

5.4.1 National Trials

Trials are problematic after mass atrocity because they depend on the state's capacity to effectively pursue justice where the perpetrators and their supporters still hold political and military power. If national trials are too narrowly focused on individual criminality their outcomes can appear too legalistic, restricted and irrelevant to the major political issues of mass atrocity. If trials are too broad they can be seen as "show trials" setting up perpetrators as scapegoats for actions beyond their actual responsibility.

In post-dictatorship Argentina in 1985 prosecutions of the junta leaders followed on the CONADEP national inquiry into the "disappeared". The new Alfonsín government expected that the transparency and impartiality of trials would serve as an antidote to the arbitrariness of dictatorship.[53] Public trials and justice would help re-establish the "force of law", reinforce public support for accountability and enhance the political legitimacy of the recently recovered democracy. Trials in Argentina responded to the organised families of the disappeared, the mass street demonstrations for justice, the desire to hold senior military accountable to demonstrate that no-one was above the law and the belief in the function of criminal jurisprudence in a liberal democratic society. But during the trials of the senior military figures in Buenos Aires protested that they were being made scapegoats for the "dirty war".[54] They complained that the crimes of the insurgents had not been addressed and that the public—many of whom had supported the military regime (or at least did not oppose them)—was now lining up to support their prosecution.

---

[52] Osiel 1997.

[53] Grandin 2005, p. 49.

[54] Malamud-Goti 1996, p. xiii.

The Argentine military's protest at being made scapegoats reveals the mechanism inherent in legal prosecutions of political crimes whereby individuals are constructed as either guilty or innocent. Prosecution of key military leaders serves to concentrate culpability on the accused and conceal the complicity of a much wider section of society. "By pinning the blame on a limited sector of society, human rights reinvent history".[55] An artificial boundary is created between degrees of culpability and makes human rights violation the criteria of responsibility. Reflecting on the outcome of the Argentine trials Jaime Malamud-Goti, who played an important role in their organisation, argued that both the supporters and opponents of the military dictatorship ultimately perceived them as political. Neither their supporters nor their opponents were satisfied with the trial outcomes. The former believed the military were made scapegoats while the latter complained that the sentences were too light and prosecutions too few. Consequently trials undermined rather than reinforced judicial authority and the force of law. The general perception was that "the trials were a ploy to draw a consensus from a compromised account of reality".[56] The "doctrine of the two demons" saw wrong on both sides and constructed political violence as the product of "illiberal intolerance".[57]

In Argentina the hope that the trials would be pedagogic and help produce a consensus about the crimes of the dictatorship did not happen.[58] The fragmented public opinion virtually ignored the actual findings of the federal court on the criminal responsibility of senior members of the junta. "The citizenry's indifference to the proceedings shows that, in Argentina, the courts' decisions lack authoritativeness, both in establishing the facts brought to trial and in evaluating the significance of these facts".[59]

Delayed justice in Latin America as a result of the drawn out process of repealing amnesty laws and initiating prosecutions was not merely the expression of the strengthening of liberal democratic institutions and human rights. Amnesty laws were eventually overturned because the political benefit of legitimacy, as the political crimes grew more distant, slowly shifted in favour of upholding human rights. An important factor in the repeal of amnesty laws was that the victims of political crimes (e.g. families of the disappeared) remained politically relevant and influential. Delayed justice in Argentina and Uruguay are contrasting cases. In the former the number of disappeared (300,000) was much larger and the families of the victims, especially the mothers organisations, became internationally renowned. In Argentina the amnesty laws that delayed justice were overcome because of the persistent political and legal pressure of victims families and key figures in human

55 Malamud-Goti 1996, p. 18.

56 Malamud-Goti 1996, p. 19.

57 Grandin 2005, p. 52.

58 Malamud-Goti 1996, p. 187.

59 Malamud-Goti 1996, p. 19.

rights NGOs. But this pressure was effective only when the government saw that it was politically safe and beneficial to do so. Thus in Argentina President Nestor Kirchner overturned the amnesty laws in 2003 when the prosecution of aging and retired military and police officers no longer represented a political risk.[60] The growing distance from events almost 20 years after the end of the dictatorship, however, diminished the imperative to forge a consensus about the past. Or put another way, the greater the distance from events the more likely political violence will be processed as a crime and their political context and import ignored, except for those directly involved. The Argentine courts were able to prosecute the military under international law without having to formally incorporate it in domestic law because the legal system is monist, as stipulated under Article 75, Section 22 of the Constitution.[61] The political benefit of the trials was to reinforce the human rights credentials of the Kirchner government and win the praise and support of local human rights groups and victim organisations. The trials did not address the transitional national consensus of the "two demons" and framed the prosecution of military leaders for crimes against humanity as occurring "in the context of genocide". O'Donnell argues that seeking to meet the expectations of victims groups for the greatest possible legal and moral condemnation of the military rather than sticking to being an arbiter of the national prosecutions can actually undermine the symbolic value of international law.[62] In the context of transitional justice trials are no longer judging the guilt or innocence of the individual but show—against Hannah Arendt's warning about the purpose of the Eichmann trial—"that questions of history, morality and conscience were not legally relevant".[63]

The complex politics over repression in Uruguay saw two referenda in 1989 and 2010 fail to repeal the amnesty laws but nevertheless saw judicial activism succeed in prosecutions on a case by case basis of senior military figures of the dictatorship.[64] The laws were eventually repealed by the leftist *Frente Amplio* (Broad Front) government under President Mujica (a former Tupamaro guerilla) in 2011, something that could have been done by the previous *Frente Amplio* governments from the time they came to power in 2004. However, rather than running the political risk of taking a stand themselves *Frente Amplio* deferred to a plebiscite which they distanced themselves from.

In practice amnesty laws actually signify delayed justice with the consequence that crimes are eventually prosecuted (if those responsible are still alive) and victims acknowledged (or at least their memory and suffering). However, delayed justice also tends to diminish the political import of the charges—crimes against humanity, genocide—and become criminal trials, except for those directly affected

---

60 Humphrey and Valverde 2007.

61 O'Donnell 2009, p. 339.

62 O'Donnell 2009, p. 373.

63 Arendt 1964.

64 Mallinder 2009.

by them. Delayed justice means national trials are not the force for mobilisation and consensus they are at transition.

5.4.2 International Trials

The establishment of international criminal tribunals to investigate war crimes and crimes against humanity and pursue accountability after large-scale atrocities has seen the emergence of a transnational juridical field which has generated its own international law professionals, case law, institutions and an imperative to respond to "legal emergencies"—the rush to get international investigators to the scene of unfolding mass crimes in "real-time" to bring international attention to atrocities and to establish the grounds for legal prosecutions.[65] All such political crises are now seen as having a legal dimension as a consequence of the expansion of international criminal law and the human rights' focus on victims. What Humphrey calls "emergency law" has become the sharp end of international criminal justice, a form of legal triage to manage critical political events.[66]

Since the establishment of the special tribunals in the mid-1990s—ICTY and ICTR—and the expansion of the field of transitional justice for conflict management international criminal law has consolidated itself as an autonomous juridical field.[67] This has happened first, through the emergence of a group of internationalised legal professions (experts on war atrocity and repression), second, through the development of special courts, procedures and legal precedent to address atrocities, and third, through the establishment of what Pierre Bourdieu calls the "force of law", the naturalisation of the court's credibility and authority based on its ability to produce legal effects—universality, neutrality and rationality.[68]

The "force of law" also is dependent upon its recognition, or in Bourdieu's terms "misrecognition".[69] The acceptance of law's authority is based on its "symbolic power" that can only be exercised "through the complicity of those who are dominated by it".[70] In other words, law's specific power as a form of "legitimised discourse" depends on it attaining recognition. It must succeed in binding people to the principle of the "jurists' professional ideology—belief in the neutrality and autonomy of the law and of jurists themselves".[71]

The formation of the ICTY highlights the special difficulties of constituting the new jurisdiction and authority of international criminal law in the states of the

[65] Humphrey 2011.

[66] Humphrey 2011.

[67] Hagan and Levi 2005.

[68] Bourdieu 1987.

[69] Bourdieu 1977.

[70] Bourdieu 1987, p. 844.

[71] Bourdieu 1987, p. 816.

former Yugoslavia. First, the ICTY was the product of a struggle between the role of law and political diplomacy in bringing peace. Human rights activists successfully undermined the "moral equivalency" argument of political diplomacy—"that Bosnians, Croats, and Serbs were equally responsible for the atrocities"—which led to the establishment of the ICTY via a Commission of Experts set up by UN Security Council Resolution 780 (1992) to investigate war atrocities in the Balkans.[72] Second, despite initial difficulties with indictments and arrests the ICTY had to assert its jurisdiction over war crimes and crimes against humanity by launching prosecutions as soon as possible.

The ICTY faced special obstacles in achieving the "force of law" and establishing a consensus about the historical narrative underlying the political crimes—crimes against humanity, war crimes and genocide. The new sovereignties of the former Yugoslavia, the compartmentalisation of Bosnia under the Dayton Agreement into "entities", and the continued political influence of the nationalist parties presented serious obstacles to trials being accepted as just and not partisan. Wilson points out that the ICTY as an international tribunal could avoid issues of national identity and by applying legal categories such as genocide and crimes against humanity which emphasise their collective character compelled "the court to situate individual acts within long-term, systematic policies".[73] International criminal trials have become important forums "at which a postconflict version of history is investigated, discussed, argued over and eventually stamped with the imprimatur of a legal judgement".[74] But they have been criticised for neither producing good history nor meeting the expectations of the universal discourse they employ. The ICTY may be able to produce (legal) facts but these by themselves were not necessarily enough to undermine the national myths that underpinned the conflict and justified the wars and ethnic cleansing.

The ICTY has faced greatest difficulty in producing a legal consensus by prosecuting individual crimes as manifestations of larger criminal political projects. This was particularly the case for political and military leaders considered to be Serbian and Croatian nationalist heroes—Milošević, Karadžić, Mladić, and Gotovina—whose detention and trials were delayed and even prevented because of continued strong nationalist support at home. The case of former Lt Gen. Ante Gotovina—a Croatian military hero of the "Homeland War" in the recovery of the Krajina in 1995—highlights the difficulty of making trials change the status of national war heroes to war criminals by international trials. In Croatia the nationalist narrative and collective memory was based on their historical victimisation of others' atrocities. In the nationalist myth his name became associated with the many martyrs dying for the national cause.[75] In this vein the ICTY was seen as yet another anti-Croatia threat to the very existence of the nation-state. Moreover the prosecution of Croatian

[72] Hagan and Levi 2005, p. 1507.

[73] Wilson 2005, p. 908.

[74] Wilson 2011, p. viii.

[75] Pavlaković 2010, p. 1725.

military generals for war crimes during the "Homeland War" was simply continuing the longer criminalisation of the Croatian nation as genocidal—i.e. the World War II accusation. For the nationalists the aim of ICTY prosecution was not simply to impose individual guilt but collective guilt. For the supporters of Gotovina represented not only "generals of Croatia's victorious army, but the Homeland War, Croatian sovereignty, the Croatian state, and ultimately all Croats".[76] Moreover his successful evasion of detention by the ICTY evoked the heroic image of the outlaw/bandit, glorified in national folklore, now repeated in the stories of soldiers who become labelled war criminals.[77] The postwar Croatian governments were ambivalent about accepting the authority of the primacy of the ICTY, especially over war crimes cases. The new Croatian state strategically complied rather than cooperated with the ICTY by detaining and transferring Croatian prisoners to the Hague for the long-term benefit of EU membership. The strategy involved cooperation with the ICTY externally and resistance to it domestically.[78]

While international criminal law has gradually forged a transnational juridical field through the emergence of experienced legal experts in war atrocities and the development of specific law and procedures through prosecutions, its legal authority remains politically contingent. International commissions of investigation and special tribunals and courts may have legitimacy in the eyes of victims (and their families and communities) but not necessarily with political groups or other sectors of the population who may still see those convicted as heroes and martyrs. International legal intervention is almost inevitably seen as political and partisan, especially if the distribution of the crimes committed are unequally discovered and/or prosecuted.

The growth of "emergency law" with the doctrine of R2P and the increased reach of international criminal law through the ICC has seen the expansion of the role of the victim in international criminal law. The victim, through the trauma lens, is used to reveal politically inflicted suffering and to justify international intervention through legal investigations to document serious human rights violations and even military action to protect civilians. The trauma lens has also become more important in international trials with the growth of international criminal law and international courts and the expansion of the role of the victim in international trial process and trial. The rights to compensation of direct victims of gross human rights violations emerged as an issue during the ICTY and ICTR trials. This led to the strengthening of victims' rights norm through the Basic Principles and Guidelines on the Rights to a Remedy and Reparation for Victims of Gross Violations of International Human Rights Law and Serious Violations of International Humanitarian Law (2006) what Cherif Bassiouni describes as an international bill of victims rights.[79] This bill of victims rights represents a shift to

[76] Pavlaković 2010, p. 1717.

[77] Pavlaković 2010, p. 1717.

[78] Lamont 2010, p. 1697.

[79] Bassiouni 2006, p. 203.

a focus on victims rights "driven by the concept of responsibility" in criminal and legal proceedings and victims rights based on "human and social solidarity reflected in social assistance and support programs".[80] In other words, the ritual structure of international trials is in some respects moving towards the truth commission victim-centred approach emphasising the truth of trauma/suffering and victims' rights following the 2006 Basic Principles. In fact Bassiouni advocates redefining international crimes by "making them dependent on the suffering experienced by the victims rather than the nature of the conflict or the context within which such violations took place".[81] In the case of some international trials this may well see the growth in the time spent on the claims of victims rather than the prosecution of perpetrators. This may well happen in the Special Tribunal for Lebanon where it is very likely that those indicted will not be apprehended and trials, if held, will be held in absentia. In this situation the claims of victims may come to dominate court business.[82]

5.5 Conclusion

Transitional justice with its focus on retributive and restorative justice has emerged as an inclusive discourse in post-conflict societies. Its inclusiveness is reflected in the universalising and individualising discourses of rights and suffering on the base of our shared humanity and our shared experience of a sentient body. Trials and truth commissions emerged as key rituals of social transformation designed to produce a separation between past and present, guilt and innocence, and unlawful and lawful. Yet these rituals confront the reality of violence at the political foundations of political orders and become implicated in them. They seek to expose the violence of preservation (based on repression and human rights violations) and turn the stories of its victims into the founding violence stories of a democratic political order. In other words instead of the heroes and martyrs it is the victims who are made the source of political legitimacy.

Yet the inclusive discourses of rights and suffering become qualified and victims and perpetrators assume different symbolic value in the production of the consensus around transition. In truth commissions the question of who deserves to be recognised as a victim shapes the official narrative and the meaning of violence—why did it happen, who was responsible? Meister provides an important insight into truth commissions as providing a counter-revolutionary political solution achieved by mediating and limiting the demands of victims and reassuring beneficiaries of previous injustice that their fears of the vengeful victim are wrong.

[80] Bassiouni 2006, p. 206.

[81] Bassiouni 2006, p. 206.

[82] Humphrey 2011, p. 17.

By reassuring the beneficiaries and recognising the victims the moral economy of trauma circumscribes the universality of rights and suffering.

In Latin America where the military—as the victors of counter-insurgency—could grant themselves amnesty their victims were often divided over accepting compensation and forfeiting justice or continuing to struggle and become victimised or blamed once again for causing trouble. In the situations of ongoing conflict where the military could still insist that security prevails over human rights, as in Algeria and Colombia, the mechanisms of inclusion and exclusion become more visible. The pattern of forging a consensus and excluding those who either insisted on justice and state accountability or wanted to continue the conflict for a more radical justice and the cementing of deals with democratic majorities has proven to be a powerful strategy for marginalising the "bad victims".

While the expansion of international criminal law has seen accountability come to the fore of transitional justice trials remain problematic in forging a consensus about the collective political projects involving crimes against humanity and genocide. The problems faced by the ICTY in the context of new sovereignties and popular nationalist military and political leaders highlight the difficulty in establishing the "force of (international) law" through trials. They have revealed the challenge of being arbiters of law while trying to situate individual criminal acts into collective and systematic projects.

References

Amnesty International (2011) The challenges of Colombia's victims' law, 15 June 2011. www.blog.amnestyusa.org/justice/the-challenges-of-colombias-victims-law. Accessed 7 March 2012

Arendt H (1964) Eichmann in Jerusalem. A report on the banality of evil. Viking Press, New York

Asad T (1997) On torture, or cruel, inhuman and degrading treatment. In: Kleinman A, Das V, Lock M (eds) Social suffering. University of California Press, Berkeley, pp 285–308

Bassiouni MC (2006) International recognition of victims' rights. Hum Rights Law Rev 6:203–279

BBC (2011) Historic Colombian victims' compensation law signed, 11 June 2011. www.bbc.co.uk/news/world-latin-america-13736523. Accessed 7 March 2012

Bell C, Campbell C, í Aoláin FN (2007) Transitional justice: (re)conceptualising the field. Int J Law Context 3:81–88

Bourdieu P (1977) Outline of a theory of practice. Cambridge University Press, Cambridge

Bourdieu P (1987) The Force of law: toward a sociology of the juridical field. Hastings Law J 38:805–813

Bittner MC (2012) Colombia's Constitutional Court broadens victims law. Colombia Reports, 9 Feb 2012. www.colombiareports.com/colombia-news/news/22110-colombian-court-broadens-victims-law.html. Accessed 7 March 2012

Comaroff J, Comaroff JL (2008) Law and disorder in the postcolony. Soc Anthropol 15:133–152

Ellyas A, Hamani H (1999) Algeria hopes and prays. Le Monde Diplomatique, 4 Sept 1999. www.mondediplo.com/1999/09/04algeria. Accessed 9 Sept 1999

Fassin D, Rechtman R (eds) (2009) Empire of Trauma: an inquiry into the condition of victimhood. Princeton University Press, Princeton

García-Godos J, Lid KAO (2010) Transitional justice and victims' rights before the end of a conflict: the unusual case of Colombia. J Latin Am Stud 42:487–516

Girard R (1977) Violence and the sacred. John Hopkins University Press, Baltimore
Grandin G (2005) The instruction of great catastrophe: truth commissions, national history, and state formation in Argentina, Chile, and Guatemala. Am Hist Rev 110:46–67
Grandin G (2007) Human rights and the empires embrace: a Latin American counterpoint. In: Wasserstrom JN, Grandin G, Hunt L, Young MB (eds) Human rights and revolutions. Rowman & Littlefield Publishers, Lanham, pp. 191–212
Guerrero L, Abramovich V, González F, Roberts C, Pinheiro PS (2009) Report on citizen security and human rights. DOC. 57. Inter-American Commission on Human Rights. www.cidh.org. Accessed 29 Feb 2012
Habermas J (1998) Remarks on legitimation through human rights. Philos Soc Crit 24:157–171
Hagan J, Levi R (2005) Crimes of war and the force of law. Soc Forces 83:1499–1534
Hastrup K (2003) Violence, suffering and human rights. Anthropol Theory 3:309–323
Hirschl R (2008) The judicialization of mega-politics and the rise of political courts. Ann Rev Political Sci 11:93–118
Human Rights Watch (2012) World report—2012: Colombia. www.hrw.org/world-report-2012/colombia. Accessed 2 March 2012
Humphrey M (2005) Reconciliation and the therapeutic state. J Intercult Stud 26:203–220
Humphrey M (2010) The politics of trauma. ARTS: J Sydney Univ Arts Assoc 32:37–54
Humphrey M (2011) The special tribunal for Lebanon: emergency law, trauma and justice. Arab Stud Q 33:4–22
Humphrey M (2012) Marginalizing "victims" and "terrorists": modes of exclusion in the reconciliation process. Renner J, Spencer A (eds) Reconciliation after terrorism: strategy, possibility, or absurdity? Routledge, London, pp. 48–68
Humphrey M, Valverde E (2007) Human rights, victimhood and impunity: an anthropology of democracy in Argentina. Soc Anal 51:179–197
Humphrey M, Valverde E (2008) Human rights politics, and injustice: transitional justice in Argentina and South Africa. Int J Transitional Justice 2:1–23
International Crisis Group (2008) Correcting course: victims and the justice and peace law in Colombia. Latin America Report N° 29, 30 Oct. www.crisisgroup.org/en/regions/latin-america-caribbean/andes/colombia/029-correcting-course-victims-and-the-justice-and-peace-law-in-colombia.aspx. Accessed 3 March 2012
Lamont CK (2010) Defiance or strategic compliance? The Post-Tuđman Croatian Democratic Union and the International Criminal Tribunal for the former Yugoslavia. Europe-Asia Stud 62:1683–1705
Malamud-Goti J (1996) Game without end: state terror and the politics of justice. University of Oklahoma Press, Norman
Mallinder L (2009) Uruguay's evolving experience of amnesty and civil society's response. www.papers.ssrn.com/sol3/papers.cfm?abstract_id=1387362. Accessed 29 Feb 2012
McDougall J (2005) Savage wars? Codes of violence in Algeria, 1830s–1990s. Third World Q 26:117–131
Meister R (2002) Human rights and the politics of victimhood. Ethics Int Aff 16:191–108
Meister R (2005) Ways of winning: the costs of moral victory in transitional regimes. In: Schrift AD (ed) Modernity and the problem of evil. Indiana University Press, Bloomington, Indianapolis, pp. 85–111
Moores EF (2011) Pensar con los pies. La Nacion (Montevideo), 25 de mayo de 2011. www.lanacion.com.ar/1376122-d. Accessed 5 Sep 2012
O'Donnell MK (2009) New dirty war judgments in Argentina: national courts and domestic prosecutions of international human rights violations. NY Univ Law Rev 84:333–374
Osiel M (1997) Mass atrocity. Collective memory and the law. Transaction Publishers, New Brunswick
Pavlaković V (2010) Croatia, the International Criminal Tribunal for the former Yugoslavia, and general Gotovina as a political symbol. Europe-Asia Stud 62:1707–1740
Robben AC (2005) Political violence and trauma in Argentina. University of Pennsylvania Press, Philadelphia

Ricoeur P (2000) The just. University of Chicago Press, Chicago

Taylor J (1994) Body memories: aide-memoires and collective amnesia in the wake of the Argentine terror. In: Ryan M, Gordon A (eds) Body politics: disease. Desire and the Family. Westview Press, Boulder, pp. 192–203

Tlemçani R (2008) Algeria under Bouteflika: civil strife and national reconciliation. Carnegie Middle East Center, Carnegie Endowment for International Peace, Washington. www.carnegieendowment.org/files/cmec7_tlemcani_algeria_final.pdf. Accessed 21 Nov 2011

UN (2006) International convention for the protection of all persons from enforced disappearance, drafted on 29 June 2006. www.ohchr.org/english/law/pdf/disappearance-convention.pdf. Accessed 22 Aug 2012

Wilson RA (2005) Judging history: the historical record of the International Criminal Tribunal for the former Yugoslavia. Hum Rights Q 27:908–942

Wilson RA (2011) Writing history in international criminal trials. Cambridge University Press, Cambridge

Chapter 6
Redressing Sexual Violence in Transitional Justice and the Labelling of Women as "Victims"

Susanne Buckley-Zistel

Abstract The chapter discusses the implications of labelling women who have experienced sexual violence in times of war and repression as "victims" in discourse and practice of transitional justice. It is based on the assumption that men and women become targets of sexual violence primarily due to their respective gender roles in a society and argues that as a consequence the prevention of future violence requires a significant modification of these gender relations (or power asymmetries) and that a focus on masculinities is essential to understanding these dynamics. This chapter marks a first attempt to conceptualise the link between masculinities, sexual violence and the advancement of gender justice through transitional justice processes. Can the focus on women in the context of crime tribunals, in particular, contribute to more gender justice in the post-conflict society?

Keywords Sexual violence • Masculinities • Transitional justice • Victims • Labelling • Gender • Women

6.1 Introduction

The objective of this chapter is to discuss the implications of labelling women who have experienced sexual violence in times of war and repression as "victims" in discourse and practice of transitional justice. Sexual violence refers to assaults of a sexual nature against both women and men. It is by no means a new phenomenon,

---

The author is Professor for Peace and Conflict Studies at the Center for Conflict Studies at the Philipps-University Marburg. I am very grateful to Henri Myrttinen for his valuable comments on an earlier draft of this chapter.

S. Buckley-Zistel (✉)
Philipps-University Marburg, Marburg, Germany
e-mail: s.buckley-zistel@staff.uni-marburg.de

T. Bonacker and C. Safferling (eds.), *Victims of International Crimes: An Interdisciplinary Discourse*, DOI: 10.1007/978-90-6704-912-2_6,

although it has recently received worldwide attention due to the widespread assault on women during the violent conflicts in *inter alia* Rwanda, Liberia and the Balkans, as well as currently in the Democratic Republic of Congo. Whereas previously, that is until the verdicts of the International Criminal Tribunal for Rwanda (ICTR) and the International Criminal Tribunal for the former Yugoslavia (ICTY), it had been treated as a by-product of war—responded to with impunity—, it now forms a central part of transitional justice processes, in particular in the context of criminal prosecution. This is based on the realisation that men and women do not become targets of sexual assaults randomly or due to the sexual drives of the perpetrators but because of political and social calculations by the opposing parties to the conflict. It is increasingly referred to as a weapon of war.[1]

The chapter is based on the assumption that men and women become targets of sexual violence primarily due to their respective gender roles in a society. It argues that as a consequence the prevention of future violence requires a significant modification of these gender relations (or power asymmetries). Can this be achieved by redressing sexual violence through transitional justice processes? Can the focus on women in the context of crime tribunals, in particular, contribute to more gender justice in the post-conflict society?

In order to respond to these questions I shall first briefly outline forms and dynamics of sexual violence during violent conflicts to then focus on the concept of masculinity to analyse the power dynamics at the heart of assaults of men against women.[2] This shall lead to a discussion of how sexual crimes are being redressed by means of transitional justice in order to then, lastly, draw some conclusions as to whether this might have a positive impact on the prevailing gender relations in a society, contribute to more gender justice, and prevent similar crimes in the future.

This chapter marks a first attempt to conceptualise the link between masculinities, sexual violence, and the advancement of gender justice through transitional justice processes. It is based on literature research only and cannot but paint a highly complex picture with very broad strokes and strong generalisations. For now, however, the purpose is to sketch out some analytical connections, rather than presenting a refined picture.

6.2 Sexual Violence During Violent Conflicts

During violent conflicts, men and women become targets of sexual violence due to their gender-specific roles within a society. In this sense, they are not always simply targeted as individual but as representatives of the respective ethnic/religious/political etc. identity group.[3] This can take various forms. Regarding women, their

---

[1] See for instance Buss 2009 and Maedl 2011.

[2] Even though violence against men is a significant occurrence for the lack of empirical data this chapter focuses on women only.

[3] For an overview of motivations of rapists see Eriksson Baaz 2009.

social (and biological) role as reproducers of ethnic, religious or national groups through childbirth can turn them into targets of sexual assault, including rape (*inter alia* to impregnate them with children from the enemy group), mutilation of their reproductive organs, and forced sterilisation, to name but a few, which all aim to undermine the reproduction of their identity group. This has been referred to as acts of ethnic cleansing (or even genocide, as ruled by the ICTR). Moreover, rape and mutilation can be understood as a symbolic attack on the "Mother of the Nation", i.e. the guardian of the respective identity group or, as Jean Elshtain puts it, on the symbolic representation of the body politic.[4] This has significant—intended—social repercussions:

> Sexual violence against women is likely to destroy a nation's culture. In times of war, the women are those who hold the families and the community together. Their physical and emotional destruction aims at destroying social and cultural stability. Moreover the psychological effects of mass rapes within the community concerned may lead to the devaluation and dissolution of the entire group. The destruction of women and/or their integrity affects overall cultural cohesion.[5]

The destruction of social and cultural cohesion within a group reduces its external value, it is humiliated and degraded in the process. This is particularly visible in incidences where husbands, brothers and sons are forced to witness the rape of female members of their family, insulting them in their socially prescribed role as the protectors of "their" women. Moreover, it produces and re-produces relations of superiority and inferiority between the parties to the conflict.

6.3 Masculinities and Violence

Recent research suggests that it is important to look at the construction of masculinities to better understand sexual assaults against women in times of crisis.[6] Masculinity, or—due to their varied expression better referred to as masculinities—broadly denotes the manifestation of widespread social norms and expectations that define what it means to be a man.[7] It has been argued that some men perform their masculine identity through the use of violence which is intrinsically connected to the assertion of social status and the value of the self, in other words: it literally "makes men".[8] This social status is subject to the particular socio-cultural background of a society in conflict and reflected in gender relations, i.e. in the way in which social practice is ordered along the lines of the reproductive arena.[9]

[4] Elshtain 1987, p. 67.

[5] Seifert 1996, p. 39.

[6] Hamber 2007; Sigsworth and Valji 2011; Theidon 2009.

[7] Hamber 2007, p. 379.

[8] Cahn et al. 2009, p. 105.

[9] Connell 2005, p. 72.

From the perspective of masculinities, men tend to assume different roles based on their *habitus*: from responsible heads of household, via protectors, to hyper-masculine action hero types,[10] to name but a few. According to R. W. Connell, this is due to the fact that men are taking a hegemonic position in society[11]: "Different masculinities exist in definite relations with each other, often relations of hierarchy and exclusion. There is generally a dominant or 'hegemonic' form of masculinity, the centre of the system of gendered power".[12]

Masculinities are socially constructed through distinction from other men (homosocial) as well as from women (heterosocial) producing and re-producing power relations.[13] This *libido dominandi*[14] is expressed in the desire to dominate other men as well as, rather secondarily, to dominate and potentially injure women as an instrument of the symbolic struggle. The injury of women is however not about the women themselves, rather, women serve as reference objects—similar to "trophies"—in the "battle" between men. This mirrors the analysis of sexual violence above, according to which the abuse of women is not necessarily about the women themselves but about insulting "their" men as well as destroying the culture and social cohesion of the other group.

This point is illustrated by a study of Wendy Bracewell on gender dimensions in the Yugoslav province of Kosovo in the 1980s. She found that in the discourses amongst Serb Kosovars on the rape of Serb women by Kosovo Albanians in the 1980s "sexual violence became a focus of public discourse [...] because of the way the subject linked assumptions and anxieties to do with gender (and especially masculinity) to a vision of Serbian nationhood under threat".[15] In other words, the perceived threat to Serbian nationhood was translated into the focus on the abuse of Serb women. Bracewell thus argues that "Serb-Albanian relations in Kosovo were presented as a matter of competing masculinities, with the bodies of women serving as the markers of success or failure".[16] Hence, the outrage about the rapes in Kosovo had little to do with violence against women as such but with the means of communication between men whilst "[i]ndividual women vanished almost entirely from the discourse of 'nationalist' rape, except as emblems of male honour and symbols of the Serbian nation".[17] One moment when women became prominent though was when demonstrating in front of army barracks in order to appeal to Serb men (armed men, i.e. soldiers) to protect them. This form of female agency reproduced the hegemonic images of Serbian "protector masculinities" amongst Serbs through stressing the strength of the men in contrast to the

[10] Meuser 2002, p. 63.

[11] For a more refined understanding of the term hegemony in Connell see Beasley 2008.

[12] Connell 2000.

[13] Meuser 2002, p. 94.

[14] Bourdieu 1997, p. 215.

[15] Bracewell 2000, p. 571.

[16] Bracewell 2000, p. 572.

[17] Bracewell 2000, p. 573.

vulnerability of the women[18]—and it illustrates that the production and reproduction of hegemonic masculinities involves both, men and women.[19]

Based on this conceptualisation of masculinities and femininities it can be summarised that, in many cases, sexual violence against women is embedded in the performance of hegemonic masculinities and the dominant position of men.[20] Or, the other way round, it is due to the inferior social position of women, and the ensuing disrespect, that they become targets.[21] In order to prevent sexual violence against women in the future it is thus paramount to change their social position from being a mere "means of communication", i.e. passive objects, to active agents, in particular in times after violent conflicts when the future composition of a society is being renegotiated. This leads us to the central question of this chapter: can this be achieved by redressing sexual violence within the framework of transitional justice?

6.4 Sexual Violence and Transitional Justice

The recent inclusion of sexual violence against women in transitional justice processes has been a significant achievement. It has led to increased awareness, new legislation, and new norms, and it has constituted a particular subject position, i.e. the women as the "victim subject". For Ratna Kapur, the discourse of violence against women has been successful "partly because of its appeal to the victim subject. In the context of law and human rights, it is invariably the abject victim subject who seeks rights, primarily because she is the one who has had the worst happen to her. The victim subject has allowed women to speak out about abuses that have remained hidden or invisible in human rights discourse".[22]

A number of benefits are connected to this subject position (if and when officially recognised), such as rights and entitlements. First, as referred to in the quote, women have the possibility to use the victim position to speak up and inform about the wrongs they have experienced. This does not only potentially restore their dignity but is also a first step of these wrongs being put right. It gives them a voice and enables them to put their abuses out in the open—if shame and the fear of stigma permit.

Moreover, "victims" may qualify for reparations, both material and symbolic. The former are significant since they might assist "victims" in improving their economic position, with a potential impact on gender relations. More recent truth

[18] Bracewell 2000, p. 574.

[19] See also Theidon 2009.

[20] This is, of course, simplified for the sake of the argument in this chapter. For an intriguing ethnographic take which comes to a somewhat different conclusion see Eriksson Baaz 2009.

[21] For the sake of the argument this is a very broad generalisation. Not only do men also become subjected to sexual violence, women also at times involved in instigating the rape of fellow females.

[22] Kapur 2002, p. 5.

commissions in Peru, Timor-Leste and Sierra Leone made explicit mention in their recommendations to financially compensate "victims" of sexual violence.[23] This is particularly significant for women who live in abject poverty due to the loss of material belongings and poor health due to assaults.[24]

Symbolic reparations in form of memorials, commemorations events or apologies may contribute to improving the standing of "victims" in a society since they single them out as a group worthy of special considerations. This might improve their social status and influence in society. Organised as lobby groups "victims" might be able to have an impact on social and political processes, such as for instance in Rwanda where women organisations achieved that sexual violence during the genocide was recognised and prosecuted as one of the most serious genocide crimes.[25]

Individually, too, women subjected to sexual violence might benefit from being labelled a "victim". Labelling can be an important step in the process of making sense of the crime and gaining control over one's life.[26] The public recognition of the deed, as well as the membership of a community of individuals with the same fate, might assist in coming to terms with the experience[27] as well as restoring the dignity of both individuals and groups. "Victims" in this sense are characterised by their innocence and consequently their moral authority over the rest of the society. As argued by Zur, "[t]he victim status is a powerful one. The victim is always morally right, neither responsible nor accountable, and forever entitled to sympathy".[28] And yet, despite these important achievements, the inclusion of sexual violence in transitional justice processes is a mixed blessing since it reproduces gender essentialisms and fixes the social position and political identity of women in the newly emerging society as perpetual "victims": passive, inferior, vulnerable and in need of (male) protection. In the sense of Gayatry Spivak, it is "[w]hite men saving brown women from brown men".[29]

Much of this is related to discursive processes of victimisation which happen in various dimensions. First, there is a risk that criminal tribunals, in particular, shift the role of women from agents in seeking justice to the category of "victims" in TJ processes. This is for instance illustrated in a study by Julie Mertus about the impact of criminal trials for wartime rape (at the ICTY) on women's agency.[30] The women's initial motivation to participate in the trials was to mobilise other survivors, to influence international opinion, and shape international norms, as well as to receive

[23] Rubio-Marin 2006, pp. 33, 34. Coming forward to claim material reparations is nevertheless a delicate issue due to stigma and shame.

[24] Goldblatt 2006.

[25] Mageza-Barthel 2012.

[26] Davis et al. 1998, p. 20.

[27] Hagemann 1992.

[28] Zur 2005, p. 20.

[29] Spivak 1988.

[30] Mertus 2004.

public recognition for their harms, to create a public historical record, and to achieve personal closure.[31] Yet, in the course of the proceedings they came to realise that they could not use the trials for their own purposes. Rather, according to Mertus, "witnesses almost universally experienced the trials as dehumanising and re-traumatising experiences" so that they became disillusioned with the adversarial process.[32] Through the particular form of questioning as practised in court—in which prosecutors appropriate the testimonies to their own schema of who did what, how, and when—the women did not have the opportunity to tell their whole story. They were not the focus of attention for their own sake but only in order to reveal something about the perpetrators.[33] This had little therapeutic impact, if any, while undermining their ambition to turn from "victims" of rape to agents in the transitional justice process. Again, they were reduced to the status of passive "victims", obstructing the development of a more gender just environment in the future.

This situation is further enhanced by what has been referred to as the "peril of representation"[34] as a consequence of international TJ entrepreneurs speaking on behalf of groups and individuals they label "victims", including women as "victims" of sexual assaults. The production of an "authentic victim" (or victim authenticity) changes the position of the person not just on the international stage, but also in her (or his) society. In this sense, "speaking for and about victims further perpetuates their disempowerment and marginality".[35] As a consequence, the "victim" produced by TJ entrepreneurs and others is passive, hapless, and dependent on others to speak on her or his behalf, reproducing relationships of (global and local) inferiority and superiority,[36] as well as undermining women who want to testify about sexual assaults and thus to turn from "victims" into agents. This, again, reduces the chances to dissent from the power asymmetries at the core of the abuses they encountered.

Furthermore, without diminishing the importance of prosecuting sexual violence, Katherine Franke directs attention to the fact that the selectivity of sexual crimes might have a counterproductive impact on broader issues of gender justice.[37] The exclusive focus on sexual crimes is based on a highly selective image of femininity—marked by peacefulness and non-aggressiveness—leading to ignoring women's role as political agents in times of crisis, and consequently also as executors of violence and cruelty. As illustrated by Kirstin Campbell with regards to the ICTY, the gendered patterns of legal practice lead to women predominately testifying to sexual violence whilst men refer to violence more generally.[38] She follows:

---

[31] Mertus 2004, p. 111.

[32] Mertus 2004, p. 112.

[33] Mertus 2004, p. 115.

[34] Kennedy 2001, p. 121.

[35] Madlingozi 2010, p. 210.

[36] Madlingozi 2010, p. 213.

[37] Franke 2006, p. 825.

[38] Campbell 2007, p. 425.

> If women only narrate rape, then they appear as passive victims of *sexual* violence. Such narrative framing reproduces traditional models of active masculinity and passive femininity. It produces the problem of the *legal representation* of women's agency, which becomes particularly important in this context of the engendering of naming and witnessing harms of conflict.[39]

The ignorance of the activity of (some) women is crucial since women, too, might play an active role in a violent conflict—yet this often remains excluded in TJ processes.[40] In Liberia, for example, the Truth and Reconciliation Commission highlighted the plight of women as "victims" of violent (sexual) attacks, while it failed to draw attention to the fact that women formed a significantly large part of the warring factions (30 % of combatants were female[41]). Accordingly, their crimes were not considered in the public eye. In doing so, the findings of the Truth and Reconciliation Commission undermined the political activities as well as the competences of women to make independent policy decisions; it constructed them as passive objects. Here, once more, there is a risk that the portrayal of women as "victims" undermines efforts to render them equal agents in the post-conflict society.

Finally, it is important to note that while sexual violence against women has become visible in transitional justice processes, sexual assaults against men have not. There is growing empirical evidence that sexual violence against men, too, is used for strategic purposes during violent conflicts. *Inter alia* raping men may serve the function of emasculating them, i.e. degrading them to the status of women, in order to undermine their position in society. Stigma, shame, and humiliation make it almost impossible for men to come forward and to seek both, medical assistance and legal advice.[42]

6.5 Conclusions

This cursory and very sketchy portrayal of how sexual violence against women is dealt with in transitional justice processes suggests that there is a threat of victimising women in the process and thus turning them into passive objects, once again. This is crucial in relation to the central question of the chapter, i.e. if the redress of sexual violence through TJ can contribute to altering the gender relations in a society. In other words, can it reduce the hegemonic status of men and the inferior position of women? This, it was stated by way of introduction, is a significant condition for advancing gender justice in a society and for preventing sexual violence against women in the future.

---

[39] Campbell 2007, p. 426.

[40] One exception is the court case against Pauline Nyiramasuhuko at the ICTR. She is accused of instigating Hutu militias to rape Tutsi women during the 1994 genocide in Rwanda.

[41] Pietsch 2010.

[42] As illustrated by the documentary "Gender Against Men" by the Refugee Law Project, Makerere University, Kampala, Uganda.

The examples referred to in this chapter suggest that, at present, the way sexual crimes are being redressed in transitional justice processes leads to the (renewed) victimisation of women, obstructing the chances of dissidence from their passive, inferior subject position. It reduces their potential to challenge the hegemonic position of men in society. The focus on the role of hegemonic masculinity in the occurrence of sexual violence suggests that it is significant to include it in the analysis of the prevention of abuses in the future.

This chapter has offered a brief exploration of the links between hegemonic masculinities, sexual violence in times of war and the chances of advancing gender justice through redressing these crimes in transitional justice processes. Due to the lack of literature its character remains suggestive, calling for more empirical research in the area. For it is only through careful analysis that the highly complex connections between these aspects can be drawn out.

References

Beasley C (2008) Rethinking hegemonic masculinities in a globalizing world. Men Masculinities 11:86–103

Bourdieu P (1997) Die männliche Herrschaft. In: Dölling I, Krais B (eds) Ein alltägliches Spiel. Geschlechterkonstruktion in der sozialen Praxis. Suhrkamp, Frankfurt am Main, pp. 153–217

Bracewell W (2000) Rape in Kosovo: masculinity and Serbian nationalism. Nations Natl 6:563–590

Buss DE (2009) Rethinking "rape as a weapon of war". Feminist Legal Stud 17:145–163

Cahn N, Ni Aolain F, Haynes DF (2009) Gender, masculinities, and transition in conflicted societies. N Engl Law Rev 44:101–122

Campbell K (2007) The gender of transitional justice: law, sexual violence and the International Criminal Tribunal for the former Yugoslavia. Int J Transitional Justice 1:411–432

Connell RW (2000) Arms and the man: using new research on masculinity to understand violence and promote peace in the contemporary world. In: Breines I, Connell RW, Eide I (eds) Male roles, masculinities and violence: a culture of peace perspective. UNESCO Publishing, Paris, pp. 21–33

Connell RW (2005) Masculinities. Polity Press, Cambridge

Davis CG, Nolen-Hoeksema S, Larson J (1998) Making sense of loss and benefiting from the experience: two construals of meaning. J Pers Soc Psychol 75:561–574

Elshtain JB (1987) Women and war. Harvester, Brighton

Eriksson Baaz M (2009) Why do soldiers rape? Masculinity, violence, and sexuality in the armed forces in the Congo (DRC). Int Stud Q 53:495–518

Franke KM (2006) Gendered subjects of transitional justice. Columbia J Gender Law 15:813–828

Goldblatt B (2006) Evaluating the gender content of reparations: lessons from South Africa. In: Rubio-Marin R (ed) What happened to the women? Gender and reparations for human rights violations. International Center for Transitional Justice, New York, pp. 48–91

Hagemann O (1992) Victims of violent crime and their coping processes. In: Viano EC (ed) Critical issues in victimology: international perspectives. Springer, New York, pp. 58–67

Hamber B (2007) Masculinity and transitional justice: an exploratory essay. Int J Transitional Justice 1:375–390

Kapur R (2002) The tragedy of victimization rhetoric: resurrecting the "native" subject in international/post-colonial feminist legal politics. Harv Hum Rights J 15:1–38

Kennedy D (2001) The international human rights movement: part of the problem? Harv Hum Rights J 15:101–125

Madlingozi T (2010) On transitional justice entrepreneurs and the production of victims. J Hum Rights Pract 2:208–228

Mageza-Barthel R (2012) Asserting their presence! Women's quest for transitional justice in post-genocide Rwanda. In: Buckley-Zistel S, Stanley R (eds) Gender in transitional justice. Palgrave, Basingstoke, pp. 163–190

Maedl A (2011) Rape as a weapon of war in Eastern Congo? A victims' perspective. Hum Rights Q 33:128–147

Mertus J (2004) Shouting from the bottom of a well. The impact of international trials for wartime rape on women's agency. Int Feminist J Politics 6:110–128

Meuser M (2002) "Doing Masculinity"—Zur Geschlechtslogik männlichen Gewalthandelns. In: Dackweiler R-M, Schäfer M (eds) Gewaltverhältnisse. Feministische Perspektiven auf Geschlecht und Gewalt. Campus, Frankfurt am Main, pp. 53–78

Pietsch S (2010) Women's participation and benefit of the liberian truth and reconciliation commission—voices from the field. MA dissertation, Center for Conflict Studies, Philipps-University Marburg (unpublished)

Rubio-Marin R (2006) Introduction. The gender of reparations: setting the Agenda. In: Rubio-Marin R (ed) What happened to the women? Gender and reparations for human rights violations. International Center for Transitional Justice, New York, pp. 20–47

Seifert R (1996) The second front. The logic of sexual violence in war. Women's Stud Int Forum 19:35–43

Sigsworth R, Valji N (2011) Continuities of violence against women in South Africa: the limitations of transitional justice. In: Buckley-Zistel S, Stanley R (eds) Gender in transitional justice. Palgrave, Basingstoke, pp. 115–135

Spivak G (1988) Can the subaltern speak? In: Grossberg L, Nelson C (eds) Marxism and the interpretation of culture. University of Illinois Press, Urbana, pp. 271–313

Theidon K (2009) Reconstructing masculinities: the disarmament, demobilization, and reintegration of former combatants in Columbia. Hum Rights Q 31:1–34

Zur O (2005) The psychology of victimhood. In: Wright RH, Cummings NA (eds) Destructive trends in mental health. Routledge, New York, pp. 45–64

Chapter 7
Everyone Wanted to be Victim: How Victims of Persecution Disappear Within a Victimised Nation

Brigitte Bailer-Galanda

Abstract For more than four decades the Allied declaration of Moscow 1943 which had stated that in 1938 Austria had been the first victim of Hitler's aggression policy stood in the centre of Austrian postwar identity. This declaration not only shaped Austria's identity dealing with her own past but also Austrian politics concerning victims of National Socialist persecution. Furthermore the impending State Treaty finally signed in 1955 influenced these politics. Austrian governments made every effort to avoid Austria being seen responsible for National Socialist crimes committed on her territory so as not to be forced to pay any reparations due to the State Treaty. Efforts of the Austrian parliament to reduce the chances for restitution were blocked up by the Allied Council. It was the Allied Council as well which had forced the Austrian parliament to stricter denazification measures in 1947. From this time on former National Socialists saw themselves as victims of Allied pressure. While Austria denied any responsibility for National Socialist crimes she cared for returning soldiers of the German Army. The legal measures for this group were built parallel to these for victims of persecution thus recognising the victim's status of these soldiers. Finally, almost all Austrians felt themselves to have unjustly suffered by National Socialism and World War II not regarding their own involvement in the regime. Thus the victims of persecution became just one small group of victims beside other much larger groups and by and by they disappeared at least from public opinion.

Keywords Victims • Denazification • Austria • National Socialism • Transitional justice • Restitution

---

The author is Academic Director of the Documentation Center of Austrian Resistance in Vienna as well as Honorary Professor at the University of Vienna for Contemporary History.

B. Bailer-Galanda (✉)
Documentation Center of Austrian Resistance, Vienna, Austria
e-mail: brigitte.bailer@doew.at

T. Bonacker and C. Safferling (eds.), *Victims of International Crimes: An Interdisciplinary Discourse*, DOI: 10.1007/978-90-6704-912-2_7,

7.1 Political and Social Settings in the First Years of the Second Republic of Austria

Austria was restored as an independent state as early as the end of April 1945. Immediately after the liberation of the city of Vienna the newly founded respectively re-established political parties—Conservatives, Social Democrats, Communists—declared Austria's independence and constituted a provisional government.[1] Conservatives (Austrian Peoples Party) and Social Democrats gained a lot of influence on all spheres of the state whereas the Communists quite soon receded to a quite unimportant small party again as they had been before 1933/1934. It had been only in the conditions of resistance first against the authoritarian state 1933–1938 and then against the National Socialist regime when the Communists had become the most important group of resistance fighters which suffered the highest number of losses.[2]

Austrian resistance had to act in an over all hostile surrounding and the number of people who actively opposed the regime stayed relatively small. Therefore this group of Austrians never was able to gain much political influence afterwards though some politicians and party representatives had formerly been politically persecuted by the National Socialist regime. But these politicians soon submitted to the necessities of gaining electoral votes—and the majority of the Austrian population had if not supported then just endured National Socialism, their memory of the past years being imprinted by the war, Allied bombing and resulting problems.

Of the approximately 200,000 Austrians having been persecuted as Jews according to the Nuremberg Laws some 66,000 were killed in the *Shoa*, the others having fled the country. At the end of 1946 the Jewish Community in Vienna counted just 6,428 members.[3]

These small groups of survivors, formerly persecuted, and resistance fighters were confronted by some 700,000 former National Socialists who (if family members and friends were included) represented more than one million voters—a number no political party could ignore in an population of over all seven million people. Even though former National Socialists were not allowed to vote in the first democratic elections in November 1945 party representatives were well aware of future developments and the votes of not registered supporters and partisans of former National Socialists who were not excluded from the elections. Since the second elections four years later former National Socialists became the target of propaganda of all three parties respectively the forth party (League of Independents) having been founded with support of the Social Democrats to collect these votes in 1948 and thereby weaken the Conservatives.[4]

---

1 Rauchensteiner 1987, p. 41.

2 For concrete numbers see the results of the registering of the names of victims of political persecution published on www.doew.at in autumn 2012.

3 Bericht des Präsidiums der Israelitischen Kultusgemeinde Wien über die Tätigkeit in den Jahren 1945 bis 1948, Wien 1948, p. 48.

4 Rathkolb 1986; Wagnleitner 1984.

Until 1955 Austria was still occupied by the four Allied forces (the USA, Great Britain, France and the Soviet Union). Its legislation was passed by the democratically elected parliament but had to be agreed upon by the Allied Council: In the case of constitutional laws the Allied Council had to pronounce its approval, the other laws could only be hindered by an unanimous veto of all four Allies. As a matter of fact the Allied Council did only seldom interfere with Austrian legislation.

7.2 The Framework for Austria's Dealing with Her National Socialist Past

Three intertwined factors constituted the background and framework for the Austrian treatment of the consequences of National Socialism:

- The Declaration of Moscow as the most important one influencing the other two
- The externalisation of any guilt and responsibility towards Germany
- The State Treaty securing Austria's full sovereignty.

Within this framework Austria dealt quite differently with the various consequences of National Socialism and World War II.

7.2.1 The Declaration of Moscow

Austria's position to her National Socialist past was mainly determined by the first part of the Declaration of Moscow of 30 October 1943 in which the Allied Forces[5] declared Austria as the first victim of National Socialist aggression and therefore should be restored as an independent state after the end of the war. Austria deliberately neglected the second part of the Declaration which saw Austria as co-responsible for taking part in the war on the side of the German Reich and stated that the Allied dealings with Austria would depend on her own contribution to her liberation. The last sentence was meant as a support for the Austrian resistance movement. In fact the western Allies did not accept Austria's position as a liberated instead of defeated and therefore a "victim" state before the autumn of 1946.[6]

7.2.2 The Externalisation of Responsibility and Guilt

Fundamentally Austria saw responsibility for Nazi crimes and thus any obligation to compensation for them as lying with the German Reich and later on its

[5] At the conference of Moscow the USA, Great Britain, and the Soviet Union passed this declaration concerning their dealing with Austria after the end of the war, France joined later on. For the origin of that declaration and its meaning see Stourzh 1998, pp. 11–28.

[6] Bailer-Galanda 2003, pp. 54, 55.

successor, the Federal Republic of Germany. The following quote may serve as an illustration: "The persecution of Jews took place during the occupation of Austria by German troops. The persecutions were ordered by German authorities and carried out with their help".[7] In 1953 the Federal Chancellor Raab responded to the claims by the Committee for Jewish Claims on Austria in the same line:

> The Federal Government of Austria regrets that after the occupation of Austria persecution took place and that it was not possible for the Federal Government to protect their citizens against the aggression of the overpowering occupant at the time, it could not do anything else but call for help the powers of the time, it could not do anything else but call for help the powers of the League of Nations, of which Austria was also a member. Its appeal remained unheard. What happened to Austria in the following years had the same effect as a natural catastrophe; Austria is not able by its own strength to make good the damages or even only soothe the want that originated in these years.[8]

Furthermore Austrian politicians claimed that Austria herself was entitled to compensation for her losses because of the German looting of her economy.[9] Therefore any payments of compensation for losses suffered during the National Socialist period had to be avoided because these might be interpreted as a confession of Austrian guilt what later on shaped the Austrian restitution measures.

7.2.3 The Future State Treaty

The absolute priority of each Austrian government in the years 1945–1955 lay on the reaching of the State Treaty on the best possible conditions, and therefore activities and demands of the Allies, especially the western Allies (led by the United States), had to be taken care of by the Austrian government.[10] That gave these demands unusual weight on one hand. On the other hand Austria could make use of the Cold War since the Western Allies avoided every weakening of Austria's position and economy in order not to play into the hands of the Soviet Union in the course of the Cold War.[11]

The denial of any responsibility for National Socialist crimes perpetrated on Austrian territory must be seen in connection with the State Treaty as the most important goal of Austrian postwar foreign policy. Fearing to get less favourable

---

[7] Memorandum der Staatskanzlei, Auswärtige Angelegenheiten: "Die außenpolitische und die völkerrechtliche Seite der Ersatzansprüche der jüdischen Naziopfer", printed in: Knight 1988, pp. 100–112. A copy of the memorandum can be found in Austrian State Archivs, AdR/06, BMF-Nachlaß Klein, box 27.

[8] Letter of Federal Chancellor Julius Raab to Nahum Goldmann, president of the World Jewish Congress, November 13, 1953. Institute of Contemporary History, University of Vienna, Legacy of Albert Loewy.

[9] See the parliamentary debate to the Nullification Law, May 15, 1946 (Stenographische Protokolle des Nationalrats, V. Gesetzgebungsperiode, pp. 186, 189, 193).

[10] See in detail Bailer-Galanda 2005.

[11] See in detail Bailer-Galanda 2003.

conditions in that treaty when being seen as a co-perpetrator instead of an innocent victim Austria avoided any possible hint of confession of co-responsibility which led to grave consequences for the Austrian victims of National Socialist persecution.

7.3 The Victims of National Socialist Persecution

In postwar Austria different groups claimed the status of a victim, victimhood promising certain material and immaterial advantages like economic support, public acceptance of personal suffering, absolution of any possible guilt, or just pity. The competition for the status of victim has to be seen in connection with the possible shame many Austrians had to suppress because they not only had been witness to crimes of the National Socialist regime but had gained profit as well. Austrians inhabited "aryanised" apartments, had got jobs formerly done by Jews in 1938, or now possessed other looted property. Being victim implied being innocent. In the debate of the war past of the former Secretary-General of the United Nations and later Federal President of Austria Kurt Waldheim one participant brought it to the point: "We all were innocent perpetrators".[12]

The inflationary use of the category of victim led to the final consequence that the victims of National Socialist crimes became an unimportant fringe group beyond the majority of the others.

According to the Declaration of Moscow the most prominent group of victims were the former resistance fighters against the National Socialist regime and the men and women who had been persecuted as political adversaries of the regime. Because these people had carried Austria's own part for her liberation the quantity and quality of this resistance was stressed in the first round of negotiations for the State Treaty in London at the end of January 1947.[13]

In consideration of its political importance it was this group which as the first got support by legal measures.

7.3.1 The Victims Welfare Act and its Selective Definition of Victim

It were the former resistance fighters and those having been persecuted because of political reasons who could get financial support by the Victim's Welfare Act in case the consequences of the persecution had made it for them impossible to earn their own living. The first form of this Act had been agreed upon by the provisional

12 Wodak et al. 1990.

13 Proceedings of the First Conference of the Deputies for Austria, held at Lancaster House, London, 16th January to 25th February 1947, pp. 68, 178 (Austrian State Archives (ÖStA), AdR/01, BMfaA, II-pol 1947, Staatsvertrag, box 50).

government as early as July 1945.[14] Until the beginning of 1946 the by far largest and most impoverished group of victims, i.e. the surviving Austrian Jews was supported only by a poor local Jewish Community and international Jewish organisations, especially the Joint Distribution Committee. Since February 1946 they were able to get some help by official relief organisations but none according to legal measures.[15] In 1947 the second Victims Welfare Act substituted the first one. It then constituted two categories of victims: on the one hand the former resistance fighters who could be granted financial help—especially maintenance pensions—if they were not able to care for their own maintenance, and on the other hand the victims of persecution, most of them Holocaust survivors who were accepted as victims but received no financial aid until amendments of the law 1948 and 1949. Though the formerly strict separation of these two categories has been softened since by numerous amendments of the law, most of them due to protests of victims' organisations and Allied pressure in the early years these two different categories of victims are upheld until now. The Austrian Historical Commission established 1998 to research expropriation by the National Socialist regime and measures of Austria for the compensation and restitution stated in a press release to its final report: "Up to the present day, the OFG's/i.e. Victims Welfare Act/selective definition of 'victim' has favoured those involved in political resistance over victims of Nazi persecution, although since 1949 some groups of victims of persecution have also been able to receive continuing pension payment. However victims of persecution who only received a Victim Identity Card are still excluded from maintenance pensions even if they are not in a position to ensure their own maintenance."[16]

Until after the turn of the century socially not accepted groups of victims were not acknowledged by the Victims Welfare Act like those having been persecuted because of their sexual orientation, because of allegedly being "asozial" (anti-social) and the handicapped who were forced to undergo sterilising surgery respectively relatives of people murdered in the "Euthanasia" programme. Only public pressure nourished by new historical research led to changes so that today (2012) all these groups are recognised as victims of National Socialism though only very few survived long enough to be able to enjoy the moderate advantages of this acceptance.

The main group excluded from the benefits of the Victims Welfare Act were those former Austrian Jews who had fled the country 1938/1939 and had taken a new citizenship in the country where they had found refuge. The Act bound most payments on a still existing Austrian citizenship, especially maintenance pensions. This was changed only in 2001.

The fact that individuals having been just persecuted and not having actively resisted National Socialism were regarded as second rate victims might be explained as follows.

---

[14] Bailer 1993a, pp. 23–28.

[15] Bailer 1993a, pp. 137–141.

[16] AHC 2003. See in detail Jabloner et al. 2003, pp. 417–419.

The surviving Jews reminded too many Austrians of the crimes which had been committed by Austrians and of the advantage many Austrians had got because of "aryanised" goods property, furthermore the Jews were sort of outside the collective memory which consisted of memories of war and not persecution and last but not least the still existing and widely spread anti-semitism worked against them. Socially disadvantaged groups like Roma and Sinti, homosexuals or handicapped had no lobby supporting them and had to fight a lot of social prejudices against them. The last group to be integrated into the Victims Welfare Act were those having been persecuted by military courts of the German Army or who had left the troop without permission. Veterans' organisations as well as public opinion had acted against them. Not long ago they were called traitors and murderers in public debates.

And last but not least the victims of persecution could not be used for aims of foreign policy.

7.3.2 Restitution of Lost Property

Many of the Jewish survivors had lost their property in the looting and expropriation measures of the National Socialist regime and were now hoping for restitution. It took until the beginning of 1946 for the Austrian government to decide on implementation of restitution measures due to international pressure and facing the first drafts of the State Treaty which stated Austria's obligation to return looted property to its former owners.[17] The denial of any (co-)responsibility for the National Socialist expropriations led to the refusal to pay any compensation therefore the seven restitution laws, passed by the Austrian parliament between 1946 and 1949, only applied the principle of restitution in kind—only still existing and traceable property was to be returned. The seven laws followed no logic or system—they applied to different categories of lost property on one hand (Restitution Law four, five, six and seven), on the other hand they oriented on the present owner of the looted property (Restitution Law one, two and three).[18] For some categories of lost property no restitution law was passed. So for instance the more than 50,000 rented apartments that had been "aryanised" in Vienna could not be reclaimed after the war.[19]

Compensatory payments were introduced only some years after the signing of the State Treaty of 1955 by pressure of the Western Allies who stated that the limitation on restitution in kind came short the intention of those articles of the State Treaty that introduced Austria's obligation to return property looted by the National Socialist regime.[20]

---

[17] Bailer-Galanda 2003, pp. 57–87; Knight 1988, pp. 43–44; Bailer-Galanda 2005, pp. 655–658.

[18] Graf 2003.

[19] Bailer-Galanda et al. 2004.

[20] Bailer-Galanda 2003, pp. 408–461.

The different laws made the situation for the victims of expropriation, most of them former Austrians now living abroad, a very difficult one. The legal procedures of the laws "necessarily put the victim in the position of plaintiff, applicant and complainant. Even if this may have been an unavoidable technical necessity after this kind of upheaval, it meant that as a result the victims had to suffer serious disadvantageous consequences. The restitution system was a confusing and partly contradictory web. /.../ Penetrating this labyrinth required an act of both financial and mental strength. For the victims of Nazism who had escaped with their lives and who wanted their plundered possessions back in order to be able to ensure some form of survival, it was extremely difficult to orient themselves."[21]

Entitled for claims according to the restitution laws were all persons whose loss of property was connected to their politically motivated persecution by the National Socialist regime notwithstanding the present citizenship or place of residence. In the case of Jews this connection was regarded as obvious, all other claimant groups had to prove it individually.[22] Approximately two-thirds of the individual claimants were Jews, a lot of the other applications came from institutions, even the Catholic Church whose property had been taken in the course of the persecution of religious institutions.[23]

7.3.3 *Different Definitions of Victims of National Socialist Persecution*

The system of restitution laws clearly defined victims of National Socialism in a much broader but less precisely drawn way than the Victims Welfare Act or the related Social Insurance Laws which were strongly connected to the Victims Welfare Act. One reason might be that restitution did not mean loads for the state's finances whereas all laws in the field of social welfare resulted in expenses for the state's budget. The exclusion of former Austrians now living abroad, the majority of them being Jewish, has to be seen in that context as well. Austria had to care for those living in Austria, for those living abroad the social system of their new home countries was to be held responsible.

Besides there were public discussions on the system of welfare for victims of National Socialism in which not only some prejudices planted by National Socialist propaganda against resistance fighters or concentration camps inmates again surfaced but feelings of social envy were expressed as well.[24] So the organisations of political victims deemed it necessary to prove that their ranks were respectable and decent people, a position which meant the exclusion of socially less accepted

[21] AHC 2003.

[22] Graf 2003, pp. 71–78.

[23] Pammer 2002, pp. 31–34; Böhmer and Faber 2003, pp. 38–39.

[24] Bailer 1993a, pp. 30–32, 49–50; Bailer-Galanda 2007, pp. 43–44.

groups like homosexuals or so called anti-social persons, i.e. people on the fringe of society. The result was a "selective definition" of victims ("selektiver Opferbegriff"), as Walter J. Pfeil stated in his analyses for the Austrian Historical Commission.[25]

In contrast to the Federal Republic of Germany Communists were not excluded from any benefits of the different laws. Their participation in the resistance movement was accepted though in the course of the Cold War the Communist oriented organisation of former resistance fighters was not well accepted by the other victim's organisation and state authorities.[26] That changed in the second half of the 1960s when all three organisations of victims of political persecution joined in an association of victims organisations ("Arbeitsgemeinschaft der Opferverbände"). Common activities became possible even a little bit earlier: Representatives of these organisations as well as functionaries of the Jewish Community and historians founded the Documentation Centre of Austrian Resistance in 1963.[27]

7.3.4 A Special Category of Victims

From 1933/1934 to 1938 there ruled a specific Austrian authoritarian regime whose precise character is still disputed by Austrian historians: the opinions reach from Austrian fascist regime to just authoritarian regime, government dictatorship or corporative state ("Ständestaat") as the regime called itself.[28] In 1933/1934 by and by all political parties were forbidden and a unified state party founded based on Catholic belief and strongly supported by the Church. Social Democrats and Communists as well as other leftist splinter groups fought the regime by means of propaganda and got persecuted for these activities by imprisonment in jail and detention camps. In June 1933 the National Socialist Party became illegal as well, their activists who resorted to violent actions as well were subject to justicial and police measures.

Since 1945 the Victims Welfare Act grants the same benefits to persons having been persecuted by the Austrian authoritarian state as to persons having been persecuted by the National Socialist regime what leads to equalisation of the unequal: time in the concentration camp of Dachau or Auschwitz cannot be equalised with time in an Austrian detention camp 1933–1938 where the prisoners were not forced to hard labour and never had to fear for their lives.[29]

---

25 Pfeil 2004, pp. 249–250.

26 That became evident in the discussions around the Mauthausen Memorial. See Perz 2006.

27 Bailer-Galanda and Neugebauer 2003, pp. 29–32.

28 Manoschek and Tálos 2005.

29 About the situation in the main detention camp Wöllersdorf see the forthcoming dissertation of Pia Schölnberger (probably finished in 2012) as well as Schölnberger 2010.

This equalisation is to be found in other legislation in favour of victims of National Socialism like the Social Insurance Laws.

In the case of looted property there were three Acts dealing with property taken from parties of the labour movement and labour unions after 1933, one of them dealing with the returning of rented apartments which had been used by these institutions.[30] Since the Social Democrats were in government 1945–1966 they were able to reach that advantage for their own interests in negotiations with the conservatives being sort of successors of the leading political ideology of 1933–1938. Functionaries of the corporate state later on became important politicians after 1945, as for instance the federal chancellor Julius Raab or the federal minister Fritz Bock.

7.4 "Aryanisers" as Victims?

The Third Restitution Act was the most contended of all the seven since it dealt with the restitution of looted property now being in private hands or in the possession of economical associations or societies and therefore intervened immediately in the economic situation of these present owners. The drafts of the Third Restitution Act had already been challenged by business interest groups. Their main argument was that restitution introduced uncertainty into the economy and should therefore be limited as far as possible. This line was pursued in the course of subsequent legislation up to the 1960s when according to the State Treaty[31] heirless property of victims of National Socialism had to be restituted or paid for to collecting agencies[32] which gave the resulting proceeds to needy survivors.

Since the end of the 1940s economically interested parts of the conservatives and the League of Independents pressed for an amendment of the Third Restitution Act in favour of the "aryanisers" who were presented as victims of the restitution claimants. An association of people being affected by restitution ("Rückstellungsbetroffene") was formed which found the political support of members of parliament. They argued that restitution were a gross injustice against the present owners who because of the legislation would have to be afraid to lose the fruits of lifelong hard work though they had never committed any injustice against anyone and were just innocent people persecuted by greedy heirs full of hate.[33] Restitution was always discussed under the flag of "aryanisation" and in connection with Jewish property, restitution for instance of property of the Catholic Church never was mentioned. Anti-Semitic stereotypes usually surfaced

[30] Graf 2003, pp. 356–365.

[31] Article 26 para 2 of the State Treaty of Vienna (1955).

[32] Sammelstelle A for heirless property of Jews and Sammelstelle B for heirless property of politically persecuted persons.

[33] Bailer-Galanda 2003, p. 170; Bailer-Galanda 2002, p. 175.

as well, as the picture of Jewish "greed" for money or conspiracy theories or the classical exchange of victims and perpetrators. In any case people claiming the restitution of their former property found themselves suddenly in the position of perpetrators who were regarded as a threat against "innocent" people who had taken Jewish property in order to enable the owners to leave the country and save their lives.

In 1949 former National Socialists were allowed to take part in the elections for all democratic institutions again. The political parties intensified their efforts to gain an as large as possible part of these potential votes. Parliament passed some motions to end the denazification measures, all of which were prohibited by the Allied Council. From today's point of view in the early fifties there was a cynical way of balanced thinking: In 1951, the conservative member of parliament Toncic-Sorinj formulated the principle like this: "At least at the same time with the pacification in the National Socialist sector, we must reach pacification in the sector of restitution, in the sector of the politically persecuted. A general settlement is the only possible way."[34]

That was the background for a motion of conservatives and Social Democrats in 1950 to create a "Compensation for Hardship"-Fund ("Härteausgleichsfonds") which should serve the elimination of all hardship caused by the National Socialist era. The draft finally intended to mix the claims of victims of National Socialism with those being inflicted by restitution. It mixed up obvious deteriorations of the Third Restitution Act against the former persecuted on the one hand with compensatory payments for imprisonment by the National Socialist regime on the other hand as well as payments in cases of "hardships" because of the obligation to restitute property. The financial means for these payments should come from heirless property of dead victims of persecution—that means former "aryanisers" were to be indemnified largely by money of murdered Jews. Because of protests of the US-occupational force whose representatives reminded the Austrian government of those passages in the draft of the State Treaty concerning Austria's duty to restitution and to use heirless property in favour of survivors the motion never became law.[35]

7.5 Soldiers of the German Army ("Deutsche Wehrmacht")

According to the logic of the "victims theory" Austria saw herself as not accountable for any measures taken by National Socialist Germany. Nevertheless Austria instantly took care of the returning soldiers of the German Army though it had not been Austria they had fought for all over Europe and in Northern Africa. While every benefit for the victims of persecution was discussed under financial aspects no such discussion took place concerning financial aid for former soldiers.

[34] Stenographische Protokolle des Nationalrats, VI. GP, 5.12.1951, p. 2426.

[35] Bailer-Galanda 2003, pp. 229–235.

The warm welcome they got on arriving on Austrian train stations returning as former prisoners of war and the fast re-integration into social and economic life for sure has to be seen as a democratic and political necessity. The political parties installed their own departments looking after the interests of these hundreds of thousand returnees because these represented a large and therefore important pool of voters. Officially these men were regarded as victims of National Socialist power—they had been forced into war, or as a Social Democrat member of parliament put it: "In front the enemy, that means attack, and behind the Gestapo spies driving people with revolvers and small arms into the war."[36]

Former soldiers not being able to care for their maintenance because of handicaps inflicted during their service got maintenance pensions, health care and other benefits through the War Victims Welfare Act ("Kriegsopferversorgungsgesetz") which was built in parallel to the Victims Welfare Act. Nevertheless the procedures for the former soldiers were definitely less strict than in the Victims Welfare Act. It was easier for applicants to get benefits granted and there were less restrictions.[37] In 1949 all former members of the Waffen-SS were included into the benefits of this Act that means they got public welfare as well.[38]

"Spätheimkehrer", i.e. the POWs who returned to Austria after the end of April 1949, received special care by the Republic of Austria. This group was very heterogeneous. It consisted of former soldiers who had been held in Soviet camps for a disproportionate long time, many of them innocent people on the one hand, as well as of persons guilty of war crimes or crimes against humanity on the other hand, like a group of Austrian men who had been charged in France for crimes against humanity and released because of a pardon in 1955. For instance Josef Weiszel former member of Eichmann's staff and responsible for rounding up of Jews in Vienna and different French cities[39] was one of this second group He and others benefited from a special amnesty from all consequences of denazification and possible persecution by the War Crimes Act.[40] This so called late returnee's amnesty ("Spätheimkehreramnestie") was passed by the National Council already in 1951 but it took two more years to reach the assent of the Allied Council to this law.[41] The Allies had tried in vain to connect their consent to an improvement of the measures for victims of National Socialism, the Austrian government was not prepared to give in to that pressure. The final consent of the Allied Council might have been caused by Soviet pressure since the Soviet Union released more than

[36] "Vorne Feind, also Angriff, und hinter ihnen die Gestapospitzeln, die mit Revolvern und Handwaffen die Leute vorwärtstrieben in den Krieg" (Stenographisches Protokoll der 11. Sitzung des Nationalrats, V. GP, 20.3.1946, p. 130).

[37] Pfeil 2004, pp. 251, 252.

[38] Das Kriegsopferversorgungsgesetz. Bundesgesetz vom 14. Juli 1949, Nr. 197 über die Versorgung der Kriegsbeschädigten und Hinterbliebenen mit den vom Bundesministerium für soziale Verwaltung erlassenen Durchführungsbestimmungen, Linz 1949, p. 3.

[39] To Weiszel see Safrian 1993.

[40] Garscha 2000, pp. 864–872.

[41] Bailer-Galanda 2003, pp. 218–222.

600 POWs and civilians at the same time.[42] Furthermore all late returnees got financial help by the state: before 1955 it was a lump sum,[43] in 1958 they got compensation for each month they had spent as POW.

Weiszel and others were special cases: they had been supported in their legal cases as well. The Austrian Ministry for the Interior had helped all Austrians being charged in France with money for attorneys and legal advice. In 1954 the government decided not to ask that money back for not to "worsen the financial distress"[44] of these men.

7.6 Mixing of Claims

After the signing of the State Treaty when all obstacles by the Allied Council had been eliminated in at least two cases claims of victims of National Socialism and victims of the war—in the broadest sense—were dealt with in one and the same law.

The financial aid for late returning POWs and persons having been indicted because of war crimes mingled that group with a very small group of victims of persecution: people who had fled to the Soviet Union in 1938 and had been interned by Stalinist repression if their internment had lasted until after the war and they too had returned as late as the end of 1949.[45] Nevertheless most of those who benefited from that law were former soldiers of the German Army and the Waffen-SS.

The War and Persecution Material Damages Act was passed in 1958. It "envisaged uniform compensation for those who had suffered damages by the war and for victims of persecution. State compensation was paid for damages caused by political persecution between 1933 and 1938 and between 1938 and 1945, but also for damages caused by the effects of war on household objects and needs for professional life."[46] That means on the side of the victims of persecution there was the usual equalisation of victims of the Austrian authoritarian regime and of the far more cruel and murderous National Socialist regime on one hand and all people having suffered material damages because of the war, e.g. by Allied bombing.

This Act in some way mirrored the public feeling of the Austrian population—all had suffered, all were victims. And it stood for the politicians' aim of the "appeasement"—similar "justice" for all who had been inflicted by National Socialism and the war. Thus they wanted to close all gaps within the Austrian population.

---

42 Bailer-Galanda 2003, p. 327.

43 First it were 500 Austrian Schilling, in 1954 the sum was raised to 2000 Austrian Schilling. As a comparison: A skilled worker earned 360 Austrian Schilling per week at that time (Bailer-Galanda 2003, pp. 347, 348).

44 In German: "um die finanzielle Notlage dieser Heimkehrer nicht noch zu vergrößern" (Ministerratsvortrag BMI Zl. 341.616-14/54, 19.8.1954, 59. Sitzung des Ministerrates, Raab I, 7.9.1954, ÖStA, AdR/04, MRp).

45 Bailer-Galanda 2003, p. 397.

46 AHC 2003. See in detail Jabloner et al. 2003, pp. 353–356.

7.7 Former National Socialists: Victims of Denazification?

The first denazification law was agreed upon by the provisional Austrian government on May 8th, 1945. Already in the forthcoming campaign for the first free parliamentary elections in November 1945 the political parties had tried to win over at least the votes of relatives and friends of former National Socialists. Because of problems with this first Act the Austrian parliament passed an amendment in 1946 that did not find the necessary consent of the Allied Council and therefore did not come into force. The Allies demanded a large number of changes most of them implementing stricter regulations than the Austrian draft. A new version had to be passed by the national council. In the accompanying discussion of the draft most members of parliament stressed the fact that this law was forced upon them by the Allied Council and did not conform to the intentions of the Austrian politicians. In 1949 the Soviet occupational force instigated an amnesty for less implicated National Socialists, these were about 90 % of all of those inflicted by the law. For them denazification had come to an end. The remaining 10 % stayed in the centre of discussions—three times the Austrian parliament passed motions in favour of this group—all attempts failed because of the resistance of the Allied Council. In all parliamentary debates including the last one in 1957 the former National Socialists were presented as victims of the Allied Forces, sometimes with anti-Semitic tendencies—implying that possibly Jewish organisations used their influence especially on the US-occupational forces.[47]

7.8 Immediate Competition Between Former National Socialists and Victims of Persecution

Besides the field of the restitution of looted property there were other fields as well where formerly persecuted people found themselves confronted by former National Socialists. After 1938 in Vienna alone more than 50,000 rented apartments were "aryanised", not all of them but quite a number was later rented to National Socialists. Though there was—as mentioned above—no legal provision for restitution of rented apartments immediately after the end of the war the Viennese housing office gave empty apartments, whose tenants mostly had fled to the west to avoid the Soviet occupation, to returning concentration camp inmates or political prisoners what was enabled by the legal provision of the National Socialist Law. Only a short time later many of these assignments had to be cancelled as Nazis—aided by law courts which did not accept these preliminary assignments—managed to expel the victims once more. In a number of cases wives of Nazis who were able to prove that they themselves had never been members of the Nazi party claimed their former apartments and reached a notice to quit

[47] Bailer 1993a, pp. 260–264; Bailer-Galanda 2003, pp. 215–225, 344–348.

for the victims who had been assigned to these apartments. In the year 1950 the minister of justice Tschadek felt obliged to call upon the courts not to permit the dislodging of victims any more.[48]

Further problems arose as the denazification was terminated 1957, as soon as possible after the State Treaty. Former attempts to do so had been blocked by the Allied Council. The denazification measures had included the forfeiting of properties of the former National Socialists as well as of allotments and furniture. Some of these allotments had been passed over to victims of National Socialism by the City of Vienna and furniture had been given to victims by the Soviet forces as a 'donation' ("Lebendenko-Schenkung") for which they had to pay rent. The amnesty of 1957 enabled the former National Socialists to reclaim their forfeited properties, allotments and furniture. Now the victims either had to return the furniture—some had done this already—to the former Nazis or they had to pay a discharge. In order to do so they were granted a credit free of interest by the City of Vienna.[49]

7.9 Conclusion: A Nation of Victims

When foreign observers stated for Germany that many Germans they had met after the war felt themselves as victims of Hitler then that might have been a precise description for the feeling of most Austrians which was politically supported by the Declaration of Moscow. After the end of the war the Austrian population in fact had suffered all the consequences of the war—shortage of food and goods, bombing, missing husbands, brothers and friends. Almost 10 % of the population had joined the Nazi Party, even many more joined organisations in the surrounding of the party. More than 1 million Austrian men joined the German Army—most forced, but many voluntarily. More than 200,000 soldiers from Austria died in the war.[50]

The fate of the victims of persecution was outside these common memories—resistance fighters had been a small minority, Jews had disappeared very soon because of their leaving the country on one hand and the anti-Jewish legislation which excluded them step by step from public life.

Immediately after the war a few memorials were built for former resistance fighters, especially due to Communist initiatives. The following years were dominated by the commemoration of soldiers killed in action, in many Austrian villages memorials were erected to honour these dead.[51] It was only in the first half of the 1960s that monuments for the victims of political persecution were built. It even took some more years until victims of racist persecution appeared in public opinion.

---

[48] Bailer-Galanda et al. 2004, p. 216; Bailer 1993b, p. 375.

[49] Bailer 1993a, pp. 264, 265.

[50] Malina 1989, pp. 145, 151.

[51] Gärtner and Rosenberger 1991.

Thus the first decades after the war were imprinted by the overall feeling of being victim—victim of Hitler, the war, the Allies. Thereby the victims of National Socialist persecution just disappeared like they had already done during National Socialism. Measures in their favour often instigated envy, prejudices planted by National Socialist propaganda reappeared. Especially victims of political persecution most of them now integrated in one of the three founding parties of the republic painfully avoided any hint that they might have any privileges or think themselves better than the rest of the Austrians.

Rosa Jochmann, Social Democrat, resistance fighter, imprisoned in the Ravensbrück concentration camp, after 1945 leader of the Social Democrat victims' organisation and member of parliament for many years stated in a radio lecture in 1949: "We were all victims of Fascism. Victim was the soldier, who experienced the war at the front in its most terrible form victim was the population who was waiting in the hinterland full of horror for the call of the cuckoo in order to flee to their shelters and who, with longing, wished for the day which would take this fright from them. Victims were those who had to leave their native country to carry the mostly sad lot of the emigrant. Finally, we were victims, who in prisons, penitentiaries and concentration camps were defenceless prey of the SS."[52] And thus they were all victims.

References

AHC (2003) Austrian Historical Commission Press Release to the Final Report (Jan 2003). www.historikerkommission.gv.at/english_home.html. Accessed 13 Jan 2012

Bailer B (1993a) Wiedergutmachung kein Thema. Österreich und die Opfer des Nationalsozialismus. Löcker, Vienna

Bailer B (1993b) "Ohne den Staat weiter damit zu belasten…" —Bemerkungen zur österreichischen Rückstellungsgesetzgebung. Zeitgeschichte 11/12:367–381

Bailer-Galanda B (2002) Die Rückstellungsproblematik in Österreich. In: Goschler C, Lillteicher J (eds) "Arisierung" und Restitution. Die Rückerstattung jüdischen Eigentums in Deutschland und Österreich nach 1945 und 1989. Wallstein, Göttingen, pp. 161–188

Bailer-Galanda B (2003) Die Entstehung der Rückstellungs- und Entschädigungsgesetzgebung. Die Republik Österreich und das in der NS-Zeit entzogene Vermögen. Oldenbourg, Vienna

Bailer-Galanda B (2005) Staatsvertrag und Rückstellungen bis 1955. In: Suppan A, Mueller W, Stourzh G (eds) Der österreichische Staatsvertrag. Internationale Strategie, rechtliche Relevanz, nationale Identität (The Austrian State Treaty. International Strategy, Legal Relevance, National Identity). Verlag der Österreichischen Akademie der Wissenschaften, Vienna, pp. 655–674

Bailer-Galanda B (2007) Der KZ-Verband. Informationen zu einer wesentlichen Quelle des Projektes der Namentlichen Erfassung der Opfer der politischen Verfolgung. In: Dokumentationsarchiv des österreichischen Widerstandes (ed) Jahrbuch 2007. DÖW Eigenverlag, Vienna, pp. 36–49

Bailer-Galanda B, Blimlinger E, Graf G, Kowarc S (2004) "Arisierung" und Rückstellung von Wohnungen in Wien. Oldenbourg, Vienna

[52] Rosa Jochmann, Aus dem Gesetz für die Opfer des Faschismus, Manuskript, Stimme zur Zeit, February 28, 1949 (Archive of the Socialdemocrat Party, quoted in Bailer 1993a, p. 58).

Bailer-Galanda B, Neugebauer W (2003) Das Dokumentationsarchiv des österreichischen Widerstandes. In: Dokumentationsarchiv des österreichischen Widerstandes (ed) 40 Jahre Dokumentationsarchiv des österreichischen Widerstandes 1963–2003. DÖW Eigenverlag, Vienna, pp. 26–70

Böhmer P, Faber R (2003) Die österreichische Finanzverwaltung und die Restitution entzogener Vermögen 1945 bis 1960. Oldenbourg, Vienna

Garscha W (2000) Entnazifizierung und gerichtliche Ahndung von NS-Verbrechen. In: Tálos E, Hanisch E, Neugebauer W (eds) NS-Herrschaft in Österreich. Ein Handbuch, Österreichischer Bundesverlag, hpt Verlagsgemeinschaft, Vienna, pp. 852–883

Gärtner R, Rosenberger S (1991) Kriegerdenkmäler: Vergangenheit in der Gegenwart. Studienverlag, Innsbruck

Graf G (2003) Die österreichische Rückstellungsgesetzgebung: eine juristische Analyse. Oldenbourg, Vienna

Jabloner C, Bailer-Galanda B, Blimlinger E, Graf G, Knight R, Mikoletzky L, Perz B, Sandgruber R, Stuhlpfarrer K, Teichova A (2003) Schlussbericht der Historikerkommission der Republik Österreich: Vermögensentzug während der NS-Zeit sowie Rückstellungen und Entschädigungen seit 1945 in Österreich. Zusammenfassungen und Einschätzungen. Oldenbourg, Vienna

Knight R (1988) "Ich bin dafür, die Sache in die Länge zu ziehen". Die Wortprotokolle der österreichischen Bundesregierung von 1945 bis 1952 über die Entschädigung der Juden. Athenäum, Frankfurt am Main

Malina P (1989) Nach dem Krieg: Österreicher/innen als Opfer und Täter. In: Bundesministerium für Unterricht, Kunst und Sport (ed) Österreicher und der Zweite Weltkrieg. Österreichischer Bundesverlag, Vienna, pp. 145–170

Manoschek W, Tálos E (2005) Aspekte der politischen Struktur des Austrofaschismus: (Verfassungs)Rechtlicher Rahmen, politische Wirklichkeit, Akteure. In: Tálos E, Neugebauer W (eds) Austrofaschismus: Politik, Ökonomie, Kultur. LIT, Vienna, pp. 124–161

Pammer M (2002) Die Rückstellungskommission beim Landesgericht für Zivilrechtssachen Wien. Die Verfahren vor den österreichischen Rückstellungskommissionen 1. Oldenbourg, Vienna

Perz B (2006) Die KZ-Gedenkstätte Mauthausen 1945 bis zur Gegenwart. Studien Verlag, Innsbruck

Pfeil WJ (2004) Die Entschädigung von Opfern des Nationalsozialismus im Sozialrecht nach 1945 in Österreich. Oldenbourg, Vienna

Rathkolb O (1986) NS-Problem und politische Restauration: Vorgeschichte und Etablierung des VdU. In: Meissl S, Mulley K-D, Rathkolb O (eds) Verdrängte Schuld, verfehlte Sühne. Entnazifizierung in Österreich 1945–1955. Verlag für Geschichte und Politik, Vienna, pp. 295–320

Rauchensteiner M (1987) Die Zwei. Die Große Koalition in Österreich 1945–1966. Österreichischer Bundesverlag, Vienna

Safrian H (1993) Die Eichmann-Männer. Europa Verlag, Vienna

Schölnberger P (2010) Wöllersdorf: Die Anfänge. In: Dokumentationsarchiv des österreichischen Widerstandes (ed) Jahrbuch 2010. Eigenverlag, Vienna, pp. 190–211

Stourzh G (1998) Um Einheit und Freiheit. Staatsvertrag, Neutralität und das Ende der Ost-West-Besetzung Österreichs 1945–1955. Böhlau, Vienna

Wagnleitner R (ed) (1984) Understanding Austria. The political reports and analyses of Martin F. Herz, Political Officer of the US-Legation in Vienna 1945–1948. Verlag Wolfgang Neugebauer, Salzburg

Wodak R, Pelikan J, Nowak R, Gruber H, De Cilia R, Mitten R (1990) "Wir sind alle unschuldige Täter": Diskurshistorische Studien zum Nachkriegsantisemitismus. Suhrkamp, Frankfurt am Main

Chapter 8
Transcending Victimhood: Child Soldiers and Restorative Justice

Mark A. Drumbl

Abstract The international community strives to eradicate the scourge of child soldiering. Mostly, though, these efforts replay the same narratives and circulate the same assumptions. This chapter, which takes a second look at these efforts, aspires to refresh law and policy so as to improve preventative, restorative, and remedial initiatives while also vivifying the dignity of youth. As a starting point, this chapter proposes that the dominant language used to characterise child soldiers—that of passive victimhood—be revisited so as to better recognise the potentiality of child soldiers to participate in and lead post-conflict reconstructive efforts. This chapter suggests a variety of reforms to the content and trajectory of law and policy in light of the complex, variegated realities of child soldiering. International lawyers and policymakers are predisposed to dissemble these complexities. Although understandable, this penchant ultimately is counterproductive. Along the way, this chapter also questions central tenets of contemporary humanitarianism, rethinks elements of international criminal justice, and aspires to embolden the rights of the child.

Keywords Child soldiers • Straight 18 position • Victims and constructions of victimhood • Agency • Transitional justice • Reintegration

It is easy to see the child soldier superficially as a contradiction in terms or simply as an anachronism. Neither childhood nor youth, after all, should be about war or weapons. Nonetheless—and however jarring—militarization suffuses the lives of many children.

The author is Class of 1975 Alumni Professor of Law and Director, Transnational Law Institute, Washington and Lee University. This contribution herein, which reflects remarks delivered at the "Victims of International Crimes" Conference held at Philipps-Universität Marburg on October 7, 2011, integrally reproduces Chapter 1 of Drumbl 2012. Full development of the arguments introduced in this contribution is found in Drumbl 2012.

M. A. Drumbl (✉)
Transnational Law Institute, Washington and Lee University, Lexington, VA, USA
e-mail: drumblm@wlu.edu

T. Bonacker and C. Safferling (eds.), *Victims of International Crimes: An Interdisciplinary Discourse*, DOI: 10.1007/978-90-6704-912-2_8,

At the very least, worldwide, tens of thousands of persons below the age of eighteen currently are associated with armed forces or armed groups. Adults who serve in such forces or groups, moreover, may have joined while younger than eighteen. In addition, the past decade has seen the demobilization of many tens of thousands more child soldiers. Although joyful, their return journey to civilian life also is bittersweet. They come back home to the communities where they initially had been recruited—at times, forcibly—and where, in some instances, they had committed terrible atrocities. While associated with armed forces or groups, many child recruits are subject to brutalities, beatings, and rape. Drug and alcohol abuse is common.

International law and policy cover considerable ground in their efforts to eradicate child soldiering and promote the well-being of current and former child soldiers. States adopt treaties and instruments, while also endorsing principles and declarations. Experts issue reports. Organizations draft best practices and 'how to' guidelines. Authorities prepare model interventions. Conscripting, enlisting, or using younger children—namely, under the age of fifteen—in hostilities is an international war crime for which adult commanders recently have been convicted. Additional verdicts are imminent, including against Charles Taylor, Liberia's former dictator.

Although international interventions have helped reduce specific incidents, the practice of child soldiering still persists. It may shift locally, and abate here and there, but it endures globally. Preventative measures, therefore, remain inadequate. Former child soldiers experience challenges in adjusting to civilian life. Reintegration is complex and eventful. The homecoming is only the beginning. Reconciliation within communities afflicted by violence committed by and against child soldiers is incomplete. Shortfalls linger on the restorative front.

What, then, to do? The reflexive response among international lawyers and transnational policymakers is to hone familiar tools and work them even faster. In practice, this means that humanitarian efforts ramp up the chorus of outrage regarding the plight of child soldiers. These efforts typically highlight themes of vulnerability, frailty, victimization, and incapacity.

The reflexive response is full of good intentions. It is rhetorically compelling. But it is becoming palliative. I urge lawmakers and policymakers to transcend what passes as conventional wisdom and encourage them to peer beyond into a more demanding space. The time is right for something new.

Meaningful reform, however, first requires the international community to *reimagine* child soldiers and the sources of child soldiering. This reimaginative exercise, in turn, calls into question habits and expectations that pervade contemporary humanitarianism, the universality of human rights, strategies for juvenile civic engagement, and post-conflict justice. Lessons learned from recent experiences with child soldiering and the improvements that can be made on this front, therefore, weave into a much broader revisionist tapestry.

This conference dedicated to victims of international crimes, which include children and child soldiers, also offers an opportunity to assess the advantages and disadvantages—and the potential and limits—to victimhood discourses generally. It also permits an exploration of the utility of transitional justice mechanisms in the process of restoring individuals and collectivities afflicted by mass atrocity.

In this vein, this chapter raises a number of admittedly tough questions. Are child soldiers necessarily well-served by formulaic stereotypes that no child ever can volunteer to participate in armed forces or armed groups? That all child soldiers are used and none wish to engage in martial activities? That no person under the age of eighteen can commit human rights abuses for reasons other than being cruelly forced to do so? That all conflicts that implicate children are innately senseless? That children associated with armed forces or groups see themselves as victims? As misled? The way international activists conceptualize an issue may morph into a self-fulfilling prophecy that, in turn, fails to concretize optimal programmatic interventions for the intended beneficiaries.

Remedial efforts currently undertaken for former child soldiers accentuate medicalized trauma recovery and psychotherapy. Although taken as obvious, is this emphasis the best way forward? Perhaps, readers may be happily surprised to learn that the mental health of former child soldiers may be less precarious and more robust than commonly believed. Hence, programmatic interventions ought to include more in the way of economic, educational, justice, and occupational efforts. Readers also may be surprised to learn that many child soldiers exit fighting factions not by way of humanitarian rescue but, rather, entirely on their own by dint of personal initiative. They escape. Or they abandon the armed force or group once they grow weary of militarized life or begin to see the futility in the putative cause for which they are fighting. In short, rescue is less common than conventional wisdom may suppose, while escape is more common.

How to effectively sanction commanders who conscript, enlist, or use children in hostilities? For the moment, entities that finance, fund, or arm groups and forces that deploy children largely fall below the radar screen. How can this blind spot be addressed? Some child soldiers are implicated in grievous acts of atrocity. Should transitional justice mechanisms be considered for them? Criminal trials are most ill-fitting in this regard. But is there not room to be more creative about engineering justice such that it involves more than just courtrooms and jailhouses? In the case of child soldiers, it is not axiomatically wise to eschew accountability conversations. Accountability measures other than criminal trials—such as truth commissions and traditional ceremonies—may facilitate reintegration, rehabilitation, restoration, and reparation. In the long term, shielding juveniles from law's obligations while conferring upon them law's beneficent protectiveness might not durably anchor them as rights-bearers.

If some children join armed forces or groups for social, economic, or political reasons, does treating them as passive or incompetent address their grievances? Is it helpful to downplay how the child entered militarized life, whether by abduction, voluntary enlistment, or because he or she was born into the armed group? Are policies that eliminate distinctions among the roles that child soldiers perform during conflict necessarily wise? At present, girl soldiers are consistently underserved by post-conflict programming. So, too, are children who are born into armed groups. What about the many children—and adults—who did not associate with armed groups but were aggrieved by the conduct of children who did? What does justice mean for them?

However embedded, perceptions of the victim status of child soldiers remain somewhat contingent upon the nationality of those persons injured by their conduct. Child soldiers who commit violence—for example, terrorist attacks—against Western targets are seen less like deluded children and more like menacing adults. On a related note, how does the West treat child soldiers affiliated with armed factions who, following their decommissioning, may seek refugee status within its borders? What actions by Western states may abet child soldiering? Law and policy do not always apply consistently. Their forward trajectory may ebb and flow depending on state power and politics.

8.1 Defining the Terms

Who, exactly, is a child soldier? A standardized—and increasingly legalized—definition has emerged, in large part through two major international conferences. The first, which was held in Cape Town in 1997, focused on the demobilization and social reintegration of child soldiers in Africa. A follow-up conference was convened in Paris in 2007. Co-hosted by the United Nations Children's Fund (UNICEF) and the French government, this event was of a larger scale and global orientation. It included representatives of fifty-eight states along with many key stakeholders.

The Cape Town and Paris conferences each led to the adoption of non-binding instruments that have since obtained widespread professional, operational, and political currency. The initial development and subsequent circulation of these influential instruments owes much to the involvement of non-governmental organizations (NGOs), United Nations (UN) agencies, donors, and activists. This constellation of actors also has sensitized a global public through media outreach, film, and literature.

These instruments include as child soldiers much more than only those persons younger than eighteen who carry weapons, engage in combat, or who take (or have taken) a direct part in hostilities. Also included are children used for auxiliary activities (for example, portering, spying, and cooking) and children forced into sexual servitude. The impetus among policymakers is to discourage distinctions from being drawn between children who serve as combatants and children who do not or who do so only incidentally. One motivation in this regard is to ensure inclusiveness toward both girl and boy soldiers. Accordingly, and responsively, official nomenclature has drifted away from *child soldier* as initially set out and defined in the Cape Town Principles.[1] The move is now toward the somewhat

[1] Cape Town Principles and Best Practices 2007 April 27–30, 1997, Definitions. Available at www.unicef.org/emerg/files/Cape_Town_Principles(1).pdf. A child soldier is 'any person under 18 years of age who is part of any kind of regular or irregular armed force or armed group in any capacity, including but not limited to cooks, porters, messengers and anyone accompanying such groups, other than family members'. The definition explicitly includes girls recruited for sexual purposes and forced marriage and affirms that it 'does not, therefore, only refer to a child who is carrying or has carried arms' (hereinafter Cape Town Principles).

tongue-tying *children associated with armed forces or armed groups*, defined in the Paris Principles to cover: 'Any person below 18 years of age who is or who has been recruited or used by an armed force or armed group in any capacity, including but not limited to children, boys, and girls used as fighters, cooks, porters, messengers, spies or for sexual purposes. It does not only refer to a child who is taking or has taken a direct part in hostilities.'[2]

Whereas *armed forces* refer to official state militaries, *armed groups* refer to non-state entities distinct from those forces (notably, rebel or protest movements, dissident factions, and insurgents).

Notwithstanding some differences between the Cape Town and Paris definitions, both still share considerable textual overlap regarding the actual persons they protect. Experts often become ensnared in debates over terms and titles.[3] Terminology matters, to be sure, but debates over it may devolve into distractions. For reasons of convenience and brevity, this chapter primarily uses the term *child soldiers*, but understands its definitional scope as based on the 2007 Paris Principles. This chapter, furthermore, understands the determination of who is considered a child soldier to arise not at the point of exit from militarized life, but at the point of entry. Hence, a *former child soldier* is a person who was initially associated with armed forces or armed groups while under the age of eighteen, even if he or she is eighteen or older at the time of release, demobilization, escape, or rescue.

At its very core, settled international law makes it unlawful to recruit or use anyone under the age of 15 in armed forces or armed groups. Actors and activists push to discard fifteen and replace it across-the-board with eighteen.[4] This push actuates the 'Straight 18' advocacy position. International law has absorbed many of the aspirations of the Straight 18 position. Armed groups, for example, are barred from recruiting anyone younger than eighteen. International law treats state armed forces more ambiguously. This means that international law has not yet absorbed every aspiration of the Straight 18 position. However, international law's trend-line arcs toward the Straight 18 horizon. Accordingly, much of settled law has become dated, if not stale, and is becoming increasingly so. The Straight 18 position has considerable momentum and portends what will be. Its advocacy efforts have exercised even

---

[2] The Paris Principles: Principles and Guidelines on Children Associated with Armed Forces or Armed Groups 2007, Prin. 2.1. Available at http://www.icrc.org/eng/assets/files/others/parisprinciples-en[1].pdf.Accessed13April2013 (hereinafter Paris Principles). As of September 2010, ninety-five states have endorsed the Paris Commitments, which the Paris Principles accompany.

[3] Yet another term of art circulated by experts is 'children associated with fighting forces.'

[4] For example, UNICEF 'joins other organizations, child rights advocates and NGOs in advocating a "straight 18 ban" on all recruitment, compulsory or voluntary and participation of children under 18 in hostilities.' UNICEF (2010) Adult Wars, Child Soldiers: Voices of Children Involved in Armed Conflict in the East Asia and Pacific Region, p. 12; see also Human Rights Watch (2007) Sold to be Soldiers: The Recruitment and Use of Child Soldiers in Burma, p. 14, calling on the Burmese government to cease recruiting and to demobilize children younger than eighteen from armed forces, and also to '[d]evelop and impose effective and appropriate sanctions against individuals found to be recruiting children under 18 into the armed forces'.

greater influence in shaping transnational policy initiatives, best practices, and persuasive authority such as the commitments and principles emerging from the Cape Town and Paris processes.[5]

As recently as 2008, it was estimated that military recruitment of children and their use in hostilities 'still takes place in one form or another in at least 86 countries and territories worldwide.'[6] Accordingly, this chapter considers evidence from an array of jurisdictions. Although many child soldiers are found within the ranks of armed groups, state actors also incorporate children into armed forces. Burma (Myanmar) is presently the largest state recruiter of child soldiers. Subject to a variety of conditions, persons under the age of eighteen may voluntarily enlist in armed forces and reserves in a number of countries, albeit a minority overall, including Australia, Bangladesh, Canada, China, Germany, India, the Netherlands, the United Kingdom, and the United States. In addition, my project examines recent and ongoing evidence of child soldiering in both armed forces and armed groups in Afghanistan, Angola, Cambodia, Colombia, Democratic Republic of the Congo (DRC), Indonesia, Liberia, Libya, Mozambique, Nepal, Papua New Guinea, Philippines, Sierra Leone, Sri Lanka, Sudan, Rwanda, Timor-Leste, and Uganda.

The focus of this chapter, and the broader book project, tilts toward the involvement of child soldiers in atrocity-producing conflicts, particularly conflicts in which international courts and tribunals indict (and, in some instances, are able to prosecute and punish) alleged offenders. Several recent conflicts that have become internationally judicialized situate in Africa, to wit, the DRC, Uganda, Rwanda, Sudan, and Sierra Leone. A number of these jurisdictions, moreover, have undertaken ambitious programmatic initiatives to reintegrate former child soldiers. So, too, have some jurisdictions whose atrocity-producing conflicts have not formally become subject to international judicialization efforts. Liberia is a case-in-point. Consequently, this project is more about child soldiering in African states than it is about child soldiering elsewhere. In this regard, it entwines with my own experiences with international justice which also, starting with my legal work in Rwanda over a decade ago, center on Africa. Persons who were minors at the time of allegedly committing acts of genocide were among the suspects I assisted in the Kigali prison. My choice to focus on child soldiers in Africa is not intended to dilute the reality that child soldiering truly is a global phenomenon. To be clear, only a plurality—reportedly, about 40 %—of the global number of child soldiers is located on the African continent. When responding to Africa, transnational narratives often

[5] The term 'best practices' (also, 'good practices') initially arose within corporate planning and has now entered the lexicon of domestic and international administrative law. Best practices are not formally binding rules. They refer to consensually agreed upon regulatory measures and processes, often informal in nature, that over time crystallize into preferential models. Because of their iterated use and replication, best practices acquire a quasi-legal character.

[6] Coalition to Stop the Use of Child Soldiers (2008) Child Soldiers Global Report 2008, p. 12.

sensationalize and objectify through intemperate depictions, distorted lenses, and paternalistic hues.[7] My aim is to transcend these pernicious impulses and the half-truths that emerge from them; and to resist tiresome tendencies that Africanise a global phenomenon and pathologize African conflicts.

More boys than girls are represented in the subgroup of child soldiers who commit acts of atrocity. One of my goals is to emphasize that these children can return to civilian life and can integrate within the community. Consequently, this project comes to talk more about boy soldiers than it does about girl soldiers. It does incorporate considerable data regarding girl soldiers, however, whose roles in communal violence are considerably more complex than may prosaically be assumed. Moreover, my recommended policy reforms would diversify post-conflict programming. They would accord greater centrality to initiatives specific to girl soldiers and implement a gender-sensitive approach.

8.2 Images of Child Soldiers

Transnational discourse typifies child soldiers in a variety of images. These portraits communicate easily with the public, but Myriam Denov is right to point out that they also inordinately simplify the complex lives and experiences of child soldiers.[8] In this regard, I would add, these images may poorly serve their subjects.

One image is that of a very young child—a guileless naïf—hued as clueless and dependent. This image telescopes the child soldier as a helpless object manipulated locally by adult malevolence, yet at the same time to be rescued transnationally by adult humanitarianism. It portrays child soldiers as forced into service, forced to fight, and forced to kill. Its visuals are of deranged militias that steal children from their families and tear them from their communities. In the hands of such militias, these children become neutered mechanical means used to fulfill nefarious ends over which they have no input. They are no more than 'instruments of war' and 'the weapon of choice.'[9] In another influential account, that of distin-

---

[7] Referencing the Lord's Resistance Army (LRA), a notorious rebel group in Northern Uganda, Ben Mergelsberg notes: 'The narrative of the LRA abducting young, innocent children, brainwashing them and forcing them to fight is common in the media. It evokes a generalized image of the child soldier as a vulnerable innocent without any agency, brutally abducted, drugged and turned into a monster.' Mergelsberg 2010, p. 156. Mergelsberg, however, adds that: '[T]he view of helpless children without agency in what has happened to them often does not correspond to their actual experiences. Passive victims on first sight, they turned out during my fieldwork to be active survivors with a good sense of why they were fighting, how they survived and what they needed most after their return.' Id. at 156–157.

[8] Denov 2010, pp. 5–14, elegantly discusses portrayals and representations of the child soldier, which she chides for their extremism and exoticism.

[9] Otunnu 2000, pp. 48, 49. Available at www2.lse.ac.uk/internationalDevelopment//pdf/WP05.pdf. Otunnu, an eminent public servant, served as the UN Special Representative for Children and Armed Conflict from 1997 to 2005.

guished human rights activist Roméo Dallaire, child soldiers are portrayed as an 'end-to-end weapon system' and as 'tools;' what is more, children 'are vulnerable and easy to catch, just like minnows in a pond,' with the involved adults depicted as 'evil.'[10] This image melds with and, in turn, disseminates a narrative—now transposed into law and policy—through which child soldiers are construed first and foremost as victims. In terms of on-the-ground practice, however, the conceptual understanding of child soldiers principally as victims tends toward operational interventions that essentialize their victimhood. This first image, therefore, typifies the child soldier as a *faultless passive victim*.

A second image, which harmonizes with the victim narrative, is that of child soldiers as *irreparable damaged goods*. Pursuant to this image, child soldiers are tormented and scarred. They form part of a 'lost generation.'[11] This image captures the pain of militarized life and the concomitant physical and emotional injuries. Yet it does so at the cost of overlooking the resilience of former child soldiers and children in war zones generally. This depiction defines expectations and sets parameters. Constructions of the child soldier as psychologically devastated and pilfered by conflict, for example, have spurred the preeminence of trauma recovery models in post-conflict programming.

A third image—somewhat antiquated, yet still in circulation—posits the child soldier as a *hero*, whose valor flows from fighting for a just cause that resists oppression or from demonstrating patriotism.[12] In contradistinction to the faultless passive victim image, the hero image plays up the independence, conviction, nobility, and enterprise of the child soldier. This portrayal also may venerate military service, however, and feed into pernicious norms of masculinity and hyper-aggression. It can lead to a parlous situation for the unpopular side. In Timor-Leste, for example, 'children who fought on the side of independence were considered heroes [while] [t]hose who fought on the opposing side were stigmatised, and some were later targeted.'[13]

A final image dramatically appears in journalistic accounts, political grandstanding, and national security circles. This image stylizes the child soldier as *demon and bandit*: irredeemable, baleful, and sinister. Pursuant to this depiction, the child soldier is a ticking time-bomb, bad seed, and warped soul incorrigibly

---

[10] Dallaire 2010, pp. 3, 12, 15, 150, also referring to former child soldiers as 'immature souls in small bodies'. Dallaire, now a Senator in Canada, is well-known for his outspoken role as commander of the UN Assistance Mission for Rwanda during the country's 1994 genocide. He recently has oriented his efforts to eradicating child soldiering. To this end, he founded the Child Soldiers Initiative.

[11] Singer 2006, p. 38.

[12] Denov 2010, pp. 9–10, noting also the celebrity status of some high-profile child soldiers viewed as heroically transcending from violence to redemption.

[13] UNICEF Innocenti Research Centre in cooperation with the International Center for Transitional Justice (2010) Children and Truth Commissions, p. 47 (citation omitted), hereinafter Children and Truth Commissions.

determined to kill with alacrity.[14] This flawed image comports with two alarming policy outputs. The first is the pointlessness of investing in the rehabilitation of former child soldiers. The second is the neglect of girl soldiers. The demon and bandit image, after all, tends to present child soldiers as wild boys, which clouds the reality that '[a]s many as 40 % of child soldiers may be girls.'[15] Girl soldiers already are poorly served by extant programming that under-appreciates the specific gender-based reintegrative challenges they face. The demon image piles onto these challenges, many of which involve recovery from abhorrent sexual violence and forced marriage. Many girls give birth while associated with armed forces or groups. Rates of HIV, AIDS, and sexually transmitted diseases are high. Upon cessation of hostilities, it is not uncommon for local communities to marginalize these young mothers and view their children with repugnance. Insofar as the fathers of these children (at times themselves teenagers) may have been abusive fighters and unit commanders, the 'bad seed' may be perceived by communities as passing down intergenerationally. Girl soldiers, assuredly, are not an indiscriminate group of interchangeable members. Girls who become 'wives' of commanders exert power over girls without 'husbands.' This latter group, in turn, comes to suffer even greater levels of sexual abuse. Some girls commit terrible acts of atrocity against other girls, boys, women, and men. The demon and bandit image also obscures the fact that boys, too, are sexually abused.

These four images are not equals. Hierarchy and ordinality can be theorized among them with regard to their operational influence in shaping official policies and sculpting conventional wisdom.

The faultless passive victim image has achieved widespread traction within—and is avidly disseminated by—influential intergovernmental organizations and UN agencies, along with NGOs and other actors that populate global civil society.[16] It has consequently come to dominate international discourse. The faultless passive victim image binds communities of conscience. This image has ascended as a metaphor for the child soldier: continuously defining the child soldier at the point of entry into conflict, during conflict, at the point of exit from conflict, and also in the aftermath of conflict. Applied top-down in a wide-range of places, this image is

[14] Denov 2010, p. 6; see also Blattman and Annan 2010, p. 882, reporting on and critiquing the use of this imagery; Wessells 2006, p. 45 (first paperback 2009) noting that 'this portrayal contradicts much evidence and does injustice to the rich interplay between personal and situational influences on decisions to become soldiers'.

[15] Wessells 2006, p. 9, citing a 2005 Save the Children Report.

[16] *Cf.* Utas 2003, pp. 7–8, noting that 'the perspective of humanitarian aid agencies (Save the Children/UNICEF, in particular) will often describe child soldiers, and deal with them, solely as victims'; Boyden and de Berry 2004, pp. xi, xv, '[C]hildren and adolescents are portrayed as the passive recipients of adult agency, the victims of wars waged by others and of brutality that is alien and imposed.... Personal volition is denied and emphasis given to their vulnerability and helplessness ...'; Ben-Ari 2009, pp. 1, 13: 'Even a cursory review of the websites devoted to young soldiers reveals the extent to which visual representations in photographs or drawings are designed to evoke images of blamelessness and helplessness.'

portable. It forms part of transnational rule of law discourse and technique. Although projections of it by communities of conscience have become more refined over time, its core attributes persist and, in fact, are hardening into law and policy. This portrait scripts official conversations about child soldiers. Accordingly, these conversations become conformist and stilted.

Global civil society, advocacy groups, donors, and activists lack the formal capacity to make international law. Although some international and intergovernmental organizations, including some UN agencies, may exercise law-making ability, most do not (including many whose mandates touch upon child soldiering). By virtue of their activities, however, all of these actors shape the content of binding international law as traditionally made by states and, what is more, often determine the legally oriented content of best practices, rule of law blueprints, and policy guidelines.[17] I refer to this normative, aspirational, and operational mix of international law, policy, and practice—constituted as it is directly and indirectly by a broad constellation of actors—as the *international legal imagination*.[18] On the topic of child soldiers, the faultless passive victim image fills the international legal imagination. This image thereby contributes to and influences the substance of international law and policy.

Attending to the scourge of child soldiering has become a portal for transnational rights discourse and its broader reformist ambitions to enter local constituencies. In this regard, the child soldier has become a site that serves broader political purposes. One purpose is the naturalization of certain characteristics of childhood. Another purpose is the universalization of a child as anyone below the age of eighteen. This chapter, and the book from which is it extracted, carefully considers the relationship between internationalized legal norms regarding coming of age, which are rooted in chronology, and diverse localized understandings, which are more malleably informed by experience, activity, relationship, and station in life.

One goal of the faultless passive victim image is to curb punitive policies and harsh measures that may flow from the demon caricature. At times, pressure may arise within post-conflict societies to pursue such policies against former child soldiers. Transnational actors may discursively respond to these pressures by even further underscoring the unwitting dependency and sacrificial nature of militarized youth. In so doing, transnational actors unhelpfully dichotomize conversational frames such that child soldiers become either 'sinners' or 'saints.'[19]

---

[17] These actors may participate in conferences in which states negotiate and adopt major multilateral treaties.

[18] The term 'international legal imagination' is not coined herein as a neologism, but no other scholarship appears to meaningfully address, define, or deploy it as an analytic tool. Among a tiny handful of unrelated references thereto in the published literature is Landauer 2011, p. 557, mentioning this term in passing without definition or deployment.

[19] For use of such language, see, e.g., Lonegan 2011, p. 71.

Because the depiction of the demon child soldier tends to hail from the global South (notably Africa), it reinforces racial stereotypes. Nor, however, are racial overtones absent from the faultless passive victim image. This portrait may inadvertently pathologize entire social structures by presenting the children as needing to be saved from their communities, from their cultures, and from their families.

Although not the doing of global civil society, the turn to victimhood narratives to thwart punitive policies and retributive measures can be selective. Owing to state behavior, the political suitability of these narratives correlates to whom, exactly, the conduct of the child soldiers aggrieves. A center/periphery divide emerges. Transnational conceptions of faultlessness do not fully reach children from the periphery who commit atrocious acts against Westerners. Whereas the child perpetrator targeting Africans tends to be held as a mindless captive of purposeless violence, the child perpetrator targeting Westerners tends to be held as an intentional author of purposeful violence.

In short, all extreme images of child soldiers run the risk, as Denov eloquently counsels, of 'reflect[ing] and reproduc[ing] enduring hierarchies between the global North and South, cementing notions of race, perversity and barbarism, alongside the dehumanisation of child soldiers and their societies.'[20]

Within post-conflict societies guided by international judicialization and administration efforts, policy initiatives generated by the faultless passive victim imagery presuppose and designate local child soldiers as programmed to commit terrible abuses over which they have neither appreciation nor control. Child soldiers are seen as forcibly coerced into military service and, in the case of atrocity-producing conflicts, compelled to commit horrific human rights abuses.[21] As a group, and *ipso facto* as individuals, they are taken to lack any volition. Seen as 'faceless,' they 'have not yet developed a concept of justice.'[22]

Is the projected image fully explanatory? If not, do its deficiencies or omissions matter? Notwithstanding accuracy in many individual cases, the portrayal of the child soldier as a faultless passive victim is unduly reductive. It belies considerably more varied actual individual experiences. This image—as do all extreme images of the child soldier—occludes, flattens, and conceals details. And, yes,

---

[20] Denov 2010, p. 14.

[21] For a typical presentation, see Spiga 2010, pp. 183, 192: 'It is common knowledge that children are often forced to take up arms and have little choice on whether or not to enlist; after their recruitment, they are coerced to commit actions, of which—in most cases—they have little understanding.'. The international legal imagination, however, stiffly balks at generalizing this explanatory account in cases of perpetrators aged 18 or older. For this group 'following orders' is a paltry defense.

[22] Dallaire 2010, pp. 3, 138, also describing some child soldiers as 'zombies'. Noting that Dallaire's book '[p]arallel[s] [his] own childhood, in which he spun fictional worlds in the forests beyond his family's log cabin … [and is] inspired by Antoine de Saint-Exupéry's *Le Petit Prince*,' one reviewer lauded it for 'perfectly captur[ing] the innocence and experience of childhood that war so savagely steals from them.' Nutt S (2005) Arms and the child, The Globe and Mail (November 5, 2010).

these details are salient. They matter. It is inadequate to generalize an overarching understanding of child soldiering based on the more extreme cases. Extrapolating from the extremes instead of the mean sensationalizes vulnerability and trauma.[23] A proportionate and inclusive process of inductive reasoning requires even-handed consideration of the full gamut of individual experiences, not only a subset of those cases most compatible with predetermined advocacy efforts. Child soldiers and child soldiering are not so simple.

In the end, I urge the international legal imagination to adopt a supple, empathetic, and dexterous approach to child soldiers that vivifies their dignity rather than the current *Zeitgeist* that encases their vulnerability. I hope for this chapter to contribute, however modestly, to that process.

8.3 Social Realities of Child Soldiering: Circumscribed Action

Accumulated knowledge about child soldiers arises from a diversity of disciplines. The richness that might flow from this diversity, unfortunately, lies fallow. These disciplines and their concomitant literatures often communicate poorly with each other. In terms of the development of law, best practices, and policy, the play of various literatures has been uneven. Child psychology and trauma studies have exerted considerable influence. So, too, have reports published by transnational pressure groups, NGOs, activists, and UN agencies. The recommendations of child rights advocates also have proven instrumental.

Other disciplines and their literatures have not resonated with the international legal imagination. In fact, the international legal imagination holds contributions from these fields at arm's length. Thus, these contributions remain untapped. This gate-keeping occasions a loss, insofar as the only way to eradicate child soldiering and promote genuine post-conflict reconciliation is to understand the phenomenon as multidimensionally as possible. Examples of undervalued contributions include ethnographic participant observation, anthropological studies, qualitative research, survey data, and feminist theory. Another is adolescent developmental neurobiology, which focuses on the social category of adolescents as distinct from young children. I hope to canvas these literatures so as to integrate them more robustly into conversations about child soldiering. In this regard, this work is both synthetic

---

[23] This impulse even arises in the work of Jeff McMahan, a leading moral philosopher, in his otherwise brilliantly nuanced discussion. McMahan 2007, pp. 9–10 (cited with permission) offering the following as an illustrative hypothetical case: an eight year-old boy, forced by a group of armed men to kill his best friend in view of his entire village, and then abducted to a camp; after several years of indoctrination, brutalisation, and training, he is administered drugs, given a light automatic weapon, and sent to fight for an unjust cause at the age of eleven or twelve.

and creative. It aims to revisit the epistemology of child soldiering. It intends to develop a less didactic and more grounded composite.

Although not monolithic, these literatures tend to perceive child soldiers neither as crushed nor as succumbing, but rather as traversing, surviving, coping, and making what they can out of bad circumstances not of their own doing. These literatures foreground individuality and adaptation, rather than aimless collective subservience. They voice a more dynamic account of child soldiers as *social navigators* interacting with, instead of overwhelmed by, their environments—even when those environments involve the most invidious of circumstances.[24] These literatures also tend to place children, adolescents, youth, and adults along a broader continuum that is less rigidly stratified by chronological age demarcations.

Presentation of this information is meant to holistically *understand* child soldiering so as to more meaningfully *prevent* its occurrence. Although the faultless passive victim image may serve as an anodyne to distressing and delicate conversations about militarized youth, the international legal imagination needs to do better. Rote deontological denunciation can only take us so far. Within transnational discourse, the seemingly inevitable obverse to the innocence of the children is the iniquity of the adult commanders of rogue armed groups. Although serving rhetorical purposes, presenting these commanders as crazed demented evildoers also obscures the reasons why they recruit children in fighting forces. Perhaps these reasons are more conventional and strategic, and less visceral, than the portrayal diffused by the international legal imagination. In any event, unraveling these reasons would help clarify the sources of child soldiering. Such clarification is necessary for the success of dissuasive efforts and the effective sanction of adult commanders.

Young children certainly are associated with armed forces or armed groups. In some instances, many young children may be forcibly recruited and, in fact, may fight. Most child soldiers, however, are not young children. Most are adolescents—often aged fifteen, sixteen, or seventeen. Overall, the young, pre-pubescent child is simply not indicative of the norm. The marketing and advertising work of charity organizations, however, still inclines toward underscoring the tender age of child soldiers. One visual, for example, involves the surrealistic juxtaposition of bullets in what looks like a Crayola crayon box.[25] Although certainly eye-catching and well-intended, this approach may neither resonate with nor strike at the heart of the problem of child soldiering.

In light of the centrality of *adolescents* (often older teenagers) to the phenomenon of *child* soldiering, is it not apposite to consider adolescent developmental psychology? This burgeoning field, which increasingly is turning to sophisticated neuroscientific and neurobiological methods, demonstrates that adolescents typically are more susceptible than adults to outside or peer influence. In comparison

---

[24] I draw the concept of social navigation from Mats Utas. See Utas 2005, pp. 403, 408, 426.

[25] See, e.g., www.warchild.org.uk/issues/child-soldiers (accessed on June 24, 2011).

to adults, adolescents are more represented in reckless behavior; they have a gauzier ability to foresee the future; are more impulsive, impetuous, and risk-taking; and have more transitory personalities. Adolescents trust more readily and their trust can be easily misplaced. But neither is the adolescent brain child-like nor prelogical. On many key metrics, in fact, available research indicates that older adolescents are much more like adults than children. Instead of pursuing rigid child/adult binaries, then, perhaps it would make sense for law and policy to engage with interstitial developmental categories.

Persons under the age of eighteen associated with armed forces or armed groups largely get there in one of three ways: (1) they are abducted or conscripted through force or serious threats; (2) they present themselves, whether independently or through recruitment programs and become enlisted/enrolled; or (3) they are born into forces or groups. The first two paths, which are the most common, are not always capable of firm demarcation. However, they are distinguishable and, moreover, should be distinguished.

Readers may find it surprising, but most child soldiers are neither abducted nor forcibly recruited. The international legal imagination, nevertheless, heavily emphasizes this path to militarization. Doing so exposes this horrific aspect of the phenomenon of child soldiering. This emphasis, however, also leads to the undertheorization and underexploration of *youth volunteerism*. The international legal imagination cannot just wish away the fact that significant numbers of children join armed forces or armed groups in the absence of evident coercion and, in fact, exercise some—and at times considerable—initiative in this regard. Even within the most maleficent of conflicts, children come forward and present themselves for service.

In response, the international legal imagination predetermines that no child has the capacity to volunteer or to consent to serve—whether innately or because of nightmarish circumstances, or both. Volunteering is presented as an illusion.[26] The international legal imagination is particularly skeptical of armed groups and, in their case, flatly views juvenile volunteerism as an impossibility or absurdity. For all intents and purposes, then, enlistment of volunteers becomes no different than abduction.

The international legal imagination is remiss to neglect the prevalence and relevance of children who volunteer for military service. To be sure, cases arise where determinations of volunteerism would be specious. Children may be offered up—like chattel—by family members or local leaders. They may be tricked into joining. They may come forward to serve as a cook, only to be given an automatic weapon and placed on the front lines. Some children may rashly present themselves for service because of excessive impulsivity.[27] That said, many children,

---

[26] Hart 2006, pp. 5, 7: 'The authors of global accounts of "child soldiers"… have little time for the idea that children may be capable of exercising any real measure of choice about recruitment….[T]he very notion of voluntary recruitment is largely an illusion.'

[27] Over time, as hardships weigh on them, these children may come to regret their decision. Some of them then exit, while others are compelled to stay; others persist and remain with the group; some advance within the ranks. Longitudinally, these latter cases become considerably more ambiguous.

notably older adolescents, come forward intentionally to join armed forces or groups. Environmental factors and situational constraints—which include poverty, insecurity, lack of education, socialization into violence, and broken families—certainly inform their decisions to enlist. Children's engagement with these factors can be more usefully understood as interactive and negotiated processes of negative push and affirmative pull.

In joining armed forces or groups, children may simply be pursuing paths of economic advancement, inclusion in occupational networks, pursuit of political or ideological reform, and professional development. Children—particularly, older adolescents—are not invariably lost on these paths. They traverse and cross them as best they can. However disturbing to outsiders, this may mean joining armed forces or armed groups. Moreover, at times child recruits deceive their parents and other commanders. They conceal their age, travel great distances, and persevere tenaciously in their quest to associate with armed forces or groups. They may join despite community and family exhortations to the contrary. These children, too, count as child soldiers. Although armed groups may seek to undermine legitimate governments through macabre methods, they may also serve as engines of protest against illegitimate rulers, state authoritarianism, and kleptocratic dictatorship.

What child soldiers actually say about their experiences may contrast with how international observers broadcast those experiences. In interviews, for example, former child soldiers often describe themselves as having volunteered for service. Some interviewers respond by discounting all such statements. They thereby massage complex data to fit a simple pre-existing theory. P. W. Singer—whose work on child soldiers has received considerable attention—finds the notion of voluntary recruitment 'misleading,' in part because children are 'of an age at which they are not capable of making mature decisions.'[28] Helping hands may prefer to believe that child soldiers are ignorant of the absence of choice in their lives and lack the cognitive capacity for discernment. This strategy, however well-intentioned, may demean by unduly accenting gullibility. This strategy, moreover, depletes the informational record and leads to misguided recommendations. It risks presenting youth inanimately as objects of study rather than vibrantly as sources of information. Although assertions of volunteer service made by child soldiers should not be immunized from contextual analysis, I believe it is wrong summarily to dismiss them. Young people may understand volunteerism within the context of their lives and apply it fairly to themselves.

Dismissing what adolescents have to say owing to their putative jejunity contrasts sharply with assumptions of juvenile capacity and autonomy that animate

---

[28] Singer 2006, p. 62. Singer's book relies heavily on humanitarian and human rights reports, journalistic accounts, psychology scholarship, and military/security studies literature. It makes only marginal reference to ethnographic or anthropological work. See also *generally* Office of the Special Representative of the Secretary-General for Children and Armed Conflict (2011) Children and Justice During and in the Aftermath of Armed Conflict (Working Paper No. 3, September 2011), p. 10: 'Children … lack the mental maturity and judgment to express consent or to fully understand the implications of their actions.' (hereinafter Children and Justice).

other areas of law and policy. For example, when it comes to bioethical debates regarding consent to medical treatment and access to reproductive rights and technologies, in many jurisdictions adolescents tend to be presumed competent. International human rights law highlights that adolescents can exercise rights of freedom of association and expression. So, too, does international family law. Protective policies predicated upon children being constructed as enfeebled *before and during* conflict may counterproductively result in children persistently being treated as enfeebled *after* conflict. I remain skeptical that atrophied delineations of capacity, and the notion that adolescents categorically require infantilising rules to protect them, actually promote the aspiration to engage them robustly as full members of society. Moreover, many persons initially recruited as children age into adulthood during conflict or before they feasibly can enroll in post-conflict programming. In these instances, infantilising aspects may become perceived both by them and the community as particularly ill-fitting.

Once associated with armed forces or groups, what do children actually do? How are they used? Children rotate among various roles, which include combat, auxiliary support, or accompanying forces as sex slaves or compelled conjugal partners.[29] These roles expose them to great danger. In contradistinction to often graphic media representations, significant numbers of children neither fight nor carry weapons.[30] Even fewer become implicated in the systematic perpetration of acts of atrocity that potentially might fall within the scope of extraordinary international crimes (such as war crimes, crimes against humanity, and genocide) proscribed by international criminal law.

The dominant explanatory account is that those child soldiers who commit extraordinary international crimes are forced by commanders and, hence, operate under extreme duress; they are incapacitated by compelled ingestion of narcotics and alcohol; they are brainwashed and resocialized by the endemic violence that envelops them; and they are plagued with fears of brutal punishment. Hence, moral responsibility should be excused, even for grievous acts of violence. Excuse begets forgiveness which, *arguendo*, establishes a firm footing for the child soldier's reintegration.

This dominant account explains many acts of atrocity perpetrated by persons under the age of eighteen. Despite their frequency, however, these cases cannot be universalized. The international legal imagination tends, once again, to wish away the fact that not all child soldiers materially implicated in acts of atrocity actually conform to this explanatory account. In this regard, the international legal imagination undertheorizes the challenge at hand, perhaps selfishly insofar as: '[T]he

---

[29] I very occasionally turn to the phrases 'child combatant' or 'child ex-combatant' specifically to refer to child soldiers who have materially (as opposed to incidentally) fulfilled combat roles.

[30] Wessells 2006, p. 71: 'Contrary to popular conceptions, many child soldiers never fight, and many neither carry their own weapon nor know how to use one.'; Ben-Ari 229, p. 1, reporting that children 'sometimes act as combatants who directly participate in hostilities [but] more often they are deployed as auxiliaries … or in various support roles'.

fact that children are capable of violence clearly falls outside entrenched modernist formulations of childhood. Children who behave violently—who rape, murder and kill—pose a conundrum because they dismantle the idea of the romantic innocence and vulnerability of childhood.'[31]

Considerable heterogeneity arises among child soldiers with regard to their relationship to violence that, in turn, underscores the ongoing salience of disposition, choice, and residual discretion to exceed or subvert command authority. Some child soldiers lie to and manipulate commanders to avoid killing. Others refuse to inflict gross human rights abuses upon third-party civilians or combatants. Other child soldiers, however, torture, rape, and kill to navigate volatile militarized hierarchies. Some do so gratuitously or to pursue lucre.

Accordingly, afflicted communities may perceive child soldiers in a considerably more individuated fashion. They may see them as actual persons known to them rather than as anonymously fungible 'beasts of no nation.'[32] These details matter. Furthermore, regardless of why they did it and the circumstances thereof, the fact remains that the acts of child soldiers do impose staggering consequences upon the lives of others, including children.[33]

Given the distortions and omissions engendered by the faultless passive victim lens (as well as the occlusions triggered by other currently circulated images), is there another way to talk about child soldiers that reflects the complexities of their experiences?

I propose to approach individual child soldiers through a *model of circumscribed action.* A circumscribed actor has the ability to act, the ability not to act, and the ability to do otherwise than what he or she actually has done. The effective range of these abilities, however, is delimited, bounded, and confined. Yet, the abilities themselves are neither evanescent nor ephemeral. Circumscribed actors exercise some discretion in navigating and mediating the constraints around them. Circumscribed actors dispose of an enclosed space which is theirs—the acreage of which varies according to an oscillating admixture of disposition and situation—in which they exercise a margin of volition. Within this space, they make short-term decisions. Circumscribed actors scale social environments they did not create. Although acted upon, they also act upon others. Oppression, after all, does not axiomatically void the oppressed's capacity for decision-making. Nor is

[31] Honwana 2005, pp. 31, 37.

[32] This is the title of a prominent novel which tracks the story of Agu, a fictional child soldier, Iweala 2005. On this note, many documentaries, movies, novels, memoirs, and autobiographies evoke the vicissitudes of the child soldier. For a handful of examples, see Kourouma 2000; Keitetsi 2002; McDonnell and Akallo 2007; Blood Diamond (2006, dir. Edward Zwick); Wit Licht (2008, recut as *The Silent Army*, dir. Jean van de Velde).

[33] Kamara with McClelland 2008, pp. 40–41, Sierra Leonean author Kamara describes how, as a child, she became a double amputee: 'Two boys steadied me as my body began to sway. As the machete came down, things went silent. I closed my eyes tightly, but then they popped open and I saw everything. It took the boy two attempts to cut off my right hand. The first swipe didn't get through the bones, which I saw sticking out in all different shapes and sizes.'.

it normatively desirable as a matter of policymaking to adopt such an arthritic and atrophied view of the oppressed.

Circumscribed action is not a metaphor, nor a photograph, nor an ideal-type, nor an image whose reification is sought and to which all *prima facie* categorized individuals are to conform. Rather, circumscribed action is presented as a *spectrum* or *continuum* that embraces the inherent diversity among the individuals aligned along its axis.[34] Presenting circumscribed action as a spectrum, instead of a singular category, facilitates procedural inquiry regarding the specific histories and experiences of these individuals.

When law internalizes the chronological watershed of the age of eighteen, and turns to it to contrast the capable adult from the incapable child, law creates an exigent situation for young adults. After all, neuroscience teaches us that, as a matter of age, cognitive functions continue to develop well into the mid-twenties. When the law draws bright-lines, outsiders may become excessively exposed to the very vicissitudes from which law aims to insulate insiders. Abusive commanders may simply shift their focus from older children to young adults. In the end, law may simultaneously protect too much and too little. Accordingly, a turn to a model of circumscribed action would abandon the current predilection for two oppositional polarities—that is, child or adult—and thereby relieve younger adults from the weight of excessive hardship and older children from the straightjacket of excessive infantilization.

8.4 An Emergent Legal Fiction and Its Effects

Where does the faultless passive victim image intend to shift international law and policy?

For starters, toward eighteen as the threshold age of permissible military service. I argue that attainment of this goal would be facilitated were its pursuit to be paired with a less judgmental and more tempered portrayal of those persons intended for protective coverage. Another intended shift involves the vitiation of the legal relevance of distinctions among kinds of recruitment or use and, correspondingly, to annul the possibility that any child ever can volunteer to serve or to perform functions within armed forces or groups.

Considerable momentum also is afoot to exclude children (including child soldiers), whether *de jure* or *de facto*, from the jurisdiction of international or internationalized courts and tribunals that adjudge extraordinary atrocity crimes. Although prosecuting child soldiers for such crimes is certainly not unlawful, such prosecutions increasingly are seen as inappropriate and, even, illegitimate.

34 Wessells 2006, p. 74: 'The lives of child combatants exhibit significant diversity, cautioning against stereotypes of child combatants as bloodthirsty predators or innocents herded onto the killing fields.'.

The push for international institutions to abjure criminal trials for child soldiers implicated in acts of atrocity conceptually seeps into the national and local court systems of post-conflict societies. As a result, national criminal prosecutions of former child soldiers become discouraged as well.

The faultless passive victim narrative also suffuses post-conflict justice modalities other than criminal trials. For example, in the case of truth-seeking and reconciliation mechanisms, ascendant best practices advise that children can only participate therein voluntarily as witnesses or victims.[35] These best practices also advocate that all child participants—including children formerly associated with armed forces or groups—be treated equally as victims or witnesses.[36] In other words, children are not to be distinguished *inter se* in terms of their individual conduct. Nor, apparently, are child soldiers to be distinguished from other children in conflict zones. Individual participation in acts of atrocity is, therefore, not approached through a *quid pro quo* dialogue of forgiveness. The elimination of distinctions among group members helps accord legal protection to as many children as possible. Nevertheless, I caution against this policy preference. Child soldiers can be treated as a generally protected class while distinctions among individual class members still remain respected.

The preferred push is to void victim-perpetrator ambiguity in the case of child soldiers. When the child inflicts horrors, responsibility passes entirely to the adult abductor, enlister, recruiter, or commander. Although abjured for child soldiers, international criminal tribunals are invoked to prosecute as war criminals those adults who conscript, enlist, or use children below the age of fifteen as active participants in hostilities. Straight 18 aspirations endeavor to expand this prohibition to cover all children, that is, all persons younger than eighteen.[37]

The international community has invested considerable resources and energy to prosecute a handful of adult militia leaders for unlawful conscription, enlistment, or use of children younger than fifteen. The Special Court for Sierra Leone (SCSL), a hybrid court created cooperatively between the UN and the Sierra Leonean government, has issued several convictions on such charges. The inaugural trial at the International Criminal Court (ICC) in The Hague—involving Thomas Lubanga Dyilo, a DRC rebel leader—is proceeding exclusively on these charges. The Rome Statute, the multilateral international treaty establishing the

[35] Paris Principles (2007) Prin. 3.8 (also adding the stipulation that child participation must be by informed consent of both the child and parent or guardian where appropriate and possible) and 8.16.

[36] Id. Prin. 8.15.

[37] See, e.g., REDRESS Trust (2006) Victims, Perpetrators or Heroes? Child Soldiers before the International Criminal Court, p. 1: 'It is recommended that the ICC should follow suit and raise the legal age of child recruitment, enlisting or "use" from fifteen to eighteen.'; UNDDR (2006) Integrated Disarmament, Demobilization and Reintegration Standards (IDDRS) Sect. 5.30, p. 23, available at www.unddr.org/iddrs/05/download/IDDRS_530.pdf: 'It is a serious breach of international humanitarian law, human rights law and international criminal law to use children as soldiers under the age of 15, and in most circumstances to use children under 18.'.

ICC, also permits victims to participate in the criminal proceedings against an accused. On this note, ICC judges have determined the class of persons harmed by child soldiers not to be direct or indirect victims of Lubanga's alleged conduct and, thus, have denied applications brought by class members to participate in the criminal proceedings against him.

Although the faultless passive victim image reflects the experiences of many child soldiers, I argue—borrowing a term of art from legal philosopher Lon Fuller—that its transposition into law spins a *legal fiction*.[38] According to Fuller, a fiction 'is neither a truthful statement, nor a lie, nor an erroneous conclusion.'[39] Fuller identifies many kinds of legal fictions. What I call the legal fiction of faultless passive victimhood most closely approximates the category of neglective or abstractive fictions.[40] For Fuller, neglective fictions constitute the 'most obvious example of the process by which our minds simplify reality.'[41]

Legal fictions are neither intrinsically malignant nor intrinsically benign. They are constructs that serve both ill and good. In the case of child soldiering, the legal fiction of faultless passive victimhood fulfills a number of valuable purposes. Because it offers a disambiguated and pointed message, it helps marshal resources and co-ordinate condemnation. Many of the reforms the fiction has impressed upon the architecture of law, policy, and best practices are salutary.

Along with a variety of gains, however, indulging this legal fiction also produces operational shortcomings.

One example arises from the prosecution of adult recruiters and users of child soldiers. These prosecutions, to be clear, help condemn child soldiering. International lawyers and policymakers, however, exaggerate their deterrent value. Such bullishness is unwise. It distracts from the need to search well beyond the architecture of the courtroom and jailhouse in order to meaningfully dissuade and, ultimately, end child soldiering. Much more than a handful of criminal prosecutions are required to promote the well-being of children in conflict zones. When international criminal law fixates on the adult recruiter or user, it flits past the multiple sources of child soldiering—institutional, power politics, commercial, and historical. State responsibility for unlawful recruitment of children, along with other forms of collective sanction, therefore remains undertheorized and underdeveloped. I hope to encourage deeper reflection and more action along these lines. As part of their goal to accentuate the moral culpability of adult recruiters or users, criminal prosecutions amplify how post-traumatic stress syndrome debilitates former child soldiers. If convicting perpetrators becomes entwined with tropes of

---

[38] Fuller 1967, p. 9, a fiction is 'either (1) a statement propounded with a complete or partial consciousness of its falsity, or (2) a false statement recognized as having utility'.

[39] Id., p. 5.

[40] Id., p. 106, citing Vaihinger 1920, p. 28. For Vaihinger, these fictions constitute 'a series of methods in which the deviation from reality manifests itself specifically as a disregard of certain elements in the fact situation.' Id., citing Vaihinger 1920, p. 28.

[41] Id.

youth helplessness, however, the upshot may be incarcerating a handful of adults while simultaneously perpetuating gerontocracy by eroding tenets of juvenile autonomy and ability.

The faultless passive victim image is conducive to several other externalities. Of greatest concern is the sidelining of *transitional justice* from post-conflict initiatives to reintegrate former child soldiers and to reconstruct their communities.[42] The phrase transitional justice designates the range of processes by which societies come to terms with histories of widespread violence, how they reckon with terrible human rights abuses, and how people within afflicted constituencies come to live together again. Transitional justice is concerned with redress, historical clarification, and reconciliation. Processes commonly associated with transitional justice include criminal trials, civil liability (for example, private tort actions, restitutionary claims, and public reparations), lustration, community service programs, truth and reconciliation commissions, endogenous mechanisms,[43] public inquiries, and restorative ceremonies. These processes vary considerably *inter se* regarding how, to whom, and to what degree they allocate responsibility for acts of atrocity. They nevertheless share the pursuit of social repair through a framework that recognizes the pain that these acts have wrought. These institutions also share the belief that there can be no durable stability if injustices and human rights abuses are left unaddressed. This does not necessarily mean that perpetrators have to confess or atone. Many endogenous ceremonies, for example, do not contemplate such methods, preferring instead to address past wrongs through future-oriented work and cultivation of relationships.

The international legal imagination's propensity is to generically ease a potential three-dimensional status of child soldiers as perpetrators, witnesses, and victims into a two-dimensional portrayal of child soldiers as victims and witnesses alone. This constriction, however, engenders some opportunity costs. In response, I advance the normative claim that transitional justice initiatives other than criminal trials—in particular, truth commissions, restorative modalities, and endogenous mechanisms—can help facilitate reintegration and reconciliation in cases of child soldiers implicated in acts of atrocity.

I do not call for former child soldiers to be criminally prosecuted for suspected violations of international criminal law before international institutions and, if

---

[42] Together with their adult counterparts, many—but certainly not all, and in some jurisdictions only few—child soldiers may return to their communities of origin through disarmament, demobilization (release), and reintegration (DDR) programs. Disarmament involves the collection of weapons. Demobilization means the discharge of individuals from fighting forces. Reintegration is the step through which the former fighter transitions to a civilian role.

[43] I borrow political scientist Phil Clark's unorthodox use of the term 'endogenous' to describe ceremonies, rites, and rituals that arise, often informally, at the local level to promote social repair and purification following wrongful conduct. I also deploy the more conventional terms 'traditional' and 'customary' in this regard. I recognize the contested meaning and use of these terms, but turn to them only descriptively and purely out of convenience. I do not aim to theorise these terms.

found guilty, to be punished through incarceration. Nor do I recommend prosecutions or imprisonment at the national level. My reservations extend even more emphatically to proceedings before military commissions or tribunals, which are particularly susceptible to procedural irregularities and political vagaries. The outrageous situation faced at Guantánamo Bay by Omar Khadr, a Canadian child soldier who, as a minor, had associated with al-Qaeda, is painfully illustrative.[44]

As a matter of outcome, then, I concur in the international legal imagination's push to discard criminal trials for child soldiers. I disagree, however, when it comes to why. My skepticism regarding criminal trials for child soldiers implicated in acts of atrocity flows from my broader circumspection regarding the ability of the atrocity trial to attain its principally avowed penological goals, especially in the case of lower-level cadres, regardless of the age of the accused.[45] These goals include retribution, deterrence, and expressivism. Penological goals of rehabilitation and reintegration, which should be particularly salient in the context of juveniles, do not centrally figure among international criminal law's aspirations. The fact that child soldiers do not serve as conflict entrepreneurs or political leaders dulls the benefits of incapacitating them. Former child soldiers and those persons harmed by their conduct require restoration, which sequestered incarceration does not provide.

To recap, this project does not turn to criminal law as a regulatory solution. Why, then, does it devote considerable space to review the interface of the international legal imagination with the question of the potential criminal culpability of child soldiers? Why be concerned with assessing how, and for which reasons, conventional wisdom has come to eschew criminal trials for child soldiers enmeshed in the commission of acts of atrocity? The answer lies in the fact that what the international legal imagination says, recommends, and exhorts ultimately bears heavily upon the reconstructive journeys of inter- and post-conflict societies. Transnational interventions matter. Although excluding child soldiers from international and national criminal trials may well be appropriate as a policy *result*, the

[44] In October 2010, a US Military Commission convicted Khadr through a plea bargain of charges that included violating the laws of war. Khadr pleaded guilty to five charges—including throwing a grenade in a 2002 firefight that killed a US combatant, Christopher Speer, in Afghanistan—as well as various other crimes in connection with terrorist activity. He was formally sentenced by a military jury to forty years' imprisonment. Because of a diplomatic agreement, however, Khadr will likely be repatriated to Canada to serve out seven years of his sentence (which the agreement capped at eight years in total) in accordance with Canadian law. Savage C (2010) Guantánamo Detainee's Guilty Plea Averts Trial, N.Y. Times (October 25, 2010), on file with author. Khadr was not credited for the eight years he had spent in detention prior to his conviction. Khadr was fifteen years old at the time of his capture by US forces. In addition to his age, his lengthy pre-trial detention by the US at Guantánamo Bay (he was twenty-four years old at the time he pleaded guilty), and the problematic conditions he faced while in custody, Khadr's situation is controversial owing to evidence that confessions he allegedly made had been secured following implicit threats of gang rape. Savage C (2010) U.S. Wary of Example Set by Tribunal Case, N.Y. Times (August 27, 2010).

[45] Drumbl 2007, pp. 149–180.

current *rationales* for so doing, and the forces that propel those rationales, have come to overshoot their mark. Fear that child soldiers may become subject to punitive criminal trials has induced a crudely fulsome protectionism that has come to insulate child soldiers from accountability processes generally, regardless of the goals or potentials of those processes. This protectionism needlessly cocoons child soldiers from the tough questions that societies must reckon with in order to come to terms with mass violence. The solution, then, is not for international criminal law to recognize the criminal culpability of children but, instead, for transnational discourse to develop a more fine-grained approach to post-conflict accountability. I have elsewhere urged the adoption of more careful approaches to victimization and perpetration as a general matter.[46] Hence, the proposals made in this chapter, and extensively discussed in the book from which it is extracted, dovetail with my overarching vision of what post-conflict justice ideally ought to look like.

Afflicted communities want their children back home. They welcome the return of former child soldiers. Transnationally motored discourses of forgiveness without reciprocal obligation may appear, at first blush, to mesh with local sentiments of forgiveness without reciprocal obligation. Impulses arise in afflicted communities to accept excuse—namely constraint enhanced by youth—in the case of the antecedent violent acts of child soldier returnees.

Transnational discourse, however, overestimates the uniformity and flexibility of community sentiment. A careful mining of the evidentiary record reveals that communities care about conduct during conflict, that is, why and how did the child join fighting forces and, once there, what did he or she do. Communities do not take all child soldier returnees to be fungible moral equals and to require identical approaches to reintegration. It is unclear whether community members unambivalently accept that the cognizability of their injuries should hew so tightly to the age of the perpetrator. The fact that community members demonstrate variable and volatile sentiments, ranging from joy to cordiality to antipathy, is understandable. In fact, it should be obvious. Regardless of who perpetrated it and why, mass atrocity invariably engenders a broad gamut of raw emotions among survivors and targeted populations. To pretend otherwise is foolhardy. To base policy on such pretension is quixotic.

Unsurprisingly, certain subgroups of former child soldiers face reintegration hurdles. Their home communities simply do not accept the suitability of the collectivized faultless passive victim narrative as applied to them as individuals. One such subgroup is child soldiers who have served for long periods of times with armed forces or groups. Another subgroup involves child soldiers suspected of having committed atrocities or believed to have been affiliated with units that inflicted atrocities. These subgroups are at risk for marginalization and a recrudescence of militarized life, crime, and violence.

The legal fiction, therefore, neither represents nor reaches a relevant number of child soldier returnees, for whom reinsertion is far from seamless or self-evident.

---

[46] Id.

For this subgroup, unconditional excuse does not resonate within afflicted communities. Instead, consideration might be given to exploring processes of forgiveness predicated upon mutual and reciprocal obligation among returnees and the community. Reintegration cannot always be assumed. The violence may be too much.

Collaterally, transitional justice measures also may relieve the child soldier's sense of injustice. The child soldier may justifiably harbor resentment toward the community that idled while forcible recruitment ensnared its youth. Transitional justice measures may enable the child soldier to tell what happened to him or her—and to identify or learn who in the community may have abetted unscrupulous warlords. Transitional justice processes create a venue to discuss much more than accountability and responsibility. They also may authenticate stories of resistance to atrocity and contestation to cruel orders.[47] In this regard, transitional justice processes may come to benefit not only subgroups of child soldiers implicated in atrocity, but all child soldiers as well. Through participation in transitional justice processes, former child soldiers even may help educate other children in the community about the perils of becoming associated with armed forces or groups.

In my work with adult atrocity perpetrators I have come to experience that many—perhaps self-servingly—view themselves as victims or tools who simply ended up on the losing side of circumstance. The international legal imagination gives short shrift to their representations of subservience and victimhood. Adults, after all, are not legally excused from choices, often exercised in times of chaos, to join armed forces or groups that commit atrocity. Their responsibility is not evacuated. Many adults are compulsorily conscripted, as well, yet this does not ab initio absolve them from the consequences of their conduct. Many adult soldiers are little older than eighteen and live in strikingly similar situations to child soldiers. They are thus contemporaries. Can so much differentiation realistically hinge upon a simple matter of chronological age? Jo Boyden and Joanna de Berry remain unconvinced: '[C]hildren and adolescents can be very active in defining their own allegiances during conflict, as well as their own strategies for coping and survival. This implies that the prevailing dichotomy between adult as active perpetrator and child as passive victim needs challenging.'[48]

According to anthropologist Susan Shepler, writing within the context of Sierra Leone, '[c]oming to terms with the participation of child soldiers … is key to post-war reconciliation and peace building.'[49] I believe that international law and policy, however, fails to demonstrate adroitness or finesse in negotiating this quandary. One way to redress this blind spot is to trim the emphasis on criminal law binaries of guilt or innocence, corruption or purity, victim or perpetrator, and adult or child.

---

47 Regarding transitional justice and resistance to atrocity, see Leebaw 2011.

48 Boyden and de Berry 2004, p. xv.

49 Shepler 2005, pp. 197, 198.

Adopting a baseline of circumscribed action might open the space necessary to effect meaningful conceptual shifts and, thereby, synergistically liaise with the work of those observers who believe that transitional justice matters for child soldiers.[50] For example, international lawyer Cécile Aptel recognizes the value of non-penal proceedings in acknowledging children's wrongdoing and diminishing stigma. She suggests that 'more thinking is required concerning the liability of children who have participated in the commission of crimes.'[51] I hope to respond to this need and inspire a framework for reform. Meaningful change cannot occur, however, until the presumptive imagery recedes from the tautness of passive victimhood and embraces something more dynamic, such as circumscribed action.[52] Efforts to engage with transitional justice will remain superficial unless liberated from the strictures of victimhood discourse. This discourse, and its correlative imagery, is simply too tendentious.

In short, then, I advise that the legal fiction of faultless passive victimhood should be dismantled and, therewith, its controlling effects deflated.

Assuredly, as is the case with any reformative process, renewal may produce fresh concerns. In reimagining the child soldier, and recommending policy shifts keyed thereto, my project is anticipatorily mindful of three sets of concerns: *pragmatics* (are the suggested reforms affordable or realistic?), *fear* (am I opening the door to harsh punishment for child soldiers, thereby leaving them worse off?), and *overreach* (instead of circumscribed action, why not just a rebuttable presumption of victimhood?).

In the end, I remain persuaded that these proposals are worthwhile. They also convey broader pedagogic value. Connections arise between reimagining child soldiers, on the one hand, and three cognate challenges, on the other. These challenges are: reforming domestic justice systems in cases of ordinary common crime committed by juveniles, rehabilitating victims of transnational crimes that fall outside the aegis of international criminal law (e.g., sex- and drug-trafficking), and revisiting the place of international criminal law within the overall framework of post-conflict justice.

---

[50] Children and Truth Commissions, pp. x–xi, 65; Parmar et al. 2010 Annex (Key Operational Principles); Children and Justice, pp. 27, 39, encouraging restorative, rehabilitative, and traditional justice processes.

[51] Aptel C (2010) International Criminal Justice and Child Protection. In Parmar et al., pp. 67, 107–111.

[52] For example, Human Rights Watch's suggestion that former child soldiers 'participat[e] in restorative justice processes to help the child acknowledge their actions and gain reacceptance by the community' is hampered by the very foundational images Human Rights Watch disseminates about children as choicelessly coerced into fighting and unthinkingly committing violent acts. Human Rights Watch (2008) Coercion and Intimidation of Child Soldiers to Participate in Violence, p. 15. The IDDRS encourages more robust connections between transitional justice and DDR programming—including for child soldiers, for whom restorative mechanisms notably are discussed. Notwithstanding their innovative nature, the IDDRS recommendations also remain cabined by the IDDRS's depiction that '[f]ormer child soldiers are victims of criminal policies for which adults are responsible.' UNDDR (2006) Integrated Disarmament, Demobilization and Reintegration Standards (IDDRS) Sect. 5.30, p. 9.

8.5 Conclusion

It is much easier to express outrage regarding the oxymoron of the child soldier than it is to interrogatively theorize the oxymoron so as to enhance preventative and remedial policies. It is considerably easier to pre-judge *ex ante* that children and adolescents bear no responsibility for the situations they find themselves in and what they interstitially do within those situations than to examine *ex post* why, exactly, they militarize and then why, exactly, some among them become involved in committing terrible crimes. The easier path that assuages transnational sensibilities, however, is not necessarily the best path to protect children or safeguard the public. Policy based on the convenient answer may simply be poor policy.

References

Ben-Ari E (2009) Facing child soldiers, moral issues, and "real soldiering": anthropological perspectives on professional armed forces. Scientia Militaria: S Afr J Mil Stud 37(1):1–24
Blattman C, Annan J (2010) The consequences of child soldiering. REStat 92(4):882–898
Boyden J, de Berry J (2004) Introduction. In: Boyden J, de Berry J (eds) Children and youth on the front line: ethnography, armed conflict and displacement. Berghahn Books, Oxford
Cape Town Principles and Best Practices (2007) April 27–30, 1997, Definitions. www.unicef.org/emerg/files/Cape_Town_Principles(1).pdf. Accessed 13 April 2013
Dallaire R (2010) They fight like soldiers, they die like children. Random House UK, London
Denov M (2010) Child soldiers: Sierra Leone's revolutionary united front. CUP, Cambridge
Drumbl MA (2007) Atrocity, punishment, and international law. CUP, New York
Drumbl MA (2012) Reimagining child soldiers in international law and policy. OUP, Oxford
Fuller LL (1967) Legal fictions. Stanford University Press, Stanford
Hart J (2006) Saving children: what role for anthropology? AT 22(1):5–8
Honwana A (2005) Innocent and guilty: child-soldiers as interstitial and tactical agents. In: Honwana A, de Boeck F (eds) Makers and breakers: children and youth in Postcolonial Africa. James Currey, Oxford, pp. 31–51
Iweala U (2005) Beasts of no nation: a novel. HarperCollins, New York
Kamara M, McClelland S (2008) The bite of the mango. Annick Press, New York
Keitetsi C (2002) Child soldier: fighting for my life. Jacana, Johannesburg
Kourouma A (2000) Allah n'est pas obligé. Seuil, Paris
Landauer C (2011) Regionalism, geography, and the international legal imagination. CJIL 11:557–595
Leebaw B (2011) Judging state-sponsored violence, imagining political change. CUP, New York
Lonegan B (2011) Sinners or saints: child soldiers and the persecutor bar to asylum after Negusie v. Holder. BCTWLJ 31:71–99
McDonnell FJH, Akallo G (2007) Girl soldier: a story of hope for Northern Uganda's children. Chosen Books, Grand Rapids, MI
McMahan J (2007) Child soldiers: the ethical perspective. Working Paper, Ford Institute for Human Security
Mergelsberg B (2010) Between two worlds: former LRA soldiers in Northern Uganda. In: Allen T, Vlassenroot K (eds) The Lord's resistance army: myth and reality. Zed Books, London
Otunnu O (2000) Keynote Address: The Convention and Children in Situations of Armed Conflict. In: Carlson L, Mackeson-Sandbach M, Allen T (eds) Children in extreme situations, Working Paper Series No. 00–05, LSE Development Studies Institute, pp. 48–57. www.lse.ac.uk/internationalDevelopment//pdf/WP05.pdf. Accessed 13 April 2013

Parmar S, Roseman MJ, Siegrist S, Sowa T (eds) (2010) Children and transitional justice: truth-telling, accountability and reconciliation. UNICEF Innocenti Research Centre and Human Rights Program at Harvard Law School

Shepler S (2005) The rites of the child: global discourses of youth and reintegrating child soldiers in Sierra Leone. JHR 4:197–211

Singer PW (2006) Children at war. University of California Press, Berkeley

Spiga V (2010) Indirect victims' participation in the Lubanga trial. JICJ 8:183–198

The Paris Principles: principles and guidelines on children associated with armed forces or armed groups (2007), Prin. 2.1. www.icrc.org/eng/assets/files/others/parisprinciples_en[1].pdf. Accessed 13 April 2013

Utas M (2003) Sweet battlefields: youth and the Liberian civil war. Uppsala University Dissertations in Cultural Anthropology, Uppsala

Utas M (2005) Victimcy, girlfriending, soldiering: tactic agency in a young woman's social navigation of the Liberian war zone. AQ 2(78):403–430

Vaihinger H (1920) Die Philosophie des Als Ob, 4th edn. Verlag Felix Meiner, Leipzig

Wessells M (2006) Child soldiers: from violence to protection. Harvard University Press, Cambridge, MA

Part III
Victim Protection and Participation in Criminal Trials

Chapter 9
The Protection of Victims in War Crimes Trials

Daniela Kravetz

Abstract International criminal courts and tribunals rely mainly on victim testimony to establish the occurrence of war crimes. These institutions face important challenges in protecting victims. Many victims are reluctant to provide testimony in fear of retaliation. For these persons, testifying requires an act of courage, especially because persons allegedly involved in the crimes still walk the streets of their villages and towns. International courts have developed protection mechanisms to address the security concerns of victims. In doing so, they have had to reconcile the conflicting rights of victims and defendants. The experience of the International Criminal Tribunal for the former Yugoslavia captures some of the challenges faced by international courts in victim protection. It also provides valuable lessons to future courts.

Keywords Victims • Protective measures • Contempt • Witness intimidation • International criminal justice • War crimes trials

---

The author is Trial Attorney, Office of the Prosecution, International Criminal Tribunal for the Former Yugoslavia. The views expressed herein are those of the author alone and do not necessarily reflect the views of the International Criminal Tribunal for the Former Yugoslavia or the United Nations in general. The author thanks Priya Gopalan for her helpful comments on an earlier version of this chapter.

D. Kravetz (✉)
Office of the Prosecution, International Criminal Tribunal for the Former Yugoslavia,
The Hague, The Netherlands
e-mail: dkravetz@yahoo.com

T. Bonacker and C. Safferling (eds.), *Victims of International Crimes: An Interdisciplinary Discourse*, DOI: 10.1007/978-90-6704-912-2_9,

9.1 Introduction

Victims play a prominent role in international war crimes trials. They are vital in establishing the occurrence of the crimes.[1] Without victims coming forward to testify, the ability to bring justice and demonstrate an end to the culture of impunity is seriously reduced.[2]

Protecting victims before international courts and tribunals involves significant challenges. Many victims are reluctant to give evidence because they fear reprisals if they speak publicly about their experiences. Others want to avoid reliving the past or stirring old antagonisms. In order to counter these apprehensions, international courts have set in place protection mechanisms to enable victims to be heard in safety. However, these institutions have a limited ability to guarantee their security outside the courtroom. Without a law enforcement capacity or witness protection programme of their own, these courts depend on the cooperation of states to enforce protective measures on the ground.

This chapter deals with the experience of the International Tribunal for the former Yugoslavia (ICTY) in victim protection. First, it explains the existing protection regime for victims at the ICTY and takes a look at the jurisprudence that has developed on this issue. Second, it addresses some of the procedural challenges faced by the ICTY in victim and witness protection, namely the due process implications of its protection regime, the limitations of its enforcement mechanisms and the difficulties in tackling witness intimidation. Finally, it explains the mechanism that will be put in place to ensure continuity in protection matters once the Tribunal closes its doors.

9.2 Protection Framework

9.2.1 General Rules Governing Victim Protection

The vast majority of the witnesses before the ICTY are victims of crimes. For these persons, the act of testifying before an international court can be a traumatic and often alienating experience.[3] In some cases, it can also expose them to acts of intimidation and retaliation by sympathisers of the accused or other persons within their communities.

---

[1] Wald 2002, pp. 217, 219. Whereas the tribunals in Nuremberg and Tokyo relied primarily on documentary evidence, the modern international tribunals make extensive use of the testimonies of survivors and eyewitnesses to establish the facts and render judgment. See May 2003, pp. 161, 165.

[2] Kippenberg 2009, p. 1.

[3] See Stover 2005, pp. 74–82.

The experience of the ICTY has shown a broad need for the protection of victims and witnesses. Since its establishment, about a quarter of the almost 4,000 witnesses who have testified in its proceedings have been granted protective measures.[4]

The ICTY was the first war crimes tribunal to acknowledge the necessity of a special unit for victims/witnesses.[5] The Victim and Witness Section (VWS) within the Registry is an independent and neutral body in charge of providing support and protection services to victims and witnesses from both prosecution and defence.[6] It is responsible not only for physical protection and security arrangements, but also provides other appropriate assistance to facilitate the testimony of victims and witnesses. In addition, it is the organ responsible for the effective implementation of protective measures outside the courtroom. It conducts an independent threat assessment for individual witnesses on the ground and has in place an immediate response system to address urgent threats.[7]

Judges at the Tribunal have produced an extensive body of jurisprudence on victim and witness protection.[8] Since its first case, the *Tadić* case, ICTY trial chambers have repeatedly recognised their statutory duty to ensure the protection of victims and witnesses.[9]

---

[4] More detailed statistics on the protective measures applied at the ICTY are available at www.icty.org.

[5] UNDP 2010, p. 27; see ICTY's 1994 Annual Progress Report, para 39, available at www.icty.org.

[6] Information Booklet for ICTY Witnesses—Victims and Witnesses Section, ICTY Registry, 2007, p. 19. See Rule 34 of the Rules. The VWS has three units: an Operations Unit, a Support Unit and a Protection Unit. In 2011, the Operations and Support Units assisted 494 witnesses travelling to The Hague to give evidence. The Protection Unit coordinated responses to threats received by witnesses before, during and after their court testimony. It also worked to relocate witnesses. See ICTY's 2011 Annual Progress Report, para 86, available at www.icty.org.

[7] Information Booklet for ICTY Witnesses—Victims and Witnesses Section, ICTY Registry, 2007, pp. 19–22.

[8] Article 20 (1) of the ICTY's Statute requires a trial chamber to ensure that proceedings are conducted with full respect for the rights of the accused and due regard for the protection of victims and witnesses. Article 21 (2) entitles the accused to a fair and public hearing, subject to Article 22, which requires the Tribunal to adopt measures for the protection of victims and witnesses.

[9] See e.g. ICTY *Prosecutor v Tadić*, TC II, IT-94-1-T, 10 August 1995, Decision on the Prosecutor's Motion Requesting Protective Measures for Victims and Witnesses, paras 13–16; ICTY *Prosecutor v Brđanin and Talić*, TC II, IT-99-36-PT, 3 July 2000, Decision on Motion by Prosecution for Protective Measures, para 7; ICTY *Prosecutor v Perišić*, TC, IT-04-81-PT, 27 May 2005, Decision on Prosecution Motion for Protective Measures for Witnesses, p. 3; ICTY *Prosecutor v Karadžić,* TC III, IT-95-5/18-T, 19 August 2011, Decision on Prosecution Motions for Protective Measures for Witnesses KDZ601 and KDZ605, para 13.

As its Rules of Procedure and Statute do not envisage the participation of victims at trial, only victims who appear as witnesses before the Tribunal are afforded protection.[10] This protection extends not only to the victims themselves, but also to family members who may be at risk on account of the testimony provided by such victims.[11]

Both prosecution and defence witnesses can benefit from protection. This protection is not only based on an equality of treatment, but is also a reflection of the risks faced by witnesses testifying before international courts. Defence witnesses often express concerns about the reactions within their communities should the fact of their cooperation with the Tribunal become known.[12]

Protective measures are not granted automatically, and the party seeking these safeguards must obtain the leave of the court and show in each case why they are warranted.[13] Trial chambers have set out the criteria to be taken into account in

---

[10] Under Rule 75(F)(i) of the Rules, once protective measures have been ordered in respect of a victim or witness in any proceedings before the Tribunal, they continue to have effect in any other proceedings before the Tribunal. At the International Criminal Court (ICC), protective measures should in principle also benefit victims participating in proceedings, as the mandate of the Victims and Witnesses Unit (VWU) covers not only witnesses, but also victims appearing before the Court. The judges in the *Lubanga* case have interpreted the expression "appearing before the court" in Article 43(6) of the ICC Statute as affording protection to victims from the moment that their completed application to participate is received by the Court. However, in their ruling, they recognised that there are limitations to the extent to which the VWU can realistically provide protection to these victims. ICC *Prosecutor v Lubanga*, TC I, ICC-01-04-01/06-1119, 18 January 2008, Decision on Victims' Participation, para 137. Similarly, the Internal Rules of the Extraordinary Chambers in the Courts of Cambodia mandate the court with the protection of "victims who participate in proceedings, whether as complainants or Civil Parties, and witnesses". See Rule 29(1) of the Internal Rules of the Extraordinary Chambers, Internal Rules (Rev. 8) as revised on 3 August 2011.

[11] See e.g. ICTY *Prosecutor v Milošević*, TC III, IT-02-54-T, 3 May 2002, First Decision on Prosecution Motion for Protective Measures for Sensitive Source Witnesses, para 8. Article 43(6) of the ICC Statute provides that the Victims and Witnesses Unit's mandate covers victims and witnesses, as well as "others who are at risk on account of the testimony given by such witnesses". Some have argued in favour of protective measures for intermediaries and lawyers acting on behalf of the victims. See Pena 2008, p. 4.

[12] See e.g. ICTY *Prosecutor v Stanišić and Simatović*, TC I, IT-03-69-T, 17 August 2011, Reasons for Granting Protective Measures to Witness DST-043, para 6; ICTY *Prosecutor v Gotovina et al.*, TC I, IT-06-90-T, 11 November 2009, Decision on Defendant Ivan Čermak's Motion for Admission of Evidence of Two Witnesses Pursuant to Rule 92*bis* and Decision on Defendant Ivan Čermak's Third Motion for Protective Measures of Witnesses IC-12 and IC-16, para 13. The ICTR has also recognised the need to protect defence witnesses. See ICTR *Prosecutor v Nyiramasuhuko*, TC II, ICTR-97-21-T, 17 June 2005, Decision on Nyiramasuhuko's Motion for Additional Protective Measures for Defence Witness WBNM; ICTR *Prosecutor v Karera*, TC I, ICTR-01-74-T, 9 February 2006, Decision on Defence Motion for Protection of Witnesses, paras 2–4. See also Sluiter 2005, pp. 962–976.

[13] In contrast to the ICTY's individualised approach to granting protective measures, the ICTR has adopted a more liberal approach when considering protection requests, which has been criticised as overly flexible. For a more detailed analysis, see Pozen 2006, pp. 281, 295–307; Sluiter 2005, pp. 962, 967–969.

assessing whether an individual should be afforded protection. These include the existence of an objectively grounded and identifiable risk to the security or welfare of the victim or the victim's family, as opposed to a subjective fear.[14] The witness' place of residence and the fact that his/her testimony may antagonise persons who reside in that territory have been considered relevant to establishing the existence of "objective grounds".[15] A minimum threshold of risk is also required, as protective measures are 'exceptional'.[16] Broad allegations of dangerous conditions for victims and witnesses in general do not meet the required threshold.[17]

Other factors to be taken into account include the length of time before the trial at which the identity of the victims and witnesses must be disclosed to the accused, and the likelihood that witnesses will be interfered with or intimidated once their identity is made known to the accused and his counsel, but not the public.[18]

Cultural issues specific to the population concerned have been taken into account in assessing perceived threats or fears of witnesses. In close-knit communities with traditional values, allegiance to the ethnic group or clan to which an individual belongs is often taken for granted, and those who speak against members of their own community are viewed as traitors.[19] In the *Limaj* case, the Chamber acknowledged that the values of honour and loyalty were particularly relevant to witnesses with Albanian roots in Kosovo. It recognised that these values may affect the willingness of witnesses to testify against defendants of their same ethnicity and should be considered when evaluating their evidence.[20]

---

[14] See ICTY *Prosecutor v Karadžić,* supra n 9, para 9; ICTY *Prosecutor v Mrkšić et al.*, TC II, IT-95-13/1-T, 25 October 2005, Decision on Prosecution's Additional Motion for Protective Measures of Sensitive Witnesses, para 5.

[15] See ICTY *Prosecutor v Karadžić,* supra n 9, para 11; ICTY *Prosecutor v Stanišić and Simatović,* TC I, IT-03-69-T-20 July 2011, Reasons for Granting Protective Measures to Witness DST-035, para 7; ICTY *Prosecutor v Vasiljević,* TC II, IT-98-32-T, 24 July 2001, Order on Protective Measures for Witnesses at Trial, p. 1. At the Special Court for Sierra Leone (SCSL), the physical location of the Court itself has been considered a compelling factor in considering the merits of protective measures application, as it increased the risks to witnesses called at trial. See SCSL *Prosecutor v Norman*, TC, SCSL-04-14-T-126, 8 June 2004, Decision on Prosecution Motion for Modification of Protective Measures for Witnesses, para 29.

[16] ICTY *Prosecutor v Mrkšić et al.*, supra n 14, para 4; ICTY *Prosecutor v Brđanin and Talić,* supra n 9, para 10.

[17] ICTY *Prosecutor v Mrkšić et al.*, supra n 14, para 5.

[18] ICTY *Prosecutor v Delić,* TC III, IT-04-83-PT, 1 December 2006, Decision on the Prosecution Motion for Protective Measures, pp. 3, 4; ICTY *Prosecutor v Milutinović et al.*, TC III, IT-05-87-PT, 1 June 2006, Decision on Prosecution Sixth Motion for Protective Measures, para 18.

[19] See expert report of Stephanie Schwandner-Sievers, cited in ICTY *Prosecutor v Limaj et al.*, TC II, IT-03-66-T, 30 November 2005, Judgement, para 13.

[20] ICTY *Prosecutor v Limaj et al.*, supra n 19, paras 13, 15.

Finally, the Tribunal has recognised the need to provide special protection to certain categories of victims, namely victims of sexual violence and children.[21] This protection seeks to reduce the risks of re-traumatisation and of rejection by the victims' families and community.[22] Moreover, ICTY judges have paid particular attention to the treatment of vulnerable victims in the courtroom. In the *Stanković* case, the Chamber denied the defendant's request to represent himself in part because the case involved charges of sexual violence and most of the witnesses on the Prosecution's list were victims of those crimes. The Chamber found that it would be "inappropriate for the accused representing himself in person to cross-examine at trial witnesses who are also alleged victims of those crimes" and required that legal counsel be imposed.[23]

9.2.2 Measures of Protection

The Tribunal uses a range of in-court and out-of-court measures to protect and support victims involved in the proceedings. Some of the measures available are:

9.2.2.1 Confidentiality

In the *Tadić* case, the Chamber held that the protection of victims and witnesses is an acceptable reason to limit an accused's rights to a public trial.[24] Trial chambers have since adopted a variety of protection measures designed to shield a witness from the public. Rule 75 of the Rules provides for various measures that limit the audience that is privy to the witness's identity, including: (a) expunging names and identifying information from the Tribunal's public records; (b) non-disclosure to the public of any records identifying the witness and (c) allowing witnesses to give testimony through image or voice distortion or in closed session. Closed session, which excludes the press and the public, can be ordered for reasons of public order or morality; safety, security or non-disclosure of the identity of a victim or witness and protection of the interests of justice.[25]

---

[21] ICTY *Prosecutor v Tadić*, supra n 9, paras 41–52. See also SCSL *Prosecutor v Sesay et al.*, TC, SCSL-04-15-T-180, 5 July 2004, Decision on Prosecution Motion for Modification of Protective Measures for Witnesses, pp. 16–17.

[22] Chinkin 1997, p. 78; Stover 2005, pp. 72–75.

[23] ICTY *Prosecutor v Janković and Stanković*, TC I, IT-96-23/2-PT, 19 August 2005, Decision Following Registrar's Notification of Radovan Stanković's Request for Self-Representation, para 21.

[24] ICTY *Prosecutor v Tadić*, supra n 9, para 36.

[25] See Rule 79 of the Rules.

To date, full anonymity has been granted with respect to only four witnesses, all in the *Tadić* case. In a rather controversial ruling, the Chamber held by majority that the identities of several witnesses could be indefinitely withheld from the accused and his counsel.[26] In determining where the balance lies between the rights of the accused to a fair and public trial and the protection of victims and witnesses, the majority took into account the individual concerns of the four witnesses, all of whom were victims of sexual violence, and found that these concerns were sufficiently serious to justify granting anonymity.[27] Judge Stephen appended a strong dissent, arguing that the decision would deny the defendant a fair trial and may lead to a conviction based on tainted evidence.[28] The decision generated extensive debate among legal scholars, some defending the majority position and others the dissent.[29] No other chamber has applied such a stringent measure since.

9.2.2.2 Delayed Disclosure

Disclosure prior to trial is necessary to allow the defence adequate time to prepare for cross-examination of witnesses. Under the ICTY's discovery rules, the Prosecution is under the obligation to disclose copies of all supporting material to the indictment within 30 days of the defendant's initial appearance. It must also disclose all statements of the witnesses it intends to call at trial during the pre-trial phase, often well in advance of the start of trial.[30]

However, these disclosure requirements are not absolute. The Prosecution at the ICTY has made extensive use of Rule 69, which allows for non-disclosure at the pre-trial stage of the identity of a victim or witness who may be in danger. This non-disclosure applies to the press, public and the accused.[31]

Trial chambers have been cautious in stressing that an order for non-disclosure of witnesses' identity will only be granted where the applicant demonstrates the

---

[26] ICTY *Prosecutor v Tadić,* supra n 9, paras 84, 85. At the ICC, the *Lubanga* trial chamber allowed victims to participate in the pre-trial proceedings in an anonymous capacity albeit with limited rights. See ICC *Prosecutor v Lubanga*, PTC I, ICC-01/04-01/06-462-tEN, 22 September 2006, Decision on the Arrangements for Participation of Victims a/0001/06, a/0002/06 and a/0003/06 at the Confirmation Hearing, p. 6. See also Jouet 2007, pp. 249, 261–266.

[27] ICTY *Prosecutor v Tadić*, supra n 9.

[28] ICTY *Prosecutor v Tadić*, IT-94-1-T, 10 August 1995, Separate Opinion of Judge Stephen on the Prosecutor's Motion Requesting Protective Measures for Victims and Witnesses.

[29] For a more detailed analysis, see Mahony 2010, pp. 8, 9; Pozen 2006, pp. 281, 287–294; Leigh 1996, pp. 235–238; Chinkin 1997, pp. 75–79.

[30] See Rules 66(A)(i) and (ii) of the Rules.

[31] Rule 69(A) of the Rules expresses the power to make a non-disclosure order in relation to a victim or witness who may be in danger or at risk "until such person is brought under the protection of the Tribunal". This rather curious wording appears to assume that the Tribunal has a witness protection programme which will render the non-disclosure order no longer necessary once it comes into operation, which is not the case.

existence of "exceptional circumstances".[32] What time frame is reasonable for such disclosure depends on the individual circumstances of each witness. As long as the defence learns of the identity of the witnesses in time to prepare a defence, the rights of the defendant are respected.[33]

The Tribunal has acknowledged the importance of limiting the length of time between the disclosure of the identity of an endangered witness and the time when the witness is to give evidence, in order to reduce the potential for witness interference. While the usual practice with respect to the time of disclosure is 30 days prior to the anticipated start of trial,[34] in exceptional cases, shorter deadlines have been imposed.[35]

9.2.2.3 Relocation

Relocation is an exceptional measure. Less than one per cent of witnesses who have testified before the ICTY have been relocated.[36] Unlike other protective measures, the decision to relocate a witness is made by the Registrar, not the judges. If the Registrar decides that a witness' concerns about his or her safety are founded, the Victims and Witnesses Section arranges for the witness' relocation to

[32] ICTY *Prosecutor v Karadžić*, TC III, IT-95-5/18-PT, 30 October 2008, Decision on Protective Measures for Witnesses, para 19, *citing* ICTY *Prosecutor v Brđanin and Talić*, supra n 9, para 11.

[33] ICTY *Prosecutor v Mladić*, TC I, IT-09-92-I, 24 June 2011, Decision on Prosecution Motion for Protective Measures for Victims and Witnesses and Documentary Evidence, paras 11–14; ICTY *Prosecutor v Karadžić*, TC III, IT-95-5/18-PT, 2 September 2008, Decision on Prosecution Motion for Non-Disclosure, paras 11, 16; ICTY *Prosecutor v Haradinaj et al.*, TC II, IT-04-84-PT, 22 November 2006, Decision on Second Haradinaj Motion to Lift Redactions of Protected Witness Statements with Confidential Annex, paras 21–23; ICTY *Prosecutor v Brđanin and Talić*, supra n 9, para 22.

[34] See ICTY *Prosecutor v Hadžić*, TC II, IT-04-75-PT, 30 November 2011, Decision on Prosecution Second Motion for Protective Measures for Victims and Witnesses and Documentary Evidence, para 12; ICTY *Prosecutor v Karadžić*, supra n 32, para 34; ICTY *Prosecutor v Delić*, supra n 18, p. 6.

[35] See ICTY *Prosecutor v Mrškić*, supra n 14, p. 8. In the *Karadžić* case, the defendant requested that the Chamber exclude the testimonies of all delayed disclosure witnesses, arguing that the prosecution had failed to disclose their identities prior to the start of trial and that this had prejudiced the preparation of his defence. In denying this motion, the Chamber noted that the well-established interpretation of Rule 69(C) allowed for delayed disclosure after the commencement of trial. See ICTY *Prosecutor v Karadžić*, TC III, IT-95-5/18-T, Decision on Accused's 66th Disclosure Violation Motion, 8 February 2012, para 20.

[36] Statistics on protective measures are available at www.icty.org/sid/158.

a third country.[37] The Section has concluded a number of framework agreements with a network of countries willing to consider accepting witnesses in their protection programmes. The agreements outline the procedure to be followed when relocation is requested and the benefits the State will provide to relocated witnesses. However, the final decision on whether to accept the witness lies with the receiving State.[38]

In some ongoing trials, the defendants have requested access to material relating to assistance provided by the prosecution to witnesses seeking relocation or asylum in third countries. These requests have been based on Rule 68, which sets out the duty of the prosecution to hand over exculpatory material to the defence. In a recent decision, the *Karadžić* Chamber ruled that such material is disclosable as it may affect the credibility of prosecution witnesses, in that it may show that the witnesses have obtained a benefit in exchange of testimony.[39] Another chamber sanctioned prosecution counsel for failing to turn over to the defence material relating to a witness' asylum application.[40] These rulings highlight the tension that exists between the protection afforded to witnesses and the accused's right to a fair trial, which is discussed below.

9.3 Challenges in Providing Protecting

9.3.1 Due Process Costs of Protective Measures

The conflict between the right of an accused to a fair and public trial and the need to provide effective protection to victims is omnipresent in ICTY trials.[41] This is an area where the Tribunal has struggled to strike a fair balance.

---

[37] Information Booklet for ICTY Witnesses—Victims and Witnesses Section, ICTY Registry, 2007, p. 22. Similarly, at the ICC, the Registrar is responsible for deciding on the relocation of witnesses. In the *Katanga* case, the ICC Appeals Chamber stressed that the Prosecutor cannot unilaterally "preventively relocate" witnesses as a provisional measure either before the Registrar has decided whether a particular witness should be relocated or after the Registrar has decided that an individual witness should not be relocated. It held that any disagreement between the Victim and Witness Unit and the Prosecutor about the relocation of a witness should ultimately be decided by the Chamber dealing with the case—and should not be resolved by the unilateral and un-checked action of the Prosecutor. See ICC *Katanga and Chui*, AC, ICC-01/04-01/07 OA 7, 26 November 2008, Judgment on the Appeal of the Prosecutor against the "Decision on Evidentiary Scope of the Confirmation Hearing, Preventive Relocation and Disclosure under Article 67(2) of the Statute and Rule 77 of the Rules" of Pre-Trial Chamber I, paras 1–2 and 93.

[38] Information obtained from VWS by the author.

[39] See ICTY *Prosecutor v Karadžić,* TC III, IT-95-5/18-T, 22 November 2011, Decision on Accused's Sixtieth, Sixty-First, Sixty-Third and Sixty-Fourth Disclosure Violation Motions.

[40] ICTY *Prosecutor v Haradinaj et al.*, TC II, IT-04-84*bis*-T, 12 October 2011, Decision on Joint Defence Motion for Relief from Rule 68 Violations by the Prosecution and for Sanctions Pursuant to Rule 68*bis*.

[41] Wald 2002, pp. 217, 224.

There is a tension between how protective measures are implemented and the preservation of the public nature of the proceedings. Where witness protection measures are imposed, witnesses' identities are withheld from the public. They are referred to by pseudonyms throughout the proceedings and in the Tribunal's judgments. Material that can potentially identify them is redacted from the public trial record. For example, during the course of their testimonies, the chamber often hears part of the evidence in private session to avoid identifying the witnesses to the public, which means that the public can see, but not hear, the court debates. These measures limit the public's ability to follow and scrutinise the fairness of the proceedings. Some legal scholars have questioned the historical usefulness of judgements that are "peppered with concealed identities of key witnesses".[42]

This issue raises the question of the purpose of international criminal trials. War crimes trials must address the needs of three key parties: the perpetrators, the victims and the communities affected by the war.[43] In order to determine the guilt or innocence of the defendants in a fair manner, due process guarantees must be respected and the trials conducted must be deemed legitimate. However, the purpose of these trials is also to ameliorate the suffering and contribute to the healing process of victims and their communities.[44] This includes allowing victims to recount their experiences in court.[45] Providing insufficient protection to victims resulting in their unwillingness to testify undercuts this purpose.

Moreover, the prosecution, as the representative of the rights and interests of victims and the community at large, is also entitled to a fair trial. The right to a fair trial obligates a judicial body to ensure that neither party is put at a disadvantage when presenting its case.[46] This means that the prosecution must be allowed to tender evidence and question witnesses to prove its case, even if this means allowing its witnesses to testify in closed session or under pseudonym.

The balance between these competing interests is a difficult one to strike. The ICTY has sought to find a fair balance on a case-to-case basis.

9.3.2 Enforcing Protective Measures

Protective measures ordered by ICTY judges would be meaningless if they were not adequately enforced. Protecting victims and witnesses also entails punishing individuals who divulge confidential information that places them at risk.

[42] See Wald 2002, pp. 217, 223. For an analysis of the implementation of protective measures in ICTR proceedings, see Pozen 2006, pp. 281, 303–308; Sluiter 2005, pp. 962, 967–971.

[43] Paterson 2003, pp. 95, 97.

[44] Haider and Welch 2008, pp. 55, 84.

[45] Paterson argues that the public acknowledgement of the crimes is more important to victims than the punishment of the perpetrators. Paterson 2003, pp. 95, 97.

[46] ICTY *Prosecutor v Tadić,* AC, IT-94-1-A, 15 July 1999, Appeals Judgement, para 48. See also Cassese 2008, p. 384. On the right of the Prosecution to a fair trial, see ICTY *Prosecutor v Haradinaj*, AC, IT-04-84-A, 19 July 2010, Appeals Judgement, paras 34–51.

At the ICTY, contempt of court proceedings have become the enforcement mechanism used to punish individuals who violate protection orders. Article 77 of its Rules gives judges the power of holding in contempt those who knowingly and wilfully interfere with the Tribunal's administration of justice. This Rule has been applied to cases where individuals have disclosed confidential information relating to proceedings before the Tribunal in knowing violation of a court order.[47] Disregarding a chamber's order to remove confidential materials from the public domain has also been found to be grounds for contempt under this Rule.[48]

Once a trial chamber has imposed protective conditions on a witness's testimony, these can only be lifted by order of the court. The orders for protective measures apply to all persons coming into possession of protected information, including those who were not party to the proceedings in which the orders were issued.

ICTY judges have been faced with several cases where individuals have published information in breach of protective measures invoking their right to freedom of expression and press. Trial chambers have held that these rights can be limited in relation to court orders. For example, in the *Margetić* case, the defendant, a freelance journalist and editor-in-chief of two Croatian publications, was found guilty of contempt of court for publishing a complete confidential witness list of witnesses from the *Blaškić* case. A large number of these witnesses were protected.[49] The defendant argued that he had published the witness list because he wanted to inform the public about who these witnesses were. While the chamber recognised the freedom of the press to report on ICTY proceedings, it noted that journalists were nevertheless bound by the Tribunal's orders on protective measures granted to witnesses.[50] It held that the defendant could not invoke the principles of freedom of expression and freedom of the press to excuse his conduct.[51] Other chambers have expressed similar views on this issue.[52]

The effectiveness of contempt proceedings depends on the imposition of sufficiently tough sanctions to deter future violations. In cases that have resulted in a conviction, judges have often imposed lenient sentences, although Rule 77 allows for tougher sanctions. To date, the sentences imposed range from fines of 7,000

---

[47] ICTY *Prosecutor v Jović*, AC, IT-95-14 & 14/2-R77-A, 15 March 2007, Appeals Judgement, para 22.

[48] ICTY *Prosecutor v Šešelj*, TC III, IT-03-67-R77.4, 24 May 2011, Public Edited Version of "Decision on Failure to Remove Confidential Information from Public Website and Order in Lieu of Indictment" Issued on 9 May 2011, p. 10.

[49] ICTY *Prosecutor v Margetić*, TC I, IT-95-14-R77.6, 7 February 2007, Judgement on Allegations of Contempt, paras 69, 70.

[50] Ibid. para 81.

[51] Ibid.

[52] See ICTY *Prosecutor v Marijačić and Rebić*, TC III, IT-95-14-R77.2, 10 March 2006, Judgement, para 39; ICTY *Prosecutor v Haxhiu*, TC I, IT-04-84-R77.5, 24 July 2008, Judgement on Allegations of Contempt, para 28; ICTY *Prosecutor v Hartman*, AC, IT-02-54-R77.5-A, 19 July 2011, Appeals Judgement, paras 158–165.

Euros[53] to custodial sentence of fifteen months.[54] These stand in stark contrast with the maximum penalties contemplated by Rule 77 (G), namely a term of imprisonment of seven years, a fine of 100,000 Euros, or both. Effective measures are required to curtail recurring violations of protection orders.

9.3.3 Countering Witness Intimidation

The protection of witnesses from intimidation or harm is imperative to the integrity and success of a judicial process.[55] The ICTY has sought to counter witness intimidation through protection and support systems, prosecuting those alleged to have intimidated witnesses. It has also introduced a new Rule that allows the parties to tender the evidence of witnesses who have been interfered with in written form.

Witness intimidation has been a prevalent feature in ICTY trials. As former Judge Wald explained, "intimidation, anonymous phone calls, and word-of-mouth threats relayed by third party intermediaries occur with some frequency when the word gets out that someone is coming to testify at The Hague".[56] In some cases, the climate of fear generated by the practice of intimidation is such that victims and witnesses are reluctant to be interviewed by members of the prosecution and refuse to testify, even when subpoenaed by the court. These cases have revealed the existence of wide networks of individuals interested in silencing witnesses.

Widespread witness intimidation has been a particularly salient factor in cases against former members of the Kosovo Liberation Army (KLA). It has significantly hampered the ability of the prosecution to prove its case at trial. In the *Limaj* case, a case against three former KLA members for crimes in the *Llapushnik* prison camp, the chamber acknowledged in its judgment that a "context of fear" among "victim witnesses" was "very perceptible throughout the trial".[57] It noted that a significant number of witnesses had requested protective measures at trial, and had expressed concerns for their lives and those of their family, in particular those living in Kosovo. A number of victims who testified only did so in response to subpoenas from the court.[58] Two of the three defendants were acquitted due to lack of evidence.

---

[53] ICTY *Prosecutor v Haxhiu*, supra n 52, para 40.

[54] ICTY *Prosecutor v Šešejl*, AC, IT-03-67-R77.2-A, 19 May 2010, Public Redacted Appeals Judgement, para 42.

[55] Mahony 2010, p. 1.

[56] Wald 2002, pp. 217, 220. Similarly, witnesses before the ICTR have been targeted for retribution after testifying. Mahony 2010, p. 64.

[57] ICTY *Prosecutor v Limaj et al.*, supra n 19, para 15.

[58] Ibid.

In the *Haradinaj* case, a case against a former Prime Minister of Kosovo and his associates for crimes in Western Kosovo, the Chamber encountered significant difficulties in securing the attendance of witnesses. Presiding Judge Orie acknowledged this when rendering judgement, observing that the chamber had gained a strong impression that the trial was held in an atmosphere where witnesses felt unsafe and were afraid.[59] Out of 100 witnesses, 34 were granted protective measures and 18 were issued subpoenas after refusing to appear in court.[60] One of the subpoenaed witnesses, Witness 55, began to testify but refused to complete his testimony, claiming that he feared for his safety.[61] The prosecution was unable to bring key witnesses to court. Two of the three defendants were acquitted.

On appeal, the Appeals Chamber admonished the trial judges for failing to exercise their powers appropriately to counter the serious witness intimidation that had permeated the trial. It held that "Countering witness intimidation is a primary and necessary function of a Trial Chamber" and that it was incumbent "upon a Trial Chamber to do its utmost to ensure that a fair trial is possible".[62] The Appeals Chamber granted an appeal by the prosecution and ordered a partial retrial, which is underway at the time of writing.

The Tribunal has tackled witness intimidation by prosecuting those responsible for contempt. In different cases, associates of the defendants,[63] members of their legal teams[64] and even the defendants themselves[65] have been tried for contempt of court for their alleged role in witness interference. These prosecutions have had varying levels of success.

The difficulties encountered in securing the evidence of intimidated witnesses have also prompted the Tribunal to revise its Rules of Procedure and Evidence. In December 2009, the judges at the ICTY amended these Rules to include a new provision, Rule 92 *quinquies*, which allows a party to tender in writing the evidence of persons subject to improper interference (including threats, intimidation, injury, bribery or coercion). This Rule specifically allows for the admission of evidence that goes to the acts and conduct of the accused without cross-examination

---

[59] ICTY *Prosecutor v Haradinaj et al.*, TC I, IT-04-84-T, 3 April 2008, Judgement Summary.

[60] ICTY *Prosecutor v Haradinaj et al.*, TC I, IT-04-84-T, 3 April 2008, Judgement, para 22.

[61] Ibid.

[62] ICTY *Prosecutor v Haradinaj et al.*, supra n 46, paras 35, 49–51.

[63] See ICTY *Prosecutor v Haraqija and Morina*, TC I, IT-04-84-R77.4, 17 December 2008, Judgement on Allegations of Contempt; ICTY *Prosecutor v Beqaj*, TC I, IT-03-66-T-R77, 27 May 2005, Judgement on Contempt Allegations.

[64] See ICTY *Prosecutor v Rašić*, TC III, IT-98-32/1-R77.2, 7 February 2012, Contempt Judgement; ICTY *Prosecutor v Brđanin*, TC II, IT-99-36/R77, 8 May 2003, Order Instigating Proceedings against Milka Maglov; ICTY *Prosecutor v Avramović and Simić*, TC III, IT-95-9-R77, 30 June 2000, Judgement in the Matter of Contempt Allegations against an Accused and his Counsel. See also ICTY *Prosecutor v Tabaković*, TC II, IT-98-32/1-R77.1, 18 March 2010, Sentencing Judgement.

[65] See ICTY *Prosecutor v Šešejl*, supra n 54; ICTY *Prosecutor v Šešejl*, TC, IT-03-67-R77.3, 31 October 2011, Public Redacted Version of 'Judgement' issued on 31 October 2011.

in the interest of justice. It remains to be seen whether, in practice, this provision will be an effective mechanism to address the issue of witness intimidation.

9.4 Conclusion

With the work of the Tribunal winding down, the need to ensure continuity in the protection of witnesses has gained significant importance. In December 2010, the UN Security Council established a new *ad hoc* body, the Residual Mechanism, which will continue the "jurisdiction, rights and obligations and essential functions" of the ICTY, as well as maintain the Tribunal's legacy.[66] One essential function of this new body will be the protection of victims and witnesses. As from 1 July 2013, the Residual Mechanism will assume these tasks both for ongoing cases before the Mechanism and for completed cases from the ICTY and the Mechanism. The ICTY will remain responsible for the protection of victims and witnesses in ongoing cases before it.

Since its first trial in 1996, the ICTY has implemented protection systems to minimise the risks posed to victims involved in its proceedings. It has strived to effectively protect victims, while safeguarding the rights of defendants to a public and fair trial. The ICTY's jurisprudence on victim and witness protection is voluminous. In addition, this Tribunal has developed special procedural mechanisms aimed at enforcing protective measures and at tackling witness intimidation. While there is much work to be done to improve victim protection in the international criminal justice system, the lessons learned by the ICTY should not go unheeded and should inform the practice adopted by other international and domestic war crimes jurisdictions in the future.

References

Cassese A (2008) International Criminal Law, 2nd edn. OUP, New York

Chinkin C (1997) Due process and witness anonymity. AJIL 91:75–79

Haider H, Welch T (2008) The prosecution of witnesses in Bosnian war crimes trials: a fair balance between the interests of victims and the rights of the accused? DLJ 20:55–86

Jouet M (2007) Reconciling the conflicting rights of victims and defendants at the international criminal court. Saint Louis Univ Public Law Rev 26:249–308

Kippenberg J (2009) Protecting child victims in sexual violence trials in the DR Congo: suggestions for the way forward. Human Rights Watch, New York. www.hrw.org

Leigh M (1996) The Yugoslav Tribunal: use of unnamed witnesses against the accused. AJIL 90:235–237

Mahony C (2010) International Criminal Court's victims and witnesses unit: a mandate to protect all? In: Mahony C (ed) Justice sector afterthought: witness protection in Africa. Institute for Security Studies, Pretoria

[66] UN Security Council Resolution 1966 (2010).

May R (2003) The collection and admissibility of evidence and the rights of the accused. In: Lattimer M, Sands P (eds) Justice for crimes against humanity. Hart Publishing, Oxford, p 161
Paterson N (2003) Silencing victims in international courts: neglecting a solemn obligation. GJIA 4:95
Pena M (2008) Time for the ICC to take on protection of intermediaries and lawyers. VRWG Access Bulletin, Issue 13
Pozen J (2006) Justice obscured: the non-disclosure of witnesses' identities in ICTR trials. JILP 38:281–322
Sluiter G (2005) The ICTR and the protection of witnesses, 3 JICJ, pp 962–976
Stover E (2005) The witnesses: war crimes and the promises of justice in The Hague. University of Pennsylvania, Philadelphia
UNDP (2010) Needs assessment in the field of support to witnesses/victims in Bih. A situation and needs assessment of the cantonal / district prosecutors' offices and courts in the field of witness/victim support and protection in war crimes cases in Bih. http://www.undp.ba/upload/publications/Needs%20Assessment%20in%20the%20Field%20of%20Support%20to%20Witness-Victims%20in%20BiH.pdf. Accessed 15 April 2013
Wald P (2002) Dealing with witnesses in war crimes trials: lessons from the Yugoslav Tribunal. YHRDLJ 5:217

Further Literature

Affolder NA (1997–1998) Tadić, the anonymous witness and the sources of international procedural law. Mich J of Int L 19:445–496
Cassese A, Gaeta P and Jones JRWD (eds) (2002) The Rome Statute of the International Criminal Court: a commentary. Oxford University Press, Oxford
Fyfe NR (2001) Protecting intimidated witnesses. Ashgate Publishing Company, Burlington
Haslam E (2004) Silencing hearings? Victim-witnesses at war crimes trials. Eur J Int L 15:151–177
Kuhner TK (2004) The status of victims in the enforcement of international criminal law. Oreg Rev Int L 6:95–152
Leigh M (1997) Witness anonymity is inconsistent with due process. Am J of Int L 91:80
Nijboer JF (2000) Children and young persons in the criminal justice system: The Council of Europe recommendation on witness protection and rights of the defence. Crim L Forum 10:443
Safferling CJM (2002) International criminal procedure and its participants: an examination of the interaction of judges, prosecutor and defence at the Yugoslav Tribunal. Yrb Int Hum L 5:219–252
Trechsel S (2005) Human rights in criminal proceedings. Oxford University Press, Oxford
Walleyn L (2002) Victimes et témoins de crimes internationaux: du droit à un protection au droit à la parole. Int Rev of the Red Cr 84(845):51–78

Chapter 10
Victims as Witnesses: Views from the Defence

Natalie von Wistinghausen

Abstract Victim participation raises the question whether a participating victim is still an adequate witness and whether such a witness can still guarantee fairness towards the accused. The principle of equality of arms is under scrutiny, as the accused is confronted with both a public and a private prosecutor. The definition of "victimhood" becomes questionable in the course of the proceedings. An accused, who has been detained for more than ten years at the ICTR and was then acquitted, as has happened, sees himself as a victim. Yet, he is still being called *génocidaire* and has no right to claim victim status. Furthermore, "story-telling" as a form of victim participation is not advisable; the trial is only concerned with charges and warrants testimony only relating to these. The right to a fair trial, it is concluded, is a right for the accused and not for victims.

Keywords Victim participation • Compensation • Witness • Trial fairness • Equality of arms • Public interest • Social identity • Mistrust • Génocidaires • Evidence • Testimonies • Credibility • Presumption of innocence • Victims as witnesses

Victim participation in criminal proceedings has been a very common institution in many civil law countries for decades (e.g. in Germany since 1975), even though frequently contested and certainly a subject of very controversial discussion by defence Bar associations and their members. However, at the International Criminal Tribunals victim participation is a relatively new phenomenon and the issues arising seem to be similar and perhaps equal to those which have emerged in national jurisdictions.

Natalie von Wistinghausen, born in Brussels, is a self-employed criminal lawyer in Berlin and has worked for the defence at the ICTR. She is admitted to the list of counsel at the ICC, STL and ICTR. Currently she is defending a Rwandan citizen before the Higher Regional Court of Frankfurt am Main who is accused of participation in the Rwandan genocide.

N. von Wistinghausen (✉)
Berlin, Germany
e-mail: office@nvw-law.com

T. Bonacker and C. Safferling (eds.), *Victims of International Crimes: An Interdisciplinary Discourse*, DOI: 10.1007/978-90-6704-912-2_10,

The Statutes and Rules of Procedure and Evidence at the *ad hoc* tribunals (International Criminal Tribunal for the former Yugoslavia [ICTY] and International Criminal Tribunal for Rwanda [ICTR]) do not accommodate the participation of victims in proceedings other than as witnesses. Victims were therefore regarded as mere source of information. Times have changed with the International Criminal Court (ICC). Both the Rome Statute[1] and the ICC Rules of Procedure and Evidence[2] incorporate victims as 'participants' in pre-trial and trial proceedings. Victims are not only allowed to claim compensation, but they can also actively participate in the proceedings at the ICC, being represented by counsel ("legal representatives")[3] even if they are called as witnesses in the same trial.

The Special Tribunal for Lebanon (STL)—guided by the necessity to ensure fair and expeditious trials—has chosen a different approach: a victim must decide at the outset of a trial whether he or she wishes to be either a participant in the proceedings, or a witness. Nonetheless, the situation may change if, for example, parties realise in the course of proceedings that a victim might be important as a witness, an application can be made to the appropriate Chamber.[4]

This article does not purport to give a detailed analysis of the rules and jurisprudence dealing with victims' participation at International Criminal Tribunals—especially the ICC[5]—but merely seeks to provide a practical view and to demonstrate the difficulties arising from victim participation in criminal proceedings as seen from the defence perspective.

What is it that concerns the defence when victims of (international) crimes participate in criminal trials? It is certainly not lack of sympathy with the narratives of victims, nor a lack of respect for pain, loss, trauma and grief or a general denial of the right of a victim to reasonable compensation. It is much more the problems generated in finding a method to incorporate, in any adequate way, the rights of the alleged perpetrator (the accused) and the rights of a victim in one and the same proceedings. A criminal trial is designed around the accused, not around the victim. Victim participation may be incompatible with the fairness of the proceedings and the principle of equality of arms. This problem is more acute when a victim is both a participant in proceedings and an active witness at the same time. As opposed to the prosecutor, who must act as an agent of Justice representing and safeguarding the public interest, victims intervene in a private capacity and their motivation is purely personal.

---

1 Rome Statute of the International Criminal Court, adopted on 17 July 1998, entry into force on 1 July 2002.

2 Rules of Procedure and Evidence of the International Criminal Court, adopted on 9 September 2002, entry into force on 9 September 2002.

3 Article 89 pp ICC RPE.

4 Article 150 (D) STL RPE (Rules of Procedure and Evidence of the Special Tribunal for Lebanon), adopted on 20 March 2009), which provides that such victim 'shall not be permitted to give evidence unless a Chamber decides that the interest of justice so require'.

5 See Baumgartner 2008, p. 409; for the STL see De Hemptinne 2010, pp. 165–179.

10.1 To Start With: Who is a "Victim"?

The provisions of the ICC statute give only a vague definition:

(a) 'Victims' means natural persons who have suffered harm as a result of the commission of any crime within the jurisdiction of the Court;
(b) Victims may include organisations or institutions that have sustained direct harm to any of their property which is dedicated to religion, education, art or science or charitable purposes and to their historic monuments, hospitals and other places and objects for humanitarian purposes.[6]

The Appeals Chamber of the ICC has limited the participation of victims in trial proceedings to those victims who are linked to the charges in a given case and where the harm suffered by a victim, whether direct or indirect, is personal.[7] This finding of the Appeals Chamber is sensibly grounded in the need to ensure that reasonable limits are in place and the same caveats would apply in domestic jurisdictions.

Taking a step back from rules and jurisprudence, one could argue that the definition of a victim should include anybody who considers him/herself as a victim.[8] One could go even further and consider that the belief in being able to differentiate objectively, and in advance of the court's judgement, between a victim and a perpetrator could lead to discriminatory truth finding.[9] A criminal lawyer would observe that many of his or her clients consider themselves as victims simply on the basis that they are prosecuted for alleged crimes that they believe they have not committed. Nobody will be surprised if defendants at the ICTR who were detained at the United Nations Detention Facility (UNDF) for more than 10 years and were then acquitted may well consider themselves as victims. However, there is no NGO fighting for compensation for these people whose rights were obviously violated, especially their right to an expeditious trial. Compensation for acquitted persons before the International Tribunals has not even been seriously contemplated in the international legal arena and has therefore not been regulated by law. Understandably for the persons concerned, this leads to a shattered sense of self and social identity and to mistrust in society and justice. They will certainly consider themselves as victims as a result of—for years—being referred to as "*génocidaires*" and treated as such in public debate, in the media etc.

The question as to who is a victim and who is not may also be dependent on the historical background of the violations of human rights with which the trial is concerned. Not every victim gets the chance or the right to be considered as

---

6 Rule 85 ICC RPE.

7 ICC *Prosecutor v Lubanga*, AC, ICC-01/04-01/06 OA 10, 11 July 2008, Judgement on the appeals of The Prosecutor and The Defence against Trial Chamber I's Decision on Victims' Participation of 18 January 2008 paras 32 and 58–66.

8 Definition by Veit Straßner, participant of the conference 'Victims of International Crimes' at the Philipps-University of Marburg on 6–8 October 2011.

9 Definition by Marcel M. Baumann, participant of the conference 'Victims of International Crimes' at the Philipps-University of Marburg on 6–8 October 2011.

such. The proceedings at the ICTR provide a stark example of this. There is no doubt that, when the history of Rwanda in the 1990s is carefully considered, there is substantial evidence to suggest that serious crimes against humanity were perpetrated by soldiers of the Rwandan Patriotic Front (RPF: initially rebel insurgents and, since 1994 the ruling government of the country).[10] That evidence may not amount to genocide, but a large number of respectable sources point to organised killings and sometimes massacres of large numbers people. No victims' organisation or NGO ever seriously considered advocating the rights of the victims of those crimes. There is surely no such thing as a civil war conflict that does not generate victims on both sides of the belligerent parties and the civil society as a whole; independently of the ethnic background of the victims. But victim's organisations in today's Rwanda have not begun to consider the violation of human rights of people belonging to the Hutu ethnic group. They and/or their relatives are rather considered "en bloc" as the "*génocidaires*" and have no right to claim a victim's status. Worse still the ICTR itself, despite having gathered a considerable quantity of evidence of such killings on its own account, has now effectively concluded its own proceedings without having indicted a single alleged RPF perpetrator. The question arises whether an individual has a higher victim status if he/she is a victim of genocide instead of a victim of "simple" war crimes and/or another species of a crime against humanity. Are there different classes of victims? Is one person more, and one less, worthy of the nomination as a "victim"?

It is difficult to deal with testimonies of victims testifying as witnesses in international trials without considering the sociocultural and historical background of the situation they have (allegedly) lived through. The word "alleged" might be considered as disturbing and rather provocative when talking about victims. But here again, who knows at the outset if the victim's story is true or not? Or if the person claiming to be a victim has a good reason to lie? There may be many such reasons: the hope for an improved social and economic status, through compensation, a wish to see "somebody" convicted for the crimes committed against close relatives, political brainwashing or simply deep trauma.

It would be unfair to minimise the possible or genuine guilt of an accused in respect of terrible war crimes and to in any way seek to attribute it to the witness. The obvious fact is that a witness is as much of a human being as the accused with all associated human weaknesses and failures. That reality cannot be disregarded if a naive approach to victims' issues in criminal proceedings is to be avoided.

Testing the credibility of a witness, which is one of the main challenges for the defence, has nothing to do with the issue of a witness being a victim. The same criteria apply to every witness or piece of evidence. Every lawyer knows that live *viva voce* witnesses provide the most compelling evidence that criminal trials ever

[10] In February 2008, Fernando Andreu, a Spanish judge, indicted 40 current or former Rwandan military officers for several counts of genocide and human rights abuses during the Rwandan Genocide; also see Desforges 1999, p. 823.

see. Indeed for many trials before the International Criminal Tribunals there has been little or no evidence in the shape of documentary, photographic or CCTV material, and where there has, the prosecution has shown a distinct aversion to using it. Often, the only direct evidence available is that adduced from witness statements and testimonies. It therefore needs to be subjected to special scrutiny, and all the more so when the witness and the victim is one and the same person.

Bearing all this in mind, there are three salient questions that highlight the doubts about the merits of victim participation in a criminal trial and even more in an international criminal trial[11] where the tension between the need to focus narrowly upon the person and the individual criminal responsibility of the accused and a concern to establish simultaneously a historical record of past events is particularly evident.[12]

Before articulating and addressing these questions, it is worth reminding ourselves that the rights of the accused are not "just" human rights guarantees; they are part and parcel of the epistemological mechanism for fact finding in criminal proceedings. The rights of the accused must be seen as an essential component of accurate and truthful fact finding on which punishment is premised. "If only one of these rights is violated, in only one aspect and in only one instance, the whole process loses credibility and is likely to fail its objective of properly establishing the truth and of therefore imposing just punishment."[13]

10.2 Is Victim Participation Fully Consistent with the Presumption of Innocence?

The adduction of testimony from persons already nominated as victims by some purportedly authoritative branch of the Tribunal responsible for the holding of a fair trial entails an underlying assumption as to the unfolding of the events (the crimes) considered to have occurred in given circumstances and that certain victims were affected by this crime, whereas in reality that remains to be proved at trial.[14]

The factual basis of any alleged crime is almost certainly one of the elements that the Prosecution has to prove beyond reasonable doubt and it is part of the fact-finding process of a criminal trial. For that good reason, the burden of proof rests with the Prosecution[15] and no reversal of the burden is allowed.[16]

Hannah Ahrendt says in her book about the proceedings against Adolf Eichmann, which she monitored: "A trial and a play have this in common: that

[11] For arguments in favour of victim participation see Trumbull IV 2008, p. 802.

[12] Dembour and Haslam 2004, p. 152.

[13] Zappalà 2010, p. 145.

[14] Jorda and de Hemptinne 2002, p. 1403.

[15] Article 66 (2) ICCSt.

[16] Article 67 (1) (i) ICCSt.

both start and end with the perpetrator and not with the victim. The focus of the trial can only be on the one who acted: if he suffers, then he must suffer for what he has done and not as a result of the sufferings of his victims."[17]

Hannah Ahrendt is in my view right. Great suffering can be caused in ways that are morally neutral (earthquakes, tsunamis etc.). The purpose of a trial is to establish the criminal actions (or otherside) of the accused. Some crimes (thwarted attempts, frustrated conspiracies) cause no suffering and have no victims. Throughout her book, she reiterates that those prosecuting Eichmann failed to concentrate on the purpose of the trial by permitting victims to recount events not directly related to the indictment.

The recounting by victims of their "stories" is widely perceived to be desirable on humane grounds even if it is not necessary to pave the way for collective peace and avoid acts of revenge. In the judicial arena, however, "story telling" can only take the form of providing legal evidence. It is constrained by the judicial endeavour to establish a legally authoritative account of "what happened".[18]

The danger with victim participation—especially in international criminal proceedings—is that the desire to create a space in which victims can become active participants, have a right to "tell their story" irrespective of its relevance to the issues before the court, undergo some measure of catharsis and feel part of a process which results in the accused being imprisoned, can lead to an indirect attack on one of the fundamental tenets of a criminal trial. The presumption of victimhood and the presumption of the accused's innocence do not sit easily together.

The concern goes even further. There is a danger that victims, called as witnesses, become a Prosecutor's tool. Assuming the witness testimony "sets the scene" for the trial, there is a potential psychological imbalance in proceedings where victims, who may have suffered terribly, influence the emotional atmosphere away from an independent and unemotional test of the evidence. All protagonists in a court are humans. Judges may do their best to be unemotional and take a balanced and "judicially distant" approach to the proceedings. That can be made all the more difficult in an emotionally charged atmosphere which is never beneficial for logical and independent evidence-based conclusions.

It happens quite frequently in a courtroom that an alleged victim is called as a witness. He or she tells their story which in the context of international crimes (crimes against humanity, war crimes or even genocide), is almost certain to be harrowing and the origin of an overall traumatic experiences. The seriousness and savagery of the events are brought right into the courtroom and stir emotions. Where, however, is the link to the accused? That is a very legitimate question for the functionaries in the court. The witness is called *"colorandi causa"*, and may have nothing to say as to any concrete participation of the accused in the alleged crimes but, nevertheless, leaves a bitter suspicion that the accused must somehow be related to what has happened or at least has failed to prevent the alleged crimes.

---

[17] Free translation from Ahrendt 1964.

[18] See *supra* note 10, p. 154.

This is even more of a problem as allegations at International Criminal Tribunals are very often based on suggestions of superior/command or joint criminal enterprise responsibility of the defendant, meaning that the Prosecution does not seek to prove a direct participation in the crime.

The tension between the need to focus narrowly upon the person of the accused and the simultaneous attempt to establish a wider record of historical events is added to the tension between adhering to the legal procedure, while attending to the sufferings of individual victims and finally the tension between the need to make horrible past events the focus of the trial whilst attempting to contribute to the creation of a more hopeful future are all present. All three certainly plague the Prosecution in international criminal trials. Tribunals tend not only to seek to establish the guilt or innocence of the accused persons, but also to establish "what actually happened" and therefore to "(re-)write history".

This leads to the next important controversial issue as to the role of witnesses, namely victims as witnesses versus witness participation in trial proceedings:

Where victims have direct knowledge of events, there is no objection to them being called as direct Prosecution or Defence witnesses. Where their knowledge is more circumstantial and they have suffered serious human rights violations, then their status as victims and the scope and nature of their participation requires more careful scrutiny. However, Rule 85 (ICC) seems over-focused on the concept of undefined "harm" and there is no clearly defined distinction between the justification for the participation of victims in the proceedings.

This critical question of victim participation in trial applies even more to the participation at an early stage in the proceedings, sometimes prior to the identification of the potential defendant. To some extent, their participation during investigations is *conditio sine qua non* as the crimes committed. Victims are at the origin of almost every initiation of an investigation. Without a victim or intended victim there is no allegation of a crime. This may lead to the conclusion that victims have a particular personal interest in the outcome of investigations and that they cannot be independent, but rather are "interested participants".

Allowing victims to participate in investigations may therefore allow them to exercise pressure on the Prosecutor, who as an independent entity, is in charge of collecting both inculpatory and exculpatory evidence during investigation.[19] Their participation may therefore impact detrimentally on the independence of the Court.

10.3 Do Victims Have a Right to a Fair Trial?

No, is the only answer. The accused alone has a statutory right to a fair trial. The accused is the one who can be held responsible for the alleged crimes and who stands liable to conviction and incarceration. It is his/her trial and nobody else's.

[19] Article 42(1) ICCSt.

A victim has rights under international law such as the right to justice, the right to the truth about what happened,[20] the right to be heard, the right to obtain compensation[21] and the right to have access to justice. However, these rights do not duplicate those which in criminal proceedings are granted to the accused person.

In international criminal proceedings, victims very often benefit from privileges—unknown in domestic trials in Germany for example—that significantly prejudice the accused. This includes protective measures without any individually scrutinised objective basis to establish the element of fear, or even being granted total anonymity as well as the permission to testify *in camera.*[22] These inevitably have an impact on the defence's ability to challenge the witness' credibility and on the necessity for the accused to know who his accuser is. Moreover, such witnesses have no obligation to expose exculpatory evidence, nor is their conduct governed by a code of professional ethics. Lastly, significant procedural rights of the accused may well be affected, as victim participation at trial can significantly prolong the proceedings.

10.4 Witnesses have far more to say than will ever be heard in court. What platform should they be given to tell those parts of their story that do not prejudice the fine focus of the law?

Paradoxically, leaving aside any hopes for compensation, it is precisely the special aura of the legal arena that motivates some witnesses to testify. Advocating an end to victim testimony because of inherent conflicts in the legal process may admittedly prejudice some genuine victims until new platforms are created where victims can recount their stories in a socially significant way. Is there the political will to provide victims with this opportunity? There are no easy answers. But these questions need to be asked in order to resolve the tensions presently prevailing at International Criminal Tribunals in a responsible way. The issue is how to treat the victims with respect and sympathy and whether it is the truth of the surrounding circumstances that gave rise to the allegations upon which the final judgement is made. Both aims are not inherently compatible.

[20] See generally Kuhner 2004.

[21] Basic Principles and Guidelines on the Right to a Remedy and Reparations of Victims of International Human Rights and Humanitarian Law, Comm'n on Hum. Rts. Res. 2005/30, U.N. Doc. E/2005/23 (Apr. 22, 2005).

[22] Article 68 (1)–(2) Rome Statute.

References

Ahrendt H (1964) Eichmann in Jerusalem. Ein Bericht von der Banalität des Bösen. Piper Verlag, Munich

Baumgartner E (2008) Aspects of victim participation in the proceedings of the International Criminal Court. IJRC 90(870):409–440

De Hemptinne J (2010) Challenges raised by victims' participation in the proceedings of the Special Tribunal for Lebanon. JICJ 8:165–179

Dembour M-B, Haslam E (2004) Silencing hearings? Victim-witnesses at war crimes tribunals. EJIL 15:151–177

Desforges A (1999) Leave none to tell the story: genocide in Rwanda. Human Rights Watch, Berlin

Jorda C, De Hemptinne J (2002) The status and role of the victim. In: Cassese A, Gaeta P, Jones JRWD (eds) The Rome Statute of the International Criminal Court: a commentary. Oxford University Press, Oxford, pp. 1387–1413

Kuhner T (2004) The status of victims in the enforcement of international criminal law. ORIL 6:95–152

Trumbull IV C (2008) The victims of victim participation in international criminal proceedings. MJIL 29:777–826

Zappalà S (2010) The rights of victims v. the rights of the accused. JICJ 8:137–169

Chapter 11
Participation Rights of Victims as Civil Parties and the Challenges of Their Implementation Before the Extraordinary Chambers in the Courts of Cambodia

Silke Studzinsky

Abstract This chapter introduces the rights of Civil Parties before the ECCC which is the first Court to grant victims standing *as civil parties* to proceedings in mass crime trials. Since the Court began, the right of civil parties to participate in proceedings and seek reparations has undergone many changes. The rights of civil parties and their legal representatives have been increasingly limited through jurisprudence, the amendment of the Court's Internal Rules and decisions of the Court Administration limiting resources available to the civil parties and their representatives. The author stresses that the participation of survivors as parties to criminal proceedings and the provision of appropriate remedies are of the utmost importance and can significantly contribute to the process of ascertaining the truth and achieving justice in a post-conflict situation. Importantly, the participation of civil parties and the reparation system available to them must comply with international standards and principals as well as being consistent, coherent, transparent and respectful. Last but not least, sufficient resources must be provided. The participation of survivors in criminal proceedings and access to meaningful remedies remains a huge challenge, but is feasible if those administrating, funding and supporting the proceedings are

---

Since 1990, the author has been working as a criminal defence lawyer and as a legal representative for civil parties in criminal courts in Germany and elsewhere in Europe. Since February 2008, she has been working with the support of the Civil Peace Service of the German Development Organisation DED (now GIZ) in Cambodia to represent Civil Parties before the Extraordinary Chambers in the Courts of Cambodia.
This chapter is based on a speech held during the Conference on 'Victims of International Crimes' (6–8 October 2011) at Marburg, Germany, and reflects the author's work as International Civil Party Lawyer before the ECCC since early 2008. This chapter was concluded in December 2011.

S. Studzinsky (✉)
Berlin, Germany
e-mail: silke.eccc@googlemail.com

T. Bonacker and C. Safferling (eds.), *Victims of International Crimes: An Interdisciplinary Discourse*, DOI: 10.1007/978-90-6704-912-2_11,

willing to ensure that these objectives are realised. Importantly, the participation of survivors in criminal proceedings and access to meaningful remedies are indispensable to ensuring that a holistic response to mass atrocities is achieved.

Keywords Victims • Civil parties • Civil party lawyers • Reparations • Participation right • Legal representation • ECCC • Cambodia

11.1 Introduction

The Extraordinary Chambers in the Courts of Cambodia (otherwise known as the ECCC or the Khmer Rouge Tribunal) was established pursuant to the Agreement[1] between the United Nations and the Royal Government of Cambodia. The ECCC started in 2006 with the first preliminary investigations by the Co-Prosecutors. The mission of the tribunal is to prosecute crimes committed during the period of Democratic Kampuchea between 17 April 1975 and 6 January 1979. The ECCC has jurisdiction over senior leaders and those most responsible for serious violations of the Cambodian Penal Code, and the international crimes of genocide, war crimes and crimes against humanity. It is a hybrid court composed of national and international judges and staffing, and is based largely on civil law procedure. The Khmer Rouge Tribunal is the first internationalised court dealing with mass crimes, which allows victims to apply as civil parties and to become party to the proceedings alongside the prosecution and the defence.[2] In Case 001, against Kaing Guek Eav (alias Duch), the former director of the security center, S-21, the Trial Chamber announced its judgment in July 2010.[3] This judgment is currently under appeal by all Parties. The Supreme Court Chamber held the Appeal hearings at the end of March 2011. The Appeal decision is expected to be handed down on 3 February 2012.

---

[1] Agreement between the United Nations and the Royal Government of Cambodia Concerning the Prosecution under Cambodian Law of Crimes Committed During the Period of Democratic Kampuchea, 6 June 2003, (hereinafter: Agreement), at www.eccc.gov.kh/sites/default/files/legal-documents/Agreement_between_UN_and_RGC.pdf. The Agreement was implemented by the Law on the Establishment of the Extraordinary Chambers, with inclusion of amendments as promulgated on 27 October 2004 (NS/RKM/1004/006), (hereinafter: ECCC Law), at www.eccc.gov.kh/sites/default/files/legal-documents/KR_Law_as_amended_27_Oct_2004_Eng.pdf.

[2] See the Internal Rules (Revision 8), as revised on 12 August 2011, in particular Rule 23 and 23 *bis* - 23 *quinquies* at www.eccc.gov.kh/sites/default/files/legal-documents/ECCC%20Internal%20Rules%20%28Rev.8%29%20English.pdf. The Internal Rules reflect the Cambodian Criminal Procedure Code.

[3] ECCC *Prosecutor v Kaing Guek Eav*, 001/18-07-2007-ECCC/TC, 26 July 2010, Judgment.

In Case 002, against four senior leaders of the Khmer Rouge regime, indictments were finalised in January 2011.[4] The substantive hearing started in November 2011. The case against Ieng Thirith has been severed because she is held unfit to stand trial and the Trial Chamber ordered her unconditional release.[5] On the prosecution's appeal against the unconditional release, the Supreme Court Chamber directed the Trial Chamber to order the Accused's medical treatment in an appropriate facility to improve her fitness to stand trial.[6]

In this chapter, I will give (i) an overview on the participation rights of civil parties as parties to the proceedings and their right to request reparations, (ii) an outline of the current practical situation at the ECCC with regard to the development of civil parties' rights and the challenges arising in the implementation of reparations and (iii) lessons learnt thus far.

11.2 Overview of the Participation Rights and Right to Seek Reparation for Victims as Civil Parties Before the ECCC

11.2.1 The Legal Basis

After nearly 10 years of negotiation, the United Nations and the Royal Government of Cambodia reached an Agreement adopted by the Cambodian National Assembly.[7] It was implemented through the ECCC Law[8] and forms the Statute of the Court. According to the ECCC Law, Cambodian procedural law applies. It stipulates—like the Agreement—that "if Cambodian procedural rules do not deal with a particular matter, or if there is uncertainty regarding their interpretation or application, or a

---

[4] ECCC *Prosecutor v Nuon Chea et al.*, 002/19-09-2007-ECCC/OCIJ, 15 September 2010, Closing Order. The Closing Order was appealed by the Accused and became final with two amendments. See at www.eccc.gov.kh/en/document/court/decision-ieng-thirith-and-nuon-chea39s-appeal-against-closing-order and www.eccc.gov.kh/sites/default/files/documents/courtdoc/D427_1_26_EN.PDF. The reasoning of the Pre-Trial Chamber Decisions on IENG Thirith and NUON Chea can be found at www.eccc.gov.kh/sites/default/files/documents/courtdoc/D427_2_12_EN.PDF. See the Decision on IENG Sary at www.eccc.gov.kh/sites/default/files/documents/courtdoc/D427_1_30_EN.PDF.

[5] ECCC *Prosecutor v Nuon Chea et al.*, Case no. 002/19-09-2007-ECCC/TC, 17 November 2011, Decision on Ieng Thirith's Fitness to Stand Trial.

[6] ECCC *Prosecutor v Nuon Chea et al.*, Case no. 002/19-09-2007-ECCC/TC/SC/(09), 13 December 2011, [Corrected2] Decision on Immediate Appeal against the Trial Chamber's Order to Release the Accused IENG Thirith.

[7] See *supra* note 1.

[8] Ibid.

question regarding their consistency with international standards, guidance may be sought in procedural rules established at the international level."[9]

Despite the fact that neither documents grant judges the power to adopt their own procedural rules, as is the case in other international(ised) Courts,[10] and the Cambodian National Assembly discussed and rejected granting such power during parliamentary debates,[11] in June 2007, the plenary of the Judges adopted the first Internal Rules. The Internal Rules were orientated along the Draft of the Cambodian Criminal Procedure Code which was adopted *during* the Judges' plenary in June 2007 and set out some weeks later. According to its Preamble, the purpose—and limits—of the Internal Rules are to consolidate the Cambodian Criminal Procedure Code[12] (hereinafter: CPC).

The Cambodian criminal proceedings are similar to French proceeding and thus reflect a civil law jurisdiction which is customised in having victims as a third party in criminal proceedings unlike in common law countries where victims mainly play a role as witnesses without any rights to intervene.

This is the reason that victims were included as a third party, equal to other parties, in proceedings before the ECCC.

Departing from the Agreement and the ECCC Law, the Pre-Trial Chamber ruled that the Internal Rules are a "self-contained system of procedural law". The Pre-Trial Chamber continued that "[t]herefore, the Internal Rules constitute the primary instrument to which reference should be made in determining procedures before the ECCC where there is a difference between the procedures in the Internal Rules. Provisions of the CPC should only apply where a question arises which is not addressed by the Internal Rules."[13]

By this ruling the Pre-Trial Chamber shifted the Internal Rules to have the rank of law. In addition, they significantly changed the ranking of the procedural legal basis of the Court, deviating from the Agreement and the ECCC Law, and determined that the Internal Rules are the first and predominant procedural foundations of the Court.

This allowed the Judges of the ECCC to adopt and to amend—with seven amendments to date—the Internal Rules, in closed plenary sessions without any

[9] Article 12 of the Agreement and Article 33 of the ECCC Law.

[10] See Article 15 of the Statute of the International Criminal Tribunal for the Former Yugoslavia; Article 14 of the International Criminal Tribunal for Rwanda; Article 14 of the Statute of the Special Court for Sierra Leone.

[11] On file with author.

[12] The Criminal Procedure Code of the Kingdom of Cambodia can be accessed at www.oecd.org/dataoecd/15/46/46814242.pdf.

[13] ECCC *Prosecutor v Nuon Chea et al.*, 002/19-09-2007-ECCC/OCIJ, 26 August 2008, Decision on Nuon Chea's Appeal against Order Refusing Request for Annulment, paras 14, 15.

outside scrutiny or control. Civil Party Lawyers are excluded from submitting proposals for amendments to the Internal Rules.[14]

Attempts by Civil Party Lawyers to challenge the legality of the Internal Rules[15] were dismissed[16] early on.

Consequently, since 2007, the ECCC Judges significantly restricted and curtailed basic rights of Civil Parties and their lawyers through amendments of the Internal Rules by plenary decisions, being in the position to create and adopt procedurally binding law for the proceedings at the ECCC which do not undergo any scrutiny in relation to being consistent with international standards or/and Cambodian law.

11.2.2 Participation Rights

Victims who apply to become a civil party and, therefore, a party to the proceedings of the ECCC, have equal rights to the prosecution and the defence, at least to a large extent and when appropriate. The Internal Rules determine the purpose of Civil Party participation as, "a) to participate in criminal proceedings against those responsible for crimes within the jurisdiction of the ECCC *by supporting the prosecution*; and b) seek collective and moral reparations."[17]

Participating in this context means that Civil Parties exercise a wide range of procedural rights, as a party to the proceedings.

Civil Parties have a right to legal representation, which has been made mandatory in the trial phase.[18] They have full access to the case files, including confidential parts,[19] and may respond to all applications submitted by the other parties as well as raise any legal or factual matters *proprio motu.* Until now, Civil Parties have not been required to give reasons as to the extent of personal interest in the respective matter, unlike victims participating at the International Criminal Court

---

[14] Internal Rule 18 (1) lists those who are allowed to make proposals to the plenary. The Victims Support Section has no mandate to represent Civil Party Lawyers. Nevertheless, Civil Party Lawyers submitted proposals for amendments through the Victims Support Section (former Victims Unit) but which were regrettably completely ignored.

[15] ECCC *Prosecutor v Nuon Chea et al.*, 002/19-09-2007-ECCC/OCIJ, 13 October 2008, Civil Party Co-Layers' Joint Request for Reconsideration of the Pre-Trial Chamber's Assessment of the legal Status of the Internal Rules in the Decision on Nuon Chea's Appeal Against Order Refusing Request for Annulment.

[16] ECCC *Prosecutor v Nuon Chea et al.*, 002/19-09-2007-ECCC/OCIJ(PTC06), 25 February 2009, Decision on Civil Party Co-Lawyers' Joint Request for Reconsideration.

[17] Internal Rule 23 (1). Emphasis added.

[18] Internal Rule 23 *ter* (1). Internal Rule 23 *ter* (2) stipulates that their rights are exercised by lawyers, except when a civil party is interviewed, either by the Co-Investigating Judges during the Investigations or before the Trial Chamber. When they testify as Civil Parties they do not take an oath (like the Accused) because they are parties to the proceedings.

[19] Internal Rule 86.

(ICC). In addition, they can be interviewed during the investigative phase by the Co-Investigating Judges. Most importantly in this context is the right during the investigation phase to submit investigative requests[20] to the Co-Investigating Judges. The submissions of civil parties during the investigation phase with regard to sexual violence were one prominent and successful example of the performance of participation rights. At the beginning, cases of sexual violence were not part of the prosecutorial strategy and were therefore omitted from the Prosecution's preliminary investigations. Only through the efforts of Civil Party Lawyers were these crimes addressed and investigated at the ECCC. Civil Party Lawyers exercised the right to submit investigative requests, and submitted the first applications of victims of sexual violence, in particular of forced marriages, which were subsequently investigated and eventually became a new count in the indictment.[21]

During the trial phase, Civil Party Lawyers are able to submit their own witness/civil party/expert lists to the Trial Chamber through the new established Lead Co-Lawyers in order to ensure the Civil Parties are personally heard[22] and evidence is strengthened and supplemented. Given the high number of Civil Parties, there will only be a limited number of Civil Parties who are able to give a statement in Court on the facts of the indictment and/or their sufferings.

The most important right of civil parties during trial is the questioning of the Accused, witnesses, other civil parties and experts through their lawyers.[23] Questioning does not need to be linked to a specific personal interest.

Nevertheless, this unlimited right—unlimited in its application under both the applicable Cambodian Procedure Code and the Internal Rules—was restricted by the Trial Chamber in Case 001. The Trial Chamber ruled that Civil Parties were not allowed to question either witnesses who testify on the character of the Accused or experts who examined the mental health of the Accused and his culpability. The Trial Chamber determined the role of Civil Parties to primarily seek

[20] Internal Rule 55 (10).

[21] During the investigations Co-Lawyers for Civil Parties submitted various investigative requests to interview or re-interview witnesses and civil parties on forced marriages and sexual violence outside of the context of forced marriages, for example '[Redacted] Civil Parties' Co-Lawyers Second Request For Investigative Actions Concerning Forced Marriages and Forced Sexual Relationship', 15 July 2009, D188, at www.eccc.gov.kh/sites/default/files/documents/courtdoc/D188_Redacted_EN.pdf and '[Redacted] Co-Lawyers For the Civil Parties' Fourth Investigative Request Concerning Forced Marriages and Sexually Related Crimes', 4 December 2009, D268, at www.eccc.gov.kh/sites/default/files/documents/courtdoc/D268_Redacted_EN.pdf. A request for expert opinion was filed with regard to sexual violence and in particular forced marriages under the Khmer Rouges. Additional documents and witness statements were submitted. Most documents are classified as confidential. The Co-Investigating Judges agreed to receive *Amici Curiae* on this issue but it was impossible to submit them within the deadline from 22 December 2009 until 31 December 2009, see 'Order on Request for Investigative Actions Concerning Forced Marriages and Sexually Related Crimes', 18 December 2009, D268/2, para 14, www.eccc.gov.kh/sites/default/files/documents/courtdoc/D268_2_EN.pdf.

[22] Internal Rule 80 (2) and (3).

[23] Internal Rule 90 (1) and 91 (2).

reparations and, as a result, limited their participation rights to addressing only the guilt of the Accused but not on matters related to sentencing.[24] The Trial Chamber also limited the role of Civil Parties to making submissions only on matters related to proof the guilt of the Accused for the crimes which caused their harm and thus, are related to the issue of reparations.[25]

This ruling can be seen as a first step towards the "personal-interest-approach" as it applies at the International Criminal Court (ICC) where Victims are limited in their interventions only to matters which affect their 'personal interests'.[26]

Although this limitation has no legal basis in the Internal Rules or the Cambodian Criminal Procedure Code[27] and affects the participation rights of Civil Parties, the possibility for civil parties to intervene is still broad.

11.2.3 Reparation Scheme in Case 002

The common understanding of compensation in the domestic Cambodian system is that victims can join criminal proceedings as civil parties and submit their civil claims for financial compensation to the criminal court.[28]

Since the beginning of the ECCC, the domestic Cambodian system has been amended *qua* Internal Rules: Reparations are limited to collective and moral reparation only.

In Case 002, the reparation scheme was again amended. The Internal Rule 23 *quinquies* describes collective and moral reparations as measures that (i) acknowledge the harm suffered by Civil Parties as a result of the commission of the crimes from which an Accused is convicted and (ii) provide benefits to the Civil Parties which address this harm. Any monetary payments to Civil Parties are *explicitly* excluded.

Despite the amendments of the Internal Rules, a clear definition of collective and moral reparations is still lacking.

---

[24] ECCC *Prosecutor v Kaing Guek Eav*, 001/18-07-2007-ECCC/TC, 9 October 2009, Decision on Civil Party Co-Lawyers' Joint Request for a Ruling on the Standing of Civil Party Lawyers to Make Submissions on Sentencing and Directions Concerning the Questioning of the Accused, Experts and Witnesses Testifying on Character [Sentencing Decision]. Judge Lavergne dissented in parts and stressed that Civil Parties have the same rights like other parties if not explicitly limited, para 16.

[25] Dissenting Opinion of Judge Lavergne in the Sentencing Decision, para 22.

[26] Article 68 (3) of the Rome Statute.

[27] Judge Lavergne stated that "the decision taken by Trial Chamber tilts towards a view that is far removed both from Cambodian law and the Internal Rules of the ECCC", para 32, Dissenting Opinion of the Sentencing Decision.

[28] See Articles 14, 21 and 24 CPC.

The Internal Rules further require (i) the description of the award sought, (ii) reasoned argument as to how they address the harm and to specify, where applicable, the specific Civil Party group and (iii) the specification of the mode of implementation.[29]

The cost of reparations can also be borne by external funds. The Internal Rules stipulate that the Trial Chamber then 'recognises that a specific project gives effect to the award sought and may be implemented'.[30] The Victims Support Section is required to secure sufficient external funding, for any possibility of implementing reparations measures. In light of the limited human resources within the Victims Support Section, and due to the absence of an established funding source, the outcome in Case 002 might be even more limited because only awards for which sufficient funding is guaranteed, can be 'recognised' by the Trial Chamber. In other words, the enforceability of the order becomes a pre-condition, and an integral part of any reparation order. This seems to be quite questionable as the matter of enforceability has never been an issue of relevance for the decision of a Trial Chamber on reparations.

Likewise, it is doubtful what 'recognition' by the Trial Chamber can contribute, and even why it is needed if all the work including the financing is already implemented by the Victims Support Section and necessary assistance provided by Civil Party Lawyers or even the Civil Parties themselves.

The amended Internal Rules broaden the mandate of the Victims Support Section, which can implement so called 'non-judicial measures for victims'. The Internal Rules stipulate that the Victims Support Section 'shall be entrusted with the development and implementation of non-judicial programs and measures addressing the broader interests of victims. Such programs may be developed and implemented in collaboration with governmental and non-governmental organizations external to the ECCC'.[31]

This, of course, sounds rather promising at first glance, since two new avenues have been added which broaden the possibility for civil parties and victims to receive reparation.

In Case 002, the final reparation request has to be filed as directed by the Trial Chamber at a later stage of the hearing[32]—approximately in 2013.

Meanwhile, the Victims Support Section could, within its new mandate, establish reparation in the form of the non-judicial measure readily available.

However, the Victims Support Section struggles with limited resources after nearly 2 years of being seized with this mandate. Additionally, the new VSS mandate can only be performed by making use of strong management and organisational skills. It is quite possible that the mandate of the Victims Support Section

---

29 Internal Rule 23 *quinquies* (2).

30 Internal Rule 23 *quinquies*, (3) (b).

31 Internal Rule 12 *bis* (3).

32 Internal Rule 80 *bis* (4) and (5).

to design and implement reparations for both the reparation awarded by the Trial Chamber and the non-judicial measures, which necessarily includes full fundraising for reparation, is too ambitious. It may well prove to be more of a window-dressing exercise rather than effective reparation.

11.2.4 The Performance of Civil Party Rights in Practice

11.2.4.1 Resources

After having discussed shiny academic theory, I will now shed light on practical reality and elaborate on some major obstacles in the performance of civil party rights.

Upon my arrival in early 2008, I was keen to contribute to achieving justice for victims by representing them as full-rights civil parties in a Criminal Court dealing with mass crimes for the first time in the history of International(ised) Courts. I was hoping that the inclusion of victims as full parties into the judicial criminal process would help them shift their role from being objects to become subjects of the proceedings. I was also hoping that civil parties would achieve effective remedies such as access to truth and information through performing their participation rights; and that they would receive reparation that may effectively contribute to healing the harm that they have suffered. Last but not least, I was hoping that the process of justice and reconciliation—huge and heavy terms that are easily used in the discussion of mechanisms in transitional justice settings—could be made tangible and concrete.

I also believed that the ECCC would become a model Court for the participation of many victims as parties to the proceedings in mass crimes and hoped to increase the benefits for the victims of the Khmer Rouge Regime as well as the Cambodian society today.

I soon learned that Civil Party Lawyers and thus Civil Parties were not that welcomed at the ECCC, at least not as an active part and party to the proceedings. The Court used and still uses all means—amendments of the Internal Rules, Court decisions and decisions by the Administration—to silence civil parties and to progressively reduce their participation from the agenda of the Court. It seems to be sufficient for the so-to-speak "family album" to have some civil parties sitting and listening attentively to the proceedings in the court room, regardless of whether they understand what is going on.

In Case 002, 3,864 civil parties were admitted.[33] Their legal representation by Civil Party Lawyers is mandatory, by virtue of the latest issuance of the indictment. The role of Civil Party Lawyers during the trial stage and beyond is to

[33] Two Civil Parties withdrew because of their frustration.

substantively support the Lead Co-Lawyers in the representation of the "consolidated group of civil parties".

In order to make participation possible and meaningful, Civil Parties must be sufficiently and continually informed about the proceedings before becoming involved and able to properly perform their procedural rights. Consequently, enough resources need to be invested to regularly inform civil parties on the court proceedings for them to be able to make informed decision on how to contribute to the proceedings and on the views that they may wish to submit. Also, consideration must be given to those victims who have never been in contact with a court before and live in remote areas of Cambodia or abroad. The way that the information is provided should also correspond to the language and educational level of the victims—bearing in mind that the low level of education generally in Cambodia can be attributed to the structural destruction of the society carried out by the Khmer Rouge Regime.

Further, Civil Party Lawyers have to work full time on the case, and must have permanent access to all software and facilities that other parties have. They must be enabled and supported to draft legal submissions to a high standard and have to be trained on international criminal law, the specificities of the ECCC and the factual historical background.

Although it was clear from the beginning that civil parties will be present during the proceedings and are an important feature in this particular Court, legal representation of civil parties was not included into the court's budget. Although funds from third party resources raised in 2008 by a concerted initiative of the former Victims Unit and civil society actors improved the under-resourced legal representation slightly; Civil Party Lawyers today work on a *pro-bono* basis and/or with minimal funds that they are required to seek for themselves. Almost all International and national Civil Party Lawyers are dedicated to their work, but they need to spend most of their time and energy following up other sources of income in order to earn their living, given that the majority of victims are not in a position to pay for their legal representation.

In late 2009, two Cambodian lawyers were paid by the Court, which received earmarked funds by the German Ministry of Foreign Affairs. International posts for legal representation were advertised but never filled, although legal representation was the centerpiece of the funding coming from the German Government. Today we have a total of three Cambodian lawyers paid by the Court. This is by far not sufficient to represent nearly 4,000 civil parties who wish to participate in the proceedings. Upon my arrival, Civil Party Lawyers were provided with two small offices and after a while with access to office supplies similarly to other parties working at the court. Subsequently new offices were built and provided with computers and other facilities so that at the beginning of 2010, working conditions further improved. In addition, we had access, at least by the end of 2008, to interpretation from the Interpretation and Translation Unit (ITU) for meetings between national and international lawyers and lawyers and clients. Meetings with clients were and are financed only by NGOs and third party funding. Since 1 July 2010, the situation deteriorated. The new Chief of the Office of the Victims Support

Section moved the Civil Party Lawyers from the Court to the Information Center of the Court in Phnom Penh, and later, ordered to leave this office as political tensions grew. This resulted in Civil Party Lawyers having no permanent professional domicile, and no access to relevant software required for the daily work. Further, access to Court interpretation is no longer provided, and we are only permitted to work on a Court computer—giving us access to the court's electronic networks and legal tools three days per week. Such usage requires an advanced reservation request. Neither the Prosecution nor the Defence is treated this way, who are both provided with permanent offices and appropriate resources at the Court's premises. Civil Party Lawyers on the other hand are no longer provided with a permanent working space (except the Court funded team), even though they are the legitimate holders of powers of attorney.

11.2.4.2 Lead Co-Lawyers and the Courts Approach to Civil Parties

The new legal representation scheme,[34] which now stipulates that one national and one international Lead Co-Lawyer employed with the Court represent the 'consolidated' group of all Civil Parties, may reduce, if not hinder—the proper representation of Civil Parties through their lawyers. Because of the intermediary 'Lead Co-Lawyers', deadlines for Civil Party Lawyers are in fact shortened because of the requirement to get the approval of the Lead Co-Lawyers. Further, where the Lead Co-Lawyers do not react in a timely manner on Civil Party Lawyers' draft submissions or refuse to sign them has led to a silencing of Civil Parties.

The Trial Chamber and all Court sections now liaise only with the Lead Co-Lawyers, resulting in limited information to Civil Party lawyers, in part due to the Lead Co-Lawyers failing to transfer all relevant information in their knowledge to the Civil Party Lawyers. Furthermore, the Trial Chamber excluded Civil Party Lawyers from accessing relevant documents such as medical certificates about the accused persons, while the fitness to stand trial was discussed.[35] These reports were only accessible to the Lead Co-Lawyers. This has resulted in a different treatment of Civil Party Lawyers by the Chambers from other party representatives. Thus, it is impossible for 'ordinary' Civil Party Lawyers to perform their work when they are excluded from access to basic documents.

Moreover, the names of Civil Party Lawyers are now not mentioned in any Court document and other public information regarding representatives of Civil Parties,[36] as though Civil Party Lawyers no longer exist, even though the vast

[34] Internal Rule 12 *ter.*

[35] Civil Party Lead Co-lawyers request to the Trial Chamber to reclassify the documents put before the Chamber during the initial hearing on fitness to stand trial from strictly confidential to confidential and notify them to all Civil Party lawyers, 12 September 2011, E117, at www.eccc.gov.kh/sites/default/files/documents/courtdoc/E117_EN-1.PDF.

[36] Memorandum Trial Chamber, 27 October 2011, E128/1, at www.eccc.gov.kh/sites/default/files/documents/courtdoc/E128_1_EN.pdf.

majority of submissions are drafted by Civil Party Lawyers. The practice has so far demonstrated that the Lead Co-Lawyers comply with their duty to 'consult with civil party lawyers and endeavor to seek consensus'[37] and therefore to discuss with Civil Party Lawyers. Nevertheless, the Lead Co-Lawyers make the ultimate decisions, sometimes without giving proper reasons to Civil Party Lawyers. It is important to note that no remedy is available to Civil Party Lawyers against any unreasonable or unwarranted decisions in written or oral submissions.

The selection of the Lead Co-lawyers as coordinators instead of un-mandated representatives of Civil Parties should have been based on merit—in other words—a standard of being experienced lawyers in international criminal law and their qualifications and experience in victims' representation in mass crime trials. This was not the case. Important to note is the fact that the Lead Co-Lawyers have no powers of attorney from the civil parties and have no direct knowledge of those they purport to represent *qua* Internal Rules. They are therefore not in a proper position to express their views.

The establishment of the Lead Co-Lawyer Section, without a proper mandate, serves more to silence civil parties than to uphold their right to be heard. Thus, the civil party rights have been stunted. Civil Parties can no longer play their role as a full right pledged party to the proceedings.[38]

As a result, Civil Party Lawyers spend a huge amount of their time struggling for resources and for the recognition of civil parties as a full-right party to the proceedings—instead of using the full time representing them as such.

The latest developments at the ECCC are less promising:

In Cases 003 and 004, cases which are highly disputed and objected by the Cambodian Prime Minister,[39] applicants are rejected for outrageous reasons, without any legal basis. Some examples include: they are only indirect victims, have already enjoyed participation rights in the other cases and that their suffering is not credible.[40]

Moreover, the Trial Chamber decided to sever Case 002 to deal only with the first two forced transfers in the 'first' trial.[41] Given the old age of the accused persons, it can be argued that the separation order would allow the opportunity for the Court to reach at least to one final judgment. However, the decision came far too late from the perspective of the Civil Parties. These victims have undertaken the

---

[37] Internal Rule 12 *ter* (3).

[38] Diamond 2010–2011, pp. 34, 43–46.

[39] Reporting on the events around cases 003 and 004 see also Open Society Justice Initiative (2011) Recent developments in the Extraordinary Chambers in the Courts of Cambodia (June 2011 and November 2011).

[40] The rejection orders are classified confidential but the reasons are quoted in the appeal of the rejected Civil Party applicant, see 003/07-09-2009-ECCC/OCIJ, 15 August 2011, [Redacted] Order on the Admissibility of Civil Party Applicant, paras 27, 28, 36 and 55.

[41] ECCC *Prosecutor v Nuon Chea et al.*, 002/17-09-2007-ECCC/TC, 22 September 2011, Severance Order Pursuant to Internal Rule 89 *ter*.

process of applying as a civil party, appealing rejections and submitting witness and civil party lists with regard to all crimes and crime sites and believing for years that they would benefit from the trial, but the severance means that only approximately 30 % of Civil Parties is connected with the upcoming trial.[42]

Consequently, most of the Civil Parties, who are admitted with regard to other crimes/crime sites than the first two transfers, will not play any role in this first—and probably last trial.

However, the Trial Chamber explicitly retained—against the clear admissibility requirements in the Internal Rules[43]—the entire consolidated group in the Severance Order although the split of the group would have been the correct response. It is because in this first case only those Civil Parties can be admitted who can demonstrate a link to the charges. In fact, the Trial Chamber postponed the rejection of more than 2/3 of them until the judgment when the trial Chamber will reject all those who cannot demonstrate a link to the two forced transfers with regard to reparations. This is another non-transparent treatment of Civil Parties that makes them believe to participate although they are not eligible for the first trial. This will cause again more harm to them.

11.2.5 Lessons Learned

- Victims' representation and participation in criminal trials dealing with mass crimes costs money. To enable victims to meaningful participation in court proceedings, support staff and qualified lawyers need to be paid and provided with adequate infrastructure and logistics to carry out their work.
- Each legal representative can meaningfully represent only a limited number of clients. Otherwise basic professional duties cannot be fulfilled. Therefore, a sufficient number of lawyers according to the number of victims must be paid.
- Victims and their representatives must be treated with dignity and genuine respect for their rights. Their party status must be fully recognised and result in a common practice by all bodies of the ECCC.
- The court must be transparent and accountable to victims, and demonstrate a common and clear policy and approach with regard to victim/civil party participation. These must be predictable from the outset.
- Any reparation scheme should be in accordance with the UN Basic Principles and be a visible and effective remedy that covers the needs of victims. The UN Basic Principles do not foresee that civil society and, ultimately, the victims and their lawyers have to seek funding for the financing of any reparations. The establishment of an independent trust fund is an indispensable means to enforce any reparation order.

[42] 953 out of 3864 Civil Parties demonstrate a link to at least one of the two forced transfers.

[43] Internal Rule 23 *bis* (1).

11.3 Conclusion

The ECCC is the first internationalised court dealing with mass crimes, which grants victims the role of third parties to the proceedings. This would have been a unique chance for the ECCC to have victims actively involved and to become a model for any future international or internationalised court.

More recently, amendments to the Internal Rules, Court rulings and directions by the Office of Administration have effectively reduced the actual possibilities of Civil Parties to participate, or rendered 'participation' meaningless, due to the watered-down rights now afforded to civil parties. Effective victim participation is no longer guaranteed due to the imposition of a Lead Co-lawyer section, responsible for representing the 'consolidated group', and effectively limiting Civil Parties' rights without legal basis and denying Civil Parties' representatives the necessary access to Court facilities.

The role of Civil Parties, to obtain some remnant of justice through actively participating in this process, remains a continuing challenge and one that must be balanced against secondary harm caused to civil parties by the gaps, inadequacies and denial of rights that have resulted so far in all before the ECCC.

There is much to learn from the experience of victim participation at the ECCC—particularly what not to do, if civil party participation is to carry any meaning for the victims it purports to serve.

Reference

Diamond AF (2010–2011) Victims once again? Civil party participation before the Extraordinary Chambers in the Courts of Cambodia. Rutgers Law Rec 38:34–48

Chapter 12
The ICC's Practice on Victim Participation

Franziska C. Eckelmans

Abstract This contribution describes the current practice of victim participation at the pre-trial, trial and interlocutory appeals phases of criminal proceedings before the ICC. By briefly addressing prior developments, crucial decisions are discussed and differences in the approach of Chambers pointed out. The author analyses the application process and how, in practice, victims participate in the proceedings. It appears that there are basically two categories of victim participation. Rights granted by an affirmative decision on the application for participation belong to the first category. The second category requires a specific (second) application to participate in a particular way in the proceedings. Within the context of the latter category, the Chambers' approaches to victims as witnesses and victims and evidence are explained.

Keywords International criminal court • Victim participation • Application process • Harm suffered by victims • Direct victims • Indirect victims • Rights of victims • Legal representatives of victims • Victims as witnesses • Victims and evidence • Determination of the truth • Victims in interlocutory appeals • ICC

The author is Legal Officer in the Appeals Chamber of the International Criminal Court. Any views expressed in this contribution are those of the author alone and not those of the ICC. This contribution was delivered as a speech at the conference "Victims of International Crimes" held in Marburg, Germany, between 6 and 8 October 2011. The article refers mainly to decisions issued until September 2012. The author thanks Eleni Chaitidou for her comments and Erin Rosenberg for her careful reading. Reference is made to the decisions and judgments of the ICC by mentioning the situation or case name and the document number, and, where applicable, the Chamber (PTC, TC, AC). Reference to the Appeals Chamber jurisprudence is also made by "OA"-numbers (see regulation 26 (3) of the Regulations of the Registry).

F. C. Eckelmans (✉)
Appeals Division, International Criminal Court, The Hague, The Netherlands
e-mail: franziska.eckelmans@icc-cpi.int

T. Bonacker and C. Safferling (eds.), *Victims of International Crimes: An Interdisciplinary Discourse*, DOI: 10.1007/978-90-6704-912-2_12,

Much has been written and assured will be regarding the participation of victims in criminal proceedings at the International Criminal Court ("Court").[1] Deriving primarily from just one of six paragraphs in Article 68 of the Rome Statute under the title "Protection of the victims and witnesses and their participation in the proceedings", the participants to the Rome Conference in 1998 probably did not envisage the extensive consequences of this short paragraph.[2] Not only has civil society taken up the matter time and again,[3] but victim participation has kept the Chambers and the Court as a whole busy from the very beginning of its existence. At times, the efforts of all actors in criminal proceedings before the Court that went into the participation of victims appeared to be too extensive. All Chambers had to and have dealt with this matter and have given numerous decisions on the subject.[4] More than 11,000 persons have applied to participate in criminal proceedings before the Court as victims.[5] While only a relatively small number of victims participate(d) in the trial proceedings of *Prosecutor v. Lubanga Dyilo* (129) and *Prosecutor v. Katanga and Ngudjolo* (364),[6] more than 4,000 victims are participating in the proceedings of *Prosecutor v. Bemba Gombo*.[7] Similarly, the Extraordinary Chambers in the Courts of Cambodia ("ECCC"), a tribunal of hybrid character based on the Cambodian, French grounded, criminal procedure, concluded one trial with 90 civil parties and is conducting a second trial in which

---

1 See e.g. Van Boven 1999; Bitti and Friman 2001; Garkawe 2003; Safferling 2003; Bottigliero 2004; Heikkilä 2004; Ferstman 2005; Bock 2007, 2010; Stehle 2007; Baumgartner 2008; Donat-Cattin 2008; Trumbull 2008; Friman 2009; Johnson 2010; Ntanda Nsereko 2010; Pena 2010; Bitti 2011; Van den Wyngaert 2011.

2 See Vasiliev 2009, pp. 651, 652.

3 See e.g. Coalition for the International Criminal Court (2012) Victims and Witnesses. http://www.iccnow.org/?mod=victimswitnesses. Accessed 12 March 2012; see also Victims' Rights and Working Group (2012). http://www.vrwg.org. Accessed 12 March 2012; see also in this context, Haslam 2011, pp. 234–240.

4 See Ušacka 2011, p. 484.

5 See Speech by the ICC Registrar at the conference "Justice for all? The International Criminal Court—10 year review of the ICC" 14 February 2012, p. 3, http://www.icc-cpi.int/NR/rdonlyres/8C6B4B5B-D854-4F18-BA76-E0F687F2D60C/284274/Speech_10anniversary_Australia.pdf; e.g. within one year, between 11 October 2010 and 3 October 2011, VPRS received 5,676 applications for participation and 6,068 applications for reparations, see ICC-ASP/10/39, para 94.

6 See ICC *Prosecutor v Lubanga*, TC, ICC-01/04-01/06-2842, 14 March 2012, Judgment pursuant to Article 74 of the Statute, para 129; ICC *Prosecutor v Ngudjolo*, TC, ICC-01/04-01/12-3, 18 December 2012, Jugement rendu en application de l'article 74 du Statute, para 32; see also ICC *Prosecutor v Bemba*, TC, ICC-01/05-01/08-2140, 23 February 2012, Partly Dissenting Opinion of Judge Sylvia Steiner on the Decision on the supplemented applications by the legal representatives of victims to present evidence and the views and concerns of victims, para 22.

7 Victims' Rights and Working Group (2012). http://www.vrwg.org/documents/legal-update. (4,451 victims). Accessed 2 October 2012; see most recent decision: ICC *Prosecutor v Bemba*, TC, ICC-01/05-01/08-2219, 21 May 2012, Decision on 1400 applications by victims to participate in the proceedings.

3,866 civil parties are allowed to participate as a "consolidated group of civil parties".[8]

Yet, victim participation in criminal proceedings as envisaged by the Rome Statute is in many respects unique. It is also important to realise that the Court is still young and that to date a full cycle of judicial activities has not yet been concluded: only recently appeals were filed against the decisions of Trial Chamber I convicting Mr Lubanga Dyilo and sentencing him to 14 years of imprisonment.[9] Proceedings against nine accused are before four Trial Chambers and important questions relevant to victim participation have already been addressed by the Appeals Chamber of the Court.

The focus of this contribution is on Article 68 (3) of the Statute read in connection with rule 85 of the Rules of Procedure and Evidence (RPE), which has been given further effect by rules 89–92 RPE and regulation 86 Regulations of the Court (RoC).[10] The contribution intends to simply lay out the practice of the Court with respect to the application of those legal provisions. Other areas, such as reparation proceedings under Article 75 and appeals under Article 82 (4) of the Statute, the submission of representations pursuant to Article 15 (3), and of observations pursuant to Article 19 (3) of the Statute,[11] or the possible effect of rule 93 RPE, are not addressed.

12.1 Institutional Framework

The Court's legal texts require the establishment of a "Victims and Witnesses Unit" (VWU).[12] This section of the Registry deals with the protection of witnesses and victims.[13] It assesses the security situation whenever personal information about victims in proceedings before the Court needs to be protected, be it from the suspects or accused persons, the Prosecutor or the public. In the first proceedings before the Court, many victims were anonymous to the parties. However, victims in subsequent proceedings were often only protected from the public. Generally, victims are

[8] See ECCC *Case of Nuon et al.*, TC, Case File 002/19-09-2007/ECCC/TC, 28 June 2011, Transcript of Initial Hearing, p. 117 (3.850 Civil Parties); latest VSS Press statement refers to 3.866 Civil Parties, http://www.eccc.gov.kh/en/articles/seventh-regional-forum-350-civil-parties-case-002-be-organized-kampong-thom. Accessed on 29 March 2012.

[9] See rule 150 (1) RPE.

[10] The Regulations of the Court deal with the "routine functioning" of the Court and were adopted by a plenary session of the judges on 26 May 2004 (ICC-BD/01-02-07).

[11] See Articles 15 (3), 19 (3) of the Statute and rules 50, 59 RPE and regulation 87 RoC; for the application of Article 15 (3) of the Statute, see also ICC *Prosecutor v Kony et al.*, ICC-02/04-01/05-252, PTC, 10 August 2007, Decision on victims' applications for participation a/0010/06, a/0064/06 to a/0070/06, a/0081/06 to a/0104/06 and a/0111/06 to a/0127/06, para 93.

[12] Article 43 (6) of the Statute, rules 17–19 RPE.

[13] See Dubuisson et al. 2009, p. 573.

referred to by numbers,[14] except when they give testimony before the Trial Chamber. Victims are also usually not present in the courtroom or the public gallery. When comparing the visibility of victims at the ICC to that of civil parties at the ECCC, the difference is apparent: At the ECCC, where the alleged crimes took place nearly 40 years ago, except for a negligible number, civil parties are referred to by name and sit wherever they can in the courtroom or the public gallery during trial.

Based on rule 16 RPE and regulation 86 (9) RoC, the Victims Participation and Reparations Section (VPRS) deals with matters relevant to the participation of victims in proceedings and with reparations. This section is responsible, with the assistance of interlocutors, for developing and distributing the Court's application forms to victims in regions where the Court is exercising its jurisdiction. Importantly, VPRS is the channel through which applications for participation and reparations reach the relevant Chamber of the Court. In carrying out its functions, VPRS must work in close cooperation with the other sections of the Registry, especially the VWU, and the section dealing with counsel.[15]

The Office of Public Counsel for victims ("OPCV") is administratively within the Registry, but independent in its functioning. It is tasked with representing victims in criminal proceedings and with providing legal advice where requested, e.g. by legal representatives of victims. The OPCV was established by the judges by means of the Regulations of the Court at the same time as the Office for Public Counsel for the Defence (OPCD).[16] Since, the OPCV has focused their legal representation on unrepresented applicants, including in reparation proceedings, victims at early stages of the proceedings or those with dual status.[17] However, recently, the Chambers have more frequently requested the appointment of an OPCV counsel as common legal representative.[18] Counsel of the OPCV may also be appointed to represent legal representatives in the proceedings when the latter are unable to attend. The OPCV provides legal advice to victims and their legal

---

[14] The number indicates the year in which the person applied to be a victim and a number that is given according to the order of applications received in relation to any proceedings before the Court.

[15] The names of the sections are subject to regular change, as they carry out functions assigned to the Registrar/Registry by the Statute, the Rules and the Regulations of the Court. Currently (August 2012), those sections are called "Victims and Witnesses Section" and "Counsel Support Section". Their functions are in more detail described in the Regulations of the Registry; see e.g. regulations 79–96 for the Victims and Witnesses Section and regulations 119–142 and 112, 113 for the Counsel Support Section. The tasks of the VPRS are detailed in regulations 97–111.

[16] Massidda and Pellet 2009, p. 692.

[17] See ICC Assembly of State Parties, ICC-ASP/10/39, 18 November 2011, para 95, wherein it was reported that the OPCV represented 2119 victims as per October 2011.

[18] ICC *Prosecutor v Gbagbo*, PTC, ICC-02/11-01/11-138, 4 June 2012, Decision on Victims' Participation and Victims' Common Legal Representation at the Confirmation of Charges Hearing and in the Related Proceedings, paras 43, 44.

representatives,[19] not least by having established an extensive manual on the victim-related jurisprudence of the Court.[20]

12.2 Application Process

Before getting into the depths of victim participation, the use of terminology requires attention. The Statute and the Rules do not differentiate between victims who are applying to participate in the proceedings and victims who are allowed to participate in the proceedings. They use the term "victim" interchangeably. However, as this contribution focuses on the rights of victims who are participating in the proceedings, the term "applicant" has been introduced in order to differentiate the victim applicant from the victim who is allowed to participate.[21]

The application process developed from an "unknown" factor to a process that is based on a set of jurisprudence that can be considered the "practice" of Pre-Trial and Trial Chambers. It is based on rule 89 RPE which provides: "In order to present their views and concerns, victims shall make written application to the Registrar, who shall transmit the application to the relevant Chamber".[22] Details are addressed in regulation 86 RoC and the Regulations of the Registry.

Regulation 86 (1) RoC stipulates that standard forms should be made available and used by victims, to the extent possible. The VPRS is primarily in charge of creating, subject to the approval of the Presidency,[23] and disseminating such forms. Recently, Pre-Trial Chambers requested or encouraged the dissemination of collective application forms.[24] Dissemination requires the assistance of other relevant sections of the Court, as this happens primarily from the field offices of the Court.[25] The Court also disseminates the forms to

---

[19] See ICC *Prosecutor v Bemba*, TC, ICC-01/05-01/08-1005, 10 November 2010, Decision on common legal representation of victims for the purpose of trial, para 29.

[20] http://www.icc-cpi.int/iccdocs/PIDS/tmp/Representing%20Victims%20before%20ICC.PDF.

[21] Decisions of nearly every Chamber dealing currently with victims also refer to the use of terminology in their decisions, see ICC *Prosecutor v Bemba*, PTC, ICC-01/05-01/08-320, 12 December 2008, Fourth Decision on Victims' Participation, para 20; ICC *Situation in Uganda,* PTC, ICC-02/04-191, Decision on Victim's Participation in Proceedings Related to the Situation in Uganda, para 13.

[22] Rule 89 (1) RPE.

[23] Regulation 23 (2) RoC.

[24] ICC *Prosecutor v. Gbagbo*, PTC, ICC-02/11-01/11-33, 6 February 2012, Decision on issues related to the victims' application process; Registry, ICC-02/11-01/11-45, 29 February 2012, Proposal on partly collective application form for victims' participation; ICC-02/11-01/11-86, 5 April 2012, Second decision on issues related to the victims' application process; ICC *Situation in Uganda,* PTC, ICC-02/04-191, 9 March 2012, Decision on Victim's Participation in Proceedings Related to the Situation in Uganda, para 22.

[25] See also regulations 104, 105 of the Regulations of the Registry.

interlocutors in the field, such as non-governmental organisations that have direct access to the victims.[26]

The process of outreach to the victims in the communities where the alleged crimes were committed is of utmost importance. While this is not primarily a concern of the judicial branch of the Court, the outreach to those communities is a task of the Court and a concern to the entire state community, as confirmed at the 2010 Review Conference relevant to the Court,[27] as well as at the recent tenth Assembly of States Parties.[28]

The standard forms require a great deal of information from applicants. The required content is stipulated in regulation 86 (2) RoC. The Chambers have confirmed that the following information is essential: (i) the identity of the applicant, (ii) the date of the crime(s), (iii) the location of the crime(s), (iv) a description of the harm suffered as a result of the commission of a crime, (v) proof of identity, (vi) if the application is made by a person acting with the consent of the victim, the express consent of the victim; (vii) if the application is made by a person acting on behalf of a victim, in the case of a victim who is a child, proof of kinship or legal guardianship; or in the case of a victim who is disabled, proof of legal guardianship and; (viii) a signature or thumbprint of the applicant on the document.[29] VPRS is responsible for verifying the completeness of the applications and requesting further information should it be necessary,[30] e.g. from states, the Prosecutor or non-governmental organisations.[31] Most importantly, VPRS submits the applications to the Chamber together with a

---

[26] See ICC *Prosecutor v Bemba*, TC, ICC-01/05-01/08-1590-Corr, 9 March 2012, Decision on 471 applications by victims to participate in the proceedings, paras 26–30, stipulating the implications interlocutors may have on the applications process of victims they contacted.

[27] Resolution RC/Res. 2, The impact of the Rome Statute system on victims and affected communities reads at No. 2: "Further encourages the Court, in dialogue with victims and affected communities, to continue to optimize the Court's strategic planning process, including the Court's Strategy in relation to victims, as well as its field presence in order to improve the way in which it addresses the concerns of victims and affected communities, paying special attention to the needs of women and children."; see also Bitti 2011.

[28] ICC-ASP/10/20, Preamble, para 17.

[29] ICC *Prosecutor v Muthaura et al.*, PTC, ICC-01/09-02/11-23, 12 August 2011, Decision on the Extension of Time Limit to File Observations on Victims' Applications for Participation in the Proceedings, para 19; ICC *Prosecutor v Bemba*, PTC, ICC-01/05-01/08-320, 12 December 2008, Fourth Decision on Victims' Participation, para 81; ICC *Situation in Darfur*, PTC, ICC-02/05-110, 3 December 2007, Decision on the Requests of the OPCD on the Production of Relevant Supporting Documentation Pursuant to Regulation 86(2) (e) of the Regulations of the Court and on the Disclosure of Exculpatory Materials by the Prosecutor, para 16; see also ICC *Prosecutor v Kony et al.*, AC, ICC-02/04-179 OA, 23 February 2009, Judgment; ICC *Prosecutor v Kony et al.*, AC, ICC-02/04-01/05-371 OA 2, 23 February 2009, Judgment.

[30] See regulation 86 (4) RoC; see also ICC *Prosecutor v Muthaura et al.*, PTC, ICC-01/09-02/11-23, 12 August 2011, Decision on the Extension of Time Limit to File Observations on Victims' Applications for Participation in the Proceedings, para 18; ICC *Situation in Uganda*, PTC, ICC-02/04-191, 9 March 2012, Decision on Victim's Participation in Proceedings Related to the Situation in Uganda, para 24.

[31] Regulation 86 (4) RoC.

report on the applications and has the obligation to "endeavour to present one report for a group of victims".[32] VPRS may also submit periodic reports.[33] The organisation of the report in each specific case is subject to the Chambers' orders. The Chambers regularly request VPRS to carry out an initial assessment of whether the applicants are victims according to rule 85 RPE and whether they fall within specific groups with common interests.[34] In recent proceedings, the Chambers have proactively informed VPRS as to their specific requirements in relation to the report. They requested, e.g., that VPRS includes "one paragraph for each victim which reflects the information contained in the application analysed in respect of each of the requirements of rule 85 of the Rules".[35] Considering the importance of the task of VPRS, it is not surprising that the Chambers are also concerned with its organisation, which is demonstrated by, e.g. requiring a representative of VPRS in the field "in particular with a view to assess[ing] the completeness of victim applications within the time limit provided".[36]

The Chambers have different approaches to whether there should be time limits for victims to apply to participate in proceedings. Pre-Trial Chamber II in the cases arising from the Kenya situation and Pre-Trial Chamber III in *Prosecutor v. Bemba*, for example, set a strict deadline after which victims could not apply to participate in the confirmation hearing.[37] Regulation 86 (3) RoC stipulates that applications before the Trial and Appeals Chamber should, "to the extent possible", be filed before the start of the trial or appeal. Nevertheless, the Trial Chambers generally have allowed victims to apply to participate throughout the trial, leading to a situation where victims have continuously joined the proceedings in all ongoing trials. Only recently have the Trial Chambers started to take various measures with a view to limiting the filing of applications.[38]

---

[32] Regulation 86 (5) RoC.

[33] Regulation 86 (6) RoC.

[34] See ICC *Prosecutor v Muthaura et al.*, PTC, ICC-01/09-02/11-23, 12 August 2011, Decision on the Extension of Time Limit to File Observations on Victims' Applications for Participation in the Proceedings, paras 17–21, 24.

[35] ICC *Prosecutor v Muthaura et al.*, PTC, ICC-01/09-02/11-23, 12 August 2011, Decision on the Extension of Time Limit to File Observations on Victims' Applications for Participation in the Proceedings, para 21; see also ICC *Situation in Uganda,* PTC, ICC-02/04-191, 9 March 2012, Decision on Victim's Participation in Proceedings Related to the Situation in Uganda, para 27.

[36] ICC *Prosecutor v Muthaura et al.*, PTC, ICC-01/09-02/11-23, 12 August 2011, Decision on the Extension of Time Limit to File Observations on Victims' Applications for Participation in the Proceedings, para 25.

[37] ICC *Prosecutor v Muthaura et al.*, PTC, ICC-01/09-02/11-23, 12 August 2011, Decision on the Extension of Time Limit to File Observations on Victims' Applications for Participation in the Proceedings, paras 11, 17; ICC *Prosecutor v Bemba*, PTC, ICC-01/05-01/08-320, 12 December 2008, Fourth Decision on Victims' Participation, para 23.

[38] ICC *Prosecutor v Bemba*, TC, ICC-01/05-01/08-1590-Corr, 9 March 2012, Decision on 471 applications by victims to participate in the proceedings, para 25; ICC *Prosecutor v Lubanga,* TC, ICC-01/04-01/06-2838, 27 January 2012, Order on the applications by victims to participate and for reparations.

In the early jurisprudence of the Pre-Trial Chambers, victims were afforded the "status of victims". This status did not need to relate to concrete judicial proceedings that could arise during the investigation/situation stage. Instead, this status gave the impression that victims had an abstract interest at this early stage in any Court activities, including in the investigation of the Prosecutor.[39] Since the Appeals Chamber quashed this approach of the Pre-Trial Chambers but did confirm that victims can participate in judicial proceedings at the situation stage,[40] the Pre-Trial Chambers require VPRS to make the necessary preparations that would enable VPRS to submit the applications to the Chamber should judicial proceedings arise at the early pre-trial phases. In other words, presently VPRS has a duty to process every application that it receives in order to bring it before the relevant Chamber when judicial proceedings arise.[41]

After having received the applications, the relevant Chamber is required, pursuant to rule 89 (2) RPE, to "provide a copy of the application to the Prosecutor and the defence, who shall be entitled to reply within a time limit to be set by the Chamber".[42] Often, the Chamber first must issue the necessary protection decisions, order redactions and can only then submit redacted applications to the parties for comment.[43] The redactions should be kept to a minimum in order to allow the par-

---

[39] ICC *Situation in the Democratic Republic of the Congo,* PTC, ICC-01/04-101, 17 January 2006, Decision on the Applications for Participation in the Proceedings of VPRS 1, VPRS 2, VPRS 3, VPRS 4, VPRS 5 and VPRS 6, paras 51, 54, 55–67; further in relation to the early jurisprudence: Miraglia 2006; De Hemptinne and Rindi 2006; Stahn et al. 2006; Greco 2007; Chung 2008; Guhr 2008.

[40] ICC *Situation in Darfur,* AC, ICC-02/05-177 OA OA 2 OA 3, 02 February 2009, Judgment on victim participation in the investigation stage of the proceedings in the appeal of the OPCD against the decision of Pre-Trial Chamber I of 3 December 2007 and in the appeals of the OPCD and the Prosecutor against the decision of Pre-Trial Chamber I of 6 December 2007; ICC *Situation in the Democratic Republic of the Congo*, AC, ICC-01/04-556 OA 4 OA 5 OA 6, 19 December 2008, Judgment on victim participation in the investigation stage of the proceedings in the appeal of the OPCD against the decision of Pre-Trial Chamber I of 7 December 2007 and in the appeals of the OPCD and the Prosecutor against the decision of Pre-Trial Chamber I of 24 December 2007; see ICC *Situation in Uganda,* PTC, ICC-02/04-191, 9 March 2012, Decision on Victim's Participation in Proceedings Related to the Situation in Uganda, para 10.

[41] ICC *Situation in the Republic of Kenya,* PTC, ICC-01/09-24, 3 November 2010, Decision on Victims' Participation in Proceedings Related to the Situation in the Republic of Kenya, paras 18–21; ICC *Situation in the Democratic Republic of the Congo,* PTC, ICC-01/04-593, 11 April 2011, Decision on victims' participation in proceedings relating to the situation in the Democratic Republic of the Congo, paras 11–18; see also in this context, ICC-ASP/10/20, para 49.

[42] Rule 89 (1) RPE.

[43] See ICC *Prosecutor v Muthaura et al.*, PTC, ICC-01/09-02/11-267, 26 August 2011, Decision on Victims' Participation at the Confirmation of Charges Hearing and in the Related Proceedings, para 22; this is an recurrent issue, as the Defence and the Prosecutor often argue that they are impeded from making meaningful observations; see recently ICC *Prosecution v Bemba,* TC, ICC-01/05-01/08-2158, 6 March 2012, Order on the implementation of Decision on the supplemented applications by the legal representatives of victims to present evidence and the views and concerns of victims.

ties to submit meaningful observations.[44] The VPRS report is, however, not as such notified or disclosed to the parties.[45]

12.3 Assessment of Victims' Applications

While VPRS recently began to assess applications on a preliminary basis, the relevant chamber needs to decide whether the applicant is a victim according to the terms of rule 85 RPE that reads:

> For the purposes of the Statute and the Rules of Procedure and Evidence:
>
> (a) "Victims" means natural persons who have suffered harm as a result of the commission of any crime within the jurisdiction of the Court;
> (b) Victims may include organisations or institutions that have sustained direct harm to any of their property which is dedicated to religion, education, art or science or charitable purposes, and to their historic monuments, hospitals and other places and objects for humanitarian purposes.

The interpretation of rule 85 RPE has changed considerably since the start of ICC proceedings, not least due to a number of landmark decisions. This has led to today's rather uniform approach of the Pre-Trial and Trial Chambers to the interpretation of this norm.

In determining the required standard for proving that an applicant is a victim, the Pre-Trial and Trial Chambers have held that there is broad discretion in assessing the soundness of a given application.[46] They consider an application successful if it shows an intrinsic coherence of the alleged facts.[47] All Chambers agree that any determination of whether the person is allowed to participate in proceedings as a

---

[44] ICC *Prosecutor v Lubanga,* TC, ICC-01/04-01/06-1556-Corr-Anx1, 15 December 2008, Decision on the applications by victims to participate in the proceedings, paras 129–133; ICC *Prosecutor v Bemba*, TC, ICC-01/05-01/08-1590-Corr, 12 July 2011, Corrigendum to the Decision on 401 applications by victims to participate in the proceedings and setting a final deadline for the submission of new victims' applications to the Registry, paras 31–34; ICC *Prosecutor v Bemba,* TC, ICC-01/05-01/08-2162, 9 March 2012, Decision on 471 applications by victims to participate in the proceedings.

[45] ICC *Prosecutor v Lubanga*, TC, ICC-01/04-01/06-1022, 9 November 2007, Decision on the implementation of the reporting system between the Registrar and the Trial Chamber in accordance with Rule 89 and Regulation of the Court 86(5), para 25; ICC *Prosecutor v Al-Bashir,* PTC, ICC-02/05-01/09-62, 10 December 2009, Decision on Applications a/0011/06 to a/0013/06, a/0015/06 and a/0443/09 to a/0450/09 for Participation in the Proceedings at the Pre-Trial Stage of the Case, paras 16–18; ICC *Situation in the Democratic Republic of the Congo,* PTC, ICC-01/04-374, 17 August 2007, Decision on the Requests of the Legal Representative of Applicants on application process for victims' participation and legal representation, paras 35, 36, 38.

[46] See ICC *Prosecutor v Bemba*, PTC, ICC-01/05-01/08-320, 12 December 2008, Fourth Decision on Victims' Participation, para 31.

[47] ICC *Prosecutor v Bemba*, PTC, ICC-01/05-01/08-320, 12 December 2008, Fourth Decision on Victims' Participation, para 23; ICC *Prosecutor v Gbagbo*, PTC, ICC-02/11-01/11-138, 4 June 2012, Decision on Victims' Participation and Victims' Common Legal Representation at the Confirmation of Charges Hearing and in the Related Proceedings, para 21.

victim of the crimes is carried out on a *prima facie* basis.[48] In this context, it needs to be mentioned that Trial Chamber I, on the basis of the evidence before it at the end of the trail, decided that nine victims, who had also given testimony were not victims of the crimes committed by Mr Lubanga Dyilo.[49]

12.3.1 The Applicant's Identity as a Natural Person

It is often difficult to sufficiently prove the identity of an applicant due to missing identity cards and the general situation in the states in which the Court exercises its jurisdiction. The Chambers overcame this hurdle by requesting reports from VPRS as to the types of identification documents and other official documentation available to persons in a specific country. While the preferred forms of proof of identity were passports, national identity cards, birth certificates or driver's licences, the Pre-Trial Chamber in the Kenyan situation considered it sufficient to receive, e.g. a National ID Waiting Card or a Chiefs Identification Letter which provided information about the full name, date and place of birth, and gender of the applicant and was signed and officially stamped by the Cheif. The Chamber also accepted, e.g., birth cards, clinic cards and a Kenyan Police Abstract Form.[50] Depending on the country, possible forms of identification vary.[51] If none of these documents could be produced, some Chambers have also accepted a declaration signed by two witnesses attesting to the identity of the applicant.[52]

Where application are filed on behalf of another person, proof of identity needs to be established for both, the person applying and the applicant on whose behalf the person is applying.[53]

---

[48] ICC *Prosecutor v Lubanga*, TC, ICC-01/04-01/06-1119, 18 January 2008, Decision on victims' participation, para 99; TC, ICC-01/04-01/06-2764-Red, 25 July 2011, Redacted version of the Decision on the applications by 7 victims to participate in the proceedings, para 23; ICC *Prosecutor v Harun and Abd-Al-Rahman*, PTC, ICC-02/05-01/07-58, 17 June 2010, Decision on 6 Applications for Victims' Participation in the Proceedings, para 7; ICC *Prosecutor v Gbagbo*, PTC, ICC-02/11-01/11-138, 4 June 2012, Decision on Victims' Participation and Victims' Common Legal Representation at the Confirmation of Charges Hearing and in the Related Proceedings, para 21.

[49] ICC *Prosecutor v Lubanga,* TC, ICC-01/04-01/06-2842, 14 March 2012, Judgment pursuant to Article 74 of the Statute, paras 1362, 1363; see ICC *Prosecutor v Ngudjolo*, TC, ICC-01/04-01/12-3, 18 December 2012, Jugement rendu en application de I'article 74 du statut, para 32.

[50] ICC *Prosecutor v Muthaura et al.*, PTC, ICC-01/09-02/11-23, 12 August 2011, Decision on the Extension of Time Limit to File Observations on Victims' Applications for Participation in the Proceedings, para 9.

[51] See ICC *Prosecutor v Bemba*, PTC, ICC-01/05-01/08-320, 12 December 2008, Fourth Decision on Victims' Participation, paras 36, 37; see ICC *Prosecutor v Bemba,* TC, ICC-01/05-01/08-1017, 15 December 2011, Decision on 418 applications by victims to participate in the proceedings, para 36.

[52] ICC *Prosecutor v Lubanga*, TC, ICC-01/04-01/06-1119, 18 January 2008, Decision on victims' participation, para 88.

[53] ICC *Prosecutor v Bemba*, PTC, ICC-01/05-01/08-320, 12 December 2008, Fourth Decision on Victims' Participation, paras 14, 38.

It is noteworthy that Chambers had different approaches as to whether deceased heirs could "participate" (through their heir) in the proceedings as victims.[54] Pre-Trial Chamber II and Trial Chamber II rejected this concept and found that persons can apply only for the harm they have suffered as indirect victims (e.g. because of the death of the direct victim).[55] However, Pre-Trial Chamber III and Trial Chamber III allowed, under certain conditions, "participation" of deceased victims.[56] The situation is somewhat different if a victim dies in the course of trial proceedings. In such a situation, Trial Chamber II permitted close relatives to continue participating in the proceedings.[57]

12.3.2 An Organisation as an Applicant

Where an organisation applies to participate in the proceedings as a victim, the constitutive documents of the organisation, in accordance with the law of the country in which the organisation had its place, need to be produced. Further, the organisation needs to show that the person acting on behalf of that organisation indeed has the right to make such a request. With respect to that person, the same requirements of proof of identification as for natural persons apply.[58]

[54] See Bachvarova 2011, pp. 672–682.

[55] ICC *Prosecutor v Muthaura et al.*, PTC, ICC-01/09-02/11-267, 26 August 2011, Decision on Victims' Participation at the Confirmation of Charges Hearing and in the Related Proceedings, paras 49–57; see ICC *Prosecutor v Katanga and Chui*, TC, ICC-01/04-01/07-1737, 22 December 2009, Motifs de la deuxième décision relative aux demandes de participation de victimes à la procédure, para 30.

[56] ICC *Prosecutor v Bemba*, PTC, ICC-01/05-01/08-320, 12 December 2008, Fourth Decision on Victims' Participation, paras 39–51.

[57] ICC *Prosecutor v Katanga and Chui,* TC, ICC-01/04-01/07-3018, 14 June 2011, Décision relative aux demandes de reprise d'instance formées par les proches des victimes décédées a/0025/08, a/0051/08, a/0197/08 et a/0311/09, para 20; see also ICC *Prosecutor v Katanga and Chui,* TC, ICC-01/04-01/07-3185-Corr-tENG, 21 October 2011, Décision relative aux demandes de reprise d'instance formées par les proches des victimes décédées a/0025/08 et a/0311/09.

[58] ICC *Prosecutor v Bemba*, PTC, ICC-01/05-01/08-320, 12 December 2008, Fourth Decision on Victims' Participation, paras 53–56; ICC *Prosecutor v Lubanga*, TC, ICC-01/04-01/06-1119, 18 January 2008, Decision on victims' participation, para 89; School accepted as a victim in ICC *DRC Situation,* PTC, ICC-01/04-42-Corr, 31 January 2008, Corrigendum to the 'Decision on the Applications for Participation Filed in Connection with the Investigation in the Democratic Republic of the Congo by a/0004/06 to a/0009/06, a/0016/06 to a/0063/06, a/0071/06 to a/0080/06 and a/0105/06 to a/0110/06, a/0188/06, a/0128/06 to a/0162/06, a/0199/06, a/0203/06, a/0209/06, a/0214/06, a/0220/06 to a/0222/06, a/0224/06, a/0227/06 to a/0230/06, a/0234/06 to a/0236/06, a/0240/06, a/0225/06, a/0226/06, a/0231/06 to a/0233/06, a/0237/06 to a/0239/06 and a/0241/06 to a/0250/06, paras 142, 143; Nigerian Army rejected as a victim in ICC *Prosecutor v Banda and Jerbo*, PTC, ICC-02/05-03/09-89, 29 October 2010, Decision on Victims' Participation at the Hearing on the Confirmation of the Charges, paras 41–54.

12.3.3 Harm Suffered

Applicants also need to prove that they have suffered harm. The concept of harm encompasses physical injury, emotional suffering and economic loss.[59] According to rule 85 RPE, the harm must be personal, meaning that the applicant him/herself suffered harm.[60]

The Appeals Chamber held that "[h]arm suffered by one victim as a result of the commission of a crime within the jurisdiction of the Court can give rise to harm suffered by other victims".[61] The concept of indirect victims has therefore been acknowledged by the Court.[62] What is the standard of proof for indirect victims? Pre-Trial Chamber II found that "emotional harm may be claimed by an immediate family member of the direct victim, only insofar as the relationship between them has been sufficiently established."[63] Consequently any person claiming to have suffered harm under this category must show sufficient proof of the existence of the victim and sufficient proof of kinship with the victim.[64] The proof of kinship is necessary in order to allow the Chamber to assume that the person has indeed suffered because of the death or physical or psychological injury of a close relative. Proof of the harm, as such, will often be impossible, especially in countries where medical and psychological treatment are not available or affordable. Kinship therefore assists the judges in assuming that a person suffered (often psychological) harm because of

---

59 ICC *Prosecutor v Muthaura et al.*, PTC, ICC-01/09-02/11-267, 26 August 2011, Decision on Victims' Participation at the Confirmation of Charges Hearing and in the Related Proceedings, para 64.

60 ICC *Prosecutor v Lubanga,* AC, ICC-01/04-01/06-1432 OA 9 OA 10, 11 July 2008, Judgment on the appeals of The Prosecutor and The Defence against Trial Chamber I's Decision on Victims' Participation of 18 January 2008, paras 32, 37; see ICC *Prosecutor v Muthaura et al.*, PTC, ICC-01/09-02/11-267, 26 August 2011, Decision on Victims' Participation at the Confirmation of Charges Hearing and in the Related Proceedings, para 67.

61 ICC *Prosecutor v Lubanga,* AC, ICC-01/04-01/06-1432 OA 9 OA 10, 11 July 2008, Judgment on the appeals of The Prosecutor and The Defence against Trial Chamber I's Decision on Victims' Participation of 18 January 2008, para 32; see also the dissenting opinion of Judge Pikis, p. 38, para 3, who states that there "must be a direct nexus between the crime and the harm, in the sense of cause and effect, […] the crime itself must be the cause generating the harm, as may be the case with the destruction, violation or humiliation of persons near and dear to the victims"; see also ICC *Prosecutor v Lubanga*, TC, ICC-01/04-01/06-1119, 18 January 2008, Decision on victims' participation, para 91.

62 ICC *Prosecutor v Lubanga*, TC, ICC-01/04-01/06-1119, 18 January 2008, Decision on victims' participation, para 91.

63 ICC *Prosecutor v Muthaura et al.*, PTC, ICC-01/09-02/11-267, 26 August 2011, Decision on Victims' Participation at the Confirmation of Charges Hearing and in the Related Proceedings, para 69; based on ICC *Situation in Uganda,* AC, ICC-02/04-179 OA, 23 February 2009, Judgment on the appeals of the Defence against the decisions entitled "Decision on victims' applications for participation a/0010/06, a/0064/06 to a/0070/06, a/0081/06, a/0082/06, a/0084/06 to a/0089/06, a/0091/06 to a/0097/06, a/0099/06, a/0100/06, a/0102/06 to a/0104/06, a/0111/06, a/0113/06 to a/0117/06, a/0120/06, a/0121/06 and a/0123/06 to a/0127/06" of Pre-Trial Chamber II.

64 ICC *Prosecutor v Bemba,* TC, ICC-01/05-01/08-1017, 18 November 2010, Decision on 772 applications by victims to participate in the proceedings, para 43.

the death or injury of a closely related person. The Appeals Chamber formulated that "[harm suffered by other victims] is evident for instance when there is a close personal relationship between the victims such as the relationship between a child soldier and the parents of that child".[65] Extensive, and in approach diverse, jurisprudence on this matter as well as generally on the link between the harm suffered and the charges is available at the ECCC.[66]

Another category of persons who might suffer harm because of an attack are those who are intervening to help victims or to prevent the latter from becoming victims.[67]

12.3.4 Link Between the Harm Suffered and the Crimes

Based on rule 85 RPE, it is required that the harm suffered be due to a crime which falls within the jurisdiction of the Court. This rather broadly worded rule has been interpreted by the Chambers as only allowing those victims who have suffered harm because of crimes which are the subject of the concrete proceedings to participate, e.g. in the confirmation hearing or at the trial.[68] The basis for this limitation is the following jurisprudence of the Appeals Chamber:

> Only victims of [the charged crimes] will be able to demonstrate that the trial, as such, affects their personal interests. Therefore, only victims who are victims of the crimes charged may participate in the trial proceedings pursuant to article 68 (3) of the Statute read with rule 85 and 89 (1) of the Rules.[69]
>
> It is for the Trial Chamber to determine within this framework whether an applicant is a victim, because he or she suffered harm in connection with the particular crimes charged, and if so, whether the personal interests of the applicant are affected. If the

[65] ICC *Prosecutor v Lubanga,* AC, ICC-01/04-01/06-1432 OA 9 OA 10, 11 July 2008, Judgment on the appeals of The Prosecutor and The Defence against Trial Chamber I's Decision on Victims' Participation of 18 January 2008, para 32.

[66] ECCC *Case of Nuon et al.*, PTC, Case File 002/19-09-2007/ECCC/OCIJ/PTC D404/2/4, 24 June 2011, Decision on Appeals Against Orders of the Co-Investigating Judges on the Admissibility of Civil Party Applications, and the dissenting opinion of Judge Marchi-Uhel; ECCC *Case of Kaing*, TC, Case File 001/18-07-2007/ECCC/TC E188, 26 July 2010, Judgement, paras 639–643; ECCC *Case of Kaing,* SC, Case File 001/18-07-2007/ECCC/SC F28, 3 February 2012, Appeal Judgement, paras 487–536.

[67] See ICC *Prosecutor v Muthaura et al.*, PTC, ICC-01/09-02/11-267, 26 August 2011, Decision on Victims' Participation at the Confirmation of Charges Hearing and in the Related Proceedings, para 68; ICC *Prosecutor v Gbagbo*, PTC, ICC-02/11-01/11-138, 4 June 2012, Decision on Victims' Participation and Victims' Common Legal Representation at the Confirmation of Charges Hearing and in the Related Proceedings, para 30.

[68] See ICC *Prosecutor v Mbarushimana,* PTC, ICC-01/04-01/10-351, 11 August 2011, Decision on the 138 applications for victims' participation in the proceedings, paras 21, 22; this criterion was disputed before TC I, see ICC *Prosecutor v Lubanga,* TC, ICC-01/04-01/06-1119, 18 January 2008, Decision on victims' participation. Partly dissenting opinion of Judge Blattmann at para 17.

[69] ICC *Prosecutor v Lubanga,* AC, ICC-01/04-01/06-1432 OA 9 OA 10, 11 July 2008, Judgment on the appeals of The Prosecutor and The Defence against Trial Chamber I's Decision on Victims' Participation of 18 January 2008, para 62.

> applicant is unable to demonstrate a link between the harm suffered and the particular crimes charged, then even if his or her personal interests are affected by an issue in the trial, it would not be appropriate under article 68 (3) read with rule 85 and 89 (1) of the Rules for his or her views and concerns to be presented.[70]

Therefore, a link is required between the harm suffered and the alleged/charged crimes that are subject of the concrete judicial proceedings in which the applicant wishes to participate.[71] This link needs to be established by means of proof. The Chambers have held that it is sufficient that it appears that the harm and the occurrence of the incident overlap.[72] In this context, it has been held that this needs to be viewed *ex post* by an objective observer.[73] The Chambers also prefer to receive rather detailed information about how the harm occurred, i.e. who was the alleged perpetrator, where precisely did the crime occur etc.[74]

12.4 Legal Representation

The organisation of the legal representation is of foremost concern to Pre-Trial and Trial Chambers. It is always based on rule 90 RPE. Often, victims who are applying to participate do not have counsel. In those cases, the Chambers consistently appoint the OPCV to represent the "unrepresented" applicants.[75] This representa-

---

[70] ICC *Prosecutor v Lubanga,* AC, ICC-01/04-01/06-1432 OA 9 OA 10, 11 July 2008, Judgment on the appeals of The Prosecutor and The Defence against Trial Chamber I's Decision on Victims' Participation of 18 January 2008, para 64.

[71] See ICC *Prosecutor v Muthaura et al.*, PTC, ICC-01/09-02/11-267, 26 August 2011, Decision on Victims' Participation at the Confirmation of Charges Hearing and in the Related Proceedings, para 60.

[72] ICC *Situation in Uganda*, PTC, ICC-02/04-101, 10 August 2007, Decision on victims' applications for participation a/0010/06, a/0064/06 to a/0070/06, a/0081/06 to a/0104/06 and a/0111/06 to a/0127/06, paras 13, 14; ICC *Prosecutor v Bemba*, PTC, ICC-01/05-01/08-320, 12 December 2008, Fourth Decision on Victims' Participation, para 75; ICC *Prosecutor v Kony et al.*, PTC, ICC-02/04-01/05-252, 10 August 2007, Decision on victims' applications for participation a/0010/06, a/0064/06 to a/0070/06, a/0081/06 to a/0104/06 and a/0111/06 to a/0127/06, para 14.

[73] ICC *Prosecutor v Bemba*, PTC, ICC-01/05-01/08-320, 12 December 2008, Fourth Decision on Victims' Participation, paras 31, 75.

[74] See e.g. ICC *Prosecutor v Muthaura et al.*, PTC, ICC-01/09-02/11-267, 26 August 2011, Decision on Victims' Participation at the Confirmation of Charges Hearing and in the Related Proceedings, paras 32, 33.

[75] ICC *Prosecutor v Muthaura et al.*, PTC, ICC-01/09-02/11-23, 30 March 2011, First Decision on Victims' Participation in the Case, para 23; see also as to the role of the Office, ICC *Prosecutor v Lubanga*, TC, ICC-01/04-01/06-1211, 6 March 2008, Decision on the role of the Office of Public Counsel for Victims and its request for access to documents, paras 30–41; ICC *Prosecutor v Banda and Jerbo,* TC, ICC-02/05-03/09-231-Corr, 3 January 2012, Request for extension of time to submit complete applications, para 28.

tion however ends as soon as the application for participation (or denied) and a common legal representative for this victim is appointed.

The Chambers are aware that finding and appointing common legal representation requires time and they usually give early directions to that effect.[76] Pre-Trial Chamber II, for example, requested VPRS very soon after the initial appearance of the suspects to "take appropriate steps with a view to organising common legal representation for the purposes of the confirmation of charges hearing" and "to group victims in the course of the assessments of victims' applications".[77]

Sub-rules (2) and (3) of rule 90 RPE do not establish criteria as to the process of appointing legal representative in a specific case. Accordingly, the approach of the Chambers to the matter differs. In the case of *Prosecutor v. Lubanga* (trial),[78] two, later three, groups of victims were represented by several legal representatives. In the case of *Prosecutor v. Bemba* (trial),[79] common legal representatives for essentially two groups of victims were appointed. Common legal representatives for (at least originally) one group were appointed in the cases of *Prosecutor v. Katanga and Chui* (trial, later two groups), *Prosecutor v. Muthaura et al.* (pre-trial), *Prosecutor v. Ruto et al.* (pre-trial), and *Prosecutor v Gbagbo* (pre-trial).[80] Reasons for appointing only one common legal representative included that the different victims have no "distinct interests" and that no problems relevant to a "conflict of interest" were expected.[81]

One of the biggest challenges for legal representatives at the Court is to establish an active connection with the victims who often reside in the situation state. Only such a relationship can ensure that the victims are heard in the proceedings.

---

[76] See ICC *Prosecutor v Lubanga*, TC, ICC-01/04-01/06-1556-Corr-Anxl, 15 December 2008, Decision on the applications by victims to participate in the proceedings, para 121; see also para 122.

[77] ICC *Prosecutor v Muthaura et al.*, PTC, ICC-01/09-02/11-23, 30 March 2011, First Decision on Victims' Participation in the Case, para 24.

[78] See ICC *Prosecutor v Lubanga*, TC, ICC-01/04-01/06-T-105-t-ENG, 22 January 2009, p. 12, line 23—p. 13, line 9; in addition, four individual victims were represented by the OPCV.

[79] ICC *Prosecutor v Bemba*, TC, ICC-01/05-01/08-1005, 10 November 2010, Decision on common legal representation of victims for the purpose of trial, para 21.

[80] See also ICC *Prosecutor v Katanga and Chui,* TC, ICC-01/04-01/07-1328, 22 July 2009, Order on the organisation of common legal representation of victims, para 13, however a number of child soldier victims was grouped differently; ICC *Prosecutor v Muthaura et al.*, PTC, ICC-01/09-02/11-267, 26 August 2011, Decision on Victims' Participation at the Confirmation of Charges Hearing and in the Related Proceedings, para 79; ICC *Prosecutor v Gbagbo*, PTC, ICC-02/11-01/11-138, 4 June 2012, Decision on Victims' Participation and Victims' Common Legal Representation at the Confirmation of Charges Hearing and in the Related Proceedings, para 40.

[81] See ICC *Prosecutor v Muthaura et al.*, PTC, ICC-01/09-02/11-267, 26 August 2011, Decision on Victims' Participation at the Confirmation of Charges Hearing and in the Related Proceedings, para 79.

The Chambers therefore require that the legal representatives or at least members of their team have a strong connection with the local situation of the victims and the region in general.[82] However, after appointment, there is usually little control as to how legal representatives connect with or are tasked by their clients. In addition, a mission to the situation state is costly and victims might reside in a variety of regions or states. Assistance by the Chambers and the Registry, as well as foresightful budgeting, might be of paramount importance in order to achieve the best possible involvement of the far-away victims in The Hague proceedings. This would also avoid the perception that Chambers address rights of legal representatives rather than rights of victims.

Other criteria in deciding on a common legal representative beyond the familiarity with the situation country are the following: a reasonable assurance that they will be available throughout the trial proceedings, and that they are experienced in representing a large number of victims. If possible, they should also know the case in question.[83]

The Court provides legal aid to the common legal representatives appointed by the Court (if the clients cannot afford the costs), but not for individual counsel, e.g. representing victims in the home country.[84]

12.5 New Stage of the Proceedings

Proceedings before the Court have different stages and the crimes that a Chamber deals with may change from stage to stage.[85] The question therefore arises of what

[82] It is an important requirement when choosing a legal representative that he or she has a strong connection with the local situation of the victims and the region in general; see e.g. ICC *Prosecutor v Katanga*, TC, ICC-01/04-01/07-1328, 22 July 2009, Order on the organisation of common legal representation of victims, paras 10a, 15; ICC *Prosecutor v Bemba*, TC, ICC-01/05-01/08-1005, 10 November 2010, Decision on common legal representation of victims for the purpose of trial, para 11; ICC *Prosecutor v Gbagbo*, PTC, ICC-02/11-01/11-138, 4 June 2012, Decision on Victims' Participation and Victims' Common Legal Representation at the Confirmation of Charges Hearing and in the Related Proceedings, paras 39, 43, 44.

[83] ICC *Prosecutor v Bemba*, TC, ICC-01/05-01/08-1005, 10 November 2010, Decision on common legal representation of victims for the purpose of tria, paras 10, 12.

[84] See ICC *Prosecutor v Muthaura et al.*, PTC, ICC-01/09-02/11-267, 26 August 2011, Decision on Victims' Participation at the Confirmation of Charges Hearing and in the Related Proceedings, paras 92, 93; ICC *Prosecutor v* Bemba, TC, ICC-01/05-01/08-1005, 10 November 2010, Decision on common legal representation of victims for the purpose of trial, para 25.

[85] Apart from the pre-trial, trial and appeals stage, there are different stages in pre-trial proceedings (i.e. judicial proceedings before and after the issuance of an arrest warrant/summons to appear and the confirmation hearing stage, and there might be different stages on trial (hearing relevant to guilt or innocence and sentencing). Reparation proceedings are not considered in this contribution. See also ICC *Situation in the Republic of Kenya,* PTC, ICC-01/09-24, 03 November 2010, Decision on Victims' Participation in Proceedings Related to the Situation in the Republic of Kenya, paras 9–16.

occurs if the proceedings move from one stage to the other, e.g. when charges have been confirmed and the case is referred to a Trial Chamber.[86]

It is the practice of the Trial Chambers, based upon regulation 86 (8) RoC, to allow victims who were already participating during the confirmation hearing to continue participating in the trial. Such participation is only subject to review by the Trial Chamber.[87] The review (based on a VPRS report) focuses on excluding those victims who allegedly suffered harm that "was not *prima facie*, the result of the commission of at least one crime within the charges confirmed by the Pre-Trial Chamber".[88] The Trial Chambers also reconsider applications if they were incomplete or if new information emerged in the meantime.[89]

The Trial Chambers require VPRS to transmit only the applications "that appear, prima facie, to be linked with the charges confirmed against the accused".[90] Applications relating to other charges are not considered by a Trial Chamber.

The Trial Chambers also render new or complementary decisions relevant to the common legal representation of the victims under rule 90 RPE, but, until that time, the decisions of the Pre-Trial Chambers on legal representation would usually remain in force.[91]

---

[86] The first cases moved only recently from the trial to the appeals stage. The first decision of the Appeals Chamber on this subject is:ICC *Prosecutor v Lubanga,* AC, ICC-01/04-01/06-2951, 13 December 2012, Decision on the participation of victims in the appeals against Trial Chamber I's conviction and sentencing decisions.

[87] See ICC *Prosecutor v Katanga and Chui,* TC, ICC-01/04-01/07-1491-Red, 23 September 2009, Grounds for the Decision on the 345 Applications for Participation in the Proceedings Submitted by Victims, paras 17, 18; ICC *Prosecutor v Bemba*, TC, ICC-01/05-01/08-699, 22 February 2010, Decision defining the status of 54 victims who participated at the pre-trial stage, and inviting the parties' observations on applications for participation by 86 applicants, paras 17–20; but see ICC *Prosecutor v Lubanga*, TC, ICC-01/04-01/06-1119, 18 January 2008, Decision on victims' participation, para 112 deciding anew.

[88] ICC *Prosecutor v Bemba*, TC, ICC-01/05-01/08-699, 22 February 2010, Decision defining the status of 54 victims who participated at the pre-trial stage, and inviting the parties' observations on applications for participation by 86 applicants; ICC *Prosecutor v Banda and Jerbo,* TC, ICC-02/05-03/09-231-Corr, 3 January 2012, Request for extension of time to submit complete applications, para 16.

[89] ICC *Prosecutor v Banda and Jerbo,* TC, ICC-02/05-03/09-231-Corr, 3 January 2012, Request for extension of time to submit complete applications, para 16.

[90] ICC *Prosecutor v Bemba*, TC, ICC-01/05-01/08-699, 22 February 2010, Decision defining the status of 54 victims who participated at the pre-trial stage, and inviting the parties' observations on applications for participation by 86 applicants, para 35; ICC *Prosecutor v Banda and Jerbo,* TC, ICC-02/05-03/09-231-Corr, 3 January 2012, Request for extension of time to submit complete applications, paras 19, 20.

[91] See ICC *Prosecutor v Bemba,* TC, ICC-01/05-01/08-651, 28 January 2010, Decision on the observations on legal representation of unrepresented applicants; see also ICC *Prosecutor v Muthaura*, AC.

12.6 The Practice of Victim Participation

Participation of victims in criminal proceedings is based on the wording of Article 68 (3) of the Statute:

> Where the personal interests of the victims are affected, the Court shall permit their views and concerns to be presented and considered at stages of the proceedings determined to be appropriate by the Court and in a manner which is not prejudicial to or inconsistent with the rights of the accused and a fair and impartial trial. Such views and concerns may be presented by the legal representatives of the victims where the Court considers it appropriate, in accordance with the Rules of Procedure and Evidence.

It has fallen to the Court, through developing its jurisprudence to clarify what "personal interests" are, when participation is "appropriate", and what is meant by "views and concerns". The early jurisprudence, of the Court as well as commentators, focused on the proper definition of "personal interests", as it is the first criterion that needs to be fulfilled pursuant to Article 68 (3) of the Statute.[92] "Personal interests" of victims are considered to be an interest in reparations and in protection,[93] both clearly laid down in the Statute, or even an interest to "see[ing] justice being done".[94] With respect to the establishment of the facts, Chambers have held that victims may have an interest in contributing to the

[92] See Vasiliev 2009, pp. 653–663; ICC *Prosecutor v Lubanga*, AC, ICC-01/04-01/06-925 OA 8, 13 June 2007, Decision of the Appeals Chamber on the Joint Application of Victims a/0001/06 to a/0003/06 and a/0105/06 concerning the "Directions and Decision of the Appeals Chamber" of 2 February 2007, paras 23–29, separate opinion of Judge Pikis, p. 18, paras 13, 14.

[93] ICC *Prosecutor v Katanga and Chui,* TC, ICC-01/04-01/07-1788, 22 January 2010, Decision on the Modalities of Victim Participation at Trial, para 59; ICC *Prosecutor v Lubanga*, TC, ICC-01/04-01/06-1119, 18 January 2008, Decision on victims' participation, paras 97, 98, the latter paragraph clearly stipulating that the interests of victims go beyond an interest in reparations; ICC *Prosecutor v Lubanga*, AC, ICC-01/04-01/06-925 OA 8, 13 June 2007, Decision of the Appeals Chamber on the Joint Application of Victims a/0001/06 to a/0003/06 and a/0105/06 concerning the "Directions and Decision of the Appeals Chamber" of 2 February 2007, para 28; Judge Pikis separate opinion, p. 20, para 16; ICC *Prosecutor v Lubanga*, AC, ICC-01/04-01/06-925 OA 8, 13 June 2007, Decision of the Appeals Chamber on the Joint Application of Victims a/0001/06 to a/0003/06 and a/0105/06 concerning the "Directions and Decision of the Appeals Chamber" of 2 February 2007 and ICC *Prosecutor v Lubanga*, AC, ICC-01/04-01/06-824, 13 February 2007, Judgment on the appeal of Mr. Thomas Lubanga Dyilo against the decision of Pre-Trial Chamber I entitled "Décision sur la demande de mise en liberté provisoire de Thomas Lubanga Dyilo", paras 50–55.

[94] ICC *Prosecutor v Lubanga*, AC, ICC-01/04-01/06-925 OA 8, 13 June 2007, Decision of the Appeals Chamber on the Joint Application of Victims a/0001/06 to a/0003/06 and a/0105/06 concerning the "Directions and Decision of the Appeals Chamber" of 2 February 2007, Judge Song's separate opinion, p. 28, para 18; ICC *Prosecutor v Katanga and Chui,* PTC, ICC-01/04-01/07-474, 13 May 2008, Decision on the Set of Procedural Rights attached to Procedural Status of Victim at the Pre-Trial Stage of the Case, paras 37–44.

determination of the truth.[95] Chambers have also held that "victims have a general interest in the proceedings and in their outcome".[96] The latter makes it apparent how difficult it is to clearly distinguish between personal interests of victims and a general interest in the proceedings.[97]

The other criteria of Article 68 (3) of the Statute, i.e. the appropriateness and the effect on the rights of the accused and a fair trial, became, over time, more central to determining whether victims may participate in specific steps of the proceedings.[98] Trial Chamber I clarified, in the context of the questioning of witnesses by victims' legal representatives, that it is less of a concern whether the personal interests of the victims are affected, but whether the questioning is prejudicial to, or inconsistent with, the rights of the accused and a fair and impartial trial. The Chamber called such determination a "quintessentially fact-based issue, which cannot be determined in advance".[99] The Chambers apparently assumed that there are many areas to which the impact of victim participation cannot be determined in advance.

Rules 91 and 92 RPE also are important indicators of how victims should participate in proceedings. Rule 92 (5) and (6) RPE regulate the notification of documents and decisions to victims or their legal representatives. Rule 91 (2) clarifies that the legal representatives of victims should be allowed to participate in oral hearings or otherwise be allowed file written observations. Further, the Prosecutor and the defence should have the right to respond to the observations of the legal representatives. However, these rights have to be part of and are subject to the ruling of the Chamber as to how victims may participate in the proceedings pursuant to rule 89 RPE. Further, any such ruling is subject to modification (rule 90 (1) RPE).

---

[95] ICC *Prosecutor v Katanga and Chui,* PTC, ICC-01/04-01/07-474, 13 May 2008, Decision on the Set of Procedural Rights attached to Procedural Status of Victim at the Pre-Trial Stage of the Case, para 32; ICC *Prosecutor v Katanga and Chui,* TC, ICC-01/04-01/07-1788, 22 January 2010, Decision on the Modalities of Victim Participation at Trial, para 60.

[96] ICC *Prosecutor v Bemba,* TC, ICC-01/05-01/08-1729, 9 September 2011, Decision (i) ruling on legal representatives' applications to question Witness 33 and (ii) setting a schedule for the filing of submissions in relation to future applications to question witnesses, para 15.

[97] See e.g. ICC *Prosecutor v Lubanga,* AC, ICC-01/04-01/06-1452-Anx OA 12, 29 August 2008, Decision on the participation of victims in the appeal. Dissenting Opinion of Judge Georghios M. Pikis; see also Cohen 2009; Vasiliev 2009.

[98] See e.g. ICC *Prosecutor v Katanga and Chui,* PTC, ICC-01/04-01/07-474, 13 May 2008, Decision on the Set of Procedural Rights attached to Procedural Status of Victim at the Pre-Trial Stage of the Case, para 45.

[99] ICC *Prosecutor v Lubanga,* TC, ICC-01/04-01/06-2340, 11 March 2010, Decision on the defence observations regarding the right of the legal representatives of victims to question defence witnesses and on the notion of personal interest -and- Decision on the defence application to exclude certain representatives of victims from the Chamber during the non-public evidence of various defence witnesses, para 35.

Rule 92 (3) sets out a specific procedure that requires legal representatives of victims to apply specifically to the Chamber if they wish to question witnesses. The sub-rule sets out what the Chamber should keep in mind when ruling on such an application. Beyond that, the applicable law is silent on how victims should participate in pre-trial and trial proceedings, except for rules 143 and 144 RPE, which concerns the presence of victims or their legal representatives at the delivery of a number of specific Trial Chamber decisions.

Based on this legal framework, the Pre-Trial and Trial Chambers have developed a practice of victim participation in pre-trial and trial proceedings that is laid out below in an attempt to distinguish the exercise of the rights[100] of victims in two categories. However, before entering into the details, the reader should bear in mind that: victims' participation at the Court is currently almost exclusively based on participation through legal representatives, they do not sit in the courtroom or the public gallery, and they are referred to by numbers.

12.6.1 First Category of Victim Participation

In the first category are rights that victims attain directly upon their (preliminary[101]) recognition as victims of the crimes with which the judicial proceedings are concerned. Pre-Trial Chamber II calls them rights "*ex lege*".[102] It is the practice of all Pre-Trial and Trial Chambers to allow legal representatives of victims to

[100] That victims are considered to have rights derives e.g. from ICC *Prosecutor v Lubanga*, TC, ICC-01/04-01/06-1119, 18 January 2008, Decision on victims' participation, para 13, ICC *Prosecutor v Muthaura et al.*, PTC, ICC-01/09-02/11-267, 26 August 2011, Decision on Victims' Participation at the Confirmation of Charges Hearing and in the Related Proceedings, paras 98, 99; ICC *Prosecutor v Bemba,* TC, ICC-01/05-01/08-2138, 22 February 2012, Decision on the supplemented applications by the legal representatives of victims to present evidence and the views and concerns of victims, para 18; see also the dissenting opinion of Judge Steiner to the latter decision wherein she stipulates that "'meaningful participation' needs to be interpreted as a right conferred to the victims, and not as a useful tool for the parties or even the Chamber." (ICC *Prosecutor v Bemba,* TC, ICC-01/05-01/08-2140, 23 February 2012, Partly Dissenting Opinion of Judge Sylvia Steiner on the Decision on the supplemented applications by the legal representatives of victims to present evidence and the views and concerns of victims, ICC *Prosecutor v Bemba;* TC, ICC-01/05-01/08-2138, 22 February 2012, Decision on the supplemented applications by the legal representatives of victims to present evidence and the views and concerns of victims, para 2).

[101] See *Prosecutor v Lubanga,* TC, ICC-01/04-01/06-2842, 14 March 2012, Judgment pursuant to Article 74 of the Statute, paras 1362, 1363.

[102] See ICC *Prosecutor v Muthaura et al.*, PTC, ICC-01/09-02/11-267, 26 August 2011, Decision on Victims' Participation at the Confirmation of Charges Hearing and in the Related Proceedings, para 98.

participate in public sessions (see also rule 91 (2) RPE) and for victims to receive all public documents filed in the record in the course of the proceedings (see also rule 92 (4)–(6) RPE).[103] Further, victims have the right to file requests to the Chamber throughout the proceedings.[104] They are also allowed to make opening and closing statements, in line with rule 89 (1) RPE.[105]

Victims are usually allowed to make submissions and file responses.[106] In other words, the Chambers read the application of regulations 24, 34 RoC directly into rule 91 (2) RPE.

Victims are often anonymous to the parties or at least to the public, i.e. their identity is protected. Victims who are not known are generally not allowed to have access to the confidential parts of the record.[107] For reasons of equal treatment between anonymous and other victims, the Chambers have developed a practice according to which, not the victims, but their legal representatives may have access to confidential documents, the confidential part of the record, and to the E-court system.[108] Legal representatives are permitted to share the information in general with their clients

[103] ICC *Prosecutor v Katanga and Chui*, PTC, ICC-01/04-01/07-474, 13 June 2008, Decision on the Set of Procedural Rights Attached to Procedural Status of Victim at the Pre-Trial Stage of the Case, paras 127, 128; ICC *Prosecutor v Lubanga*, TC, ICC-01/04-01/06-1119, 18 January 2008, Decision on victims' participation paras 106, 107; ICC *Prosecutor v Muthaura et al.*, PTC, ICC-01/09-02/11-267, 26 August 2011, Decision on Victims' Participation at the Confirmation of Charges Hearing and in the Related Proceeding, paras 103, 108.

[104] ICC *Prosecutor v Lubanga*, PTC, ICC-01/04-01/06-462, 22 September 2006, Decision on the Arrangements for Participation of Victims a/0001/06, a/0002/06 and a/0003/06 at the Confirmation Hearing.

[105] ICC *Prosecutor v Gbagbo*, PTC, ICC-02/11-01/11-138, 4 June 2012, Decision on Victims' Participation and Victims' Common Legal Representation at the Confirmation of Charges Hearing and in the Related Proceedings, para 51.

[106] ICC *Prosecutor v Abu Garda*, PTC, ICC-02/05-02/09-136, 06 October 2010, Decision on victims' modalities of participation at the Pre-Trial Stage of the Case, para 18; but see ICC *Prosecutor v Muthaura et al.*, PTC, ICC-01/09-02/11-267, 26 August 2011, Decision on Victims' Participation at the Confirmation of Charges Hearing and in the Related Proceeding, paras 105, 118.

[107] ICC *Prosecutor v Lubanga*, TC, ICC-01/04-01/06-1119, 18 January 2008, Decision on victims' participation, paras 106, 107; ICC *Prosecutor v Lubanga*, PTC, ICC-01/04-01/06-462, 22 September 2006, Decision on the Arrangements for Participation of Victims a/0001/06, a/0002/06 and a/0003/06 at the Confirmation Hearing.

[108] ICC *Prosecutor v Katanga and Chui*, PTC, ICC-01/04-01/07-537, 30 May 2008, Decision on Limitations of Set of Procedural Rights for Non-Anonymous Victims, paras 25, 26; ICC *Prosecutor v Katanga and Chui*, TC, ICC-01/04-01/07-1788, 22 January 2010, Decision on the Modalities of Victim Participation at Trial, paras 122, 123; ICC *Prosecutor v Abu Grada*, PTC, ICC-02/05-02/09-136, 06 October 2010, Decision on victims' modalities of participation at the Pre-Trial Stage of the Case, para 20.

except for personal details about protected witnesses.[109] In other words, as a rule, the Pre-Trial and Trial Chambers exclude victims from confidential information and retain power to exclude legal representatives of victims from participating in closed sessions and from the confidential part of the record.[110]

If parties and participants to proceedings or the Chamber wish for the legal representatives (not necessarily the victims) to receive a filing or decision/order that is filed confidentially, they should include the name of the legal representative on the notification page of their filings.[111]

12.6.2 Second Category of Victim Participation

With respect to other more specific procedural steps, such as those relating to evidence, the Pre-Trial and Trial Chambers, following the example set by rule 91 (3) RPE, require the legal representatives of victims to make a motivated request to the Chamber, "specifying why and how the victims' personal interests are affected by the issues concerned".[112] In deciding the matter, the Chambers take, *inter alia*, "due account of the stage of the proceedings, the nature of the issue(s) concerned,

[109] ICC *Prosecutor v Katanga and Chui*, PTC, ICC-01/04-01/07-537, 30 May 2008, Decision on Limitations of Set of Procedural Rights for Non-Anonymous Victims, paras 13–26; see also ICC *Prosecutor v Lubanga,* TC, ICC-01/04-01/06-2340, 11 March 2010, Decision on the defence observations regarding the right of the legal representatives of victims to question defence witnesses and on the notion of personal interest -and- Decision on the defence application to exclude certain representatives of victims from the Chamber during the non-public evidence of various defence witnesses, paras 36–39.

[110] See ICC *Prosecutor v Muthaura et al.*, PTC, ICC-01/09-02/11-267, 26 August 2011, Decision on Victims' Participation at the Confirmation of Charges Hearing and in the Related Proceeding, paras 103, 109; ICC *Prosecutor v Gbagbo*, PTC, ICC-02/11-01/11-138, 4 June 2012, Decision on Victims' Participation and Victims' Common Legal Representation at the Confirmation of Charges Hearing and in the Related Proceedings, paras 53, 57. It is, however, understood that where the legal representative participates in closed sessions, he/she will also have access to the transcript of those sessions and confidential documents relating thereto.

[111] See ICC *Prosecutor v Lubanga*, TC, ICC-01/04-01/06-1119, 18 January 2008, Decision on victims' participation, para 107; ICC *Prosecutor v Muthaura et al.*, PTC, ICC-01/09-02/11-267, 26 August 2011, Decision on Victims' Participation at the Confirmation of Charges Hearing and in the Related Proceeding, para 113; ICC *Prosecutor v Abu Grada*, PTC, ICC-02/05-02/09-136, 06 October 2010, Decision on victims' modalities of participation at the Pre-Trial Stage of the Case, para 14.

[112] See e.g. ICC *Prosecutor v Muthaura et al.*, PTC, ICC-01/09-02/11-267, 26 August 2011, Decision on Victims' Participation at the Confirmation of Charges Hearing and in the Related Proceeding, para 99; the partly dissenting opinion of Judge Blattmann, ICC *Prosecutor v Lubanga*, TC, ICC-01/04-01/06-1119, 18 January 2008, Decision on victims' participation, paras 22, 32.

the rights of the suspects and the principle of fairness and expeditiousness of the proceedings".[113]

12.6.2.1 A Right to Challenge and Present Evidence?

The Appeals Chamber's judgment in the appeals OA 9, OA 10 in the case of *Prosecutor v. Lubanga Dyilo* clarified that victims may present and challenge evidence (a) if they could show that this would affect their personal interests, (b) if this would be considered appropriate by the Trial Chamber, and (c) if further conditions were met, as those stipulated in rule 91 (3) RPE.[114]

It is noteworthy that the Appeals Chamber as well as the Trial Chambers linked this role of victims in the proceedings to the Trial Chamber's power to "request the submission of all evidence that it considers necessary for the determination of the truth" as provided for in Article 69 (3) of the Statute.[115] Trial Chamber II expressly stated that, in this context, that victims are not parties to the trial and have no role in supporting the case of the Prosecutor.[116] Considering this jurisprudence, there is ground for the argument that the victims have the right to assist the Chamber in the pursuit of the truth, rather than a right to present and challenge evidence.

---

[113] ICC *Prosecutor v Muthaura et al.*, PTC, ICC-01/09-02/11-267, 26 August 2011, Decision on Victims' Participation at the Confirmation of Charges Hearing and in the Related Proceeding, paras 105, 118.

[114] ICC *Prosecutor v Lubanga,* AC, ICC-01/04-01/06-1432 OA 9 OA 10, 11 July 2008, Judgment on the appeals of The Prosecutor and The Defence against Trial Chamber I's Decision on Victims' Participation of 18 January 2008, paras 97–104; this was a majority judgment, Judges Kirsch and Pikis dissented; see also ICC *Prosecutor v Katanga and Chui,* AC, ICC-01/04-01/07-2288 OA 11, 16 July 2010, Judgment on the Appeal of Mr Katanga Against the Decision of Trial Chamber II of 22 January 2010 Entitled "Decision on the Modalities of Victim Participation at Trial", paras 37–48, 110–114.

[115] See Article 69 (3) of the Statute, see also ICC *Prosecutor v Lubanga*; TC, ICC-01/04-01/06-2127, 16 September 2009, Decision on the Manner of Questioning Witnesses Representatives of Victims by the Legal, para 27; ICC *Prosecutor v Katanga and Chui*, TC, ICC-01/04-01/07-1665-Corr, 01 December 2009, Directions for the conduct of the proceedings and testimony in accordance with rule 140, para 82; ICC *Prosecutor v Bemba,* TC, ICC-01/05-01/08-2138, 22 February 2012, Decision on the supplemented applications by the legal representatives of victims to present evidence and the views and concerns of victims, see also the dissenting opinion of Judge Steiner to the latter decision wherein she stipulates that "'meaningful participation' needs to be interpreted as a right conferred to the victims, and not as a useful tool for the parties or even the Chamber." (see ICC *Prosecutor v Bemba*, TC, ICC-01/05-01/08-2140, 23 February 2012, Partly Dissenting Opinion of Judge Sylvia Steiner on the Decision on the supplemented applications by the legal representatives of victims to present evidence and the views and concerns of victims, para 25).

[116] See ICC *Prosecutor v Katanga and Chui,* TC, ICC-01/04-01/07-1788, 22 January 2010, Decision on the Modalities of Victim Participation at Trial, para 75.

The Chambers decide on a case-by-case basis how to proceed in relation to each witness.[117] Trial Chamber III, for example, held that it required submissions by victims' legal representatives seven days before the questioning, responses (objections) thereto by the Prosecutor and the Defence four days before the questioning and a reply two days before.[118] The Chambers also held that legal representatives of victims who were allowed to question witnesses should also participate in the process of familiarising those witnesses with the Court and the persons questioning them.[119]

The precise scope of the victims' right to put questions to witnesses is not yet east in stone. Trial Chamber III's majority held that there is not only a personal interest of victims where a witness discusses the "physical commission of the alleged crimes" but also where the "question of the person or persons who should be held liable for those crimes" is at issue.[120] They justified this by reasoning that "victims have a general interest in the proceedings and in their outcome" and therefore an interest in making sure that "all pertinent questions are put to witnesses".[121] Trial Chamber II held, as formulated by the dissenting judge of Trial Chamber III:

> With regard to the use of statements in the objective of testing a witness's credibility, in line with the approach adopted by Trial Chamber II, I am of the view that Legal Representatives should in principle "not be allowed to ask questions pertaining to the credibility and/or accuracy of the witness's testimony, unless the Victims' Legal

---

[117] ICC *Prosecutor v Katanga and Chui*, TC, ICC-01/04-01/07-1665-Corr, 01 December 2009, Directions for the conduct of the proceedings and testimony in accordance with rule 140, paras 82–90; ICC *Prosecutor v Bemba*, TC, ICC-01/05-01/08-1729, 09 September 2011, Decision (i) ruling on legal representatives' applications to question Witness 33 and (ii) setting a schedule for the filing of submissions in relation to future applications to question witnesses; see as an example, ICC *Prosecutor v Katanga and Chui,* TC, ICC-01/04-01/07-2517, 09 November 2010, Decision authorising the appearance of Victims a/0381/09, a/0018/09, a/0191/08, and pan/0363/09 acting on behalf of a/0363/09.

[118] ICC *Prosecutor v Bemba*, TC, ICC-01/05-01/08-1729, 09 September 2011, Decision (i) ruling on legal representatives' applications to question Witness 33 and (ii) setting a schedule for the filing of submissions in relation to future applications to question witnesses, paras 14, 15.

[119] ICC *Prosecutor v Lubanga,* TC, ICC-01/04-01/06-1049, 30 November 2007, Decision Regarding the Practices Used to Prepare and Familiarise Witnesses for Giving Testimony at Trial; ICC *Prosecutor v Katanga and Chui,* TC, ICC-01/04-01/07-1788, 22 January 2010, Decision on the Modalities of Victim Participation at Trial, paras 79, 80.

[120] ICC *Prosecutor v Bemba*, TC, ICC-01/05-01/08-1729, 09 September 2011, Decision (i) ruling on legal representatives' applications to question Witness 33 and (ii) setting a schedule for the filing of submissions in relation to future applications to question witnesses, para 15.

[121] ICC *Prosecutor v Bemba*, TC, ICC-01/05-01/08-1729, 09 September 2011, Decision (i) ruling on legal representatives' applications to question Witness 33 and (ii) setting a schedule for the filing of submissions in relation to future applications to question witnesses, para 15.

> Representative can demonstrate that the witness gave evidence that goes directly against the interests of the victims represented."[122]

Trial Chamber I, however, has previously stated that victims' legal representatives should take a neutral approach to the questioning of witnesses, except if otherwise approved by the Chamber upon a request to that effect during the questioning.[123] Such exceptions applied "where the views and concerns of a victim conflict with the evidence given by that witness, or when material evidence has not been forthcoming".[124] Trial Chamber I held that the "Chamber must take a global view for each witness, to ensure that the overall effect to the questioning by victims does not undermine the rights of the accused and his fair and impartial trial".[125]

Victims may also request to present evidence, including calling witnesses other than victims.[126] However, it remains within the Trial Chambers,[127] authority to decide whether any such witness or other evidence genuinely contributes to the determination of the truth.[128] Victims must also disclose the material they are allowed to present according to the modalities set by the Chamber.[129] They are not generally obliged to disclose exculpatory materials in their possession, except when ordered by the Chamber to do so.[130]

---

[122] ICC *Prosecutor v Bemba,* TC, ICC-01/05-01/08-1471, 31 May 2011, Partly Dissenting Opinion of Judge Kuniko Ozaki on the Order on procedure relating to the submission of evidence, para 13, citing ICC *Prosecutor v Katanga and Chui,* TC, ICC-01/04-01/07-1665-Corr, 01 December 2009, Directions for the conduct of the proceedings and testimony in accordance with rule 140, para 90 (c).

[123] ICC *Prosecutor v Lubanga,* TC, ICC-01/04-01/06-2127, 16 September 2009, Decision on the Manner of Questioning Witnesses Representatives of Victims by the Legal, para 29; see also ICC *Prosecutor v Katanga and Chui,* TC, ICC-01/04-01/07-1665-Corr, 01 December 2009, Directions for the conduct of the proceedings and testimony in accordance with rule 140, para 91.

[124] ICC *Prosecutor v Lubanga,* TC, ICC-01/04-01/06-2127, 16 September 2009, Decision on the Manner of Questioning Witnesses Representatives of Victims by the Legal, para 28.

[125] ICC *Prosecutor v Lubanga,* TC, ICC-01/04-01/06-2340, 11 March 2010, Decision on the defence observations regarding the right of the legal representatives of victims to question defence witnesses and on the notion of personal interest -and- Decision on the defence application to exclude certain representatives of victims from the Chamber during the non-public evidence of various defence witnesses, para 35.

[126] See Friman 2009, pp. 496–498.

[127] For the Pre-Trial Chamber's approach, see e.g. ICC *Prosecutor v Katanga and Chui,* PTC, ICC-01/04-01/07-474, 13 May 2008, Decision on the Set of Procedural Rights attached to Procedural Status of Victim at the Pre-Trial Stage of the Case, paras 100–114.

[128] ICC *Prosecutor v Katanga and Chui,* TC, ICC-01/04-01/07-1788, 22 January 2010, Decision on the Modalities of Victim Participation at Trial, paras 82–84, 94–97.

[129] ICC *Prosecutor v Katanga and Chui,* TC, ICC-01/04-01/07-1788, 22 January 2010, Decision on the Modalities of Victim Participation at Trial, paras 105–107.

[130] ICC *Prosecutor v Katanga and Chui,* AC, ICC-01/04-01/07-2288 OA 11, 16 July 2010, Judgment on the Appeal of Mr Katanga Against the Decision of Trial Chamber II of 22 January 2010 Entitled "Decision on the Modalities of Victim Participation at Trial", paras 72–86.

12.6.2.2 Victims as Witnesses

In the practice of the Chambers, victims have appeared as witnesses primarily in trial proceedings.[131] When they appear, they are treated like any other witness, meaning they have to take an oath and are questioned by the Defence and the Prosecutor.[132] The Appeals Chamber confirmed that victims may appear as witnesses and testify on matters relevant to the guilt and innocence of the accused by holding that this must be decided,

> on a case-by-case basis, [and] that the right of the accused to a fair trial is respected. Therefore, whether a victim will be requested to testify on matters relating to the conduct of the accused will depend on the Trial Chamber's assessment of whether such testimony: (i) affects the victim's personal interests; (ii) is relevant to the issues of the case; (iii) contributes to the determination of the truth; and (iv) whether the testimony would be consistent with the rights of the accused, and in particular the right to have adequate time and facilities to prepare his defence (article 67 (1) (b) of the Statute), and a fair and impartial trial.[133]

Trial Chamber III left the choice in the first place with the legal representative to decide which victims should appear as witnesses. It was, however, important for the Chamber to point out that these should be the victims who are best-placed to assist the Chamber in determining the truth, who are able to present evidence that affects the personal interests of the greatest number of participating victims and that will not be cumulative of evidence already presented, and who are willing to

---

[131] Three victims gave evidence before TC I, but their right to participate was withdrawn at the end of the trail together with the rights of six dual status witness (see *Prosecutor v Lubanga, TC*, ICC-01/04-01/06-2842, 14 March 2012, Judgment pursuant to Article 74 of the statute, paras 21, 1363), TC II initially authorised four victims out of 370 to give evidence (see *Prosecutor v Bemba,* TC III, ICC-01/05-01/08-2140, 23 February 2012, Partly dissenting opinion of Judge Steiner on the Decision on the supplemented applications by the legal representatives of victims to present evidence and the views and concerns of victims, para 22), TC III authorized two victims out of 2287 to give evidence and three victims to present their views and concerns (see ICC *Prosecutor v Bemba,* TC, ICC-01/05-01/08-2138, 22 February 2012, Decision on the supplemented applications by the legal representatives of victims to present evidence and the views and concerns of victims, ICC *Prosecutor v Bemba,* TC, ICC-01/05-01/08-2138, 22 February 2012, Decision on the supplemented applications by the legal representatives of victims to present evidence and the views and concerns of victims, para 55).

[132] See ICC *Prosecutor v Katanga and Chui,* TC, ICC-01/04-01/07-1665-Corr, 01 December 2009, Directions for the conduct of the proceedings and testimony in accordance with rule 140, paras 31, 32; ICC *Prosecutor v Katanga and Chui,* TC, ICC-01/04-01/07-1788, 22 January 2010, Decision on the Modalities of Victim Participation at Trial, paras 88–91.

[133] ICC *Prosecutor v Katanga and Chui,* AC, ICC-01/04-01/07-2288, 16 July 2010, Judgment on the Appeal of Mr Katanga Against the Decision of Trial Chamber II of 22 January 2010 Entitled "Decision on the Modalities of Victim Participation at Trial", para 114; the appealed decision is ICC *Prosecutor v Katanga and Chui,* TC, ICC-01/04-01/07-1788, 22 January 2010, Decision on the Modalities of Victim Participation at Trial.

disclose their identity to the parties.[134] Trial Chambers also required written, signed and comprehensive statements of these victims.[135]

Trial Chamber I discussed the possibility of victims simply expressing their views and concerns without a need for them to testify as witnesses under oath. The same Trial Chamber also concluded that the expression of views and concerns, although perhaps assisting the Chamber in its approach to the evidence, could not be considered in the same way as evidence.[136] Nevertheless, it remained as an option that individual victims would express their views and concerns orally (without an oath) or in writing.[137] Two years later, Trial Chamber III recently allowed three victims to express their views and concerns, not by way of testimony but by an oral statement.[138]

The Appeals Chamber confirmed Trial Chamber II's finding that, in specifically defined circumstances, victims can request that incriminating evidence be produced in the course of a trial even if such evidence was not disclosed before the start of the trial. The Appeals Chamber thereby again gave weight to Article 69 (3) of the Statute by stipulating that the Trial Chamber can request the submission of evidence that it considers necessary for the determination of the truth in the course of the trial.[139]

Victims who are also witnesses are considered to be of "dual status". They can either be first witnesses and then become victims or *vice versa.* Trial Chamber I held that VWU should also advise witnesses as to their rights as victims, i.e. that

---

[134] ICC *Prosecutor v Bemba.* TC, ICC-01/05-01/08-2027, 21 December 2011, Second order regarding the applications of the legal representatives of victims to present evidence and the views and concerns of victims, para 12; see also ICC *Prosecutor v Bemba,* TC, ICC-01/05-01/08-1935, 21 November 2011, Order regarding applications by victims to present their views and concerns or to present evidence; ICC *Prosecutor v Katanga and Chui,* TC, ICC-01/04-01/07-1788, 22 January 2010, Decision on the Modalities of Victim Participation at Trial, paras 92, 93.

[135] ICC *Prosecutor v Katanga and Chui,* TC, ICC-01/04-01/07-1665-Corr, 01 December 2009, Directions for the conduct of the proceedings and testimony in accordance with rule 140, paras 25–29; ICC *Prosecutor v Bemba,* TC, ICC-01/05-01/08-2027, 21 December 2011, Second order regarding the applications of the legal representatives of victims to present evidence and the views and concerns of victims, para 15.

[136] ICC *Prosecutor v Lubanga,* TC, ICC-01/04-01/06-2032-Anx, 26 June 2009, Decision on the request by victims a/0225/06, a/0229/06 and a/0270/07 to express their views and concerns in person and to present evidence during the trial, paras 25–27; see also ICC *Prosecutor v Katanga and Chui,* TC, ICC-01/04-01/07-1788, 22 January 2010, Decision on the Modalities of Victim Participation at Trial, para 84.

[137] ICC *Prosecutor v Bemba,* TC, ICC-01/05-01/08-1935, 21 November 2011, Order regarding applications by victims to present their views and concerns or to present evidence, para 3c.

[138] ICC *Prosecutor v Bemba,* TC, ICC-01/05-01/08-2138, 22 February 2012, Decision on the supplemented applications by the legal representatives of victims to present evidence and the views and concerns of victims, para 55.

[139] ICC *Prosecutor v Katanga and Chui,* AC, ICC-01/04-01/07-2288 OA 11, 16 July 2010, Judgment on the Appeal of Mr Katanga Against the Decision of Trial Chamber II of 22 January 2010 Entitled "Decision on the Modalities of Victim Participation at Trial", paras 37–48; 110–114.

they can apply to participate in the proceedings.[140] The Trial Chambers confirmed that dual status is not legally problematic.[141] However, such witnesses do not get access to confidential material through their victim status.[142] The Prosecutor and the Defence might have an interest in knowing that a certain witness is a victim in the proceedings.[143] They might also wish to contact or interview dual status victims. Trial Chambers I and II have ruled that the legal representatives should be informed of any such interviews and be allowed to be present if the victim agrees.[144] While Trial Chamber I held that such statements should, as a rule, be disclosed to the legal representatives,[145] Trial Chamber II ruled that this is not the case in relation to the Defence, except if the Defence omitted to inform the legal representative that such interview was about to take place.[146]

12.6.2.3 Others

Victims' legal representatives can also trigger other decisions of the Chamber in areas where a Chamber has *proprio motu* powers. Victims may not conduct investigations relevant to the charges, but only those with a view to collecting information that establishes the existence, nature and extent of the harm suffered by them.[147]

---

[140] ICC *Prosecutor v Lubanga,* TC, ICC-01/04-01/06-1379, 5 June 2008, Decision on certain practicalities regarding individuals who have the dual status of witness and victim, para 54 (e).

[141] See ICC *Prosecutor v Lubanga,* TC, ICC-01/04-01/06-1119, 18 January 2008, Decision on victims' participation, paras 132–134.

[142] ICC *Prosecutor v Katanga and Chui,* PTC, ICC-01/04-01/07-632, 23 June 2008, Decision on the Application for Participation of Witness 166; see also ICC *Prosecutor v Katanga and Chui,* PTC, ICC-01/04-01/07-717, 30 September 2008, Decision on the confirmation of charges, paras 200–209; ICC *Prosecutor v Katanga and Chui,* TC, ICC-01/04-01/07-1788, 22 January 2010, Decision on the Modalities of Victim Participation at Trial, para 114.

[143] ICC *Prosecutor v Lubanga,* TC, ICC-01/04-01/06-1379, 5 June 2008, Decision on certain practicalities regarding individuals who have the dual status of witness and victim, paras 54–56.

[144] ICC *Prosecutor v Lubanga,* TC, ICC-01/04-01/06-1379, 5 June 2008, Decision on certain practicalities regarding individuals who have the dual status of witness and victim, paras 59, 60.

[145] ICC *Prosecutor v Lubanga,* TC, ICC-01/04-01/06-1379, 5 June 2008, Decision on certain practicalities regarding individuals who have the dual status of witness and victim, paras 63, 68.

[146] ICC *Prosecutor v Katanga and Chui,* TC, ICC-01/04-01/07-2571, 23 November 2010, Décision relative aux modalités de contact entre des victimes représentées et les parties, paras 16–28.

[147] See ICC *Prosecutor v Katanga and Chui,* PTC, ICC-01/04-01/07-474, 13 May 2008, Decision on the Set of Procedural Rights attached to Procedural Status of Victim at the Pre-Trial Stage of the Case, paras 80–83; ICC *Prosecutor v Katanga and Chui,* TC, ICC-01/04-01/07-1788, 22 January 2010, Decision on the Modalities of Victim Participation at Trial, paras 102, 103.

12.7 Victims and Sentencing

Trial Chamber I, when holding its very short sentencing hearing, in the case of *Prosecutor v. Lubanga Dyilo*, treated victims who participated in the same manner as it has during the trial. Victims' legal representatives were heard orally and in writing, made closing statements but did not request a specific sentence.[148] A short consideration of the ECCC proceedings is of merit as it shows the differences between the ICC victim participation and the ECCC Civil Party scheme. Because civil parties are pursuing a civil action against the accused that could lead to reparations, they are perceived as only having an interest in the finding on guilt or innocence and in reparations, but not in sentencing. It follows that they are not allowed to request a specific sentence or make submissions on the matter or to question character witnesses who are perceived to be relevant only to sentencing.[149] In all other instances, Civil Parties are allowed to fully question witnesses.

12.8 Victims Participation Before the Appeals Chamber

The presentation of the Appeals Chamber's jurisprudence is limited to appeals under Article 82 (1) of the Statute, as the first appeals pursuant to Article 81 (1) and (2) of the Statute are currently underway.[150] For those [for the purpose of this article called] interlocutory appeals, the Appeals Chamber established a procedure for victims to apply to participate in the proceedings.[151] Legal representatives of victims have to file an application specifying whom they are representing and that

---

148 ICC *Prosecutor v Lubanga*, TC, ICC-01/04-01/06-T-360-Red2-ENG, 13 June 2012, Transcript of the hearing of 13 June 2012, pp. 19, 20, 30, 36–43.

149 See ECCC *Case of Kaing*, TC, Case File 001/18-07-2007/ECCC/TC, E72/3, 9 October 2009, Decision on Civil Party Co-lawyers' joint request for a ruling on the standing of Civil Party lawyers to make submissions on sentencing and directions concerning the questioning of the accused, experts and witnesses testifying on character.

150 But see the recent Appeals Chamber decision: ICC *Prosecutor v Lubanga*, ICC-01/04-01/06-2951, 13 December 2012, Decision on the participation victims in the appeals against Trial Chamber I's conviction and sentencing decisions, para 5..

151 ICC *Prosecutor v Lubanga*, AC, ICC-01/04-01/06-824, 13 February 2007, Judgment on the appeal of Mr. Thomas Lubanga Dyilo against the decision of Pre-Trial Chamber I entitled "Décision sur la demande de mise en liberté provisoire de Thomas Lubanga Dyilo", paras 37–49; ICC *Prosecutor v Lubanga*, AC, ICC-01/04-01/06-925 OA 8, 13 June 2007, Decision of the Appeals Chamber on the Joint Application of Victims a/0001/06 to a/0003/06 and a/0105/06 concerning the "Directions and Decision of the Appeals Chamber" of 2 February 2007; ICC *Prosecutor v Lubanga*, AC, ICC-01/04-01/06-1335 OA 9 OA 10 16 May 2008, Decision, in limine, on Victim Participation in the appeals of the Prosecutor and Defence against Trial Chamber I's Decision entitled "Decision on Victims' Participation", paras 12–15.

the victims have standing before the Pre-Trial Chamber or Trial Chamber.[152] Further, victims have to set out "how their personal interests are affected by this appeal, indicating why it is appropriate for the Appeals Chamber to permit their views and concerns to be presented at this stage of the proceedings and why the presentation of such views and concerns would not be prejudicial to or inconsistent with the rights of the Defence".[153] The applications should be submitted latest when the response to the document in support of the appeal is due.[154]

Upon receiving an application, the Appeals Chamber hears the appellant and the respondent and analyses the submissions on a case-by-case basis.[155] If the application is granted, the victims are allowed to file their observations within a time limit set by the Appeals Chamber and the appellant and respondent also have

---

[152] ICC *Prosecutor v Bemba,* AC, ICC-01/05-01/08-2098 OA 10, 6 March 2012, Decision on "Application of Legal Representative of Victims Mr Zarambaud Assingambi for leave to participate in the appeals proceedings following the Defence appeal of 9 January 2012 and addendum of 10 January 2012", paras 12, 13; ICC *Prosecutor v Bemba,* AC, ICC-01/05-01/08-1597 OA 7, 14 July 2008, Decision on the Participation of Victims in the Appeal against the "Decision on Applications for Provisional Release" of Trial Chamber III, para 14; ICC *Prosecutor v Katanga and Chui,* AC, ICC-01/04-01/07-2124 OA 7, 24 May 2010, Decision on the Participation of Victims in the Appeal of Mr Katanga Against the "Decision on the Modalities of Victim Participation at Trial", para 6.

[153] ICC *Prosecutor v Lubanga,* AC, ICC-01/04-01/06-1335 OA 9 OA 10 16 May 2008, Decision, in limine, on Victim Participation in the appeals of the Prosecutor and the Defence against Trial Chamber I's Decision entitled "Decision on Victims' Participation", para 36; ICC *Situation in the Democratic Republic of the Congo,* AC, ICC-01/04-503 OA 4 OA 5 OA 6 30 June 2008, Decision on Victim Participation in the appeal of the Office of Public Counsel for the Defence against Pre-Trial Chamber I's Decision of 7 December 2007 and in the appeals of the Prosecutor and the Office of Public Counsel for the Defence against Pre-Trial Chamber I's Decision of 24 December 2007, para 35; see also ICC *Prosecutor v Lubanga,* AC, ICC-01/04-01/06-824 OA 7, 13 February 2007, Judgment on the appeal of Mr. Thomas Lubanga Dyilo against the decision of Pre-Trial Chamber I entitled "Décision sur la demande de mise en liberté provisoire de Thomas Lubanga Dyilo", para 44, wherein it was merely required that victims address the personal interests and the appropriateness criteria.

[154] ICC *Situation in the Democratic Republic of the Congo,* AC, ICC-01/04-503, 30 June 2008, Decision on Victim Participation in the appeal of the Office of Public Counsel for the Defence against Pre-Trial Chamber I's Decision of 7 December 2007 and in the appeals of the Prosecutor and the Office of Public Counsel for the Defence against Pre-Trial Chamber I's Decision of 24 December 2007, para 39; ICC *Prosecutor v Bemba*, AC, ICC-01/05-01/08-2098 OA 10, 6 March 2012, Decision on "Application of Legal Representative of Victims Mr Zarambaud Assingambi for leave to participate in the appeals proceedings following the Defence appeal of 9 January 2012 and addendum of 10 January 2012", para 10.

[155] ICC *Situation in the Democratic Republic of the Congo,* AC, ICC-01/04-503 OA 4 OA 5 OA 6, 30 June 2008, Decision on Victim Participation in the appeal of the Office of Public Counsel for the Defence against Pre-Trial Chamber I's Decision of 7 December 2007 and in the appeals of the Prosecutor and the Office of Public Counsel for the Defence against Pre-Trial Chamber I's Decision of 24 December 2007, paras 32–34; ICC *Prosecutor v Lubanga,* AC, ICC-01/04-01/06-824 OA 7, 13 February 2007, Judgment on the appeal of Mr. Thomas Lubanga Dyilo against the decision of Pre-Trial Chamber I entitled "Décision sur la demande de mise en liberté provisoire de Thomas Lubanga Dyilo", paras 43, 47, 48.

a right to respond thereto.[156] As a rule, and if the formal and substantiation requirements are met, the Appeals Chamber grants victims the right to participate in an interlocutory appeal as their personal interests are often affected by the nature or the possible outcome of the appeal and the impugned decision.[157] Exceptionally, when the rights of the accused were at stake, the procedure was abbreviated or victim participation excluded.[158]

The Appeals Chamber jurisprudence is based on the understanding that interlocutory appeals are a separate stage of the proceedings in the sense of Article 68 (3) of the Statute, requiring an additional layer of scrutiny by the Appeals Chamber,[159] similar to the second category of victim participation described above. A minority is of the opinion that a new application of victims should not be necessary as regulations 64 and 65 RoC allow them to directly participate in an appeal. However, they would require the victims to have participated in the proceedings that led to the impugned decision.[160]

---

[156] Ibid.

[157] ICC *Prosecutor v Lubanga,* AC, ICC-01/04-01/06-824 OA 7, 13 February 2007, Judgment on the appeal of Mr. Thomas Lubanga Dyilo against the decision of Pre-Trial Chamber I entitled "Décision sur la demande de mise en liberté provisoire de Thomas Lubanga Dyilo", paras 54, 70; but see: ICC *Prosecutor v Lubanga*, AC, ICC-01/04-01/06-925 OA 8, 13 June 2007, Decision of the Appeals Chamber on the Joint Application of Victims a/0001/06 to a/0003/06 and a/0105/06 concerning the "Directions and Decision of the Appeals Chamber" of 2 February 2007, paras 26–29, ICC *Situation in Uganda*, AC, ICC-02/04-164 OA, 27 October 2008, Decision on the participation of victims in the appeal, para 13; ICCC *Prosecutor v. Kony et al.*, AC, ICC-02/04-01/05-324 OA 2, 27 October 2008, Decision on the participation of victims in the appeal, para 15.

[158] ICC*Prosecutor v Mbarushimana*, AC, ICC-01/04-01/10-483 OA 3, 24 January 2012, Reasons for "Decision on appeal of the Prosecutor of 19 December 2011 against the 'Decision on the confirmation of the charges' and, in the alternative, against the 'Decision on the Prosecution's Request for stay of order to release Callixte Mbarushimana' and on the victims' request for participation" of 20 December 2011, paras 33–35.

[159] ICC *Prosecutor v Lubanga,* AC, ICC-01/04-01/06-824 OA 7, 13 February 2007, Judgment on the appeal of Mr. Thomas Lubanga Dyilo against the decision of Pre-Trial Chamber I entitled "Décision sur la demande de mise en liberté provisoire de Thomas Lubanga Dyilo", paras 40–43; ICC *Prosecutor v Bemba*, AC, ICC-01/05-01/08-566 OA 2, 20 October 2009, Reasons for the "Decision on the Participation of Victims in the Appeal against the 'Decision on the Interim Release of Jean-Pierre Bemba Gombo and Convening Hearings with the Kingdom of Belgium, the Republic of Portugal, the Republic of France, the Federal Republic of Germany, the Italian Republic, and the Republic of South Africa'", para 16; see also Vasiliev 2009, pp. 656, 657.

[160] ICC *Prosecutor v Lubanga,* AC, ICC-01/04-01/06-824 OA 7, AC, 13 February 2007, Judgment on the appeal of Mr. Thomas Lubanga Dyilo against the decision of Pre-Trial Chamber I entitled "Décision sur la demande de mise en liberté provisoire de Thomas Lubanga Dyilo", Dissenting Opinion of Judge Sang-Hyun Song Regarding the Participation of Victims, pp. 55–57, paras 4–8; *Prosecutor v Muthaura et al.*, TC, ICC-01/09-02/11-400, 20 February 2012, Decision on the "Observations on the 'Directions on the submission of observations pursuant to Article 19 (3) of the Rome Statute and rule 59 (3) of the Rules of Procedure and Evidence'", Separate Opinion of Judge Sang-Hyun Song, paras 2, 3.

12.9 Conclusion

This contribution shows that the jurisprudence of the ICC on the topic of victim participation in criminal proceedings has developed considerably over the past years. Victim participation in criminal proceedings has taken on a clearer shape. Victims indeed have a place in the proceedings before the Court and their rights therein are given effect. This contribution, however, also points to many issues that are still in development. A prime example for such developments is, for example, Trial Chamber V's very recent decision on victim participation.[161] The legal challenge of Article 68 (3) of the Statute lies in ensuring the proceedings' fairness and timeliness, while also providing victims a role in the proceedings that goes beyond that of a close onlooker. The practical challenge of giving victims a place in the Court's proceedings lies in allowing them to participate effectively, despite their distance from the seat of the Court and their often difficult, crisisridden living environments.

References

Bachvarova T (2011) Victims eligibility before the International Criminal Court in historical and comparative context. ICLR 11:665–706

Baumgartner E (2008) Aspects of victim participation in the proceedings of the International Criminal Court. IRRC 90(870):409–440

Bitti G (2011) Les victimes devant la Cour pénale internationale. Les promesses faites à Rome ont-elles été tenues? RSC 2:293–341

Bitti G, Friman H (2001) Participation of victims in the proceedings. In: Lee RS (ed) The International Criminal Court: elements of crimes and rules of procedure and evidence. Transnational Publishers, Leiden, pp 456–474

Bock S (2007) Das Opfer vor dem Internationalen Strafgerichtshof. ZStW 119(3):664–680

Bock S (2010) Das Opfer vor dem Internationalen Strafgerichtshof. Duncker & Humblot, Berlin

Bottigliero I (2004) Redress for victims of crimes under international law. Martinus Nijhoff Publishers, Leiden/Boston

Chung C H (2008) Victim participation before the International Criminal Court: are concessions of the court clouding the promise? NJIHR 6(3):459–545

Cohen M (2009) Victim participation rights within the International Criminal Court: a critical overview. DJILP 37:351–377

De Hemptinne J, Rindi F (2006) ICC Pre-Trial Chamber allows victims to participate in the investigation phase of proceedings. JICJ 4(1):342–350

Donat-Cattin D (2008) Article 68. In: Triffterer O (ed) Commentary on the Rome Statute of the International Criminal Court—Observers' Notes, Article by Article. C.H. Beck, Munich

Dubuisson M, Bertrand A, Schauder N (2009) Contribution of the Registry to greater respect for the principles of fairness and expeditious proceedings before the International Criminal Court. In: Stahn C, Sluiter G (eds) The emerging practice of the International Criminal Court. Brill, Leiden, pp. 565–584

Ferstman C (2005) The role of victims at the International Criminal Court: key prospects'. In: Vetere E, Pedro D (eds) Victims of crime and abuse of power. United Nations, Vienna, p. 159

[161] ICC *Prosecutor v Muthaura et al.*, TC, ICC-01/09-02/11-498 (see also ICC-01/09-01/11-460), 3 October 2012, Decision on victims' representation and participation. This decision was rendered when this contribution was in the final stages.

Friman H (2009) The International Criminal Court and participation of victims: a third party to the proceedings? LJIL 22:485–500

Garkawe S (2003) Victims and the International Criminal Court: three major issues. ICLR 3:345–367

Greco G (2007) Victims rights overview under the ICC legal framework: a jurisprudential analysis. ICLR 7:531–547

Guhr AH (2008) Victim participation during the pre-trial stage at the International Criminal Court. ICLR 8:109–140

Haslam E (2011) Subjects and objects: International Criminal Law and the institutionalization of civil society. IJTJ 5:221–240

Heikkilä M (2004) International criminal tribunals and victims of crimes, Turku, Institute for Human Rights, Abo Akademi University. http://www.edoc.hu-berlin.de/dissertationen/burkhardt-maren-2010-01-13/PDF/burkhardt.pdf. Accessed 20 March 2012

Johnson ST (2010) Neither victims nor executioners: the dilemma of victim participation and the defendant's right to a fair trial at the International Criminal Court. ILSAJICL 16:489–496

Massidda P, Pellet S (2009) Role and practice of the Office of Public Counsel for Victims. In: Stahn C, Sluiter G (eds) The emerging practice of the International Criminal Court. Brill, Leiden, pp. 691–706

Miraglia M (2006) The first decision of the ICC Pre-Trial Chamber: international criminal procedure under construction. JICJ 4:188–195

Ntanda Nsereko DD (2010) The role of victims in criminal proceedings—lessons national jurisdictions can learn from the ICC. CLF 21:399–415

Pena M (2010) Victim participation at the International Criminal Court: achievements made and challenges lying ahead. ILSAJICL 16:497–516

Safferling CJM (2003) Das Opfer völkerrechtlicher Verbrechen: Die Stellung der Verbrechensopfer vor dem Internationalen Strafgerichtshof. ZStW 115:352–384

Stahn C, Olasolo H, Gibson K (2006) Participation of victims in pre-trial proceedings of the ICC. JICJ 4(1):219–238

Stehle S (2007) Das Strafverfahren als immaterielle Wiedergutmachung. Die aktiven Beteiligungsrechte des Verletzten im Verfahren vor dem Internationalen Strafgerichtshof und in ausgewählten nationalen Strafverfahren. Verlag Dr. Kovac, Frankfurt am Main

Trumbull IV CP (2008) The victims of victim participation in international criminal proceedings. MJIL 29(277):777–826

Ušacka A (2011) Promises fulfilled? Some reflections on the International Criminal Court in its first decade. CLF 22:473–492

Van Boven T (1999) The position of the victims in the statute of the International Criminal Court. In: Von Hebel H (ed) Reflections on the International Criminal Court: essays in honour of Adrian Bos. TMC Asser Press, The Hague, pp. 77–89

Van den Wyngaert C (2011) Victims before the International Criminal Courts: some views and concerns of an ICC Trial Judge. Case West Reserv J Int Law 44:475–495

Vasiliev S (2009) Article 68 (3) and personal interests of victims in the emerging practice of the ICC. In: Stahn C, Sluiter G (eds) The emerging practice of the International Criminal Court. Brill, Leiden, pp. 635–690

Chapter 13
Victims' Rights and Peace

Hans-Peter Kaul

Abstract The contribution provides an overview of the ICC victims' participation and reparations system. It analyses the origins of the system—the French system of victims' participation in criminal proceedings—and examines its potential to alleviate and to acknowledge the sufferings of the victims but also the many challenges or even risks for errors it presents. The article refers in particular to the problem of establishing standards of evidence sufficient to ascertain that a person has suffered harm as a result of the commission of a crime under the jurisdiction of the Court and the related issue of establishing a person's identity. It also refers to the Court's obligation to guarantee the victims a genuine and authentic participation in the proceedings through a legal representative. The article highlights the significant contribution to promote reconciliation and peace in regions affected by mass crimes the ICC system of victims' participation and reparations can make. In the second part of this article, the author turns the attention to several key questions concerning the relationship between victims' rights and peace: what are the factors and risks leading time and again to mass victimisation of human beings? Is it not a fundamental and urgent necessity for all concerned to exhaust all ways and means to prevent developments that lead to mass victimisation? Given this question, the author finds that the most serious dangers and grave risks to make thousands of men, women and children victims of international crimes are brought about by war-making, illegal or questionable uses of armed force or outright crimes against peace as defined in the Nuremberg principles. The conclusion is that the best chance to prevent mass victimisation is determination and resolve in the prevention of questionable uses of

---

The author is a judge at the International Criminal Court. From 1996 to 2003, he has been the head of the German delegation for the negotiations for the ICC, before being elected in February 2003 as the first German judge to the ICC for a period of three years. He was re-elected in 2006 for another period of nine years. From March 2009 to March 2012, Judge Kaul has served for three years as the Second Vice-President of the ICC. He is assigned to the Pre-Trial Division.

The form of an oral presentation as actually delivered has been largely maintained also for reasons of authenticity.

H.-P. Kaul (✉)
Pre-Trial Division of the International Criminal Court, The Hague, The Netherlands
e-mail: Hans-Peter.Kaul@icc-cpi.int

T. Bonacker and C. Safferling (eds.), *Victims of International Crimes: An Interdisciplinary Discourse*, DOI: 10.1007/978-90-6704-912-2_13,

armed force, including possible future crimes against peace, crimes of aggression as defined in Articles 8 *bis* and 15 *bis* and 15 *ter* of the Rome Statute, as, according to experience, they inevitably lead to widespread human suffering and victims.

Keywords Victim participation • Standards of evidence • Proof of identity • Legal representative • Domestic legal community • Nuremberg principles • Kampala • Rome Statute

It is very much appreciated that the International Research and Documentation Center for War Crimes Trials, in cooperation with the Center for Conflict Studies of Marburg University has taken the initiative to organise this important international conference on "Victims of International Crimes". It is a pleasure and an honour to be given the opportunity to submit and to share with you, as a Judge of the International Criminal Court (ICC), some experiences and general thoughts on the rights of victims and peace.

In this contribution, I will deal with two sets of issues:

(1) What are some observations and impressions of an ICC Judge with regard to victims' issues? What are some more general aspects of the system of victims' participation as practiced at our Court?
(2) What are some of the underlying reasons that so many—women, children and men—time and again, become victims of international crimes in so many parts of the world? How important is the existence of peace for victims' rights?

To a certain extent, this approach and structure of my contribution builds on the pertinent and comprehensive presentation of the system of victims' participation and reparations under the Rome Statute[1] of the ICC which was made yesterday[2] by Franziska Eckelmans from the Appeals Division of the ICC.

13.1 Observations and Impressions Regarding Victims' Issues

It is well-known and widely acknowledged that the system of victims' participation at the International Criminal Court and the possibility for victims to receive, under certain conditions, reparations for the harm suffered, is one of the many positive and quite significant innovations introduced by the Rome Statute.[3] In the following, let me at first share, from the perspective of a Pre-Trial Judge, some personal

[1] For a comprehensive monography on the rights of victims before the International Criminal Court see Bock 2010.

[2] See Eckelmans, Chap. 12 in this volume, pp. 189–222.

[3] Stahn et al. 2006, p. 220.

observations made during the work of Pre-Trial Chamber II of the ICC with regard to victims issues.

Already in the first cases in which victims' applications had to be examined, a number of challenging legal and practical issues became apparent. We had to determine standards of evidence sufficient to establish that a person has suffered harm as a result of the commission of a crime under the jurisdiction of the Court. As our situations concern developing African countries, at times still affected by conflict, a number of difficulties arose with regard to the question of establishing a person's identity. In the absence of a proper identity card, which document may be considered to be sufficient? It would take me too long to recall all the solutions which were found by the Judges to solve this problem. But it is fair to say that meanwhile there is a consolidated practice and jurisprudence of Chambers with regard to the question of proof of identity.[4]

The particularities of international criminal law present an important challenge to victims' participation in the ICC proceedings. The innovative system of victims' participation and reparations as set out in the Rome Statute was largely inspired by the French system of victims' participation in criminal proceedings. Cases under French criminal law regularly involve one perpetrator and a limited number of victims. Thus, a criminal judge or a criminal chamber in France will generally not be confronted with important difficulties in the admission of victims. It is obvious that the situation before the ICC is entirely different: its cases concern mass crimes committed in countries at a great distance from The Hague with usually hundreds or thousands of victims.[5]

The unavoidable consequence is that victims regularly cannot be present at the hearings. They must be represented by an intermediary, namely a legal representative. This is a serious handicap which reduces the positive effects of victims' participation at the ICC. Thus, the only instances of genuine victims' participation are the cases in which they appear as direct witnesses before the Court. In times of modern technology, these negative effects can be mitigated. We have, for example, heard that some victims in the Kenya situation are able to follow the proceedings of our Chamber on video screens which may even be available in public spaces or in supermarkets.

Many Chambers were faced with the further problem that various victims participating in the proceedings had given mandates to different legal representatives who all

---

[4] See for example ICC *Prosecutor v Bemba*, PTC, ICC-01/05-01/08-320, 12 December 2008, Fourth Decision on Victims' Participation; ICC *Prosecutor v Bemba*, TC, ICC-01/05-01/08-1862, 25 October 2011, Decision on 270 applications by victims to participate in the proceedings; ICC *Situation in Darfur*, PTC, ICC-02/05-110, 3 December 2007, Decision on the Requests of the OPCD on the Production of Relevant Supporting Documentation Pursuant to Regulation 86(2)(e) of the Regulations of the Court and on the Disclosure of Exculpatory Materials by the Prosecutor; ICC *Situation in Uganda*, PTC, ICC-02/04-191, 9 March 2012, Decision on Victim's Participation in Proceedings Related to the Situation in Uganda. For an overview see Chung 2008, pp. 459–545.

[5] With a critical remark: Van den Wyngaert 2012.

wished to appear in Court. In an important decision taken in December 2008, I ruled as a Single Judge in the *Bemba* case that 54 victims admitted by the Chamber to participate should be represented jointly by a common legal representative.[6] It should be noted that also other Chambers, including Trial Chamber II and Trial Chamber III, have subsequently followed this decision.[7] In the Kenya cases,[8] of which my Chamber was seised, the 327 admitted victims in Case 1 and the 233 admitted victims in Case 2, were represented in each case by one common legal representative.

Another critical aspect related to the legal representation of victims is the issue of communication. Counsel should be in close contact with the victims in order to genuinely represent their views and concerns. Further, it is the legal representatives' task to inform the victims regularly on the proceedings. However, we have had problematic cases in which the communication between the victims and their representative was not realised satisfactorily. After receiving the mandate to appear before the ICC, some lawyers did not find it necessary to maintain contact with the victims and to seek their views; they seemed to be primarily interested in representing their own interests. This is, in my view, an untenable situation as we must guarantee the victims a genuine and authentic participation. One possible option could be to ensure a meaningful participation through the appearance of Elders or self-chosen representatives of African villages affected by the crimes in question.

My experience in the two Kenya cases was that the common legal representatives of victims managed to convey to the Chamber and to the public the concerns and sufferings of the victims convincingly. However, I felt that the legal representatives of victims at times acted in the courtroom like a second prosecutor, which is not their legitimate role.[9]

Another major issue of victims' participation is the question of reparations. The conclusion of the *Lubanga* trial[10] and the subsequent conclusion of the *Katanga and Ngudjolo* trial will provide an understanding of the reparation scheme at the ICC.

[6] ICC *Prosecutor v Bemba*, PTC, ICC-01/05-01/08-322, 16 December 2008, Fifth Decision on Victims' Issues Concerning Common Legal Representation of Victims.

[7] ICC *Prosecutor v Katanga and Chui*, TC, ICC-01/04-01/07-1328, 22 July 2009, Order on the organisation of common legal representation of victims; ICC *Prosecutor v Bemba*, TC, ICC-01/05-01/08-1005, 20 November 2010, Decision on common legal representation of victims for the purpose of trial.

[8] ICC *Prosecutor v Ruto and Sang*, ICC-01/09-01/11; ICC *Prosecutor v Muthaura and Kenyatta*, ICC-01/09-02/11.

[9] ICC *Situation in the Democratic Republic of the Congo*, PTC, ICC-01/04-101-tENG, 17 January 2006, Decision on the Applications for Participation in the Proceedings of VPRS 1, VPRS 2, VPRS 3, VPRS 4, VPRS 5 and VPRS 6, para 51; ICC *Prosecutor v Katanga and Chui*, PTC, ICC-01/04-01/07-474, 13 May 2008, Decision on the Set of Procedural Rights Attached to Procedural Status of Victim at the Pre-Trial Stage of the Case, para 155; ICC *Prosecutor v Bemba*, PTC, ICC-01/05-01/08-320, 12 December 2008, Fourth Decision on Victims' Participation, para 90. On the role of the legal representatives see also for example McGonigle Leyh 2011, p. 505 et subs.

[10] ICC *Prosecutor v Lubanga*, TC, ICC-01/04-01/06-2842, 14 March 2012, Judgment pursuant to Article 74 of the Statute.

Article 75 of the Statute reads that the Court shall establish general principles relating to reparations. As no principles have been established so far, this question is left to the Trial Chambers. The two Trial Chambers dealing with the abovementioned cases will be challenged with the important task of establishing principles for reparations and rendering the first decisions on victims' reparations.[11]

All in all, it is my view that the ICC system of victims' participation and reparations can make a significant contribution to promote reconciliation and peace in regions affected by mass crimes. Victims who feel part of the judicial process may accept more easily the outcome of ICC judgments. They can also provide the Judges with useful information for their decisions which otherwise may not be available to them. Furthermore, there is a possibility to strengthen the domestic legal community by involving local lawyers in the common legal representation of victims.[12] Taken together, these effects may facilitate reconciliation and peace.

The ICC system of victims' participation and reparations is an entirely new, unique, complex and holistic system. On the one side, it represents progress and an inherent potential to alleviate and to acknowledge the sufferings of the victims. On the other side, it cannot be overlooked that the system and its implementation present many challenges or even risks for errors. Thus the Judges of the International Criminal Court and all parties concerned continue to be faced with the task to make the best out of this far-reaching concept.

13.2 Underlying Reasons

In the second part of this contribution, I turn to some questions which in my view have not yet been discussed at this conference. There are several questions which we also should consider:

What are the factors, what are the risks that according to our experience lead time and again to the depressing phenomenon that large numbers of innocent human beings become victims of international crimes? As we are considering the topic of victims' rights and peace, it is my suggestion that States, the international community, continue to be faced with a rather obvious necessity. All ways and means must be exhausted to prevent and to stop possible developments which may lead to mass victimisation. In this respect I would like to emphasise a principle, which might seem almost obvious or even commonplace—which it is not.

It is necessary to recall and to be fully aware that the best protection of human rights is the absence of violence, armed conflict and war-making. The conclusion out of this simple truth is obvious. There is an urgent necessity—and it is probably the best approach to victims' issues—to avoid and to prevent mass victimisation through violence, armed conflict and war-making.

---

[11] Van den Wyngaert 2012; McKay 2008, p. 4.

[12] Boyle 2006, p. 307.

This is a reality and experience which must be seen quite clearly: the greatest risks of mass victimisation, the greatest risks to make thousands of men, women and children victims of international crimes stem from war-making, illegal or questionable uses of armed force or outright crimes against peace as defined in the Nuremberg principles.[13] As I have stated already many times, we should bear in mind a cruel reality. Experience shows that war, the injustice of war in itself begets massive war crimes and crimes against humanity, thus leading time and again to human suffering and victims. There is no armed conflict without murder, killing of innocent civilians and children. There is no war without rapes and other sex crimes. We have seen this in World War II, in Vietnam, in the former Yugoslavia, in Iraq and also in practically all African situations and cases with which the ICC is currently seised. As in the past century, a terrible law seems to hold true: war, the ruthless readiness to use military force, to use military power for political interests regularly leads to wide-spread victimisation, to massive and grievous crimes of all kinds.

People around the world, men and women in every country, share a desire not to become victims of brutal force and violence. They share a desire for justice and peace. People around the world agree that the highest value and best protection for human dignity and human rights is the absence of armed force.

Thus, when we discuss the issue of victims of international crimes the conclusion seems obvious: All ways and means must be exhausted to contain, to avert the risk of future war-making. All must be done to reduce and to eliminate, if possible, the risks emanating from future illegal or questionable uses of armed force, including possible future crimes against peace, crimes of aggression as defined in Articles 8(bis) and 15(bis) and 15(ter) of the Rome Statute.

Since Nuremberg, to wage war without recourse to self-defence pursuant to Article 51 of the UN Charter is no longer a national right but an international crime. The Kampala break-through of 11 June 2010 on the crime of aggression offers also a chance to avoid future mass victimisation through illegal uses of armed force. Once again, determination and resolve in the prevention of the use of armed force offers in my view the best chances to prevent ab initio mass victimisation.

It is time for a new impetus to promote a culture of peace and non-use of force in international relations. As Benjamin Ferencz, the last surviving Nuremberg Prosecutor has often told us, "you have to begin very early to educate young minds that war is not glorious. War is an abominable crime, no matter what the cause". Consequently, one way of preventing future mass victimisation is to incorporate the reasons and necessity of the common task to discredit or even outlaw, in the curricula of schools, universities and all kinds of educational organisations, the use of aggressive or questionable armed force.

---

[13] Doc. A/CN.4/SER.A/1950/Add.1 (1950). United Nations International Law Commission: Principles of International Law Recognized in the Charter of the Nürnberg Tribunal and in the Judgement of the Tribunal, 5 June–29 July 1950.

This is my conviction. As a Judge of the International Criminal Court, I felt it important to underline this point for the record of this important conference.

References

Bock S (2010) Das Opfer vor dem Internationalen Strafgerichtshof. Duncker & Humblot, Berlin

Boyle D (2006) The rights of victims. JICJ 4:307–313

Chung CH (2008) Victims' participation at the International Criminal Court: are concessions of the court clouding the promise? NJIHR 6:459–545

McGonigle Leyh B (2011) Victim participation and the ICC. In: Letschert R, Haveman R, de Brouwer A, Pemberton A (eds) Victimological approaches to international crimes: Africa. Intersentia, Antwerp, pp. 493–524

McKay F (2008) Victim participation in proceedings before the International Criminal Court. Hum Rights Brief 15(3):2–5

Stahn C, Olásolo H, Gibson K (2006) Participation of victims in pre-trial proceedings of the ICC. JICJ 4:219–238

Van den Wyngaert C (2012) Victims before International Criminal Courts: Some views and concerns of an ICC trial judge. Case West Reserv Univ J Int Law 44:475–496

Part IV
Victims in Transitional Justice Processes

Chapter 14
Victims, Excombatants and the Communities: Irreconcilable Demands or a Dangerous Convergence?

Chandra Lekha Sriram

Abstract In recent years, scholars and practitioners of transitional justice and international criminal justice have increasingly emphasised the role of victims in post-atrocity justice processes, not only as witnesses but as active participants and beneficiaries of related reparations processes. At the same time, internationally run peacebuilding processes have developed detailed proceedings for disarmament, demobilisation and reintegration of excombatants, which include education and training, as well as frequent cash or other benefits. Yet, while these processes pertain to the same conflict, practitioners of each are not always sufficiently aware of the real or potential clashes between them, or the risks of overlap or linking them. Based on empirical evidence from a range of post-atrocity processes, this chapter seeks to outline these risks.

Keywords Victim-centred justice • Restorative justice • DDR • Transitional justice • Peacebuilding • International criminal tribunals

14.1 Introduction

In this chapter, I deal with one particular dimension of the treatment of victims in transitional justice processes, situating them in the larger interplay of transitional justice and peacebuilding processes in conflict-affected societies. Specifically, I discuss the competing and possibly irreconcilable demands facing many post-conflict societies of addressing the needs of victims, demobilising former fighters and returning them to communities. This chapter builds upon a recently completed collaborative research project supported by the United States Institute of Peace on victim-centred justice and

---

The author is Professor of Law at the School of Oriental and African Studies at the University of London, UK.

C. L. Sriram (✉)
University of London, London, UK
e-mail: chandra.sriram@soas.ac.uk

T. Bonacker and C. Safferling (eds.), *Victims of International Crimes: An Interdisciplinary Discourse*, DOI: 10.1007/978-90-6704-912-2_14,

disarmament, demobilisation and reintegration of excombatants (DDR).[1] The research in that project, as well as other recent studies on transitional justice and DDR, illustrates the tensions between the demands to address the needs of victims and those of excombatants who may also have perpetrated serious human rights violations. Nonetheless, processes dealing with both take place alongside one another, in the same territories, dealing with many of the same people, and often such processes are designed by the same or overlapping national and international actors. Further, as is well known, many individuals within conflicts may be both victims and perpetrators; this may be more rather than less true of combatants. The distinction between victims and excombatants may be necessary for postconflict programming, but it is also often artificial. However, it has consequences, as the two sets of actors receive different treatment and different modes of benefits. Victims are often treated as objects of processes, receiving reparations in response to their victimhood, although their right to reparation and remedy is increasingly emphasised in scholarship and practice. At the same time, excombatants are subjects of processes, with articulated entitlement to certain processes and benefits by virtue of their status.[2]

I argue that it is unrealistic to consider these processes in isolation, and that scholars and practitioners should recognise these connections in order to avoid unintended consequences. At the same time, however, I caution against the risks of linking DDR and victim-centred justice processes without reflection, not least because victim and combatant identities are more fluid than programming often assumes. I begin with a discussion of victim-centred approaches to justice, focussing on their goals and justifications, followed by a brief account of excombatants and DDR processes in countries emerging from conflict. I then discuss the linkages, including tensions and overlaps, between the processes and turn to lessons from my field research in Sierra Leone and Colombia as well as that of others to illustrate my arguments. As other chapters in this volume deal with victims' rights and treatment of victims before specific courts, tribunals and truth commissions, I deal with these topics in a relatively limited fashion, focussing instead on the relationship between victims, excombatants and communities. I argue that the promotions of victim-centred justice and DDR programmes often intersect and contradict one another and that greater attentiveness to these intersections, as well as the complexity of identities of beneficiaries, might improve the practice of each.

14.2 The Context: Justice Versus Peace

The challenges which this chapter will elaborate upon are but one element of the wider "justice versus peace" debate. As this is a well-worn debate, I will not discuss it in great detail, but a brief summary is merited. In the wake of abusive

---

1 Sriram et al. 2012.

2 I am grateful to Amy Ross for this point and her insightful comments on an earlier draft of this chapter. I am also grateful to Thorsten Bonacker for comments on an earlier draft of this chapter. Any errors are mine alone.

authoritarian rule or violent conflict, societies face conflicting demands. On the one hand, domestic and international human rights advocates, other civil society actors, society at large and/or victims may demand accountability for past atrocities, particularly for core international crimes such as genocide, war crimes and crimes against humanity. On the other hand, those at risk from accountability processes including members of the security services and of non-state armed groups as well as those tasked with building peace, including DDR programmers and others in United Nations peacekeeping and peacebuilding missions, will see accountability processes as a threat to their own interests or to stability. Peace agreements may also have imposed limits upon options for accountability in order to secure participation by one or more warring factions. Each side in this debate offers a very different account of the choice that should be made in the wake of atrocities. On the one hand, advocates of accountability insist that this principle is essential for victims, for society, for democratisation and the rule of law, and ultimately that any peace will not be stable without it. On the other hand, advocates of prioritising peace will insist that attempts at accountability, particularly although not only through criminal justice measures, will disrupt any fragile peace and make longer term stability which may promote rule of law and human rights difficult, if not impossible.[3]

In reality, of course, the situation is more complex. States and societies do not simply choose between peace and justice, but from a range of options for accountability, including amnesties, prosecutions, vetting, truth-telling, reparations and memorials. And they may choose a variety of these over time, shifting strategies according to the demands of different constituencies. Thus the choices are not always as stark as they initially appear. Nonetheless, there are real tensions between and amongst processes designed to promote accountability and those designed to promote peace. This chapter will focus on just one of these tensions—that between victim-centred approaches to justice and reintegration of former combatants.

14.3 Victim-Centred Justice

I do not seek in this chapter to define victims, either in a legal or social-scientific sense, although I do draw upon legal and normative principles which guide the treatment of victims in the wake of mass atrocities.[4] As will become clear throughout this chapter and as is evident throughout this volume, defining victims and victimhood are not simple matters—an individual's victim status may be challenged by other putative victims, victims may also be perpetrators and victims have very different and often conflicting needs and demands. Indeed, while there is a turn, particularly although not only with respect to child soldiers, to a narrative of what

[3] There is a vast literature on the subject. See, for example, Sriram 2004; Teitel 2000; Kritz 1995.

[4] The chapter by Eckelmanns addresses victims' rights in greater detail.

Drumbl refers to as "faultless passive victims", identities and statuses are far more complex.[5] I thus focus not on victims and who they are, but rather on the turn to victim-centred approaches to justice in the wake of conflict and its relationship to reintegration of former combatants.

Many practitioners and scholars have argued that justice in the wake of mass atrocity requires far more than retributive justice. They argue for the need to be attentive to the needs of victims and of wider affected communities. This may entail a range of non-retributive responses, from truth-telling to reparations and memorials.[6] Victim-centred approaches to justice may of course not be limited to non-retributive approaches—victims and their advocates may emphasise the importance of retributive justice as well. Victim-centred approaches to justice are increasingly promoted in the transitional literature, sometimes relying upon claims about legal or emergent legal rights of victims, sometimes emphasising normative claims about victimhood and restoration and sometimes highlighting what victims "want". I thus use the term "victim-centred justice" in an attempt to emphasise the scope of concerns beyond victims' rights which are often expected to be addressed. However, I will briefly outline the turn to victims' rights at the international level, in legal and normative terms. The trend towards victim-centred approaches to justice is wide-ranging; I note here the development of provisions for victims in international criminal tribunals and the development of draft principles on the right to remedy and reparation at the United Nations, the attendant scholarship on and practice of reparations, as well as the widespread expectations of truth and reconciliation commissions to attend to the needs of victims.

Traditionally, in international criminal tribunals, victims' participation was primarily limited to their role as witnesses. However, at institutions such as the International Criminal Tribunal for the Former Yugoslavia (ICTY) and the Special Court for Sierra Leone (SCSL), victims and witnesses sections were created to ensure protection of those victims engaged directly with the courts as witnesses. This has gone beyond the necessary provisions for witness protection; at the SCSL the section has provided medical support, both psychological and physical, including reconstructive, to victim-witnesses. However, these sections were not mandated to address victims' needs more broadly.[7]

By comparison, at the Extraordinary Chambers in the Courts of Cambodia (ECCC), victim participation is clearly enshrined through their role as civil parties, as explained in the chapter by Studzinsky in this volume. The Statute of the International Criminal Court (ICC), similarly, provides for greater roles for, and responses to, victims, providing for both participation in proceedings and material reparations to victims, as discussed in the chapter by Eckelmans in this volume. The ICC Statute establishes a Trust Fund for Victims and provides for fines as well

---

[5] The chapter by Drumbl illuminates the difficulty, in the context of child soldiers, of assigning simple labels such as victim or perpetrator.

[6] De Feyter et al. 2005; de Greiff 2006.

[7] Author's interviews at the Special Court for Sierra Leone, Freetown, July 2011.

as imprisonment and penalties, the former of which may be provided to identified victims.[8] Indeed, the court can order individual and/or collective reparations from perpetrators to victims via the Trust Fund. To date, the Trust Fund has disbursed funds to affected communities through voluntary contributions from member states. And the Statute of course also provides for the participation of victims in court proceedings via two units—the Victims' Participation and Reparation Section provides information on reparation proceedings and applications, and the Office of Public Counsel for Victims provides legal support and assistance to the victims or their legal representatives.

At the same time, there is an emergent set of norms which describe developing sets of rights of victims of serious human rights violations to remedy and reparations. These include the UN's Basic Principles and Guidelines on the Right to Remedy and Reparation (Basic Principles), approved by the UN General Assembly in 2005, and the Draft Updated Set of Principles for the Protection and Promotion of Human Rights through Action to Combat Impunity of 2005 (Draft Principles).[9] These principles enshrine some existing obligations within international human rights and international humanitarian law to prosecute and punish certain violations as well as emergent rights to truth, reparations and remedy for victims.[10] Reparations processes have now been developed in and for many transitional societies, although the resources come from a range of sources. Reparations may be one mode where the state has been responsible of "making the government pay", since the state cannot be prosecuted as such.[11] However, the state is not the only source of reparations. In Colombia, convicted individuals may provide reparations to victims; in Sierra Leone the reparations programme has been funded largely by the international community; and as noted above at the ICC reparations may come via the trust fund from either perpetrators or the international community.[12] However, to the degree that victims want reparations not only for material reasons but as compensation from perpetrators, where the international community is the source of the money, reparations may not serve the latter goal and may not, for many, be easy to distinguish from humanitarian or development assistance.

Truth and reconciliation commissions have a wide range of ostensible purposes, including developing a historical account of past abuses and their causes and the prevention of future abuses, chiefly through recommendations for reforms, and in some cases, criminal responses.[13] However, they are also often explicitly about victims, in

[8] García-Godos 2006, p. 116.

[9] United Nations 2005a, b.

[10] Shelton 2006, p. 20.

[11] Laplante and Theidon 2007, p. 245.

[12] See de Greiff 2006 for detailed discussions of the range of types of reparations.

[13] Hayner 2000; Wiebelhaus-Brahm 2010. Other purposes include the promotion of future human rights protections and the promotion of democracy but their records on these are decidedly questionable.

at least two senses. First, the processes are meant to be *for* victims: they are meant to provide the "truth" to victims, to allow victims to tell their stories and to acknowledge victims and their suffering.[14] Advocates of such commissions argue that the very act of telling the truth to an official body helps a victim with his/her recovery.[15] At the same time, truth commissions may be expected to partially fulfil some elements of the emergent rights to the truth and to a remedy, the former in obvious ways and the latter through recommendations of commissions promoting specific reparations or other measures. Second, the processes *rely upon* victims: to feed into a narrative for a report which may inform and instruct the wider society, to confront and be the recipients of apologies by perpetrators, and to perform the act of forgiveness. While many early truth commissions omitted the term "reconciliation", the majority of recent commissions includes the term, signifying an attempt to bring together victims, perpetrators and societies, rather than simply reconstructing a historical "truth". Whether, in fact, these commissions help victims to heal or are in fact harmful, whether they satisfy victims' needs and expectations or engender expectations (such as expectations of reparations) that are not met, remains a matter of some debate.[16]

14.4 Restorative Justice

Restorative justice is of course by no means identical to victim-centred justice. Victim-centred justice may involve greater participation by victims in retributive processes as well as a range of other measures. Nonetheless, much current practice and literature in transitional justice has emphasised victim-centred justice as restorative justice, suggesting in particular that it will contribute to reconciliation.[17] This phenomenon is not new. Some advocates and some streams in the transitional justice literature have long advocated a victim-centred, rather than solely retributive justice, and/or communally rather than individually focussed accountability. However, specific measures to incorporate victims into transitional justice processes, including through participation in retributive processes as well as through the use of local or traditional justice and conflict resolution mechanisms, have increased in recent years.[18]

Victim-centred justice is thus not, as is clear from the UN Basic Principles and Draft Principles and the ICC statute, purely about restorative justice, although it is sometimes so understood. Certainly, the inclusion of reparations procedures within the ICC Statute may encourage that understanding, despite the inclusion of victim

---

[14] I use the term "truth" advisedly, as it is contested in such situations. See García-Godos 2008.

[15] Laplante and Theidon 2007.

[16] Laplante and Theidon 2007, p. 237.

[17] For a critique see Humphrey 2003.

[18] I use the word "traditional" advisedly here, recognising that it is a contested term.

participation in proceedings and the primarily retributive functions of the court.[19] At the same time, retributive justice processes may not be expected to serve all of the goals of restorative justice.

What are the expectations of restorative justice? Restorative justice is strongly linked to victim-centred justice because of its emphasis on restoring victims, that is to say responding to the harms which they have experienced in an effort to repair the damage they have suffered, whether that damage is physical or psychological, or more broadly, social. These goals are partly articulated in the UN Basic Principles on Restorative Justice Programmes in Criminal Matters.[20] But restorative justice is often not concerned only with victims. It is also concerned with return and social reintegration of offenders into communities and facilitating reconciliation between victims and perpetrators, perpetrators and communities, and victims and communities.[21] Restorative processes such as reparations programmes have increased in number, at the same time a lot of truth and reconciliation commissions have been created and expected to provide not only an accounting of the past, but some form of social, emotional and moral benefits to victims. Thus transitional justice mechanisms often invoke restorative, and indeed reconciliation goals, and promote the participation of victims, perpetrators and communities. They are also, I will argue, increasingly used in tandem with efforts to promote reintegration of ex-combatants. There are at least two types of arguments that might be made in favour of restorative, victim-centred approaches to justice, either instead of, as part of, or as a complement to retributive justice. One is a normative goal of promoting a specific non-retributive form of justice which rebuilds social relationships. The other is the somewhat more pragmatic role of promoting stable social relations and returning former combatants who might also be perpetrators to communities.

Normative arguments for a restorative approach to victim-centred justice emphasise the harm done to victims and the need to repair relationships. From this perspective, because victims have suffered a harm, attempts should be made to restore them, and because perpetrators have caused that harm they have the responsibility to attempt to repair the harm. Further, the repair aimed at is not just that of the relationships between perpetrators and victims, but also between perpetrators and communities. Restorative processes are expected to facilitate the reintegration of perpetrators into communities and to promote the restoration of social trust.[22] Advocates and scholars of restorative justice argue that it is not merely an alternative mode of doing justice, or a second-best option when criminal justice is

---

[19] McCarthy 2009. McCarthy uses the term "reparative justice" to refer to what is commonly known in the literature as "restorative justice". For a discussion of "reparative justice" as a concept that emphasises "the principle of reparation, as the origin and core of the need for justice in times of violent and brutalizing transition" see Mani 2006. See also Baumgartner 2008; Rauschenbach and Scalia 2008; Henham 2004.

[20] United Nations 2005c, 2006a; Gillett 2009; García-Godos 2008; Nwogu 2010; Findlay 2009; Rubio-Marín and de Greiff 2007; McCarthy 2009; Robins 2011.

[21] Beck et al. 2010, p. 48.

[22] Stovel and Valiñas 2010, pp. 4–7. Both explicate and critique this perspective.

not viable, but rather that it is based in an "alternative vision of justice".[23] They argue that human beings are relational, that is to say that they are connected by a web of relationships. Thus any justice response needs to recognise that connectedness, addressing not only individual victims, but wider affected actors. Justice on this account seeks the transformation of relationships, not necessarily only to their state prior to violence and violations, but in many cases even to something better, to a state of peaceful or even positive relationships.[24] This conception is, according to one proponent, forward-looking and focussed on reintegration over isolation and must involve not only victims, wrongdoers and communities but also focus on restoring relations among all of these.[25]

Practical arguments for restorative justice are related to the above normative goals, but have pragmatic, security- and stability-oriented goals. They emphasise the need for victims to accept the return of former perpetrators into their communities, or as normalised members of society at large, in order to build a stable and secure post-transition society. Advocates and practitioners developing these processes hope to prevent victims exacting vengeance and generating new cycles of violence, but also to facilitate not only perpetrators' but also victims' social rehabilitation where victims may have been stigmatised because of their own victimisation. The goal is secure physical return to communities, and also the restoration of functional trust, if not the wider normative goal of reconciliation, a contested concept.[26]

Of course, victim-centred approaches to justice are not simple to design or effect—just who the victims are is contested within and across communities, just as who is a genuine perpetrator may be contested. In interviews I conducted recently in Sierra Leone on the reparations programme, many interviewees challenged the concept of identifying victims, stating that everyone who lived in the country during the war is a victim.[27] Further, in conflicts involving mass atrocities, many individuals are both victims and perpetrators; this is perhaps most notoriously the case with child soldiers. As some scholars have noted, there is a risk that the concept of the victim may be reified, defining individuals by nothing other than their victimhood and against those who are not victims. This approach may, in emphasising the individual victim, miss the collective impact of mass atrocities on not only direct victims, but also on their families, immediate communities and on the wider community.[28] It may also disempower victims by treating them as

---

[23] Llewellyn 2008, p. 4.

[24] Llewellyn 2008, pp. 5, 6.

[25] Llewellyn 2008, pp. 7, 11. See also Teitel 2000.

[26] Stovel and Valiñas 2010, pp. 2–4; Sriram 2005, pp. 55, 56. Compare Bennett 2006.

[27] Author's interview with Sierra Leonean NGO and government officials, not for attribution, Freetown, July 2011.

[28] See generally Humphrey 2003.

though victimhood defines their identity, and it may disempower those who are not designated victims in reparations registries or of specific perpetrators at the ICC.

As discussed above, advocates promote restorative justice processes as measures to restore dignity to victims, a normative goal, but also often argue that they can serve the pragmatic goals of return and acceptance of perpetrators, including through, as will be discussed below, the return of former combatants who may be perpetrators. This is often presented under the wider rubric of reconciliation, a problematic term which I will not explore here.[29] What is critical, however, for my analysis, is that such processes often necessarily entail increased interaction between victims and their specific victimisers or perpetrators of serious crimes more generally.

This interaction between victims and victimisers, again often an artificial dichotomy, is essential to many contemporary transitional justice processes, in particular, in truth and reconciliation commissions and in so-called traditional justice processes, as well as increasingly in international and internationalised criminal tribunals. Thus for example, *gacaca,* a local traditional practice to manage local, relatively low-level, disputes and conflicts has been used to address crimes committed during the 1994 genocide in Rwanda. This has not been without controversy, including claims that it is a significant deviation from traditional practice, that it coerces participation in many cases of both victims and perpetrators and that victims' forgiveness is also coerced in the process.[30]

However, restorative processes that seek to promote reconciliation by bringing together victims and perpetrators, and often expecting forgiveness or at least acceptance, may have deleterious side effects. Encouraging or even coercing victims to engage with perpetrators for the sake of larger goals such as reintegration and reconciliation runs the risk of re-traumatising victims or imposing a new stigma of victimhood upon them. There is a real risk in many circumstances that victims are used to serve the purposes of reintegration of perpetrators and are coerced into "reconciling", and there is the risk that processes simply coerce participation of victims in the name of restorative justice which is itself contradictory to the ostensible goals of restorative justice.[31] At the same time, perpetrators may also be stigmatised through their inclusion in certain processes and reified purely as perpetrators rather than also as victims. Such outcomes would seem to run counter to the ostensible goals of victim-centred justice, specifically the goal of addressing the needs of victims and restoring their dignity.[32]

---

[29] Quinn 2009.

[30] See generally Straus and Waldorf 2011.

[31] Stovel and Valiñas 2010, p. 15; Thomson 2011, pp. 331–339.

[32] This does not mean that the risk of re-traumatising victims is not present in restorative justice, although restorative justice professionals are possibly more aware of this risk.

14.5 Excombatants and DDR

In countries emerging from conflict, particularly, although not only those hosting UN peacekeeping and peacebuilding missions, rank and file excombatants (of non-state armed groups and in many cases of state fighting forces) are processed through DDR programmes.[33] DDR programmes necessarily create classes of excombatants and non-excombatants. Early programmes relied heavily on the surrender of a weapon, often excluding women and girls associated with fighting forces, while current programmes take a broader view of who constitutes an excombatant. Nonetheless, some excombatants may be excluded from programmes, "false" participants in DDR programmes are frequent and individuals may choose not to participate in programmes out of fear of being stigmatised as an excombatant.

DDR programming tends to follow a relatively set procedure, whether it is managing the reduction of state armed forces or the partial or complete demobilisation of non-state armed groups. These are now spelt out in the comprehensive guidance provided by the United Nations, the UN Integrated DDR Standards.[34] Combatants are first disarmed—small arms, ammunition, explosives, light and heavy weapons are collected from former combatants and in many cases civilians and catalogued, afterwards they are destroyed or placed in secure facilities. Combatants are then demobilised or discharged from their groups and placed in cantonment or assembly areas. At this stage, former combatants are given a variety of forms of assistance, as incentives for remaining in the process, but also to enable their transition to civilian life, gainful employment in non-combatant roles or reinsertion assistance. This reinsertion assistance can include a range of benefits, including cash payments and food and shelter as well as training and education designed to enable former fighters to obtain employment. The reintegration stage is perhaps the most challenging, certainly it is the stage which experts agree DDR programmes have been least successful at: the return of excombatants to peaceful civilian life with the capacity to make a living within former or new communities.[35]

In many postconflict countries, efforts at pursuing victim-centred justice intersect with efforts at DDR. They do so where initial efforts to disarm and demobilise excombatants may require promises of amnesty, or where such efforts may be resisted because excombatants fear they may face prosecution. They intersect particularly in subsequent efforts at longer term social reintegration of those former combatants, including perpetrators of atrocities, into communities, and alongside victims whom they have harmed in many instances. It was for this reason that the project on which this chapter draws focussed upon victim-centred justice and DDR, a pairing seldom studied academically or carefully scrutinised by policymakers.

---

[33] Of course, this may only be true of the rank and file fighters. Leaders of fighting forces on one or more sides may benefit from peace agreements which guarantee them political and economic power, particularly through power-sharing arrangements.

[34] United Nations 2006b.

[35] Muggah 2009; Waldorf 2012.

However, it is essential in transitional situations to understand the relationship between efforts at justice and efforts at stabilisation. In particular, DDR processes are frequently prioritised temporally in transitional situations, because they are essential to stabilising security and limiting the risks of a return to violence. However, at the same time these processes are often in tension with victim-centred approaches to justice, as DDR processes involve prioritising the security and sustenance concerns of former combatants, frequently also perpetrators of serious crimes over the concerns and demands of victims. The former are provided with secure facilities, training and education and often cash payouts and work-specific "DDR kits", while the demands of the latter for either criminal justice, truth-telling or reparations are often deferred. Further, subsequent efforts to promote reintegration of former combatants into communities necessarily involve engagement with victims and/or affected communities. Nonetheless, DDR processes are central to major, particularly UN-led, peacekeeping and peacebuilding operations.[36]

14.6 Victims and Excombatants in Transition

14.6.1 Tensions and Contestations

DDR benefits in transitional countries are likely to be controversial and often at odds with transitional justice processes. Further, many communities will be resistant to the return of former combatants who have committed abuses against them or others, or who are presumed to do so, making longer term social reintegration difficult. This difficulty may be exacerbated by the perception that former combatants have already been unfairly privileged. Victims and conflict-affected communities who themselves may have received no reparations and perhaps limited reconstruction assistance, or minimal humanitarian and development assistance, may resent the provision of training and education, DDR kits and cash payouts to former combatants. Specifically, they may see these benefits as not only inequitable but also as compensation to the very people who perpetrated violence and abuses and destroyed their homes and businesses, while victims often gain no form of reparation or receive them far later. In order to ease return of former combatants, some DDR programmers may offer community incentives (often development benefits) to accept return of former combatants or, as we turn to next, may engage or utilise transitional justice mechanisms to promote return.

Whether by design or by necessity, DDR processes interact with and can be in tension with transitional justice processes. This may occur not only because victims and communities critically compare benefits given to possible perpetrators and identified victims. In addition, ex-combatants, whether perpetrators or not, may be expected to participate in transitional justice processes, including truth

[36] United Nations 2006c, para 9b.

commissions, trials and traditional justice mechanisms, often shortly after the demobilisation process, but in some instances transitional justice processes will loom large in the calculations of combatants.[37] Not surprisingly, former combatants, particularly negotiating parties to peace processes, will resist any accountability and may seek to enshrine amnesties in peace agreements; the prospect of accountability may cause them to exit demobilisation processes or at least threaten to do so. Further, peace agreements may, particularly via power-sharing arrangements, guarantee posts in government for leaders of parties to the conflict, which may ensure in turn the presence of large numbers of individuals responsible for abuses in positions of power and able to resist accountability and reform processes, in tension with calls for victim-centred justice.[38]

However, while the demands of former combatants, frequently including the demands for limitations on or bars to accountability, may be strong and take precedence in peace negotiations and peacebuilding processes, victims and human rights advocates will frequently demand accountability. As a result, and usually following quite contested processes, peace agreements and/or post-transition legislation may provide for a range of accountability (or non-accountability) mechanisms, including vetting, exclusion from certain official functions of those responsible for serious abuses, prosecutions, truth commissions, reparations and amnesties. So an evident tension between demands of these two groups arises. While the UN Draft Principles reject blanket amnesties and amnesties for the most serious international crimes (such as genocide, war crimes and crimes against humanity), compromises are nonetheless often struck, with limited amnesties or other protections of possible accused put in place.

At the same time, modes of justice demanded by victims, whether formal retributive justice processes or vetting and reparations processes, may undermine the incentives for former combatants to return to civilian life. They may fear criminal trials or being ordered to pay reparations from their own limited resources (or simply not wish to sacrifice the spoils of conflict in some cases), and they may be afraid of being shunned by communities or being excluded from employment by virtue of their status as excombatants and frequently presumed perpetrators. Here, DDR and transitional justice activities may clearly be in conflict, but until recently there has been relatively little discussion of the relationship between them.[39] The connection between DDR and transitional justice generally has been recognised in more recent UN policy documents, with the addition of a transitional justice module to the United Nations Integrated Disarmament, Demobilisation, and Reintegration Standards (IDDRS). The 2006 original draft of the standards simply emphasised the need for DDR measures to be developed which would encourage communities to accept excombatants, such as development incentives, while the

[37] Muggah 2010.

[38] Vandeginste and Sriram 2011.

[39] Vandeginste and Sriram 2011, pp. 465, 466.

transitional justice module emphasised the need to respect human rights standards and the constraints on amnesties for core crimes, and advocates greater coordination between DDR and transitional justice processes.[40] This is already taking place on the ground, but often without self-reflection by programmers.

14.6.2 Intentional and Unintentional Linkages

Despite the evident intersections and tensions between victim-centred approaches to justice and DDR processes, programmers often do not acknowledge them. This is because these activities are conducted, in theory, by distinct sets of actors: transitional justice programmers and human rights advocates on the one hand, and peacemakers and peacebuilders on the other.[41] While these processes involve distinct activities and have differing goals, it becomes clear that they nonetheless overlap, as each relies upon the (re)integration of persons, whether victim or perpetrator, into communities. However, this does not mean that the processes are complementary—far from it. Rather, as discussed above, they are likely to be in tension, not least because DDR processes are generally prioritised, financially and temporally, by international peacebuilders, for pragmatic reasons. The apparent prioritisation of excombatants perceived to be victims, over identified victims, may not only appear unfair but also links the fate of the two groups at least in the minds of victims and communities. The situation is complicated further because many excombatants may also have been victims, having been kidnapped or otherwise forcibly recruited, and because these identities are not singular or stable, the same individual may seek to self-identify with one or the other at the end of a conflict.

DDR and transitional justice processes engage not only overlapping sets of beneficiaries but are also increasingly engaged in by overlapping sets of actors, as peacebuilding missions engage more extensively in activities beyond immediate DDR and security and engage in rule of law and human rights promotion. Further, DDR and transitional justice processes may even draw on and modify similar mechanisms and concepts, in particular, invoking concepts such as restorative justice, processes such as traditional justice and traditional conflict resolution, reconciliation and social reintegration—in essence they operate in the same space and with the same tools. They do so, however, often without fully acknowledging that they are. This approach, I will suggest, is deeply problematic, failing as it does to recognise the purposes and limitations of such concepts and the ways in which they may have been altered through the course of conflicts. In particular, processes which link, intentionally or otherwise, victim-centred justice and DDR, may

[40] United Nations 2006b, module 6.20.

[41] Sriram and Herman 2009.

coerce victims to engage with and "forgive" perpetrators for the purposes of short-term reconciliation processes in ways which do not promote longer term acceptance and coexistence.[42] Even if victims are not coerced, they may feel that they have been used for a process which does not benefit them or help in their own healing.[43]

For a variety of reasons, victims and excombatants, as well as the postconflict activities designed to address their needs, may be difficult to disaggregate. First, they cannot be separated because their needs and demands are articulated and addressed (or not) simultaneously in countries emerging from conflict. Historically, they were designed by different actors without a clear understanding of the relationship or interaction of processes addressing victims and excombatants, although with the expanding remit of peacekeeping and peacebuilding operations. Those developing programmes may increasingly overlap.[44] Further, these processes are not solely in contradiction. They may also have overlapping goals.

DDR processes clearly aim to disarm former combatants, but their goals are wider. Specifically, they also seek to transform them from fighters to civilians or members of legitimate state security forces, and importantly seek to promote their return to their own former communities or to new communities, which will include victims in most instances. At the same time, DDR processes must provide incentives to encourage members of fighting forces to give up the security and access to resources which remaining armed may provide. DDR programmes thus usually offer training and education, and in some cases cash payments, in order to enable their transition to civilian life. And in some instances, the packages, including cash payments, are expected to make former combatants more attractive returnees to communities, which otherwise might resist the return of individuals either suspected of committing, or known to have committed, serious abuses.

At the same time, victim-centred approaches to justice seek to address the needs or demands of victims in a variety of means, as discussed above, and may entail far more than retributive criminal justice. They may include processes which recognise the harm which victims have suffered, including material and symbolic restorative justice processes, and which may assist in victims feeling themselves to be part of a community again. They may also involve processes of reconciliation which include former perpetrators of abuses. The question is whether they can or should be linked. While there has been little intentional linkage to date, some lessons from recent experiences, where the processes have interacted in the absence of any clear design, may be instructive.

---

[42] Stovel and Valiñas 2010, p. vi.

[43] Laplante and Theidon warn of this risk with truth commissions (Laplante and Theidon 2007, pp. 240, 241).

[44] Sriram and Herman 2009.

14.7 Victims and Excombatants in Recent Transitional Justice Practice

As I have discussed in the chapter, there are evident tensions between victim-centred approaches to justice and DDR processes. However, there is a turn to greater engagement between the two, in part by design, with the promotion by the IDDRS of greater coordination, but largely not by design, even where the two sets of processes may use the same "tools" and actors. The relatively limited recent experience in this area demonstrates both the tensions resultant from parallel practice, but also the potential limitations in attempting greater coordination. I consider a few recent examples illustrating these phenomena.

The tensions I have discussed abound, but the experience of Sierra Leone may be illustrative.[45] The country's conflict ended in 2000/2001, with DDR processes initiated rapidly. Those processes demobilised 70,000 former combatants (many more than expected, which is not unusual given underestimates of genuine numbers of fighters and fraudulent participants in DDR). Those who completed the DDR process received vocational training and/or educational support, typically involving carpentry, masonry and computer education for male demobilised, and hair weaving for female demobilised.[46] They also received a small cash payout and "kits", largely for future prospective employment in construction. The DDR process was completed relatively quickly. Victims and civil society have been extremely critical of the fact that former combatants received such support, while calls for reparations went unanswered until the creation of a reparations programme in 2009. That programme ran for only one year and provided, in addition to direct medical assistance for some victims, a small one-time cash payout to some 20,000 of about 30,000 registered victims. The bulk of international assistance for the programme has expired, with a comparatively small amount of assistance still provided, largely via UN Women, and a tiny amount via a national trust fund. Meanwhile, victims not only complain about the delay in assistance but also the comparative scale; many have spent years unable to make a living.

At the same time, the training element of DDR has not been a resounding success. There is evidence that many female former fighters chose not to go through the DDR process even where it was accessible in order to avoid stigma, registering as victims many years later instead. With few construction or computing jobs available, former combatants rapidly sold their DDR kits, enabling many to set up business as taxi or motorcycle drivers. This enabled them to begin to earn money, while victims, most notably amputees, continue to face difficulties earning a living in one of the poorest countries in the world. Former fighters, particularly

[45] This discussion draws upon Sriram 2012.

[46] While it is beyond the scope of this chapter, it is worth recognising that such gendered training might well have been unsuitable for female demobilised. Further evaluations indicate that females associated with fighting forces are often excluded from DDR processes, either because they lack weapons to turn in or because they decline to participate because of the stigma attached.

former Revolutionary United Front (RUF) members, have not returned to their former communities, but are concentrated in urban populations and are still socially demarcated: recklessly driving motorcycle and taxi drivers in Freetown rapidly have the invective "DDR driver" hurled at them. The Sierra Leonean experience illustrates the tensions when the relationship between dealing with the needs of excombatants and dealing with the needs of victims is not taken into consideration.

But what happens when these processes are more directly connected? It is possible to have processes which link criminal accountability, truth-telling and reparations, all of which may be considered at least in part victim-centred, with DDR, as in Colombia.[47] The process initiated by the Justice and Peace Law in Colombia involves a truth-telling process linked to a demobilisation process for excombatants, criminal justice proceedings and a reparations process, thus connecting not only victims and victimisers but also restorative and ostensibly reconciliatory and retributive justice processes.[48] However, as Theidon argues, despite this institutional linkage amongst processes, many former paramilitary members reject it, as it was not part of the original agreement regarding demobilisation, and other members are unaware of the linkage. Further, the return of excombatants is not always welcomed by communities in Colombia that have not been consulted.[49] The processes now in place in Colombia were not designed in a holistic fashion, with the intention of coordinating all of these processes, but have emerged through the amendment of the 2005 Justice and Peace Law and the evolution of institutions and passage of new laws, most recently a Victims' Law.[50]

Beyond state-sponsored or internationally driven processes of transitional justice such as commissions of inquiry, DDR processes also operate alongside, and sometimes seek to utilise, non-state or traditional justice and conflict resolution mechanisms, often without recognising that they may have an impact on these processes. They also rely openly on these processes to aid "reintegration", but without any critical reflection. Thus, for example, returning fighters may take part in community or "traditional" cleansing or reconciliation ceremonies, as with some former members of the Lord's Resistance Army (LRA) in Northern Uganda through the Acholi *mato oput* traditional justice or conflict resolution practices. While such processes may ease reintegration, it is worth recalling not only that traditional practices are not designed to cope with ordinary killing, much less mass atrocities, but also that the practices themselves may be inconsistent with international human rights standards. There are no formal guidelines for assessing which non-state practices of justice merit support, or to determine how they should interface with DDR processes. Because traditional systems are frequently utilised in post-conflict

47 Theidon 2007, p. 73.

48 The very title of the Comisión Nacional de Reparación y Reconciliación, a core institution in the process, speaks to the purported goals. See Theidon 2007; García-Godos and Lid 2010.

49 Theidon 2007, pp. 79, 80, 83.

50 García-Godos 2012. I do not discuss the Victims' Law because it is too recent for its operation to be assessed.

situations, practitioners need a greater understanding of how they engage communities, victims and perpetrators.

The convergence of transitional justice and DDR processes is perhaps most evident in the context of child soldiers, not least because they are often both victims and perpetrators. Programmes also expect, rightly or wrongly, that former child soldiers particularly need to be returned to former communities and family structures, given that they may still be minors.[51] Further, the emphasis on reintegration rather than punishment is strong with respect to former child soldiers in part because, as Drumbl explains eloquently, they are cast as innocent victims. This is reinforced by the legal proscription of child recruitment: while there are discrepancies with regard to the appropriate age threshold, child recruitment is a crime in international law.[52] However, despite the emphasis on returning child soldiers to former communities, they often still face a stigma, even where they have gone through ceremonies of cleansing or forgiveness. Thus in Sierra Leone, some former child soldiers are reported to be taunted in villages of return with calls of "rebel girl".

14.8 Conclusions

The distinction between victims and excombatants may be a necessary one for programmers of both transitional justice and peacebuilding in the field, but may also obscure the fact that these identities are somewhat mutable and imposed by international programmers and/or adopted by individuals in countries emerging from conflict despite the multifarious identities individuals may have. Victim-centred approaches to justice and DDR programmes have largely engaged these two sets of actors as though they were easily distinguishable, and treated them separately—they have been beneficiaries of distinct types of support and material assistance (if any), engaged by different international actors, and afforded distinct roles or agency in processes designed for or around them. Yet, as this chapter has discussed, the processes engaging victims and excombatants are often in conflict with one another and increasingly engaging the same sets of international programmers and local beneficiaries. And whether by design or by accident, the same processes, whether traditional justice activities, truth and reconciliation commissions, or prosecutions and reparations, may engage both victims and excombatants at once, with the risk of satisfying neither. Policy recommendations are beyond the scope of this chapter, but policymakers would do well to attend to the risks and challenges outlined here.

---

[51] With Drumbl I use this as a term of convenience, recognising that many are in fact (in the language of the Paris Principles) children associated with fighting forces and may not have engaged in direct combat.

[52] McKnight 2010; McKay 2004.

References

Baumgartner E (2008) Aspects of victim participation in the proceedings of the International Criminal Court. Int Rev Red Cross 90:409–440
Beck E, Kropf NP, Blume Leonard P (eds) (2010) Social work and restorative justice: skills for dialogue, peacemaking, and reconciliation. Oxford University Press, Oxford
Bennett C (2006) Taking the sincerity out of saying sorry: restorative justice as ritual. J Appl Philos 23:127–143
de Feyter K, Parmentier S, Bossuyt M, Lemmens P (eds) (2005) Out of the ashes: reparation for victims of gross and systematic human rights violations. Intersentia, Antwerpen
de Greiff P (ed) (2006) The handbook of reparations. Cambridge University Press, Cambridge
Findlay M (2009) Activating a victim constituency in International Criminal Justice. Int J Transitional Justice 3:183–206
García-Godos J (2006) Citizenship, conflict and reconstruction: a case-study of the effects of armed conflict on peasant-state relations in Tambo, Peru. Unipub forlag, Oslo
García-Godos J (2008) Victim reparations in the Peruvian Truth Commission and the challenge of historical interpretation. Int J Transitional Justice 2:62–83
García-Godos J (2012) Colombia: accountability and DDR in the pursuit of peace? In: Sriram CL, García-Godos J, Herman J, Martin-Ortega O (eds) Transitional justice and peacebuilding on the ground: victims and excombatants. Routledge, London
García-Godos J, Lid K AO (2010) Transitional justice and victims' rights before the end of a conflict: the unusual case of Colombia. J Latin Am Stud 42:487–526
Gillett M (2009) Victim participation at the International Criminal Court. Aust Int Law J 16:29–46
Hayner P (2000) Unspeakable truths: confronting state terror and atrocity. Routledge, London
Henham R (2004) Some reflections on the role of victims in the international criminal trial process. Int Rev Vict 11:201–224
Humphrey M (2003) From victim to victimhood: truth commissions and trials as rituals of political transition and individual healing. Aust J Anthropol 14:171–187
Kritz N (1995) Transitional justice: how emerging democracies reckon with former regimes. US Institute of Peace, Washington
Laplante LJ, Theidon K (2007) Truth with consequences: justice and reparations in post-truth commission Peru. Hum Rights Q 29:228–250
Llewellyn J (2008) Restorative justice and peacebuilding in post-conflict societies. Paper presented at the annual conference of the International Studies Association San Francisco. www.humansecuritygateway.com/showRecord_fr.php?RecordId=23155. Accessed 31 May 2012
Mani R (2006) Reparations as a component of transitional justice: pursuing "reparative justice" in the aftermath of violent conflict. In: de Feyter K, Parmentier S, Bossuyt M, Lemmens P (eds) Out of the ashes: reparation for victims of gross and systematic human rights violations. Intersentia, Antwerpen, pp. 53–82
McCarthy C (2009) Reparations under the Rome Statute of the International Criminal Court and Reparative Justice Theory. Int J Transitional Justice 3:250–271
McKay S (2004) Reconstructing fragile lives: girls' social reintegration in northern Uganda and Sierra Leone. Gender Dev 12:19–30
McKnight J (2010) Child soldiers in Africa: a global approach to human rights protection, enforcement, and post-conflict reintegration. Afr J Int Comp Law 18:113–142
Muggah R (2009) Security and post-conflict reconstruction: dealing with fighters in the aftermath of war. Routledge, London
Muggah R (2010) Innovations in disarmament, demobilization and reintegration policy and research: reflections on the last decade, NUPI Working Paper 774, Norwegian Institute of International Affairs, Oslo. www.english.nupi.no/Publications/Working-Papers/2010/Innovations-in-disarmament-demobilization-and-reintegration-policy-and-research. Accessed 31 May 2012
Nwogu NW (2010) When and why it started: deconstructing victim-centered truth commissions in the context of ethnicity-based conflict. Int J Transitional Justice 4:275–289

Quinn JR (2009) Reconciliation(s): transitional justice in postconflict societies. McGill-Queens University Press, Montreal

Rauschenbach M, Scalia D (2008) Victims and international criminal justice: a vexed question? Int Rev Red Cross 90:441–459

Robins S (2011) Towards victim-centred transitional justice: understanding the needs of families of the disappeared in postconflict Nepal. Int J Transitional Justice 5:75–98

Rubio-Marín R, de Greiff P (2007) Women and reparations. Int J Transitional Justice 1:318–337

Shelton D (2006) The United Nations draft principles on reparations for human rights violations: context and content. In: de Feyter K, Parmentier S, Bossuyt M, Lemmens P (eds) Out of the ashes: reparation for victims of gross and systematic human rights violations. Intersentia, Antwerpen, pp. 11–33

Sriram CL (2004) Confronting past human rights violations: justice versus peace in times of transition. Routledge, London

Sriram CL (2005) Globalizing justice for mass atrocities: a revolution in accountability. Routledge, London

Sriram CL (2012) Victim-centred justice and DDR in Sierra Leone. In: Sriram CL, García-Godos J, Herman J, Martin-Ortega O (eds) Transitional justice and peacebuilding on the ground: victims and excombatants. Routledge, London, pp. 159–177

Sriram CL, Herman J (2009) DDR and transitional justice: bridging the divide? J Confl Sec Dev 9:455–474

Sriram CL, García-Godos J, Herman J, Martin-Ortega O (eds) (2012) Transitional justice and peacebuilding on the ground: victims and excombatants. Routledge, London

Stovel L, Valiñas M (2010) Restorative justice after mass violence, UNICEF Innocenti Working Paper, Florence. www.unicef-irc.org/publications/pdf/iwp_2010_15.pdf. Accessed 31 May 2012

Straus S, Waldorf L (eds) (2011) Remaking Rwanda: state building and human rights after mass violence. University of Wisconsin Press, Madison

Teitel R (2000) Transitional justice. New York, Oxford

Theidon K (2007) Transitional subjects: the disarmament, demobilization, and reintegration of former combatants in Colombia. Int J Transitional Justice 1:66–90

Thomson S (2011) Reeducation for reconciliation. In: Straus S, Waldorf L (eds) Remaking Rwanda: state building and human rights after mass violence. University of Wisconsin Press, Madison, pp. 331–339

United Nations (2005a) Basic principles and guidelines on the right to a remedy and reparation for victims of gross violations of International Human Rights Law and Serious Violations of International Humanitarian Law, UN General Assembly Resolution 147, UN GA, 60th Session, UN Doc A/RES/60/147

United Nations (2005b) Draft updated set of principles for the protection and promotion of human rights through action to combat impunity, UN Doc. E/CN.4/2005/102/Add.1

United Nations (2005c) Basic principles on the use of restorative justice programmes in criminal matters, United Nations Economic and Social Council, UN Doc. E/CN.15/2002/5/Add.1

United Nations (2006a) Handbook on restorative justice programmes. United Nations Office on Drugs and Crime, Vienna

United Nations (2006b) Integrated disarmament, demobilization, and reintegration standards, module 6.20. www.unddr.org/iddrs/06/20.php. Accessed 3 April 2012

United Nations (2006c) Report of the secretary general on disarmament, demobilization and reintegration, UN Doc. A/60/75

Vandeginste S, Sriram C L (2011) Power sharing and transitional justice: a clash of paradigms? Glob Gov 17:489–505

Waldorf L (2012) Just peace: integrating transitional justice and DDR. In: Sriram CL, García-Godos J, Herman J, Martin-Ortega O (eds) Transitional justice and peacebuilding on the ground: victims and excombatants. Routledge, London, pp. 62–80

Wiebelhaus-Brahm E (2010) Truth commissions and transitional societies: the impact on human rights and democracy. Routledge, London

Chapter 15
Victims of Genocide and Crimes Against Humanity

Boris Barth

Abstract The first part of this chapter gives a very short overview of the historiography of the concept of genocide. Some of the problems and controversies caused both by the term and by the definition of victim groups are put into a historical perspective. The second part deals with the consequences for the research on victims of genocide and crimes against humanity. In the third part, the question is discussed whether the concept of genocide is still useful for the analysis of mass violence in the 20th century, because a considerable gap exists between the expectations of victim groups and the need to find clear and scientific definitions for mass violence.

Keywords Victims • Genocide • Ethnic cleansing • Crimes against humanity • Mass violence • Twentieth century • Modernity

15.1 Definitions

As I am not a scholar of international law but a historian, I would like to focus on some of the historical aspects of the topic. First of all it is striking that the terminology we are using today is relatively new, and this might explain why debates about definitions are still leading to sharp controversies. The term genocide was coined in 1944. Since 1992, the term "ethnic cleansing" has been introduced in most of the Western languages, and the term "crimes against humanity" might have existed already before the Second World War, but was not common before the Nuremberg Trials. Obviously in the second half of the 20th century, a necessity was felt both by scholars and by public opinion at least in the West to define new

---

The author is Professor of Modern and Contemporary History at the University of Konstanz, Germany.

B. Barth (✉)
University of Konstanz, Konstanz, Germany
e-mail: boris.barth@uni-konstanz.de

T. Bonacker and C. Safferling (eds.), *Victims of International Crimes: An Interdisciplinary Discourse*, DOI: 10.1007/978-90-6704-912-2_15,

concepts. The historiography of the terminology is already showing how difficult it was and is to find terms for the new wave of crimes committed by governments which arose during the 20th century.

Before the 20th century, in the European languages no specific term was known to describe extreme forms of violence. In the 19th century, massacres in the colonies or especially during the wars on the Balkans were described as cruelties, or in the German language as "Gräueltaten" (atrocities or horrors of war). Massacres inflicted on civilians during military conflicts were often regarded as a pre-modern phenomenon which would disappear during the ongoing process of civilisation. Despite the European behaviour in some colonial wars and the invention of new lethal weapons, most of the contemporaries were convinced that European progress would also lead automatically to more civilised forms of warfare. This optimism was based on facts. The International Red Cross was founded to improve the fate of both prisoners of war and wounded soldiers in hospitals. In 1899 and 1907, for the first time in world history, the Hague Conventions established international laws on war and war crimes and tried to regulate the rights and the obligations of neutral states. Additionally, since the middle of the 19th century, the European experience seemed to show that modern wars were short and could be controlled—as cabinet wars—by the political institutions. Today this optimist view has disappeared completely—historians and sociologists are now discussing the question whether genocide and ethnic cleansing are integral parts of 20th century modernity, and whether a direct connection exists between new forms of mass violence on the one hand and the wave of democratisation accompanied by nationalist aggression on the other.[1] Analysing the example of Eastern Anatolia Mark Levene further asserts a direct connection between nation building and state formation on the one hand and ethnic cleansing and huge massacres of minorities on the other.[2]

The horrors of World War I changed the perception of civilisation and inevitable progress. However, this war did not really stimulate a general debate about new forms of mass killings of civilians. The *entente*'s attempts to instigate legal proceedings against the leadership of the Young Turks, which was responsible for the Armenian genocide, failed for different reasons after World War I. It is still an open research question why hardly anybody was interested in this problem after 1918, although the facts of the mass violence were well known and had already been sharply criticised by the *entente* powers during the war. In 1933 at the conference on international criminal law in Madrid, organised by the legal council of the League of Nations, the young lawyer Raphael Lemkin argued that the sovereignty of the state could not include the right to kill hundreds of thousands of its citizens, but at this time he was not able to raise any debate among the scholars of international law.[3] The Holocaust changed the situation. As early as December 1944, the Washington Post published an article about the gas chambers in Auschwitz and

---

1 See Mann 2005; Naimark 2001; Snyder 2000.

2 See Levene 1998.

3 Gilbert 2003, p. 22.

came to the conclusion that it would be a mistake to use the term "atrocities"—it would be something new.[4]

During the negotiations which led to the famous UN Genocide Convention in 1948 different interests of the respective states had to be taken into account. The convention, which was closely connected with the Universal Declaration of Human Rights, created a new approach towards international law and limited the sovereignty of the state. However, at the same time the convention was a political compromise aiming at the punishment and the prevention of genocide, but it contains no precise definitions of possible victim groups.[5] According to the convention national, racial, ethnic and religious groups can become the object of genocide and need special protection. In 1948, in view of the Holocaust, the inclusion of racial and ethnic groups seemed to be obvious and did not need more detailed explanation, but today the definition of a racial or ethnic group is much more difficult, if not impossible. Most scholars would refuse to use the term "racial" groups, because this would mean at least indirectly accepting some kind of racist interpretation of differences between human beings. The same can be said about the concept of "ethnic" groups. Ethnicity is a widely used and popular term; however, from a scientific and historical perspective it is impossible to define. Ethnicity is not an objective category, but—to use Benedict Anderson's famous statement about the nation state—ethnic groups are "imagined communities".[6]

In 1948 both the United States and the Soviet Union pressed successfully for the exclusion of political groups. The Soviet motivation was obvious, because otherwise the Stalinist terror of the 1930s, the hunger catastrophe in the Ukraine, and the policies towards the different nationalities within the Soviet Union could have been suspected of being genocidal. The US position was less clear, but obviously it was designed to prevent topics like the former racial slavery, the displacements of the native Americans, or other dark chapters of American history becoming subjects of international discussion. The exclusion of political groups has therefore often been subjected to harsh criticism, but despite the respective interests which led to this decision it made sense in the long run. The proper definition of political groups is impossible and would only provoke endless propaganda battles in the context of conflicts and wars. Helen Fein points out that the Khmer Rouge, the SS, the NKWD, and other organisations were also without doubt political groups or political organisations which did not need any special international protection—on the contrary.[7] A single person can become a member of a political group and leave it voluntarily. Leaving an ethnic group—whether real or imagined—which is threatened by a potential perpetrator, however, is impossible. One way to find a solution which is leading out of these definition problems could be the idea in the French Criminal Law Code which refers to "a group determined by any other

[4] Washington Post, 3 December 1944. See also the letters to the editor in the following days.

[5] For details see Schabas 2000.

[6] Anderson 2006.

[7] Fein 1999, pp. 13, 14.

arbitrary criterion".[8] However, the consequence would be that every group which is threatened by any perpetrator is protected by the genocide convention—in theory this might be a way to avoid massacres and mass violence against civilians in the future, in political reality it might cause many fruitless debates about both political issues and power politics. Additionally, other problems of definition are caused by the fact that historians, scholars of international law, and politicians have to distinguish between "arbitrary" and "non-arbitrary" criteria which might become difficult as well.

Today historians, anthropologists, social scientists and some scholars of international law are reading the genocide convention in rather different ways, and this is also the result of different national research traditions. After 1948, the convention was almost forgotten and hardly anybody cared about it between the 1950s and 1970s. When the problem was rediscovered in the USA in the 1980s, no historians or scholars of international or criminal law took part in the debate, which was initiated mainly by anthropologists and some social scientists. Without deeper historical analysis, they identified many cases of genocide and set up scales of atrocities. Several authors like Frank Chalk, Kurt Jonassohn or Alexander Hinton were and are using very broad and extended definitions of genocide.[9] For them genocide started with the destruction of ancient Carthage by the Romans, and every big massacre and many cases of mass killings were simply classified as genocidal. In this tradition, the terms mass murder, massacre, and genocide are used as synonyms, and some authors claim to have found more than 30, sometimes even 50 examples of genocide in world history. The recently published Oxford Handbook of Genocide Studies gives no precise definition either. Genocide seems to be a global phenomenon which has existed since Adam and Eve left paradise.[10]

Australian historians like Colin Tatz have raised the issue of the so-called stolen generation, i.e. children of Aborigines who were taken away from their mothers.[11] In Australia during the 20th century many children of Aborigines were taken away from their mothers by the state authorities and—no doubt—seen from today's perspective this was a criminal act caused by racism. If one reads the convention literally (especially Article II.e. concerning the transfer of children) one really can argue like Tatz, and genocide can even happen if no one is killed. The consequence would be to add ten or twenty more cases to the already long list of genocides in history, because the stealing of children happened rather often in the past, starting with the transatlantic slave trade and ending with the deportation of children to communist countries after the Greek Civil War in 1948/1949. The number of genocides becomes endless and so does the number of potential or real groups of victims. Additionally, the question arises whether it makes sense to put the racist but democratic Australian Government on the same level with Hitler's Nazi regime.

[8] FIDH 2012, p. 5.

[9] Chalk and Jonassohn 1990; Hinton 2002.

[10] Bloxham 2010.

[11] See Tatz 2003, p. 69.

One more general problem remains: Should one distinguish conceptually between, for example, the Tianmen massacre in Bejing and National Socialist annihilation camps like Treblinka? Was Auschwitz something new? On Tianmen Square, the Chinese democratisation movement was suppressed, but the Holocaust meant an attack on every concept of humanity and civilisation as such!

In Germany, in Israel of course, and to some extent in France as well until the end of the 1990s, the field was dominated by historians who used a very strict and narrow definition due to the fact that the annihilation of the European Jews during World War II was regarded as the ultimate and sometimes as the only case of real genocide. Especially in Germany, every attempt to start comparative genocide research at an international level was faced with the suspicion of playing down the meaning of the Holocaust. This attitude was the result of the long and very difficult process of coming to terms with one's own past, which was a major preoccupation of German public opinion for several decades. Additionally, in the 1980s, some revisionist German historians had started a debate, the so-called "historians dispute", about the historical meaning of the Holocaust.[12] However, the attempt to qualify the meaning of Auschwitz and to establish a new relativistic view of the annihilation of the European Jews failed; nearly all German and international historians then agreed about the "uniqueness" of the Shoah. Additionally, in the German language, the term genocide is used as a synonym for "Völkermord" (murder of people) or for final solution, and this fact already limits the use of broader concepts.

Since the late 1990s a new debate about the concept of genocide has started, caused by the conceptual confusion mentioned above. A general feeling of discontent with the definition in the UN convention has arisen among many scholars from different disciplines. For some authors, the existing terminology is too narrow to integrate very brutal forms of suppression and mass murder, like, for example, the Stalinist crimes in Russia; for others, it is too far-reaching. As a result, an inflation of new concepts has appeared. Alongside "genocide" one finds terms like "genocidal massacre", "self-genocide" (Cambodia), "ethnocide", "politicide" (Soviet Union), "democide", "feminicide", "ecocide", "economicide", and many more. This inflation of new concepts—whether useful or not—is always a certain indicator that the extension of an older concept does not work properly any more. Apart from this inflation the term "genocide" has been used in the public for a huge variety of different cases which have nothing to do with extreme forms of mass killings, sometimes not even with mass violence. To give only a few examples taken from daily domestic politics: The misuse of drugs, methadone programs, birth control, medical treatment of fundamentalist Christians, the closing of synagogues in the Soviet Union, or the abortion of children in the USA have been regarded as genocidal in the past. Again in the words of Helen Fein: "If this is awful it must be genocide."[13] One can also distinguish between a broad "social" and a more limited "legal" concept of genocide, but the problem is that both the so-called social and the legal concept as well only refer to the genocide convention. The problem does not lie in the different ways of reading

---

[12] See the documents in Augstein 1987.

[13] Fein 1994, p. 95.

the convention, but in the text of the convention itself. It does not give a precise scientific analysis, but is a political compromise aiming at the prevention of mass murder, if necessary by a military intervention organised and led by the United Nations.

15.2 Victim Groups

All of these debates were mainly focused on definitions, states, the role of governments, new forms of violence, or the question of sovereignty, but the victims played hardly any role at all. In the past, the scapegoat argument has been stressed to explain waves of violence against minority groups, but it is obviously not suited to analyse mass violence in the 20th century. If Jews had been killed as scapegoats, Auschwitz would have been a rather popular enterprise and it would have been used openly for Nazi propaganda purposes. However, both the Armenian genocide and the Nazi mass murder in the East were kept secret. No government ever used the murder of millions of people to legitimate its rule openly.[14]

When focusing on victims a first and general problem is caused by the very fact that the victim groups are arbitrarily defined by the perpetrator. Genocide in the 20th century always had an ethnic dimension or was based on racist ideas. For victims who are threatened by murderous violence it is impossible to re-define their ethnic, religious or cultural identity. The second problem arises from the fact that most of the victims are dead and unable to speak for themselves, while the culture of remembrance is constructed either by a small number of survivors or by interest groups. If victims are represented by a state like Israel, the formation of a collective culture of mourning and the concern for the interests of the survivors is much easier than in the case of the Armenians, who could hardly develop their own national traditions during the time of the Soviet Union. Other groups, i.e. the Romani people, the handicapped or the homosexuals, who had become victims of the National Socialist genocides as well, had to lead a long and exhausting struggle until their status as victims was respected by both the German state and German society.

The traumatic experience of collective victimisation often caused a reinterpretation of self-definitions, of one's own history, or of the respective national traditions. Genocide and mass violence have transferred or destroyed existing group identities and have also created new perceptions among the survivors. The German case is well known: Before 1933 many German Jews felt extremely patriotic, a considerable number of young Jewish men volunteered in World War I, and the self definition of being Jewish was not determined by ideas about ethnicity, but by religion, which was regarded as a private affair. Something similar can be said about many Jews in Western Europe, who defined themselves as patriotic, sometimes even as nationalist members of the respective nation states, and they had little in common with much more traditional East European communities—despite

[14] Valentino 2004, pp. 23, 31, 32.

a vague feeling of solidarity. In Rwanda, Hutu and Tutsi were originally African social categories and it is a matter of historical controversy whether and when exactly a kind of ethnic feeling among the Tutsi was formed. However, it is clear that this ethnic redefinition of social groups was a direct consequence of colonialism and decolonisation. Both the German and, later, the Belgian colonial rulers were obsessed by the idea of classifying the population in their colonies along racial or ethnic lines. Ethnicity was not historically given, but it was created by the interest of the coloniser. During the process of decolonisation eager African politicians discovered the advantages of using the growing ethnic hatred for their own nationalist purposes, and they stimulated outbreaks of violence.

Something similar could be said about many other groups which became victims of massive violence. However, to this day the genocide concept has to follow at least indirectly the racist logic and/or the ethnic motivation of the murderer and not the perspective of the victims, which might differ a lot. Perhaps this is not a problem for criminal law, which is primarily interested in the motivation of the individual perpetrator, but it causes difficulties for the general historical analysis of violence.

Much more comparative historical research is still necessary concerning cultures of remembrance which were directly and indirectly formed by mass violence. The case of Israel is obvious, because the modern identity of the Jewish state is directly linked with the Shoah. The same is true for the Republic of Armenia and for the modern Armenian identity. The Armenian genocide in World War I is still seen as the most important historical event in the Armenian past, and the cults of remembrance are extremely important for the creation of a unified nation. Something similar can be said about the Ukrainian identity, even if hardly any official culture of remembrance was established.[15] After the break-down of the Soviet empire history became a kind of a raw material to legitimate the creation of a new and unified nation state. Since then the history of the people of the Ukraine is often interpreted as a history of suffering with the climax of the *holodomor* (Ukrainian for "hunger catastrophe") in 1932/33, which led to at least three million victims. Even if some international historians refuse to use the term genocide in this case, because no single document has been found which proves a genocidal intention of the Soviet leaders, the hunger catastrophe was caused by the Stalinist regime and was—no doubt—a crime against humanity. However, such a nationalisation of historical violence sometimes creates difficulties. The official nationalist view on the *holodomor* stresses the "Soviet" or "Russian" responsibility, but ignores the fact that Ukrainian troops prevented the peasants from escaping from the regions of starvation and that communist Ukrainian party organisations were fully integrated into the execution of the murderous plans. In Ukraine, the racist or ethnic component is missing which is typical of many other cases of mass violence. That makes it difficult to construct a "national" or patriotic narrative of victimhood which is also convincing for Western scholars.

---

[15] See Öhman 2003.

No national narrative exists in the case of Rwanda. In this country only very few serious historical and comparative studies were written about the traumatic experiences of the victims. The lack of research on victims in Africa was mainly caused by the new Government of Rwanda, which is trying to build a new post-genocidal society but at the same time suppresses in an authoritarian way any public debate about the state's racist past. Historians might doubt whether such a policy will be successful in the long run. One might expect new conflicts in the future, because the repression of memories has seldom contributed to the stabilisation of societies. It is a striking fact that we have only very few scientific attempts to write comparative histories from the perspective of the survivors. Nearly all the respective narratives are told within a national frame and the traumatic experiences are mixed up with new forms of defensive nationalism. However, to this day no categories for comparative analysis have been established which are accepted by the majority of scholars.

15.3 Conclusion

The term genocide carries a strong moral message, but this has caused unpleasant debates of another kind. If one comes to a general definition—no matter whether it is a narrow or a broad one—one must necessarily exclude some groups of victims. This does not mean a denial of crimes, but it means that in accordance with the respective definition the killings in "XYZ-state" are not classified as genocide or as genocidal. Normally, this causes a storm of protest among some of the groups concerned and the rather aggressive accusation of playing down horrifying crimes. If one uses a narrow definition of genocide it is necessary to exclude many colonial massacres from the concept. Colonial armies sometimes killed tens of thousands of indigenous women and children, but for a number of reasons it can make sense to avoid the genocide terminology.

Why do people react in such an aggressive way just because of an academic classification? Some recent polemical publications deal with the so-called competition of the victims as well, i.e. a kind of scramble of victim groups competing for the genocide trophy.[16] The refusal to apply the genocide terminology does not necessarily mean a denial of crimes. For the victim it is not important whether he or she was killed during a genocide or "only" in an "ordinary" massacre. However, a huge gap is often visible between the scientific attempts to develop a precise definition and the public expectations which are aiming for a clear moral evaluation.

Some historians doubt that the genocide concept is really suited to come to a deeper understanding of massacres and state violence in the 20th century, because the legal definition which is formulated by international law is not really helpful to understand the historical dimension. For example, Jacques Semelin, who shares this

[16] See Novick 2000; Chaumont 2001.

opinion, has written about the massacre in history and comes to extremely fascinating conclusions. Beyond all debates about genocide the massacre itself is a highly complex phenomenon and deeper historical, sociological, and psychological scrutiny is still necessary. The analysis of massacres touches upon topics like the dynamics of mass murder, the problem of bystanders and collective ignorance, the international situation, the role of media, collective paranoia, hate and imagined concepts of an enemy, the collective psychology of the perpetrators and the dehumanisation of perpetrators and victims.[17] Additionally, gender aspects like sexual violence or male/female stereotypes on violence deserve special attention. Such an integrated approach proves to be much more fruitful than endless debates on definitions.

Despite all of these weak points many authors believe that the genocide concept should not be given up until something better has been created. The term still carries a very strong message, and the UN convention might either deter potential perpetrators in the future or protect potential victims. However, to this day no research study exists which analyses the deterrent effect of the convention. It is an open question whether any dictator ever gave up ideas about mass killings because he was afraid of a reaction of the UN Security Council.

Obviously, it is impossible to discuss these matters on a university level alone, because public and published opinions and political interests are always present. In these public and political debates hierarchies of norms are set up. Many historians, sociologists, journalists, and scholars of international law are working with hierarchies of crimes. Torture, slave labour and forced prostitution are put on a high level in the pyramid of crimes; genocide is at the very top. Even if scholars try to remain as neutral as possible it is hard to prevent the analytical comparative discussion from suddenly acquiring a classifying character. This is also the result of a semantic problem. If genocide is seen as the worst possible crime, it is a superlative which can no longer be compared with anything else. A formulation that one genocide was more genocidal than another is definitely nonsense. However, if one compares genocides linguistically, the comparative form is impossible to avoid. This problem cannot be solved; one can only try to be aware of it.[18]

No doubt Lemkin was the leading pioneer in the field of the analysis of genocide, and the genocide convention marks a milestone in the history of international law. However, today its limits are clearly visible. Obviously by now Lemkin's definition of genocide has created such confusion that it makes sense to give it up. Lemkin deserves an honourable place in the history of research on mass violence, but he and his convention should not be treated as a holy cow. Recently, a new tendency in international law is becoming visible which is of interest for the historians as well. The Rome Statute for the International Criminal Court has been created to punish war crimes and crimes against humanity. The ICTR (International Criminal Tribunal for Rwanda) has stated that no hierarchy of norms exists in cases of genocide and

17 Semelin 2007.

18 Barth 2006, p. 48.

crimes against humanity.[19] It refers to the definitions which were used during the Nuremberg Trials, but improves some of the weak points which were caused by the genocide convention. Therefore, the term "crimes against humanity" is better suited to avoid international controversies and endless debates about definitions, because every persecution should be punished by international law.

References

Anderson B (2006) Imagined communities. Reflections on the origins and spread of nationalism. Verso, London

Augstein R (1987) Historikerstreit. Die Dokumentation der Kontroverse um die Einzigartigkeit der nationalsozialistischen Judenvernichtung. Piper, München

Barth B (2006) Genozid. Völkermord im 20. Jahrhundert. Geschichte, Theorien, Kontroversen. C.H. Beck, München

Bloxham D (2010) The Oxford handbook of genocide studies. Oxford University Press, Oxford

Chalk F, Jonassohn K (1990) The history and sociology of genocide: analyses and case studies. Yale University Press, New Haven

Chaumont J (2001) Die Konkurrenz der Opfer. Genozid, Identität und Anerkennung. Zu Klampen, Lüneburg

Fein H (1994) Genocide, terror, life integrity, and war crimes: the case for discrimination. In: Andreopoulos G (ed) Genocide. University of Pennsylvania Press, Philadelphia, pp. 95–107

Fein H (1999) Definition and discontent. labelling, detecting, and explaining genocide in the twentieth century. In: Förster S, Hirschfeld G (eds) Genozid in der modernen Geschichte. LIT, Münster, pp. 11–21

FIDH (2012) Implementing the principle of universal jurisdiction in France. www.fidh.org/IMG//pdf/universal_juris.pdf. Accessed 9 Aug 2012

Gilbert M (2003) Twentieth-century genocides. In: Winter J (ed) America and the Armenian genocide of 1915. Cambridge University Press, Cambridge, pp. 9–36

Hinton A (2002) Annihilating difference. University of California Press, Berkeley

Levene M (1998) Creating a modern "zone of genocide": the impact of nation- and state-formation on Eastern Anatolia 1878–1923. Holocaust Genocide Stud 12:393–433

Mann M (2005) The dark side of democracy: explaining ethnic cleansing. Cambridge University Press, Cambridge

Naimark N (2001) Fires of hatred: ethnic cleansing in twentieth century Europe. Harvard University Press, Boston

Novick P (2000) The holocaust and collective memory: the American experience. Bloomsbury, London

Öhman J (2003) Holodomor and the Ukrainian identity of suffering. The 1932–1933 Ukrainian famine in historical culture. Canadian-American Slavic Stud 37:27–44

Schabas W (2000) Genocide in international law: the crimes of crimes. Cambridge University Press, Cambridge

Semelin J (2007) Purify and destroy: the political uses of massacre and genocide. Columbia University Press, New York

Snyder J (2000) From voting to violence: democratization and nationalist conflict. Norton, New York

Tatz C (2003) With intent to destroy: reflecting on genocide. Verso, London

Valentino B (2004) Final solutions: mass killing and genocide in the twentieth century. Cornell University Press, New York

[19] See Barth 2006, pp. 208, 209.

Chapter 16
Victims of Civil War

Stefanie Bock

Abstract Large-scale international crimes always have a profound impact on both the individual victims and the society as a whole, i.e., the victimisation has an individual and a collective dimension. Civil wars or non-international armed conflicts are characterised by the fact that they take place within a society. Accordingly, the belligerent parties are often connected in language, history and culture. With the outbreak of the conflict, the need arises to stress the differences between them in order to construct clearly distinguishable opposing groups. This process is often accompanied by a systematic discrimination, dehumanisation and degradation of the adversary creating a general atmosphere of hate which furthers an escalation of violence and a brutalisation of the conflict. In addition, civil wars are often asymmetric conflicts with a strong imbalance of power between the conflicting parties—a critical situation which entails an increased risk of non-compliance with international humanitarian law. Moreover, the fighting may result in a circle of violence in which the positions of victims and victimisers become interchangeable. The main challenge of a transitional process in the aftermath of the atrocities is to meet the needs of all persons affected by the violence—be they civilians, soldiers or fighters—and to heal the divide of the society.

Keywords Victims • Civil war • Neutralisation techniques • Asymmetrical warfare • International humanitarian law • Traumatisation

16.1 Introduction

All international crimes share some common features. In contrast to 'normal' national crimes there is not only one victim facing one perpetrator. Rather, the victimisation forms part of an overall conflict which affects the whole society.[1]

The author is Senior Research Assistant of Professor Dr. Kai Ambos, Department for Foreign and International Criminal Law, and assistant professor at the Georg-August Universität Göttingen, Germany.

[1] Ewald 2002, pp. 90, 93, 94; Rauschenbach and Scalia 2008, pp. 441, 450.

S. Bock (✉)
Department for Foreign and International Criminal Law, Georg-August Universität, Göttingen, Germany
e-mail: stefanie.bock@jura.uni-goettingen.de

T. Bonacker and C. Safferling (eds.), *Victims of International Crimes: An Interdisciplinary Discourse*, DOI: 10.1007/978-90-6704-912-2_16,

Violence is omnipresent and becomes an integral part of the social reality. This collective dimension increases the impact of the crimes on the individual victims.[2] To properly address the needs of victims in court proceedings and during a transitional process it is important to be aware of this interrelation between individual and collective victimisation. In the following, I would like to highlight some structural characteristics of victimisation in civil wars.

16.2 The Notion of Civil Wars and Their Treatment in International Law

Civil wars respectively non-international armed conflicts have been defined by the Appeals Chamber of the International Tribunal for the former Yugoslavia (ICTY) in the groundbreaking *Tadić* decision as 'armed violence between governmental authorities and organised armed groups or between such groups within a State'.[3] Traditionally, such intra-state conflicts have been regarded as internal affairs of the affected state, which were not and could not be subject of international regulations.[4] Even after the adoption of the Geneva Conventions[5] in 1949, whose common Article 3 provides for minimum guarantees applicable in non-international armed conflicts, it was widely accepted that a breach of this norm does not give rise to individual criminal responsibility.[6] Since the territorial state is often unwilling or unable to prosecute atrocities committed during a civil war, the reluctance to criminalise and investigate the respective conducts on an international level has deprived many victims of legal protection.[7]

This has, however, changed in the 1990s with the creation of the *ad hoc* Tribunals. With a particular emphasis on the need to protect civilians against the

---

[2] In more detail and with further references Bock 2010 pp. 166–168; see also Ewald and von Oppeln 2002 pp. 39, 44.

[3] ICTY *Prosecutor v Tadić*, AC, IT-94-1, 2 October 1995, Decision on the Defence Motion for Interlocutory Appeal on Jurisdiction, para 70. This definition was adopted by Article 8 para 2 lit. f) of the Statute of the International Criminal Court (hereafter, ICC Statute), adopted on 17 July 1998, entered into force on 1 July 2002.

[4] Cryer et al. 2010, p. 275; Fleck 2008, mn 1202/2; Kolb and Hyde 2008, p. 257; Robinson and von Hebel 1999, pp. 193, 194; Werle 2009, mn 967; Sivakumaran 2011, pp. 219, 220, 222.

[5] Convention (I) for the Amelioration of the Condition of the Wounded and Sick in Armed Forces in the Field; Convention (II) for the Amelioration of the Condition of Wounded, Sick and Shipwrecked Members of Armed Forces at Sea; Convention (III) relative to the Treatment of Prisoners of War and Convention (IV) relative to the Protection of Civilian Persons in Time of War, Geneva, 12 August 1949.

[6] Cryer et al. 2010, p. 275; Cottier 2008, mn 3; Kreß 2000, pp. 103–105; Robinson and von Hebel 1999, p. 195.

[7] In this vein also Kolb and Hyde 2008, pp. 257, 258. Cf. also Ambos 2001, p. 327 who criticises that the distinction between international and non-international armed conflicts has led to a different legal treatment of similar conducts.

effects of armed hostilities the ICTY Appeals Chamber argued in the above mentioned *Tadić* Decision that '[w]hat is inhumane, and consequently proscribed, in international wars, cannot but be inhumane and inadmissible in civil strife.'[8] This was the beginning of the increasing equalisation of internal and international conflicts—a process which has reached its current culmination in the adoption of the ICC Statute.[9] Although Article 8 ICC Statute is still based on the traditional two box approach[10] and has thus not led to a full equal treatment of both types of conflicts,[11] it has improved the protection of victims in civil wars.[12] Thus, from a purely legal point of view the differentiation between international conflicts and civil wars has become less important. In structural regard, however, the core difference between them remains[13]: While in international conflicts two opposing states are fighting each other, civil wars take place within a society, i.e., they directly affect the social proximity of victims and perpetrators.

16.3 Structural Characteristics of Civil Wars

16.3.1 The Outbreak of the Violence: Divide of a Society

In all kinds of gross violence and systematic human rights abuses one central question arises: 'Why start people killing each other?'[14] or—from the perspective of a (rational) military leader 'How does one make soldiers or fighters engage in combat?'.[15] In principle, all people know and accept that killing is legally and morally wrong.[16] Humans have a profound reluctance to kill its own species[17] which has to be overcome in times of armed conflicts.[18]

---

[8] ICTY *Prosecutor v Tadić,* AC, IT-94-1, 2 October 1995, Decision on the Defence Motion for Interlocutory Appeal on Jurisdiction, para 119. Cf. also Fleck 2008, mn 1201/4.

[9] Kreß 2000, p. 102.

[10] Ambos 2001, p. 326; Ambos 2011, § 7 mn 232; Safferling 2011, § 6 mn 128. Cf. also Olásolo 2008, p. 55.

[11] Cf. the overview on the different levels of protection by Ambos 2011, § 7 mn 248. Critically thereto *inter alia* Olásolo 2008, p. 57; Cryer et al. 2010, p. 278.

[12] See also Bock 2010, p. 114; Kreß 2000, p. 107; Politi 2001, p. 11; Werle 2009, mn 971 and SCSL, *Prosecutor vFofana* and Kondewa, AC, SCSL-04-14-PT-101, 25 May 2004, Decision on preliminary motion on lack of jurisdiction—nature of the armed conflict, para 25.

[13] In more detail Sivakumaran 2011, pp. 237 et seq.

[14] See Neubacher 2008, p. 26.

[15] Lavie and Muller 2011, pp. 155, 157. Cf. also Grossman 2009, pp. 177 et seq.

[16] Neubacher 2008, p. 33 who refers to the prohibition to kill as a *minima moralia*.

[17] In more detail Grossman 2009, pp. 2 et seq., 30 et seq. With a special view on imposing and executing death penalties Adcock 2010, p. 314; Moses 1996, p. 52.

[18] Some armies use computer games to reduce the soldiers' reluctance to kill, see Mixon 2010, pp. 327, 364; Saunders 2003, pp. 51, 77.

One explanation of how even worst crimes are made possible,[19] is offered by *Sykes* and *Matza*'s theory on techniques of neutralisation.[20] According to this approach, the individual in principle accepts the dominant normative system, but neutralises its imperatives in certain situations by arguing that in this concrete context the violation of a (criminal) norm was acceptable or even right. In doing so, the perpetrator may commit crimes without having to break with fundamental rules of his society and thus without seriously damaging his self image.[21]

One important neutralisation technique is the denial of the victim. In this case, the perpetrator claims that the injury caused is not wrong, but a form of self-defence or punishment the victim deserves.[22] This technique is relatively easily applied in international armed conflicts since there is (or is said to be) a malicious external aggressor to fight against.[23] In case of civil wars, however, the situation is more difficult, since the adversaries are not unknown and foreign strangers.[24] Rather, they are part of the same society and have been in constant touch over years and decades. Thus, they share some common features like nationality, language and at least in part history and culture. Moreover, the members of the conflicting parties may know each other personally. In civil wars, neighbours, colleagues and sometimes even family members may become a deadly danger.[25] Thus, intra-state conflicts require in the first place the existence or construction of distinguishable (adversary) groups.[26]

Civil war societies are characterised by ethnic, religious or social-cultural tensions.[27] After the outbreak of the violence these intra-societal conflicts and differences become dominant.[28] This contributes to a de-individualisation of the opponents who are not regarded as individuals but primarily as members of a certain group. The main targets of the violent acts are not the individual victims but

---

[19] Cf. also the application of the neutralisation theory on international crimes by Jäger 1989, pp. 187 et seq.; Neubacher 2008, pp. 35 et seq.

[20] Sykes and Matza 1957, p. 664.

[21] Sykes and Matza 1957, p. 667.

[22] Sykes and Matza 1957, p. 668. The other neutralisation techniques are 'denial of responsibility', 'denial of injury', 'condemnation of the condemners' and the 'appeal to higher loyalties'. Although all this techniques may become relevant in civil wars (see Bock 2010, pp. 120 et seq.; Neubacher 2008, pp. 35 et seq.), I will focus on the denial of victims because of its fundamental social consequences.

[23] Bock 2010, p. 122 with further references. See also Jäger 1989, p. 194; Neubacher 2008, p. 37.

[24] Illustrative Grossman 2009, p. 161 who states that '[i]t is so much easier to kill someone if they look distinctly different from you'.

[25] Cf. for example Ajdukovic and Corkalo 2004, p. 287; Corkalo et al. 2004, p. 145; Ewald 2002, p. 96 and Bock 2010, p. 127 with fn. 561.

[26] As to the development of the ethnic tensions in the former Yugoslavia see Ajdukovic and Corkalo 2004, pp. 290 et seq.

[27] Waldmann 1998, p. 142. Cf. also Corkalo et al. 2004, pp. 145, 146.

[28] Corkalo et al. 2004, pp. 145, 146; Waldmann 1998, p. 142.

the group they belong to. This collective dimension of the victimisation is reflected in the rhetoric of civil wars. Typically, both sides express fear to be suppressed, discriminated or even exterminated by their hostile opponents. Thus, crimes committed against members of the adverse party become acts of self-defence[29] or even heroism, which are aimed at the protection of the own social, ethnical, religious etc. group.[30] This line of argument may also be used to cover less 'respectable' grounds for initiating or furthering the conflict, in particular the financial interests pursued by at least some of the main actors.[31] The justification and glorification of the atrocities is often accompanied by the systematic devaluation of the victims, who are regarded as 'scum', 'rats' or 'virus'—a labelling which finally results in a complete dehumanisation of the victims, to whom—as non human beings—the prohibition of killing does not apply.[32] In sum, the denial of the victim—one of the major neutralisation techniques used during civil wars[33]—enforces thinking in categories of 'them' and 'us' and thus contributes to a long-lasting divide of the society into separate groups.[34] In addition, the permanent discrimination, dehumanisation and degradation of both the individuals and their social group create a general atmosphere of hate which furthers an escalation of violence and a brutalisation of the conflict.[35]

16.3.2 Asymmetrical Warfare

The second important characteristic of civil wars relates to the imbalance between the belligerent parties. International humanitarian law is based on the presumption that the conflict takes place between two more or less equal parties,[36] i.e., two sovereign states with comparable military strength and organisational structure.[37]

---

29 Neubacher 2008, p. 143; Waldmann 1998, p. 143.

30 Cf. also Bassiouni 2008, pp. 711, 780.

31 Cf. in more detail Lavie and Muller 2011, p. 155; also Waldmann 1998, pp. 114, 145 and the example by Neubacher 2008, p. 47. In the war in the Democratic Republic of the Congo, for example, the control over natural resources like gold, oil, timber and diamonds played an important role, cf. only ICC *Prosecutor* v *Lubanga,* PTC I, ICC-01/04-01/06-803, 29 January 2007, Decision on the confirmation of charges, paras 2 et seq.

32 Jäger 1989, pp. 194, 195; Neubacher 2008, p. 37; Grossman 2009, pp. 158, 161, 190. Cf. also Bassiouni 2008, p. 779; Bock 2010, p. 125.

33 In this vein also Bassiouni 2008, p. 780.

34 Cf. the example given by Ajdukovic and Corkalo 2004, p. 294; see also Ewald 2002, p. 95.

35 Bassiouni 2008, pp. 780, 781. Cf. also Waldmann 1998, pp. 148 et seq. and the example given bei Grossman 2009, p. 190.

36 As to imbalances between the belligerent parties in modern *international* armed conflicts see, however, Heinsch 2010, pp. 133, 140; Pfanner 2005, pp. 149, 152, 153.

37 Instructive Münkler 2008, pp. 309 et seq. Cf. also Geiß 2006, pp. 757, 760, 762; Pfanner 2005, p. 152.

The parties of non-international armed conflicts, to the contrary, are not equal—neither in law nor in fact.[38] In particular, size, equipment, training and tactics of the adversaries may differ significantly.[39] This holds especially true if the government is fighting an armed rebel group.[40] The latter are almost always military inferior and thus not able to effectually combat their opponent if they comply with international humanitarian law, especially with its limitations on means and methods of warfare.[41] Thus, armed oppositional groups may resort to alternative and unlawful tactics to compensate the power-imbalance.[42] Typical means in asymmetric conflicts are suicide attacks—which are often directed directly against civilians—, hijacks, hostage-taking, launching attacks from protected buildings, use of human shields and perfidious attacks.[43] With the increasing use of asymmetric means, the situation of the state party gets more and more complicated.[44] It is very difficult to fight an enemy who has no clear territorial basis, eludes direct confrontation, strikes unexpectedly and is sometimes hard to distinguish from (protected) civilians.[45] Thus, the state party as well has strong incentives to defy the limitations and restrictions of humanitarian law.[46] Countermeasures to the rebel's actions may include indiscriminate attacks, illegal interrogation techniques or targeted killings.[47] This escalation is, of course, no automatism. To the contrary, a state may consciously decide to comply strictly with humanitarian law to minimise superfluous and unnecessary suffering and thus to gain public acknowledgement and support.[48] Nevertheless, it seems safe to conclude that asymmetric intra-state conflicts entail a high risk of non-compliance with international humanitarian law or—to put it the other way round—an increased risk of gross human rights violations.

---

[38] Cf. also Geiß 2010, p. 758; Somer 2007, pp. 655, 659. The differences between the actors of international and non-international armed conflicts are also stressed by Sivakumaran 2011, p. 237.

[39] Bassiouni 2008, p. 785; Fleck 2008, mn 1201/1; Geiß 2006, p. 758; Bock 2010, p. 114.

[40] Geiß 2010, pp. 122, 123; Pfanner 2005, p. 153.

[41] Bassiouni 2008, p. 714; Geiß 2006, p. 758.

[42] Austin and Kolenc 2006, pp. 291, 293; Bassiouni 2008, pp. 714, 715; Bock 2010, p. 114; Geiß 2010, p. 122; in more detail on reasons why armed groups may decide not to respect international humanitarian law Bangerter 2011, pp. 368–383.

[43] Austin and Kolenc 2006, p. 293; Geiß 2006, p. 758; id. 2010, p. 123. I focus only on means that are in breach of humanitarian law. Such unlawful attacks may, however, be complemented by lawful strategies like 'media war' (the well-directed manipulation of the population through mass media, cf. thereto Austin and Kolenc 2006, pp. 305, 306) and 'law-fare' (the use of judicial processes to challenge the stronger opponent, in more detail Austin and Kolenc 2006, pp. 306 et seq.; Ziolkowski 2010, p. 112).

[44] Bassiouni 2008, p. 770.

[45] Geiß 2006, pp. 763 et seq.; id 2010, p. 123; Pfanner 2005, p. 154.

[46] Hankel 2008, pp. 418, 419. Cf. also Bassiouni 2008, p. 770.

[47] Geiß 2006, p. 758.

[48] Geiß 2010, p. 124; in more detail Bangerter 2011, pp. 358–368.

16.4 The Victims of Civil Wars

These structural characteristics influence the nature and extent of victimisation in civil wars.

16.4.1 The Fine Line Between Victims and Perpetrators

According to common Article 3 of the Geneva Conventions, victims of civil wars are 'persons taking no active part in the hostilities'.[49] In the same vein, Article 4 of the Additional Protocol II grants protection to 'all persons who do not take a direct part or who have ceased to take part in hostilities'. This corresponds to Article 8 para 2 lit. c) of the ICC Statute according to which civil war crimes can be committed against 'persons taking no active part in the hostilities, including members of armed forces who have laid down their arms and those placed *hors de combat* by sickness, wounds, detention or any other cause'. The central aim of all these provisions is to protect those who are in middle of the civil war but do not engage in the fighting.[50] Apart from the crucial questions when, whereby and how long a person takes active part in the hostilities,[51] the differentiation between perpetrators and victims seems in principle to be clear-cut: dangerous fighters on the one and (by now) innocuous, harmless, uninvolved third parties on the other side. This corresponds to the general perception of 'ideal victims' who are weak, pure, and blameless and thus easy to identify with.[52] The social reality is, however, often more complicated. To quote the simple but telling words of Simon Green: 'Victims are not always entirely good and offenders are not always entirely bad'.[53] This holds also true in civil wars. In the course of the fighting, the line between victims and perpetrators becomes blurred; the positions of victims and victimisers are often interchangeable.[54] Prime examples are child soldiers who are deployed in internal conflicts with particular frequency.[55] Their recruitment and use in combat, which in the words of the Appeals Chamber of the Special Court for Sierra Leone (SCSL) 'bears the most

[49] Kreß 2000, p. 123.

[50] ICTY *Prosecutor* v *Mucić et al.*, AC, IT-96-21-A, 20 February 2001, Appeals Chamber Judgement, para 420.

[51] Cf. only the comprehensive study of the ICRC (2009) Interpretive Guidance on the notion of direct participation in hostilities under International Humanitarian Law. Available at www.icrc.org/eng/assets/files/other/icrc-002-0990.pdf.

[52] Chuter 2003, p. 105; Green 2007, p. 91.

[53] Green 2007, p. 91.

[54] Bock 2010, p. 448; Ewald and von Oppeln 2002, p. 40.

[55] Helle 2000, available at www.icrc.org/eng/resources/documents/misc/57jqqe.htm.

atrocious consequences for the children',[56] constitutes a war crime punishable under Article 8 para 2 lit. e) (vii) of the ICC Statute. In this regard, the recruited children certainly qualify as victims. In fulfilling their assigned military tasks, however, they sometimes show an increased willingness to use violence and to commit grave crimes.[57] Thus, at least some child soldiers are both victims and perpetrators.[58] Generally, civil wars may give rise to a circle of violence: the killing or abuse of loved-ones, for example, may produce feelings of hate and a desire for revenge, which finally makes the victim take up arms.[59] Moreover, in a war-torn society with a high level of violence and poverty, joining an armed group may become a survival strategy[60] and a chance to overcome feelings of helplessness and vulnerability.[61] All in all, in civil wars victims and perpetrators are not always easy to distinguish and one should be cautious in making general categorisations. In particular, the fact that some persons do not conform to the high ideal of the perfect victim must not lead to disregarding their suffering or to prematurely denying them the status of a victim.[62] Rather, civil wars have a serious impact on civilians and fighters.

16.4.2 Civilians

As a consequence of the asymmetric nature of the conflict, civilians are extremely vulnerable since they may become a main target of military attacks.[63] The conflict takes place in the middle of the society which means that it is almost impossible to stay away from the fighting. Rather, civilians are directly exposed to high level of violence over a long period of time. The situation is uncontrollable and unpredictable. There is no safe place to hide; the victims expect the next military attack at any time and thus live in a daily fear of death. Moreover, they are often confronted with the death,

---

56 SCSL *Prosecutor v Norman,* AC, SCSL-2004-14-AR72, 31 May 2004, Decision on preliminary motion based on lack of jurisdiction (child recruitment), para 29. As to the heinous recruitment methods, the often hard and brutal training and the specific tasks assigned to child soldiers see Cohn and Goodwin-Gill 1994, pp. 93 et seq.; Davison 2004, pp. 124, 137 et seq.; Happold 2005, pp. 4 et seq. Cf. also Bock 2010, p. 448 and the historical overview on child participation in armed conflicts by Palomo Suárez 2008, pp. 17 et seq.

57 Happold 2005, pp. 141 et seq.; Maystre 2010, pp. 193 et seq.; cf. also Werle 2009, mn 1137.

58 Bock 2010, p. 448; Maystre 2010, p. 139; Happold 2008, p. 56. Another question is, however, if the children are criminally responsible for their actions. The ICC, for example, has no jurisdiction over any person who was under the age of 18 at the time of the alleged commission of the crime (Article 26 of the ICC Statute), cf. thereto in more detail Maystre 2010, pp. 193 et seq.; Happold 2005, pp. 141 et seq.

59 Bock 2010, p. 165; Cohn and Goodwin-Gill 1994, pp. 32, 42; Ewald and von Oppeln 2002, p. 44; Happold 2005, p. 13.

60 Lavie and Muller 2011, p. 171. Cf. also Happold 2005, pp. 12, 13.

61 Cohn and Goodwin-Gill 1994, pp. 40 et seq.

62 With a special on the view on victim participation in the proceedings before the ICC Bock 2010, pp. 447, 448.

63 Ewald and von Oppeln 2002, p. 41; in a similar vein in more detail Bangerter 2011, p. 374.

serious injury or sudden disappearance of family members, friends or neighbours.[64] To escape (further) victimisation, many people leave their homes and become refugees.[65] To give but one example: in the war in the Democratic Republic of the Congo, more than 2 million people have been internally displaced.[66] Flight, life in refugee camps and asylum seeking involve additional stressors[67]: Families and friends get separated; refugees lose their possessions, their homes and livelihoods and with it an important part of their social identity. Moreover, they are often the target of ongoing attacks.[68] The situation in refugee camps is difficult as well, since the inhabitants often have only very limited access to food, water and health care.[69] In sum, civil wars present a serious physical, psychological and social danger for civilians and may have long-lasting negative effects on the victims.

In principle, the impact and psychological consequences of victimisations depend *inter alia* on the personality of the victims, their sex, age and cultural background, their ability to cope with the situation and the availability of social support.[70] This holds also true if the crime qualifies as a traumatic event,[71] i.e., if it involves death or threatened death, actual or threatened serious injury, or actual or threatened sexual violation.[72]

---

[64] Dyregrov et al. 2002, p. 59 at p. 66; Rosner et al. 2003, p. 41 at p. 50; Bock 2010, p. 123 with further references. Cf. also ICTR, *Prosecutor* v *Akayesu,* Trial Judgement, 02.09.1998, ICTR-96-4-T, para 142.

[65] Waldmann 1998, p. 146.

[66] www.unhcr.org/cgi-bin/texis/vtx/page?page=49e45c366&submit=GO. Cf. also Human Rights Watch (2010) Always on the Run—The Vicious Cycle of Displacement in Eastern Congo. Available at www.hrw.org/sites/default/files/reports/drc0910webwcover.pdf, p. 8.

[67] In more detail Spasojević et al. 2000, p. 205.

[68] Human Rights Watch, supra note 66, at pp. 8, 22 et seq.; Bock 2010, pp. 144 et seq.

[69] Bock 2010, pp. 146 et seq. with further references. Cf. also Eisenbruch et al. 2004, p. 123.

[70] Kilpatrick and Acierno 2003, p. 119 at pp. 128 et seq.; Bock 2010, pp. 67, 68 with further references. With a particular focus on social support Irving et al. 1997, p. 465; Andrews et al. 2003, pp. 421, 424 et seq.

[71] See only Rosner et al. 2003, p. 42 who emphasise that 'that regardless of cultural origin, the majority of those surviving traumatic events usually do not develop a long-lasting psychiatric disorder'. In the same vein Ewald 2002, p. 97.

[72] The American Psychiatric Association defines a traumatic event as follows (definition proposed for the fifth edition of the diagnostic and statistical manual of mental disorders which shall be released in May 2013, available at www.dsm5.org/ProposedRevisions/Pages/proposedrevision.aspx?rid=165): T he person was exposed to one or more of the following event(s): death or threatened death, actual or threatened serious injury, or actual or threatened sexual violation, in one or more of the following ways:

1. Experiencing the event(s) him/herself
2. Witnessing, in person, the event(s) as they occurred to others
3. Learning that the event(s) occurred to a close relative or close friend; in such cases, the actual or threatened death must have been violent or accidental
4. Experiencing repeated or extreme exposure to aversive details of the event(s) (e.g., first responders collecting body parts; police officers repeatedly exposed to details of child abuse); this does not apply to exposure through electronic media, television, movies or pictures, unless this exposure is work related.

The probability of post traumatic stress disorders or comparable serious mental health problems, however, grows in proportion to the scale of the violence.[73] In the 'multi-traumatisation of war situation',[74] where almost everyone experiences serve and multiple traumatic events,[75] the likelihood of traumatisation is considerably increased.[76] The negative effects of the persistent victimisations are further strengthened by the fact that the victims may know the perpetrators personally which may result in a deep distrust in one's ability to distinguish friend from foe.[77] To overcome the traumatisation is hardly possible since a war-torn society lacks the necessary resources and structural conditions to assist victims in the coping process.[78]

As a consequence of the systematic nature of the crimes their impact is not limited to the individual victims. Rather, they also destabilise the whole society by shattering its social and cultural foundations.[79] This explains why reconciliation in the aftermath of civil wars must take place on an individual and collective level, i.e., it must include a form of social healing and reconstruction of the society.[80]

16.4.3 Soldiers and Fighters

Turning to soldiers and fighters, one have to keep in mind that persons taking active part in the hostilities are not protected by international humanitarian law so that acts harming soldiers and fighters in principle do not constitute war crimes.[81] Nevertheless, being in combat is a highly stressful experience. Just as civilians, soldiers and fighters are exposed to a high level of violence. They witness killings, injuries and destruction first hand,[82] have to be on guard all time and often suffer from a permanent fear of death and exhaustion. This situation in itself causes extreme mental stress which might have serious psychological consequences even

---

73 Irving et al. 1997, p. 475; Rauschenbach and Scalia 2008, p. 450.

74 Dahl et al. 1998, pp. 137, 142.

75 Dahl et al. 1998, p. 142. Cf. also Rauschenbach and Scalia 2008, p. 450 and Rosner et al. 2003, who state that 'after 8 years of war in Sri Lanka, *93 %* of respondents of a representative sample of civilians reported being subject to at least one direct traumatic stressor, *40 %* hat experienced between five and nine traumatic stressors' (emphasises added).

76 Rosner et al. 2003, p. 52. Ewald 2002, p. 97 even argues that 'traumatisation is almost unavoidable'. Cf. also ICTR *Prosecutor v Akayesu,* TC I, ICTR-96-4-T, 2 September 1998, Trial Judgement, para 142.

77 Bock 2010, p. 127 with further references.

78 Ewald 2002, p. 96; Bock 2010, p. 168.

79 Ewald and von Oppeln 2002, p. 44; Rauschenbach and Scalia 2008, p. 451. See in more detail Barsalou 2005, available at www.usip.org/files/resources/sr135.pdf, pp. 4 et seq.

80 Rauschenbach and Scalia 2008, p. 451. Cf. also Barsalou 2005, p. 1.

81 Zimmermann 2008, mn 278 et seq.; Werle 2009, mn 1027; Cryer et al. 2010, p. 287.

82 Cf. only Beckham et al. 1998, pp. 777, 780.

if all participants comply with humanitarian law.[83] Moreover, some provisions of Article 8 para 2 of the ICC Statute are aimed to protect soldiers and fighters from unnecessary sufferings and inappropriate risks. The most obvious example is the prohibition of killing or wounding treacherously a combatant adversary (Article 8 para 2 lit. e] [ix] of the ICC Statute). In addition, special provisions apply to arrested soldiers and fighters like the prohibition of mutilation, cruel treatment and torture (Article 8 para 2 lit. c] [i] of the ICC Statute) or the restrictions on executions (Article 8 para 2 lit. c] [iv] of the ICC Statute). Thus, under certain circumstances international criminal law recognises (former) soldiers and fighters as victims. At the same time, however, they are also participants in traumatic events.[84] They have to fight and kill—an extreme experience which is for most people hard to conceal with their self-perception and which might give rise to deep feelings of guilt and remorse. In particular, soldiers may suffer from a form of survivor guilt, i.e., guilt about the behaviour required for survival.[85] Such feelings may occur even if the relevant conduct was consistent with international humanitarian law, but are often increased if the perpetrator 'has crossed a line' and regards his action as morally wrong.[86] Another source of guilt which overshadows the lifes of many veterans relates to the belief that they could have done more in order to prevent the suffering of people they feel responsible for like comrades and innocent civilians.[87]

16.4.4 Indirect Victims

The social implications of civil war crimes are increased by the fact that their impact is not limited to the direct victims. Rather, the atrocities might substantially affect their close relatives even if these have never been directly exposed to the violence. For example, partners of combat veterans who suffer from a chronic psychological disease as a result of their wartime experiences have an increased risk to develop depression, anxiety and obsessive–compulsive symptoms. Moreover, they are often confronted with anger, hostility and even acts of interpersonal violence committed by the veteran.[88] Generally, traumatic experiences may reduce the ability of the victims to engage in personal relationships and to enjoy interactions with other people,

---

[83] Cf. for example Grossman 2009, pp. 43 et seq. and the study of Schnurr et al. 2003, p. 545 with further references.

[84] Irving et al. 1997, p. 475; Beckham et al. 1998, p. 777; Grossman 2009, p. 86; Bock 2010, p. 121.

[85] Kubany et al. 1997, pp. 235, 236; Grossman 2009, p. 88.

[86] Cf. the case studies by Grossman 2009, pp. 88 et seq., 92, 198 et seq.; 224 et seq.

[87] Kubany et al. 1997, p. 246; Grossman 2009, p. 74.

[88] Calhoun et al. 2002a, pp. 205, 208–210. Cf. also Bock 2010, p. 161 with further references and the study by Calhoun et al. 2002b, p. 133.

which may result in a serious dysfunction of their whole family.[89] There is even evidence that a traumatisation may be passed to the next generation, i.e., that it may lead to behavioural disturbances or psychological disorders in the children of the survivors, who were born after the traumatic events.[90]

16.5 Conclusion

Civil wars have a serious impact on all persons affected by the violence—be they civilians, soldiers or fighters. At the same time, the committed crimes and the associated de-individualisation and de-humanisation of the victims shutter the very foundations of the society. The main challenge of a transitional process in the aftermath of the atrocities is to heal the divide of the society and to lay the foundation for a peaceful togetherness and coexistence of the social groups.

References

Adcock CF (2010) The collateral anti-therapeutic effects of the death penalty. Fla Coast L Rev 11:289–320.

Ajdukovic D, Corkalo D (2004) Trust and betrayal in war. In: Stoverand E, Weinstein HM (eds) My neighbor, my enemy. CUP, Cambridge, pp. 287–302.

Ambos K (2001) Zur Bestrafung von Verbrechen im internationalen, nicht-internationalen und internen Konflikt. In: Hasse J, Müller E, Schneider P (eds) Humanitäres Völkerrecht—Politische, rechtliche und strafgerichtliche Dimensionen. Nomos, Munich, p. 325.

Ambos K (2011) Internationales Strafrecht, 3rd edn. Beck, Munich.

Andrews B, Brewin CR, Rose S (2003) Gender, social support, and PTSD in victims of violent crime. JTS 16:421–427.

Austin WC, Kolenc AB (2006) Who's afraid of the big bad wolf? The International Criminal Court as a weapon of asymmetric warfare. VJTL 39:291–335.

Bangerter O (2011) Reasons why armed groups choose to respect International Humanitarian Law or not. IRRC 93:353–384.

Barsalou J (2005) Trauma and transitional justice in divided societies. Special Report No. 135. www.usip.org/files/resources/sr135.pdf.Accessed 14 April 2013.

Bassiouni MC (2008) The new wars and the crisis of compliance with the law of armed conflict by non-state actors. JCLC 98:711–810.

Beckham JC, Feldman ME, Kirby AC (1998) Atrocities exposure in Vietnam combat veterans with chronic posttraumatic stress disorder: relationship to combat exposure, symptom severity, guilt and interpersonal violence. JTS 11:777–785.

Bock S (2010) Das Opfer vor dem Internationalen Strafgerichtshof. Duncker & Humblot, Berlin.

Calhoun PS, Beckham JC, Bosworth HB (2002a) Caregiver burden and psychological distress in partners of veterans with chronic posttraumatic stress disorder. JTS 15:205–212.

[89] See in more detail Ruscio et al. 2001, p. 351; Riggs et al. 1998, p. 87; Samper et al. 2004, pp. 311, 313, 314; Bock 2010, pp. 159–161.

[90] Cf. thereto Bock 2010, pp. 161–164; Rosenheck and Fontana 1998, p. 731; van IJzendoorn et al. 2003, p. 459; Rosenthal 2002, p. 174; Rauschenbach and Scalia 2008, p. 451.

Calhoun PS, Beckham JC, Feldman ME, Barefoot JC, Haney T, Bosworth HB (2002b) Partners' ratings of combat veterans' anger. JTS 15:133–136.
Chuter D (2003) War crimes: confronting atrocity in the modern world. Lynne Rienner Publishers, Boulder.
Cohn I, Goodwin-Gill GS (1994) Child soldiers—the role of children in armed conflict. Clarendon Press, Oxford.
Corkalo D, Ajdukovic D, Weinstein HM, Stover E, Djipa D, Biro M (2004) Neighbors again? Intercommunity relations after ethnic cleansing. In: Stover E, Weinstein HM (eds) My neighbor, my enemy. CUP, Cambridge, pp. 143–161.
Cottier M (2008) Article 8. In: Triffterer O (ed) Commentary on the Rome Statute of the International Criminal Court, Beck/Hart/Nomos, Munich, mn. 1–234.
Cryer R, Friman H, Robinson D, Wilmshurst E (2010) An introduction to International Criminal Law and procedure, 2nd edn. CUP, Cambridge.
Dahl S, Mutapcic A, Schei B (1998) Traumatic events and predictive factors for posttraumatic symptoms in displaced Bosnian women in a war zone. JTS 11:137–145.
Davison A (2004) Child soldiers: no longer a minor incident. WJILDR 12:124–157.
Dyregrov A, Gjestad R, Raundalen M (2002) Children exposed to warfare: a longitudinal study. JTS 15:59–68.
Eisenbruch M, de Jong J, van de Put W (2004) Bringing order out of chaos: a culturally competent approach to managing the problems of refugees and victims of organized violence. JTS 17:123–131.
Ewald U (2002) Victimization in the context of war—some aspects of a macro-victimological research project. EJCCLCJ 10:90–97.
Ewald U, von Oppeln C (2002) War—victimization—security: the case of the former Yugoslavia. EJCCLCJ 10:39–44.
Fleck D (2008) The law of non-international armed conflicts. In: Fleck D (ed) The handbook of International Humanitarian Law, 2nd edn. OUP, Oxford, pp 605–633.
Geiß R (2006) Asymmetric conflict structures. IRRC 88:757–777.
Geiß R (2010) The conduct of hostilities in asymmetric conflicts: reciprocity, distinction, proportionality, precautions. HuV-I 23:122–132.
Green S (2007) Crime, victimisation and vulnerability. In: Walklate S (ed) Handbook of victims and victimology. Willan, Cullompton, pp. 91–118.
Grossman D (2009) On killing—the psychological cost of learning to kill in war and society, little. Brown and Co., New York.
Hankel G (2008) Eroberung, Widerstand und Radikalisierung—Überlegungen zum Kombattantenstatus im asymmetrischen Krieg. In: Hankel G (ed) Die Macht und das Recht. Hamburger Edition, Hamburg, pp. 414–460.
Happold M (2005) Child soldiers in international law. Manchester University Press, Manchester.
Happold M (2008) Child soldiers: victims or perpetrators. Univ La Verne L Rev 29:56–87.
Heinsch R (2010) Der Wandel des Kriegsbegriffs - Brauchen wir eine Revision des humanitären Völkerrechts? HuV-I 23:133–141.
Helle D (2000) Optional protocol on the involvement of children in armed conflict to the convention on the rights of the child, 30-09-2000 Article, IRRC, No. 839. www.icrc.org/eng/resources/documents/misc/57jqqe.htm. Accessed 14 April 2013.
Irving LM, Telfer L, Blake DD (1997) Hope, coping, and social support in combat-related posttraumatic stress disorder. JTS 10:465–479.
Jäger H (1989) Makrokriminalität. Suhrkamp, Frankfurt/Main.
Kilpatrick DG, Acierno R (2003) Mental health needs of crime victims: epidemiology and outcomes. JTS 16:119–132.
Kolb R, Hyde R (2008) An introduction to the international law of armed conflicts. Hart Publishing, Oxford.
Kreß C (2000) War crimes committed in non-international armed conflict and the emerging system of international criminal justice. Israel Yearb Hum Rights 30:103–177.
Kubany ES, Abueg FR, Kilauano W, Manke RP, Kaplan A (1997) Development and validation of the sources of trauma-related guilt survey—war-zone version. JTS 10:235–258.

Lavie M, Muller C (2011) Incentives and survival in violent conflicts. GoJIL 3:155–174.
Maystre M (2010) Les enfants soldats en droit international. Pedone, Paris.
Mixon J (2010) Neoclassical economics and the erosion of middle-class values: an explanation for the economic collapse. Notre Dame J Law Ethics Pub Poly 24:327–366.
Moses R (1996) Persuading the sentencing body not to return a death verdict. Champion 20:52.
Münkler H (2008) Reziprozität, Asymmetrie und die neuerliche Moralisierung des Krieges. In: Hankel G (ed) Die Macht und das Recht. Hamburger Edition, Hamburg, pp. 300–322.
Neubacher F (2008) Die Relativierung von Normen bei Verbrechen des Staates - wie selbst schwerste Verbrechen möglich (gemacht) werden. In: Hankel G (ed) Die Macht und das Recht. Hamburger Edition, Hamburg, pp. 23–49.
Olásolo H (2008) Unlawful attacks in combat situations—from the ICTY's case law to the Rome Statute. Martinus Nijhoff Publishers, Leiden.
Palomo Suárez G (2008) Kindersoldaten und Völkerstrafrecht - Die Strafbarkeit der Rekrutierung und Verwendung von Kindersoldaten nach Völkerrecht. Berliner Wissenschaftsverlag, Berlin.
Pfanner T (2005) Asymmetrical warfare from the perspective of humanitarian law and humanitarian action. IRRC 87:149–174.
Politi M (2001) The Rome Statute of the ICC: rays of light and some shadows. In: Politi M, Nesi G (eds) The Rome Statute of the International Criminal Court—a challenge to impunity. Ashgate, Aldershot, pp 7–16.
Rauschenbach M, Scalia D (2008) Victims and international criminal justice: a vexed question? IRRC 90:441–459.
Riggs DS, Byrne CA, Weathers FW, Litz BT (1998) The quality of the intimate relationships of male Vietnam veterans: problems associated with posttraumatic stress disorder. JTS 11:87–101.
Robinson D, von Hebel H (1999) War crimes in internal conflicts: article 8 of the ICC Statute. Yearb Int Humanit Law 2:193–209.
Rosenheck R, Fontana A (1998) Transgenerational effects of abusive violence on the children of Vietnam combat veterans. JTS 11:731–742.
Rosenthal G (2002) Transgenerationale Folgen von Verfolgung und Täterschaft. In: Streeck-Fischer A, Sachsse U, Özkan I (eds) Körper, Seele, Trauma. Vandenhoeck und Ruprecht, Göttingen, pp. 174–206.
Rosner R, Powell S, Butollo W (2003) Posttraumatic stress disorder three years after the siege of Sarajevo. JCLP 59:41–55.
Ruscio AM, Weathers FW, King LA, King DW (2001) Male war-zone veterans' perceived relationships with their children: the importance of emotional numbing. JTS 15:351–357.
Safferling CJM (2011) Internationales Strafrecht. Springer, Heidelberg.
Samper RE, Taft CT, King DW, King LA (2004) Posttraumatic stress disorder symptoms and parenting satisfaction among a national sample of male Vietnam veterans. JTS 17:311–315.
Saunders KW (2003) Regulating youth access to violent video games: three responses to first amendment concerns. Law Rev Mich State Univ Detroit Coll Law 51:51–114.
Schnurr PP, Lunney CA, Sengupta A (2003) A descriptive analysis of PTSD chronicity in Vietnam veterans. JTS 16:545–553.
Sivakumaran S (2011) Re-envisaging the international law of internal armed conflict. EJIL 22:219–264.
Somer J (2007) Jungle justice: passing sentence on the equality of belligerents in non-international armed conflict. IRRC 89:655–690.
Spasojević J, Heffer RW, Snyder DK (2000) Effects of posttraumatic stress and acculturation on marital functioning in Bosnian refugee couples. JTS 13:205–277.
Sykes GM, Matza D (1957) Techniques of neutralization: a theory of delinquency. ASR 22:664–670.
van IJzendoorn MH, Bakermans-Kranenburg MJ, Sagi-Schwartz A (2003) Are children of Holocaust survivors less well-adapted? A meta-analytic investigation of secondary traumatization. JTS 16:459–469.
Waldmann P (1998) Gesellschaften im Bürgerkrieg - Zur Eigendynamik entfesselter Gewalt. In: Lüderssen K (ed) Aufgeklärte Kriminalpolitik oder Kampf gegen das Böse? Band III, Makrodelinquenz. Nomos, Baden–Baden, pp. 139–169.

Werle G (2009) Principles of International Criminal Law. TMC Asser Press, The Hague.
Zimmermann A (2008) Art. 8. In: Triffterer O (ed) Commentary on the Rome Statute of the International Criminal Court. Beck, Hart, Nomos, Munich, mn 270.
Ziolkowski K (2010) "Lawfare" - die Theorie von der Fortsetzung des Krieges mit "rechtlichen Mitteln". HuV-I 23:112–121.

Chapter 17
Valorising Victims' Ambivalences in Contemporary Trends in Transitional Justice

Thorsten Bonacker, Anika Oettler and Christoph Safferling

Abstract Since the 1990s we can observe both an increasing inclusion of victims as participants in transitional justice processes and a still ongoing debate on the opportunities and risks of such an inclusion. In this chapter we first illustrate several ways in which victims become more integrated into transitional justice. We argue that the valorisation of the victim can basically be traced back to the institutionalisation and dissemination of human rights, which served as a central reference point for social movements in order to demand victims' rights in the context of dealing with past macro violence. Institutionally, victim participation is visible in transitional justice efforts of international criminal law. Since the present debate about the possibilities and risks of transitional justice is strongly focused on the proceedings of the International Criminal Court (ICC), this example seems particularly well suited to discuss the specific form of victim participation. After the reconstruction of the enhancement of victim participation we will conclude by discussing the ambiguities that result from this enhancement for both the victims and transitional justice processes.

Keywords Transitional justice • Victim participation • Human rights movement • Victim-centred transitional justice • International criminal law • Post-conflict transition

Thorsten Bonacker is Professor of Peace and Conflict Studies at the Center for Conflict Studies at the University of Marburg, Germany. Anika Oettler is Professor of Sociology at the University of Marburg. Christoph Safferling is Professor of Criminal Law, Criminal Procedure, International Criminal Law and Public International Law at the University of Marburg as well as Director of the International Research and Documentation Center War Crimes Trials.

T. Bonacker (✉) · A. Oettler · C. Safferling
University of Marburg, Marburg, Germany
e-mail: thorsten.bonacker@staff.uni-marburg.de

A. Oettler
e-mail: anika.oettler@staff.uni-marburg.de

C. Safferling
e-mail: christoph.safferling@jura.uni-marburg.de

T. Bonacker and C. Safferling (eds.), *Victims of International Crimes: An Interdisciplinary Discourse*, DOI: 10.1007/978-90-6704-912-2_17,

17.1 Introduction

Transitional justice is now considered an integral part of political transitions which mark the end of civil wars or dictatorships. Institutions such as criminal proceedings and truth commissions organise standardised patterns of dealing with the past, recurring to an ever growing set of norms. The requirement that a society addresses past mass violence so that it is not repeated and that the dignity of victims may be restored, has long since become the international standard.[1] Victims have over the course of a decade-long process fought for a change of roles, turning them from passive recipients of reparations and public apologies into active and institutionalised actors in the process of addressing previous human rights violations.

The active participation of victims can take different forms: (a) in the context of retributive justice by participating in criminal proceedings, (b) within the framework of restorative justice through participation in truth commissions and (c) by participation in the design and organisation of memorials and memorial sites, or the development of school curricula through institutionally recognised representation. In particular, the participation of victims in international or hybrid criminal proceedings has given rise to a lively debate about the significance and problems of the active inclusion of victims and victim groups.[2]

In the following we will illustrate different ways in which victims become ever more integrated into transitional justice. We presume that the appreciation of victims can basically be traced back to the institutionalisation and dissemination of human rights, which served as a central reference point for social movements in order to demand victims' rights in the context of dealing with past macro violence (17.2). Institutionally, the enhancement of victim participation is visible in transitional justice efforts of international criminal law (17.3). Since the present debate about the current and future possibilities and limits of transitional justice is strongly focused on the proceedings of the International Criminal Court (ICC), this example seems particularly well suited to discuss the specific form of victim participation. After the reconstruction of the enhancement of victim participation we will conclude by discussing the ambiguities that result for both the victims and transitional justice processes (17.4).

17.2 The Enhancement of Victim Participation in Transitional Justice

In her reconstruction of the evolution of the concept of transitional justice, Teitel distinguishes three phases, which at the same time reveal a change of focus from the perpetrator to the victim.[3] According to Teitel, the origins of modern transitional jus-

---

1 Bell et al. 2004; Bonacker et al. 2011; Oettler 2008.

2 Safferling 2012.

3 Teitel 2003.

tice can be traced back to the First World War, but are usually associated with post-war history after 1945. Above all, the Nuremberg Tribunal is considered to be the moment of birth of the legal processing of international crimes. The second phase begins in the mid to late 1980s with the transitions from dictatorship to democracy, beginning with Latin America, especially Chile and Argentina, to the revolutions in Eastern Europe. This phase has also been referred to as the "Third Wave of Democratization".[4] In the third phase, which lasts until the present, transitional justice processes are primarily concerned with civil wars and genocides—such as in Sierra Leone, Rwanda and Cambodia. While the Nuremberg Military Tribunal (1945/46) can be identified with the prosecution of crimes committed during the Second World War in general, creating the normative framework for law enforcement and the development of a code of criminal law in order to guarantee, as far as possible, due process, in the second and third phases, transitional justice mechanisms were developed that focused more strongly on the needs of victims and the desire for national reconciliation. Both the Nuremberg and the Tokyo tribunals sought primarily to determine individual responsibility for crimes against humanity and therefore focused on perpetrators.[5] In the processes themselves, victims played only a minor part in their role as witnesses. This changed, however, with the second phase of democratic transition in Latin America, Africa and Eastern Europe. Although at this stage no international jurisdiction emerged, the principles of international law established in Nuremberg were advanced *inter alia* through UN conventions, and international treaties were also of importance for the legal ways of dealing with the past. However, according to Teitel, this phase brings with it the problem of aligning the needs of victims (that is, truth-finding) with the social goal of political stability, which may include amnesty provisions.[6] "These profound dilemmas were recognized in the deliberations preceding the decisions in many countries to forgo prosecutions in favour of alternative methods for truth-seeking and accountability".[7] This phase focused mainly on approaches of restorative justice, especially truth and reconciliation commissions, first in Argentina and then, in particular, in South Africa. The main concern of restorative justice is national reconciliation between perpetrators and victims, on the one hand, and truth-seeking, which is to be achieved primarily through public testimony made by victims, on the other hand.[8] The participation of victims and the dialogue between victims and perpetrators thus turn into important tools of transitional justice. The perpetrator-centred focus of the first phase transforms into a victim-centred one in the second phase:

> The choice between trials and truth commissions as mechanisms of transitional justice involves a shift in the focus of truth production from perpetrator to victim. Although victims are necessarily involved in both trials and tribunals they are so in very different ways with different purposes. In trials they are one source of evidence, amongst others, to establish the

---

[4] Huntington 1991.

[5] Ainley 2008, pp. 37–60.

[6] Teitel 2003.

[7] Teitel 2003, p. 77.

[8] Oettler 2008.

> facts of criminal acts, whereas in truth commissions they are the centre-piece of truth production and the most credible and authoritative source for empathic witnessing. In the truth commissions, private individual memory is transformed into shared public knowledge as part of the basis of the political legitimacy and authority of the successor state, re-establishing the rule of law and promoting reconciliation. The victim has been put in the centre of the states' post-atrocity strategies to reform governance, rehabilitate state authority and promote reconciliation.[9]

Truth and reconciliation commissions continue to play a major role in the third phase of transitional justice following civil wars and genocides. However, this is complemented by the international criminal proceedings through the tribunals established by the UN Security Council, the ICTY[10] and the ICTR,[11] as well as the hybrid courts in Sierra Leone and Cambodia, and finally the establishment of the ICC, which serves not only as a link to the Nuremberg trials but also as a milestone in international criminal law and the establishment of the principle of international accountability for crimes against humanity. In particular, criticism of the international criminal proceedings of the Yugoslav and Rwanda tribunals—specifically because the victims and local population had not been offered participation—resulted in victims and the general population being more deeply involved in the process, also to increase the legitimacy of proceedings. If, at the time, criminal proceedings were primarily considered to be an instrument of social control and governance, a process through which the voices of the victims were marginalised, they are now supposed to play an active role in the process itself.[12]

The development of an international norm for victim participation in the legal and social approaches of coming to terms with serious human rights abuses has mainly been driven by transnational victim advocacy groups, which have emerged in the second and third phases of the development of the concept of transitional justice.[13] These groups were able to draw on globally institutionalised human rights as well as the charismatic authority of the victim.

17.3 The Institutionalisation of Human Rights

From the beginning, transitional justice was closely associated with the global institutionalisation of human rights and the transnational human rights movement.[14] Along with this global diffusion of human rights came the normative compulsion for states not to let massive human rights violations go unpunished. This global institutionalisation which took place primarily in and through international

[9] Humphrey 2003, p. 72.

[10] International Criminal Tribunal for the former Yugoslavia.

[11] International Criminal Tribunal for Rwanda.

[12] Safferling 2011.

[13] Bonacker 2012.

[14] Arthur 2009.

law also changed the relationship between the individual and the state. Whereas the Westphalian system was built around the idea of absolute state sovereignty, the legal codification of human rights has turned the individual into an international legal subject, whose fundamental rights the state must not infringe in the name of state sovereignty. "To better protect the individual from state interference, the recognition of state sovereignty was successively made conditional on the acceptance of value-rational expectancy structures giving charismatic status to the individual person"[15] Important stages of this development, in addition to the UN Charter and the Nuremberg Principles of 1946, were the Universal Declaration of Human Rights of 1948, the Genocide Convention in 1948, the human rights covenants of 1966 and the Additional Protocols of the Geneva Convention in 1977. The so far last step on the global level was marked by the founding of the ICC in July 2002. The first proceedings at the ICC began in early 2009 against Thomas Lubanga. So far, 123 victims represented by seven lawyers have participated in the proceedings. The importance of victim participation in international criminal proceedings for the development of international criminal law is repeatedly emphasised, in particular, by NGOs. In addition to these developments at the global level, also the regional anchoring of norms is of relevance for the worldwide diffusion of human rights, in particular, through the importance of regional jurisdictions such as the jurisdiction of the European Court of Human Rights, the Inter-American Court of Human Rights and the Inter-American Human Rights Commission.

A crucial step for the global institutionalisation of victims' rights was the 1985 UN General Assembly Resolution 40/34 (Declaration of Basic Principles of Justice for Victims of Crime and Abuse of Power). The worldwide recognition of victims' rights embodies two main principles: "Victims should be treated with compassion and respect for their dignity" and "are entitled to access to the mechanisms of justice and to prompt redress".[16] The principles of the UN resolution call on states to allow victims to present their views and concerns during proceedings, to take the concerns of the victim into account, and to avoid delays in proceedings. In 2005, the UN Human Rights Commission adopted the Basic Principles and Guidelines on the Rights to a Remedy and Reparation of Victims of Violations of International Human Rights and Humanitarian Law in accordance with the General Assembly Resolution 40/34. These guidelines also call on states to grant similar rights to the victims of international crimes. "Most importantly, the Guidelines state that victims of violations of international human rights law have the right to 'equal and effective access to justice', 'reparation for harm suffered', and 'access to relevant information concerning violations and reparation mechanisms'".[17] The guidelines emphasise that they follow a victim-centred approach as the international community has declared its solidarity with the victims of human rights violations.

[15] Koenig 2008, p. 99.

[16] United Nations 1985.

[17] Trumbull 2008, p. 784.

17.4 Social Movements and the Diffusion of Victim Rights

In the process of establishing a new normative standard, social movements played a decisive role as norm entrepreneurs. Even before the institutionalisation of victim participation in international criminal law, a development had taken place in Latin America and sub-Saharan Africa that led to a new victim-centred approach of dealing with the past and that was closely intertwined with the dynamics of national and international human rights movements. Through the establishment of truth commissions, beginning in the 1980s in countries such as Argentina, Uganda, Chad and Chile, the concept of restorative justice has asserted itself worldwide.[18] On a global scale, the public perception of some flagship commissions was supportive, if not enthusiastic. Up to this point, the view prevailed that an active form of the state's handling of massive human rights abuses, atrocities and war crimes is primarily a matter of justice. The Nuremberg trials in Europe were followed by a wave of national criminal convictions and amnesties. In the 1970s, however, many transitions were accompanied by amnesties. The normative turn of the 1980s and 1990s was highly influenced by the Latin American experience.[19] The "move from the courtroom to the hearing room"[20] was a response to three historical challenges faced by Latin American societies. First, the practice of mass violence by Latin American dictatorships in the twentieth century was characterised both by clandestine repression (the "disappearances") and a systematisation of impunity. Second, variously strong opposition and human rights movements emerged, representing two key challenges: public awareness of the crimes and an end to impunity. Third, the social power relations, and, in particular, the position of the military, were a crucial factor.[21] Faced with the veto power held by the perpetrators, the political elite sought an alternative path for political transition that took into account the interests of victims organisations while at the same time avoiding a renewed coup.

A milestone in the history of the human rights movement was the establishment of the Argentine *Madres de Plaza de Mayo*, which with its first public appearance in April 1977 demanded the "living reappearance" of their disappeared relatives. In the following years, it increasingly called for the criminal prosecution of human rights violations. Thus, both demands began to merge. When the military withdrew to its barracks in 1983, President Alfonsín pursued a dual strategy to deal with the history of the dictatorship. On the one hand, the National Commission on the Disappearance of Persons (*Comisión Nacional sobre la Desaparición de personas*, CONADEP) was established, while on the other hand, the amnesty scheme was repealed in the same year, a prerequisite for

---

[18] Teitel 2003, p. 78. On the history of truth commissions see Hayner 2001.

[19] Oettler 2012.

[20] Teitel 2003, p. 83.

[21] Barahona de Brito et al. 2001; Oettler 2012.

criminal proceedings against military personnel. The *Madres de Plaza de Mayo*, which had quickly become an icon of resistance against the dictatorship and was quickly replicated in other countries, together with the *Abuelas de Plaza de Mayo* and the *Familiares de Detenidos Desaparecidos*, formed an important wing of the Argentine human rights movement. The *Madres de Plaza de Mayo* saw itself as an organisation of relatives (*familiares*) or affected (*afectados*)—and at the same time as the authoritative voice in the fight for displaced relatives.[22] In addition to this wing of the human rights movement, there were also civil rights and faith-based wings that were formed out of solidarity groups such as the *Centro de Estudios Legales y Sociales* (CELS), the *Asamblea Permanente los Derechos Humanos* (APDH) and the *Servicio Paz y Justicia*.[23] Over time, the Argentine human rights movement—especially through its international network—was able to develop a strong discursive influence. In this regard, of relevance were both continental networking initiatives such as the umbrella organisation *Federación Latinoamericana de Asociaciones de Familiares de Detenidos-desaparecidos* (FEDEFAM) founded in 1981, and the support of international human rights organisations and European and North American groups and institutions.[24] Political demands in terms of how society deals with mass violence have, since the 1980s, been formulated against the background of local conditions. At the same time, they were increasingly influenced by a progressively differentiated set of norms that did not only underpin the basic requirements for transitional justice, but also the modes of its implementation.[25] Not only in Argentina, but also in many other countries around the world, organisations of relatives and national human rights groups were the driving force behind transitional justice initiatives. At the same time, their position was strengthened by the global spread of an inclusive way of dealing with the past: Since the creation of the truth commission in the late 1970s, the double objectives of trauma work and public catharsis were an integral part of transitional justice. When the character of the victim acquired a prominent position within the discourse of transitional justice, the number of national and international human rights organisations increased dramatically.[26] As the global history of the practice of dealing with the past shows, a revision of the policy of pardon and blanket amnesty would not have been possible in many places without the political engagement of national human rights movements and transnational advocacy networks. The political agenda of coming to terms with the past was not conditioned by the perpetrators but by political elites who sought to negotiate, in consultation with human rights movements, a new culture of democracy and the rule of law.

[22] Jelin 2007.

[23] Brysk 1993.

[24] Brysk 1993.

[25] Oettler 2008.

[26] Keck and Sikkink 1998, p. 92.

17.5 Victim-Centred Transitional Justice: The Example of International Criminal Law

The enhancement of the victim participation in approaches to dealing with the past is exemplified by the growing importance of the victim's perspective in international criminal law, which is not least due to successful lobbying by NGOs. The institutionalisation of criminal law at the international level was fully implemented with the establishment of the ICC in 2002. The Court is based on the adoption of the 1998 so-called Rome Statute, which came about due to the enormous participation of NGOs.[27] The ICC provides the opportunity for victims to participate directly in criminal proceedings for mass crimes to an extent which was not previously available.[28]

17.5.1 The Increased Importance in Structured Criminal Law and International Criminal Law

In traditional national criminal law, as it has developed since the Enlightenment, the victim of an offence is mediated or rather neutralised by the criminal process.[29] The public interest in the prosecution is represented by the prosecutor. The interests of the victim appear only indirectly. The procedural role of the victim is confined to the position of a witness to the offence. Organisations for the protection of victims' rights, such as the German *Weisser Ring*, have long pointed to the plight of victims and call for greater attention to the injured party in criminal proceedings, with the aim of giving the victim "a voice" in criminal proceedings.[30] The involvement of the victim is based on two reasons: (1) the victims can be compensated for participating in the criminal proceedings by civil law,[31] (2) the victims may overcome their trauma by participation in the criminal proceedings, through offering them the possibility of a forum which gives form to their suffering, leading to the public acceptance of their role as victims.[32] Another less frequently expressed importance of the victim's participation in the prosecution of macro crimes consists in the symbolic effect on both the general public and the defendant. The mass victimisation of which the defendant is accused can be expressed by the participation of victims in addition to the public prosecution.

In 1980, calls for the establishment of an international criminal justice were raised primarily by non-governmental organisations in relation to the unpunished

---

[27] Pearson 2006.

[28] Safferling 2011.

[29] Hassemer 1990, p. 72.

[30] Neubacher 2005, p. 209.

[31] Walther 2000.

[32] Möller 2003, pp. 600–606.

human rights violations of dictatorial states. The "end of impunity" was called for by Amnesty International and Human Rights Watch, largely in order to articulate victims' rights and their situation. The creation of the first international criminal tribunal since Nuremberg by the United Nations Security Council in 1993, the so-called Yugoslav-Tribunal, (still) followed the traditional approach under which criminal law is used to maintain or restore public safety and to sanction serious misconduct against humanity, i.e. it serves the requirements of public criminal prosecution and thus only indirectly the protection of the victims' interests. The ensuing debate over the establishment of a permanent criminal court was dominated by NGOs and the idea of victims' interests. In 1995, in order to concentrate their effort and political influence, a group of 25 large NGOs created the Coalition of the ICC (CICC), which was not only fighting for the establishment of an international criminal court, but also for influencing its organisational and procedural structure. At the time of the Rome Conference in July 1998 the CICC comprised 450 organisations; today there are over 2,500 from 150 countries. With almost 500 delegates present at the Diplomatic Conference in Rome, the CICC was the strongest group represented.

17.5.2 Victim Participation in the International Criminal Court

The ICC is not only an international institution that symbolises the "end of impunity", it is also intended to be a contact point for victims and victims' organisations to protect themselves against criminal injustice and to provide them with the opportunity to participate actively in the proceedings.[33] In addition, Article 75 of the Rome Statute[34] allows for the victim to apply for compensation via a reparations fund (the so-called trust fund).

In RPE[35] Rule 85 "victims" are defined as "natural persons who have suffered harm as a result of the commission of any crime within the jurisdiction of the Court".[36] This definition differs—as otherwise stipulated by many NGOs—not insignificantly from the UN definition of the victim as contained in Article 1 of the Annex of the Declaration of Basic Principles of Justice for Victims of Crime and Abuse of Power.[37] The Rome Statute follows a narrow definition of the victim, since relations of the victim are not covered by this definition. The interpretation of "harm" has yet

[33] Rome Statute, Article 68, para 3 (ICC 2002b, p. 38).

[34] ICC 2002b, p. 42.

[35] Rules of Procedure and Evidence.

[36] ICC 2002a, p. 31.

[37] "'Victims' means persons who, individually or collectively, have suffered harm, including physical or mental injury, emotional suffering, economic loss or substantial impairment of their fundamental rights, through acts or omissions that are in violation of criminal laws operative within Member States, including those laws proscribing criminal abuse of power" (United Nations 1985).

to be clarified, so that it remains questionable whether psychological effects and the emotional suffering of a person are sufficient to qualify as a victim before the ICC.[38]

According to Article 68, para 3 of the Rome Statute[39] and RPE Rule 89,[40] the victim must first be proven within the meaning of the above definition, and it has to be furthermore established that the "personal interests" of the applicant are met by this particular criminal proceeding or this stage of the proceeding.[41] The Registry Office provides the application forms.[42]

Participation is possible at each stage of the process. Victims participate in the pre-trial proceedings,[43] in the interim proceedings,[44] in the main proceedings, and in any appeal.[45] In the *habeas corpus* proceedings representatives of the victims are permitted.[46]

The involvement of the victim occurs through written statements[47] and through participation in the proceedings.[48] The latter can only be made through a representative and covers attendance, submission of comments and requests and—after the approval of the chamber—also the right to ask questions. This gives the victim, via their representatives, a position similar to that of the other parties.

Within the court, the institutionalisation of the victims' participation by the ICC is organised by the Office of Public Counsel for Victims (OPCV), which was established by the Registry Office on the basis of Regulation 81 of the Regulations of the Court.[49] This office is a first for international legal organisations, whereby the prominent position of victim participation in the process requires appropriate

38 See also the chapter of Michael Kelly in this volume.

39 ICC 2002b, p. 38.

40 ICC 2002a, p. 34.

41 Compare ICC, The Prosecutor v. Thomas Lubanga Dyilo, 01/04-01/06 (OA7), from 13.02.2007, § 44. On this point the Appeals Chamber was not unanimous. While the status of victim remains in place, once they are so recognised, the "personal interests" are to be considered again in each case; Judge Sang Hyun Song, the current president is, however, in favour of a one-time recognition for all the instances, which, however, can be revoked or modified. That would certainly be a more practicable solution.

42 Regulations of the Court, Regulation 86, para 1 (ICC 2004, p. 51).

43 ICC Pre-Trial Chamber I, Situation in the Democratic Republic of Congo, ICC-01/04-101, Pre-Trial Chamber I, Ruling from 17.01.2006, § 54. See also RPE 50 (ICC 2002a, p. 18).

44 Rome Statute, Article 17, para 3 (ICC 2002b, p. 12).

45 Rome Statute, Article 68, para 3 (ICC 2002b, p. 38); RPE Rules 89–91 (ICC 2002a, pp. 34, 35).

46 ICC, The Prosecutor v. Thomas Lubanga Dyilo, 01/04-01/06 (OA7), from 13.02.2007. The Extraordinary Chambers in the Courts of Cambodia (ECCC) also relied on this decision in re Nuon, 002/19-09-2007-ECCC-OCJI (PTC01), Pre-Trial Chamber, Ruling from 20.03.2008, Victims admitted to habeas corpus proceedings.

47 RPE Rule 102 (ICC 2002a, p. 40).

48 RPE Rules 89 and 91 (ICC 2002a, pp. 34, 35).

49 ICC 2004, p. 48.

representation. Thus, it is the task of this office to promote the effective participation of victims at every stage of the proceedings. The staff of the OPCV are to assist the victims' lawyers in their work; they can also represent victims or victim groups in the proceedings.

17.6 The Ambivalence of Victim-Centred Transitional Justice

All of the mechanisms of transitional justice (criminal proceedings, truth commissions, reparations, lustration, memory politics) have in common that they stabilise social norms and produce historical "truths". The focus of transitional justice is always also an attempt to conduct official fact-finding and to sanction previously denied or disputed crimes. On this foundation, historical narratives are also produced that reflect present social needs and that do not only mirror the ideological convictions of "post-conflict" societies, but at the same time create and reinforce these.[50] The public ways of dealing with the past of mass violence are strongly influenced by social relations of power and taboos and inevitably produce discursive inclusions and exclusions. This begins on the performative level with the selection of victims and survivors, whose suffering is given a hearing, and tapers to the discursive level, where what can be said is highly selective and simultaneously the testimonies themselves are restricted by the limits of the sayable. The hearing of victims' relatives, exiles, the tortured and survivors of terror is an endeavour that is often severely restricted due to a lack of time, personnel and financial resources. In Argentina, CONADEP heard 7,000 victims in nine months, in Chile 3,400 people used the opportunity of the truth commission as a chance to talk about their suffering and in Guatemala 7,338 individual and 500 collective testimonies have been documented. In the further course of the work of truth commissions (or legal proceedings), what is said is transformed into "facts" and quotable fragments. In this process, the experience of terror is reduced to classifiable events (such as beatings, arbitrary executions, massacres), leaving the unspeakable core of the horror inevitably excluded. In this context, it is useful in particular to refer to the decades-long debate over the memory of the Holocaust, which has shown again and again the impossibility of a "precise" memory.[51] Thus, while any attempt of the public rectification of mass violence necessarily leaves a number of dimensions of experience untouched, the extent of dealing with the past is mapped out by social taboos, the legal layout of criminal proceedings or truth commissions and the contemporary relevance of transitional justice.

---

[50] Oettler 2006.

[51] Adorno 1973, p. 237; Agamben 2003.

17.6.1 Exclusionary Mechanisms in International Criminal Law

The dark side of mobilising victims is also reflected in international criminal proceedings. On the one hand, victims' participation at the ICC, as described above and as praised in large parts, leads to an insufficiently justified structural shift, raising questions of legitimacy. On the other hand, it is evident that there are problems in the practical process of victim selection and participation in proceedings that still need to be verified empirically.[52]

The integration of victims in public criminal proceedings leads to different problems on the structural level. Defendants' rights are jeopardised by the enhancement of opportunities for participation by victims, and the party-like status of victims as a private plaintiffs causes a doubling of the indictment. This implies a shift of the sensitive balance in criminal proceedings to the detriment of defendants. These changes, however, have an impact on the justification of criminal proceedings as a whole.[53] Whereas previously the primary purpose of criminal proceedings was to affirm norms in the society—especially in German criminal law and criminology literature—the establishment of a victim position which resembles the prosecution leads in contrast to moving the idea of retribution to the forefront. These effects can be absorbed in the micro-criminal, usually bilateral, context of conflict by emphasising the compensatory function in the disputed legal relationship, which consists in the committing of an offence. Here, due to a reduction of the stigmatising effect and the restorative approach, de-formalisation and de-criminalisation can lead to a lasting healing of the violation of rights.

In the macro-criminal context, especially regarding the frequently observed crimes, which are conducted from a distance, as performed by long-range weapons or from behind a desk, there is a lack of personal relations between perpetrator and victim, which would be a requirement for restorative compensation. The victimisation is usually only indirectly connected with the identity of the perpetrator—a political or military leader—and the relationship remains abstract. Due to the required systematic or massive violation of personal rights on the part of the perpetrator, the de-individualisation of the victim becomes a characteristic of international crimes.

The institutionalisation of victim participation through their activation in the criminal proceedings also carries risks for the victims themselves. A fundamental problem is the random, and therefore arbitrary, selection of the victims participating. In respect of mass-victimisation under Article 5 of the Rome Statute,[54] comprehensive accessibility of the (potential) victims cannot be guaranteed, especially in countries with underdeveloped infrastructure.[55] From experience, the activation

[52] Safferling 2012.

[53] Safferling 2011.

[54] ICC 2002b, p. 4.

[55] Rome Statute, Article 5 (ICC 2002b, p. 4).

follows from victim NGOs. Their areas of activities, geographically and thematically, are accidental and provide no consistent information about victims. The fragmentary, possibly biased, composition of the victims involved has an impact on the legitimacy of the criminal trial as a whole; the acceptability of the procedure and of the outcome does not suffer from the involvement of victims as a whole, but from the partial participation of victims, especially among those who do not participate.

Moreover, the participation in criminal proceedings presents the acute danger of frustration for the victims. In their involvement lies the hope for healing through the process of participation and individual compensation. However, any criminal procedure following the rule of law and the presumption of innocence[56] also contains the imminent danger of an acquittal. Thus the possibility to participate in and have an influence on the criminal proceedings may be frustrating. However, even in the event of a conviction, the healing power of participation is equivocal. For a great many participating victims there remains the risk of the individual becoming marginalised once more and participation degenerates into a mere formality. What was at first the inclusion of the individual victim threatens to turn into a new exclusion.

An exclusion of individual victims or victim groups can also arise during the proceedings if individual charges in relation to a specific group of victims (e.g. victims of sexual violence) must be dropped. This may also lead to conflicts among different groups of victims if, and when, their interests diverge during the course of the proceedings. Here, too, there remains enormous potential for frustration.

A further risk to the extensive participation of victims is the straining of criminal proceedings and that it will raise hopes that cannot be fulfilled. To date, this can only be demonstrated empirically in proceedings before the ECCC, where in Case No. 002, the participation of victims brought the court to its organisational limit; and in the Case No. 001, compensation for the victims was rejected.[57]

17.6.2 National and Local Perspectives

The politics of difference and identity create and maintain political ambiguity within transitional justice processes. In his book "La Concurrence des Victimes", Chaumont has described the dilemmas of recognition, resulting from the differences that divide the groups of the victims of the Nazi regime.[58] Whose names

[56] Article 14, para 2 of the International Covenant on Civil and Political Rights (United Nations 1966, p. 176); Article 6, para 2 of the European Convention on Human Rights (Council of Europe 2010, p. 9); Article 66 of the Rome Statute (ICC 2002b, p. 37).

[57] See Hoven and Studzinsky 2010 in this volume.

[58] Chaumont 2001, p. 42.

should be named, whose suffering matters? The social construction of victim groups in many "post-conflict" societies is particularly embedded in the debate about guilt and innocence. Victims are primarily associated with those who are innocently caught in the crossfire of warring groups (in Latin America: guerilla vs. state; in sub-Saharan Africa: competing rebel groups). Ambiguous figures are indigenous patrols and child soldiers, situated in a grey zone between guilt and innocence. In Guatemala, for example, men who were forcefully recruited into "civilian self-defence patrols" in the 1980s, which served as an extended arm of the military, began in June 2002 to demand compensation for their services. Under President Portillo 250,000 *patrulleros* received the first instalment of payment, while his successor Berger introduced a compensation policy. Thus, in Guatemala a group of perpetrators-victims, 20 years after the crime, six years after the end of armed conflict and nearly three years after the presentation of the Guatemalan truth report, benefited from individual compensation payments—and this before the survivors of state terror. Paradoxically, this development only brought new impetus to the debate on a national compensation programme. While in this case the question of the inclusion or exclusion of groups from the category of "victim" was directly linked to the question of guilt, in other cases the primary difficulty is the breaking of taboos. It was only well into the 1990s that the offence of (systematic) sexual/gender-based violence went beyond the level of "truth reporting". If sexual violence was mentioned it was often in the context of other crimes: Both commissioners and affected women tended to treat systematically exercised sexual violence as a "secondary experience".[59] However, from the 1990s a new understanding of the importance of the taboo experience of sexual violence gradually began to emerge. In the aftermath of the South African Truth and Reconciliation Commission (TRC) it was pointed out that much of the experience of female victims heard before the commission had not been appropriately included in the final report. This discussion, which took place against the double background of the compact between the transnational transitional justice movement and the boom of feminist discourse in the context of the UN Conference on Women in Beijing, led to this aspect of history now being given more attention. In Latin America the issue of sexual/sexualised violence was, in two cases, an important element of truth reporting. In Guatemala and Peru, the engagement was led by feminists, who were encouraged by the discursive developments at the international level, yet less by the national or local circumstances, and led to sexual/sexualised violence becoming the subject of public dealing with the past. While here female victim groups became increasingly heard, the experience of male victims of sexual/sexualised violence remained banished from public discourse. One exception was the final report of the Argentine CONADEP, which exposed the widespread practice by the military junta of enforced homosexual acts in its torture facilities.

In many countries, victim groups have been excluded *per se* from the process of institutional truth finding, namely, where the mandate of a truth commission is to

[59] Goldblatt, cited in Hayner 2001, p. 77.

pursue a capital offence. A good example is the Chilean transitional justice process which began in April 1990 with the establishment of the National Commission for Truth and Reconciliation. This commission was tasked to investigate human rights violations resulting in death committed during the dictatorship. Following the publication of the report, which documented more than 3,000 cases of disappearances and extra-judicial executions, the television address by President Aylwin and comments on the armed forces in public debates dominated.[60] Only in the late 1990s—in the wake of the arrest of Pinochet in London—the fate of the surviving political prisoners became subject to official transitional justice. The *Agrupación de Ex-Presos Políticos de Chile*, founded in 1999, managed to take advantage of the public boom in dealing with the past and to place the issue of recognition and compensation for victims of torture on the political agenda.[61] Subsequently, in 2003 President Lagos established the National Commission on Political Detention and Torture (*Comisión Nacional sobre Prisión Política y Tortura*, CNPT), which was chaired by Bishop Sergio Valech and which presented its findings in late 2004. 30 years after the coup of 11 September, 35,868 people had felt the need to testify before the commission—a fact which cannot be attributed to the prospect of material compensation alone. As such, 27,255 persons were granted victim status and the fate of 11 infants born in custody and 102 persons who had been imprisoned as minors with relatives was determined. However, a total of 6,845 people (19 % of all cases) were not recognised as victims of political imprisonment and torture.[62] These people were excluded, because some attacks, such as in the house of the victim or during active military service, did not fall within the mandate of the commission. Enforced exile was also not recognised as an offence. It also excludes those cases in which the arrest and torture was not politically motivated.[63] The fact that the burden of proof lay here with the victims, may indicate that the effort of the Valech Commission was psychologically speaking rather ambivalent. While the suffering of 27,255 people was officially recognised, 6,845 people found themselves confronted with the negation of their experience. The exclusion of victims' experiences such as exile creates, at the same time, the possibility for a new cycle of investigative transitional justice.

17.7 Conclusion

Global normative and institutional changes have meant that mass crimes—and especially those committed by state actors—were and are being regarded as human rights violations. For this reason, individual human rights have become the central

[60] Hayner 2001, p. 37.

[61] Straßner 2007, p. 45.

[62] CNPT 2004, p. 77.

[63] CNPT 2004, p. 76.

reference in the framework of transitional justice approaches. This is even more true for the second and third phases of the development of the concept of transitional justice, especially for the transition processes in Latin America.[64] In this chapter, we have argued that in the second and third phases of this development a more victim-centred way of dealing with past human rights abuses occurs. This enhancement of victim participation, we argue, is based on the one hand on the institutionalisation of human rights and on the other on their dispersion in national and local contexts of dealing with the past by norm entrepreneurs, primarily by NGOs. Tsutsui has shown in detail how the global diffusion of human rights norms has allowed social movements, activists and citizens to reconsider past atrocities as human rights violations.[65] "This shared understanding facilitates construction of actorhood among those who were resigned to the status quo, encouraging them to engage in activism".[66] This is accompanied by a construction of the victim through the lens of human rights as an individual whose fundamental rights have been violated. The victim is not a universal or natural category, but it is a social and cultural construction that has undergone modification due to global institutional change: from passive recipients of justice to actors.[67] In other words, the agency of victims becoming actors results from the global diffusion of human rights which has been generated by the legitimate actors—individual victims acting as co-plaintiffs, victim groups or social advocacy movements.[68] Humphrey elucidated this relationship for the South African Truth and Reconciliation Commission.[69] This participation precluded that apartheid could be comprehended as a human rights violation and that individual victims could become agents, since they have become victims of such a violation. This also forms the basis for the emergence of collective actors who represent the interests of victims, publicly represent victims, or unite them as a collective actor. To qualify as a legitimate actor these groups—as well as individuals and institutions such as courts and commissions—refer to the human rights status of the victim. "Human rights law and discourse have made the fate of human rights abuses of victims the primary focus of political and legal intervention in societies that have experienced mass atrocities".[70]

This observable enhancement of victims' inclusion in transitional justice is of course not without ambivalence—for the victims as much as for the process of dealing with the past. Institutions are inclined to include and exclude actors according to specific rules. This can be shown by the inclusion of victims: Only certain groups are institutionally recognised as victims, while others are excluded. The strong

64 Oettler 2008; Arthur 2009.

65 Tsutsui 2006.

66 Tsutsui 2006, p. 335.

67 Findlay 2009.

68 Bonacker 2012.

69 Humphrey 2003.

70 Humphrey 2003, p. 184.

participation of victims for instance in criminal proceedings may indeed meet victims' needs, but it can also lead to a prolongation of the process and to secondary victimisation. With this contribution we wanted to demonstrate that victims' rights have found a greater currency in transitional justice approaches. We have attempted to show the consequences of a more victim-centred transitional justice. Further empirical studies are required to show to what extent one can speak of a global norm for victim participation and what such a global norm means for, and in, local transitional justice processes.

References

Adorno TW (1973) Minima Moralia. Suhrkamp, Frankfurt am Main
Agamben G (2003) Was von Auschwitz bleibt. Das Archiv und der Zeuge. Suhrkamp, Frankfurt am Main
Ainley K (2008) Confronting evil in international relations: ethical responses to problems of moral agency. Palgrave, Basingstoke
Arthur P (2009) How "transitions" reshaped human rights: a conceptual history of transitional justice. Hum Rights Q 31:321–367
Barahona de Brito A, González-Enriquez C, Aguilar P (2001) The politics of memory: transitional justice in democratizing societies. Oxford University Press, Oxford
Bell C, Campbell C, Ni Aoláin F (2004) Justice discourses in transition. Soc Legal Stud 13:305–328
Bonacker T, Form W, Pfeiffer D (2011) Transitional justice and victim participation in Cambodia: a world polity perspective. Global Soc 25:113–134
Bonacker T (2012) Globale Opferschaft. Zum Charisma des Opfers in Transitional-Justice-Prozessen. Zeitschrift für Internationale Beziehungen 19:1–35
Brysk A (1993) From above and below: social movements, the international system, and human rights in Argentina. Comp Political Stud 26:259–85
Chaumont J-M (2001) La concurrence des victimes. Génocide, identité, reconnaissance. La Découverte, Paris
PT CN (2004) Informe. Ministerio del Interior, Santiago
Council of Europe (2010) European Convention on Human Rights as amended by the provisions of Protocol No. 14 (CETS no. 194) as from its entry into force on 1 June 2010. www.book.coe.int/sysmodules/RBS_fichier/admin/download.php?fileid=3502. Accessed 14 August 2012
Findlay M (2009) Activating a victim constituency in international criminal justice. Int J Transitional Justice 3:183–206
Hassemer W (1990) Einführung in die Grundlagen des Strafrechts. C.H Beck, München
Hayner PB (2001) Unspeakable truths. Confronting state terror and atrocity. Routledge, London
Hoven E (2010) Opfer im Völkerstrafrecht – Probleme der Nebenklägerbeteiligung am Rote-Khmer Tribunal. ZStW 122:706–722
Humphrey M (2003) From victim to victimhood: truth commissions and trials as rituals of political transition and individual healing. Austr J Anthropol 14:171–187
Huntington SP (1991) The third wave: democratization in the late twentieth century. University of Oklahoma Press, London
ICC (2002a) Rules of procedure and evidence, Official Records ICC-ASP/1/3, 3–10 Sept 2002. www.uclalawforum.com/media/background/general/2002-09-09_ICC_Rules_of_Procedure_and_Evidence_%28English%29.pdf. Accessed 14 August 2012
ICC (2002b) Rome Statute of the International Criminal Court, Text of the Rome Statute circulated as document A/CONF.183/9 of 17 July 1998 and corrected by procès-verbaux of 10 November 1998, 12 July 1999, 30 November 1999, 8 May 2000, 17 January 2001 and 16 January 2002. www.untreaty.un.org/cod/icc/statute/english/rome_statute%28e%29.pdf. Accessed 14 Aug 2012

ICC (2004) Regulations of the Court, Adopted by the judges of the Court on 26 May 2004, Official documents of the International Criminal Court, ICC-BD/01-01-04. www.icc-cpi.int/NR/rdonlyres/B920AD62-DF49-4010-8907-E0D8CC61EBA4/277527/Regulations_of_the_Court_170604EN.pdf. Accessed 14 August 2012

Jelin E (2007) Víctimas, familiars y ciudadanos/as: las luchas por la legitimidad de la palabra. Cadernos pagu 29:37–60

Keck ME, Sikkink K (1998) Activists beyond borders: advocacy networks in international politics. Cornell University Press, New York

Koenig M (2008) institutional change in the world polity. International human rights and the construction of collective identities. Int Soc 23:95–114

Möller C (2003) Völkerstrafrecht und Internationaler Strafgerichtshof—kriminologische, straftheoretische und rechtspolitische Aspekte. LIT, Münster

Neubacher F (2005) Kriminologische Grundlagen einer internationalen Strafgerichtsbarkeit. Mohr, Tübingen

Oettler A (2006) Encounters with history. Dealing with the present past in Guatemala. Eur Rev Latin Am Caribb Stud 81:3–19

Oettler A (2008) Staatliche Initiativen zur Ahndung von Massengewalt: Perspektiven einer transnationalen Geschichte und Gegenwart. Peripherie 28:83–109

Oettler A (2012) Truth commissions. Online Dictionary Social and Political Key Terms of the Americas: Politics, Inequalities, and North-South Relations, Version 1.0. www.elearning.uni-bielefeld.de/wikifarm/fields/ges_cias/field.php/Main/Unterkapitel202. Accessed 14 August 2012

Pearson Z (2006) Non-governmental organizations and the International Criminal Court: changing landscapes of international law. Cornell Int Law J 39:243–284

Safferling C (2011) The role of the victim in the criminal process: a paradigm shift in national German and international Law? Int Crim Law Rev 11:183–215

Safferling C (2012) International criminal procedure. Oxford University Press, Oxford

Strassner V (2007) Die offenen Wunden Lateinamerikas. Vergangenheitspolitik im postautoritären Argentinien, Uruguay und Chile. Verlag für Sozialwissenschaften, Wiesbaden

Teitel RG (2003) Transitional justice genealogy. Harv Hum Rights J 16:69–94

Trumbull C (2008) The victims of victim participation in international criminal proceedings. Mich J Int Law 29:777–826

Tsutsui K (2006) Redressing past human rights violations: global dimensions of contemporary social movements. Soc Forces 85:331–354

United Nations (1966) International covenant on civil and political rights. Adopted by the General Assembly of the United Nations on 19 Dec 1966. www.unhcr.org/refworld/docid/3ae6b3aa0.html. Accessed 14 August 2012

United Nations (1985) Declaration of basic principles of justice for victims of crime and abuse of power. General Assembly Resolution 40/34, 29 Novemb 1985. www.un.org/documents/ga/res/40/a40r034.htm. Accessed 14 August 2012

Walther S (2000) Vom Rechtsbruch zum Realkonflikt. Duncker & Humblot, Berlin

Chapter 18
A Reflection on Transitional Justice in Guatemala 15 Years After the Peace Agreements

Raquel Aldana

Abstract This chapter is a reflection of what the wartime prosecutions in Guatemala have achieved in the past fifteen years since the signing of the peace agreements. Through their participation in emblematic wartime cases in Guatemala, victims have infused the justice system with accountability to make it harder for individual prosecutors or judges to dismiss the cases; they have brought resources that have resulted in better investigations, better trials and better evidence and even more protection for the brave prosecutors and judges and they have creatively pushed the boundaries of law to advance criminal law and procedural doctrines in accordance with international legal developments. However, these heroic efforts in important individual cases have yielded few lasting reforms in the judicial system of Guatemala. It is time for Guatemala to acknowledge that it has asked too much from the victims and to consider alternative models for addressing the persistent and endemic problems of transitional justice in the country.

Keywords Guatemala • Transitional justice • Post-conflict transition • Victims • Prosecution • Amnesty

The author is Professor of Law and Director of the Inter-American Program at the Pacific McGeorge School of Law. I thank the support of my scholarship by my law school Pacific McGeorge School of Law and the research assistance of Erika González, JD 2012. I dedicate this chapter to the many victims and lawyers of the wartime cases in Guatemala for their valour and tenacity, and in particular Jennifer Harbury who over the years has also become a friend.

R. Aldana (✉)
McGeorge School of Law, University of the Pacific, Sacramento, USA
e-mail: raldana@pacific.edu

T. Bonacker and C. Safferling (eds.), *Victims of International Crimes: An Interdisciplinary Discourse*, DOI: 10.1007/978-90-6704-912-2_18,

18.1 Introduction

On January 14, 2012, retired General Otto Pérez Molina took office as President of Guatemala. This political moment speaks volumes about Guatemala's persistent challenges with transitional justice fifteen years after the signing of the peace agreements that ended a 36-year-long civil war. During Guatemala's civil war, President Pérez served in the brutal special military forces known as the Kaibiles and was also director of military intelligence and inspector-general of the army. The nature of Guatemala's civil war which left 200,000 victims of massacres, forced disappearances and torture strongly indicates that President Pérez at a minimum must have known of the atrocities when he held high office in the military.[1] Yet, President Pérez, whose campaign motto was to rule with an "iron fist", reveals the country's desperation with violence and impunity, which trumped warnings that President Pérez's election could mean a return to a repressive past.

In contrast to General Efraín Rios Montt, whose wartime role has been copiously documented and pursued in wartime prosecutions for genocide,[2] prior to his bid for the presidency, President Pérez had remained largely under the radar for wartime human rights prosecutions in Guatemala. In fact, President Pérez has even been portrayed as someone who played a positive role to uphold the rule of law and an end to the war. For example, President Pérez is reported to have been a member of a group of army officers who backed Defense Minister Óscar Mejía's 1983 coup d'état against *de facto* president Efraín Ríos Montt.[3] President Pérez is also considered a leader of the Guatemalan Army faction that favoured a negotiated resolution to the war who also represented the military in the negotiations with military forces that led to the signing of the 1996 peace accords.[4] More recently, human rights groups, however, place President Pérez as being in a command position in the Ixil triangle in 1982 when acts of torture, terror and genocide were daily events in that region.[5] In 2011, Jennifer Harbury also amended her criminal complaint in Guatemala to include the names of additional military defendants, including that of then presidential candidate Pérez, in the case involving the torture and forcible disappearance of her husband Efraín Bámaca Velásquez.[6] Not surprisingly, President Pérez and his supporters question the timing of the allegations. In response, human rights groups explain the delay in bringing charges against President Pérez as a result of the under-resourced, necessarily selective and full of obstacles journey towards accountability for the wartime cases in Guatemala and President Pérez's own careful cover-up of his involvement.

---

[1] Guatemalan Commission for Historical Clarification 1997, Conclusions, Part I.

[2] Alvarado 2012.

[3] Fauriol and Loser 1991, p. 56.

[4] Cerigua Weekly Briefs 1994.

[5] Rights Action 2011a.

[6] Bird 2012.

President Pérez obtained 53.74 % of the vote from about the 4.5 million Guatemalan voters who participated in the election.[7] His victory was an affirmation of his consistent and persistent electoral promise to the Guatemalan citizenry of utilising the entire state apparatus, including the military, to wage war on gangs, narcotraffickers and other violent criminals. His message proved defining, which was expected given the state of terror that most Guatemalans experience daily from common crime. Guatemala still reports one of Latin America's highest rates of crime: 23.3 % reported having been victims in 2010.[8] Guatemala's 2010 homicide rate of 41.2 per every 100,000 residents is among the highest in the world.[9] According to the Office of the Catholic Archbishop of Guatemala (ODHAG) study, in 2010, 14 years since the signing of the peace agreements, Guatemala reported 64,200 homicides in a country with fewer than 14 million residents. To put this in perspective, during the civil war period in Guatemala spanning 36 years, on average, there had been 5,556 murders per year, as compared to 4,585 murders during the post-conflict years, a mere 17 % reduction.[10] Considering also the brutality of certain crimes, such as femicide and drug-related massacres, not much has changed in terms of victimisation in Guatemala.[11] Moreover, and despite significant criminal justice reforms, including the intervention of the United Nations Commission Against Impunity (CICIG), Guatemala remains a killer's paradise, suffering single-digit rates of prosecutions (3–4 %).[12]

Guatemala's story of spiralling violence is hardly atypical of post-conflict societies and yet it might have been different. The blueprint for transitional justice included in the peace agreements, while still a product of a negotiated settlement, had many of the right ingredients for the transformation of a nation. Guatemalans aimed ambitiously to begin to address the root causes of violence and included such factors as land and tax reform alongside issues of respect for multiculturalism, strengthening institutions of justice, as well as more direct victim reparations.[13] Unfortunately, even when Guatemala is largely democratic, it is hard to measure much progress in the implementation of the peace agreements. Aside from violence, it remains a nation of significant wealth inequality with dire poverty still experienced particularly among indigenous communities who remain largely excluded.[14] Guatemala has grave problems and feeble means to combat

---

[7] Tribunal Supremo Electoral de Guatemala 2012.

[8] Azpuru 2010, p. 74.

[9] United Nations Office on Drugs and Crime 2010.

[10] Oficina del Arzobispado de Guatemala 2010.

[11] Programa de las Naciones Unidas para el Desarrollo Guatemala 2007, pp. 20–32.

[12] Fundación Myrna Mack 2009, p. 10 (citing Movimiento Pro Justicia study of 998 femicide cases from 2006 and finding that only 3.7 % had led to charges).

[13] Secretaría de la Paz de la República de Guatemala 1996.

[14] Brett 2009.

them. Government revenues are just over a tenth of GDP, the region's lowest share; moreover, Guatemala has one of the lowest rates of public expenditure in social programs in Latin America.[15]

President Pérez's election has meant for Guatemala a return to military-style efficiency to combat crime. So far, there appears to be a honeymoon mood in the country, with Guatemalans resigned and even grateful to experience several traffic roadblocks with police and military united against crime.[16] In contrast, to many of the victims of war crimes in Guatemala, particularly those fighting still for truth and justice through Guatemala's criminal courts, President Pérez's election is a tough pill to swallow. They fear not only the return of repression but a concerted effort to shut down the war time cases that had finally been winding their way through Guatemala's criminal courts.[17]

This chapter aims to offer a reflection of the complex and challenging journey towards transitional justice in Guatemala at a time when the nation is at an important crossroads. Guatemala, unlike most nations in Latin America transitioning from conflict or dictatorial regimes, did not adopt a general blanket amnesty. As such, it left open the possibility for the criminal prosecution of at least some of the horrendous crimes committed during the war. The UN supported a significant truth commission process that shed some light on the brutality of the war and the collective institutional responsibility of largely the military as culprit. But no international criminal trials ensued, and with the exception of a few Guatemalan wartime cases brought in Spain,[18] the project has largely been domestic, *ad hoc*, and the result of a tenacious group of victims who have pushed against all odds in a handful of cases, supported by the judgements of international human rights tribunals and at times by a few brave prosecutors and judges. What broader lessons about best practices on transitional justice can we glean from Guatemala's journey not only for other nations but also for Guatemala moving forward? More specifically, what can we learn about the role of victims in wartime prosecutions in Guatemala and in other countries in post-conflict transition?

18.2 Preliminary Reflections About Transitional Justice in Guatemala

Guatemala took the unusual step of not precluding prosecutions entirely through an amnesty. Instead, the Law of National Reconciliation exempted from prosecution only political crimes and further established that the crimes of genocide, forced disappearance, torture and any other crime without a statute of limitations

[15] World Bank 2009, pp. 35–61.

[16] Paredes 2012.

[17] Bird 2012.

[18] Rights Action 2011b; Center for Justice and Accountability 2011.

could not qualify for an amnesty.[19] This was a negotiated yet principled choice that, at least in theory, affirmed the importance of prosecutions as part of reparations for the victims. Guatemala's negotiated peace came only four years after El Salvador opted for amnesty which remains today.[20] In Latin America, at the time, were plenty of other examples of amnesties: Argentina, Brazil, Chile, Paraguay, Peru and Uruguay. Guatemala, however, largely enjoys *de facto* amnesty with very few criminal prosecutions for wartime cases and even fewer actual convictions. And ironically, today a dwindling list of nations, Brazil and El Salvador, appear to remain steadfastly committed to forgetting.[21] Moreover, at least in some of these amnestied nations, transitional justice has made greater progress than in Guatemala when measured in terms of prosecutions or even simply the destitution of wartime leaders, such is the case of Chile, Argentina and Peru.[22]

However, Guatemala's mistake was not to reject an amnesty. This was a nation where unspeakable horrors had transpired. True, prosecutions were imperfect for constructing the more comprehensive story of institutional guilt that the UN Truth Commission brought to bear. The Truth Commission process interviewed more than 1,000 key witnesses to document 7,517 cases involving massacres, extra-judicial executions, torture and forced disappearance with 200,000 victims, many of them civilians, Mayans, who were not discriminated between young and old.[23] Through this process, the Commission was able to uncover not only patterns of victimisation and abuses but to situate them in a historically-rooted understanding of racial and economic violence in Guatemala. Unfortunately, the UN Truth Commission Report, an impressive voluminous publication, remains largely unread in Guatemala.[24] Moreover, important sectors of society dismiss its findings and especially question the quantification of 93 % of the responsibility for the atrocities in the military. That is, the story of the war continues to polarise Guatemalan society, often across similar divisions of race and class, in their explanation of the war. The alternative story would significantly elevate the agency of the guerilla forces and the alleged victims, deny the racialised motivations of violence and hence that genocide happened in Guatemala and justify what transpired as necessary acts of war in defence of the nation.[25] The UN Truth Commission, moreover, did not assign individual guilt nor mete out punishment. And sure, 1996, the year Guatemala negotiated peace, was before the International Criminal Court but not before Nuremberg, Rwanda and Yugoslavia. By this time, the international community understood that prosecutions, even as imperfect instruments, were the only mechanism for assessing individual

[19] Leonardo Segura 2011, p. 167.

[20] Amnesty International 2011.

[21] Padget 2011.

[22] Padget 2011.

[23] Guatemalan Commission for Historical Clarification 1997, Conclusions, Part I.

[24] Impunity Watch 2009, p. 10.

[25] Impunity Watch 2009, p. 11.

blame and apportioning punishment, even if only in selecting emblematic cases that either targeted the worst offenders or prioritised the worst crimes.

In this chapter, I elaborate on the significant limitations of what wartime prosecutions in Guatemala have achieved and the reasons why. Guatemala's mistake, or strategy if viewed more cynically, was to guarantee the near failure of wartime prosecutions by expecting the victims largely to carry the burdens of prosecutions, often while having to fight the state apparatus along the way. This has come at a huge cost to victims, although there have also been some gains.[26] The problem is that these small gains, while significant to the individual victims, could not have produced the type of systemic change in the administration of justice of Guatemala that was required to restore or even start to build the public's faith in justice or respect for the rule of law.[27]

Still, I remain convinced that prosecuting war crimes and crimes against humanity must be a part of transitional justice, and it should remain an important goal in Guatemala. This is true even today when decades have transpired since most of the crimes being prosecuted were committed and even despite, and perhaps because of, Guatemala's intractable modern problems with crime. Raquel Zelaya, Secretary of Peace in 1999 in Guatemala, disagreed with this assessment ten years after the publication of the UN Truth Commission Report. In her estimation, if a general amnesty had been adopted in Guatemala, the alleged perpetrators and the state would have been more willing to share information about the disappeared, for example, and victims would, at least, know more about their remains.[28] I am sceptical of this claim. In Guatemala's neighbouring country of El Salvador, for example, a general amnesty did not yield truth nor a reckoning with the past. Victims there, too, continue to ask for truth and justice, without the possibility for an investigation and trials.[29] The same is true in Brazil where a blanket amnesty has not promoted significant efforts to look for the disappeared.[30]

In Guatemala, moreover, the face of not prosecuting unspeakable horrors shows up in unsettling ways. In fact, following the UN Truth Commission Report, aside from some temporary increased reporting of its findings by the Guatemalan media, life in Guatemala remained business as usual. Perhaps the most notorious example of the largely unchanged landscape is the prominent political role that Efraín Ríos Montt continued to play in Guatemala as congressman, twice serving as President of Congress, despite knowledge that some of the worst atrocities of the war occurred during his reign as *de facto* President of the country for 17 months of war (1982–1983). The influence of Ríos Montt extended even to whether and how the young learned about the war. Demetrio Cojtí, who was Vice Minister of Education

[26] See Sect. 18.3 infra.

[27] See Sect. 18.4 infra.

[28] Impunity Watch 2009, p. 16.

[29] Cuéllar 2011.

[30] Aldana 2011.

during the Alfonso Portillo government (2000–2004) said in a 2008 interview that while the administration had prepared didactic materials to teach the UN Truth Commission Report in the public schools, these were pulled at the eleventh hour and replaced with a version that was kinder to the military and kinder to Ríos Montt who was then the secretary of the president's political party (the FRG).[31]

On January 26, 2012, however, after a long day of heady hearings, a Guatemalan court opened a criminal case for genocide against Ríos Montt and ordered him detained under house arrest. Now 85, the retired general must face trial accused of being responsible for 100 massacres, which produced a death toll of 1,771 victims. When asked in court if he understood the charges he faced, Ríos Montt said into the microphone "I understand perfectly". Then, instead of making a formal declaration of guilt or not guilt, he stated a preference for silence. Outside the courthouse, indigenous Guatemalans laid red rose petals spelling "impunity no more".[32] Undoubtedly, an open criminal hearing in a domestic court attended by retired General Ríos Montt which resulted in a criminal investigation being opened against the ex-*de facto* wartime President is itself a historic event in Guatemala. The irony, however, is that this hearing is occurring during the Presidency of another wartime former general, Otto Pérez Molina, who days prior to this inauguration had his own eleventh hour wartime charges against him dismissed for alleged lack of evidence in court, an outcome human rights groups challenge.[33] Guatemalans did debate the morality of electing a former high wartime official, who (as the head of military intelligence) must have known what was going on. Guatemala's desperation with crime, however, has made many Guatemalans tolerate and acquiesce a tough reign on crime. Even private justice in the form of public lynchings as a response to crime is all too common in Guatemala.[34]

It is difficult to prove empirically that more effective wartime prosecutions in Guatemala would have remedied modern impunity; however, there is a nexus between those who committed crimes in the past and those who commit crime today.[35] The nexus is sometimes direct, with similar actors and similar *modi operandi* for crime. Indirectly, the message is terribly wrong when unspeakable crime goes unpunished, yesterday and today. Institutions of justice lose credibility, victims are revictimised and the moral fabric of society comes undone.[36] In the end, the potential for transformation in Guatemala through fair wartime prosecutions cannot be overstated, and their significance should not be dismissed. For the victims, prosecutions are a type of reparation and satisfy their right to truth

[31] Impunity Watch 2009, p. 18.

[32] Alvarado 2012.

[33] Bird 2012.

[34] Fernández García 2004.

[35] Fundación Myrna Mack 2009, p. 1.

[36] Aldana-Pindell 2002, pp. 1457–1498.

and justice.[37] For Guatemalans collectively, they are an opportunity to confront and reject the evil that transpired in their nation and to vindicate the victims. It is also an opportunity to start to cleanse the state apparatus from those who come to it with "dirty hands".[38]

18.3 Lessons from the Victims of the Wartime Trials in Guatemala

The wartime trials in Guatemala have been a largely decentralised effort driven by the priorities and dictated by the resources of victims. This is not to say that victims have acted alone in the wartime prosecutions in Guatemala. Victims ultimately depend on the willingness of state prosecutors and judges to support the prosecutions. In Guatemala, victims are able to participate as co-prosecutors or *querellantes adhesivos*.[39] The term "victims" is defined broadly to include the direct victim of the crime, the husband or co-habiting partner at the time of the crime, parents and children of the victim, representatives of an organisation affected by the crime and the members of the group when the crime is a collective or generalised crime.[40] Under this definition, human rights groups in Guatemala have been able to act as co-prosecutors in the wartime cases. Once constituted as co-prosecutors, victims may seek to initiate a criminal investigation or join a pre-existing one. The victims may also appeal to a judge if the prosecutor fails to investigate the crime. Victims may collaborate with the prosecutor during the criminal investigation by presenting evidence for the prosecutor's consideration. The victim has the right to be notified of any proceedings in the prosecution and may also participate in the hearings but only after making a formal request to the trial judge, which could be denied. Unfortunately, once denied, the victim is powerless to appeal any adverse decision taken at the hearings. The victim may also seek protection from the judge if he or she feels in danger and may seek reparations for the harm resulting from the crime.[41] In Guatemala, the Human Rights Unit (established in 2005 to handle the wartime cases) has processed an approximate 1,749 cases.[42] The reality, however, is that unless victims persistently push these cases, most lay dormant and inactive, largely due to limited resources.[43] The few documented successes have been the result of often strained and largely

---

[37] Aldana-Pindell 2002, pp. 1437–1456.

[38] Aldana-Pindell 2002, pp. 1437–1456.

[39] Leonardo Segura 2011, p. 170.

[40] Leonardo Segura 2011, p. 171.

[41] Leonardo Segura 2011, pp. 172, 173.

[42] Galis Patiño 2011, p. 8.

[43] Impunity Watch 2010b, p. 27.

co-dependent partnerships between the state prosecutors and victims.[44] The state, too, has needed the victims. Victims have infused the process with external political pressures that push for accountability and have improved the protection of state actors willing to take a stand. Furthermore, victims have multiplied resources to improve the discovery of evidence or have themselves provided evidence to the state for use in the criminal prosecutions. Victims, moreover, have simply persisted to elevate the priority of the wartime cases when a multitude of pressing modern demands from violence would dictate other priorities for the prosecutors or judges.

There have been notable limits, however, to the reliance on victims for the wartime prosecutions in Guatemala. Foremost, the burdens on the victims have simply been too steep. The end result is an uneven participation by a few victims that has hardly been the result of a meaningful choice to forgive and "move on".[45] Most of the wartime cases either depend on military secrets the government refuses to turn over or require investigation that would take enormous resources of money and time.[46] Consider, for example, that in Guatemala since 1992 the Forensic Anthropology Team of Guatemala (FAFG) has opened 1,169 cases of crimes committed during the civil war, many of which have involved the digging of mass graves in the 669 documented massacres committed during the war and having to collect bones and DNA evidence to hope for a match.[47] In one massacre alone in 1982, Las Dos Erres, during which in three ill-fated days, more than 500 men, women and children were brutally executed and then dumped into mass graves, to date the FAFG has exhumed only 75 bodies from mass graves.[48] Yet, while the criminal procedural code of Guatemala accords victims certain participatory rights, it provides absolutely no funding for their involvement. Further aggravating the lack of resources is that many rural areas where war crimes occurred still have no courts or prosecutors near them and victims must travel long distances to attend any of the multitude of proceedings in their cases.[49] As a result, few victims have actually participated, at least beyond the filing of their initial complaint with the state.

Furthermore, the degree of valour it takes for victims to stand up to justice in Guatemala is at once exceptional and unreasonable. War victims and victim representatives in Guatemala have constantly been the target of threats and constant harassment.[50] Moreover, while valour can be a human quality that is independent of resources, undoubtedly, the ability to act on valour is also largely contingent on being able to tap into resources for protection or to take action. Considering the

44 Leonardo Segura 2011, p. 175.

45 Impunity Watch 2010b, pp. 29, 32.

46 Leonardo Segura 2011, p. 182.

47 Fundación de Antropologia Forense de Guatemala 2012.

48 Fundación de Antropología Forense de Guatemala 2012.

49 Leonardo Segura 2011, p. 179.

50 Fundación Myrna Mack 2007.

trauma of victimisation alone it would take an enormous amount of resources, time and dedication to provide victims with a space to heal, to make them speak or even fight. Not all victims are emotionally prepared and most cannot afford to exercise this unreasonable valour. For some, their own basic necessity of sheer survival has dictated different priorities, as they have their largely untreated emotional traumas. There is one story that will always haunt me. As a young human rights lawyer working with a team of lawyers in the Las Dos Erres case, we failed one of the survivors whom we brought to testify as a witness to a hearing before the Inter-American Commission on Human Rights. The victim, eight when the massacre happened, was then in his mid-thirties. I am unsure how many times he had to tell the story; regardless, we did not prepare him well for the resurgence of trauma. After telling his testimony, it was almost as if he reverted back to that horror in that moment in time. He became paranoid and would not eat for days, afraid to be poisoned, and would not return to his family in Guatemala, afraid of being killed.

There is also a requirement of relentless tenacity and persistence not to give up in the prosecutions of wartime cases in Guatemala, which has been enormously taxing on even the boldest wartime victims. The Guatemalan justice system is wrought with corruption and under-resourced weak institutions.[51] Moreover, the criminal justice system is notorious for significant delays caused by constant frivolous petitions filed by the defence counsel or by failure to comply with established procedural deadlines.[52] Since the signing of the peace agreements, significant justice reforms have been attempted and undertaken in Guatemala, each requiring tremendous political pressure and an influx of resources; and yet, the results are not what many had hoped.[53]

Of course, through their participation in emblematic wartime cases in Guatemala, victims have infused the justice system with accountability to make it harder for individual prosecutors or judges to dismiss the cases; victims have brought resources that have resulted in better investigations, better trials and better evidence and even more protection for the brave prosecutors and judges and victims have creatively pushed the boundaries of law to advance criminal law and procedural doctrines in accordance with international legal developments. However, it is more difficult to assess whether these heroic efforts in the individual cases have yielded lasting reforms in the judicial system of Guatemala beyond important albeit limited victories in a few of the cases. The model of pushing for broader systemic reforms through emblematic high-impact litigation has merit. This approach, of course, requires inordinate resources of time and money to coordinate not only the victims' efforts but also to identify common needs of reforms and then a concerted, sustained and organised effort to push for reforms and, then, to assess their effectiveness. Several prominent human rights groups in Guatemala, such as the Myrna Mack Foundation, the Centre for Human Rights Legal Action

[51] Impunity Watch 2010b, pp. 29–32.

[52] Leonardo Segura 2011, p. 181.

[53] See Sect. 18.4 infra.

and more recently Lawyers Without Borders, have commendably been working to support and coordinate the efforts in the wartime cases in an effort to produce through them more sustainable changes beyond the outcomes in the individual cases. But the task remains daunting, and while victims should remain a vital part of continuing to push for justice reform in Guatemala, a better model could be one similar to that of the United Nations Commission Against Impunity in Guatemala to assist in the prosecution of the wartime cases. This recommendation is taken up in Sect. 18.4 of this chapter.

Lastly, the *ad hoc* nature of victim-dictated persecutions necessarily has meant the decentralisation of difficult choices that must or should be made in the prosecution of wartime cases, either based on pragmatic considerations or on principles of legality. The reality is that Guatemala could not viably prosecute all of the wartime cases, even if it wanted to. The UN Truth Commission estimated that more than 160,000 extra-judicial executions, including 669 massacres, and more than 40,000 forced disappearances occurred.[54] For nearly twenty years, the Forensic Anthropology Foundation of Guatemala has been able to document an impressive 1,169 cases involving wartime crimes in Guatemala, which has led to the exhumation of thousands of human remains, mostly bones.[55] Yet, only a small percentage of the remains have been identified and returned to their families while many other remains have yet to be recovered and may never be recovered. Prosecutions in Guatemala, thus, must be selective and must consider such factors as the availability of condemnatory evidence as well as assessments of agency, such as the choice to go after low-level soldiers who were themselves co-opted into military or paramilitary service. In addition, principles of legality must also dictate considerations for the due process of criminal defendants, including the apportionment of punishment. Other choices that must be made are even more difficult to assess given their political implications. Consider, for example, the decision of whether to press charges against now President Otto Pérez Molina. President Otto Pérez Molina certainly held high office in Guatemala's military ranks during the war and could face charges under a command responsibility doctrine. The problem is that until 2010, President Pérez Molina had not been named in any of the wartime cases. There are probably a number of legitimate explanations for this omission, including the simple fact that the at once deficient and overwhelming nature of the wartime cases will mean that many potential criminal defendants will have unintentionally escaped being named. Now, however, the country of Guatemala has democratically elected President Pérez Molina as their leader. Should principles of immunity shield him from prosecution to allow him to govern? Should strategic considerations justify the exercise of prosecutorial discretion to defer his prosecution in order to allow other wartime cases to continue while he is in power? These questions are enormously difficult to answer, even with preexisting legal principles.

[54] Guatemalan Commission for Historical Clarification 1997, Conclusions, Part I.

[55] Fundación de Antropología Forense de Guatemala 2012.

What is clear is that victims have not (and should not have been) expected to consider principled, strategic or pragmatic reasons for prioritising the wartime prosecutions in Guatemala, beyond their own self-interest in the cases. Of course, what each victim wants and should want is truth and justice in their own individual cases. This is a principled and morally justified position for each of the victims. The point is that principled and pragmatic considerations will sometimes conflict in ways that demand resolution that is probably best achieved in a more centralised process, rather than through victim-dictated priorities as it has largely been the case in Guatemala. Let me be clear. This statement is not at all against victim participation in the wartime cases in Guatemala. Victims should continue to play a central and important role in the wartime prosecutions in Guatemala. They should remain the consciousness and the heart of justice pursuits in Guatemala, especially now when the country appears content or resigned to return to a military-style reign to control violence. However, it is also time for Guatemala to acknowledge that it has asked too much from the victims.

In the end, the victories for the wartime victims, while significant in themselves, have been numerically too few. Of the over 600 massacres committed during the conflict in Guatemala, only three have resulted in the conviction of some of the material perpetrators, which are still subject to appeal.[56] These include guilty verdicts in the case of the Rio Negro Massacre against 5 members of the Civil Self-Defence Group, a paramilitary group and most recently in the case of the massacre of Las Dos Erres against 4 members of the special military forces known as Kaibiles (more than 6000 years).[57] In addition, firm guilty sentences have been rendered in only a handful of additional wartime cases: in the execution of Myrna Mack Chang against the material authors in 1994 and the intellectual authors in 2004; in the forced disappearance of eight residents of El Jute against an Army Colonel and four members of the military commissions (53 years); in the forced disappearance of eight indigenous residents of Choatalum against a member of the military commissions (150 years); in the execution of Bishop Juan José Gerardi Conedera against Colonel and Captain Lima (30 years)[58]; in the execution of the parents of Anabela Garniga; and in the crimes committed by Cándido Noriega.[59]

18.4 One Recommendation: Expanding the CICIG to Include the Wartime Trials

Ultimately, transitional justice seeks more than the prosecution and punishment of the perpetrators of war crimes or crimes against humanity. It also seeks to achieve structural changes related to the administration of justice to replace what was once

---

[56] Impunity Watch 2010b, p. 27.

[57] Galis Patiño 2011, p. 17.

[58] Galis Patiño 2011, p. 17; Bathanti 2008.

[59] Paz y Paz Bailey 2006, p. 117.

a system or instrument of repression with institutions, norms and practices that embrace and contribute to a fair democracy. In Guatemala, the UN Truth Commission documented that during the armed conflict, the inefficiency and weaknesses of the judiciary contributed to the existence of a systematic pattern of denials of justice that, in turn, promoted violence.[60] One of the urgent recommendations of the UN Truth Commission, thus, was the need to address the challenges in the administration of justice in Guatemala.

Some important reforms to the administration of justice were undertaken in Guatemala.[61] In 1994, for example, the justice system abandoned the inquisitorial in favour of the adversarial model, which not only modified the role of the prosecutor and the police in criminal investigations but also expanded the role of victims.[62] Guatemala also established in its constitution that common crimes committed by the military should be tried in civilian, not military courts.[63] Also, Guatemala has passed laws, such as the codification of the crime of forced disappearance in 1996 that has facilitated the prosecution of these crimes beyond their treatment as kidnappings. Then in 2009, the Constitutional Court of Guatemala treated the crime of forced disappearance as an ongoing crime, thereby permitting the application of the 1996 laws to the forced disappearances that occurred during the war.[64] Moreover, Guatemala established in 2005 a Human Rights Unit to prosecute the wartime cases.

Still, additional justice reforms are needed in the country. Impunity Watch has identified several persistent weaknesses in the administration of justice in Guatemala. These include the lack of effective mechanisms of supervision over those charged with the administration of justice; violations of existing norms related to selection, promotion, evaluation and destitution of those charged with the administration of justice; weak disciplinary systems, as well as too much discretionary power in the hands of those who administer justice.[65] Furthermore, the fact that there is turnover every five years in the judges selected by the congress to the Supreme Court and Appellate Courts of Guatemala makes the courts susceptible to political interests.[66] There is also the need to reform the *amparo* legislation (*habeas* law), which currently allows criminal defendants to abuse it to unnecessarily delay and obstruct the criminal process.[67] Moreover, what studies of transitional justice have shown is that the reforms themselves, while important, are insufficient to achieve transitional justice. Key to the success of the reforms is the

---

60 Guatemalan Commission for Historical Clarification 1997, Conclusions, Part I.

61 Impunity Watch 2010b, p. 26.

62 Leonardo Segura 2011, p. 164.

63 Leonardo Segura 2011, pp. 166, 167.

64 Leonardo Segura 2011, p. 178.

65 Impunity Watch 2010a, p. 15.

66 Impunity Watch 2010a, p. 15.

67 Impunity Watch 2010b, p. 28.

sheer political will to eradicate impunity.[68] In Guatemala, more than any deficiencies in the reforms undertaken, political obstacles have obstructed justice insofar as top military or political leaders have used threats and intimidation or relied on corruptible judges and prosecutors to delay or shut down the cases.[69] Unfortunately, the office charged with offering protection to judges, prosecutors, witnesses, victims and any other person involved in a case is largely underfunded and ineffective.[70]

Interestingly, parallels exist in the explanation for impunity in the post-conflict violence, this time with pressure against prosecutions on the administration of justice coming from organised crime. In Guatemala, the national police is known to be infiltrated and largely co-opted by organised crime, for example.[71] This led the Government of Guatemala to agree to enter into a cooperation agreement with the United Nations to form an unprecedented Commission Against Impunity. The CICIG is a hybrid organ that enjoys international status and possesses autonomy to conduct criminal investigations but it also depends on the intervention of Guatemalan prosecutors and courts to file a charge and prosecute members of organised crime.[72] Its funding comes almost exclusively from UN Member States, with the Guatemalan government simply providing the local office space.[73] Its staff consists of 207 national and international employees.[74] The CICIG investigates crimes committed by illegal organised groups, such as narcotraffickers and gangs. Its mandate included not only the liquidation of organised crime entities but also the strengthening of the administration of justice in Guatemala.[75]

Not unlike victim participation in the wartime cases, the CICIG provides evidence that can be used in criminal investigations against organised crime, although not every case it chooses to investigate will lead to a prosecution.[76] In fact, also not unlike the wartime victims, the CICIG can join a prosecution as a *querellante adhesivo*. The CICIG, moreover, has other powers that victims in the wartime cases do not have. Under Article 3 of the 2006 agreement between the United Nations and Guatemala to form the CICIG,[77] the CICIG, for example, can solicit information from the state that could be relevant to one of its ongoing investigations, which Guatemala is required to provide promptly. Furthermore, under Article 6 of the agreement, the CICIG enjoys freedom of movement within the country, the right to have unrestricted access to state offices, the right to conduct

---

68 Galis Patiño 2011, p. 11.

69 Leonardo Segura 2011, pp. 164, 165.

70 Impunity Watch 2010a, p. 15.

71 Impunity Watch 2010a, p. 17; Briscoe and Stappers 2012, pp. 13, 14.

72 Impunity Watch 2010a, p. 11.

73 Impunity Watch 2010a, p. 11.

74 CICIG 2011, p. 4.

75 Impunity Watch 2010a, p. 16.

76 Impunity Watch 2010b, p. 27.

77 CICIG 2006.

interviews, including with state officials, and the right to free access to all information and documents in the hands of the state that are relevant to an investigation. Also under Article 6 of the agreement, the Office of the Prosecutor of Guatemala may name special prosecutors as needed to work in collaboration with the CICIG, while the national police had to create a special unit in order to assist the collaboration between the CICIG and prosecutors. Moreover, following a 2004 judgement of the Constitutional Court of Guatemala and the approval of the congress in 2007, the CICIG can denounce administrative infractions (not criminal ones) and can even participate as an interested third-party in disciplinary proceedings against public functionaries charged with the administration of justice in the country.[78] Finally, of course, the CICIG has access to significant resources and enjoys political clout by virtue alone of being a UN organ that is, moreover, acting with the ratification of the Guatemalan congress.

So far, reactions to the work of the CICIG in Guatemala are understandably mixed. The CICIG has stirred deep and powerful antagonisms within the country, including from the economic elite, the judiciary and parts of the political establishment.[79] However, the assessment, at least from groups that have fought against impunity in Guatemala has been very positive. Impunity Watch observes that one notable change in Guatemala is that public officials charged with the administration of justice feel watched for the first time, especially after a number of very visible disciplinary proceedings taken against some.[80] Impunity Watch also acknowledged the development of mechanisms of collaboration in the criminal investigations between the prosecutor and the CICIG, particularly with the establishment of special prosecutors and the provision of technical assistance for the investigation of cases.[81] Similarly, the trainings occur when members of the national police co-investigate cases with the CICIG, which is a positive development.[82] Moreover, Impunity Watch sees the centralisation of high profile cases in the capital (away from under-resourced and vulnerable rural justice systems) as progress against the influence that organised crime could exert on judges.[83] The CICIG also has provided technical support to the Office for the Protection of Witnesses to improve the participation of key witnesses in the investigations or trials.[84] Furthermore, the CICIG has pushed for stronger legislation to deal with organised crime.[85] In terms of concrete outcomes in cases, in just four years, the CICIG has opened a total of 62 investigations, becoming a *querellante adhesivo* in 20 prosecutions.[86] There

[78] Impunity Watch 2010b, pp. 29, 30.

[79] Briscoe and Stappers 2012, p. 8.

[80] Impunity Watch 2010b, pp. 35, 36.

[81] Impunity Watch 2010b, p. 36. See also Briscoe and Stappers 2012, p. 15.

[82] Impunity Watch 2010b, p. 37.

[83] Impunity Watch 2010b, p. 36.

[84] CICIG 2011, p. 5.

[85] Briscoe and Stappers 2012, p. 15.

[86] CICIG 2011, p. 4.

have been final judgements rendered in six paradigmatic high profile cases, five of which reached guilty verdicts,[87] and a number of other cases are being readied to go to trial.

Based on political opposition, the CICIG's mandate did not include the investigation of the wartime cases,[88] and it is unlikely that this political opposition to expand its mandate to include them has changed. There are ways, of course, that the work of the CICIG could contribute to transitional justice, at least indirectly, insofar as its work includes broader systemic reforms to the way justice is administered in Guatemala and a challenge to a culture of corruption and impunity.[89] There is also the nexus between the modern actors of organised crime in Guatemala and members of the military or paramilitary groups who committed crimes in the past, which means some of them could be targeted by the CICIG for modern crimes.[90] More direct support of the current largely decentralised and victim-driven model of transitional justice, however, is needed, and the CICIG offers an interesting model for Guatemala to consider adopting the treatment of wartime cases. For one, given that the wartime cases are handled by a special Human Rights Unit of the prosecutor's office, the direct involvement of the CICIG under its current mandate does not directly impact the work of that office.

One possibility is to expand the CICIG's mandate to include the prosecution of emblematic wartime cases against high officials. It should be noted, however, that the work of the CICIG against organised crime raises unique criminal trends that may not translate as well to the investigation of wartime cases.[91] Alternatively, another hybrid entity with international (e.g., by the Organisation of American States) and domestic participation and resources could be created to address the wartime cases. To be meaningful, any expansion of the CICIG or creation of a new hybrid entity must be accompanied by significant resources from external sources.

Admittedly, these types of proposals must acknowledge the challenges that the new global economic reality means to the dwindling donor base, including the current work of the CICIG.[92] However, the creation of a purely domestic model to assist the victims is likely not to work in Guatemala, at least not without significant reform first to Guatemala's tax revenues.[93] A looming problem in Guatemala

---

87 CICIG 2011, p. 4.

88 Impunity Watch 2010b, pp. 13, 59.

89 Impunity Watch 2010b, p. 60.

90 Briscoe and Stappers 2012, pp. 12, 13.

91 Briscoe and Stappper 2012, pp. 21–26 (describing the new criminal trends: complexity and collusion).

92 Brioscoe and Stappers 2012, p. 19.

93 Brioscoe and Stappers 2012, p. 37.

is the inability of the State to fund even basic government programmes. Since 1996, Guatemala already has had a law for the assistance of victims of crime[94] and Units for the Assistance of Victims have also been created in some of prosecutor's offices to attend to the needs of crime victims.[95] However, the programme is largely underfunded and relies on volunteers to focus on addressing psychological issues related to victimisation as well as the secondary victimisation that victims experience from having to be a part of the criminal justice system.[96] There also have been legal reforms introduced to create an institute for the rights to victims, which contemplates granting victims a right to a lawyer to represent their interests in criminal trials.[97] These efforts, while laudable, are oriented to address all violent crimes and would not be sufficiently funded to adequately address the needs of all victims in Guatemala. The model suggested here would aim to be selective in targeting paradigmatic cases likely to have an impact beyond the individual verdict in the case.

Whether any of the efforts undertaken by the CICIG will be lasting beyond their presence in Guatemala remain to be seen. The unfortunate reality is that in Guatemala significant international investments of money and time to improve the institutions of justice have not proven to be sustainable in the long term.[98] The CICIG, for example, continues to fault principally the judiciary for obstructing many of the prosecutions in cases undertaken by the CICIG.[99] The CICIG also laments that the Guatemalan congress has failed to approve any of its proposed legislative reforms, particularly those related to anti-corruption.[100] These critiques, however, point for the need of the CICIG to remain and for its work or the work of a similar entity to be extended to include the wartime cases. As Impunity Watch has noted, any limitations of the work of the CICIG in terms of short-term gains in the cases have at least the potential to lead to more permanent and lasting change in the institutions of justice of Guatemala.[101] There are lessons to be learned from past failed experiences in justice reforms in Guatemala and some recommendations for best practices have developed that should be considered for Guatemalans to have any hope for lasting peace.[102]

---

[94] Ley para la Protección de Sujetos Procesales y Personas viculadas a la Administración de Justicia Penal (Decreto no. 70-96).

[95] González Leche 2002.

[96] González Leche 2002, pp. 224–228.

[97] Ley del Instituto de Atención y Protección a Víctimas y Ofendidos de Delito (2005).

[98] Briscoe and Stappers 2012, p. 35.

[99] CICIG 2011, p. 5.

[100] CICIG 2011, p. 6.

[101] Impunity Watch 2010b, p. 47.

[102] Briscoe and Stappers 2012, pp. 39–43; Zunino 2011, pp. 99–108.

18.5 Conclusion

As of this writing, Guatemalan courts will hear yet another historical case on February 23, 2012, this time against Pedro Pimentel, leader of the armed forces said to have committed the massacres in the Dos Erres.[103] Pimental was extradited from the United States and more than a dozen others implicated in the Dos Erres may be extradited as well either from Canada or the United States.[104] The accused coming back to a nation that has already sentenced to over 6,000 years, even though only a few of the defendants have already faced trial. Behind these herculean efforts are the victims, led by Aura Elena Farfán, Director of the Friends and Family of the Disappeared of Guatemala. Aura Elena's story is also one of victimisation, as her own brother, Rubén Amílcar Farfán, was disappeared in 1984.[105] For nearly 30 years, Aura Elena has not stopped looking for truth and justice for herself or for others who were victims of the war. Aura Elena went from being a nurse, as well as a mother and a wife, to becoming one of the most tenacious and persistent leaders in the wartime trials in Guatemala.[106] This chapter is above all a celebration of the heroism of the many victims in Guatemala who like Aura Elena will not let us forget.

References

Aldana R (2011) Repairing the past and healing the present: Gomes Lund et al. v. Brazil. Int Justice 1:55–60

Aldana-Pindell R (2002) In vindication of justiciable victim's rights to truth and justice for state-sponsored crimes. Vanderbilt J Transnatl Law 35:1399–1500

Alvarado H (2011) Deniegan Cambio de Delito a Acusaso en Caso Dos Erres, Prensa Libre, 29 Sept 2011. www.prensalibre.com/noticias/justicia/Deniegan-cambio-delito-acusado-Erres_0_563343877.html. Accessed 12 February 2012

Alvarado H (2012) José Efraín Ríos Montt queda ligado a proceso por genocidio, Prensa Libre, 27 January 2012. www.prensalibre.com/noticias/Rios-Montt-queda-ligado-proceso_0_635336490.html. Accessed 12 February 2012

Amnesty International (2011) El Salvador Massacre: a 30-Year Fight for Justice. www.amnesty.org/zh-hant/node/28684. Accessed 11 February 2012

Archila O (2011) Víctimas Piden Condena a Militares por Masacre en Aldea Dos Erres, Prensa Libre, 21 July 2011. www.prensalibre.com/noticias/justicia/masacre-justicia-ejercito_0_521348011.html. Accessed 12 February 2012

Azpuru D (2010) Political culture of democracy in Guatemala. LAPOP-Vanderbilt University, Nashville

---

[103] Alvarado 2011.

[104] Archila 2011.

[105] Fundación de Antropología Forense de Guatemala 2009.

[106] Fundación de Antropología Forense de Guatemala 2009.

Bathanti J (2008) Bishop Gerardi: a life devoted to social justice. www.ghrc-usa.org/AboutGuatemala/TimelineGerardiWebsite.pdf. Accessed 10 February 2012

Bird A (2012) Otto Perez Molina elected President of Guatemala days earlier a court improperly dismissed charges against him of forced disappearance and torture. www.rightsaction.org/action-content/new-guatemalan-president-article-1-annie-bird. Accessed 10 February 2012

Brett R (2009) Etnicidad y Ciudadanía, Programa de las Naciones Unidas para el Desarrollo Guatemala. www.pnud.org.gt/data/publicacion/Etnicidad_y_ciudadania.pdf. Accessed 10 February 2010

Briscoe I, Stappers M (2012) Breaking the wave: critical steps in the fight against crime in Guatemala, Impunity Watch. www.impunitywatch.org/upload/UserFiles/file/Breaking%20the%20wave.pdf. Accessed 9 February 2012

Center for Justice and Accountability (2011) The Guatemala Genocide case before the Spanish National Court. www.cja.org/section.php?id=83. Accessed 11 February 2012

Cerigua Weekly Briefs (1994) Military shake-up reveals power struggle, Cerigua Weekly Briefs, 21 February 1994. www.tulane.edu/~libweb/RESTRICTED/CERIGUA/1994_0221.txt. Accessed 10 February 2012

CICIG (2006) Acuerdo entre la Organización de Naciones Unidas y el Gobierno de Guatemala relative al establecimiento de una Comisión Internacional Contra la Impunidad en Guatemala (CICIG). www.cicig.org/uploads/documents/mandato/01_cicig_acuerdo.pdf. Accessed 6 February 2012

CICIG (2011) Informe Ejecutivo Cicig: Cuatro Años de Labores. www.cicig.org/uploads/documents/2011/COM-052-20111005-DOC02.pdf. Accessed 6 February 2012

Cuéllar B (2011) El Salvador. In: Fundación para el Debido Proceso Legal (ed) Las Víctimas y las Justicia Transicional: ¿Están Cumpliendo los Estados Latinoamericanos con los Estándares Internacionales? Fundación para el Debido Proceso Legal, Washington, pp. 127–156

Fauriol GA, Loser E (eds) (1991) Guatemala's political puzzle. Transaction Publishers, London

Fernández García MC (2004) Lynching in Guatemala: legacy of war and impunity. www.wcfia.harvard.edu/fellows/papers/2003-04/fernandez.pdf. Accessed 11 February 2012

Fundación de Antropología Forense de Guatemala (2009) Entrevista con Aura Elena Farfán. www.fafg.org/entrevistas/EntrevistaFarfan.html. Accessed 12 February 2012

Fundación de Antropología Forense de Guatemala (2012) Investigaciones Antropológico Forense Realizadas en Guatemala de 1992-2010. www.fafg.org/paginas/casos.htm. Accessed 6 February 2012

Fundación Myrna Mack (2007) Una Aproximación al Uso de la Violencia Política contra la Búsqueda de Verdad y Justicia. www.myrnamack.org.gt/index.php/analisis/159-una-aproximacion-al-uso-de-la-violencia-politica-contra-la-busqueda-de-verdad-y-justicia. Accessed 11 February 2012

Fundación Myrna Mack (2009) Una Aproximación de los Rasgos de la Violencia en Guatemala. www.myrnamack.org.gt/index.php/analisis/168-una-aproximacion-a-los-rasgos-de-la-violencia-en-guatemala. Accessed 11 February 2012

Galis Patiño M C (2011) Informe Comparativo. In: Fundación para el Debido Proceso Legal (ed) Las Víctimas y las Justicia Transicional: ¿Están Cumpliendo los Estados Latinoamericanos con los Estándares Internacionales?, Fundación para el Debido Proceso Legal, Washington, pp. 1–34

González Leche RA (2002) Modelo de Atención a la Víctima del Delito, Implementado en el Ministerio Público de de Guatemala, Centro América. www.ilanud.or.cr/A116.pdf. Accessed 4 October 2012

Guatemalan Commission for Historical Clarification (1997) Guatemala, Memory of Silence Tz'Inil Na' Tab'Al: Report of the Commission for Historical Clarification Conclusions and Recommendations. www.shr.aaas.org/guatemala/ceh/report/english/toc.html. Accessed 10 February 2012

Impunity Watch (2009) La Persistencia de la Verdad: A Diez Años del Informe de la CEH. www.impunitywatch.org/en/publication/33. Accessed 11 February 2012

Impunity Watch (2010a) Cambiar la Cultura de la Violencia por la Cultura de la Vida: Los Primeros dos Años de la Comisión Internacional contra la Impunidad en Guatemala. www.impunitywatch.org/upload/UserFiles/file/CICIG%20Report%20(IW,%20ICTJ,%20Dutch%20Platform).pdf. Accessed 10 February 2012

Impunity Watch (2010b) Reconociendo el Pasado: Desafíos para Combatir la Impunidad en Guatemala: Resumen y Recomendaciones. www.impunitywatch.org/upload/UserFiles/file/IW%20Guatemala%20BCR,%20Spanish.pdf. Accessed 10 February 2012

Leonardo Segura M (2011) Guatemala. In: Fundación para el Debido Proceso Legal (ed) Las Víctimas y las Justicia Transicional: ¿Están Cumpliendo los Estados Latinoamericanos con los Estándares Internacionales?, Fundación para el Debido Proceso Legal, Washington, pp. 157–190

Oficina del Arzobispado de Guatemala (2010) Violencia en Guatemala: Estudio Estadístico en Cinco Departamentos. www.odhag.org.gt/pdf/Violencia%20en%20Guatemala.pdf. Accessed 10 February 2012

Padget T (2011) Sins of the past: will all of Latin America find justice for cold war atrocities Guatemala. www.globalspin.blogs.time.com/2011/11/03/sins-of-the-cold-war-when-will-all-of-latin-america-find-justice/. Accessed 11 February 2012

Paredes E (2012) President Pérez Molina Ignaura plan de Recuperación Vial, Prensa Libre, 12 January 2012. www.prensalibre.com/escuintla/Presidente-Otto_Perez-inaugura-carreteras_3_632366758.html. Accessed 11 February 2012

Paz y, Paz Bailey C (2006) Guatemala: gender and reparations for human rights violations. In: Rubio-Marín R (ed) What happened to the women? Gender and reparations for human rights violations. Social Science Research Council, New York, pp. 92–135

Programa de las Naciones Unidas para el Desarrollo Guatemala (2007) Informe Estadístico de la Violencia en Guatemala. www.who.int/violence_injury_prevention/violence/national_activities/informe_estadistico_violencia_guatemala.pdf. Accessed 10 February 2012

Rights Action (2011a) Allegation letter from rights action, Guatemala Human Rights Commission, and Jennifer Harbury to Juan Méndez U.N. Special Rapporteur on Torture, 11 July 2011. www.rightsaction.org/articles/Letter_to_United_Nations_082411.html. Accessed 10 February 2012

Rights Action (2011b) Juez Español Santiago Pedraz, Investigará Crímenes de Género www.rightsaction.org/articles/rape_trials_in_Spain_072911.html. Accessed 11 February 2012

Secretaría de la Paz de la República de Guatemala (1996) Acuerdos de Paz en Guatemala. www.arias.or.cr/publicaciones/FA05035107.pdf. Accessed 10 February 2012

Tribunal Supremo Electoral de Guatemala (2012) Magistrados el TSE Oficializaron Resultados de la Segunda Elección Presidencial, 17 November 2012. www.elecciones2011.tse.org.gt/noticias.php?num=1469. Accessed 10 February 2012

United Nations Office on Drugs and Crime (2010) Homicide statistics. www.elecciones2011.tse.org.gt/noticias.php?num=1469. Accessed 10 February 2012

World Bank (2009) Guatemala Poverty Assessment: good performance at low levels. www.wds.worldbank.org/external/default/WDSContentServer/WDSP/IB/2009/07/08/000333038_20090708235221/Rendered/PDF/439200ESW0GT0P1IC0Disclosed07171091.pdf. Accessed 11 February 2012

Zunino M (2011) Releasing transitional justice from the technical asylum: judicial reform in Guatemala seen through Technē and Phronēsis. Int J Transitional Justice 5:99–118

Chapter 19
The Role and Mandates of the ICC Trust Fund for Victims

Katharina Peschke

Abstract The chapter provides a brief overview of the mandates and role of the Trust Fund for Victims as an unprecedented *sui generis* mechanism in the context of transitional justice. It elaborates on how the interplay between its two mandates make it a key element of the Rome Statute system that can add in an important way to its success in the eyes of victims and the international community as a whole. In particular, it will provide examples of how the activities it supports enable the empowerment of victims with a view to reintegrating them back into society and promoting reconciliation. The chapter will also highlight some of the challenges still ahead, including first and foremost the Trust Fund's dependency on long-term financial and political support from States, civil society, victims' groups and individuals. Such support will be essential if the Trust Fund is to reach its full potential and set an inspirational example for how a victims-centred approach to transitional justice can function.

Keywords Transitional justice • ICTJ • Trust Fund for Victims • Reintegration • Reparations mandate • General assistance mandate • Physical rehabilitation • Psychological rehabilitation • Material support • Individual level • Collective level

---

Legal Advisor of the Trust Fund for Victims. This chapter is written in a personal capacity and the view expressed reflect those of the author and not necessarily those of the Trust Fund for Victims or the International Criminal Court.
The author would gratefully like to acknowledge that she has used in this chapter analysis and research conducted on program and gender issues by Kristin Kalla, Senior Program Officer and Peter Dixon, Senior Research and Evaluation Fellow. More detailed information on these and other topics relevant to the Trust Fund can be found online at www.trusfundforvictim.org and in particular in the Trust Fund's biannual Programme Progress Reports of the Trust Fund for Victims. The author would further like to thank Pieter de Baan, Executive Director of the Trust Fund, for his helpful comments and Ms. Daisy Schmidt, intern with the Trust Fund, for her input.

K. Peschke (✉)
Trust Fund for Victims, The Hague, The Netherlands
e-mail: Katharina.Peschke@icc-cpi.int

T. Bonacker and C. Safferling (eds.), *Victims of International Crimes: An Interdisciplinary Discourse*, DOI: 10.1007/978-90-6704-912-2_19,

Practitioners and academics agree that addressing the legacies of past violence and human rights abuses is necessary for fostering sustainable peace. Transitional justice is aimed at bringing about positive change to a society emerging from conflict. "Transitional justice", it has been claimed by the International Center for Transitional Justice, "is not a special form of justice but justice adapted to societies transforming themselves after a period of pervasive human rights abuse."[1] Indeed, countries emerging from long-term violent conflict are often troubled and unstable societies. If the massive abuses of the past are not properly addressed, this may lead to cyclical recurrence of violence: the need for justice does not disappear.

The adoption of the Rome Statute was a major step in the global acknowledgment of the importance of transitional justice at an international level. Moreover, the Rome Conference also acknowledged that restoring the balance in the aftermath of mass atrocities involves at its core the support for victims of international crimes. As expressed by some, "a clear theme that runs through the ICC is that of justice for victims where reparations were seen as the hope of bringing justice to the victims of the gravest forms of atrocities."[2] Accordingly, the Rome Statute (hereafter "the Statute") embodies a system that makes a marked shift from trials focused on perpetrator and retribution towards a process that focuses also on the needs of victims.

As a manifestation of this change in approach, the Rome Statute created the Trust Fund for Victims (hereafter the "Trust Fund") as a new and unique mechanism "for the benefit of victims of crimes within the jurisdiction of the Court, and of the families of such victims."[3] The Trust Fund in many ways "affirms the importance and centrality of victims' claims to reparation in international justice efforts."[4] Its evolving role will be seminal in how victim-sensitive the Rome Statute system will be in practice and in the eyes of the world.

The purpose of this short chapter is to provide a brief overview of the mandates and role of the Trust Fund for Victims as an unprecedented *sui generis* mechanism in the context of transitional justice. It elaborates on how the interplay between its two mandates make it a key element of the Rome Statute system that can add in an important way to its success in the eyes of victims and the international community as a whole. In particular, it will provide examples of how the activities it supports enable the empowerment of victims with a view to reintegrating them back into society and promoting reconciliation. The chapter will also highlight some of the challenges still ahead, including first and foremost the Trust Fund's dependency on long-term financial and political support from States, civil society,

[1] International Centre for Transitional Justice (2012) What is transitional justice? www.ictj.org/about/transitional-justice.

[2] McGoldrick et al. 2004, pp. 464 et subs.

[3] Article 79 of the Rome Statute.

[4] De Greiff and Wierda 2006, pp. 225 et subs.

victims' groups and individuals. Such support will be essential if the Trust Fund is to reach its full potential and set an inspirational example for how a victims-centred approach to transitional justice can function.

19.1 Short background

The Trust Fund as an operative entity was established by the Assembly of States Parties in September 2002.[5] In late 2007, it began carrying out its first activities for the benefit of victims in countries where the International Criminal Court (hereafter "the ICC") is active and has widened its operations ever since.

The Trust Fund benefits from the leadership and guidance of a five-member Board of Directors elected by the Assembly of States Parties, which represents the member States of the Rome Statue, for three-year terms. The five seats are distributed on the basis of equitable geographic and gender distribution. Each member serves in an individual capacity on a pro bono basis. The Trust Fund Secretariat manages the day-to-day operations of the Fund and is located at the ICC's headquarters in The Hague. There are also currently two field offices, located in Uganda and the Democratic Republic of the Congo, and it is planned that a field office in the Central African Republic will take up operations in 2012.

19.2 The Two Mandates of the Trust Fund

The Trust Fund for Victims fulfils two mandates for the benefit of victims of crimes under jurisdiction of the ICC and their families.

The first mandate of the Trust Fund is its reparations mandate. Under this mandate it is tasked with implementing Court-ordered reparations awards against a convicted person when directed by the Court to do so. This mandate has not been activated yet: while several cases are pending before the ICC, none has reached the reparation stage to date.

The Trust Fund's reparations mandate is linked to a criminal case against an accused before the ICC. Resources are collected through fines or forfeiture and awards for reparations and complemented with "other resources of the Trust Fund" if the Board of Directors so determines.[6] Reparations to, or in respect of victims, can take many different forms, including restitution, compensation and rehabilitation, and they can be individual or collective or both. This broad mandate leaves room for the ICC to identify the most appropriate forms of reparation in light of the context of the situation and the wishes of the victims and their communities.

---

5 ICC-ASP/1/Res. 6.

6 This is set out in Regulation 56 of the Regulations of the Trust Fund.

The second mandate of the Trust Fund, in which it has already been active for four years, is its general assistance mandate. Under this mandate, the Trust Fund is using voluntary contributions from donors to provide victims and their families in situations before the Court with three legally defined categories of assistance:

- Physical Rehabilitation, which includes reconstructive surgery, general surgery, bullet and bomb fragment removal, prosthetic and orthopaedic devices, referrals to services like fistula repair and HIV and AIDS screening, treatment, care and support;
- Psychological Rehabilitation, which includes both, individual and group-based trauma counselling; music, dance and drama groups to promote social cohesion and healing; community sensitisation workshops and radio broadcasts on victims' rights; information sessions and large-scale community meetings. Community awareness responses may include broad-based community education on sexual and gender-based violence and the links between peace, justice, reconciliation and rehabilitation and
- Material Support initiatives, which may include livelihood activities, vocational training or access to referral programmes that offer income generation and training opportunities to focus on longer term economic empowerment. Material support may also include education grants for victim survivors and their children.

The general assistance mandate is not linked to a trial and does not require a conviction to take place. Rather, general assistance is provided to victims within the broader situations where crimes are alleged to have occurred and can engage with victims outside of the scope of any particular trial and prior to as well as after the conclusion of Court proceedings. However, procedurally the Trust Fund must notify the respective Pre-Trial Chamber of its intention to undertake activities for the benefit of victims so as to ensure that its activities will "not pre-determine any issue to be determined by the Court", including the determination of jurisdiction and admissibility. Furthermore, Trust Fund activities shall not violate the presumption of innocence, or be prejudicial to or inconsistent with the rights of the accused and a fair and impartial trial.[7] Unless the Chamber has given an indication to the contrary, the Board may then proceed with the specified activities of which it has notified the Chamber.

The Trust Fund provides its assistance to victims through partnerships with national and international implementing partners.[8] In this context, it is noteworthy that in the Trust Fund's experience many victim-survivors receiving rehabilitation assistance from the Trust Fund view this support as a form of recognition by the

[7] Regulation 50 (a) (ii) of the Regulations of the Trust Fund.

[8] These partners include international non-governmental organisations, local grassroots organisations, women's associations, faith-based organisations and the private sector. The Fund aims to ensure that they have the financial resources, technical expertise and oversight they need to adequately rehabilitate victims.

International Criminal Court, which in turn, impacts the way they viewed the Court and its role in ending impunity in their communities.[9]

19.3 The Trust Fund as an Agent for Transformation and Empowerment of Victims

In the ideal-case scenario, the assistance that the Trust Fund provides to victims under both its mandates will enable the empowerment of victims. In this way, the Trust Fund may contribute not only to improving the life of an individual victim but also to stabilising communities affected by conflict. In other words, it may assist in positive transformation at an individual and collective level. Pablo De Greiff highlights this inherent political potential of transitional justice efforts, stating that "[i]n transitional periods, reparations seek, in the last analysis, as most transitional measures do, to contribute (modestly) to the reconstitution or the constitution of a new political community."[10]

The Trust Fund benefits "victims". It does not provide humanitarian assistance *per se*, but because of the link of its mandate to the Rome Statute system, the assistance it gives has an added immaterial level: assistance by the Trust Fund implies the recognition of the fact that the beneficiary is a victim-survivor of the worst crime of humanity, war crimes, crimes against humanity or genocide. Having suffered harm from such a crime, he/she may benefit from Trust Fund assistance. This adds a symbolic dimension to Trust Fund assistance under both its mandates.

At the collective level, transitional justice mechanisms often aim at creating an official record of the human cost of atrocities, e.g. through trials and truth seeking mechanisms, encouraging resistance to a return to conflict or oppressive rule.[11] At the individual level, however, and this is in particular true for survivors of atrocities and violence, a society which allows all members to participate in dignity and with equal opportunities can only be achieved if victim-survivors are empowered again and regain their place within their communities.[12] The assistance granted to victims by the Trust Fund is there to directly benefit victims of international crimes at both levels with a view of bringing about positive change: at an individual level

[9] For more details on this argument see Trust Fund for Victims' Programme Progress Report Fall 2010, available online at www.trustfundforvctims.org.

[10] De Greiff 2006, pp. 451–477.

[11] For more details on this argument, see Van Zyl 2005, p. 217.

[12] Arenhövel 2008, pp. 572, 573, claims for example that "a basic precondition for a democratic society lies in the "self-evident truth", that everybody acknowledges everybody else as a free and equal citizen, regardless of religion, ethnicity, gender, age, sexual orientation, social status or heritage. Democratic procedures (one person, one vote) only make sense when this democratic promise is unquestioned by all citizens and all conflicting parties, and when it is guaranteed by political institutions and procedures."

the Trust Fund supports the empowerment and restoration of dignity of victims through concrete activities which directly benefit them; and at a collective level, the Trust Fund supports efforts to promote reconciliation within affected communities and to restore the social fabric that has been torn by conflict.

At an individual level, for example, the Trust Fund supports medical rehabilitation of victims of mutilation (e.g. by providing prosthetic limbs) that enables the victims to take up or increase income-generating activities. Another, maybe more complex illustration of a Trust Fund supported empowering rehabilitation project is a project addressing the needs of former child soldier girls who leave the armed forces and groups with children that were born during their time as child soldiers. These girls are given assistance to return to the school system.[13] This process is started by attending a special class for one year, during which the teachers try to bring these former child soldiers up to an educational standard corresponding to their age. If they succeed, these girls will join the classes at their level.[14] Implementing partners then provide scholarships for each of the girls. The project also established a day-care centre for their children of the former girl child soldiers where childcare workers help the girls to develop a motherly relationship with their babies—reconciling the bond between mother and children is particularly important because often the babies were born as a result of sexual abuse. In fact, many of the girls face stigmatisation because of their past within their communities and are often not even supported by their own parents. Rehabilitation has therefore also focused on sensitising parents of the former girl child soldiers to their responsibilities towards their daughters and grandchildren, including by encouraging their efforts aimed at income-generating activities in order to generate funds for school fees. The importance of such activities can be seen from explanation offered by one of the beneficiaries who stated that wearing a school uniform has given her back her dignity and enabled her to proudly walk down the street and be an active and respected member of her community. Moreover, in the Trust Fund's view this project is also a good example of how it aims at integrating the various categories of assistance it may offer in accordance with local needs.

To bring about positive change at the collective level, the Trust Fund, for example, currently supports two community reconciliation projects in the Eastern Democratic Republic of the Congo where the situation is still unstable and local conflict persists. One of these projects is a Trust Fund sponsored project called "*A l'école de la paix*",[15] which seeks to restore a culture of peace among children who have been victims of violence in Eastern DRC. Its objective is to promote dialogue between child and adolescent victims and their community to ensure a better understanding and expression of past events, with the ultimate goal

[13] TFV/RDC/2007/R2/029.

[14] In case they fail to achieve the necessary educational level to join their class at school, the girls are reoriented towards vocational training.

[15] This project is implemented in Ituri, North and South Kivu and directly benefits over 14,000 children. In Ituri, activities are carried out in Bunia, Bogoro, Mongwalu, Komanda, Mahagi, Badiya and Gety.

of coming together to build a future free of violence. Through peace education activities, adapted instructional material is used to teach children about the underlying causes of the conflicts and develop plans for resolving these issues. The young people who graduate from the "*A l'école de la paix*" become peace ambassadors tasked with propagating and transmitting messages of peace within their families, neighbourhoods and communities using various media such as drama, poetry, music and community work.

The "*A l'école de la paix*" project has had a large impact with little funding needed to support such an intervention. The positive impacts that the Trust Fund has observed include the establishment of a "conflict resolution committee" set up in a playground; children addressing adults who act violently, asking them to change their behaviours; the willingness of students who some months ago showed reluctance to interact with another ethnic group to live together with members of this other ethnic group; and the fact that children began to contribute to school fees for other vulnerable children and started to smile again after months of post-traumatic depression.

19.4 The Advantages of the Trust Fund's Dual Mandate

The dual mandate of being able to offer both assistance and Court-ordered reparations at the end of a criminal trial provides the Trust Fund with key strengths for meeting the needs of victims of the gravest crimes, enabling it to contribute to transformative change.

First, it allows the Trust Fund to act timely. Throughout its brief history the Trust Fund has provided assistance to the most vulnerable victims before trials have started before the Court and while trial proceedings are ongoing. In the case of the situation of Northern Uganda, for example, so far the arrest warrants issued by the ICC in May 2005 have not been executed to date, almost six years later. This has not prevented the Trust Fund from undertaking activities for the benefit of victims in Northern Uganda. In practice this means for example that five Trust Fund projects have been providing physical rehabilitation to victims of mutilation. During the conflict, amongst other atrocities, the Lord Resistance Army (the "LRA") mutilated people. Trust Fund support for LRA victims includes e.g. prosthetic limbs, reconstructive surgery and operations like post-burn contractures and lip/nose reconstructions.

The Trust Fund is also flexible, especially in its ability to target victims of crimes within a situation beyond those defined by particular trials. In other words, it can assist a much larger scope of victims than those who may eventually be eligible for Court-ordered reparations. Indeed, the International Criminal Court can only address specific and often very limited cases, in part due to the strategy of the Prosecution to focus on particular events (as the attack on the village of Bogoro in the Katanga Ngojolo Chui case) or crimes (as on child soldier crimes in the case against Lubanga). In Ituri district in Eastern Congo for example, the Trust Fund has been supporting girls forcibly conscripted into, and sexually abused, by armed groups. Crimes of sexual violence are not included in the charges against Thomas Lubanga, the first ICC accused in the DRC situation.

Lastly, the Trust Fund is a valuable source of operational knowledge for the International Criminal Court, especially *vis-à-vis* the design and implementation of awards for reparation. With its field experience it can help the Court, to move towards a better understanding of both what victims need, and how the ICC can best engage with victims and give them a voice in the process of justice. To better analyse its lessons-learnt, the Trust Fund initiated a multi-method, quasi-experimental, longitudinal impact evaluation with its implementing partners in early 2010.[16] Overall results of the study show a variety of important and interesting results.

One important finding made is that of a gender dimension related to the impact of violence. Violence impacts men and boys differently than it impacts women and girls; and findings suggested that among the Trust Fund's beneficiaries, female victims had experienced more severe psychological and social consequences. In reply to all questions, except one, women reported experiencing more severe psychological symptoms and more negative relations vis-à-vis their families and communities. Women and girls were twice as likely to report that their family was "not at all" caring. Twice as many women as men reported feeling "sad" a lot of the time, and just under twice as many reported feeling "lonely" a lot of the time. A third of women and girls said they felt "distant or cut off from others" a lot of the time, compared to a fifth of men and boys. Overall, ten per cent of female respondents said they did not trust their community at all. And just as many said they did not feel important in their community at all.

In line with these findings, the Trust Fund, in its activities under its general assistance mandate, has supported programmes designed to offer assistance by supporting economic empowerment of women and of survivors of sexual violence (who may be both male and female). In doing so, the Trust Fund hopes to place these particularly vulnerable victims in a better position to break with historic patterns of subordination and social exclusion. In addition, the Trust Fund also actively advocates with a view to possible upcoming reparation proceedings before the International Criminal Court that in designing and administering reparations it will be important for the Court to consider the importance of integrating a gender dimension. The Court will have to ensure that women are involved in the design, implementation and monitoring of the reparation process; and that reparations are responsive to the particularities of women's vulnerability and their roles *vis-à-vis* their communities. The Trust Fund argues that, if appropriately designed and delivered, reparations may be able to play a significant role in bringing about transformative change to the lives of women and girls.

---

[16] A detailed analysis of the research, conducted by Kristin Kalla and Peter Dixon will be forthcoming before the end of 2011 and made publically available through the Trust Fund. Some first results of the study are already available in the Programme Progress Reports, Fall 2010 and Summer 2011, available online at www.trustfundforvctims.org.

Other important findings include the danger of treating victims as a homogenous groups or category. The Trust Fund has learnt the lesson that it shares with the Court that in designing assistance and eventually also Court-ordered reparation awards there is a need to take into account the diversity of victims' experiences, both in terms of the violence that they have suffered and the consequences with which they still live. For example, assistance needs to take into consideration the special needs, vulnerability and diversity of children and youth, including those abducted into fighting forces, those made vulnerable by war and those victimised by sexual violence.

The experience of the Trust Fund also provides lessons-learnt about the importance and interdependence of rehabilitation and reconciliation in transitional justice processes. The Trust Fund has furthermore learnt about the value of combining and integrating individual and collective approaches to assistance and reparations to simultaneously recognise individual harm and repair social ties. Finally, it has learnt about the value of outreach and meaningful involvement of victims in processes to ensure, first, that affected communities understand the different between assistance and reparations, and second, that they have a meaningful stake and ownership in the process.

19.5 An Outlook to Future Developments: Challenges and Opportunities

The International Criminal Court has gained momentum and is moving into more and more situations: in the present year, 2011, it has already become active in two new situations. On 26 February 2011, the United Nations Security Council decided unanimously in its resolution 1970 to refer the situation in Libya since 15 February 2011 to the ICC. Accordingly, on 3 March 2011, the ICC Prosecutor announced his decision to open an investigation in Libya. In addition, on June 2011, the ICC Prosecutor submitted to Pre-Trial Chamber III a request for authorisation to open investigations *proprio motu* into the situation in *Côte d'Ivoire* since 28 November 2010. Furthermore, already on 31 March 2010, Pre-Trial Chamber II authorised the Prosecutor to open an investigation *proprio motu* in the situation in the Republic of Kenya, in relation to the 2007–2008 post-election violence in that country.

For the Trust Fund these developments mean that it has the mandate and responsibility to respond under its general assistance mandate to the needs of an increasing number of victims, located in more and more countries. After having been active in Uganda and the Democratic Republic of the Congo since late 2007, in 2011, it has launched a public tender to launch activities for victims of sexual and gender-based violence in the Central African Republic. It will also be in the near future assess the needs in the new situations.

In addition, the important role that the Trust Fund has to play in the reparations regime before the International Criminal Court will become clear once there will be a conviction before the Court and the first reparations begin, something that is likely to happen in 2012. Many questions are still open on how this judicial reparations process will work.

It seems clear already at this stage, however, that the Trust Fund will have an important role to play in the implementation as well as the financing of Court-ordered reparations awards. Moreover, it seems likely that the Court in many cases will also not be able to trace sufficient assets from the convicted persons for the purpose of reparations. Accordingly, the Trust Fund has at present reserved €1 million for complementing reparation orders in the cases currently pending before the Court. This amount translates roughly into one-third of the voluntary contributions currently available to the Trust Fund. The other two-thirds have been budgeted to assist up to 42,300 direct victim beneficiaries under the general assistance mandate in the DRC and Northern Uganda, and for the upcoming programme to benefit victims of sexual and gender-based violence in the Central African Republic.

What seems also clear already now is that reparations awarded in proceedings before the International Criminal Court will be limited if compared with the high number of victims and the enormous scale of their needs. As explained above, the interplay between the Trust Fund's two mandates may help to overcome some of the inherent narrowness of the reparations system set out in Article 75 of the Statute that is limited by its direct link to individual criminal responsibility.

If the Trust Fund is to play its key role in the Rome Statute regime it will depend on sustained voluntary contributions from donors. In fact, for both its mandates the Trust Fund relies on donations which are its main source of funding. In 2010, the Trust Fund received 1 Million 555,000 euros in donations, a sum which is likely to be exceeded in 2011. At present, the bulk of money donated comes from States, with Germany, Finland, the UK and Norway so far the biggest donors.[17] But while the trend is positive, there is still a mismatch between the (increasing) needs of the victims and the available resources at the Trust Fund's disposal.

Finally, whether the Trust Fund can play an important role in "giving a human face" to the International Criminal Court in the eyes of victims depends and will depend largely on the manner in which the International Criminal Court, the Trust Fund and implementing partners communicate and brand the support provided under both mandates, i.e. whether the link of Trust Fund supported activities to the Rome Statute system is publically explained and acknowledged. However, because of the difficult security situations in some of the regions where the Trust Fund operates (e.g. the persistent instability in Eastern Congo) as well as for more global concerns (international NGOs with operations e.g. in Darfur/Sudan may have an interest not to be seen close to the ICC), some of the Trust Fund's implementing partners have been reluctant to be too publically associated with the

[17] The Trust Fund has also received donations from non-European countries, including Senegal, Namibia, the DRC, South Korea, Jordan, Mexico, South Africa and Trinidad and Tobago which show the global support for the idea of such an institution. Moreover, private individuals have contributed money.

International Criminal Court and therefore also with the Trust Fund. Accordingly, they have asked to keep their link to the Trust Fund confidential. This problem might in fact be further exacerbated in the context of the first Court-ordered reparations that the International Criminal Court will award to victims because such reparations will necessarily create much public interest.

19.6 Conclusion

The Trust Fund is a concrete manifestation of the promise of the Rome Statute system towards victims. It is in a position to act effectively because of the advantages of its dual mandate and its ability to effectively restore the dignity of victims at the individual and collective level. It has been claimed that "the institutionalisation of victim reparations as an integral part of the work of the ICC brings the rights of victims to the highest level, and can be expected to have a strong effect upon national criminal courts, both in protecting the right to remedy as well as fighting impunity."[18] It is the Trust Fund's hope that this claim will become a tangible reality for victims and that its work in assisting victims under its two mandates will inspire others to support victims of the gravest crimes wherever they are. In the Trust Fund's view, empowerment of victims will transform communities and societies in which these victims live in a most positive way. For the Trust Fund to act as a catalyst for change and fulfil its two mandates it will, however, need sustained support both financially and morally from States, civil society and individuals.

References

Arenhövel M (2008) Democratization and transitional justice. Democratization 15(3):572–573

De Greiff P (2006) Justice and reparations. In: De Greiff P (ed) The handbook of reparations. Oxford University Press, Oxford, pp. 451–477

De Greiff P, Wierda M (2006) The trust fund for victims of the International Criminal Court: between possibilities and constraints. In: Feyter K, Parmentier S, Bossuyt M, Lemmens P (eds) Out of the ashes: reparations for victims of gross human rights violations. Intersentia, Antwerp, pp. 225 et subs.

Garcia-Godos J (2008) Victims reparations in transitional justice—What is at stake and why? NJHR 26(2):111–130

McGoldrick D, Rowe P, Donnelly E (2004) The permanent International Criminal Court—legal and policy issues. Hart Publishers, London, pp. 464–468.

Van Zyl P (2005) Promoting transitional justice in post-conflict societies. In: Bryden A, Hanggi H (eds) Security governance in post-conflict peacebuilding. Geneva Center for the Democratic Control of Armed Forces, Geneva, p. 217

[18] Garcia-Godos 2008.

Part V
The Role of Civil Society Actors

Chapter 20
From Victimhood to Political Protagonism: Victim Groups and Associations in the Process of Dealing with a Violent Past

Veit Strassner

Abstract This chapter focuses on the organised victims as collective political actors in post-conflict-societies. After proposing a typology of victim groups and pointing out the particularities of post-authoritarian human rights policies the political role of the victim organisations will be analysed. It will be argued, that the existence of political relevant victim groups is a necessary pre-condition for broader attempts to deal with the past human rights violations. Victim groups are essential for putting the issue on the public and political agenda. But while the existence of these groups is a necessary condition, it is by no means a sufficient one. Whether they are able to succeed or not depends on a variety of different aspects. Finally, it will be pointed out that the victim groups also play a tragic role, since their fundamental goals can never be realised.

Keywords Latin America • Victims • Victims organisations • Transitional justice • Post-conflict transition • Political action • Civil society

20.1 Introduction

> Madres y Familiares de Uruguayos Detenidos Desaparecidos (henceforth 'Familiares') came into being in the middle of the 1970s when the relatives of disappeared people in Uruguay and Argentina started the first enquiries and filed the first complaints. The group was consolidated in 1983 [...]. From the beginning Familiares tried to discover the truth about the fates of their sons, husbands, and parents. [...] When democracy was re-established, the competent government agencies did not investigate the human rights violations. Nevertheless, the search for the truth about what had happened to the people

He holds a M.A. and a Ph.D. in political science and a postgraduate degree (Lic. theol.) in theology.

V. Strassner (✉)
Kurt Schumacher School, Ingelheim, Germany
e-mail: vstrassner@hotmail.com

T. Bonacker and C. Safferling (eds.), *Victims of International Crimes: An Interdisciplinary Discourse*, DOI: 10.1007/978-90-6704-912-2_20,

who had been detained/disappeared was carried on by Familiares together with broad sectors of society that understood and shared Familiares' objectives. Familiares did this in a peaceful way and tried to bring forward the institutional mechanisms of the state of law. The objectives of the group are to find out about the fate of these people, promote truth and justice, and to prevent the repetition of these crimes. Familiares provides legal advice, reflects on the changing political circumstances, evaluates and takes decisions. They obtain and organise public support.[1]

This introductory quotation—a kind of self-description of a Uruguayan victim-group—already provides a set of aspects that characterise the particularities of victims' associations: Founded at the height of the violence their principle aim is to provide direct relief for those suffering from repression. Initially, they have the important function of mutual help, endorsement and support. But then, in many cases, things change: Some groups become more formalised and consolidated. These groups do not concentrate only on direct relief of the symptoms of repression. As they also want to get to root causes of the issues, they soon start political activism and campaigning. They become part of the broader movement that struggles for an end to violence, repression and dictatorship. They wait impatiently and with great expectations for the return to democracy and rule of law, because they hope that the democratic government will fulfil their claims. But the transition to democracy often brings serious disappointments: Governments will not and cannot fulfil all the demands of the victim-groups—sometimes not even some of them. Instead of having their mission accomplished the struggle goes on, but this time against a *democratic* government and in different social contexts. The role of the victims' organisations and their aims change as time passes and the political and social context changes.

The purpose of this chapter is to take a closer look at the particularities of victim associations as political actors. After proposing a typology of victims organisations, I would like to show that these groups are the *crucial* actors in the policy of dealing with the past. The very existence of victim groups is a *necessary* precondition for an active way of coming to terms with the past, but not a *sufficient* one. Their success depends on a number of different aspects. After examining

[1] Spanish Original: "Madres y Familiares de Uruguayos Detenidos Desaparecidos (en adelante Familiares) se fue conformando a partir de la segunda mitad de los años '70, a raíz de las denuncias y las primeras investigaciones realizadas por familiares de personas detenidas desaparecidas en Uruguay y en Argentina. El grupo se consolida en el año 1983 [...]. Desde sus comienzos, los familiares intentaron llegar a la verdad respecto a la situación de sus hijos, hermanos, esposos, padres. [...] Una vez recuperada la democracia, las violaciones a los derechos humanos quedaron sin ser investigadas por los organismos competentes [...]. Sin embargo, la búsqueda de la verdad sobre lo ocurrido a los detenidos desaparecidos ha sido mantenida y sostenida por Familiares, acompañados de amplios sectores de la sociedad que comprenden y comparten nuestros fines, recorriendo caminos pacíficos y alentando los mecanismos institucionales del Estado de Derecho. Los objetivos del grupo son conocer la suerte de estas personas, procurar la verdad y la justicia y la no reiteración de estos crímenes. Familiares es el lugar donde se busca asesoramiento, se piensa cada situación política, se evalúa y se decide, se logran y se organizan los apoyos." (Madres y Familiares de Uruguayos Detenidos Desaparecidos 2010).

some of these factors I will look more closely at the logic of political action employed by the victim groups. Finally I will point out that the victim groups not only play a crucial role but also a *tragic* one.

This will be illustrated by theoretical considerations as well as by empirical evidence. The examples are all taken from Latin American sources and therefore are somewhat contextual. Nevertheless, a set of more general conclusions can be drawn that can be adapted to other cases in different cultural and historical settings.

20.2 Victims and Victim Groups: A Typology

There is a broad legal, moral and philosophical debate about who and what is a victim. Especially in complex and long-lasting conflicts the distinction between victim and offender may become difficult and blurred. From a political scientist's point of view we can start with a broad—and simple—definition: A victim of a human rights' violation is everyone who considers himself a victim. I am aware of the problem of this self-adscription and self-victimisation.[2] But examining the political role of victim groups we can neglect this point, because as even "real" victims do have problems with receiving legal, social or political recognition, "self-declared" victims will not be recognised if there is no real basis for their status as victims. And furthermore, if we ask about the political role of these groups, the question whether they are "real" victims or not is a secondary one. As soon as they become relevant political actors and as soon as they are able to take influence on political decision-making, they are in the focus of politological analysis.

For our purposes a victim group can be defined as an association of people who consider themselves victims and who organise themselves in order to achieve certain goals related to the status of being a victim. Only those groups that approach the government or society to realise their goals are of political relevance. So when talking about victims organisations, I am not referring to self-help groups, but to collective civil society actors with clearly defined social and political interests as well as political strategies to accomplish these goals.

---

[2] I follow the definition of the United Nations—but without insisting upon empirical or criminal evidence. According to the United Nations victims of human rights violations are "persons who, individually or collectively, have suffered harm, including physical or mental injury, emotional suffering, economic loss or substantial impairment of their fundamental rights, through acts or omissions that are in violation of criminal laws operative within Member States, including those criminal laws proscribing criminal abuse of power" (United Nations 1985). According to the United Nation's Basic Principles and Guidelines on the Right to a Remedy and Reparation for Victims of Gross Violations victims are also relatives or friends of direct victims who were affected by the primary violations (United Nations 2006).

Thus, different types of victims and victim groups can be distinguished according to their involvement[3] and their victim status[4]:

Victim status involvement	Temporary	Definitive
Direct	Former political prisoners Victims of torture Victims of relegation Exiles Survivors ...	Fatalities People executed (extra-legally) People disappeared ...
Indirect	Relatives of political prisoners Relatives of exiles Relatives of victims of torture Relatives of survivors ...	Relatives of the disappeared Relatives of the executed Relatives of other casualties ...

All these different types of victims categories—for obvious reasons without the direct-definitive ones—can become organised in victim associations. This leads to the following typology:

Victim status involvement	Temporary	Definitive
Direct	Associations of ... ... former political prisoners ... victims of torture ... victims of relegation ... exiles ... survivors ...	–/–
Indirect	Associations of ... ... relatives of political prisoners ... relatives of exiles ... relatives of victims of torture ... relatives of survivors ...	Associations of ... ... relatives of the disappeared ... relatives of the executed ... relatives of other causalities ...

Apart from the common ground of being composed of people who consider themselves victims of human rights violations, these groups can be quite diverse. As political actors they play different roles—and they do it at different times:

The *groups indirectly involved* like the associations of relatives of people imprisoned, tortured, disappeared, killed etc. normally start their public and political activities during the time of repression. The difference between the two categories (temporary and definitive indirectly involved) is basically that the ones with a temporary victim status are in principle able to reach their primary goals (return of the exiles, release of the prisoners ...). Their political actions are focused on primary objectives and their main time of activism is while repression is still executed.

[3] This distinction is taken from Huyse 2003, pp. 54–55.

[4] See Strassner 2007, pp. 35–37, 58–62.

As this political involvement entails a high personal risk,[5] relatives of the direct victims stop their commitment when their family member is freed, returned from exile etc. As a consequence these groups tend not to be very stable. When the acute conflict ceases or when authoritarian rule ends these groups normally disperse after having reached their goals. In post-conflict-situations they normally play a minor role or no role at all.

The other victim groups remain: The ones *indirectly involved to "definitive victimisation"* cannot reach their original objectives (return of the disappeared, saving the lives of their loved ones). As they do not disperse, they can become very important political actors in the process of coming to terms with the past. Their political goals change over the course of time as will be shown below. Society sees them in an ambiguous way: On the one hand they are inconvenient, annoying and somewhat irritating because they disturb the apparent post-conflict peace. On the other hand—especially for those sympathetic to the human rights agenda—they are the ones with the highest degree of moral authority. They are struggling for a just cause. They are the ones who suffered from repression and still go on suffering. And they are not asking for themselves, but for others who cannot claim their own rights any more.

The groups of *temporarily involved direct victims* face a different and difficult situation: While they are still in exile or in prison, others campaign for them. And when they are freed, the victim groups their relatives were involved in, stop their political activities, because their primary goals are reached. These groups normally disappear.[6] The direct victims and survivors themselves have to struggle to cope with their new situation. They have to come to terms with their everyday life, have to find employment, care for their families and so on. Very often they are traumatised by the experiences they went through. Some of them refrain from further political involvement. However, among them there is usually still no *political* consciousness that they have been the victims of human rights violations and that they do have legitimate claims. While the public debate focuses on those who were killed or disappeared, former political prisoners or exiles are unlikely to start claiming *their* rights. Although they have suffered, they feel somehow fortunate, because they survived repression. After a couple of years in many cases these people started to organise themselves to demand their rights.

In public perception there is always a certain distrust because they are asking for something—usually money—and at the same time they are somehow suspicious, because people do not always make a clear distinction between political prisoners and "normal criminals". Another prejudice they may have to face is the suspicion that they have only survived, because they collaborated with the regime or because of betrayals.[7]

[5] See Loveman 1998.

[6] See Strassner 2005, pp. 40–41.

[7] See Longoni 2005; da Silva Catela 2001.

These groups usually start their political activities relatively late, but they can become important political actors in post-conflict-situations, even though they may have to face certain reservations by society.

20.3 Victims Organisations: Crucial Actors in a Difficult Policy

To understand the role of the victims organisations as political actors it is essential to have a closer look to the particularities of the policy itself, where these groups develop their activities.

20.3.1 Coming to Terms with the Past: A Dangerous Policy

Post-conflict or post-authoritarian dealing with former human rights violations is a very dangerous, difficult and challenging topic. Tackling this matter is the "most explosive transitional issue"—as Alexandra Barahona de Brito puts it—"and even its hasty burial because of fears of polarization and instability testify to the political importance of the problem".[8] It is the problem that entails "the greatest potential to destabilize a transition process".[9] There is only little to win for a young democratic government—but there is a lot to lose.[10]

German scholar Adrienne Windhoff-Héritier proposed a typology of policies. The one that suits best the policy of coming to terms with the past is what she calls a "social regulative policy": It is a policy where essential moral issues of human behaviour and fundamental rules of social coherence are debated. It is an emotionally-charged topic where deeply rooted matters of value are touched. Therefore ideological convictions play an important role—especially because most of the key actors in these debates have formerly been involved in some way in the conflicts. These policies are—according to Windhoff-Héritier—also characterised by the appearance of single issue-groups as well as by the importance of the judiciary.[11]

Coming to terms with past human rights violations deals with fundamental value questions. It is an emotionally (and often ideologically) charged debate on moral concerns in which compromises are hardly possible, or, as David Pion-Berlin puts it:

> Normally the policies under authoritarian rule polarised the society to such an extent, that finding a win-win strategy is virtually impossible. Decisions to prosecute would have relieved the families of the victims, while creating anxiety and fear within the armed

---

[8] Barahona de Brito 1997, p. 213.

[9] Barahona de Brito et al. 2001a, p. 1.

[10] See Fuchs and Nolte 2004, pp. 68–69.

[11] See Windhoff-Héritier 1987, pp. 50–51.

> forces. Decisions not to prosecute would have calmed the armed forces but would have left old wounds unhealed and justice not served. Retribution could have fuelled military animosities; exoneration could have lowered the costs to future acts of terror. Midpoints between the two options were not necessarily the most desirable, because less than satisfactory solutions could have easily caused the government to lose margins of political support and military cooperation simultaneously.[12]

How do these characteristics of the policy influence the political process and the behaviour of the political actors? The inherent difficulties in finding political compromise, the emotional implications and the point in time at which these issues erupt (often in instable transitional situations) make the policy dangerous and potentially destabilising. It is a policy with potentially high political costs (and little prospect of political benefit).

20.3.2 The Arrangement of Actors

One major reason for the complexity of this policy is the arrangement of political actors in this field. Who are the central political actors in this field? Apart from some prominent individuals there are basically collective actors.

First of all, there is the (often young) *democratic* or *post-conflict-government*. Its principle aim is to avoid political frictions and instabilities. The government tries to mediate and reduce the level of confrontation. It will not touch this highly explosive topic without necessity or without the prospect of political benefits. The executive usually tends to be reluctant or indifferent towards the victims' claims. It wants to keep the political costs as low as possible.

The *armed forces* are the ones basically responsible for high political costs. Their resistance against such politics is very persistent. Their concrete power may vary depending on the actual situation, the mode of transition from authoritarian rule and the balance of powers. But their monopoly of war weapons and their potential for violent military interventions makes them a threatening actor in internal politics. Their behaviour is very often determined by the conviction to have acted appropriately (and heroically) during the time of military rule to defend the nation and its values. In some cases there is even a kind of messianic sense of mission.[13]

So the only actor permanently interested in advancing in this issue is the *human rights movement*. The victims organisations form part of the broader human rights movement. Particularly in issues related to past violations the victim associations are the ones with the highest degree of moral legitimacy. Human rights organisations can support the victim groups but they will not act without their mandate or

---

[12] Pion-Berlin 1994, p. 106.

[13] See Loveman 1999.

even against their will. Considering the policy's characteristics and the actors' constellation and interests it becomes obvious that the human rights movement and the victim groups as the key actors will have a central role—specially in respect to the agenda-setting as the first and necessary step. The existence of these groups is the *conditio sine qua non* for an extensive way of coming to terms with the past: "The more pressure a new democratizing elite is under from mobilized human rights organizations or other bodies, such as opposition parties and churches and even from public opinion, the more likely it is to adopt some sort of policy to deal with the past."[14]

20.3.3 Victims Organisations and Agenda-Setting

Examining the politics of coming to terms with the past in three Southern Cone-countries (Argentina, Chile, Uruguay) it stands out that in the great majority of the cases the political measures were initiated by the victim groups with the active support of the human rights organisations. The dominating model of agenda-setting was what Cobb et al. called the "outside initiative model": Actors outside the government try to place their demands first in the public debate and then by different mechanisms onto the political agenda.[15]

It was nearly always the human rights movement that initiated the political measures. The mechanisms employed were for example public and political pressure, direct influence on decision takers, the use of international pressure, mass mobilisations, legal devices etc. The differences between the cases analysed basically lay in the degree of confrontation the human rights movement had to use to put their issues on the political agenda. But it was nearly always them who pushed the topics and so ensured that the past would not be buried.

One concrete example: The Chilean dictatorship practised extensive political imprisonment. For decades there were no clear figures; estimations varied from 10,000 up to 400,000 political prisoners.[16] The relatives of the imprisoned were campaigning in order to free them. After the return to democracy in 1989 when the last political prisoners were set free, the issue vanished from the political debate and from the public consciousness. For more than a decade nobody spoke about political imprisonment and torture. It was almost a taboo. The public debate centred around the fate of the more than 2,000 *desaparecidos*, people who had been arrested and then "disappeared" without a trace. The victim groups of the relatives of the disappeared were very well organised and had good links to other civil society actors. The former political prisoners were not organised at all. They had no public voice, they did not have any lobbying strength. Ten years later (1999), when

14 Barahona de Brito et al. 2001b, p. 307.

15 See Cobb et al. 1976.

16 See King 1989, p. 1045; Comisión Ética contra la Tortura 2004, p. 2.

Pinochet was caught in London, the first political ex-prisoners organised themselves. Due to frictions between members of different leftist parties the group split up into different organisations according to their party-political affiliation. The movement grew: Several groups of former political ex-prisoners emerged, and more and more victims organised themselves into these groups. Their concerns received increasing public recognition. Talking about their experiences in prison and about torture was no longer considered a taboo. The groups of former political ex-prisoners started demanding *truth* (i.e. the appointment of a truth commission), *justice* (i.e. punishing the guilty) and *reparation*. In 2003, after some time of campaigning, the Lagos administration (middle-left coalition led by the socialist Ricardo Lagos; 2000–2006) set up a truth commission. The two volumes of reports of this commission documented more than 27,000 cases of political imprisonment and torture. At the end of 2004 a reparation law was passed for those who had been victims of prison and torture.[17]

20.3.4 Victim Groups: Dynamic Actors in a Changing Policy

Dealing with the past is not a static policy, but a dynamic one. Challenges and needs change with the course of time depending on the balance of powers and the varying political contexts.[18] Usually there is a great need for truth-seeking in the direct aftermath of conflict and repression. Society wants to know what happened. The call for reparatory measures for the victims of massive abuses usually comes later. The importance of trials may differ from case to case; as pointed out above, the judiciary plays an important role in social regulative policies. Very often, however, there is a strong political influence on the judiciaries. In post-conflict-societies the rule of law is normally not (yet) established to its full extent.[19] Therefore criminal justice and legal investigations depend on how the legal system recovered its autonomy and how the rule of law is realised. Years later demands for criminal justice are ebbing, because the ones legally responsible for the crimes die as well as the direct victims or their relatives. But there is a shift in topics and focal points: Politics and measures of remembrance become more important. These politics of memory can be seen as an attempt to reach at least historical reparation and influence the collective memory and the historiography for one's own ends. Victim groups respond to these changes in policy, but at the same time they themselves and their political activities have an influence on the changes in the policy.[20]

---

[17] For a more detailed analysis see Strassner 2005.

[18] See Fuchs and Nolte 2004, pp. 85–86.

[19] See O'Donnell 1999.

[20] See Jelin 2002.

Let's have a closer look at one concrete example: The Argentine dictatorship (1976–1983) was one of the most bloody dictatorships in Latin America; thousands of people disappeared,[21] 1,200 people were executed, more than 30,000 suffered political imprisonment and torture, half a million escaped into exile. About 500 children were abducted and given up for adoption under a false identity.[22] Due to the magnitude the issue of the *desaparecidos* was and still is the dominant topic when dealing with the human rights legacy of military rule. Also the search for the "children", today in their mid-1930s, is still ongoing.

Let me focus on the issue of the disappeared.[23] At the beginning the major objective of the victims' organisations (mainly relatives of the *desaparecidos*) was the return of their loved ones. As they had to recognise that in most cases there will not be an *aparición con vida,*[24] the focus shifted to *verdad y justicia* (truth and justice). As the Argentine military left power after their regime collapsed, they faced the new democratic government from a weak position. The first democratic government put a series of high-ranking generals on trial and established a truth commission. When the number of charges against military personnel grew, the armed forces became more and more concerned about this development and started to put pressure on the executive to pass an amnesty law. The victim groups started—unsuccessfully—to campaign against this amnesty. For years the struggle for criminal justice seemed to be blocked. The victims' political struggle for truth and justice became a legal struggle against the amnesty laws. Victims and their lawyers tried to find breaches in this legislation by filing suits before national and international courts. Over the years, as the Argentine judiciary gained more and more independence, the victims began to be able to celebrate their first successes.

But as the years went by and it became obvious that at best only a small number of the responsible will be charged for their crimes during military rule, the victim groups shifted their focus. If the dictatorship was not to be held responsible by the courts, it should at least be judged by history. An impressive struggle for collective memory started and still goes on. The victim groups try to anchor their interpretation of history and their memories in the public discourse and in collective memory of the nation: Together with an NGO they established an audio-visual archive with the filmed testimonies of many protagonists of the victim movement. A wide range of testimonial literature by the victims has been published. Regional committees for the memory were established, in which the victims are represented. Memorials were inaugurated. The famous *Madres de Plaza de Mayo*, an association of mothers of the disappeared, even founded a university in order to

[21] Following official figures, almost 14,000 cases of forced disappearance are documented; in the victims' (and in public) discourse one very often hears the figure of 30,000 *desaparecidos* (see Strassner 2007, pp. 77–78).

[22] For an overview see Novaro and Palermo 2004.

[23] See also Strassner 2006.

[24] Some of the victim groups never gave up this claim or slogan to show that they ask for a complete restitution of the *status quo ante* and that they are not willing to accept any compromises.

keep not only the memory of their disappeared children alive but also their ideas and political projects.[25]

20.3.5 The Victims Organisations as Crucial Actors

As has been shown, the victim groups play a central role in the policy of coming to terms with past human rights' violations. Without organised victims, there will hardly be an in-depth debate on the violent past or—even less—on criminal justice. The only ones who will place this topic on the public agenda are the victim groups. The topics they try to put on the political agenda change as the policy itself is a dynamic one.

The existence of victims organisations is a necessary condition for an active way of dealing with the past. But whether they are really able to articulate their demands and to bring them into the public sphere as well as the political arena, depends on a series of different variables.

20.4 The Existence of Victim Groups: A Necessary But Not Sufficient Condition

Whether victims organisations are able to put their demands successfully onto public and political agendas or not, depends on a variety of different factors. I will only name some of them: How large are they? How sophisticated is their degree of organisation? What financial and personal resources (staff, funding, volunteers, infrastructure, offices etc.) do they have? Can they count on members who are working full time for the organisation? Can they afford paid employees? Do they have access to the media? Or do they even have their own means of communication? Do they have prominent members—"public faces"—of the organisation? Can they count on good lawyers and on victims willing to have their cases used for political purposes?

As victims organisations usually do not have high numbers of members, they need allies. Can they build coalitions with other civil society groups such as trade unions, social movements, churches etc.? Or do they have direct access to political decision makers by close links to political parties? Do they get support from abroad? Do they have (inter)nationally known sympathisers or prominent people supporting them and helping them to bring their cause to a broader public?

As victim groups act in concrete political and social circumstances these aspects also influence their possible success. How did violence or authoritarian rule come to an end? What was the mode of transition? What does the balance of

---

[25] The *Universidad Popular Madres de Plaza de Mayo—Universidad de Lucha y Resistencia* (Popular University of the Mothers of Plaza de Mayo—University of Struggle and Resistance) was founded in 2000, holds treaties with several national universities, and gives degrees in Social Work, History, Teaching, Education, Journalism etc. In 2010 the university received the provisional authorisation as a university by presidential decree.

powers look like? Are they able to influence this balance of powers? How favourable is society to the victims' demands? And so forth …

The success of the victim groups depends on a variety of external factors, but also on their ability to adapt to the circumstances and to develop political strategies to reach their goals.

20.5 The Logic of Political Action

What if they succeed? It has been an interesting result of my research to see that there is no clear correlation between what a government does to deal with past human rights violations and the degree of satisfaction of the victim groups.[26] The relationship between these two variables is an asymmetric one. If, on the one hand, the government ignores the victims' demands or even takes measures to impede the search for truth, justice or reparations, the victim groups will—unsurprisingly—criticise these policies harshly. But if, on the other hand, government takes the victims' demands into consideration and implements measures to foster truth, justice, reparation and memory, the victim groups will appreciate these measures—but they will never be satisfied.

There are several explanations for these findings. I will mention only four of them: Firstly, the victims are biographically inseparably linked to what happened to them. Being a victim of massive human rights violations has become part of their identity. Especially if they struggled for a long time for their rights, giving up is nearly impossible—in particular when their demands have not been fulfilled completely.

This leads to a second important point: As the damage caused is often overwhelming, the compensation or the reparation must be infinite as well. The magnitude of the damage makes total satisfaction for the victim almost impossible. The damage done cannot be repaired.

Another point has to do with the logic of political actions employed by the victim groups: As the government is not in favour of responding to their demands normally and the political adversaries try to obstruct retroactive policies, the victim groups have formulated maximal demands in order to achieve at least *something*. Normally they ask for the punishment of *all* those responsible and involved in human rights violations, being aware at the same time that not all of them will be punished. In many cases there is a certain progression in the demands of the victim groups, a kind of dialectic of the things *already reached* and those *still due*: As soon as they realise that political goals become reachable or are even reached, that which has seemed unreachable so far becomes more realistic and realisable. So victims' demands will expand. This dialectical relationship of accomplished goals and desired goals, requires a—what I would call—"strategic discontent or dissatisfaction": In order to go on demanding you *cannot* be satisfied. This is an

[26] See Strassner 2007, pp. 331–339.

inherent logic of political bargaining. It is part of the political strategy to criticise and to challenge the government by insisting in the gap between what they rightfully ask for and what the government was prepared to concede.

Another explanation refers to the sociology of groups: Asserting claims for (more) truth, justice and reparation is the *raison d'être* of the victims organisations. Being satisfied with fulfilled goals and not asking for more would mean to admit that there is no more reason for the group to exist.

To sum up: Whatever a government does to deal with the past, victim groups will not be satisfied. But there may be differences in the degree of discontent. This leads to my last point: Victim groups not only play a crucial role, but also a *tragic* one.

20.6 The Tragic Role of the Victim Groups

I showed that the victim groups play a—or more precisely *the*—central role in the political processes of coming to terms with the past. They are the central agenda-setter, the ones that push forward the search for truth, justice and reparation. If they do not pressure the government, there will hardly be a broad policy of dealing with the past.

Besides being a central political actor they have a crucial social task: Post-conflict-societies tend to forget their violent past and to repress the memories. The victim groups have a *memento* function: By their mere existence and by their political actions they try to keep the past in the public consciousness. They are a thorn in the side of the society's self-approval and complacency. In this way they play an important role for the society: They challenge society, they question the way society deals with its own past, and they push society to get to the bottom of what happened and why it happened. This critical debate on the past will help to prevent a repetition of that past.

Society profits in some way from the victims' unwillingness and inability to forgive and to forget. The victims' sufferings and their dolefulness with the current situation of not reaching truth and justice helps society to handle its past.

The tragic role of the victim groups consists in their ongoing suffering and their inability to come to terms with the past. It is exactly the victims' inability to come to terms with the past that helps society to do so. Figuratively speaking one could say that the open wounds of the victims help to heal the wounds of the society.

References

Barahona de Brito A (1997) Human rights and democratization in Latin America: Uruguay and Chile. Oxford University Press, Oxford

Barahona de Brito A, González-Enríquez C, Aguilar P (2001a) Introduction. In: Barahona de Brito A, González-Enríquez C, Aguilar P (eds) The politics of memory. Transitional Justice in Democratizing Societies. Oxford University Press, Oxford, pp. 1–39

Barahona de Brito A, González-Enríquez C, Aguilar P (2001b) Conclusion. In: Barahona de Brito A, González-Enríquez C, Aguilar P (eds) The politics of memory. Transitional Justice in Democratizing Societies. Oxford University Press, Oxford, pp. 303–314

Cobb R, Ross J-K, Ross MH (1976) Agenda building as a comparative political process. APSR 70:126–138

Comisión Ética contra la Tortura (2004) Tortura nunca más, por el derecho a vivir en paz. Comisión Ética contra la Tortura, Santiago

da Silva Catela L (2001) No habrá flores en las tumbas del pasado. La experiencia de reconstrucción del mundo de los familiares de desaparecidos. Ediciones Al Margen, La Plata

Fuchs R, Nolte D (2004) Politikfeld Vergangenheitspolitik: Zur Analyse der Aufarbeitung von Menschenrechtsverletzungen in Lateinamerika. Lateinamerika Analysen 9:59–92

Huyse L (2003) Victims. In: Bloomfield D, Barnes T, Huyse L (eds) Reconciliation after violent conflict. A handbook. International Institute for Democracy and Electoral Assistance, Stockholm, pp. 54–66

Jelin E (2002) Los trabajos de la memoria. Siglo Ventiuno, Madrid

King PJ (1989) Comparative analysis of human rights violations under military rule in Argentina, Brazil, Chile, and Uruguay. Stat Abstr Lat Am 27:1043–1065

Longoni A (2005) Traiciones. La figura del traidor (y la traidora) en los relatos acerca de los sobrevivientes de la represión. In: Jelin E, Longoni A (eds) Escrituras, imágenes y escenarios ante la represión. Siglo Ventiuno, Madrid, pp. 203–240

Loveman B (1999) For La Patria. Politics and the armed forces in Latin America. Scholarly Resources, Wilmington

Loveman M (1998) High-risk collective action: defending human rights in Chile, Uruguay and Argentina. Am J Sociol 104:477–525

Madres y familiares de Uruguayos detenidos desaparecidos (2010) Nuestra historia. www.desaparecidos.org.uy/madresyfamiliara.html. Accessed 21 October 2011

Novaro M, Palermo V (2004) La dictadura militar 1976/1983. Del golpe de estado a la restauración democrática. Paidós, Buenos Aires

O'Donnell G (1999) Polyarchies and the (Un)rule of law in Latin America: a partial conclusion. In: Méndez J, O'Donnell G, Pinheiro PS (eds) The (un)rule of law & the underprivileged in Latin America. Helen Kellogg Institute for International Studies, Notre Dame, pp. 303–337

Pion-Berlin D (1994) To prosecute or to pardon? Human rights decisions in the Latin American Southern Cone. Hum Rights Q 16:105–130

Strassner V (2005) Die Comisión Nacional sobre Prisión Política y Tortura – ein neues Kapitel in der Aufarbeitung des Staatsterrorismus in Chile. Lateinamerika Analysen 12:37–62

Strassner V (2006) ¡La lucha continúa! Der Kampf um die Erinnerungen an die Verschwundenen der argentinischen Militärdiktatur. Totalitarismus und Demokratie 5:345–368

Strassner V (2007) Die offenen Wunden Lateinamerikas. Vergangenheitspolitik im postautoritären Argentinien, Uruguay und Chile. Verlag für Sozialwissenschaften, Wiesbaden

United Nations (1985) Declaration of basic principles of justice for victims of crime and abuse of power. General Assembly Resolution 40/34, 29 Nov 1985. www.un.org/documents/ga/res/40/a40r034.htm. Accessed 8 August 2012

United Nations (2006) Basic principles and guidelines on the right to a remedy and reparation for victims of gross violations of international human rights law and serious violations of international humanitarian law. General Assembly Resolution 60/147, 21 March 2006. www.daccess-dds-ny.un.org/doc/UNDOC/GEN/N05/496/42/PDF/N0549642.pdf?OpenElement. Accessed 8 Aug 2012

Windhoff-Héritier A (1987) Policy-Analyse. Eine Einführung. Campus, Frankfurt am Main

Chapter 21
The Role of Cambodian Civil Society in the Victim Participation Scheme of the Extraordinary Chambers in the Courts of Cambodia

Christoph Sperfeldt

Abstract One of the most interesting features of the ECCC is that it combines an extensive victim participation scheme with a collective reparations mandate. However, it has been a gradual learning curve for the ECCC to manage the participation of more than 8,000 victims in its proceedings. Benefiting from its in-country location, the ECCC has been able to rely on collaboration with relatively strong and proactive local civil society organisations. Working primarily at the intersection between the Court and society, these NGOs have assumed various roles in support of the ECCC's victim participation process, some of which would more commonly fall within the responsibility of a court. This chapter explores the main roles Cambodian NGOs play in the ECCC's victim participation scheme and draws some preliminary observations at a point where the Court has completed its first case and is in the midst of trial hearings in its second case.

Keywords ECCC • Victim participation • Civil society • NGOs • Hybrid courts • Transitional justice

21.1 Introduction

The twentieth century has seen many violent conflicts and mass atrocities in Cambodia, the worst occurring in the period of Democratic Kampuchea, often referred to as the era of the Khmer Rouge regime, from 1975 to 1979. The 1991

Christoph Sperfeldt is Regional Program Coordinator at the Asian International Justice Initiative (AIJI), a collaborative project between the East–West Center and UC Berkeley's War Crimes Studies Center.

C. Sperfeldt (✉)
Asian International Justice Initiative, East–West Center and UC Berkeley's War Crimes Studies Center, Honolulu, USA
e-mail: csperfeldt@gmail.com

T. Bonacker and C. Safferling (eds.), *Victims of International Crimes: An Interdisciplinary Discourse*, DOI: 10.1007/978-90-6704-912-2_21,

Paris Peace Agreements, which, through the United Nations Transitional Authority in Cambodia (UNTAC), provided for one of the largest peacekeeping missions in the history of the United Nations, did not mention bringing to justice those responsible for these crimes. However, in 1997, the then two Cambodian Co-Prime Ministers wrote to the Secretary-General requesting United Nations assistance to the Royal Government of Cambodia, to bring to justice those most responsible for the crimes committed during the reign of the Khmer Rouge regime. It was only in 2003, after many years of protracted negotiations, that both parties were able to conclude an agreement to establish the Extraordinary Chambers in the Courts of Cambodia (ECCC), often referred to as the Khmer Rouge Tribunal.

The ECCC is a mixed hybrid court of national and international composition, applying both international and Cambodian national law. Five individuals have initially been tried in two cases before the ECCC, referred to as Case 001 and Case 002.[1] Additional prosecutions are considered but remain stagnant.[2] From the outset, the Court has faced criticism common to other internationalised courts, including high costs and slow proceedings. Additional difficulties arising from the hybrid nature of the Court include allegations of corruption and political interference in the manner of its conduct of cases.[3] The United Nations and international donors supporting the ECCC have made multiple attempts to contain these problems, all the while attempting to ensure that trial proceedings are in accordance with international standards of justice.

Despite these problems, the pronouncement in July 2010 of the first verdict against Kaing Guek Eav, alias "Duch", the former head of the Khmer Rouge prison site S-21, was for many Cambodians a visible milestone, marking that the ECCC was beginning to deliver justice. Against the benchmark of other international(-ised) criminal courts, trial monitors in that case found "the Accused Person's right to a fair trial to have been upheld".[4] Population-based surveys by the Human Rights Center, University of California, Berkeley, indicate that Cambodians generally have positive attitudes towards the Court, with over 80 % believing that the ECCC should be involved in responding to what happened during the Khmer Rouge regime.[5]

One of the most distinct features of the ECCC is its extensive victim participation scheme.[6] Victim participation, beyond that of pure witness, is a novel and fairly recent development for international criminal courts. The ECCC has introduced, through its Internal Rules in 2007, victim participation provisions based on

[1] Case 002 currently proceeds only against two defendants after Ieng Thirith was found by the Trial Chamber not be fit to stand trial and a second defendant, Ieng Sary, passed away in March 2013.

[2] See for instance OSJI 2011.

[3] See more at Bertelman 2010.

[4] AIJI 2009, p. 6.

[5] Pham et al. 2011a, After the First Trial, p. 26.

[6] For more specific information, see the chapter of Silke Studzinsky in this book.

Cambodian national law. These provisions allow survivors either to file a complaint with the Co-Prosecutors or to apply to the Co-Investigating Judges to become a civil party and to claim collective and moral reparations.[7] The possibility for victims to join the proceedings as civil parties in particular is, so far, an unprecedented mechanism in comparison with other internationalised tribunals.[8] Accordingly, victims are permitted to play an active role in proceedings with full procedural rights, similar to those afforded to a charged person. These participation rights confer upon survivors, themselves key beneficiaries of the ECCC process, direct access to justice and the opportunity to present their personal experiences, views and concerns.

There has been much writing about the role of civil society in transitional justice processes.[9] Although there seems to be general agreement that civil society actors can make vital contributions to these settings, only few examine this claim by looking at concrete case studies. Based on numerous informal discussions over the past years with NGO and ECCC staff, government and donor officials, combined with participation in outreach and survivor meetings, this chapter explores the main roles local civil society actors have played in the ECCC's victim participation scheme. The focus is here on Cambodian NGOs and not on the contributions of the many international NGOs. Based on this overview, some preliminary observations will be drawn at a point where the Court has completed the appeals stage in its first trial and continues trial proceedings in its second case.

21.2 The Roles of Civil Society in the ECCC's Victim Participation Process

Following the withdrawal of the UNTAC, the country witnessed a significant influx of development aid that was inefficiently absorbed by the rudimentary state structures at the time. Therefore, many donors began channelling large parts of the funding through newly established local NGOs. As a consequence, the number and capacity of those NGOs increased considerably throughout the 1990s.[10] These developments led to the creation of a comparatively strong and diverse local NGO community in Cambodia, distinguishing the country from other neighbours in the Mekong region.

The transitional justice process, as revived through the establishment of the ECCC, was thus able to build upon the strength of Cambodia's NGO community. Around 10–15 Cambodian NGOs have engaged at different times with the ECCC process,[11] although a number of NGOs abstained from engaging with the Court

---

7 Refer to Rule 23 of the ECCC Internal Rules.

8 See for instance Boyle 2006; McGonigle 2009; Thomas and Chy 2009, pp. 214–293.

9 See for instance Backer 2003; Brahm 2007; Duthie 2009; Roht-Arriaza 2002.

10 For more about Cambodia's post-UNTAC development, see, for example, Hughes 2003; Sorpong 2007.

11 See, for example, Penh et al. 2006.

for the reasons of flaws in the ECCC's hybrid structure and the need to focus on other development priorities.[12] Many local NGOs that began to develop activities in support of the ECCC's process concentrated their work on victim assistance following the adoption of Internal Rules in 2007 permitting civil party participation. The following section provides an overview of the main roles these NGOs have assumed in the ECCC's victim participation scheme.[13]

21.2.1 The Messengers: Outreach

Whilst the ECCC was established with a mandate to try the senior leaders and those most responsible for crimes committed under the Khmer Rouge regime, many NGO activists on the ground also hope it could make a positive contribution to national reconciliation, healing and the rule-of-law in Cambodia. For this to happen, it is important to ensure that the Court and its proceedings are known to the Cambodian public. The UN Office of the High Commissioner for Human Rights' (OHCHR) rule-of-law tool on hybrid courts argues that "a hybrid court may be seen as largely irrelevant unless there is a robust outreach programme that informs the public about its activities".[14] In the Cambodian context, this is a difficult task given that most Cambodians live in rural areas often with limited access to information. The complexities in understanding and participating in internationalised criminal proceedings makes it all the more difficult.[15]

At the ECCC, the Public Affairs Section (PAS) and the Victims Support Section (VSS) are the main sections responsible for reaching out to the general public and victims. No separate unit exclusively dedicated to outreach exists at the Court. The activities of these two sections have mainly been directed towards providing public information about the ECCC and its legal proceedings to the population. During the Court's early years, however, these outreach programs were under -prioritised within the Court and lacked necessary resources, rendering their operations and capacities quite limited. Without access to information, survivors of the Khmer Rouge regime would know very little about the potential to participate in the ECCC's proceedings. As a consequence, Cambodian NGOs were at the forefront of ECCC-related outreach to victims, dominating the field at least until the beginning of the first trial in 2009. During the first trial, the Court paid more attention to outreach and played a more active role in reaching out to the public.[16]

---

[12] See for instance Human Rights Watch 2003.

[13] These roles are described in relation to the ECCC more generally at Sperfeldt 2012b, pp. 150–152.

[14] OHCHR 2008a, p. 18.

[15] Sperfeldt 2012b, p. 151.

[16] See more at ICTJ 2010.

Since the ECCC's establishment, more than a dozen Cambodian NGOs have been involved at different stages in victim outreach activities. Each NGO has taken a different approach to outreach, with some focusing more on victims of crimes than others. Activities such as designing and distributing specialised information materials and newsletters, radio call-in shows, websites, films, public forums, and community-based outreach sessions are largely aimed at informing Cambodians about the Court's judicial processes, but a number of activities also provide opportunities for two-way communication. Many local NGOs adapted their existing community and communication structures for the purposes of ECCC-related outreach, including the Cambodian Human Rights and Development Association (ADHOC) through its offices in each of the Cambodian provinces; the Documentation Center of Cambodia (DC-Cam) through provincial missions from the capital; the Center for Social Development (CSD) through public forums in provincial capitals; the Khmer Kampuchea Krom Human Rights Association (KKKHRA) with its targeted outreach programs for minority victims.[17]

The case of the Khmer Institute of Democracy (KID) is one clear example of a local NGO utilising its established networks for ECCC outreach activities. For more than ten years, KID had been coordinating a network of approximately 120 "Citizen Advisors" who are engaged community members operating in nine Cambodian provinces. With the establishment of the ECCC, KID began using its extended community-based network for ECCC-related outreach. Citizen Advisors received basic training on the work of the Court, its mandate and procedures, with specific focus on the Court's rules on victim participation and witness protection. On average, each of the Citizen Advisors carried out one workshop per month at the community level, interacting with groups of 30–50 community members at each event. The methodology of outreach activities depended on the focal topic, but utilised an interactive learning style including ample time for discussion and the use of materials often developed by KID itself. Between October 2007 and the beginning of 2009, KID's network has held around 2,200 workshops with a total number of 66,000 participants, a number that rose to approximately 100,000 people at the beginning of 2010.[18]

More than five years into the judicial process, it could be said that a majority of Cambodians know of the existence of the ECCC. Results of the International Republican Institute's survey conducted in 2009 indicate that 82 % of respondents were aware of the Court, an increase from 71 % in 2008.[19] More detailed population-based surveys conducted in 2008 and 2010 by the Human Rights Center, University of California Berkeley, indicated, respectively, that 61 % and 75 % of Cambodian people had some limited knowledge about the Court.[20] Both sets of

[17] Sperfeldt 2012b, pp. 158–159.

[18] Information provided by KID, on file with author.

[19] IRI 2009, pp. 32–40.

[20] Pham et al. 2011a, After the First Trial, p. 21.

data suggest that awareness of the ECCC has increased over time, but that knowledge of the Court and its judicial process remains limited. Much of this relative accomplishment is due to the combined activities of Cambodian NGOs and the ECCC's expanded outreach program post-2009.

21.2.2 The Middlemen: Intermediary Functions

After the adoption of the Internal Rules in 2007, which for the first time incorporated provisions on victim participation, NGOs began to gradually integrate more information about the rights of victims at the Court into their general ECCC-related outreach programs. As the ECCC, in its formative years, had failed to include victim participation in any of its operational strategies, the Court's Victims Unit (later renamed as the Victims Support Section, VSS) began its work with inadequate funding and very limited capacities in late 2007. It took almost two years, near the end of the first trial in late 2009 after having received earmarked funding from the German Foreign Office that the Unit could operate at a more considerable threshold.[21] Prior to this, Cambodian NGOs filled the gap. Throughout this process, some organisations gradually assumed the role of "intermediaries", playing an important role as middlemen between the ECCC and victims who sought to participate in its proceedings.[22] Similar interactions have evolved with NGOs at the International Criminal Court (ICC). Such intermediary functions relate predominantly to facilitating communication between the Court and victims, as well as enabling active victim participation in the pre-trial and trial proceedings.

Generally, some of these activities are specific to the application phase, while others are more pronounced during the trial stage. During the application stage, the main task carried out by NGOs was informing interested victims about the ECCC's rules and procedures and assisting them to complete the complex Victim Information Form provided by the Court. This was an important function as the average Cambodian survivor was generally unable to complete these forms without assistance. However, this assistance was a time-consuming process and required much preparation for NGO staff involved. Further, and in echo of similar challenges occurring at the ICC, the VSS encountered considerable processing problems when it began receiving the first applications at the end of 2007, mostly through these NGO intermediaries.

Observing these obstacles, NGOs feared that only few victims would be able to participate, given that the judicial process was further progressing. As a consequence, a number of them begun to further remodel their outreach programs, design more specific outreach materials for this purpose and provide further training to staff assisting in the application process. Within only one year, between the

[21] ECCC 2008.

[22] Sperfeldt 2012b, pp. 155–157.

end of 2007 and the end of 2008, Cambodian NGOs and various diaspora groups enabled the participation of more than 90 civil parties in the first trial against the former director of the Khmer Rouge's most notorious prison centre at Tuol Sleng. In the ECCC's second case, the contribution of intermediaries was even more evident: Approximately 84 % of the more than 8,200 forms had been submitted through intermediary NGOs, underlining the significant role Cambodian NGOs have played in the ECCC victim participation scheme.[23]

Once civil parties were preliminarily recognised by the Co-Investigating Judges, they had the right to be represented by a lawyer and to be informed about the proceedings. In Case 001, the ECCC administration announced that it would not provide legal aid to civil parties. In addition, the VSS, Co-Investigating Judges, and Co-Prosecutors struggled to notify civil parties and complainants about the status of their applications and other matters of relevance to their participation. In this situation, intermediary NGOs' initial outreach projects further expanded to include comprehensive victim support activities including notifying survivors about the status of their application, making requests for protective measures, facilitating legal representation to civil parties, and regularly informing and supporting admitted civil parties in the process of their participation.[24] In addition, intermediary NGO support at trial stage was vital to ensure an active participation of civil parties in the hearings.

The case of the Cambodian Human Rights and Development Association (ADHOC), one of the largest human rights organisations in Cambodia, is one example of a particularly active intermediary NGO that was able to rely on its extensive provincial office structure.[25] Between the late 2006 to the beginning of 2010, some 103,000 women and men from virtually all districts of the country, including multipliers such as local officials, teachers, and monks, had participated in ADHOC's outreach workshops. Various print materials and regular radio broadcasts—considered one of the most effective tools to reach into rural areas—had disseminated information about the ECCC. Since the end of 2007, ADHOC increasingly focused its program on victim participation, particularly promoting the civil party mechanism. In doing so, it organised direct support and various forms of logistical assistance (transport, food, accommodation for meetings of civil parties with lawyers and trial attendance), facilitated legal advice and representation, and provided regular information to civil parties and other victims, many of whom live in remote provincial areas. Overall, more than 1,800 of all victims applying for civil party status in the Tribunal's second case have applied through ADHOC.[26]

---

[23] According to data provided by the VSS as at 26 August 2010, the most significant intermediary NGOs are KID (2,486 forms), ADHOC (1,848 forms), DC-Cam (1,744 forms), KKKHRA (325 forms), the Applied Social Research Institute (ASRIC) from the Cambodian-American diaspora (170 forms), and the Center for Justice and Reconciliation (CJR, 165 forms). The numbers combine complaints and civil party applications.

[24] See more at Hermann 2010.

[25] The other primary intermediary organisations were KID, DC-Cam, KKKHRA, ASRIC, and CJR.

[26] Raab and Poluda 2010.

21.2.3 The Providers: Victim Support Services

Apart from intermediary functions, local NGOs also began to deliver significant support services to victims participating in the ECCC's proceedings. Much of the need for such complementary activities arose from an early lack of service provision by the Court. The most significant areas of NGO victim support services have been legal representation and psychosocial support.[27]

As mentioned earlier, the procurement of legal representation became a necessary part of NGO support, since the Court did not initially offer an ECCC-funded legal aid scheme for civil parties. In a country where most survivors lacked the means and an appropriate education to follow the proceedings by themselves, this was a major obstacle to active participation. As a consequence, intermediary organisations, fearing that civil parties were not able to exercise their right to participate, reached out to external partners. Some of these NGOs actively looked for national and international *pro bono* lawyers. During the early phases of the ECCC proceedings, other NGOs, many of them working in the field of human rights, mobilised their traditional relationship with Cambodian legal aid NGOs such as the Cambodian Defenders Project (CDP) and Legal Aid of Cambodia (LAC). These two organisations and their Cambodian lawyers were the first to represent civil parties before the ECCC, offering a unique framework for learning and capacity building for Cambodian lawyers, typically in cooperation with international *pro bono* civil party lawyers. Without any substantive assistance from the Court, this joint national-international collaboration was instrumental in providing legal representation to the more than 90 civil parties in Case 001. Even in Case 002, which sees a much larger civil party participation, a majority of civil parties is currently represented by *pro bono* legal teams—the remaining unrepresented civil parties were largely taken on by a few court-funded lawyers recruited towards the end of pre-trial stage in Case 002.

In addition to legal representation, Cambodian NGOs were quick to realise the need for psychosocial support to survivors of the Khmer Rouge regime. Various recent studies have found high rates of post-traumatic stress disorder among Cambodian people, particularly among those who lived during the Khmer Rouge period.[28] The Transcultural Psychosocial Organization (TPO) has been offering psychosocial support services to survivors since the beginning of the proceedings, while the ECCC itself does not retain any in-house expert capacity. So far, TPO is the only organisation providing comprehensive mental health and psychological services to survivors participating in the Court's proceedings. In May 2007, TPO and the ECCC signed a Memorandum of Understanding outlining TPO's responsibilities with the Court. Working in close cooperation with the Witness and Expert Support Unit and the VSS, TPO's Cambodian mental health experts provide a variety of psychological services. Importantly, TPO counsellors delivered

[27] Sperfeldt 2012b, pp. 151–152.

[28] See Sonis et al. 2009, pp. 527–536; Stammel et al. 2009.

psychological support to approximately 90 civil parties and 31 witnesses during the first trial. TPO has also collaborated closely with intermediary organisations in their outreach programs and provided specific training on torture and its after-effects to staff of the VSS, civil party lawyers and NGO staff.[29]

21.2.4 The Benefactors: Restorative Justice and Collective Reparations

As elsewhere, victim participation in judicial proceedings has reinforced demands for reparations. Alongside the ICC, the ECCC is now one of the few international (-ised) criminal courts with an explicit reparations mandate.[30] However, the Court's Internal Rule 23 limits the scope of reparations in that civil parties are only allowed to seek "collective and moral reparations"—presumably as opposed to individual or material reparation. In addition, the first Internal Rules provided that these reparations were to be borne exclusively by the convicted person.[31] Largely because of these limitations in the first Internal Rules, no substantial reparations were afforded to victims participating in the first trial.[32] Although this has created some discontent among civil parties, many local NGOs still hope that the symbolic nature of the reparations could provide some acknowledgment and recognition to survivors beyond the constraints of the judicial process.

It was only in 2010 that the Judges of the ECCC amended the Internal Rules with a view to providing for more flexibility in designing and implementing moral and collective reparations in relation to Case 002 and beyond. This has come about in two important ways. Firstly, the Internal Rules now provide that the VSS shall endeavour to identify and design projects, which would give effect to the reparations awards sought by civil parties. Secondly, the VSS is entrusted with the development and implementation of non-judicial measures, which benefit not only civil parties but the broader interests of victims generally.[33] In both cases, the VSS will need to collaborate closely with governmental and non-governmental organisations.

Local NGOs and survivors alike have put much hope in the reparations process, and it is foreseeable that the ECCC will not be able to satisfy all expectations. Apart from judicial reparations, Cambodian NGOs have already begun to implement restorative projects with no direct link to the judicial process, aimed at providing

---

[29] Strasser et al. 2011a, Engaging Communities.

[30] See about the ECCC's collective reparations at Sperfeldt 2012a.

[31] See more on the ECCC's reparations mandate prior to the recent amendments at Sperfeldt 2009 and Sperfeldt 2012a, pp. 460–462; see also Ramji 2005, pp. 359–376.

[32] The Trial Chamber granted only two reparations requests in Case 001: to include in its judgment the names of civil parties and their relatives who died at S-21, and to compile statements of apology by the convicted person.

[33] See ECCC Internal Rules (Rev.6), 17 September 2010, Rule 12bis (2) and (3); and Rule 23quinquies.

benefits to victims. These include memorialisation initiatives, documentation, education, and psycho-social support. The case of Youth for Peace (YfP) demonstrates how a local NGO combines its original work with Cambodian youth in its creation of new programs aimed at involving the survivors of the Khmer Rouge regime. Since 2009, a new memory culture project focuses on participatory approaches to local remembrance and memorialisation by forming community-based committees in half a dozen villages from different Cambodian provinces. One interesting example here is Kraing Ta Chan, Takeo province, where YfP has supported the local committee to develop a mapping of the former prison site and to begin construction of a small museum at the same location.[34] These and other NGO activities help to engage communities and promote localised approaches to remembrance beyond national commemoration sites in the capital. Numerous other NGO initiatives involve restorative measures, such as victim-perpetrator dialogues, self-help groups, and oral history.

Throughout the 1990s, coverage of the Khmer Rouge regime had disappeared from school texts. In this context, DC-Cam has offered assistance to the Ministry of Education in providing supplementary educational materials about the Khmer Rouge regime. As part of its Genocide Education Project, in 2007, the Center published the textbook "A History of Democratic Kampuchea (1975–1979)" and has distributed, up to 2010, 300,000 copies to over 1,300 secondary schools across Cambodia. The book was endorsed by the Ministry of Education as a reference for teaching Khmer Rouge history in Cambodian secondary schools. Moreover, DC-Cam developed a teachers' guidebook to accompany the textbook and has now trained more than 1,800 national, provincial, and commune teachers on its use.[35] DC-Cam plans to establish a permanent documentation centre, called the Sleuk Rith Institute, which will include a research and training institute, a library, and a museum.[36]

These innovative programs led by Cambodian NGOs bear many interesting lessons in developing restorative projects for survivors of the Khmer Rouge. They also have the potential to be linked in various ways with the recently amended collective reparations mandate of the ECCC and the VSS' corresponding project development mandate.[37]

21.2.5 The Watchdogs: Monitoring and Advocacy

The difficult political negotiations leading to the establishment of the ECCC provided early indications of a need for continuous and independent Court monitoring to assess whether the new institution meets international standards in its practice,

---

34 Youth for Peace 2010.

35 Refer to www.dccam.org/Projects/Genocide/Genocide_Education.htm.

36 See more at www.dccam.org/Sleuk_Rith_Institute/index.htm.

37 Sperfeldt 2012a, pp. 485–487.

including upholding the rights of victims and exercising judicial decisions free from political interference. As monitoring of judicial proceedings in the field of international criminal justice is a fairly novel and complex activity, international NGOs and institutions have dominated this process during the early years. The leading monitor of the ECCC is provided through a local project of the Open Society Justice Initiative (OSJI) which has been monitoring the Court since 2006. The Asian International Justice Initiative (AIJI), a collaboration between the East–West Center and the U.C. Berkeley War Crimes Studies Center, is another international organisation that provides a focused trial monitoring program while integrating Cambodian and ASEAN[38] monitors into its monitoring teams.[39] In addition, a number of Cambodian NGOs began monitoring the ECCC when it became operational. For instance, DC-Cam, in collaboration with the Northwestern University School of Law, set up the Cambodia Tribunal Monitor.[40] These activities have also assisted in increasing transparency on victim participation matters at the ECCC.

Further, many NGOs have engaged in advocacy activities, such as those in response to corruption allegations or instances when the ECCC's independence appeared to be threatened by political interference. Those NGOs involved in the ECCC's victim participation scheme have made advocacy around victims' rights a priority in their campaigns by focusing public attention on the lack of outreach and other assistance measures to victims. For the infamous Cases 003 and 004, civil party participation even acted as a trigger for further judicial responses to an otherwise non-transparent handling of the investigations at the Court.[41] In addition, many Cambodian NGOs have advocated strongly for making the ECCC's collective reparations mandate meaningful for the participating survivors, despite the many challenges in the Cambodian context.[42] These NGOs have organised numerous advocacy events and radio call-in shows, and set up specialised websites to inform the public and advocate for changes.

21.3 The ECCC, Survivors and Civil Society

This overview has illustrated the main roles that Cambodian NGOs play in relation to the ECCC's victim participation scheme. What follows are some observations regarding the consequences of such an extensive engagement by local civil society. In making these observations, the chapter explores the different experiences between Cases 001 and 002. Whereas NGOs were able to provide

---

[38] Association of Southeast Asian Nations.

[39] See more at www.forum.eastwestcenter.org/Khmer-Rouge-Trials.

[40] See more information at www.cambodiatribunal.org.

[41] OSJI 2012.

[42] See, for instance, CHRAC and ECCC Victims Unit 2009.

extensive services to civil parties in Case 001, leading by and large to satisfaction among victims about their participation, the sheer number of civil parties in Case 002 poses new and unprecedented challenges. After examining these experiences, the chapter considers the collaboration between the ECCC and NGOs as well as the relationship between civil society and key stakeholders of this judicial accountability process, namely the Cambodian government and international donors. Lastly, some views are presented on the longer-term effects of civil society involvement in the ECCC's victim participation scheme. It is hoped that these observations will provide some useful insight for institutions involved in similar processes and encourage future research.

21.3.1 Case 001: Extensive Support by Cambodian NGOs

Cambodian NGOs' engagement with victim participation in Case 001 demonstrated how far-reaching NGO support can be, as well as demonstrating the extent to which an internationalised criminal court has ultimately relied on such assistance. The fact that a number of NGOs gradually took on roles as intermediaries compensated, to some extent, for the lack of preparedness and services from the ECCC. Despite their initial willingness, many of these local NGOs struggled at first to engage in more complex judicial matters, as the right expertise was not readily available within these organisations and limited information or guidance was forthcoming from the Court. Moreover, these NGOs simply had not anticipated that after the initial application stage, they would be left to deal with numerous follow-up activities relating to complainants and civil parties, which were expected to be within the responsibility of the Court.

Nonetheless, the more than 90 civil parties in Case 001 were able to benefit from various forms of NGO assistance ranging from assistance with their initial application process and visits to the ECCC, to facilitating their legal representation and arranging regular meetings with their lawyers. Although all civil parties in Case 001 eventually found a legal representative, without much assistance from the Court and mostly through NGO facilitation, the lawyers often worked on a *pro bono* basis and had no further resources available to meet with their clients. Thus, it was largely left to NGOs to organise regular meetings between lawyers and their clients and to provide support for civil parties and other victims who wished to attend the trial hearings. These meetings and Court visits proved vital for enabling the active participation of civil parties, particularly by facilitating the regular presence of civil parties throughout the entire Case 001 hearings. This direct attendance in the courtroom increased knowledge among civil parties about the issues at trial and provided a forum for consultations. In addition, on-site and follow-up psychological care through TPO's Cambodian mental health workers assisted in minimising negative side-effects from the participation process.

More recent surveys among civil parties in Case 001 after the conclusion of trial hearings substantiate the importance of this comprehensive support inside and outside the courtroom. A first survey conducted by Pham and colleagues among most of the Cambodian civil parties in Case 001, found that 63 % of the respondents felt "extremely" supported by the NGOs during the application process, and 68 % received information from NGOs at least once a month. Similarly, 72 % interacted with either an NGO or their lawyers at least once a month during the trial stage, and 67 % felt "adequately" supported throughout the hearings.[43] The authors of this study conclude that "despite some disappointments in the Duch trial outcomes, civil parties felt positive about their overall participation, suggesting the importance of that process".[44] These results tend to suggest that a satisfactory participation process could, to some extent, mitigate even negatively perceived judicial outcomes, such as the lack of tangible reparations in Case 001. Based on these results, the authors recommend that "NGOs who have been the backbone of victim participation should be further supported and recognized in their role as intermediaries between the court and the victims".[45]

Likewise, in a more qualitative study conducted by Eric Stover and his colleagues, among more than 20 civil parties who testified at the trial in Case 001, "all of the civil parties said that their primary connection to the court was not through the Victims Unit but through their lawyers and local NGOs".[46] In their conclusion, the authors found that

> civil party lawyers and local NGO activists, through their outreach and support services to victims, can provide vital assistance to international criminal courts. Indeed, we found that Cambodian NGO activists and civil party lawyers, especially those with an in-country presence, filled a huge void in the Duch trial by providing legal, emotional, and psychosocial support to victims. With limited funding, these activists and lawyers mobilized networks throughout Cambodia to encourage civil party participation at the Court, and did their best to ensure that those who entered the system understood its laws and procedures. Our interviews suggest that the attention that the TPO and other NGOs and lawyers paid to the informational, psychological, and cultural needs of civil parties positively influenced their views of the tribunal.[47]

Despite this far-reaching, and in some aspects dominant, involvement of NGOs, some limitations became apparent during Case 001. For instance, NGOs were not able to compensate for the lack of guidance from the ECCC regarding the application process. This cumulated in the Trial Chamber's late admissibility decision, in their judgment, denying civil party status to 24 applicants who had actively participated throughout the entire trial, on the basis of a preliminary admissibility decision by the court's Co-Investigating Judges. This resulted in numerous misunderstandings and disappointment among civil parties.[48] Aside from this,

---

[43] See Pham et al. 2011b, Victim Participation and the Trial of Duch, pp. 273–277.

[44] Pham et al. 2011b, Victim Participation and the Trial of Duch, pp. 284–285.

[45] Pham et al. 2011b, Victim Participation and the Trial of Duch, p. 285.

[46] Stover et al. 2011, p. 14.

[47] Stover et al. 2011, p. 42.

[48] In their final judgment on appeals, issued on 3 February 2012, the Supreme Court Judges admitted an additional 10 civil party applicants.

intermediary NGOs did not have much influence on encouraging collaboration among the four civil party legal teams in Case 001, who lacked a coordinated approach in representing civil parties' interests. These are just two examples which highlight the limitations of NGO engagement and draw attention to areas where earlier action would have been required from the Court and its officials.

21.3.2 Case 002: Reaching the Limits

In the Court's second, and arguably most important case, victim participation has reached a new level. Overall, the Victims Support Section received more than 8,200 forms from victims—roughly half of them, almost 4,000, applying for civil party status. Out of those, 2,123 civil parties were admitted by the Co-Investigating Judges in the Case 002 Closing Order. However, following appeals on admissibility before the Pre-Trial Chamber, Judges overturned the vast majority of the previous rejections, bringing the total number of civil parties admitted to join Case 002 to 3,866.[49] This makes Case 002 one of the largest cases of victim participation in contemporary international criminal justice.

These numbers were above many of the initial estimates when victim participation was introduced; and they can be attributed largely to local intermediary organisations' extensive outreach activities. However, some NGOs had set themselves even more ambitious targets. DC-Cam, for instance, had aimed to assist at least 10,000 Khmer Rouge victims fill out their victim participation requests, either as complainants or civil parties.[50] NGOs had initially underestimated the time and efforts needed to complete and submit the long and complex victim information forms provided by the ECCC. A lack of guidance from the Court on matters such as what constitutes a complete application, clarify over admissibility criteria, and what constitutes protective measures and under what circumstances these measures are appropriate, rendered it necessary for NGOs to go back and forth between victims and the Court to seek supplementary information or further proof of identity—an unfortunate loss of scarce resources. There was no doubt that for many non-legally trained intermediary staff, the whole process was also a learning curve into what complex victim participation processes entail. Whilst the information in the forms played an important part in the civil party admissibility process, its utility at trial phase has been the subject of many objections and debate, mainly due to inaccuracies of the record, and the subsequent multiple levels of interpretation engaged to ensure that the information can be made of use to the court.

Managing victim participation at such a large scale poses challenges, particularly relating to logistical and trial managements aspects. The trial monitoring team of the AIJI noted in particular the ECCC's lack of advanced planning insofar as "the Court

[49] Number of civil parties as of November 2011. See also ECCC 2011.

[50] Refer to DC-Cam's Victim Participation Project (VPA) at www.dccam.org.

did not budget for the inclusion of a victims' participation process—a process which would inevitably be costly if rights afforded to victims (such as the right to apply for civil party status, to legal representation, and to seek collective and moral reparations) were to be meaningfully upheld".[51] Similarly to the Victim Participation and Reparations Section (VPRS) at the ICC, the VSS at the ECCC encountered considerable problems when it began receiving the first applications from victims at the end of 2007 due to inadequate structures and human resources. The years 2008 and 2009 saw an accumulation of a sizable backlog of unprocessed forms in relation to Case 002, which was only overcome once additional earmarked funding from Germany to the VSS allowed for the recruitment of additional staff and the creation of a suitable database system. This led to a situation where numerous applicants did not hear about their application until two or more years after submission.

Because of the early limited capacities at the VSS, NGOs had to rely on their own management structures to administer such large participation. Member organisations of the Cambodian Human Rights Action Committee (CHRAC), a coalition of local human rights NGOs, established in February 2008 a support scheme coordinating member organisations' activities relating to victim participation ranging from provincial outreach and administration of information through a database system to facilitating legal representation. More than half of all victims applying for participation before the ECCC received assistance through this coordinated scheme and its participating NGOs.[52]

Given the problems that occurred during the trial proceedings of Case 001, the ECCC Judges considered the re-organisation of legal representation of civil parties as their main response to ensure effective proceedings.[53] Successive amendments to the Internal Rules in 2009 and 2010 introduced common legal representation in the form of two Civil Party Lead Co-Lawyers at the trial stage for Case 002 and beyond. The Civil Party Lead Co-Lawyers draw their powers from the Internal Rules and do not come from among the existing civil party lawyers. This system maintains the lawyer-client relationship between civil parties and their lawyers, even though the ultimate representation at trial is in the hands of the Lead Co-Lawyers.[54] However, the early lack of an ECCC-funded legal aid scheme for civil parties has led to a situation where most civil parties are currently directly represented by 11 *pro bono* legal teams—the remaining unrepresented civil parties were largely taken on by a few Court-funded lawyers recruited towards the end of pre-trial stage in Case 002. Despite these challenges, this hybrid scheme was able to provide all civil parties with a legal representative, even before the Lead Co-Lawyers were instituted.

---

[51] AIJI 2009, pp. 28–35.

[52] Among the intermediary NGOs in Cambodia, ADHOC, KID, CSD and KKKHRA, as well as the legal aid NGOs CDP and LAC were part of this support scheme. See more at Oeung and Sperfeldt 2010.

[53] See for instance Werner and Rudy 2010, pp. 301–309.

[54] ECCC Internal Rule (Rev.8) 12ter.

The early lack of legal representation for civil parties and the backlog at the VSS in processing victims' applications limited civil parties' impact on the investigative stage of the proceedings. Although civil parties have the right to request additional investigations, this right could only be effectively executed through a lawyer. Nevertheless, civil parties still managed to influence the judicial investigations in Case 002 to some extent. Some civil party lawyers, supported by NGOs, advocated for the inclusion of gender-based crimes into the investigations, focusing in particular on the widespread phenomenon of forced marriages under the Khmer Rouge.[55] Forced marriages were eventually included into the charges against the accused in Case 002 and over 600 civil parties were admitted on this basis alone. In addition, the NGO CDP created a specialised gender-based violence project dedicated exclusively to providing assistance to civil parties and other survivors of gender-based crimes and continuing advocacy on the matter. Similarly, and building on preparatory work of an intermediary NGO, civil party lawyers of Khmer Krom and ethnic Vietnamese minority victims made requests for supplementary investigations regarding the genocide of these two groups, highlighting the suffering of both minority groups and providing further momentum for the inclusion of genocide charges against the accused.[56] Both initiatives demonstrate that civil society engagement and close collaboration with legal representatives can contribute to raising awareness, within and outside the legal proceedings, of the suffering of marginalised victim groups who might otherwise have been forgotten.

However, with almost 4,000 civil parties in Case 002, this low-budget scheme has reached its limits and it is likely that these civil parties will not experience the same level of assistance as the 90 civil parties in Case 001. Under such circumstances, achieving participation meaningful to survivors will be challenging. The NGO ADHOC tried to respond to those challenges by establishing a civil party representative network to manage communication with the more than 1,790 admitted civil parties to whom it has provided assistance. Over 120 civil party representatives were elected from among those civil parties to act as a communication focal point between the Court and ADHOC and the civil parties in their respective regional areas. Such a representative network represents an interesting model for large-scale victim participation. However, its performance has not yet been proven, and much will depend on whether this NGO can secure sufficient funding to build the capacities of those representatives and activate this network throughout the trial proceedings in Case 002.[57]

[55] See more in Silke Studzinky's contribution contributions to this volume. Refer to the press release by the Co-Lawyers of Civil Parties, Ny and Studzinsky 2008, as well as of the Co-Lawyers for Civil Parties (Mohan et al. 2009).

[56] Civil Parties' Request for Supplementary Investigations Regarding Genocide of the Khmer Krom and the Vietnamese, ECCC Doc D250/3, 3 December 2009, submitted by Civil Party Co-Lawyers Ny Chandy, Mahdev Mohan and Lyma Nguyen (Mohan et al. 2009).

[57] FIDH et al. 2011, pp. 17–18.

21.3.3 *Coordination and Collaboration Between the ECCC and Civil Society*

Coordination among NGOs and between NGOs and courts is not an easy task, since NGOs are by their nature independent organisations, each with their specific goals and approaches. Although it was argued elsewhere that "NGOs were able to coordinate reasonably well"[58] amongst themselves, the only systematic effort of coordination among NGOs around the ECCC took place within the CHRAC network and its extended membership, although no strategic approach to collaboration developed, and coordination remained at the level of regular exchange of information. This is also illustrated by the fact that no venue for regular coordination exists, as is the case through the civil society Special Court Working Group in Sierra Leone. In Cambodia, such a forum could have, for instance, facilitated coordination of NGO activities in certain regional areas or ensured more coherence in information disseminated to victims.

Similarly, despite the reliance on local civil society actors in various areas, the ECCC itself has not engaged in strategic coordination with NGOs.[59] Sporadic meetings between the VSS and intermediary NGOs were only replaced at the beginning of 2010 by more regular monthly outreach coordination meetings with the Court's Public Affairs Section. It appears that the Court had initially failed to recognise that it would benefit from playing a lead role in coordinating NGO activities of relevance for the completion of its mandate on victim participation. As a result, the civil party process lacked a joint outreach and victim strategy from the both ECCC and civil society. Had such a strategy existed, it could have provided guidance in ensuring consistency in the formulation and dissemination of messages about the Court. Without such a strategic approach and a regular exchange of information, the process saw numerous difficulties associated with survivors' understanding of the ECCC's role and its limitations. Inadequate management of victim and civil party expectations was most visible in the areas of civil party admissibility and reparations.[60] Pham and colleagues conclude from their research that

> [t]he court should provide early and clear guidance to NGOs on civil party application process and requirements as well as establishing effective communication channels between the court and civil society. The later is especially essential so that NGOs get updated information on rules, process and requirements on a regular basis and thus are able to inform civil party applicants in a timely manner. Additionally, a clear and direct communication channel would facilitate coordination of activities and thus maximize resources.[61]

With regard to communication, local NGOs have found it difficult to engage in a strategic dialogue with the ECCC, due to the lack of a focal point within the Court who could lead the planning and make the necessary decisions. Likewise,

---

[58] Hermann 2010, p. 5.

[59] See more at Sperfeldt 2012b, pp. 152–153.

[60] ICTJ 2010, pp. 11–18; Sperfeldt 2012b, pp. 152–153.

[61] Pham et al. 2011b, Victim Participation and the Trial of Duch, p. 285.

ECCC staff may have found it difficult to engage with such a diverse setting of organisations. The fact that a number of local NGOs have simultaneously engaged in critical monitoring of the Court led from time to time to tensions in the communication between the two sides. In addition, there have been differences in language and perspectives, making it difficult to combine the Court's legal discourses and the requirements of a judicial process with the NGOs' imperative of social reconstruction and reconciliation.[62] Acknowledging these challenges, the OHCHR tool on the legacy of hybrid courts argues that "it will be important for a court to map the general state of civil society and to understand the dynamics from conception and through the period of its mandate. In this regard, it would be helpful to create an NGO liaison position within hybrid courts that will act as a regular forum for interaction between the court and civil society."[63]

Beyond coordination and an exchange of information, the ECCC has not sought more far-reaching collaboration with those NGOs most deeply involved with the victim participation process, namely the intermediary NGOs. For instance, a more structured and formalised collaboration is currently under discussion at the ICC in the form of guidelines for intermediaries, as seen during the 10th session of the Assembly of States Parties—although admittedly it has taken that court almost ten years to recognise the necessity of such an approach.[64] Also, there are differences in the problems these courts have encountered, as the ECCC is not operating in a conflict zone—making protection matters less prominent—and has been able to conduct its investigations mostly independently from NGO support. However, such guidelines are certainly necessary, as the ECCC, ICC, and other internationalised courts will continue to rely on collaboration with intermediaries, particularly in the field of victim participation. This would apply even more so to the ICC which does not have the same in-country presence as the ECCC. Therefore, Stover and colleagues suggest in their conclusion of the ECCC experience in Case 001 that "it may even behove courts to formalize their relationship with such NGOs and facilitate the creation of an official or unofficial network of local organizations to meet the needs of victim participants".[65]

One such area of extended collaboration could be capacity building. Many intermediary NGOs did not initially have the necessary expertise to properly complete the court's victim information forms or to deal with matters such as requests for protective measures for unrepresented civil parties. Despite its increasing reliance on intermediary NGO support, the ECCC provided little guidance or training, particularly during the formative years of the Court's victim participation scheme, so as to build upon the capacities of these intermediaries to enable them to engage more effectively with the Court's process. From the outset, many Cambodians had

---

[62] Sperfeldt 2012b, p. 153.

[63] OHCHR 2008a, p. 20.

[64] See for instance ICC Assembly of States Parties, Report of the Bureau on Victims and Affected Communities and Trust Fund for Victims, ICC-ASP/10/31, 22 November 2011.

[65] Stover et al. 2011, p. 43.

hoped that the ECCC would contribute to domestic capacity building, which arguably should also extend to local civil society actors. In light of the limited resource capacities at the Court itself, building upon the capacities of intermediaries could significantly assist to multiply outreach efforts and ensure that these activities meet the specific requirements of the judicial process. It can fairly be assumed that a lot of time and resources could have been saved had there been a more proactive approach by the ECCC towards local NGOs in the area of victim participation.[66]

Taking into account the ECCC experience thus far, it can be seen that local NGOs have much to contribute to support a victim participation process, including their proximity to the population, local knowledge, and their generally less cost-intensive activities. For courts to be able to make use of these comparative advantages of local NGOs, they need to establish more effective channels of communication and engage in a structured collaborative process.[67] Developing such collaboration is not easy and requires much effort and trust-building from both sides. In addition, there is a need to recognise the importance of assistance *outside* the courtroom, even more so in cases of large-scale victim participation. The two above-mentioned research projects among civil parties in Case 001 seem to confirm this assessment. In Case 002 only a few civil parties will only ever be allowed to provide testimony, while for the vast majority, the benefits of participation will be less visible.

21.3.4 The State, Donors, and Civil Society

The relationship between the state and civil society is one of the key variables in any transitional justice process. The political history of post-conflict Cambodia led to a mushrooming of civil society organisations, many of which take an activist approach in their work. The government generally seems reluctant to engage widely with this diverse NGO body and is sensitive to critical reporting and advocacy. Thus, both sides often keep each other at arm's length even if some links have evolved regarding certain aspects of the country's development agenda.[68] Given the ECCC's national-international hybrid structure, these domestic dynamics in the relationship between the government and civil society have a direct impact on the Court and its relationship with local NGOs.

Moreover, many of the local civil society actors engaging with the ECCC's victim participation scheme have been human rights NGOs, often simultaneously playing a role as a critical monitor of the ECCC and its work. The prevailing distance between those NGOs and government stakeholders in the domestic public policy setting has thus somewhat influenced the prospects for collaboration,

---

[66] Sperfeldt 2012b, pp. 152–153.

[67] Sperfeldt 2012b, p. 160.

[68] These explanations are inspired by David Backer's theoretical framework on the trends of collaboration between civil society and governments. See Backer 2003, pp. 306–310.

particularly between NGOs and the Court's national side, whose staff members predominantly come from offices of the national government or judiciary. Nonetheless, the ECCC's trials and its victim participation scheme continue to enjoy support among local civil society, as shown by the extensive support of NGOs to civil party participation in Case 002.[69] Similarly, the government appears to give more attention to the involvement of survivors in the proceedings and has also recognised the need to proceed at the Court with the development of restorative measures for victims.[70] These developments indicate that there is ground for a constructive relationship between the government and local NGOs in the context of the ECCC's victim participation and reparations process.

Apart from the state, another determining factor for NGOs' performance and capacity in the field of victim participation is the attitude and the support of international donors. This is particularly so because most funding for Cambodia's transitional justice process comes from external sources and all local stakeholders depend significantly on those contributions. Until the end of 2011, these donors had contributed more than USD 140 million to the ECCC, both to the UN and the national side of the Court.[71] With another almost USD 90 million approved for the ECCC budget in 2012 and 2013, this amount is expected to increase to around 230 million by the end of 2013.[72] The vast majority of the money goes into funding the judicial process, with only small amounts being committed to victim participation and reparations. In addition, and as in most other transitional justice settings involving international or hybrid courts, funding to local NGOs working at the periphery of the Court is only a fraction of what the ECCC itself receives.[73]

The strength of local NGOs, combined with the delays experienced in the time it has taken the ECCC to become functional in its work, enabled those NGOs to fundraise in the early phase for a number of important projects, beginning in the field of outreach then extending into victim participation post-2007. Several partnerships with international NGOs and other partners provided further knowledge and expertise. Although some donor states channelled their funding exclusively to the ECCC, others complemented their engagement with additional funding to NGO actors working at the intersection between the Court and Cambodian society. Multi-year projects, such as those provided through European Commission funding, offered some stability and a more adequate timeframe for transferring existing local knowledge into a new, complex criminal justice setting. Other development partners, such as the Civil Peace Service program of the German Development Service (now merged into the GIZ), provided expert advisors on a longer-term basis to various NGOs around the ECCC to support capacity building.[74] This and

69 Sperfeldt 2012b, pp. 155–158.

70 Mom Kunthear 2011.

71 ECCC 2012a.

72 ECCC 2012b.

73 Sperfeldt 2012b, pp. 154–155.

74 Dosch et al. 2010.

other donor assistance during the early years of the Court made it possible for local NGOs to provide extensive support to victim participation at the ECCC.[75]

However, after a number of noteworthy projects had been implemented, in particular in preparation of the first trial, the initial enthusiasm of donors for both the ECCC and NGO activities began to fade after 2009, with consequences for the victim participation process. Although this was partly compensated by additional services provided by the Court, such as legal representation, the overall number of Cambodian NGOs with ECCC-related projects and thus the capacity for services to civil parties decreased. Following the commencement of the ECCC's second trial, this situation poses major challenges, in particular for ensuring a meaningful participation of almost 4,000 civil parties. This phenomenon of dwindling funding over time, following the successes initially experienced in reviving a transitional justice process from donor support, has been observed in similar situations.[76] Hermann argues that "a small investment in this area will maximize any other money put into the ECCC".[77] The lack of continued engagement over the entire lifespan of the Court threatens the ability of this institution to successfully complete its work and leave a positive legacy. In this context, it is important for donors to recognise that NGO involvement is vital for the sustainability of the ECCC's victim participation process—otherwise it may well do more harm than good to the survivors if they are forgotten after they have filed their initial application.[78]

21.3.5 Local Ownership and Sustainability

More generally, the ECCC provides an example of how involving local NGOs in a court's victim participation scheme can potentially contribute to increasing local ownership of an internationalised justice process, which in turn is indispensable if one wishes to achieve a more sustainable impact of such efforts. Since the inception of the ECCC, many Cambodian NGOs have regarded the participation of victims in the judicial process as crucial to Cambodia's longer-term process of dealing with its violent past. In particular, many of those NGOs hope that victim participation may help to narrow the gap that exists elsewhere between internationalised criminal courts and the societies in which they operate and support reconciliation in the country.[79] Taking into account that the ECCC is currently Cambodia's only official transitional justice mechanism, such an inclusion of restorative justice principles into the ECCC's process may promote a more holistic approach to justice.[80]

---

75 Sperfeldt 2012b, pp. 154–155.

76 Sperfeldt 2012b, p. 155.

77 Hermann 2010, p. 7.

78 Strasser et al. 2011b, Justice and Healing.

79 See ICTJ et al. 2009.

80 Sperfeldt 2012b, pp. 155–156.

In this process, mobilising local knowledge and other comparative advantages of local NGOs can help to maximise the impact of an internationalised court. The proximity of these NGOs to the universe of survivors and their communities provides these actors with access where an official institution would not be able to go. The OHCHR rule-of-law tool on reparations programs notes that "civil society organizations may, on their own and, particularly, collectively, have more information about that universe than official institutions".[81] In the case of Cambodia, NGOs are able to reach a large number of survivors in Cambodia's rural communities through their longstanding local presence in the provinces and established relations of trust. Since an internationalised court, such as the ECCC, exists only for a short period time, it cannot rely on a similar network.[82]

By engaging in such activities, local NGOs have in many ways helped to bring to Cambodia's communities an accountability initiative that originated largely at the national level. Victim participation and expanded networks, such as ADHOC's civil party representative scheme, have the potential to contribute to the emergence of local initiatives dealing with the specific consequences of the Khmer Rouge past in the context of each community. It has been argued elsewhere that such "local-level initiatives can tailor their strategies to the unique experiences of each geographic region and community. They can foster the integration of cultural practices and promote participation and a sense of ownership, which makes such initiatives sustainable beyond the short window of external project financing."[83] Although local-level initiatives in dealing with Cambodia's violent past remain limited and under-researched, a few NGOs, such as YfP and TPO, have begun to initiate pilot projects with local communities. Notable examples include the incorporation of Buddhist ceremonies and Buddhist monks, such as practiced in TPO's Testimonial Therapy, also referred to as Narrative Exposure Therapy, a culturally adapted short-term psychosocial intervention with survivors. These projects bear interesting lessons for a more culturally sensitive approach to Cambodia's process of dealing with its past, beyond the ECCC.[84]

Moreover, the survivor-centred work of intermediary NGOs can contribute to transforming victims into active stakeholders of a justice process. In Cambodia, the regular NGO-facilitated interactions of civil parties around the ECCC led to the establishment of two new victims associations, indicating the emergence of an empowerment process among those participating in the legal proceedings and corresponding NGO activities.[85] One of the new associations, Ksem Ksan, now with a membership of several hundred, has proposed plans to build a memorial for the victims of S-21 at the premises of the Tuol Sleng museum.[86] Despite these positive side-effects of NGO support,

---

81 OHCHR 2008b, p. 12.

82 ICTJ 2010, pp. 10–12.

83 Arriaza and Roht-Arriaza 2008, p. 170.

84 Sperfeldt 2012b, pp. 158–159.

85 The Ksaem Ksan Association and the Association of Khmer Rouge Victims in Cambodia.

86 See Ksaem Ksan Association 2010.

one needs to be careful in underestimating the differences within the relationship between NGOs and survivors. Even though local NGOs and survivor groups often share a number of common objectives, they are rarely unified in their opinions.[87]

Finally, the establishment of the ECCC was also expected to contribute to building domestic legal and judicial capacities, in particular by serving as a model for improving the performance of the national judiciary.[88] Generally speaking, however, civil society engagement with an internationalised court and its victim participation scheme can also build specific capacities among the NGOs involved in such processes. In addition, the extensive engagement of local NGOs may, in many areas, prove more sustainable than placing most of the responsibilities on a court which exists only temporarily. The OHCHR rule-of-law tool therefore acknowledges that "the influx of international legal actors that a hybrid can bring may further yield extremely important benefits for civil society in terms of building technical capacity and augmenting political standing".[89]

For instance, the involvement of Cambodian lawyers from local legal aid NGOs has provided them with an important professional learning experience alongside their international peers. Strengthening the role and capacities of independent defence and legal aid lawyers is a vital element in Cambodia's legal and judicial reform process.[90] Likewise, civil society monitoring of the ECCC's criminal proceedings, often with support of international legal actors, may contribute to extending similar programs with the national judiciary where court monitoring remains limited. Other significant capacity building around the ECCC has taken place in the field of mental health, such as through TPO's psychosocial support services to the ECCC and other stakeholders. In recent years, these and other activities have led to an increase in awareness of trauma and other psychosocial consequences of the Khmer Rouge violence. However, a few years into the ECCC process, it can also be observed that the transfer of knowledge and the strengthening of local NGO capacities rarely happen automatically. The victim participation process at the ECCC has demonstrated that without concerted efforts and specific capacity-building activities for intermediary and other NGOs, the potential for collaboration and a positive legacy beyond the Court cannot be fully exploited.

21.4 Conclusion

The roles local NGOs play in Cambodia illustrate how local civil society organisations can support and complement the work of an internationalised criminal court in the field of victim participation. Importantly, many weaknesses in the ECCC's

[87] Sperfeldt 2012b, pp. 156–158.

[88] See for instance Un and Ledgerwood 2010.

[89] OHCHR 2008a, p. 20.

[90] See for instance Sperfeldt et al. 2010.

outreach and victim participation scheme were compensated for during the early years, by extensive contributions of local NGOs. Without this support, most civil parties would not have been able to access information about the Court, file applications, access legal representation, meet with their lawyers or receive psychosocial support.[91] The OHCHR tools support this point by arguing that "hybrid courts [...] should seek to engage local civil society directly in their work. Such involvement can yield important benefits, including access to valuable information and evidence, additional technical expertise, political support, and an additional medium of outreach and public engagement."[92]

However, the ECCC's overreliance on local NGOs in the field of victim participation can be problematic, as NGOs were assuming roles which are normally within the responsibility of a court. Tasks closely associated with the judicial process should be more appropriately dealt with by a court and cannot be left to civil society alone. At the very least, the ECCC should have assured from the beginning, a legal aid scheme for civil parties, particularly on account of knowing that most victims have a low level of education and are unable to afford their own legal representation.[93] In this regard, the ECCC experience shows that if a court decides to allow for provisions on victim participation, it should ensure that an adequate organisational infrastructure is in place and sufficient resources are made available to implement the mandate. This is even more important in cases of mass victim participation, such as in Case 002 at the ECCC, which has illustrated the extent to which a strong civil society can contribute to an internationalised criminal justice process, and at the same time, demonstrate where the major limitations of such an engagement lie.

These observations suggest that internationalised courts dealing with mass crimes and large-scale victim participation must recognise that "intermediaries" play an indispensable role in support of the courts' work. Considering the disproportional advantage that most of these courts have in terms of expertise and knowledge of the judicial process, courts must take a leading role in fostering coordination and collaboration of activities relating to these processes. The case of the ECCC demonstrates that not only do these courts need to develop a structured and forward-looking approach to collaboration with civil society beyond a pure exchange of information; they must also lead the strategic planning and capacity-building process. This may require additional resources, but more so political will in a court's administrations, as well as dedicated staff with the requisite qualifications and expertise to interact effectively with such a diverse setting of actors. Likewise, donors need to be aware that short-term funding attention and corresponding shifts in NGO priorities may endanger adequate support to participating survivors. Hence, a consistent application of the "do no harm" principle must continue to guide the actions of courts, NGOs and donors alike.

---

[91] Sperfeldt 2012b.

[92] OHCHR 2008a, p. 20.

[93] Thomas and Chy 2009, pp. 234–250.

Finally, with increasing numbers of survivors seeking to participate in international(-ised) criminal proceedings, courts will likely find it increasingly challenging to accomplish a participation process that is meaningful to survivors of mass crimes. At the same time, it is clear that the main priority at these courts is to safeguard the effectiveness of the judicial proceedings and ensure a fair trial for the accused. At the ECCC, judges have therefore gradually resorted to introducing more collective modes of participation, mainly through common legal representation and reparations limited exclusively to collective measures. While these responses are understandable, such a shift in policy and practice demands more attention to be paid to the work and communication with survivors outside the courtroom.

Similarly, Stover concludes from his interviews with civil parties in Case 001 that "international courts and NGOs might want to explore mechanisms for victims to tell their story in a setting other than the trial and develop alternatives for involving participants".[94] Such propositions allude to the need to explore more integrated forms of participation and restorative measures for participating survivors. Considering the ECCC's combined mandate on reparations and non-judicial measures, there is a chance that a few symbolic measures could be implemented which would contribute to a positive legacy for the ECCC.[95] However, if courts are not willing or able to afford the required comprehensive assistance to participating victims—either because they do not see it as part of their mandate or they have to focus scarce resources on other parts of the judicial process—then they need to communicate about the institutional limitations clearly with their stakeholders, and establish effective partnerships with external actors, such as local civil society, to assist in this endeavour. In the case of Cambodia, local civil society organisations have proven that they can take on such responsibility.

References

AIJI (2009) Lessons learned from the "Duch". A comprehensive review of the first case before the extraordinary chambers in the Courts of Cambodia. Report produced by the Asian International Justice Initiative's KRT Trial Monitoring Group. www.ocf.berkeley.edu/~changmin/documents/Lessons%20Learned%20from%20the%20Duch%20Trial_MRSK_FINAL.pdf. Accessed 29 September 2012

Arriaza L, Roht-Arriaza N (2008) Social reconstruction as a local process. Int J Transit Justice 2:152–172

Backer D (2003) Civil society and transitional justice: possibilities, patterns and prospects. J Hum Rights 2:297–313

Bertelman H (2010) International Standards and National Ownership? Judicial Independence in hybrid courts: The Extraordinary Chambers in the Courts of Cambodia. Nord J Int Law 79:341–382

[94] Stover et al. 2011, p. 44.

[95] Sperfeldt 2012a, pp. 487–489.

Boyle D (2006) The rights of victims: participation, representation, protection, reparation. J Int Crim Justice 4:307–313

Brahm E (2007) Transitional justice, civil society, and the development of the rule of law in post-conflict societies. Int J Not-for-Profit Law 9:62–72

CHRAC, ECCC Victims Unit (2009) Reparations for victims of the Khmer Rouge Regime. Conference report, 26–27 November 2008, Phnom Penh. www.chrac.org/eng/KRT%20NL%20June%202005-%20May%202008/Conference%20Report%20on%20Reparations%20for%20the%20Victims%20of%20the%20Khmer%20Rouge%20Regime.pdf. Accessed 29 September 2012

Dosch J, Doung V, Kim S (2010) The German Civil Peace Service. Case study of Cambodia. Unpublished evaluation report for the Federal Ministry for Economic Cooperation and Development, Bonn, Oct 2010

Duthie R (2009) Building trust and capacity: civil society and transitional justice from a development perspective. International Center for Transitional Justice, New York

ECCC (2008) Germany pledges 1.5 million Euro to victim support unit, media alert, 6 November 2008. www.eccc.gov.kh/sites/default/files/media/Media_Alert_German_contribution-En.pdf. Accessed 10 October 2012

ECCC (2011) Pre-trial chamber overturns previous rejection of 98 percent of appealing civil party applicants in Case 002, media release, 24 June 2011 (on file with author)

ECCC (2012a) ECCC Financial outlook, ECCC Budget and Finance Offices, 30 June 2012. www.eccc.gov.kh/sites/default/files/5-Financial%20Outlook%20-%2030%20June%202012.pdf. Accessed 29 September 2012

ECCC (2012b) Proposed budget for 2012–2013, 17 February 2012. www.eccc.gov.kh/sites/default/files/ECCC%20Budget%202012-2013.pdf. Accessed 29 September 2012

Hermann J (2010) Reaching for justice: the participation of victims at the extraordinary chambers in the Courts of Cambodia. Centre on Human Rights in Conflict Policy Paper No. 5, University of East London, London. www.uel.ac.uk/chrc/documents/CHRCReachingforJustice2010.pdf. Accessed 29 September 2012

Hughes C (2003) The political economy of the Cambodian transition, 1991–2001. Routledge, London

Human Rights Watch (2003) Serious flaws: why the U.N. General assembly should require changes to the Draft Khmer Rouge Tribunal Agreement. Report dated 30 April 2003. www.hrw.org/reports/2003/04/30/serious-flaws-why-un-general-assembly-should-require-changes-draft-khmer-rouge-tr. Accessed 29 September 2012

ICTJ (2010) Outreach strategies in international and hybrid courts. Report of the ICTJ-ECCC Workshop in Phnom Penh, 3–5 March 2010, New York. www.ictj.org/sites/default/files/ICTJ-Outreach-ECCCWorkshop-Report-2010-English.pdf. Accessed 29 September 2012

ICTJ, ECCC Victims Unit, Cambodian Human Rights Action Committee (2009) Leaving a lasting legacy for victims: practical workshop for ECCC victims' representatives. Workshop report, 10 March 2009, Phnom Penh. www.ictj.org/sites/default/files/ICTJ-ECCC-Cambodia-Victims-Workshop-2009-English.pdf. Accessed 29 September 2012

FIDH, ADHOC, CJA (2011) Opening of the trial in Case 002. Expectations of victims from here and abroad, press kit, November 2011. www.fidh.org/IMG/pdf/draftagenda21novconf.pdf. Accessed 29 September 2012

IRI (2009) Survey of Cambodian public opinion, July/August 2009, Phnom Penh. www.iri.org/sites/default/files/2010%20February%202%20Survey%20of%20Cambodian%20Public%20Opinion,%20July%2031-August%2026,%202009%20–%20Khmer%20and%20English%20version.pdf. Accessed 29 September 2012

Ksaem Ksan Association (2010) United in the quest for justice, social harmony, a culture of peace and spiritual healing, public statement, 20 March 2010, Phnom Penh. www.ksaemksan.info/index.php?nav=home&lang=en&statement=detail. Accessed 29 September 2012

McGonigle B (2009) Two for the price of one: attempts by the extraordinary chambers in the Courts of Cambodia to combine retributive and restorative justice principles. Leiden J Int Law 22:127–149

Kunthear M (2011) KR tribunal mulls reparation plan with Culture Ministry, Phnom Penh Post, 8 March 2011. www.publicinternationallawandpolicygroup.org/wp-content/uploads/2011/04/wcpw_vol05issue25.html#cam1. Accessed 29 September 2012

Mohan M, Nguyen L, Ny C (2009) Civil parties' request for supplementary investigations regarding genocide of the Khmer Krom and the Vietnamese, ECCC Doc D250/3, 3 December 2009. www.eccc.gov.kh/sites/default/files/documents/courtdoc/D250_3_EN.PDF. Accessed 29 September 2012

Ny C, Studzinsky S (2008) Four victims of forced marriage under the Khmer Rouge Regime file their complaint to the ECCC, press release, 14 October 2008 (on file with author)

Oeung J, Sperfeldt C (2010) Victim participation in the ECCC: third CHRAC monitoring report. Cambodian Human Rights Action Committee, 30 November 2010, Phnom Penh. www.chrac.org/eng/KRT%20NL%20June%202005-%20May%202008/11_30_2010_CHRAC%203rd%20Monitoring%20Report_FINAL.pdf. Accessed 5 October 2012

OHCHR (2008a) Rule-of-law tools for post-conflict states: maximizing the legacy of hybrid courts, New York. www.ohchr.org/Documents/Publications/HybridCourts.pdf. Accessed 29 September 2012

OHCHR (2008b) Rule-of-law tools for post-conflict states: reparations programmes, New York. www.ohchr.org/Documents/Publications/ReparationsProgrammes.pdf. Accessed 29 September 2012

OSJI (2011) Recent developments at the extraordinary chambers in the Courts of Cambodia, November 2011. www.soros.org/sites/default/files/eccc-developments-20111114.pdf. Accessed 29 September 2012

OSJI (2012) Recent developments at the extraordinary chambers in the Courts of Cambodia, February 2012. www.soros.org/sites/default/files/cambodia-eccc-20120223.pdf. Accessed 29 September 2012

Penh B, Chhouk K, Men C, Invong S, Chea P (2006) Report on NGO activities related to the Khmer Rouge tribunal in Cambodia: National Reconciliation after the Khmer Rouge, Center for Advanced Studies, Phnom Penh (on file with author)

Pham P, Vinck P, Balthazard M, Hean S (2011a) After the first trial: a population-based survey on knowledge and perception of justice and the extraordinary chambers in the Courts of Cambodia, Human Rights Center, UC Berkeley. www.law.berkeley.edu/files/HRC/Publications_After-the-First-Trial_06-2011.pdf. Accessed 29 September 2012

Pham P, Vinck P, Balthazard M, Strasser J, Om C (2011b) Victim participation and the trial of Duch at the extraordinary chambers in the Courts of Cambodia. J Hum Rights Pract 3:273–277

Raab M, Poluda J (2010) Justice for the survivors and for future generations: ADHOC's ECCC/ICC Justice Project, December 2006–March 2010. Evaluation report, Phnom Penh (on file with author)

Ramji J (2005) A Collective Response to Mass Violence: Reparations and Healing in Cambodia. In: Ramji J, van Schaack B (eds) Bringing the Khmer Rouge to justice: prosecuting mass violence before the extraordinary chambers in the Courts of Cambodia. Edwin Mellen Press, Lewiston, pp. 359–376

Roht-Arriaza N (2002) Civil society in processes of accountability. In: Bassiouni C (ed) Post-conflict justice. Transnational Publishers, New York, pp. 98–114

Sonis J, Gibson JL, de Jong JT, Field NP, Hean S, Komproe I (2009) Probable posttraumatic stress disorder and disability in Cambodia: associations with perceived justice, desire for revenge, and attitudes toward the Khmer Rouge trials. JAMA 302:527–536

Sorpong P (2007) International democracy assistance for peacebuilding: the Cambodian experience. Palgrave Macmillan, London

Sperfeldt C (2009) Reparations for victims of the Khmer Rouge, OTJR working paper series. www.csls.ox.ac.uk/documents/SperfeldtFinal.pdf. Accessed 29 September 2012

Sperfeldt C (2012a) Collective reparations at the extraordinary chambers in the Courts of Cambodia. Int Crim Law Rev 12:457–489

Sperfeldt C (2012b) Cambodian civil society and the Khmer Rouge tribunal. Int J Transit Justice 6:149–160

Stammel N, Bockers E, Taing S, Knaevelsrud C (2009) Mental health and readiness to reconcile in the context of the Khmer Rouge trials. Conference presentation, 3 December 2009, Phnom Penh (on file with author)

Stover E, Balthazard M, Koenig A (2011) Confronting Duch: civil party participation at the extraordinary chambers in the Courts of Cambodia. Int Rev Red Cross 93:1–44

Strasser J, Poluda J, Balthazard M, Om C, Yim S, Im S, Eng K-T, Sperfeldt C (2011a) Engaging communities—easing the pain: outreach and psychosocial interventions in the context of the Khmer Rouge tribunal. In: Lauritsch K, Kernjak F (eds) We need the truth. Enforced disappearances in Asia. ECAP, Colonia Bran, pp. 146–159

Strasser J, Poluda J, Chhim S, Pham P (2011b) Justice and healing at the Khmer Rouge tribunal: the psychological impact of civil party participation. In: van Schaack B, Reicherter D, Chhang Y (eds) Cambodia's hidden scars. trauma psychology in the wake of the Khmer Rouge. Documentation Center of Cambodia, Phnom Penh, pp. 149–170

Thomas S, Chy T (2009) Including survivors in the tribunal process. In: Ciorciari J, Heindel A (eds) The Khmer Rouge accountability process. Documentation Center of Cambodia, Phnom Penh, pp. 214–293

Un K, Ledgerwood J (2010) Is the trial of "Duch" a catalyst for change in Cambodia's Courts?, AsiaPacific Issues, Analysis from the East-West Center, No. 95, June 2010. www.asiapacificedcrossings.org/wp-content/uploads/2011/11/Un-and-Ledgerwood-Change-in-Cambodias-Courts-6-2010.pdf. Accessed 29 September 2010

Werner A, Rudy D (2010) Civil party representation at the ECCC: sounding the retreat in international criminal law? Northwest J Int Hum Rights 8:301–309

Youth for Peace (2010) Memory culture project. Unpublished narrative report from January–April 2010

Chapter 22
Critical Memory Studies and the Politics of Victimhood: Reassessing the Role of Victimhood Nationalism in Northern Ireland and South Africa

Marcel M. Baumann

Abstract This chapter examines the role of victimhood nationalism in post-conflict societies. It elaborates on the advancing discipline of "memory studies" by reassessing the roles of memories in societies like Northern Ireland and South Africa. Based on extensive field research in both case studies, this chapter makes the case for the establishment of so-called "critical memory studies". Such an approach would take into account the contentious and conflict-ridden nature of "victim" and "victimhood": The definition of a "victim" is bound to be dominated by victimhood nationalism in post-conflict societies, while victimhood nationalism is interrelated with the demand for dealing with the past. Critical memory studies may, thus, add a new perspective to the conventional wisdoms of transitional justice because they challenge the very concept of "victimhood" and its applicability. As a key analytical consequence, this chapter wants to draw awareness of the inherent dialectic of memory: On the one hand, there is the possibility of exploitation of memory through acts of memoralisation; while on the other hand, memory practices can acquire transformative quality in themselves. In order to analyse this dialectical nature of memory, critical memory studies will have to interpret violence as embedded within a collective memoralisation by the referent communities.

Keywords Memory • Victims • Victimhood nationalism • Transitional justice • Post-conflict transition • Northern Ireland • South Africa

The author is Lecturer and Senior Researcher at the Department of Political Science at the Albert-Ludwigs-University of Freiburg, Germany.

M. M. Baumann (✉)
Albert-Ludwigs-University of Freiburg, Freiburg, Germany
e-mail: marcel.baumann@politik.uni-freiburg.de

T. Bonacker and C. Safferling (eds.), *Victims of International Crimes: An Interdisciplinary Discourse*, DOI: 10.1007/978-90-6704-912-2_22,

22.1 Introduction: Who Defines a Victim?

In this chapter, I want to contribute to the growing and advancing discipline of memory[1] studies. Broadly speaking, memory studies can be described as a discipline that tries to analyse the social, cultural, cognitive, political and technological shifts which affect how, what and why individuals, groups and societies remember or forget.[2] Eminent pioneering work has been done drawing on the classical foundations of Maurice Halbwachs, Henri Bergson and others. Within the emerging discipline, there is an ongoing and fundamental as well as critical debate on the basis and substance of memory studies.[3] The significance of memory in conflicts[4] and the collective determination of public memory is largely undisputed within scholarly debates.[5] In particular, the importance of memory practices for post-conflict societies has been emphasised, i.e. societies which are in the process of dealing with the past. The "historical truth" is considered to have great ethical and transformative power.[6] Crucially, Assmann and Short claim that memory is not only subject to changes; it is itself a powerful agent of change.[7] Thus, memory has a transformative quality by itself.[8] Recognising the contingent and contentious nature of memory (destructive *and* transformative) amounts to a severe challenge to the conventional orthodoxy regarding the analysis of processes of dealing with the past. For this reason, the growing discipline of memory studies needs to embrace the notion and premises of what I would call "critical memory studies". Critical memory studies have to challenge conventional wisdom and analyses of dealing with the past. A good and representative example of the conventional science of memory is the recent work of Christian Meier, who is a famous German historian. He argued that it is the ability to forget which should be considered the cultural achievement; remembering is only to be recommended under exceptional circumstances such as

---

[1] The term "memory" shall be defined as the creation of meaning and significance to the past in order to reconstruct the past, but also to be able to sequence the presence and the future (see Assmann 1999b).

[2] This definition is adopted from the "rationale" of a journal named "Memory Studies" (see www.mss.sagepub.com/).

[3] Assmann A 2011a, b; Assmann and Shortt 2011; Margalit 1997, 2002; Brown 2008; Sutton 2009; Wright and Davies 2010.

[4] Cairns and Roe 2003; Diner 1996.

[5] Assmann A 1996, 1999a, 2006, 2011a, b; Assmann J 1999b, 2000, 2005; Hamber and Wilson 2003.

[6] Assmann and Shortt 2011, p. 1. See also the comments by Jay Winter: "Memory has power [...] only when people come together in political life and transform representations of the past into matters of urgent importance in the present. Words are weapons, and like all other weapons, on occasion they misfire, or they get hijacked by those who are their target. But they have been powerful agents of change, in the two generations which separate us from World War II." (Winter 2011, p. xi).

[7] Assmann and Shortt 2011, p. 4.

[8] Assmann and Shortt 2011, p. 3.

Auschwitz.[9] In a sophisticated critique of Meier's analysis, Aleida Assmann claimed that remembering and forgetting should not be perceived as diametrical concepts or strategies as Meier does.[10] Assmann argues that the crucial questions to be asked should focus on who profits and who suffers from forgetting: "Can a fresh start really be achieved on an equal basis or is the price too high which one group has to pay?".[11]

Thus, rather than focusing on the negative side of memory, the dialectic of memory should become the focal point. Such a perspective tries to analyse those who profit *and* those who suffer from memory practices within post-conflict societies. Public memory and memory politics involve processes of social integration and conflict (with reference to a "shared history"), of myth creation by specific groups and of reinterpretation and selection of past collective experiences. The concept of the collective memory of a community goes back to Halbwachs. To him, social memory refers to events that can be experienced publicly as well as communally. Accordingly, remembering and forgetting are always social processes; within a given society, there are as many collective memories as there are communities or ethnic groups.[12] Halbwachs emphasised the enormous significance of the community as a context of communication and symbolisation of memories and the role that memories play for the cohesion of the communities. Social memory becomes a central facet of the ideological armoury of the group, helping it to legitimise and rationalise difference. Memory is therefore neither individual nor inherited; rather, it is woven into the social fabric and is bound to the process of social construction.

Through collective imprinting, memory is not just reduced to mere immediate first-hand experience. Rather, a major part is made up of the individual experiences of others in one's own community as well.[13] These are experiences which have been passed on, told in stories and have become tradition. Remembrance is therefore an active cultural process and the memory must always be recreated and kept alive. The memories are monitored, tested and evaluated in an ongoing process in order to transform the past to fit in with the present needs of the community. Consequently, certain historical events and symbols are removed from the collective memory. Additionally, a process of simplification takes place in which the chosen events are mystified and de-contextualised, i.e. they are taken out of their concrete historical context. For that reasons, public memory may be said to rely on the translation of experiences or historical records into societal myths.[14]

---

[9] Meier 1996, 2010.

[10] Assmann A 2011b, p. 68.

[11] Assmann A 2011b, p. 68.

[12] Halbwachs 1966, 1967.

[13] I have elaborated on these arguments in Baumann 2008 as well as Baumann and Kößler 2011.

[14] Baumann 2008; Baumann and Kößler 2011.

The aim of this chapter is to analyse the politics of victimhood that are predominant in post-war societies. It will illustrate that the concept of victimhood is contentious by nature. The concept is contentious because post-war societies are engaged in a competition around the question "who is a victim?". Victimhood is only accepted for their own communities. In cases like Northern Ireland, there are state-led initiatives—or we should say "non-initiatives"—aimed at forgetting and leaving the past behind. In response, civil society actors make the case for remembering and dealing with the past. However, there is no agreement on the definition or understanding of victimhood in the post-conflict society. The "victimhood competition" is played out at the level of civil society.

This chapter starts with two stories from Northern Ireland. The key question that will be asked regarding these stories is: Are they stories of perpetrators or victims? Are the individuals described victims or perpetrators—or both? Or are they neither victims nor perpetrators?

The first story is about Billy Giles who wrote: "I was a victim, too. Please let our next generation live normal lives. Tell them about our mistakes and admit to them our regrets. I have decided to put an end to this now, I am tired."[15] Giles was a member of the Ulster Volunteer Force (UVF), which was founded in 1966 and perceived itself as an army waging a war in defence of the Protestant community against the Irish Republican Army (IRA). As part of that "war", in November 1982 Giles killed a Catholic man, who was his friend and workmate. Giles was charged with murder and served 14 years of his life sentence in prison. He was released on 4 July 1997, having completed a degree in prison. Despite his degree, he was unable to obtain a proper job that paid a decent salary. In the early hours of 25 September 1998, after composing the letter of explanation cited above, Giles hanged himself. In a TV documentary called "Loyalists" by the famous British journalist Peter Taylor,[16] Giles described how he was unable to cope with his actions that led to the killing of his workmate and friend. Because of that he hanged himself. This leads to the questions: Does Billy Giles, who murdered a Catholic civilian, qualify as a victim?

The second story is about Margaret Robinson. Her son was Brian Robinson, like Billy Giles, a member of the UVF. On 2 September 1989, Brian was shot dead by an undercover Army patrol. He was shot while on his motorbike driving home together with a friend. He had just finished a paramilitary "mission": He had killed Patrick McKenna, a Catholic living in North Belfast. When Robinson's mother was told of her son's death, Margaret Robinson suffered a heart attack and died. The two were buried on the same day. This leads to the following question: Does Margaret, who's son was killed while "on action", qualify as a victim?

These stories highlight the contentious nature of the victim-perpetrator formula and put the clear-cut distinction between victims and perpetrators into question. Thus, the necessary prerequisite for any post-conflict society to put a definite end

[15] BBC 1999.

[16] The documentary was also published as a book (see Taylor 2000).

to its violent conflict and start a process towards reconciliation is to abandon existing "hierarchies of victims"; no one can claim ownership of "victimhood" for himself.[17] The theoretical implications that will be developed in this chapter cannot simply be transferred to all cases where violence happened on a massive, organised scale, for example in the case of genocide or in those conflict settings where many of the victims were not on any "side". The argument of this chapter is linked to post-war societies where former enemies have to live together, i.e. "divided societies". Put simply, in "divided societies" the communities will have to live together in the future and cannot risk being divided over the past. This argument is not based on any romantic version of truism. Rather, it becomes essential for the success of conflict transformation processes in "divided societies", in which former enemies have to live together when the "war" is over to reach a consensus on dealing with the past that enables the conflicting communities to recognise and understand the other's communities "understanding" of violence.[18]

22.2 Comparative Victimhood Nationalism, State-Led Amnesia and Civil Society Responses

The cases of Northern Ireland and South Africa are quite illustrative for the analysis of comparative victimhood nationalism. Jie-Hyun Lim uses the term "victimhood nationalism" as a working hypothesis to explain the competing national memories in "memory wars".[19] Memory wars are fought for the position of "legitimate" or "real" collective victim status: "What is most stunning in victimhood nationalism is the magical metamorphosis of the individual victimizer into the collective victim. It is through this process that individual perpetrators can be exonerated from their own criminal acts."[20] Having successfully completed this metamorphosis, individuals hide themselves behind the "memory wall of national victimhood".[21] This wall allows the individual to block any sceptical and critical reflection of the memory content and practices: "By not allowing outsiders any chance to understand 'our own unique past,' sacralized memories keep a monopoly of understanding the past. In this unique past, nationalists can find a mental enclave where they can enjoy morally comfortable position".[22]

This means that nations or communities remain almost unable to accept the "legitimate" victim status of their former enemies; they cannot empathise with the other community and remain divided over the past. The moral distinction between

[17] I have made this argument before (see Baumann 2010, 2011).

[18] Baumann 2009, p. 109.

[19] Lim 2010, p. 139.

[20] Lim 2010, p. 139.

[21] Lim 2010, p. 139.

[22] Lim 2010, p. 139.

victims and perpetrators becomes flawed, the traditional victim-perpetrator-formula becomes seriously eroded through victimhood nationalism. Coming back to Aleida Assmann's critique of Meier's study on forgetting, the crucial question to be asked will focus on who profits and who suffers from forgetting. Profiteers and losers of victimhood nationalism will be analysed in the case studies in Northern Ireland and South Africa.

22.2.1 Northern Ireland: Mothers' Tears and the Peace Process Contradiction

It was yet another historic moment for the peace process when the new Government of Northern Ireland was formed in May 2007. For the first time in the history of Northern Ireland, the new government included the two former enemies: the Democratic Unionist Party (DUP), the most radical Unionist party which strongly argues the case for the Union of Northern Ireland with Great Britain and the Sinn Fein party, the political wing of the IRA. Northern Ireland can be seen as a case in which a political peace settlement has been reached but the process of dealing with the past has not even started yet. While the political conflict transformation process seems to be stable, the question of dealing with the past remains an open wound of the peace process. As a consequence, the possibility of instrumentalisation of the divided past still exists. This is done on a regular basis on the societal level and, mostly, by civil society actors. Acts of commemoration, for example, are based on what was described above as the collective imprinting of memory. Using simplification they uphold the existing ethno-political separateness between the two communities because they are constructed as constant reminder of the suffering inflicted on "our community" by the "other community".

Looking at the new political dispensation and the consolidated post-war elite of Northern Ireland, it becomes very clear that the new political elite is all too eager to ignore or leave the past behind. Their macro-political strategy is one of "chosen amnesia",[23] because they want to move forward with the political consolidation while ignoring the evident structural divisions on societal level. Through chosen amnesia, the political elite are the profiteers of victimhood nationalism. This argument might be difficult to comprehend, but it becomes feasible if we consider that the governmental "inaction" regarding dealing with the past provokes civil society responses. On the one hand, these responses are able to initiate debates surrounding the violent past, but on the other hand, they sustain victimhood nationalism because the debate is used as a platform for civil society actors from both communities to compete on the question of "who is a victim?".

Given the fact that 1,800 of the nearly 4,000 killings that took place since 1969 have not yet been accounted for, the community's desire for disclosure has a

[23] The term was coined by Buckley-Zistel (see Buckley-Zistel 2006, 2011).

particular relevance.[24] Norman Porter distinguishes two sides which have dominated the Northern Irish "reconciliation debate": the "cynics" and the "enthusiasts".[25] Although there is a strategy of chosen amnesia by the political establishment, there is at the same time a vibrant debate about the legacy of the past on the level of civil society. Porter considers himself as being part of the "enthusiasts" and argues for an empathetic embrace of reconciliation, although it might be difficult and dangerous.[26] He issues strong criticism against the current political leadership as well as against the churches for lacking any willingness or substantial incentives to facilitate meaningful reconciliation. His critique seems credible, since there is not enough strength in the political leadership to support or lead a social reconciliation process. At the national level, the necessary degree of political leadership does not exist. This distinguishes the situation in Northern Ireland greatly from that pertaining in South Africa (see below).[27] In Northern Ireland, a "double consensus" can be identified which might sound contradictory: On the one hand, a negative "common sense" prevails which claims that Northern Ireland is not ready to cope with the full disclosure of the truth about the violent past; however, on the other hand, a positive sign might be that there is a consensus on the level of civil society that the past cannot be simply left "untouched" and that it has to be dealt with at some stage of the conflict transformation process. Yet there is no plausible agreement on how to do this at all. Thus, this may indeed be seen as the great "peace process contradiction": The political elite tries to ignore the past for the sake of *political* stability whereas the communities seem to agree on the necessity of dealing with the past *in principle*—however, the post-war is not ready to cope with the remedies of the violence they had to suffer. Regarding this obvious contradiction, Bernadette Devlin McAliskey, who was a prominent human rights campaigner in the 1960s, spoke of "two peace processes"[28]: the political one which seems to be stable and the peace process at the level of society which has not really started yet—because the two communities are too much divided over the legacy of the past. They are fighting the sheer endless battle of victimhood nationalism.

In response to the civil society-led debates and "victimhood competition", the so-called "Consultative Group on the Past" was established in 2007 as an independent group to seek different opinions across the community. Co-chaired by Lord Robin Eames, the former archbishop of Armagh and Primate of All Ireland, and Denis Bradley, former vice-chairman of the Police Board, the group produced a report on 28 January 2009. The report recommended the establishment of a Legacy Commission, a Reconciliation Forum to aid the existing commission for victims and survivors and a new historical case review body. Additionally, it was

---

[24] Detailed victim statistics can be found in Smyth and Fay 2000.

[25] Porter 2003, pp. 13–15.

[26] Porter 2003, p. 21.

[27] Burton 1999.

[28] In an interview with the Swiss Weekly (see Die Wochenzeitung 2007).

proposed that no new public inquiries should be held, and an annual Day of Reflection and Reconciliation should be established. The most controversial proposal of the report was a £12,000 "recognition payment" to the nearest relatives of all victims killed in the Troubles: "The suffering of families from Northern Ireland and Great Britain should be recognised. The nearest relative of someone who died as a result of the conflict in and about Northern Ireland, from January 1966, should receive a one-off ex-gratia recognition payment of £12,000."[29]

Unsurprisingly, a storm of anger followed. For example, Maurice Morrow of the DUP argued as quoted in an article for the "News Letter" on 3 February 2009, that "mother's tears are not the same": "The question has been asked, 'Are the tears of the mother of a paramilitary killer any different from the tears of the mother of a victim who had no involvement whatsoever in violence?' I happen to think there is a difference, in particular, when that mother declares her support for the murderous activities her offspring was engaged in."[30]

Northern Ireland's civil society NGOs do act as proxies for their communities' desire to perpetrate victimhood nationalism. In today's post-conflict society, the perceptions and rationalisations of violence are irreconcilably opposed. An example that illustrates the Protestant community's lack of understanding and recognition with regard to the Republican justification of violence was represented on a symbolical level when a mural with the following title was formally inaugurated: "30 Years of Indiscriminate Slaughter by So-Called Non-Sectarian Irish Freedom Fighters". Beneath the title, there are pictures portraying five large IRA bomb attacks that struck the Protestant community of the Shankill Road area (in West Belfast). For example, nine Protestants lost their lives during the attack, known as the "Shankill Bombing", when the fish store "Fizzel's Fish Shop" was bombed on 23 October 1993. The mural includes two straightforward messages from the Protestant community directed towards the IRA and equally to the British government: "No Military Targets! No Economic Targets! No Legitimate Targets! Where are our inquiries? Where is our truth? Where is our justice?"[31] (Fig. 22.1).

Two declarations by the IRA can be seen as indirect responses to the Protestant claim, which is epitomised by the mural, namely that their victims are "forgotten" and not recognised in the same way as Catholic victims.

First, on 16 July 2002 the IRA declared publicly: "While it was not our intention to injure or kill non-combatants, the reality is that on this and on a number of other occasions, that was the consequence of our actions. [...] We offer our sincere apologies and condolences to their families."[32] This apology was valued as a "historical" step at the international level. Yet, as they explicitly made that apology only with respect to "non-combatants" it becomes implicitly clear that the military

29 Consultative Group on the Past 2009, p. 16.

30 News Letter 2009.

31 See also Flickr 2012.

32 IRA 2002.

Fig. 22.1 Mural Shankill Road, Belfast (© M.M. Baumann)

targets of the IRA—institutions and symbols of the British state—were legitimate targets and therefore required no apology.

The second "historical" IRA statement that occurred on 28 July 2005 was done in the same ideological manner. The organisation announced the end of their armed campaign, but at the same time stated that the armed struggle had been legitimate: "We are very mindful of the sacrifices of our patriotic dead, those who went to jail, volunteers, their families and the wider republican base. We reiterate our view that the armed struggle was entirely legitimate. We are conscious that many people suffered in the conflict. There is a compelling imperative on all sides to build a just and lasting peace."[33]

There are diametrical interpretations of violence which resulted in diametrical views and judgements of the past in the post-war society. By and large the prevailing conditions are those of self-chosen, "voluntary apartheid",[34] in which there is a strong perception of one-sided victimhood and a moral competition for primary victim status: "A political culture that is based on competing claims to victimhood is likely to support and legitimise violence, and unlikely to foster an atmosphere of political responsibility and maturity."[35]

There are numerous examples, where these competing claims to victimhood came to the public surface. For example, when the Eames-Bradley report was officially launched in the Europa Hotel in Belfast, there was a group of protesters

---

33 IRA 2005.

34 Baumann 2008.

35 Smyth 1999, p. 37.

from the organisation called FAIR (Families Acting For Innocent Relatives) showing their opposition to the recommendations of Eames and Bradley. During this public launch, a sharp confrontation between Michelle Williamson, a member of FAIR, and Daniel Bradley occurred. Ms. Williamson's parents were among the nine people killed in the Shankill bomb in October 1993, while Mr. Bradley's brother, Seamus, was a member of the IRA. Seamus Bradley was shot dead in 1972 during a British Army offensive against the IRA. Williamson and Bradley confronted each other in an angry exchange. Both claim to be victims, but deny the victim's status of the other. Indeed, both individuals represent the larger picture of discontent between the Protestant and the Catholic community: Who defines a victim? This is the unanswered and probably unanswerable question of the post-conflict society. Related to that is the critical challenge that can be directed towards the justification of violence by groups like the IRA: Is it possible to distinguish between civilians and non-civilians, between civilian victims and military "targets" at all? It is a difficult task to explain to the family of a murdered RUC[36] policeman that their murdered father is not a civilian. However, the state forces, like the police and the army, must also face similar critical questions: How do you explain to a mother of a 12-year-old child, who was killed by a police plastic bullet, that the police was not a part of the "occupation force"?

Inevitably, dealing with the past in Northern Ireland will be faced with what was called the danger of "discriminatory truth-seeking".[37] Bernhard Moltmann made the accusation of discriminatory truth-seeking against the Bloody Sunday Tribunal. The tribunal was set up by Tony Blair in January 1998 and presided over by Judge Lord Saville of Newdigate. It had been tasked to find out the "truth" about events from 30 January 1972 when 14 Catholic civilians were shot dead by British paratroopers. Over the years, almost 1,000 witnesses had been heard. Throughout the lifetime of the tribunal, serious criticism was directed against it, for example, because of the total costs which added up to ca. 150 million British pounds. The central point of criticism directed towards the tribunal was, however, that the victims from Bloody Sunday came exclusively from the Catholic community. There are increasing demands that IRA attacks resulting in the loss of thousands of Protestant lives, have to be investigated with the same attention and the same financial investment as the events from Bloody Sunday. In making that case, it is usually referred to the attacks in Enniskillen or what is commonly known as "Bloody Friday" (21 July 1971), when the IRA launched 26 bomb attacks in Belfast killing nine people. There is a growing danger of discriminatory truth seeking, if cases like Bloody Friday are ignored. The Protestant community will feel victimised by the peace process.

If discriminatory truth-seeking is not avoided, a hierarchy of victimhood will be maintained within the post-war society. This would simply re-enforce victimhood

[36] "Royal Ulster Constabulary" (RUC) was the name of the police force in Northern Ireland from 1922 to 2000.

[37] Moltmann 2002, p. 43.

nationalism. Who profits? It would be the political elite with its desire to leave the past behind. The families suffering from the loss of relatives and people left behind on both sides will only lose from victimhood nationalism.

22.2.2 South Africa: Amnesty Decisions and the Freedom Park Controversy

Similar to the developments within Northern Ireland's post-conflict society, post-apartheid South Africa could not avoid "victimhood competitions". This can be shown with a view to the amnesty provisions of the Truth and Reconciliation Commission (TRC) and also, to the quite recent Freedom Park controversy.

The example of Victor Mtembu can be used to illustrate the contentious propositions of the amnesty arrangements of the TRC. Mtembu was a member of the Inkatha Freedom Party (IFP).[38] He applied for amnesty for his part in the Boipatong Massacre.[39] IFP combatants attacked the Boipatong township, which was inhabited by supporters of the African National Congress (ANC), and killed 46 ANC supporters: "the world witnessed the image of a nine-year-old child impaled by a spear, and grief-stricken families and angry young comrades vowing revenge on the Inkatha inmates of the KwaMadala hostel from which the attack had originated".[40] Mtembu killed an eight-month-old baby along with the baby's mother in the course of the massacre. During his amnesty application he used the following phrase for his defence: "a snake gives birth to a snake".[41]

Mtembu and 16 other IFP combatants were granted amnesty on the basis that they had fulfilled the necessary requirements that were established by the TRC.[42] One key requirement was that the violent acts had been committed with a

---

[38] The IFP was founded in 1975 and has been led by Mangosuthu Buthelezi since. Buthelezi used a structure rooted in Inkatha, a cultural organisation of the Zulu ethnic group that has been established by Zulu King Solomon kaDinuzulu in the 1920s. The party was founded as the Zulu-dominated Inkatha movement by Buthelezi with explicit aim to counter the Xhosa-dominated ANC. Unlike the ANC, which sought to overthrow the apartheid system through armed struggle, Inkatha was pledged to represent Zulu interests by working within the Bantu homeland system established by the white apartheid regime (see Maré 1992). As a result of this conflict, the IFP and the ANC clashed politically as well as militarily, leading to a massive increase of deaths in the period between 1990 and 1994 (see the summary of the events in Baumann 2008, pp. 47–50).

[39] The Boipatong massacre took place on 17 June 1992 in the township called "Boipatong" when IFP combatants killed 46 people who were perceived as being associated with the ANC. The massacre caused the African National Congress to a temporary walk-out of the negotiations to end apartheid (see the summary of the events in Simpson 2004 as well as Baumann 2008, pp. 47–49).

[40] Pauw 1997, p. 128.

[41] Simpson 2002, p. 244; Simpson 2004.

[42] Simpson 2004.

political motive.[43] The case of Mtembu has shown that the TRC had far-reaching semi-legal authority. This was also the crucial factor for which the TRC gained its enormous international recognition. The South African version of amnesty was deemed an innovative feature: "Our amnesty process has been quite unique in the world. We have conditional amnesty. We would not have had all of these revelations if we had just gone for a blanket amnesty and families would still have been deprived of the knowledge."[44] Amnesty was granted as an exchange for "truth": "Applicants had to make a 'full disclosure' of their human rights violations in order to qualify for amnesty. In most instances applicants would appear before the Amnesty Committee, and these hearings would be open to the public."[45]

As indicated in the case of Mtembu, one additional essential requirement to be granted amnesty was the political motivation of the violent act. The bottom line was that the South African "invention" of amnesty was a limited version[46] of what was termed "qualified amnesty".[47] Granting amnesty was conditional upon "truth", publicly declared by the applicant, i.e. the perpetrator of violence.[48] The amnesty provision led to a heavy storm of criticism challenging the very institution of the TRC and its legitimacy in principle: Robert Price, for example, who was an UN Election Observer in 1990, described the amnesty process as "soft ball" because its provisions were in fact too weak to be challenged sufficiently.[49] Because of cases like Mtembu, Graeme Simpson, who is the director of the Institute for Justice and Reconciliation based in Johannesburg, has reached a negative judgement of the amnesty process: "At best, amnesty decisions were unpredictable and arbitrary."[50]

In the analysis of Simpson, the amnesty process relied on the ability to distinguish between politically motivated and criminal violence during the apartheid era.[51] This was a challenging and extremely difficult exercise: "What the Boipatong massacre example clearly demonstrates are the dramatic dilemmas presented by the reality that the dividing line between politics and crime under apartheid was blurred and cannot easily be navigated either by reference to near theoretical distinctions or by means of the clumsy quasi-judicial proceedings of the TRC's Amnesty Committee."[52]

---

[43] Simpson 2004.

[44] Wildschut 2000.

[45] Boraine 2003, p. 165.

[46] Boraine 2003, p. 165.

[47] Personal Interview with Charles Villa-Vicencio, Cape Town, 17 June 2003 (quoted in Baumann 2008, p. 214).

[48] Hayner 2000, p. 37.

[49] Personal Interview with Robert Price, Berkeley, 9 March 2004 (quoted in Baumann 2008, p. 217).

[50] Simpson 2002, p. 244.

[51] Simpson 2004.

[52] Simpson 2004, p. 2.

The TRC amnesty provisions are an illustrative case which helps to understand the contentious nature of the "victimhood" concept. The decision to grant amnesty to Inkatha combatants like Mtembu puts the well-established victim-perpetrator formula into question: He was granted amnesty because his violent act was politically motivated.

Beyond the TRC, South Africa is also a case where victimhood nationalism has predominated in the post-apartheid era. The dialectical nature of memory practices came to the surface again during the so-called Freedom Park controversy. The Freedom Park is situated on Salvokop in Pretoria and was officially opened in December 2007. It includes memorial walls with a list of the names of those killed in the Boer Wars, World War I, World War II and apartheid: "The Freedom Park is a national monument and memorial. Our guiding principle is creating inclusivity and ownership amongst the nation to ensure that every South African is able to identify with the Park and what it represents."[53]

In total, more than 37 million dollars were spent on the Freedom Park. The concept of the park is based on a monumental scheme, one that wishes to symbolise a reconciled nation.[54] Former President Thabo Mbeki labelled it the "legacy project"; one important influence was the ideological narrative of the TRC.[55] The leading theme was the so-called "struggle of humanity".[56] However, the park is still a far shot from being a "legacy project" for all South Africans. In early 2007—more than 10 months before the official opening of the Freedom Park—a severe controversy had erupted because the memorial wall excluded the names of soldiers of the South African Defence Force (SADF) who died in the Border War in Angola and occupied Namibia. The resulting controversy became a telling example for victimhood nationalism. The disputed question was: Are SADF soldiers, who died during apartheid "legitimate victims"?

This controversy has been fostered by Steve Hofmeyr, a former SADF soldier and well-known Afrikaans singer and actor. Hofmeyr canvassed for the inclusion of the names of SADF soldiers on the memorial wall.[57] As a response, the Freedom Park Trust organised a series of public discussions in which both positions were aired. However, the Trust failed to reconcile both positions and could only reach a rhetorical compromise: "the research and names collection process is ongoing. The Park is a living monument and will continue to grow and evolve".[58]

[53] Freedom Park Trust 2007, p. 2.

[54] Noble 2011, p. 213.

[55] Noble 2011, p. 213.

[56] Noble 2011, p. 215.

[57] See the report in Cape Argus, 9 February 2007.

[58] Freedom Park Trust 2007, p. 1.

The Freedom Park Trust issued a carefully drafted press release, in which the possibility was left open that SADF soldiers' names may be put on the memorial wall:

> It is from this principle that the names of those who laid down their lives for humanity and freedom will be recorded on the Wall of Names. We are, however, in the process of collecting the names of the SADF soldiers who died during the war, based on the principle of inclusivity and representivity. The question of inscribing the names on the Wall of Names needs further debate within the context of reconciliation and nation building.[59]

On 9 August 2008, the Freedom Park Trust tried to go one step further and hosted a function in honour of the families of the SADF soldiers who died in the Border War during the period between 1966 and 1994. The function included a wreath laying ceremony as well as the launch of a memorial book inscribed with the names of the deceased SADF soldiers. This step, however, could not defuse the debate either. By contrast, the controversy accelerated, when on 24 March 2009 deceased "liberation struggle heroes" were proposed for inclusion into the memorial.[60] These included Steve Biko, Oliver Tambo and other national and international leaders. International names were Che Guevara and Fidel Castro. This gesture led the Freedom Front Plus (FF Plus) party to call for a boycott of Freedom Park because in their view, the Afrikaner leaders were still neglected.[61] Willie Spies, a member of parliament of FF Plus, claimed that Afrikaner freedom fighters, for example Paul Kruger, were not part of the Freedom Park's wall of names: "These Afrikaner heroes were freedom fighters in every sense of the word for their resistance to British hegemony in South Africa. [...] The park that aimed to promote reconciliation in South Africa transformed into a monstrosity whereby tax money is used to glorify the ANC and to insult others."[62]

The central criticism against the park claims that it is used "to promote a one-sided viewpoint of history".[63] In other words, we might say that the park could sustain perceptions and strategies of victimhood nationalism. This danger became eminent, when acts of "counter-memoralisation" were initiated: On 25 October 2009, the South Africa's Defence Force "Wall of Remembrance" was inaugurated at the Voortrekker Monument in Pretoria.[64] The rationality of that move was that the wall of remembrance should honour 2,500 members of the South African Defence Force who died between 1961 and 1994—because they would not appear on the Freedom Park memorial. As one pro-Afrikaner blogger commented: "The Wall was erected without any state finance, after it became clear that management

---

59 Freedom Park Trust 2007, p. 1.

60 See the comment in Portfolio Collection Travel Blog 2011.

61 See the report in Mail & Guardian 2009.

62 Mail & Guardian 2009.

63 Mail & Guardian 2009.

64 Tia Mysoa 2009.

of Freedom Park were not going to change its stance on adding former SA Defence Force dead to its Wall of Remembrance."[65]

That this act of counter-memoralisation was done at the Voortrekker Monument is quite significant because the monument can be qualified as the "infamous symbol of Afrikaner nationalism".[66] The foundation stones of the Voortrekker Monument, which is of "critical significance for the foundational myth of Afrikaner nationalism",[67] were laid on a hill outside Pretoria in December 1938.[68] The monument was inaugurated in 1949. According to the analysis of Coombes, not least the inaugural speech by the then Prime Minister Daniel Francis Malan made clear that the "theatrical orchestration of national unity"[69] was not the only thing the South African leaders had borrowed from the Nazis. Malan said in his speech:

> Exclusively, and bound by their own blood ties, they had to be children of South Africa. Further, there was the realization that as bearers and propagators of Christian civilization, they had a national calling which had set them and their descendants the inevitable demand on the one hand to act as guardians over the non-European races, but on the other hand to see to the maintenance of their own white paramount cry of their white race purity.[70]

The Voortrekker Monument and the Freedom Park are situated geographically quite close, the monument can be seen from the Freedom Park:

> Within minutes, a turn to the left captures a dramatic view of Freedom Park situated on a hilltop to one's right. [...] Located here at Salvokop, Freedom Park has initiated an explicit dialogue with the apartheid legacy of the Voortrekker Monument.[71]

This "explicit dialogue" has not yet been transformed into a serious dialogue about dealing with the past of the apartheid legacy. Indeed, Coombes argues that the Voortrekker Monument is an illustrative example showing the complexities of the debates around the appropriate form for commemorating the past.[72] The arguments ranged from destroying all apartheid monuments to keeping some of them like the Voortrekker Monument as a reminder of oppression of the apartheid era.[73] Indeed, key ANC spokespeople, who were involved in outlining cultural policy argued for keeping of most Afrikaner monuments, including the Voortrekker Monument.[74]

---

65 Tia Mysoa 2009.

66 Noble 2011, p. 218.

67 Coombes 2003, p. 28.

68 Coombes 2003, p. 26.

69 Coombes 2003, p. 26.

70 Coombes 2003, p. 26.

71 Coombes 2003, p. 26.

72 Coombes 2003, p. 20.

73 Coombes 2003, p. 20.

74 Coombes 2003, p. 20.

While I am neither in a position to judge the claims and counter-claims surrounding the Freedom Park controversy and the Voortrekker Monument nor to say which side is "right" and which is "wrong", the controversy nevertheless validates the relevance and dangers of victimhood nationalism. It is upheld by ongoing "victimhood competitions" which inhibit any serious progress of dealing with the past. Here, the question "Who profits?" becomes relevant, too.

In South Africa, there seems to be a different style of leadership evolving—in sharp contrast to Northern Ireland—which wants to see an end to the politics of victimhood. This became obvious, when the ANC argued that the Freedom Park and the Voortrekker Monument should be linked. In March 2010, the ANC secretary general Gwede Mantashe maid that claim publicly: "We must systematically own all our history and heritage and undo the appropriation of parts of our history and heritage to individual nationalities in the country. [...] So we link them, in a big way, into a single precinct. Even if you call that precinct the Freedom precinct, you can even call it that. Because that history is our history."[75]

In a similar vein, ANC spokesman Jackson Mtembu said that all South Africans should take ownership of the country's heritage: "We must take ownership of everything that is South African so that there is no history and heritage that belongs to a particular grouping and history and heritage that belongs again to another grouping."[76] If this linkage of Freedom Park and the Voortrekker Monument is achieved, it would mark a valuable step towards the end of the politics of victimhood because it would remove the ideological basis of victimhood nationalism.

22.3 Conclusions

Critical memory studies seek to reassess the role or *roles* memories play in post-conflict societies. It wants to draw awareness of the inherent dialectic of memory: On the one hand, there is the possibility of exploitation of memory. Acts of remembrance can be misused for political gains. Indeed, the reality of such acts of remembrance is that people do remember events they have not witnessed themselves. On the other hand, memory practices can acquire transformative quality in themselves.[77] In order to analyse this dialectical nature of memory, critical memory studies will have to interpret violence as embedded within a collective memoralisation by the referent communities. Violent acts by groups like the IRA and others were directed against the "institutions" of the British crown and according to their "discourse" and rhetorical strategies, violent acts were not directed against individual members of the Protestant community in Northern Ireland or that community as such. Thus, violence has to be seen as a way of communication, distributing (symbolic) meaning which is

[75] Times Live 2010.

[76] Times Live 2010.

[77] Assmann and Shortt 2011, p. 4.

open for interpretation. This interpretational or discursive basis of violence may lead to very critical questions to be asked: Are there reasons or "rationalisations" that could convince or persuade the surviving families, whose members fell "victim" to violent acts "perpetrated" by the IRA and others, that the armed groups and their families can be recognised as victims, too? Or in other words: Is it feasible to classify armed combatants not only as "terrorists" or "perpetrators" but also as "victims"?

This point might become comprehensible if we look at the living conditions and the biographies of the individuals involved in violence. Most individuals who decided to join the IRA felt that they *had* to fight against an oppressive British "occupying force". Most of those who joined the IRA had personal experiences of violence by the British security forces. The IRA's aim was to force British withdrawal from Ireland and a unification of the island. They perceived their violent "struggle" as being the only alternative open to them. It was the "perpetrators" and their families, too, who had to suffer the consequences of their actions. Not only did members of the IRA serve very long prison sentences for their acts of violence, but their families were destroyed, "innocent" lives were ruined. In addition, many family members, who had no IRA connection, were murdered by the IRA or the security forces. Civilian family members of the armed groups were drawn into the civil war and many of them were killed.

Similarly, those groups who fought against the IRA—like the UVF—thought that they *had* to defend their Protestant-British identity and community from the IRA. People like Giles felt that they were not given any other chance than to use "violence". They became "victims" of the circumstances. The same circumstances also "victimised" Brian and Margret Robinson.

Billy Giles and Brian Robinson were "perpetrators", but they were also "victims of circumstances". These examples show that the demand for an "inclusive" definition of "victimhood" becomes unsustainable—and this is the "final conclusion" of this chapter: If everybody becomes a "victim" the value of the category becomes questionable because the analysis cannot distinguish between perpetrators and victims anymore. As a result, the category of "victimhood" is in danger to become irrelevant. Thus, the perspective of critical memory studies leads us to question the concept of victimhood. In cases like Northern Ireland, the clear distinction between victims and perpetrators is blurred; therefore, the concept of victimhood itself is limited of use. It keeps the post-conflict society stuck into a "victim-bond society" unable to embark on a constructive conflict transformation process.

Regarding the application of the concept of victimhood, Northern Ireland stands in obvious contrast to the South African case. The Nazi-inspired ideology honoured at the Voortrekker Monument and the racial apartheid system produced "victims" and "perpetrators". Although, it should not be forgotten that ANC members were, in many instances, perpetrators, too. Most notably, the transition from 1990 to 1994 was accompanied by a "war" in the KwaZulu Natal province, in which Inkatha and the ANC fought each other.[78] During that "war", over 14,000 people were killed; thus, the transition period from apartheid to democracy

[78] See the summary in Baumann 2008, pp. 47–50.

became the most "bloodiest" in the history of South Africa.[79] This war was called the "unofficial war" by Rupert Taylor and others,[80] because the TRC avoided to reach a deeper analysis and understanding of the reasons and underlying factors of that "war".[81] The war had to remain "unofficial": "It is evident that the violent power struggle between the African National Congress (ANC) and the Inkatha Freedom Party (IFP) that took place during the era of negotiations fits uncomfortably within the moral tale of the fall of apartheid that the TRC wishes to tell."[82]

The TRC report followed a different agenda and moral "project", and therefore largely ignored the "war" in KwaZulu Natal.[83] During that war, which remained "unofficial", the ANC and the IFP were involved in violence and killings—they were perpetrators *and* victims of violence.

However, what can still be learned from the South African debates like the Freedom Park controversy is that political leadership and courage may overcome victimhood nationalism in the post-conflict society. The political elite in Northern Ireland lacks such courage, while the ANC leadership used the Freedom Park controversy to air a spirit of recognition for all traditions in South Africa, even those which caused the most deaths and sufferings. Political leadership is desperately needed in order to make post-war societies aware and able to (re-)claim ownership of their own "common" or "united" heritage. This will contribute to the end of the politics of victimhood.

References

Assmann A (1996) Erinnerungsorte und Gedächtnislandschaften. In: Loewy H, Moltmann B (eds) Erlebnis—Gedächtnis—Sinn. Authentische und konstruierte Erinnerung. Campus, Frankfurt am Main, pp. 13–29

Assmann A (1999a) Erinnerungsräume Formen und Wandlungen des kulturellen Gedächtnisses. C.H Beck, Munich

Assmann J (1999b) Das kulturelle Gedächtnis. Schrift, Erinnerung und politische Identität in den frühen Hochkulturen. Wilhelm Fink, Munich

Assmann J (2000) Religion und das kulturelle Gedächtnis. Zehn Studien. Wilhelm Fink, Munich

Assmann J (2005) Das kollektive Gedächtnis zwischen Körper und Schrift. Zur Gedächtnistheorie von Maurice Halbwachs. In: Krapoth H, Laborde D (eds) Erinnerung und Gesellschaft. Mémoire et Société. Hommage à Maurice Halbwachs (1877–1945). Leske + Budrich, Opladen, pp. 65–81

Assmann A (2006) Trauma und Tabu. Schattierungen zwischen Täter- und Opfergedächtnis. In: Landkamer J, Noetzel T, Zimmerli WC (eds) Erinnerungsmanagement. Systemtransformation und Vergangenheitspolitik im internationalen Vergleich. Wilhelm Fink, Munich, pp. 235–255

[79] Figures of the Human Rights Commission (see TRC 2003, p. 579).

[80] Taylor 2002.

[81] Guelke 2000, p. 240.

[82] Guelke 2000, p. 240.

[83] Guelke 2000, p. 240; Baumann 2008, p. 216.

Assmann A (2011a) Vergessen oder Erinnern? Wege aus einer gewaltsamen Gewaltgeschichte. In: Ferhadbegovic S, Weiffen B (eds) Bürgerkriege erzählen: Zum Verlauf unziviler Konflikte. Konstanz University Press, Constance, pp. 303–319

Assmann A (2011b) To remember or to forget: Which way out of a shared history of violence? In: Assmann A, Shortt L (eds) Memory and political change. Palgrave, Basingstoke, pp. 53–71

Assmann A, Shortt L (2011) Memory and political change: introduction. In: Assmann A, Shortt L (eds) Memory and political change. Palgrave, Basingstoke, pp. 1–14

Baumann M (2008) Zwischenwelten: Weder Krieg Noch Frieden. Über den konstruktiven Umgang mit Gewaltphänomenen im Prozess der Konflikttransformation. VS, Wiesbaden

Baumann M (2009) Understanding the other's "understanding" of violence: legitimacy, recognition, and the challenge of dealing with the past in divided societies. Int J Confl Violence 3:107–123

Baumann M (2010) Contested victimhood in the Northern Irish peace process. Peace Rev 22:171–177

Baumann M (2011) Verabschiedung von den Opfern? Die namenlose Tragik des Friedens in Nordirland. In: Buckley-Zistel S, Kater T (eds) Nach Krieg, Gewalt und Repression: Der schwierige Umgang mit der Vergangenheit, AFK-Friedensschriften, vol 35. Nomos, Baden–Baden, pp. 39–57

Baumann M, Kößler R (2011) Contested "Amnesias": Remembering, Forgetting or "Non-Addressing"? The "Victim-Perpetrator-Formula" and the Normative Dimension of Dealing with the Past, Presentation at the 6th ECPR General Conference, University of Iceland, 25–27 Aug 2011. www.ecprnet.eu/MyECPR/proposals/reykjavik/uploads/papers/275.pdf. Accessed 5 August 2012

BBC (1999) Changing voices: Billy Giles. www.bbc.co.uk/northernireland/learning/eyewitness/changing/voices/giles.shtml. Accessed 7 Aug 2012

Boraine A (2003) South Africa's amnesty revisited. In: Villa-Vicencio C, Doxtader E (eds) The provocations of amnesty: memory, justice and impunity. New Africa Books, Cape Town, pp. 165–180

Brown S D (2008) The quotation marks have a certain importance: prospects for a 'memory studies'. Mem Stud 1:261–271

Buckley-Zistel S (2006) Remembering to forget: chosen amnesia as a strategy for local coexistence in post-genocide Rwanda. Africa: J Int Afr Inst 76:131–150

Buckley-Zistel S (2011) Between pragmatism, coercion and fear: chosen amnesia after the Rwandan genocide. In: Assmann A, Shortt L (eds) Memory and political change. Palgrave, Basingstoke, pp. 72–88

Burton M (1999) The South African Truth and Reconciliation Commission: looking back, moving forward. In: Hamber B (ed) Past imperfect: dealing with the past in Northern Ireland and countries in transition. INCORE, Londonderry, pp. 13–24

Cairns E, Roe MD (2003) Why memories in conflict? In: Cairns E, Roe MD (eds) The role of memory in ethnic conflict. Palgrave, Basingstoke, pp. 3–8

Consultative Group on the Past (2009) Report of the Consultative Group on the Past, 23 January 2009. www.healingthroughremembering.org/images/j_library/lib/NI%20Consultative%20Group%20on%20the%20Past%20Report.pdf. Accessed 4 August 2012

Coombes AE (2003) History after apartheid visual culture and public memory in a democratic South Africa. Duke University Press, Durham

Die Wochenzeitung () Operation Schweiz, 16 Aug . www.woz.ch/0733/nordirland/operation-schweiz. Accessed 7 Aug 2012

Diner D (1996) Massenvernichtung und Gedächtnis. Zur kulturellen Strukturierung historischer Ereignisse. In: Loewy H, Moltmann B (eds) Erlebnis – Gedächtnis – Sinn. Authentische und konstruierte Erinnerung. Campus, Frankfurt am Main, pp. 47–55

Flickr (2012) Jan 10—"No military targets! No economic targets! No legitimate targets!", mural off the Shankill road, Belfast. www.flickr.com/photos/97924400@N00/4378171056/. Accessed 7 August 2012

Freedom Park Trust () Press Release, 11 January . www.freedompark.co.za/cms/index.php?option=com_docman&task=doc_download&Itemid=3&gid=92. Accessed 4 August 2012

Guelke A (2000) Interpretations of political violence during South Africa's transition. Politikon 27:239–254
Halbwachs M (1966) Das Gedächtnis und seine sozialen Bedingungen. Suhrkamp, Frankfurt am Main
Halbwachs M (1967) Das Kollektive Gedächtnis. Enke, Stuttgart
Hamber B, Wilson R (2003) Symbolic closure through memory, reparation and revenge in post-conflict societies. In: Cairns E, Roe MD (eds) The role of memory in ethnic conflict. Palgrave, Basingstoke, pp. 144–168
Hayner PB (2000) Same species, different animal. How South Africa compares to truth commissions worldwide. In: Villa-Vicencio C, Verwoerd W (eds) Looking back reaching forward. Reflections on the Truth and Reconciliation Commission of South Africa. UCT Press, Cape Town, pp. 32–41
IRA (2002) Irish Republican Army (IRA) Statement of Apology, 16 July 2002. www.cain.ulst.ac.uk/events/peace/docs/ira160702.htm. Accessed 7 August 2012
IRA (2005) Irish Republican Army (IRA) Statement on the Ending of the Armed Campaign, 28 July 2005. www.cain.ulst.ac.uk/othelem/organ/ira/ira280705.htm. Accessed 29 July 2005
Lim J-H (2010) Victimhood nationalism in contested memories: national mourning and global accountability. In: Assmann A, Conrad S (eds) Memory in a global age. Discourses Practices and Trajectories. Palgrave, Basingstoke, pp. 138–162
Mail & Guardian (2009) FF Plus calls for Freedom Park boycott, 20 March 2009. www.mg.co.za/article/2009-03-20-ff-plus-calls-for-freedom-park-boycott. Accessed 11 November 2011
Maré G (1992) Brothers born in warrior blood. Politics and Ethnicity in South Africa. Zed Books, Atlantic Highlands
Margalit A (1997) Gedenken, Vergessen, Vergeben. In: Margalit A, Smith D (eds) Amnestie oder Die Politik der Erinnerung in der Demokratie. Suhrkamp, Frankfurt am Main, pp. 192–205
Margalit A (2002) The ethics of memory. Harvard University Press, Cambridge
Meier C (1996) Erinnern—Verdrängen—Vergessen. Merkur 50:937–52
Meier C (2010) Das Gebot zu vergessen und die Unabweisbarkeit des Erinnerns. Vom öffentlichen Umgang mit schlimmer Vergangenheit. Siedler, Münich
Moltmann B (2002) 'Es kann der Frömmste nicht im Frieden bleiben:' Nordirland und sein kalter Frieden. Peace Research Institute Frankfurt, Frankfurt am Main
News Letter (2009) All mother's tears are not the same, 2 Feb 2009. www.newsletter.co.uk/news/politics/all-mother-s-tears-are-not-the-same-lord-morrow-1-1881119. Accessed 7 August 2012
Noble JA (2011) African identity in post-apartheid public architecture. White skin, black masks. Ashgate, Farnham
Pauw J (1997) Into the heart of darkness confessions of apartheid's assassins. Jonathan Ball Publishers, Johannesburg
Porter N (2003) The elusive quest: reconciliation in Northern Ireland. Blackstaff Press, Belfast
Portfolio Collection Travel Blog (2011) Monument Monday—Freedom Park, 14 Nov 2011. www.travelblog.portfoliocollection.com/Blog/Monument-Monday—Freedom-Park. Accessed 1 December 2011
Simpson G (2002) 'Tell no lies, claim no easy victories:' a brief evaluation of South Africa's Truth and Reconciliation Commission. In: Posel D, Simpson G (eds) Commissioning the past: understanding South Africa's Truth and Reconciliation Commission. Witwatersrand University Press, Johannesburg, pp. 220–251
Simpson G (2004) A snake gives birth to a snake: politics and crime in the transition to democracy in South Africa. www.csvr.org.za/docs/crime/snake.pdf. Accessed 1 October 2011
Smyth M (1999) Remembering in Northern Ireland: victims, perpetrators and hierarchies of pain and responsibility. In: Hamber B (ed) Past imperfect: dealing with the past in Northern Ireland and countries in transition. INCORE, Londonderry, pp. 31–49
Smyth M, Fay M-T (eds) (2000) Personal accounts from Northern Ireland's troubles: public conflict, private loss. Pluto Press, London
Sutton J (2009) Looking beyond memory studies: comparisons and integrations. Mem Stud 2:299–302

Taylor P (2000) Loyalists. Bloomsbury, London
Taylor R (2002) Justice denied: political violence in KwaZulu-Natal after 1994. www.csvr.org.za/wits/papers/papvtp6.htm. Accessed 1 December 2011
Tia Mysoa (2009) SA Defence Force Wall of Remembrance, 26 Oct 2009. www.tia-mysoa.blogspot.com/2009/10/sa-defence-force-wall-of-remembrance.html. Accessed 1 December 2011
Times Live (2010) ANC wants Freedom Park, Voortrekker Monument linked, 30 March 2010. www.timeslive.co.za/local/2010/03/30/anc-wants-freedom-park-voortrekker-monument-linked. Accessed 1 December 2011
TRC (2003) Truth and Reconciliation Commission of South Africa Report, vol 6 (Final Report). www.info.gov.za/otherdocs/2003/trc/. Accessed 5 August 2012
Wildschut G (2000) Statement of Glenda Wildschut in the Documentary "Long Night's Journey Into Day" (2000). www.newsreel.org/transcripts/longnight.htm. Accessed 13 May 2004
Winter J (2011) Foreword: remembrance as a human right. In: Assmann A, Shortt L (eds) Memory and political change. Palgrave, Basingstoke, pp. vii–xi
Wright P, Davies J (2010) Just start digging: memory and the framing of heritage. Mem Stud 3:196–220
Wuhrer P (2007) Operation Schweiz. Woz 3312007, 16 August 2007. www.woz.ch/0733/nordirland/operation-Schweiz . Accessed 7 August 2012

Index

T. Bonacker and C. Safferling (eds.), *Victims of International Crimes: An Interdisciplinary Discourse*, DOI: 10.1007/978-90-6704-912-2,

MIX
Papier aus verantwortungsvollen Quellen
Paper from responsible sources
FSC® C105338

If you have any concerns about our products,
you can contact us on
ProductSafety@springernature.com

In case Publisher is established outside the EU,
the EU authorized representative is:
Springer Nature Customer Service Center GmbH
Europaplatz 3, 69115 Heidelberg, Germany

Printed by Libri Plureos GmbH
in Hamburg, Germany